China and Southeast Asia

Spanning over a millennium of history, this book seeks to describe and define the evolution of the China–Southeast Asia nexus and the interactions which have shaped their shared pasts.

Examining the relationships which have proven integral to connecting Northeast and Southeast Asia with other parts of the world, the contributors of the volume provide a wide-ranging historical context to changing relations in the region today – perhaps one of the most intense re-orderings occurring anywhere in the world. From maritime trading relations and political interactions to overland Chinese expansion and commerce in Southeast Asia, this book reveals rarely explored connections across the China–Southeast Asia interface. In so doing, it transcends existing area studies boundaries to present an invaluable new perspective to the field.

A major contribution to the study of Asian economic and cultural interactions, this book will appeal to students and scholars of Chinese history, as well as those engaged with Southeast Asia.

Geoff Wade researches Asian connections and interactions, both historical and contemporary. His recent publications include *Asian Expansions* (2015) and *Anthony Reid and the Study of the Southeast Asian Past* (ed. with Li Tana, 2012).

James K. Chin is Chair Professor in the School of Overseas Chinese Studies at Jinan University, China. His recent English language publications include *Mapping Ming China's Maritime World: The Selden Map and Other Treasures from the University of Oxford* (ed. with Tianlong Jiao, 2015).

Routledge Studies in the Modern History of Asia

125 **The Economy of Colonial Malaya**
Administrators versus Capitalists
Sivachandralingam Sundara Raja

126 **Secularism, Decolonisation, and the Cold War in South and Southeast Asia**
Clemens Six

127 **Chinese Middlemen in Hong Kong's Colonial Economy, 1830–1890**
Kaori Abe

128 **World War Two Legacies in East Asia**
China Remembers the War
Chan Yang

129 **Civil Society and Postwar Pacific Basin Reconciliation**
Wounds, Scars, and Healing
Edited by Yasuko Claremont

130 **Korean National Identity under Japanese Colonial Rule**
Yi Gwangsu and the March First Movement of 1919
Michael D. Shin

131 **English Language Teaching during Japan's Post-war Occupation**
Politics and Pedagogy
Mayumi Ohara and John Buchanan

132 **China and Southeast Asia**
Historical Interactions
Edited by Geoff Wade and James K. Chin

For a full list of available titles please visit: www.routledge.com/Routledge-Studies-in-the-Modern-History-of-Asia/book-series/MODHISTASIA

China and Southeast Asia

Historical Interactions

Edited by Geoff Wade and James K. Chin

LONDON AND NEW YORK

First published 2019
by Routledge
2 Park Square, Milton Park, Abingdon, Oxon OX14 4RN

and by Routledge
711 Third Avenue, New York, NY 10017

Routledge is an imprint of the Taylor & Francis Group, an informa business

© 2019 selection and editorial matter, Geoff Wade and James K. Chin; individual chapters, the contributors

The right of Geoff Wade and James K. Chin to be identified as the authors of the editorial matter, and of the authors for their individual chapters, has been asserted in accordance with sections 77 and 78 of the Copyright, Designs and Patents Act 1988.

All rights reserved. No part of this book may be reprinted or reproduced or utilised in any form or by any electronic, mechanical, or other means, now known or hereafter invented, including photocopying and recording, or in any information storage or retrieval system, without permission in writing from the publishers.

Trademark notice: Product or corporate names may be trademarks or registered trademarks, and are used only for identification and explanation without intent to infringe.

Every effort has been made to contact copyright holders for their permission to reprint material in this book. The publishers would be grateful to hear from any copyright holder who is not here acknowledged and will undertake to rectify any errors or omissions in future editions of this book.

British Library Cataloguing-in-Publication Data
A catalogue record for this book is available from the British Library

Library of Congress Cataloging-in-Publication Data
Names: Wade, Geoff, editor. | Chin, James K., editor.
Title: China and Southeast Asia : historical interactions / edited by Geoff Wade and James K. Chin.
Description: First edition. | London ; New York, NY : Routledge/Taylor & Francis Group, 2019. | Series: Routledge studies in the modern history of Asia ; 132 | Includes bibliographical references and index.
Identifiers: LCCN 2018018345| ISBN 9780415589970 (hardback) | ISBN 9780429489518 (ebook)
Subjects: LCSH: China–Foreign relations–Southeast Asia. | Southeast Asia–Foreign relations–China.
Classification: LCC DS740.4 .C354523 2019 | DDC 303.48/251059–dc23
LC record available at https://lccn.loc.gov/2018018345

ISBN: 978-0-415-58997-0 (hbk)
ISBN: 978-0-429-48951-8 (ebk)

Typeset in Times New Roman
by Wearset Ltd, Boldon, Tyne and Wear

Contents

List of figures	viii
List of tables	xii
Notes on contributors	xiii
Acknowledgements	xvi

1 **China and Southeast Asia: historical interactions**   1
GEOFF WADE AND JAMES K. CHIN

PART I
Trading relations   19

2 **Hainan and its international trade: ports, merchants, commodities (Song to mid-Ming)**   21
RODERICH PTAK

3 **China in India: porcelain trade and attitudes to collecting in early Islamic India**   44
JOHN GUY

PART II
Political interactions in the maritime realm and overland   85

4 **Ming China and Southeast Asia in the fifteenth century**   87
GEOFF WADE

5 **The Portuguese occupation of Malacca in 1511 and China's response**   130
LIAO DAKE

6   The Chinese factor in the shaping of Nguyễn rule in
    Southern Vietnam during the seventeenth and eighteenth
    centuries   156
    DANNY WONG TZE KEN

7   King Taksin and China: Siam–Chinese relations during the
    Thonburi period as seen from Chinese sources   174
    JAMES K. CHIN

8   Upland peoples and the 1729 Qing annexation of the Tai
    polity of Sipsong Panna, Yunnan: disintegration from the
    periphery   188
    CHRISTIAN DANIELS

PART III
Chinese commerce in Southeast Asia   219

9   The rise of Chinese mercantile power in maritime Southeast
    Asia, c.1400–1700   221
    CHANG PIN-TSUN

10 Chinese traders in the Malay Archipelago, 1680–1795   241
    M. RADIN FERNANDO

11 Cang hai sang tian (沧海桑田): Chinese communities in the
    Mekong delta in the eighteenth century   264
    LI TANA

PART IV
China–Southeast Asian interactions during the age of
European imperialism   279

12 Shifting categorisations of Chinese migrants in Burma in
    the nineteenth and twentieth centuries   281
    MICHAEL W. CHARNEY

13 Revenue farming and the Chinese economy of colonial
    Southeast Asia   303
    CARL A. TROCKI

14 Towards a connected history of Asian Communism: the case of Sino-Vietnamese revolutionary overlaps 314
CHRISTOPHER E. GOSCHA

Bibliography 335
Index 373

Figures

3.1, 3.2, 3.3 Chinese porcelain and other treasures being transported by cart, displayed and used; details of manuscript paintings preserved in the Istanbul Album, Aqqoyunlu Tabriz, later fifteenth century   45–47

3.4 Jar decorated with qilin, phoenixes and peonies in underglaze cobalt blue. Early Ming period, second-half fourteenth century, likely reign of Hongwu (1368–98). Ht. 48 cm. From the collection of William Cummins formed in India 1864–83   48

3.5 Turkic nobleman with cloud collar robe, being offered wine from a blue-and-white porcelain ewer; detail of a manuscript painting from the Istanbul Album, Aqqoyunlu Tabriz, later fifteenth century   49

3.6 Fragment of a jar, Yuan polychrome and applied decoration in ogival cartouche, mid-fourteenth century. Recovered from the Java Sea, Indonesia   54

3.7 Yuan porcelain jar with underglaze copper red and cobalt blue and applied decoration. Jingdezhen, mid-fourteenth century, ht. 41.3 cm   55

3.8 Porcelain bowl with underglaze cobalt blue design of a pair of ducks in aquatic landscape. Yuan period, second-quarter of the fourteenth century. Excavated at the Tughlaq Palace of Firuz Shah Kotla, Delhi. Archaeological Survey of India, New Delhi   57

3.9 Porcelain bowl with lotus bloom scrolling and a band of lotus petal cartouches in underglaze cobalt blue. Yuan period, second-quarter of the fourteenth century. Excavated at the Tughlaq Palace of Firuz Shah Kotla, Delhi. Archaeological Survey of India, New Delhi   58

3.10 Celebrations in honour of the birth of Humayun in the Chahar Bagh of Kabul (1508), depicting the Mughal emperor Babur and couriers dining from blue-and-white and greenware dishes. Folio from an illustrated edition of the *Baburnama*, the life of emperor Babur, commissioned by his grandson, Akbar, *c*.1590   59

3.11 Celadon dish with incised lotus bloom and scrolls. Yuan period, *c*.1350. Excavated at the Tughlaq Palace of Firuz Shah Kotla, Delhi. Archaeological Survey of India, New Delhi   62

Figures ix

3.12 Detail of a celadon dish glazed base with drilled *naskh* script inscription *matbah-e khas*, 'royal kitchen'. Yuan period, c.1350. Excavated at the Tughlaq Palace of Firuz Shah Kotla, Delhi. Archaeological Survey of India, New Delhi   63

3.13 Fragments of porcelain dishes with underglaze cobalt blue design, left with moulded monochrome cartouche, and right with cloud-collar lappet design. Yuan period, second-quarter of the fourteenth century excavated from Jingdezhen, Jiangxi (*After* Liu Xinyuan, 1999)   63

3.14 Detail of porcelain dish with reserved white-on-blue ground of four lappets ('cloud collar') design framing a central floral meander. Yuan period, second-quarter of the fourteenth century. Excavated at the Tughlaq Palace of Firuz Shah Kotla, Delhi. Archaeological Survey of India, New Delhi   64

3.15 Porcelain dish with underglaze cobalt blue design of eight-petalled medallion and reserved white lotus scroll with five blooms in the cavetto, Yuan period, second-quarter of the fourteenth century. Excavated at the Tughlaq Palace of Firuz Shah Kotla, Delhi. Archaeological Survey of India, New Delhi   64

3.16 Porcelain dish with underglaze cobalt blue design of a chrysanthemum surrounded sixteen auspicious motifs in lappets, reversed white moulded cavetto and wave pattern cusped rim. Yuan period, second-quarter of the fourteenth century   65

3.17 Porcelain dish with underglaze cobalt blue design of six-petalled medallion reserved in white-on-blue, enclosing circle with textile grid pattern, six cartouches in cavetto. Yuan period, second-quarter of the fourteenth century. Excavated at the Tughlaq Palace of Firuz Shah Kotla, Delhi. Archaeological Survey of India, New Delhi   65

3.18 Detail of porcelain dish with underglaze cobalt blue design of the auspicious Eight Buddhist Treasure in lotus petal cartouches imitative of metalwork (cf. Figure 3.19), with central medallion of a crane in flight, repeated in eight cartouches in cavetto. Yuan period, second-quarter of the fourteenth century. Excavated at the Tughlaq Palace of Firuz Shah Kotla, Delhi. Archaeological Survey of India, New Delhi   66

3.19 Cup stand decorated with the Eight Buddhist Treasures, silver with repoussé decoration. Yuan period, fourteenth century. Diam. 15.6 cm   66

3.20 Detail of porcelain dish with underglaze cobalt blue design of eight panelled design with floral motifs reserved in white-on blue, cusped edges imitative of metalwork. Yuan period, second-quarter of the fourteenth century. Excavated at the Tughlaq Palace of Firuz Shah Kotla, Delhi. Archaeological Survey of India, New Delhi   67

Figures

3.21 Detail of porcelain dish with underglaze cobalt blue design of moulded peony bloom and floral meanders reserved in white-on-blue hatched ground. Yuan period, second-quarter of the fourteenth century. Excavated at the Tughlaq Palace of Firuz Shah Kotla, Delhi. Archaeological Survey of India, New Delhi   67

3.22 Porcelain dish with underglaze cobalt blue design of two phoenix in flight amidst lotus and vines, repeated on the cavetto. Yuan period, second-quarter of the fourteenth century. Excavated at the Tughlaq Palace of Firuz Shah Kotla, Delhi. Archaeological Survey of India, New Delhi   68

3.23 Porcelain dish with underglaze cobalt blue design of an aquatic bird in garden landscape, with melon, grapevine and plantain; terrace wall in foreground. Yuan period, second-quarter of the fourteenth century. Excavated at the Tughlaq Palace of Firuz Shah Kotla, Delhi. Archaeological Survey of India, New Delhi   69

3.24 Porcelain dish with underglaze cobalt blue design of garden landscape of plantain, melon and grapevine. Yuan period, second-quarter of the fourteenth century. Excavated at the Tughlaq Palace of Firuz Shah Kotla, Delhi. Archaeological Survey of India, New Delhi   70

3.25 Detail of Figure 3.24, plantain and grapes. Archaeological Survey of India, New Delhi   71

3.26 Porcelain dish with underglaze cobalt blue design of a carp swimming amidst waterweed. Yuan period, second-quarter of the fourteenth century. Excavated at the Tughlaq Palace of Firuz Shah Kotla, Delhi. Archaeological Survey of India, New Delhi   72

3.27 Detail of Figure 3.26, tonal modelling of fish and pooling of cobalt in waterweed visible. Archaeological Survey of India, New Delhi   72

3.28 Detail of a porcelain dish with underglaze cobalt blue design of a mythical winged *qilin* amidst foliate landscape. Yuan period, second-quarter of the fourteenth century. Excavated at the Tughlaq Palace of Firuz Shah Kotla, Delhi. Archaeological Survey of India, New Delhi   73

3.29 Akbar receiving the Iranian ambassador Sayyif Beg. Right-hand folio from a double-page composition, from the *Akbarnama*. Composition by La'l, painting by Ibrahim Kahar, Mughal, *c.*1586–89. Gouache on paper; 30.8 × 19.1 cm   73

3.30 Wine ewers, monochrome white and underglaze cobalt blue. Early Ming – Yongle and Xuande periods – early fifteenth century. Excavated from the Zhushan Ming imperial kiln site, Jingdezhen, Jiangxi (*After* Liu Xinyuan, 1999)   75

3.31	Porcelain wine ewer with blue-and-white floral meander decoration. Xuande (1426–35), Jingdezhen. Inscribed and dated Shah Jahan AH 1038, equivalent to 1628	75
3.32	Detail of cartouche of Figure 3.31, inscribed in Persian *nasta'liq* script	76
3.33	Monk's cap ewer of white monochrome, Yongle period (1402–24), Jingdezhen. Inscribed in *nasta'liq* script the property of Shah Jahan and dated AH 1052, equivalent to 1643	77
3.34	Detail of ogival cartouche of Figure 3.33, inscribed in Persian *nasta'liq* script	78
3.35	Porcelain dish (so-called Mahin Banu dish), with underglaze cobalt blue grapes and vine design, Ming dynasty, Yongle (r. 1402–24). Jingdezhen, *c.*1420. Inscribed with a *vaqf* cartouche recording donation by (Princess) Mahin Banu to the Shrine of Ali al-Ridha, Mashad, Iran, and subsequently in *nasta'liq* script the property of Shah Jahan in AH 1053, equivalent to 1643	78
3.36	Detail of Iranian ownership inscriptions of base of Figure 3.35. The Shah Jahan inscription appears on the foot exterior	79
3.37	Detail of Shah Jahan inscription on the foot exterior of Figure 3.35	79
3.38	Porcelain dish with blue-and-white *qilin* design, Yuan dynasty, Jingdezhen, mid-fourteenth century. Inscribed in *nasta'liq* script the property of Shah Jahan and dated AH 1063, equivalent to 1653	80
3.39	Detail of inscription of Figure 3.38, inscribed in Persian *nasta'liq* script	80
10.1	The proportion of Chinese traders of all traders, 1682–1792	245

Tables

8.1	Activities of the outlaws of Lukui Mountain, 1671–1724	203
8.2	Han migrants massacred by Woni (6 and 7/ 04/ Yongzheng 5) (May 26 and 27 1727)	207
9.1	Trade model: China, Southeast Asia and India	222
9.2	Trade model with transaction cost: China, Southeast Asia and India	223
9.3	Chinese communities in Southeast Asia thirteenth–early seventeenth century	228
10.1	Spatial distribution of Chinese population in Melaka, 1677	244
10.2a	Base of operation of Chinese traders, 1682–1742	246
10.2b	Base of operation of Chinese traders, 1761–1792	247
10.3	Examples of merchant voyaging 1682–1742	249
10.4	Examples of merchant voyaging 1760–1792	250
10.5	Number of trips per trader	251
10.6	Types of vessels used in particular years	252
11.1	Remittances from Southeast Asia to China (via Hong Kong) in 1930	265
11.2	Period of arrival of Hokkien persons in Southern Vietnam	268
A11.1	Percentages of Chinese in Cochinchina and Cambodia in 1937	274

Contributors

Chang Pin-tsun received his Ph.D from the Department of East Asian Studies, Princeton University, in 1983. He returned to his native country of Taiwan, worked at the Research Center for the Humanities and Social Sciences, Academia Sinica, and taught at the Economics Department of National Taiwan University. He is interested in economic history, especially maritime economic history. He retired in August 2015.

Michael W. Charney is Professor of Asian and Military History, SOAS, the University of London. He is the author of three monographs, *Southeast Asian Warfare, 1300–1900* (Brill), *Powerful Learning: Buddhist Literati and the Throne in Burma's Last Dynasty* and *History of Modern Burma*. His research focuses on mainland Southeast Asia and West Africa in the areas of warfare, transportation, and mobile populations and their impact on religious, cultural, and ethnic formation in the precolonial and colonial periods.

James K. Chin is a professor and Deputy Dean at Research School of Silk Roads of Jinan University, China. He is also Vice President of China's Association for Maritime History Studies, and chief editor of *Haijiaoshi yanjiu* (*Journal of Maritime History Studies*). He worked at Xiamen University, National University of Singapore and the University of Hong Kong for more than thirty years and recently joined Jinan University. His research focuses on the maritime history of Asia and Chinese transnational migration and diaspora. He has published more than eighty scholarly journal articles and book chapters in the fields.

Christian Daniels was professor of Chinese history at the Research Institute for Languages and Cultures of Asia and Africa, Tokyo University of Foreign Studies from 1996 to 2014. He is now Professor and head of the Division of Humanities, Hong Kong University of Science and Technology. He has published in Chinese, Japanese and English on the history of Southwest China and northern Continental Southeast Asia. Recently he guest edited the 'Special Issue: Upland Peoples in the Making of History in Northern Continental Southeast Asia' for *Southeast Asian Studies* (Vol. 2, No. 1, April 2013) published by Kyoto University.

M. Radin Fernando received his early education in Sri Lanka, where he began his career as a lecturer in 1972. Following his graduate studies at Monash University, he became a researcher in the Research School of Pacific Studies at the Australian National University (1980–1994) and subsequently taught at University of Science Malaysia in Penang (1995–2001) and Nanyang Technological University in Singapore (2002–2011). He is now retired and continues his studies as a senior research fellow in the School of History at Monash University.

Christopher E. Goscha is associate professor of international history at the Université du Québec à Montréal. He has published widely on Southeast Asia and Vietnam. His primary interests focus on colonial Indochina and the wars for Vietnam. He has recently published, *Vietnam: Un Etat né de la guerre, 1945–1954* (2011) and is finishing the *Penguin History of Modern Vietnam* (2016). He teaches international relations and world history.

John Guy, FSA, is the Florence and Herbert Irving Curator of the Arts of South and Southeast Asia at The Metropolitan Museum of Art, New York, and an elected Fellow of the Society of Antiquaries, London and of the American Academy of Arts and Sciences. He was formerly Senior Curator of Indian Art at the Victoria and Albert Museum, London, and has served on the Councils of the European Associations of South Asia and Southeast Asian Archaeology and various editorial boards. He has worked on a number of archaeological excavations, both land and maritime sites, and served as an advisor to UNESCO on historical sites in Southeast Asia. Widely published, his most recent books are *Indian Temple Sculpture* (2007), *Wonder of the Age: Master Painters of India* (2011), and *Lost Kingdoms. Hindu-Buddhist Sculpture of Early Southeast Asia* (2014).

Li Tana is a visiting Senior Fellow of School of Culture, History and Language, College of Asia and Pacific Studies, the Australian National University. She is interested in the maritime history of Vietnam and the history of overseas Chinese. Her recent project is the environmental history of the Red River delta of the last 1000 years. Her works include *The Nguyen Cochinchina* (SEAP, Cornell, 1998), *Water Frontier* (Rowman and Littlefield, 2004, co-edited with Nola Cooke), *Tongking Gulf through History* (University of Pennsylvania Press, 2010, co-editors Nola Cooke and James A. Anderson); *Anthony Reid and the Study of the Southeast Asian Past*, co-edited with Geoff Wade (Institute of Southeast Asian Studies, Singapore, 2012).

Liao Dake is a professor at Nanyang (Southeast Asian) Research School of Xiamen University, China. He is also Vice President of China's Association for Maritime History Studies. His research interests include the maritime history of imperial China, history of Sino-foreign relations, and history of Overseas Chinese. He is the author of *Zhongguo gudai haiwai maoyi shi* (History of China's Maritime Trade, 1985, with LI Jinming) and *Fujian haiwai jiaotong shi* (Maritime History of Fujian, 2002), in addition to over fifty scholarly journal articles in Chinese.

Roderich Ptak has been Professor of Chinese in Heidelberg, then in Mainz-Germersheim and, since 1994, in Munich, where he is also chair of the Institut für Sinologie. He has been a Heisenberg scholar, and served as a visiting lecturer in Paris, Lisbon and Macau. His publications centre on maritime Chinese history, Macau, Chinese literature, and animals in Chinese texts.

Carl A. Trocki is a senior scholar of Southeast Asian history. He has published on the history and politics of Singapore, Malaysia, Thailand, the Chinese diaspora, and the drug trade in Asia. He has held appointments at Georgetown University in Washington, DC as the Jacobson Visiting Associate Professor in Southeast Asian History and the Queensland University of Technology as the Professor of Asian Studies. His recent books include *Opium, Empire and the Global Political Economy: A Study of the Asian Opium Trade, 1750–1950*, and *Singapore: Wealth, Power and the Culture of Control*, both by Routledge. He was also an editor of *Paths Not Taken: Political Pluralism in Postwar Singapore*, NUS Press. He is a member of the Australian Academy of the Humanities.

Geoff Wade is engaged in the study of Asian interactions, historical and contemporary, with a focus on China–Southeast Asia links. He is the creator of the online database *Southeast Asia in the Ming shi-lu* (www.epress.nus.edu.sg/msl/). Recent works include the six-volume collection *China and Southeast Asia* (Routledge, 2009) and *Asian Expansions: The Historical Experiences of Polity Expansion in Asia* (Routledge, 2015).

Danny Wong Tze Ken is Professor of History at the Department of History, Faculty of Arts and Social Sciences, University of Malaya where he teaches the history of Indochina and Southeast Asia. His research interests include the history of Vietnam, history of Sabah and the Chinese in Malaysia. Among his publications are: *The Chinese Overseas in Malaysia in an Era of Change* (co-edited, 2018), *The Diaries of G.C. Woolley, 1901–1907* (2015), *Vol. II: 1907–1913* (2016), *Vol. III: 1913–1919* (2018), *The Nguyen and Champa during 17th and 18th Century* (2007), and *The Transformation of an Immigrant Society: a Study of the Chinese of Sabah* (1998).

Acknowledgements

The editors wish to thank Professor Anthony Reid, Professor Wang Gungwu, Professor Wong Siu-lun, Deborah Chua, Jiang Na and Saharah Abubakar for their assistance in the production of this volume.

1 China and Southeast Asia

Historical interactions

Geoff Wade and James K. Chin

Introduction

The decline in the study of national histories over the last several decades has been mirrored by the growth in works which examine linkages between polities, societies and regions. Linkages, connections, interactions and flows across regions, continents and oceans have become the focus of new histories, in attempts to reveal the processes of change over the *longue durée* and the historical connectivities of peoples and societies beyond the borders of modern nation states. Even with the very contemporary political resurgence of stress on national borders, such writing has become necessary to explore and explain our increasingly collective condition and how we have arrived here. The histories of economic systems, trading networks, human movement, and the spread of ideas and religions – almost always involving interactions across national and imperial borders – have become key topics of research in new historical writing, as have tracts on ecological and environmental histories.

The avenues through which such studies have been pursued go under various names – depending on scope – and include "world history" "global history", or "transnational history",[1] "connected history",[2] "shared history", "regional history", "transcultural history",[3] and most recently "entangled history" (*histoire croisée*).[4] These terms often overlap, however, in terms of the scope over which they engage, and the types of stories they tell.

The Mediterranean world, for example, is a sphere where regional histories have burgeoned and brought fame to various scholars, including particularly Fernand Braudel.[5] The stress which Braudel assigned to geographical time, to the sea and to the long-term social, economic, and cultural historical processes, created a new form of history in which interactions across regions assumed an importance as great as events within individual polities. Studies of the interactions which constituted the Atlantic world[6] and the Indian Ocean world[7] have also now been steadily incorporated into scholarly debate and teaching. Further, in a related phenomenon, with the aim of reversing the current trend towards increasingly shorter periods being examined in historical studies, Jo Guldi and David Armitage have laid out in *The History Manifesto*, the range of reasons for – and indeed desirability of – the new attention being paid to longer-term histories.[8]

In comparison to studies of the Mediterranean, the Atlantic and the Indian Ocean "worlds", far fewer studies have been conducted on the interconnected maritime (or indeed other) realms in East and Southeast Asia, where the Pacific Ocean meets the East China Sea, the Sea of Japan, the South China Sea and, through it, the Indian Ocean. Cultural links, trading networks, human movements, and political aspirations have linked these regions for millennia. While there have been some efforts to describe this maritime realm as an "Asian Mediterranean", not all are convinced of the validity of the comparison.[9]

While studies of the interconnectedness of East Asia[10] through maritime connections are not absent, the realm has certainly not been as fully treated as other areas of the globe. Some works addressing this sphere have taken China as the key element of a realm where the maritime is but periphery,[11] while others have deliberately focused on interactions across a maritime realm where China is one of several bordering polities.[12]

The obvious deficiencies of studying Asian pasts solely through nation-state perspectives have been widely examined and need not be underlined here. In many ways, regional studies might also be criticized for the same deficiencies, albeit writ large. What then validates a collection such as the current volume, which examines historical interactions simply between the regions we today know as China and Southeast Asia? Why is such a range of relations informative beyond either more limited or larger rubrics of study? As in most history-writing, the period in which we live provides the context. In our current age – post-colonial and post-Cold War – global relations remain in rapid flux and the interactions between the People's Republic of China and the states of Southeast Asia in the early 21st century are undergoing profound change, perhaps one of the most intense reorderings occurring anywhere in the world today. It is thus that the historical contexts of these relations command our attention.

The regions which we today know as China and Southeast Asia have, for millennia, been linked through a wide range of political, economic, and social interactions. From the earliest times, the two regions have been tied by human movement, commercial interactions and political aspirations, and been woven together through technological and cultural interflows. However, the patterns by which these aspects were manifested have varied enormously over time. In recent centuries we saw the links being again repatterned, initially by the expansion of European mercantile interests and imperialist powers into both these regions, and subsequently by the revolutions which occurred and the regimes which emerged in twentieth-century Asia during decolonization. Today, in the early decades of the twenty-first century, the situation is undergoing change again, as we witness a resurgent China, a divided Association of Southeast Asian Nations (ASEAN), new capital resources, powerful external forces acting on both regions, and global ecological and technological changes which affect us all.

The essential importance of contemporary China–Southeast Asia relations and their genealogies requires us to reverse the neglect which the study and cognizance of intra-Asian historical links have suffered as a result of the creation of several political and intellectual borders. The first is the entrenchment, between the sixteenth and the nineteenth centuries, of the political borders between China and areas to the south of China which we today refer to as Southeast Asia,[13] as the latter became politically subject to (or, in the case of Siam, greatly influenced by) European empires. The nineteenth-century establishment of British control of Upper Burma, and French control of Northern Vietnam and Laos, saw a firming of this political boundary between China (during the nineteenth century included in the Qing empire) and the Southeast Asian polities, and in fact bequeathed to us many of the modern boundaries of the nation-states of today. These political boundaries have been a major obstacle to the study and understanding of the historical links which had long tied and transcended the two regions. They have also, through the "area studies" field of scholarship, which developed in Western societies in the nineteenth and the twentieth centuries, resulted in two distinct fields of scholarship – Chinese studies (Sinology) and Southeast Asian studies, the latter usually subdivided into the fields delimited by the various colonial (and then nation state) administrations.

In some ways, however, even the dichotomy represented when we speak of "China" vis-à-vis "Southeast Asia" is somewhat misleading given the modernity of the definitions and borders assigned to the terms. Areas of what is today southern China were long parts of a larger "Southeast Asian" world, with the speakers of Tai and Austroasiatic languages having emerged in areas south of the Yangzi River, regions now considered parts of "China".[14] The processes by which these areas "became China" are an element of the larger story told by some of the essays contained within this collection.

That said, this collection is intended to help describe and define the evolution of the China–Southeast Asia nexus relationships which have been such an integral element in connecting both Northeast Asia and Southeast Asia with other parts of the world through time. By examining the modes and forms by which Chinese polities and societies interacted with their Southeast Asian counterparts, and vice versa, through approximately the last 1,000 years, we can perhaps begin to understand some of the contexts of contemporary East Asian relations. While the essays presented in this volume cannot of course provide a comprehensive history of China–Southeast Asia historical interactions, they will provide readers with a useful range of vignettes which plot points on the overall graph of these interactions.

If we are to classify the interactions which have tied the regions we today term China and Southeast Asia, we might employ five general categories, and it is within these categories that the chapters contained within the volume can be introduced.

1 *Economic interactions* have always been key in the relations between Southeast Asia and China. These ranged from trade in diverse products and commodities through to remittance transfers, and included economic activities extending from primary agricultural production and mining to the financing of revolutions.

Roderich Ptak's contribution to this volume, which examines the role of Hainanese ports as major entrepôts linking Southeast Asian and East Asian traders, reflects the importance of intermediate ports in facilitating maritime trade between these two regions. It carries forward Ptak's earlier studies of ports and navigation routes connecting China and Southeast Asia.[15] The relationships between port and polity in Southeast Asia has also been examined by Kathirithamby-Wells and Villiers,[16] while Mills[17] and Manguin[18] have contributed valuable studies on the maritime trade routes connecting these regions.

The economic roles of ethnic Chinese persons in Southeast Asian societies have been topics of much research over more than a century.[19] However, few scholars have addressed the issue as directly as Chang Pin-tsun who has contributed an essay to this volume on the rise of Chinese mercantile power in maritime Southeast Asia between 1400 and 1700. He sees this process as developing after the decline of the dominance of the South and West Asians in Southeast Asian commerce, which extended up until the end of the fourteenth century, and lasting until the emergence of the maritime dominance of the Dutch in the region from the seventeenth century. James Chin Kong's doctoral thesis on the Hokkiens[20] also provides a useful overview of the development of Hokkien communities abroad during this period, while both the Tagliacozzo and Chang collection[21] and the volume edited by Wang and Ng[22] offer a wide range of studies on the activities of Chinese persons in Southeast Asia and their roles in the economic links between that region and China.

The trade goods which flowed between the ports of Southeast Asia and China are perhaps some of the best recorded aspects of the economic links between these regions. Paul Wheatley's study of such trade goods during the tenth–thirteenth centuries[23] remains a key work for studying the commodities traded during this period. Later trade goods are detailed by Stephen Chang Tseng-hsin using listings in Zhang Xie's 張燮 *Dongxiyang kao* 東西洋考 of 1618.[24]

One of the foremost categories of trade goods traded out of China in commercial quantities from at least the Song period was ceramics. Almost all archaeological sites across Southeast Asia bear evidence of the range and quantity of Chinese ceramics imported into Southeast Asia over the last 1,000 years.[25] John Guy offers to this volume a paper which looks at the export of Chinese ceramics to the sultanates of early Islamic India over the fourteenth–seventeenth centuries, primarily through Southeast Asian ports which were closely tied to the subcontinental Islamic polities. Guy explores why the Indian subcontinent never provided a mass market for Chinese ceramics in the way that Southeast Asia clearly did, and instead saw select consumption of high quality wares at a succession of Indian courts.[26]

The period following European colonization of various Southeast Asian polities and some China coast port cities was marked by European colonial administrations adopting many pre-colonial practices. One of these was the practice of sub-contracting tax collection to private operators, through farming out monopolies over commodities, a practice the British termed "revenue farming".[27] Carl Trocki's contribution to this volume explores the opium revenue farms under British-controlled colonies in Southeast Asia and Southern China.[28] He examines acculturalized Southeast Asian Chinese (Baba/Peranakan) families and individuals who played a key role as compradors between the colonial administrators and the local populations and who acquired most of the revenue farms available in the Straits Settlements.[29] This study investigates the growing links between the Singapore, Saigon and Hong Kong opium farm holders in the second half of the nineteenth century and how Penang and Singapore Chinese persons continued to be involved in the opium farms of Hong Kong and the China coast treaty ports right into the early twentieth century. Again the intimate links between economic activities in Southeast Asia and southern China are underscored.

2 The *political interactions* between China and Southeast Asia constitute another key aspect of the relationships between these two regions, encompassing diplomatic engagement, military endeavours, political influence and empire extension.

Pre-modern political relations between China and Southeast Asia remains a debated sphere. A range of scholars including John King Fairbank,[30] Wang Gungwu,[31] Hamashita Takeshi,[32] David Kang[33] and David Shambaugh[34] argue for the "Chinese tribute system" as having institutionalized a benevolent if hierarchical inter-state order in East Asia. An insightful critique of this acceptance of Chinese traditional rhetoric – of the idea that "because of its Confucian culture, China has not behaved aggressively toward others throughout history" – is provided by Wang Yuan-kang.[35] Contrasting Confucian pacifism with cultural realism and structural realism, Wang examines imperial China's realpolitik behaviour and concludes that "Ming China's Confucian culture did not constrain its decisions to use force", that "structural realism provides a better explanation of Chinese strategic behaviour than Confucian pacifism does", and that "the presence of the tribute system did not translate into peaceful interstate relations".[36] Regardless of the interpretation one adopts, it is clear that political interactions between the polities of Southeast Asia and of China extended long before the modern era.

Liao Dake offers a study in this volume which examines interactions between the Melakan sultanate, the Ming court and the Portuguese who had attacked and occupied Melaka (Malacca) in 1511. Noting how the deposed Melakan ruler had sought assistance from China following his flight, the work records Chinese reactions to these events beyond its borders and to the arrival of Portuguese envoys in Ming China. Liao assigns the failure of China to militarily respond to the Portuguese occupation of Melaka to dynastic decline, the later Ming's retreat from the sea and a general ineptitude in Ming foreign policy making. This study is unusual in that, while we have works which examine Melaka-Ming relations,[37] Portuguese-Ming links[38] and Portuguese-Melaka relations,[39] there are few studies like this which examine the triangular relationship.

Overall political relations between China and the states of Southeast Asia are explored more broadly in Geoff Wade's chapter in this volume. It comprises a chronological review of the policies pursued in respect of Southeast Asian polities by successive Ming emperors, and examines their effects on Southeast Asia through changes in Southeast Asia's political, economic, technological and cultural topographies.[40]

It is clear that nascent and developing polities in Southeast Asia often pursued relations with Chinese courts, and several essays within this volume look at some of these political interactions between Southeast Asian and East Asian polities. Danny Wong Tze Ken offers here a chapter which examines the emergence of the Nguyễn polity in southern Vietnam, the perceived role of Chinese courts as a source of authority and legitimation, and the role of Guangdong officials as frequent mediators in the interactions.[41]

James Chin examines another Southeast Asian polity, the new Thai state which was established by Taksin in the late eighteenth century, and its relations with the Qing court,[42] as well as with the Mạc polity of Ha-tien,[43] the descendants of the Ayudhyan court, and the Burmese polity. This is a truly novel and revealing study which demonstrates how wide were the diplomatic links of the polities of mainland Southeast Asia, and how frequently they engaged with the Qing court through Overseas Chinese intermediaries.[44] It is also a useful study for examining how the Qing court used the Thai polity to pursue its political aims in Burma.[45]

A different form of political interaction between the Manchu Qing state and Southeast Asian polities is investigated by Christian Daniels in his chapter. Looking at the changes which occurred among northern Southeast Asian polities, and especially Tai polities, during the seventeenth and eighteenth centuries, Daniels explores the processes by which the Qing expanded their control over polities on their southern borders. In particular, he looks at the expanding *gaitu guiliu* 改土歸流 process in Sipsong Panna under E'ertai in the 1720–30s, launching "the polity on the path towards full absorption into the Chinese state, a long journey that did not end until the 1950s".[46]

Bringing the volume into the modern era is Christopher Goscha's study of the interactions between Chinese and Vietnamese communism as part of a broader interrogation of the transnational nature of early Asian communism. His contribution overtly manifests the intent of this volume, to encourage scholars to explore histories beyond national boundaries. He does this by demonstrating "how regional linkages flowing out of the 'pre-colonial period' continued to exist in the late 19th and right into the 20th century", and how such links are crucial to understanding the present relations between Northeast and Southeast Asia.[47]

3 *Human movement* marks many of the interactions between the two regions, with traders, entrepreneurs, labourers, migrants, military personnel and others moving between the two areas. Almost all of the contributions to this volume address this issue to varying degrees, generally examining the flow of Chinese person into Southeast Asia. Chang Pin-tsun's chapter, for example, looks at factors such as population pressure in China, economic opportunities overseas, shipping technologies, maritime prohibitions, and Zheng He's voyages, as elements in the rise of an ethnic Chinese diaspora in Southeast Asia. Danny Wong's chapter also looks at the role of the Nguyễn rulers in facilitating the settlement of migrants from China within their realm, particularly following the end of Ming rule in China. Some of these persons went on to serve the Nguyễn court and, as James Chin shows, persons of Chinese descent such as Taksin assumed even the highest levels of political power in some Southeast Asian polities.

The activities of Chinese persons who moved to Southeast Asia are the subject of several of the contributions within this volume. Radin Fernando brings together the results of his decades of researching the Harbourmaster's records of Dutch Melaka over the seventeenth and eighteenth centuries.[48] By extracting from this collection – one of the largest archives on maritime trade in Southeast Asia over this period – the materials relating to Chinese traders, Fernando provides a valuable vignette of Chinese maritime operators trading through the port of Melaka. Li Tana's chapter, under the title of "Cāng hǎi sāng tián" 滄海桑田, which is a Chinese idiom referring to great changes occurring through time, examines the evolution of Chinese communities in Vietnam, particularly in the Mekong delta region from the seventeenth to early nineteenth centuries, in the context of the Southeast Asian "water frontier".[49] This story connects with movements of Chinese persons to and from Batavia, Bangka, the Philippines, Cambodia, Siam and Terengganu based on an examination of Hokkien genealogies, Nguyễn chronicles, Minh Hương materials and European works.

The ways in which Chinese immigrant communities were categorized within a European colonial regime in Southeast Asia is the subject of the contribution by Michael Charney.[50] Within the chapter, the growing awareness among colonial officials of differences among Chinese persons of diverse origins is examined. The evolution of British perceptions of Overseas Chinese in Lower Burma, as well as the Overland Chinese in Upper Burma, as economic tools to assist British expansion, provides a useful focus on the new European forces which were mediating relations between Southeast Asia and China during the nineteenth century.

4 *Technological flows* have long been another key aspect of relations between China and Southeast Asia, often coextensive with human flows. Three spheres which provide useful vignettes of such transfers are ship-building, firearms and ceramic technologies. Southeast Asian and Chinese ship-building traditions have been detailed by Manguin[51] and Needham[52] respectively, while Manguin has also looked at the cross-influences between the Southeast Asian and Chinese shipbuilding traditions, and posits a hybrid South China Sea junk as resulting from interflow between the two traditions.[53] Reid has also examined the role of hybrid ship-building in the broader scope of Sino-Javanese shipping.[54] In this volume, Danny Wong notes that ship-building was a Chinese specialty in southern Vietnam. The confession made by Li Wenguang to Qing officers in 1756 mentions that he went to Huế in 1744 with some friends to trade Chinese medicine, but soon they were sent to Đồng Nai to do logging and ship-building for the Nguyễn lord. One of the newly discovered Minh Hương materials from Vĩnh Long lists the names of 31 heads of this Chinese community from 1783 to 1847, and describes certain tasks carried out by each of them. Among the duties of the Chinese were tailoring robes for the officers, and ship-building and ship repairing.

One of the most original recent theses of Chinese influence on Southeast Asia during the fifteenth century is that of Sun Laichen, who has posited that Ming China greatly affected Southeast Asian historical trajectories through the introduction of firearms.[55] He has concluded that "the founding of the Ming dynasty in 1368 started the 'military revolution' not only in Chinese but also world history in the early modern period". These weapons were certainly used in the Ming wars against the Vietnamese and the Tai polities in the fifteenth century and were particularly effective against the elephants which the Tai relied upon. Sun sees a significant transfer of Chinese military technology (specifically firearms) to the Vietnamese in the early Ming, particularly through the Ming occupation of the Việt polity. Subsequently, he suggests, the Vietnamese used this new technology to mount major military expeditions in the 1470s, into Champa, and then across through the Tai heartlands as far as the Irrawaddy. The adoption of firearms by most major Southeast Asian traditions followed soon thereafter. Similarly, in later centuries, as noted by Michael Charney in this volume, the Chinese whom the Burmese settled at Bassein were "made to manufacture gunpowder and fireworks".

Chinese ceramics have been major products traded into Southeast Asia for well over a millennium. The obvious appeal of Chinese ceramics to the rulers and markets of Southeast Asia both before and during the early Ming, frequently gave rise to imitators within the region. The Si Satchanalai and Sukothai celadons of the fourteenth and fifteenth centuries appear to have drawn from Chinese ceramic technologies, as did Vietnamese wares of the fourteenth and fifteenth centuries.[56] Sharon Wong Wai-yee's recent thesis on the connectivities between the Guangdong and Khmer ceramic traditions[57] also shows clearly how Chinese and Southeast Asian technologies interacted, reflecting "technological choices and cross-craft interaction between Khmer and Chinese ceramic production".

5 *Cultural flows* constituted yet another aspect of interaction, whereby linguistic influences, food, religious beliefs and other aspects of social practice also travelled with people who moved between these regions.

The direct political interventions mentioned above brought with them intense cultural influence. During the Ming occupation of Đại Việt in the first quarter of the fifteenth century, for example, the Ming introduced to Vietnamese society a wide range of practices which changed society in diverse ways. John Whitmore has discussed a number of these.[58] The establishment of Confucian schools, as well as geomancy schools and medical schools in the Ming colony would certainly have had some impact on the population. However, it was the overall Ming administrative structure and procedures which existed for these 20 years, along with the presence of a huge number of Chinese persons which would have had most effect in changing society. However, whether all of the Ming policies – including the proposal during the occupation that the Vietnamese should adopt Chinese mourning customs[59] – actually had long-lasting effect on the society is an issue which needs to be subject to much further study.

But much Chinese social influence in societies beyond China was not state-sponsored. Rather it was effected by Chinese persons who moved to Southeast Asia. Certainly, the use of Chinese languages would have increased in the major port cities of Southeast Asia from the fifteenth century onwards. The adoption of Chinese terms for a range of food and other daily products in many of the major languages of the archipelago has also been a continuing process since then. Kong Yuanzhi has done much work on identifying Chinese lexical items borrowed into

Malay and Indonesian,[60] while Russell Jones has also made a valuable contribution through his study of Chinese borrowings in Indonesian.[61] However, determining the periods during which such borrowings were made is nigh impossible.

The spread of religions across Southeast Asia has also involved Chinese actors. The role of the Zheng He voyages in the early fifteenth century, and Chinese Muslims more generally, as being carriers of Islam throughout Southeast Asia is a topic which has continued to attract attention.[62] Many of the members of the eunuch commanders' retinues were Muslims and their voyages to the Middle East are likely to have also involved the *hajj* pilgrimage. The Parlindungan/Poortman text,[63] which appears to be derived at least in part from Chinese local accounts in Java, claims that there was a network of Chinese Hanafi Muslims throughout Southeast Asia in the fifteenth century, and that this network, which had emerged from the Zheng He voyages, established the first Islamic communities in Palembang, Sambas and in various ports along the north coast of Java. It seems wise to concur with Reid's opinion that "More systematic work needs to be done, however, before [the Parlindungan/Poortman text] can be accepted as a credible source for the fifteenth century".[64]

The role of Chinese monks in the southward spread of Mahayana Buddhism is also engaged with in some of the studies in this volume. Danny Wong's study makes reference to Nguyễn Phúc Trăn (r. 1687–1691), a pious Buddhist, who promoted the religion in what is today southern Vietnam by inviting Buddhist monks from China. The role of the Chinese monk Da Shan in spreading Chinese variants of Buddhism to the area around the Mekong delta is also examined.

The rise of Sino-Southeast Asian societies as a result of fairly large-scale migration of Chinese persons to Southeast Asia from the fifteenth century, with the consequent creation of hybrid food, hybrid languages and hybrid cultural expression has been discussed elsewhere by Reid.[65] He notes the marked contrast between Ma Huan's account of Java in the early fifteenth century, which describes influential Chinese and Sino-Javanese communities, with the picture given by the Portuguese a century later. The Portuguese authors reported no resident Chinese or Sino-Southeast Asian communities of substance in Java. Reid suggests that:

> the Ming abandonment of state trading and progressive loss of interest in tribute after the 1430s, left Chinese communities little alternative than assimilation, while Islam provided a bond for the new identities being formed in the maritime cities.... The reabsorption of this creatively syncretic and newly Muslim element into a modern middle-Javanese identity was a long story of the sixteenth and early seventeenth centuries.[66]

Li Tana's chapter also posits acculturation as one of the reasons for the apparent disappearance of Chinese from southern Vietnam.

It appears that Chinese weights and measures also had some impact in the archipelago. In 1404, an envoy from Siam to the Ming court requested that Chinese "weights and measures be conferred upon them".[67] Is there any evidence of subsequent changes to Southeast Asian metrological standards? This is difficult to assess, but business interactions certainly affected the weights and measures being used in Southeast Asia. In the middle of the sixteenth century, in a Portuguese text of 1554, we read that "In Malacca the weight used for gold, musk, &c., the *cate*, contains 20 *taels*, each tael 16 *mazes*, each maz 20 cumduryns; also 1 paual 4 mazes, each maz 4 *cupongs*; each cupong 5 cumduryns".[68] The "cate" and "tael" are the Malay terms for the Chinese *jin* (斤) and *liang* (兩) respectively.

The centuries of Sino-Southeast Asian interactions which are sketched within this volume, comprise a huge range of diverse phenomena but also a number of constancies. First, the sources on which our reconstructions have had to be based, particularly pre-1500, are far more often Chinese than Southeast Asian. This obviously conditions how we see and can represent these pasts. In a more concrete vein, the massive cultural, technological and economic strengths of successive Chinese states have frequently provided capacities for extensions – political and economic – to the south, whereas one of the very few examples of a cultural "push" northwards from Southeast Asia was that provided by the spread of Theravada Buddhism into what is today Southern China. Human flows have also generally been southward, with more Chinese persons settling in Southeast Asian realms than vice versa. This phenomenon has, throughout time, been partly driven by economic imperatives and, on occasions, by political maelstroms in China. Migration of Southeast Asians to China has generally been less significant. The histories of Vietnamese persons and their roles in Chinese societies in both the fifteenth and twentieth centuries as described within these pages are examples of such northwards human movement. The nature of trade goods flows between the two regions is another constant characteristic. The pattern has, until today, mainly involved raw or unprocessed materials being shipped northwards to China, and manufactured commodities being traded south. Capital flows are more recent and are less easy to characterize, with massive Southeast Asian investments flowing into China in the decades following Deng Xiaoping's reform and opening up from the early 1980s.[69] In 2017, Singapore was the largest foreign investor in China. Since 2013, large amounts of capital have also flowed from China to Southeast Asia[70] under President Xi Jinping's externally-oriented agenda known as the "One Belt, One Road" or "Belt and Road Initiative", whereby the Chinese state is attempting to create economic corridors across Eurasia, one maritime and one overland.[71]

How useful is the past for understanding the many changes now taking place in both Southeast Asia and China, and the links that are binding these places ever closer? The modernity which has already appeared in – or is in the process of visiting itself upon – all the societies of Northeast and Southeast Asia, along with the ever-evolving technologies, will undoubtedly produce many new modes of interaction between these regions. Some of the current interactions are cooperative, while others such as the intense disputes over suzerainty in the South China Sea are obviously competitive.[72] Examining and comprehending the many facets involved in the historical processes which have linked these two regions will, it is hoped, provide contexts for, or otherwise illumine, aspects of the contemporary and future relations between China and Southeast Asia.

Notes

1 With precursors including Arnold Toynbee's *A Study of History* (Oxford: Oxford University Press, 1934–39); William McNeill's *The Rise of the West: A History of the Human Community* (Chicago: University of Chicago Press, 1992 [1963]); and more recent volumes including Christopher Bayly's *The Birth of the Modern World, 1780–1914: Global Connections and Comparison* (Oxford: Blackwell, 2004); and Jürgen Osterhammel's *The Transformation of the World: A Global History of the Nineteenth Century* (Princeton: Princeton University Press, 2014). Pat Manning examined the historiography in *Navigating World History: Historians Create a Global Past* (New York: Palgrave Macmillan, 2003).
2 Such as the works by Sanjay Subrahmanyam, including *Explorations in Connected History: From the Tagus to the Ganges* (Delhi: Oxford University Press, 2004); and *Explorations in Connected History: Mughals and Franks* (Delhi: Oxford University Press, 2004).
3 Joachim Berger, Jennifer Willenberg, and Lisa Landes: "EGO | European History Online: A Transcultural History of Europe on the Internet", (Mainz: Institute of European History, 2010). www.ieg-ego.eu/introduction-2010-en.
4 Sönke Bauck and Thomas Maier, "Entangled History" (2015). www.uni-bielefeld.de/cias/wiki/e_Entangled_History.html.
5 Fernand Braudel, *La Méditerranée et le monde méditerranéen à l'époque de Philippe II*, 3 vols. (Paris: Armand Colin, 1949). An English translation by Sian Reynolds is available as *The Mediterranean and the Mediterranean World in the Age of Philip II*, 2 vols. (Berkeley: University of California Press, 1995).
6 Described in works including: Bernard Bailyn, *Atlantic History: Concept and Contours* (Cambridge Mass: Harvard University Press, 2005); Ida Altman, *Transatlantic Ties in the Spanish Empire: Brihuega, Spain, and Puebla, Mexico, 1560–1620* (Stanford: Stanford University Press, 2000); David Armitage and Michael J. Braddick, eds., *The British Atlantic World, 1500–1800* (Basingstoke: Palgrave Macmillan, 2002); Betty Wood and Martin Lynn, eds., *Travel, Trade and Power in the Atlantic, 1765–1884* (Cambridge: Cambridge University Press, 2003); and John K. Thornton, *Africa and Africans in the Formation of the Atlantic World, 1400–1680*, 2d expanded ed. (Cambridge: Cambridge University Press, 1998).
7 Represented by writings including: K.N. Chaudhuri, *Trade and Civilization in the Indian Ocean from the Rise of Islam to 1750* (Cambridge: Cambridge University Press, 1985); Philippe Beaujard, *Les Mondes de l'Océan Indien*, 2 volumes (Paris: Armand Colin, 2012); Ravi Palat, *The Making of an Indian Ocean World-Economy, 1250–1650: Princes, Paddy fields, and Bazaars* (New York: Palgrave Macmillan, 2015); Michael Pearson (ed.) *Trade, Circulation, and Flow in the Indian Ocean World* (New York: Palgrave Macmillan, 2015); Giancarlo Casale, *The Ottoman Age of Exploration* (Oxford: Oxford University Press, 2010); and Gwyn Campbell (ed.), *Early Exchange Between Africa and the Wider Indian Ocean World* (New York: Palgrave Macmillan, 2016).
8 Jo Guldi and David Armitage, *The History Manifesto* (Cambridge: Cambridge University Press, 2014).
9 See Heather Sutherland, "Southeast Asian History and the Mediterranean Analogy", *Journal of Southeast Asian Studies*, Vol. 34, No. 1 (February 2003), pp. 1–20; François Gipouloux, *The Asian Mediterranean: Port Cities and Trading Networks in China, Japan and Southeast Asia, 13th–21st Century*, translated by Jonathan Hall and Dianna Martin (Cheltenham and Northampton, MA: Edward Elgar Publishing, 2011); and the various essays in Angela Schottenhammer (ed.), *The East Asian Mediterranean: Maritime Crossroads of Culture, Commerce and Human Migration* (Wiesbaden: Harrassowitz Verlag, 2008).
10 Referring collectively to the regions generally known as Southeast Asia and Northeast Asia.

11 Wang Gungwu and Ng Chin-keong (ed.), *Maritime China in Transition 1750–1850* (Wiesbaden: Harrassowitz, 2004); Xing Hang, *Conflict and Commerce in Maritime East Asia: The Zheng Family and the Shaping of the Modern World*, c.*1620–1720* (Cambridge: Cambridge University Press, 2015); Li Kangying, *The Ming Maritime Trade Policy in Transition, 1368 to 1567* (Wiesbaden: Harrassowitz, 2010); Roderich Ptak, *China's Seaborne Trade with South and Southeast Asia, 1200–1750* (Aldershot: Ashgate, 1999).

12 Angela Schottenhammer (ed.), *The East Asian Maritime World 1400–1800: Its Fabrics of Power and Dynamics of Exchanges* (Wiesbaden: Harrassowitz, 2007); Fujita Kayoko, Momoki Shiro, and Anthony Reid (ed.), *Offshore Asia: Maritime Interactions in Eastern Asia Before Steamships* (Singapore: Institute of Southeast Asian Studies, 2013); Tonio Andrade and Xing Hang (ed.), *Sea Rovers, Silver, and Samurai: Maritime East Asia in Global History, 1550–1700* (Honolulu: University of Hawaii Press, 2016); Geoffrey Gunn, *History Without Borders: The Making of an Asian World Region, 1000–1800* (Hong Kong: Hong Kong University Press, 2011).

13 For a description of the process by which the name "Southeast Asia" came to be used and applied, see Donald Emmerson, "Southeast Asia–What's in a Name?", *Journal of Southeast Asian Studies* Vol. 15, No. 1 (1984): 1–21.

14 Wang Gungwu has distinguished modern "Southeast Asia" from an earlier "Southeastern Asia", which included modern South China. See his *The Nanhai Trade: Early History of Chinese Trade in the South China Sea* (Singapore: Eastern Universities Press, 2003), p. 4, Map 1. Christian Daniels, following Shintani Tadahiko (新谷忠彥), speaks of the region extending from northern Southeast Asia into Southern China as the "Tai Cultural Area". Sun Laichen posits a region which he calls "Northern Mainland Southeast Asia" in "Military Technology Transfers from Ming China and the Emergence of Northern Mainland Southeast Asia", *Journal of Southeast Asian Studies* Vol. 34, No. 3 (2003). pp. 495–517, while Yang Bin writes of this region as part of a "Southern Silk Road" (Yang Bin, "Horses, Silver, and Cowries: Yunnan in Global Perspective" *Journal of World History*, Vol. 15, No. 3, September 2004, pp. 281–322. Wilhelm G. Solheim II, in his "'Southeast Asia:' What's in a Name, Another Point of View", *Journal of Southeast Asian Studies* XVI (1985), pp. 141–7 sees the Yangzi River as being the northern boundary marker for Southeast Asia. In the linguistic sphere, speakers of Austroasiatic and Tai languages extend across the China–Southeast Asia interface. Mei Tsu-lin and Jerry Norman have presented evidence for an Austroasiatic element in Hokkien, suggesting a former Austroasiatic presence in that region. See "The Austroasiatics in Ancient South China: Some Lexical Evidence", *Monumenta Serica* 32 (1976): pp. 274–301. Robert Bauer, meanwhile, has suggested that Cantonese has a Tai substratum. See R.S. Bauer, "Identifying the Tai substratum in Cantonese", in *The Fourth International Symposium on Language and Linguistics*, Thailand, Institute of Language and Culture for Rural Development, Mahidol University, 1996, pp. 1806–44.

15 See R. Ptak, "Die Paracel- und Spratly-Inseln in Sung-, Yüan- und frühen Ming-Texten: Ein maritimes Grenzgebiet?" in *China and Her Neighbours. Borders, Visions of the Other, Foreign Policy. 10th to 19th Century*, ed. Sabine Dabringhaus and R. Ptak, Wiesbaden: Harrassowitz Verlag, 1997, pp. 159–81; R. Ptak, "From Quanzhou to the Sulu Zone and Beyond: Questions Related to the Early Fourteenth Century", *Journal of Southeast Asian Studies*, Vol. 29, No. 2 (Sep. 1998), pp. 269–94; R. Ptak, "Yuan and Early Ming Notices on the Kayal Area in South India", *Bulletin de l'École Française d'Extrême-Orient 80* (1993), pp. 137–56; R. Ptak, "The Northern Trade Route to the Spice Islands: South China Sea-Sulu Zone-North Moluccas (14th to early 16th century)", *Archipel*, No. 43 (1992), pp. 27–56; and the various studies in R. Ptak, *China, the Portuguese, and the Nanyang: Oceans and Routes, Regions and Trade (c.1000–1600)* (Aldershot: Ashgate, 2004).

16 Jeyamalar Kathirithamby-Wells and John Villiers (ed.), *The Southeast Asian Port and Polity: Rise and Demise* (Singapore: Singapore University Press, 1990).
17 J.V.G. Mills, "Chinese Navigators in Insulinde About A.D. 1500", *Archipel*, 18 (1979), pp. 69–83; J.V.G. Mills, "Arab and Chinese Navigators in Malaysian Waters in about A.D. 1500", *Journal of the Malaysian Branch of the Royal Asiatic Society* Vol. 47, No. 2 (1974), pp. 1–82.
18 P.Y. Manguin, *Les Portugais sur les Côtes du Viêt-Nam et du Campá* (Paris: EFEO, 1972).
19 Including: Wang Gungwu, *Community and Nation: Essays on Southeast Asia and the Chinese* (Sydney: Published for the Asian Studies Association of Australia by Heinemann Educational Books (Asia) Ltd. and George Allen & Unwin, 1981); Wang Gungwu, *The Chinese Overseas: From Earthbound China to the Quest for Autonomy* (Cambridge, MA: Harvard University Press, 2000); Victor Purcell, *The Position of the Chinese in Southeast Asia* (New York: Institute of Pacific Relations, 1950); Victor Purcell, *The Chinese in Southeast Asia* (London: Oxford University Press, 1965); Yen Ch'ing-huang, *The Chinese in Southeast Asia and Beyond: Socioeconomic and Political Dimensions* (New Jersey: World Scientific Publishing, 2008); Zhu Jieqin 朱傑勤, *Dongnanya Huaqiao shi* 東南亞華僑史 [A History of the Overseas Chinese in Southeast Asia] (Beijing: Tertiary Education Publishers, 1990); Anthony Reid (ed.) *Sojourners and Settlers: Histories of Southeast Asia and the Chinese in Honour of Jennifer Cushman* (St Leonards, NSW: Allen & Unwin, 1996); C.P. Fitzgerald, *The Southern Expansion of the Chinese People: 'Southern Fields and Southern Ocean'* (Canberra: Australian National University Press, 1972); Jennifer W. Cushman and Wang Gungwu (ed.), *Changing Identities of the Southeast Asian Chinese since World War II* (Hong Kong: Hong Kong University Press, 1988); Henry Yeung Wai-Chung, *Chinese Capitalism in a Global Era: Towards Hybrid Capitalism* (London: Routledge, 2004); and Jomo Kwame Sundaram and Brian C. Folk (ed.) *Ethnic Business: Chinese Capitalism in Southeast Asia* (New York: Routledge, 2003).
20 James Chin Kong 錢江, "Merchants and Other Sojourners: the Hokkiens Overseas, 1570–1760". Ph.D. dissertation, University of Hong Kong, 1998.
21 Eric Tagliacozzo and Wen-chin Chang (ed.), *Chinese Circulations: Capital, Commodities, and Networks in Southeast Asia* (Durham: Duke University Press, 2011).
22 Wang Gungwu and Ng Chin-keong (ed.), *Maritime China in Transition 1750–1850* (Wiesbaden: Harrassowitz, 2004).
23 Paul Wheatley, "Geographical Notes on Some Commodities Involved in Sung Maritime Trade", *Journal of the Malayan Branch of the Royal Asiatic Society* Vol. 32, No. 2 (1959): pp. 1–140.
24 Chang Tseng-hsin, "Commodities Imported to the Chang-chou Region of Fukien During the Late Ming Period: A Preliminary Analysis of the Tax Lists Found in Tung-hsi-yang k'ao", in Roderich Ptak and Dietmar Rothermund (eds.), *Emporia, Commodities, and Entrepreneurs in Asian Maritime Trade, c.1400–1750* (Stuttgart: Steiner Verlag, 1991). pp. 159–194.
25 John Miksic, "Chinese Ceramic Production and Trade", *Oxford Research Encyclopaedia of Asian History*, (Oxford: Oxford University Press, June 2017). http://asianhistory.oxfordre.com/view/10.1093/acrefore/9780190277727.001.0001/acrefore-9780190277727-e-218.
26 This study carries forward Guy's earlier works on ceramics in Asian trade, including *Oriental Trade Ceramics in South East Asia: Ninth to Sixteenth Centuries* (Singapore: Oxford University Press, 1986) and his work on Southeast Asia as a vector of cultural and material transmission between South Asia and East Asia, including "Tamil Merchant Guilds and the Quanzhou Trade," in *The Emporium of the World: Maritime Quanzhou, 1000–1400*, ed. A. Schottenhammer (Leiden: Brill, 2001), pp. 283–317.
27 For a useful compendium of studies of these practices, see Howard Dick, Michael Sullivan and John Butcher (ed.), *The Rise and Fall of Revenue Farming: Business*

Elites and the Emergence of the Modern State in Southeast Asia (Basingstoke: Palgrave Macmillan, 1993).
28 Trocki's chapter carries forward his earlier work on this topic: C.A. Trocki, "The Internationalization of Chinese Revenue Farming Networks", in *Water Frontier: Commerce and the Chinese in the Lower Mekong Region, 1750–1880*, eds. N. Cooke and Li Tana (Singapore: Singapore University Press, 2004), pp. 159–173.
29 The earlier history of Straits Settlements revenue farms can be found in Wong Lin Ken, "The Revenue Farms of Prince of Wales Island, 1805–1830", *Journal of the South Seas Society*, Vol. 19, No. i (1964), pp. 56–127.
30 John King Fairbank, "A Preliminary Framework" in *The Chinese World Order: Traditional China's Foreign Relations*, ed. John King Fairbank (Cambridge, Mass.: Harvard University Press, 1968), pp. 1–19.
31 Wang Gungwu suggests that "The [tributary] system was never used for territorial expansion, only for extending influence and affirming China's interpretation of its central place in the universe". See Wang Gungwu, "China and Southeast Asia: Myths, Threats and Culture", EAI Occasional Paper No. 13 (Singapore: World Scientific, 1999), p. 32.
32 Hamashita, Takeshi, "The Tribute Trade System and Modern Asia", *Memoirs of the Research Department of the Toyo Bunko*, No 46 (1988), pp. 7–23.
33 David C. Kang, *East Asia Before the West: Five Centuries of Trade and Tribute* (New York: Columbia University Press, 2010).
34 "China does not have a significant history of coercive statecraft.... The tribute system may have been hegemonic, but it was not based on coercion or territorial expansionism." See David Shambaugh, "China Engages Asia: Reshaping the Regional Order", *International Security* Vol. 29, No. 3 (Winter 2004/05): pp. 64–99. See p. 95.
35 Wang Yuan-kang, *Harmony and War: Confucian Culture and Chinese Power Politics* (New York: Columbia University Press, 2010).
36 Wang Yuan-kang, *Harmony and War*, pp. 143, 179.
37 Wang Gungwu, "The Opening of Relations Between China and Malacca" in J.S. Bastin and R. Roolvink (eds) *Malayan and Indonesian Studies: Essays Presented to Sir Richard Winstedt* (Oxford: Clarendon Press, 1964), pp. 87–104; Wang Gungwu, "The First Three Rulers of Melaka", *Journal of the Malaysian Branch of the Royal Asiatic Society*, Vol. 41, No. 1 (July 1968b), pp. 11–22.
38 Chang T'ien-tse, *Sino-Portuguese Trade from 1514 to 1644: A Synthesis of Portuguese and Chinese Sources* (Leiden: Brill, 1934); Donald Ferguson, *Letters from Portuguese Captives in Canton, Written in 1534 and 1536: With an Introduction on Portuguese Intercourse with China in the First Half of the Sixteenth Century* (Bombay: Educ. Steam Press, Byculla, 1902); Geoff Wade, "The Portuguese as Represented in Some Chinese Sources of the Ming Dynasty" in *Portugal e a China. Conferências nos Encontros de História Luso-Chinesa*, ed. Jorge M. dos Santos Alves (Lisbon: Fundação Oriente, 2000).
39 Such as João Paulo de Oliveira e Costa and Vítor Luís Gaspar Rodrigues, *Campanhas de Afonso de Albuquerque: Conquista de Malaca, 1511* (Lisbon: Tribuna da Historia, 2011); Luís Filipe F. Reis Thomaz, *Nina Chatu and the Portuguese Trade in Malacca*, translated from the Portuguese by M.J. Pintado, with a foreword by A. Kalimuthu (Melaka: Luso-Malaysian Books, 1991); Luís Filipe F. Reis Thomaz, *Early Portuguese Malacca* (Macau: CTMCDP/IPM, 2000).
40 Related works include: Geoff Wade, "The Zheng He Voyages: A Reassessment", *Journal of the Malaysian Branch of the Royal Asiatic Society*, Vol. 77, No. 1 (2005), pp. 37–58; Geoff Wade, "Domination in Four Keys: Ming China and its Southern Neighbours 1400–1450" in Craig Clunas, Luk Yu-Ping & Jessica Harrison-Hall (ed.), *Ming China: Courts and Contacts 1400–1450* (London: British Museum Press, 2016).
41 Building on earlier work, including Chen Ching-ho, "Minh Hương Xa Village and Thanh Ha Pho in Thua Thien Province (Central Viet-Nam)", *The New Asia Journal*, Vol. 4, No. 1, (August 1959), pp. 305–329; Shiqiba shiji zhi Huian zhi Tangrenjie ji

qi Shangye <十七、十八世紀之會安唐人街及其商業> [The Chinese Town of Hoi An and its Trade During the 17th and 18th Centuries] *Xinya Xuebao* [*New Asia Journal*], Vol. 3, No. 1, (1960), pp. 273–332.

Nguyễn Thế Anh, "L'Immigration Chinoise et la Colonisation du Delta du Mékong", *The Vietnam Review*, No. 1 (Autumn–Winter 1996), pp. 154–177; and Li Tana, *Nguyễn Cochinchina: Southern Vietnam During the Seventeenth and Eighteenth Centuries* (Ithaca: Cornell University, Southeast Asian Program, 1998).

42 Which have also been explored by Sarasin Viraphol, *Tribute and Profit: Sino-Siamese Trade, 1652–1853* (Cambridge: Harvard University Press, 1977); and by Jennifer Cushman, *Fields from the Sea: Chinese Junk Trade with Siam During the Late Eighteenth and Early Nineteenth Centuries* (Ithaca: Cornell University, Southeast Asia Program, 1993).

43 This polity is examined in Chen Ching-ho 陳荊和, "Hexian Zhen Yezhen Mo shi jiapu zhushi 河仙鎮葉鎮鄭氏家譜注釋 [Notes on the Genealogy of the Mac Family from Hà Tiên]", *Wen Shi Zhe Xue Bao* (Bulletin of the College of Arts of Taiwan National University), No. 7 (1956), pp. 77–140.

44 See, for example, Dhiravat Na Pombejra, "Administrative and Military Roles of the Chinese in Siam during an Age of Turmoil, circa 1760–1782", *Maritime China in Transition 1750–1850*, ed. Wang Gungwu and Ng Chin-keong (Wiesbaden: Harrassowitz Verlag, 2004), pp. 335–354.

45 Also examined in Dai Yingcong, "A Disguised Defeat: The Myanmar Campaign of the Qing Dynasty", *Modern Asian Studies*, Vol. 38, No. 1 (2004), pp. 145–189.

46 Other studies which examine this process include Leo Shin, *The Making of the Chinese State: Ethnicity and Expansion on the Ming Borderlands* (Cambridge: Cambridge University Press, 2006); C. Patterson Giersch, *Asian Borderlands: The Transformation of Qing China's Yunnan Frontier* (Cambridge MA: Harvard University Press, 2006); John Herman, "The Cant of Conquest: Tusi Offices and China's Political Incorporation of the Southwest Frontier'", in Pamela Crossley, Helen Siu, and Donald Sutton, ed., *Empire at the Margins* (Berkeley: University of California Press, 2006), pp. 136–157; and the various contributions to James A. Anderson and John K. Whitmore (ed.), *China's Encounters on the South and Southwest: Reforging the Fiery Frontier* (Leiden: Brill, 2015).

47 Other Goscha works addressing similar trans-borders issues include *Thailand and the Southeast Asian Networks of the Vietnamese Revolution (1885–1954)* (London: Routledge/Curzon, 1999); and Christopher E. Goscha and Christian Ostermann (ed.), *Connecting Histories: Decolonization and the Cold War in Southeast Asia 1945–1962* (Stanford, Stanford University Press, 2009).

48 Buiding on earlier works including M.R. Fernando, "Early Settlers in the Land of Promise; Chinese Traders in the Malay Archipelago in the Seventeenth and Eighteenth Centuries" in Wang Gungwu and Ng Chin-keong (eds), *Maritime China in Transition 1750–1850* (Wiesbaden: Harrassowitz Verlag, 2004), pp. 227–244; and M.R. Fernando, "The Lost Archives of Melaka: Is It Really Lost?", *Journal of the Malaysian Branch of Royal Asiatic Society*, Vol. 78, No. 1 (2005), pp. 1–36.

49 For which see Nola Cooke and Li Tana (ed.), *Water Frontier: Commerce and the Chinese in the Lower Mekong Region, 1750–1880* (Lanham: Rowman & Littlefield Publishers, Inc. and Singapore University Press, 2004).

50 This extends his earlier studies on this topic including: Michael W. Charney, "Problematics and Paradigms in Historicizing the Overseas Chinese in the Nineteenth- and Twentieth-century Straits and Burma", *Journal of the South Seas Society*, Vol. 54 (1999), pp. 93–106; and Michael W. Charney, "Chinese Business in Penang and Tenasserim (Burma) in the 1820s: A Glimpse from a Vietnamese Travelogue", *Journal of the South Seas Society*, 55 (2002a), pp. 48–60.

51 See, for example, Pierre-Yves Manguin, "The Southeast Asian Ship: An Historical Approach", *Journal of Southeast Asian Studies*, Vol 11, No. 2 (1980): pp. 266–276; and

his "The Vanishing *Jong*: Insular Southeast Asian Fleets in Trade and War (Fifteenth to Seventeenth Centuries)", in Anthony Reid (ed.) *Southeast Asia in the Early Modern Era: Trade, Power and Belief* (Ithaca: Cornell University Press, 1993), pp. 197–213.

52 Joseph Needham, *Science and Civilization in China, Vol. 4, No. 3 – Civil Engineering and Nautics* (Cambridge: Cambridge University Press, 1971).

53 P.-Y. Manguin, "Relationships and Cross-influences between Southeast Asian and Chinese Shipbuilding Traditions", *SPAFA Final Report on Maritime Shipping and Trade Networks in Southeast Asia* (Bangkok: SPAFA Coordinating Unit, 1984).

54 Anthony Reid, "The Rise and Fall of Sino-Javanese Shipping" in Anthony Reid (ed.), *Charting the Shape of Early Modern Southeast Asia* (Chiang Mai: Silkworm Books, 1999), pp. 56–84.

55 See Sun Laichen "Chinese Military Technology and Dai Viet: c.1390–1497", Asia Research Institute Online Working Paper No. 11 (September 2003a), www.ari.nus.edu.sg/docs/wps/wps03_011.pdf.

56 See Roxanna M. Brown, *The Ceramics of South-East Asia, Their Dating and Identification* (Kuala Lumpur: Oxford University Press, 1977); John Guy, *Ceramic Traditions of South-East Asia* (Singapore: Oxford University Press, 1989); and Dick Richards, *South-East Asian Ceramics: Thai, Vietnamese, and Khmer, from the Collection of the Art Gallery of South Australia* (Kuala Lumpur: Oxford University Press, 1995). For an excellently illustrated collection of the Chinese blue and white wares and their Vietnamese equivalents, see Larry Gotuaco, Rita C. Tan and Allison I. Diem, *Chinese and Vietnamese Blue and White Wares Found in the Philippines* (Manila: Bookmark Inc. 1997).

57 Sharon Wong Wai-yee, "A Preliminary Study on some Economic Activities of the Khmer Empire: Examining the Relationship between the Khmer and Guangdong Ceramic Industries during the 9th–14th Centuries" PhD. dissertation, National University of Singapore, 2009. http://scholarbank.nus.edu.sg/handle/10635/17643.

58 See John Whitmore, *Vietnam, Hồ Quý Ly, and the Mîng (1371–1421)* (New Haven: Yale University Press, 1985).

59 *Taizong shilu*, juan 214.1b.

60 See Kong Yuanzhi 孔遠志, "Zhongguo yindunixiya wenhua jiaoliu" 中國印度尼西亞文化交流 [Cultural Exchanges between China and Indonesia], (Beijing: Beijing daxue chubanshe, 1999). The listing of borrowed lexical items can be seen on pp. 128–156.

61 Russell Jones, *Chinese Loan-Words in Malay and Indonesian. A Background Study* (Kuala Lumpur: Universiti Malaya, 2009).

62 See Geoff Wade, "Early Muslim Expansion in Southeast Asia, Eighth to Fifteenth Centuries" in David O. Morgan and Anthony Reid (eds.), *The New Cambridge History of Islam, Vol. 3: The Eastern Islamic World Eleventh to Eighteenth Centuries* (Cambridge: Cambridge University Press, 2010), pp. 366–408.

63 For which see H.J. de Graaf and Th. G. Th. Pigeaud (edited by M.C. Ricklefs), *Chinese Muslims in Java in the 15th and 16th Centuries* (Melbourne: Monash Papers on Southeast Asia, 1984).

64 Reid, "Rise and Fall of Sino-Javanese Shipping", p. 68.

65 See Reid, "Rise and Fall of Sino-Javanese Shipping"; and Anthony Reid, "Hybrid Identities in the Fifteenth-Century Straits of Malacca", Asia Research Institute Working Paper Series No. 67 (Singapore: Asia Research Institute, 2006). www.ari.nus.edu.sg/wps/wps06_067.pdf.

66 Reid, "Hybrid Identities", pp. 28–29.

67 *Taizong shilu*, juan 34.3a.

68 Henry Yule and A.C. Burnell, *Hobson Jobson: Glossary of Colloquial Anglo-Indian Words & Phrases, & of Kindred Terms Etymological, Historical, Geographical & Discursive*, New edition edited by William Crooke, Fourth edition (Delhi: Munshiram Manoharlal Publishers, 1984). See entry for 'Candareen', p. 155.

69 Krislert Samphantharak, "The Rise of China and Foreign Direct Investment from Southeast Asia", *Journal of Current Southeast Asian Affairs*, Vol. 30, No. 2 (2011): 65–75.
70 Avery Goldstein, "A Rising China's Growing Presence: The Challenges of Global Engagement", in Jacques Deslisle and Avery Goldstein (eds.), *China's Global Engagement: Cooperation, Competition, and Influence in the 21st Century* (Washington, D.C.: Brookings Institution Press, 2017), pp. 1–34; and Mark Grimsditch, "Chinese Agriculture in Southeast Asia: Investment, Aid and Trade in Cambodia, Laos and Myanmar" (Bangkok: Heinrich-Böll-Stiftung Southeast Asia, June 2017). https://th.boell.org/en/2017/06/22/chinese-agriculture-southeast-asia-investment-aid-and-trade-cambodia-laos-and-myanmar.
71 Peter Cai, "Understanding China's Belt and Road Initiative" (Sydney: Lowy Institute, 2017).
72 Jacques Delisle, "China's Territorial and Maritime Disputes in the South and East China Seas: What Role for International Law?" in Jacques Deslisle and Avery Goldstein (eds.), *China's Global Engagement: Cooperation, Competition, and Influence in the 21st Century* (Washington, D.C.: Brookings Institution Press, 2017), pp. 235–290; and Barthélémy Courmont, Frédéric Lasserre and Éric Mottet (eds.) *Assessing Maritime Disputes in East Asia: Political and Legal Perspectives* (Abingdon, Oxon: Routledge, 2017).

Part I
Trading relations

2 Hainan and its international trade
Ports, merchants, commodities (Song to mid-Ming)

Roderich Ptak

Introduction

Written sources on the early history of Hainan do not abound, which also means that information on Hainan's external trade and its links to Southeast Asia is scarce. It is only with the Song period (960–1279) that more data begin to appear. These materials are scattered in ethnographic accounts such as Zhou Qufei's 周去非 *Lingwai daida* (1178) and Zhao Rugua's 趙汝适 *Zhufan zhi* (1225), but are also found in more official works – for example, the dynastic annals of that dynasty, as well as the *Song huiyao jigao*, *Yudi jisheng*, *Taiping huanyu ji*, *Guihai yu heng zhi*, *Yuanfeng jiuyu zhi*, and so forth.[1] Further references are contained in literary sources, especially the poems by Su Shi 蘇軾, but they are not especially relevant to the history of Hainan's maritime trade. Yuan dynasty works are less detailed. Hainan is mentioned in the official annals and several other texts, but the picture one can draw of that period remains rather incomplete.

With the Ming dynasty more details become available. The earliest extant local gazetteer, the *Qiong tai zhi* 瓊台志 (hereafter *QTZ*) from the Zhengde period (1506–21), presents information on almost every aspect of Hainan's society. This includes local production, taxes, coastal defence, piracy, and other relevant matters. Foreign trade, however, is not adequately presented. The *QTZ* is partly based on earlier sources that have since been lost.[2] It influenced many later gazetteers, which often repeated the details found in this work. These later gazetteers are essential for our knowledge of the mid- and late-sixteenth century and the early Qing period for which they often provide original information. One such work is the 1561 edition of the *Guangdong tongzhi* (hereafter *GDTZ*). It looks at the entire province of Guangdong and also covers events in and around Hainan until the mid-sixteenth century.[3] Other Ming texts containing relevant data include the *Ming shilu* (hereafter *MSL*) and several chronologies of a similar nature, the Ming dynastic history, some geographic accounts, and certain other works.

Non-Chinese sources are also worth referencing. Medieval Persian and Arabic materials mention Hainan, but rarely go beyond that. Portuguese texts contain more details, although the early works – for example Fernão Mendes Pinto's *Peregrinação* – are often difficult to interpret. Later texts, mostly written by missionaries, are chiefly interested in religious matters.⁴ Spanish and Dutch sources must also be mentioned, although, as far as I know, no research has ever been made on how Hainan is presented in these texts. Vietnamese works, I believe, are more important for later periods, especially the Qing dynasty.⁵

In view of the existence of so many different materials, several of which have remained nearly untouched by Western scholars (one example being the *QTZ*), any survey of Hainan's foreign trade sector will, of course, remain incomplete. Indeed, this survey comes at an almost premature stage, as there is no up-to-date Western monograph on Hainan's history – the existing literature comprising only Schafer's *Shore of Pearls*, some specialized studies, and certain accounts written by anthropologists, geographers, natural scientists and missionaries in the late nineteenth and early twentieth centuries.⁶

A second initial point one has to consider, in the context of Hainan's foreign trade, is the system of sea routes linking the island to both China and Southeast Asia. In the age of sail, ships going south would closely follow the Guangdong coast and then steer in a southwesterly direction, eventually bypassing the Qizhou 七洲 Islands off Hainan's eastern tip. They would usually stay at some distance from Hainan's eastern and southern shores and proceed to the central Vietnam area, for example to Culao Rè. Both the Paracel Islands and the Macclesfield Banks and Reefs had to be avoided on this route. Hainan thus lay near but not on the main trade artery connecting Fujian, Guangdong and Vietnam with the ports and harbours around the Gulf of Siam, along the Malay peninsula, and so on.⁷

Sailing through the Gulf of Tonkin was a different matter. Several local routes connected various ports on the western side of Hainan with ports along the coasts of Vietnam and the Chinese mainland, particularly in the areas of Qinzhou 欽州, Lianzhou 廉州 (near modern Beihai 北海) and Xuwen 徐聞. Xuwen, on the Leizhou 雷州 peninsula, lay almost directly opposite the Qiongshan 瓊山/ Qiongzhou 瓊州 area on northern Hainan. Going through the narrow passage between Hainan and the mainland remained a dangerous undertaking, due to unpredictable currents and seasonal winds. These were different from those encountered on the "international" route off Hainan's eastern coast. Therefore, the Gulf of Tonkin was like a separate scenario not directly linked to the trade and traffic following the great trade artery through the South China Sea.

Theoretically, ships could also sail directly from Hainan's east coast to Luzon and Taiwan, via the Dongsha 東沙 or Pratas Islands. But Song, Yuan and Ming sources do not refer to such direct passages, although they do of course mention Luzon and other places in the Philippines and – at least in the case of Ming works – the Pratas group.

In sum, Chinese nautical treatises of the Ming and early Qing periods mostly look at the main trade axis connecting Fujian, Guangdong and Southeast Asia via Vietnam, i.e., the so-called "western trade route" or *xi hanglu* 西航路. The route around the western coast of Hainan, through the Gulf of Tonkin, is also described, but it was probably always considered as a subordinate segment in international sailing. Direct trade between Hainan and places along the great eastern trade artery linking Fujian via Taiwan to Luzon and the Sulu zone – "the eastern trade route" or *dong hanglu* 東航路 – likely did not play a significant role in the early days. The eastern route gradually emerged during the Song and became important during the Yuan, but Hainan was at no point involved in it.[8] Therefore, as the present chapter discusses Hainan's position between China and Southeast Asia, it mostly refers to trade and traffic along the great western route outlined above.

A further point which requires mention concerns the many coral islands and reefs in the South China Sea, particularly the Paracel, Macclesfield and Pratas groups. These places posed substantial threats to all ships sailing back and forth between East and Southeast Asia. Moreover, geographically they were responsible for the existence of the double route system sketched above. Direct passage from Hainan to, say, the north coast of Borneo rarely occurred – if it occurred at all. And yet, one cannot totally exclude the possibility of Hainanese and other fishing vessels sailing into the central segments of the South China Sea, which were clearly avoided by commercial vessels involved in long-distance trading. These observations can be related to the ongoing discussion of the history of the Paracel Islands and other archipelagos in the area. Chinese historians maintain that Chinese vessels regularly explored these waters, and there are even claims to a continued Chinese presence on the islands in question, but Song, Yuan and Ming sources do not really suggest this. It is only during the Qing that some evidence begins to appear.[9] Therefore, the present note will not deal with the central part of the South China Sea. It would however be interesting to explore early Iberian maps and to link their perception of China's maritime space to contemporary Chinese accounts – and perhaps also the history of Hainan.

Having referred to some of the more important sources and the geographical scope of the present note, I shall now summarize the more essential observations in relation to Hainan's maritime links with both China and Southeast Asia. The chapter will follow a chronological order and it will also address some questions which remain unanswered; it will not be based on theories, models, or typologies.

The Song period

In Song times, Hainan was still among China's remotest frontiers. As in earlier periods, immigrant groups moved to the many small villages and towns, which had gradually emerged all around the island. It is not known where these groups came from, but probably many originated from what are today Fujian and Guangdong. Furthermore, it is usually assumed that Shiqiu 石 蠟, Haikou(pu) 海口(浦) and Baisha(jin) 白沙津, all on the northern coast of Hainan, were then among the leading ports of that island. Regarding Baisha, the *Yudi jisheng* reports, for example, that foreign ships would often call there, but large vessels had to moor off the coast, at some distance from the port.[10]

Here we can directly turn to foreign trade. During the Song, China's maritime relations were controlled through a number of "supervisorates," the so-called *shibosi* 市舶司, which were located in China's leading ports. The duties of these offices have been described in many modern studies and do not need to be repeated here. What is of concern in the present context is that in 1173 a proposal was made to expand the *shibosi* structure to Hainan. This was rejected, but Zhao Rugua tells us, there were several *shibo* officers placed in Qiongshan, Chengmai 澄邁, Lin'gao 臨高 (also along the northern coast), and Wenchang 文昌 and Lehui 樂會 (both on the eastern coast).[11] Thus, Hainan appears to have been placed under the *shibosi* regime in some form or the other, albeit perhaps with a less formal system. If so, this implies that foreign ships anchoring at Hainan would have been subjected to import duties. Certain goods were graded and taxed accordingly, with the grading standards being adjusted from to time, probably not only in the ports of Guangdong and Fujian, but also on Hainan. On the mainland, the two ports of Guangzhou and Quanzhou in particular profited from this system.[12]

Placing *shibo* officers on Hainan meant that the provincial authorities (and central authorities as well) were expected to generate additional income. It is possible that many vessels had previously evaded tax payments on the mainland by sailing to Qiongshan and other Hainanese ports instead; thus the presence of *shibo* officers on the island may have helped to redirect some foreign trade back to Guangzhou and the Fujian coast. But this is no more than an assumption that cannot be verified through the sources.

Assuming that it was mostly immigrant groups from Fujian and Guangdong who became involved in Hainan's local trade and port administration, it also seems likely that a certain share of the island's income from the maritime sector flowed back to these two provinces – although this remains again a hypothesis. By and large, however, trade in and around Hainan must have been attractive because migration to the island continued. "Push factors" in Fujian and Guangdong may certainly have been of some significance as well.

Some figures on tax generated in Hainan have survived in written sources. These are aggregated numbers, which include duties on all kinds of local products. There was also a shipping toll (*chuanboshui* 船舶稅) and it is reported that vessels sailing to Hainan were normally charged according to their size. The exact amount of income generated in this way is not known, but Lu Wei thinks that it may have constituted a high share in total tax revenues.[13] If indeed so, then Hainan's maritime trade may have been more substantial in volume than one is normally inclined to think.

Much has been written on Hainan's own products. Less is known about its imports from Southeast Asia and the China mainland, and its exports to these regions. To begin with, Hainan produced all kinds of fruits and vegetables. But more important were gharuwood (*chenxiang* 沉沈香), betel-nut, coconuts, wax, sapanwood, pearls, tortoise-shell, and other such products. Both the *Lingwai daida* and *Zhufan zhi* enumerate a range of items, although in one or two cases it is not clear which specific products were meant. *Dingxiang* 丁香, for example, normally refers to cloves. In mediaeval times "true cloves" only came from the Moluccan Islands and not from Hainan or mainland Southeast Asia, and therefore this term may have referred to a different product.[14]

Most tropical products "produced" in Hainan were also available in other tropical areas. Gharuwood, especially its most expensive variety, namely calambac (*jia'nan xiang* 伽楠香 and various other terms), came from Indochina, tortoise-shell was obtained in many parts of modern Indonesia and the Philippines, sapanwood was a major export from Siam, while pearls were associated with the Sulu Islands, the Gulf of Manar, and the Persian Gulf. Some products, pearls being a case in point, were even available on or near the China mainland. Ramie, diverse kinds of cotton, and other such products were also produced and sold in other parts of Asia. All this leads to an important question: To what extent did Hainan compete with others in the Chinese market? Were its tropical resources marketed in Guangzhou and Quanzhou at lower prices than "rival" products coming in from Southeast Asia? Did Hainanese products replace certain foreign imports to China at any point in time? Zhao Rugua provides one or two details, saying, for example, that Hainanese gharuwood was better than that from Champa and Cambodia and that Hainanese wax was inferior to that from Srivijaya. But how representative are these remarks?

Trade in and out of Hainan also implied the transportation of local tribute goods, provided by different ethnic Li 黎 groups, to the China mainland, and bringing back to Hainan rice and silks, mostly for the Chinese population. Salt and certain metals were produced on the island itself, as were other daily necessities, but some manufactured goods also had to be brought in from Guangdong and Fujian. Zhao Rugua, for example, refers to the shipment to Hainan of lacquer, ceramics and other things from Quanzhou. Whether locally bred horses were already being sent to the China mainland during the Song period is rather uncertain; but under the Ming they were a frequently mentioned tribute item.[15]

Hainan's exports to the non-Chinese world are nowhere presented in any systematic way. We are told that Champa needed horses from Hainan, but this is all that is said and nothing can be drawn from this about the island's local horse market.[16] In the Yuan period more details emerge. *Hainan bu* 海南布 (or Hainan cloth/cottons) and betel, to mention just two examples, now appeared in various Southeast Asian locations.[17] Perhaps export of these commodities was already occurring during the Song; Zhao Rugua observes that betel-nut and cotton (*jibei* 吉貝) were "extraordinarily plentiful" on Hainan, adding that "the Quanzhou traders look principally to the latter as a profitable article."[18] But it is not clear whether Fujianese merchants took most of these "items" back to China, or whether they carried them to Southeast Asia. Earlier, Zhou Qufei also refers to cotton products from Hainan, which apparently had an exotic touch, and he complains about the unpleasant habit of chewing betel-nut, although not with explicit reference to Hainan.[19]

Ceramics probably played no significant role in Hainan trade during this period – quite in contrast to ceramics from the China mainland, which circulated to many parts of Asia – although small quantities were produced on the island. Copper coins and other metal products were not exported either; one gets the impression that most metals were in that period brought in from the mainland. Moreover, at that time cowries were still an important local currency.[20] There thus arises a second question: What products did foreign merchant ships load in the ports of Hainan on their return voyages to Southeast Asia? Betel-nut and cotton products? Or might it have been – as Hainan had so few special things to offer – that foreign ships avoided calling there during the homebound voyage? Were the supervisorates designed as a kind of counterweight against this imbalance? Again, I am afraid that there are no definite answers to these crucial questions because the sources do not supply sufficient information. But it would be important to reconcile these issues with the image of Hainan having had some weight in international commodity flows.

Who were the foreign merchants going through Hainan? Sources collected by Kuwabara and others indicate they mostly came from or via Champa. Many professed the Muslim faith and were in touch with other Islamic groups in the foreign quarters (*fanfang* 番坊) of Guangzhou and certainly also with groups active in Fujian. Some of the foreign merchants trading to these ports hailed from West Asia, especially Persia and the Arabian Peninsula. Often, however, references are vague and toponyms such as Dashi 大食 should perhaps be understood as general expressions for all kinds of Muslim traders, without clear specification. Many of these merchants, particularly those from Champa, carried the name Pu 蒲.[21]

Relations between Champa and Hainan under the Song are difficult to fully evaluate. It is noted above that Champa wanted to obtain horses from Hainan in 1172. When Hainan declined the request, this led to violence. In 1175 it was decreed that no further horse exports were allowed from the island. In the following year Champa tried to settle its dispute with Hainan. All of this is reported in the *Qiong tai zhi* 瓊台志. Unfortunately, the text is somewhat ambiguous here, but it can be interpreted to mean that at this time Champa also requested to do some trade with the "local barbarian" (*benfan* 本番) residents on the island. Two observations may be added: First, there may have been a link between these events and the proposal to establish a trade supervisorate in 1173. Second, obviously there were two kinds of foreigners dealing with the people of Hainan: those based abroad, in this case Champa, and those *in situ*, on the island itself.[22]

The presence of foreigners on Hainan during the Song is mostly associated with the area of Yazhou 崖州 where, according to some sources, one or two small *fanfang* had come into existence, the remnants of which can be traced through later periods as well.[23] This in turn can be linked to the Champa Muslims just mentioned above. Other foreign groups, probably also mostly from Champa, appeared in Danxian 儋縣 (in the northwestern part of Hainan) and in Baisha, as mentioned above.[24] Furthermore, according to Zhao Rugua, trading ships would also pass through the military districts of Wan'an 萬安 (east coast), Jiyang 吉陽 (in the Yazhou area) and Changhua 昌化 (west coast).[25]

Here we may briefly consider wind patterns and the other natural phenomena on which all ships depended in one way or the other: Vessels following the great Western trade artery from Fujian and Guangdong to Southeast Asia or, sailing in the other direction, could easily make a stopover near Yazhou (the Jiyang area) or at the ports along Hainan's east coast. Stopovers at the ports of northern and western Hainan required additional time and certainly incurred higher costs because these areas were far off the main route. This did not apply to local traffic through the Gulf of Tonkin. Regular merchants and even refugees leaving Champa and Annam could reach any place along the southern, western and northern coasts of Hainan, be that Yazhou, Danxian, Changhua, or Baisha. One might thus expect more traders from Indochina in these ports and a rather mixed and more international group of merchants near Yazhou and along Hainan's eastern coast. If so, the *shibo* officers placed along the northern coasts were probably mostly concerned with trade from Annam to Guangzhou, Quanzhou, etc., while those along the east coast would chiefly have looked after vessels sailing along the great western trunk route. But why then, it may be asked, was there no *shibo* officer in Yazhou? Is Zhao Rugua's failure to mention any *shibo* in that place reliable or significant?

Regarding other foreign groups on Hainan, nothing is certain for the Song period, not even in the context of tribute shipments to China.[26] By and large, the story of Hainan's "permanent" foreign communities during the Song – and the temporary presence of itinerant merchants – is the story of traders from Champa, especially those belonging to the Pu "clan," and their links to both Indochina and the China mainland, as was noted above. Secondary sources are not clear as to whether these merchants should be equated with or distinguished from the Persian and Arab groups. The literature on the foreign communities of Quanzhou and Guangzhou, when referring to Islamic groups, mostly seems to imply Persian and Arab traders, but there is much room for interpretation.[27] Be this as it may, it seems plausible to assume that merchants from Champa, operating out of Hainan, or regularly calling at Hainan, had some influence in mainland China's trading ports and that these groups were in close touch with, competed against or even cooperated with other Islamic communities and the Fujianese. At a more general level – and following the arguments presented by Chang Pin-tsun – one may say that this "symbiosis" became a crucial element in Fujian's commercial rise.[28] Furthermore, if the presence of foreign communities on Hainan, especially near Yazhou, is seen as one element within a chain of foreign "posts" along the China coast, then Hainan's role in international maritime trade must indeed have attained a certain importance in this period.

The Yuan period

Mongol rule over Hainan began in the late 1270s and lasted for *c.*90 years. After the occupation of the island by the general Ma Chengwang 馬成旺, a new administrative structure was gradually established, one distinctive element of which being that Hainan was now placed under the so-called *xuanweisi* 宣尉司 or pacification offices. Other changes concerned the military. The Mongol rulers saw in Hainan an important stepping stone on the way to Southeast Asia. Hainan, they thought, would be of use in future campaigns against Annam and Champa. Troops stationed on the island included Han Chinese, but probably also several Khitan and Jurchen contingents.[29] Since the military on the island also had to its disposal some gunners, it is very likely that there existed plans to deploy these units in combat against external enemies.[30]

The Mongols did indeed conduct war against Annam and Champa. During these campaigns Hainan was used as a logistics base and Hainanese soldiers were sent to the mainland. One result of these campaigns was that a sizeable group of Cham soldiers, who had surrendered to the Yuan, were settled near Haikou, together with their families. These soldiers were later referred to as "Nanfan bing" 南番兵.[31] They were likely Muslims and thus classified as *semu* 色目 by the Mongol rulers. Another new development involved the ethnic Li groups of Hainan. The Mongols made use of them in many ways because they were non-Han and had little sympathy for their former overlords, the Chinese. According to the Yuan annals, some 15,000 Li soldiers were employed abroad, even in the costly campaigns against Japan. Within the *tuntian* 屯田 (military farm) system we find Li contingents as well.[32] All these developments point to regular naval transports from and to Hainan, through the Gulf of Tonkin, and along the great western trade artery, in the direction of Guangdong, Fujian, and farther north.

Although the Yuan must have been quite open towards the Li and other non-Han groups, several Li rebellions were recorded under Mongol rule. Excessive economic pressure, too many military obligations and a chain of natural disasters, especially in the fourteenth century, may have been among the chief reasons for these rebellions.[33]

The economic situation of Hainan at this time is worthy of some attention. Hainan's population, there can be no doubt, grew during the Yuan period. Agricultural output also improved. During the Song period, grain still had to be imported. In Mongol times rice production expanded and Hainan had so much rice – perhaps due to the introduction of new crops from Champa which yielded up to three harvests per year – that supplies were sent to the soldiers campaigning against Annam and Champa.[34]

Apparently, rice shipments were largely restricted to the military sphere and were mostly sent through the Gulf of Tonkin. What is more interesting in the context of the present volume, is of course Hainan's connections beyond China. Generally, across China, the Mongol rulers placed foreign trade under the regime of the *shibosi* offices, more or less following the earlier Song system. However, in 1285 major changes were introduced and the so-called *guanben* 官本 system became popular. This was a type of state-private commercial arrangement with profits nominally being shared between the government and the merchant in a ratio of 7:3. The new rules were not always observed, therefore the government issued several prohibitions on the export of certain commodities. Most of these and other restrictions were instituted from the 1290s. The third period of trade in Mongol times was marked by the abolition of the *guanben* system and the permitting of free private trade. This began in *c.*1323.[35] It is normally to this third period that historians refer when they write about Yuan China's maritime relations and the flourishing foreign communities in Chinese ports.

Regarding Hainan during this period, there are few sources in the available texts. In 1293 a branch of the *shibosi* was established on the island, but it was closed again in the following year. It was then revived in 1308, and continued until 1311. The reasons for these ups and downs are not reported. However, it can be affirmed that the changes in 1308 and 1311 also affected other supervisorates, namely those in Guangzhou, Quanzhou and Qingyuan 慶元. However, in 1314, when the latter were reinstalled for a third period (until 1320), Hainan did not benefit from this new regulation.[36]

Presumably, the various small Champa communities continued to exist on Hainan through the Yuan period, although practically no additional details of any significance – other than the ones related to the above-mentioned Cham soldiers – are reported in the sources. The destruction of Guangzhou towards the end of the Song period and the temporary presence of Song refugees on Hainan may have had some more general implications for these Cham groups and international trade being pursued through the island. It has been assumed that, as Guangzhou had suffered so badly during this period, Quanzhou became China's leading port. Perhaps, and this is necessarily speculative, this strengthened the links between the foreign communities in Fujian and on Hainan to the effect that the latter directed more activities to Quanzhou, rather than to Guangzhou.

Another point to be considered in this context is, once again, the system of trade routes. Under Mongol rule China's second major trade axis to Southeast Asia, the eastern route linking Fujian via Taiwan with Luzon, the Sulu zone and modern eastern Indonesia, begins to emerge very clearly. This is accompanied by a changed perception of maritime space. The seas associated with the eastern route were now called Dongyang 東洋 (or Xiao Dongyang 小東洋, etc.), while those associated with the western trunk route were placed in the Xiyang 西洋 (Xiao Xiayang 小西洋, etc.) category.[37]

To what extent these changes affected Hainan remains unknown. The initial period of Mongol rule over and around the island, and in southern Guangxi, was marked by a range of military activities, including the dispatch of fleets against Java and the Vietnamese coast, as we have noted already. These naval activities may have disturbed purely commercial ventures, and indeed, they may have contributed to the shifting away of some international trade from the western to the eastern trunk route – to the temporary disadvantage of Hainan. Yet, Hainan must have had its place in international trade because it is mentioned in one or two Arabic sources of this same period and it also appears on the Catalan atlas of 1375, which was based on earlier information, likely from Mongol times.[38] Finally, we also know that there was much ship-building on the island during this period. Although these ships were mainly used for military purposes in the Gulf of Tonkin, some commercial vessels may have been among them.[39]

Hainan's exports during the Yuan were probably much the same as during the Song. Cotton has already been mentioned. Betel-nut and certain precious woods were also likely exported. The *QTZ* contains a long list of local products and trade items (*huo* 貨), and although this list is from the early sixteenth century and does not distinguish between "export *huo*" and locally traded goods, many of the items contained therein may have been exported beyond the island during the Yuan.[40] Ceramics, it may be surmised, were of no export importance yet – as under the Song. Hainan continued to receive its ceramic supplies from the mainland, and indeed, it was an importer of many other manufactured goods. Possibly it also received some ceramic products from the Indochina region, including Champa wares.[41]

The early to mid-Ming period

The transition from Yuan to Ming rule brought about many changes in China's coastal areas. Quanzhou was devastated through the so-called Isfahan rebellion and its foreign community disappeared almost completely. Now, once again, Guangzhou became the leading port in southern China. Guangzhou was also placed in charge of Hainan, which had been subject to the Guangxi government in late Yuan times. The internal structure of Hainan's administration also underwent certain readjustments. Thus, by 1370 the island comprised three counties (zhou 州) – Yazhou, Wanzhou, Danzhou – and several districts (xian 縣). By and large, this structure was maintained until the end of the dynasty.[42]

Hainan's supervision through the Guangdong authorities probably led to a greater measure of bureaucratic control over the island. The early Ming court intended to centralize China's internal administration; therefore, placing Hainan under Guangdong may have been one step in that direction. Since the first few Ming emperors also tried to tightly control foreign relations, particularly along the maritime periphery, the period of liberal trading, which Hainan had enjoyed during the late Yuan, was definitely ended by this time. Whether the decline of Quanzhou and its Muslim community had further effects on the island, especially its Cham "colonies," is not revealed by the sources. We shall return to these groups again below.

To facilitate control, the early Ming placed maritime trade again in the hands of maritime supervisorates. In 1370 there were three such shibosi, namely in Ningbo, Quanzhou und Guangzhou. Smaller locations were often supervised by so-called bay masters (shou'aoguan 守澳官), one such post being assigned to the Haikou area (Qiongshan). Technically, the only legal way in and out of China during this period was through tribute trade.[43] The rules governing this type of trade were adjusted from time to time and inscribed in the Ming codex. But these regulations were not always observed. Moreover, tribute delegations normally had many opportunities to do some non-official trading on the side.

As in other parts of China, the central government sought to enforce its regulations by strengthening coastal controls. This entailed the installation of many new military posts all around Hainan island, including watch towers and some fortifications. But these installations and the naval units assigned to them were rather weak and not always able to ward off smugglers and armed gangs.[44]

Smuggling and banditry had its roots in excessive economic pressure on and tension between Chinese settlers and non-Han groups, particularly the Li. "Structural" problems, for example inadequate supplies, mismanagement, corruption and bad treatment of government troops, aggravated the situation. In several cases this led to larger uprisings. The Ming shilu (MSL) and other sources frequently refer to such clashes which involved both armed gangs operating on the island itself as well as "maritime" groups from the mainland. The latter in particular could easily abscond to the many bays and inlets of Hainan. Contemporary terms used for such groups were *shanzei* 山賊, *haikou* 海寇, *haizei* 海賊, *wokou* 倭寇, etc. Although it is not possible to make a sharp distinction between them, at least twenty to thirty clashes with a maritime element can be identified during the first part of the Ming period, i.e., between 1368 and c.1500. These were reported in the *MSL* and local gazetteers.[45]

While Hainan's military was often called on to subdue coastal gangs and internal uprisings, it rarely became involved in warfare against Vietnam. Indeed, war in Vietnam had little to do with Hainan; moreover, it was costly and, in the end, did not pay for the early Ming government. One wonders why then the Ming court, unlike its Mongol predecessor, did not develop Hainan into an operational base against Vietnam.[46] True, occasionally troops fighting on the mainland would receive logistical support from the island, but references to the shipment of grain and other supplies are not numerous.[47] Even later in the century, after the formidable defeat of Champa by Annam in 1471, there is little evidence that Hainan was seen as a major naval or military outpost by Ming China in its relations with Vietnam.[48] Interestingly, however, there are quite a few references to administrative staff being transferred from Hainan to other parts of China as if Hainan had become a major supplier of civil servants to the mainland.[49]

Militarily, Hainan was thus somewhat divorced from the mainland. To a certain extent it was also not connected with the foreign trade sector. No major *shibosi* office existed on the island, as was mentioned above. Moreover, Zheng He's 鄭和 famous expeditions and the official missions directed by other court eunuchs nearly always bypassed Hainan.[50] Possibly there was a very practical reason for this: Ports along the southern and eastern coasts were too small to accommodate large naval units and furnish supplies to thousands of men. Even a single squadron under Zheng He – a group of, say, seven to ten *baochuan* 寶船 (or "treasure ships" under Zheng He's command) plus some additional convoy vessels – would have been enough to put enormous logistic stress on a coastal settlement like Yazhou, which would have had a population of not more than 20,000 to 30,000. Hainan's only major town "along" the great western trunk route was Wenchang, but in terms of its abilities to furnish supplies this place may not have been better off than most other ports in the area.[51]

Thus, while other regions of coastal China profited from the passing through of the great armadas dispatched under the Yongle and Xuande emperors – in the sense that at least some trade in these regions was maintained by absorbing commercial activities into the state sector – Hainan could not derive any major benefit thereof. Essentially it was excluded from the 'Zheng He scenario.'

Tribute missions, which came to China in the wake of the returning Ming fleets, or by themselves, did occasionally stop in Hainan, but, once again, the extant sources suggest that they were not numerous (as compared to the hundreds of arrivals in Nanjing and Beijing). The *QTZ* indicates arrivals in Hainan from Siam in 1397, 1445 and 1459, from Champa in 1429, 1437, 1447, 1449, 1463, 1471, 1480, 1504 and 1518, and from Melaka in 1505. In some cases, local Hainanese officials were put in charge of these envoys and assisted them on their onward journey to the capital; examples are also found in the *QTZ*. The tribute items brought to China in this way included ivory, elephants, horses, rare animals and all kinds of tropical products.[52]

Some of the above missions are not mentioned under their respective dates in other contemporary documents, not even in the *MSL*.[53] The *MSL* in turn carries two or three additional entries not included in the *QTZ*. One 1374 entry refers to a Siamese envoy, who claimed he had been shipwrecked off Hainan; however, his tribute offerings were later rejected by the imperial court.[54] Two further cases relate to Champa. In 1460 an envoy from that country came through Yazhou, his mission being linked to the plan of sending a Champa prince to China.[55] The second episode goes much beyond regular tribute relations: Gulai 古來, another Champa prince, had fled to Yazhou in 1486, taking with him more than 1,000 followers in all. The Ming court, he suggested, might start a campaign against his enemies in Annam, but China opted to stay out of the conflict.[56] Not too many additional details are known, nor are we informed on how these refugees were sheltered and supplied in or near Yazhou and whether they were in touch with the local Cham communities, which, as mentioned earlier, still existed during the early Ming.

Indeed, local gazetteers and other Ming sources contain scattered references to these communities and, more generally, to the presence of foreigners on Hainan. But the evidence is scarce and often indirect. One example pertains to a certain Pu Sheng 蒲盛, a literatus, who was of Cham descent.[57] We are also told of a shrine, called Fanshen miao 番神廟, which existed in Wanzhou, the modern Wanning 萬寧. Its name suggests that a foreign deity was worshipped, perhaps again related to the Cham community, but little else is known.[58] Another case is that of Hai Rui 海瑞. He was an outstanding scholar who, and this is often forgotten, also came from a Champa family.[59]

A further aspect of Hainan's contacts with the outside world concerns the frequent shipping disasters occurring near its shores. The Siamese delegate, mentioned above, is one example. According to Huang Zuo, vessels from the Ryukyu Islands were also driven off course and forced to seek shelter in Hainan's ports.[60] One case is reported in a *MSL* entry for the year 1503: On its way to Melaka, a delegation from Naha, comprising 152 persons in all, landed on Hainan; some time thereafter, the emperor decreed that these mission members be brought back to Fujian; from there, they were to embark on a regular Ryukyuan tribute vessel and return to their native land.[61] The *QTZ* lists a further incident, which could be related to that in the *MSL*: In 1503, four ships appeared off Hainan. They were stopped by Hainanese forces and the crew was handed over to the island's authorities. Among the persons detained was a certain Cai Bowu 蔡伯烏 from Ryukyu – perhaps their leader. If indeed both sources refer to the same incident, then the presentation is quite different in tone. The local perspective, mirrored in *QTZ*, would be rather rigorous; the official view, given in *MSL*, would be more conciliatory – certainly because of the long-lasting and generally much appreciated relations between the Ming court and the Ryukyu Islands.[62] Unfortunately Ryukyuan sources provide no additional data on this issue.[63]

Two further cases may be mentioned here. In 1495 a group of Siamese landed on Hainan. The *anchasi* 按察司 (surveillance commission) of Guangdong Province investigated their case and finally orders were issued that they be supplied with daily necessities and sent back to Thailand.[64] An earlier incident occurred in the Hongwu period. In 1383, several foreigners, including some from Shepo 闍婆 (Java), were caught by Hainan's coast guard. They were brought to the imperial capital but were then released and sent back to their native lands.[65]

The second episode, in particular, seems to indicate that Hainan's officials were very strict with foreign merchant vessels, especially if these could not identify themselves as tribute ships. Some foreigners, we may presume, were active in contraband trade, and therefore Hainan, like other coastal areas, would persecute them. It is even possible that vigilance on the island was stricter than elsewhere along the China coast.

In the early sixteenth century, when so-called *wokou* groups began to become more active in Zhejiang, and later on in Jiangsu and Fujian, we also find references to them in the context of Hainan.[66] In 1519, for example, the port authorities of Yulin 榆林 caught and executed twenty-four individuals, among whom was one from Patani. In 1556 foreign "pirates" were reported to have landed in the area of Danxian, and in 1573 they threatened Gan'en 感恩. He Yaba 何亞八 and his group, who maintained good connections to Southeast Asia, is a further case in point, where a Chinese "piratical" element had become connected with foreign maritime operators. There was also an incident which involved some sailors from Borneo (likely Brunei). Other groups active on or near Hainan were those led by Zeng Yiben 曾一本, Wu Ping 吳平, Lin Rong 林容, Su Da 蘇大, Li Mao 李茂, etc. Many of these leaders came from Guangdong, and especially from the Chaozhou region. During the Jiajing and early Longqing reigns, the groups they led pillaged Wenchang, Qiongshan and other parts of Hainan.[67]

Here we have already entered the mid-Ming period and therefore the heyday of *wokou* activities. The mechanics underlying these activities have been examined in countless studies and do not need to be repeated in the present note. Suffice it to say that, by and large, the Hainan scenario – during the mid-Ming – was probably not too different from the rest of coastal China, although the degree of violence and the number of reported incidents may have been lower than in other parts of the country. Furthermore, several *wokou* leaders were originally active farther to the north; but persecuted by the coast guard in these areas, they gradually moved south, eventually reaching Hainan. Put differently, the economic and structural causes leading to the *wokou* problem on and near Hainan were not all "home-made"; in part at least the problem was imported from the mainland.

Two or three further points must still be considered in the context of Hainan's maritime relations. First, during the early and mid-Ming periods, several ethnic Li groups sent regular tribute missions to the Ming capital. In all likelihood these missions would have followed the short route from Hainan's northern coast to the Leizhou peninsula or the longer route to Guangzhou. Curiously, the most frequently mentioned tribute item is horses.[68] Whether this implies that Hainan's local horse production had grown since the Song period cannot be affirmed, because the Ming are known to have imported horses from almost everywhere; moreover, sending horses to China often had a purely symbolic function, hence the economic dimensions of these shipments cannot really be estimated.[69]

Next, sources do not provide any clear picture of the commodities which Hainan received from and exported to Southeast Asia. As was noted above, the *QTZ* and other works list many local products, but their destinations are rarely specified.[70] There is only some information on local products being shipped to Guangdong.[71] Military provisions would have gone across the sea as well, and in some years Hainan sent salt taxes to the mainland; however, the effects of these shipments on the domestic economy are not really understood.[72] Other questions relate to the *wokou* problem. Some *wokou* groups based in Zhejiang and Fujian were involved in the lucrative silk-for-silver trade, which became important in the middle of the sixteenth century; Hainan's role in this constellation is nowhere discussed, at least not with respect to that period.

The last point brings us to the arrival of the first few Europeans who actively participated in the silk-for-silver business. Portugal had made its appearance in the Far East well prior to the well-known relaxation of trade prohibitions in 1567, which brought *wokou* smuggling and violence down to "regular" levels along most sections of the China coast. However, Portuguese trade, at first from Melaka to central Guangdong, then to the Ningbo and Fujian areas and finally again to the Pearl River estuary, where Macau was founded in the mid-1550s, did not really touch Hainan. Portuguese vessels would bypass the island, although involuntary stops could not always be avoided, due to unfavorable currents and winds. This was the experience of, for example, Baltasar Gago in the 1560s. Yet, during the Ming no regular connections were established either between Macau and Hainan, or between that place and Portuguese Melaka.[73]

Spanish sources also mention Hainan. Towards the end of the sixteenth century, when some influential groups in Manila thought about conquering parts of China, especially Fujian, it was also proposed to take Hainan for the Spanish Crown. Francisco de Ortega, an Augustinian, was among the ones who favored this project. But none of these plans ever came near to being carried out.[74] Taiwan was the only nearby area where Spain undertook efforts to secure a number of small posts.

As noted, the relaxation of trade prohibitions in 1567 brought about a certain "détente" along the China coast. Some pirates were still active in the last two or three decades of the sixteenth century, but this was of minor concern. Essentially, Chinese private trade could now flourish without too many obstacles. Fujian was the province which profited most from these new regulations. Henceforth, dozens of Fujianese junks sailed to Nagasaki, Manila and other destinations each year. Both the western and eastern trunk routes were fully developed by private Chinese traders under these favorable conditions. To what extent

Hainan profited thereof, from the rising presence of sailors and emigrants from Fujian – and perhaps from bypassing Japanese vessels sailing to the Vietnam coast – is another question that must be investigated separately.

Conclusion

In spite of the sources cited above, evidence for Hainan's foreign relations during the Song, Yuan and first part of the Ming period remains rather fragmentary. Clearly, Hainan was involved in trade between China and Southeast Asia at all times, but whether this occurred within the framework of government trade, as during the early Ming, or in the context of tribute trade, *guanben* trade, smuggling or free trade, is difficult to ascertain. The same applies to Hainan's foreign communities, especially the ones from Champa. Most data stem from the Song dynasty; but whether this in itself shows that these communities were more influential during the Song than in later times is rather doubtful. Imperial policy towards Hainan poses further questions. Apparently, there were periods, when the government kept Hainan out of international commodity flows, but just why this was so, remains a matter of speculation. Likewise, there were some periods in which Hainan should have profited from deregulation efforts. However, our sources do not provide enough evidence to suggest that this translated into clear growth of the foreign trade sector.

Due to its geographical location, Hainan was of course in close contact with the Vietnamese coast. Although the present note did not offer a systematic survey of this linkage, it is clear that imperial policy vis-à-vis Annam and Champa always required certain adjustments on the part of the people of Hainan. In terms of its functions, Hainan was a subordinated entity. Being part of China's periphery, it had to serve the mainland, and not vice versa. At the same time, it was busy with its own internal problems, especially the local Li population. This constellation may have contributed to the fact that Hainan never became a major commercial hub along the great western trunk route in the period considered here, although it certainly drew modest profits from the trade which followed this route.

Notes

1 See Almut Netolitzky, *Das Ling-wai tai-ta von Chou Ch'ü-fei. Eine Landeskunde Südchinas aus dem 12. Jahrhundert*, Münchner Ostasiatische Studien 21 (Wiesbaden: Franz Steiner Verlag, 1977), especially pp. 32–5; Zhou Qufei, *Lingwai daida jiaozhu*, ed. Yang Wuquan 楊武泉, in Zhongwai jiaotong shiji congkan, (Beijing: Zhonghua shuju, 1999), j. 2, pp. 70–4; Friedrich Hirth and W. W. Rockhill (trans., ed.), *Chau Ju-kua: His Work on the Chinese and Arab Trade in the Twelfth and Thirteenth Centuries, Entitled Chu-fan-chï* (Taipei: Ch'engwen Publishing Company, 1967 reprint), pp. 175–90; Zhao Rugua, *Zhufan zhi jiaoshi*, ed. Yang Bowen 楊博文, in Zhongwai jiaotong shiji congkan (Beijing: Zhonghua shuju, 1996), j. xia, pp. 216–24. Parts of the other texts translated in Angela Schottenhammer, "Hainan's politisch-ökonomische Anbindung an das chinesische Festland während der Song-Dynastie," in *Hainan: de la Chine à l'Asie du Sud-Est; von China nach Südostasien*, eds. Claudine

Salmon and Roderich Ptak, assoc. ed. Shing Müller, *South China and Maritime Asia 10* (Wiesbaden: Harrassowitz Verlag, 2001), pp. 35–83. Additional sources are provided in *Zhufan zhi zhubu*, which is vol. 2 in the collection *Han Zhenhua xuanji* 韓振華選集, Centre of Asian Studies Occasional Papers and Monographs 134, 2 (Hong Kong: The University of Hong Kong, 2000), pp. 447–79.

2 Tang Zhou 唐胄, (*Zhengde*) *Qiong tai zhi*, 2 vols., Tianyi ge cang Mingdai fangzhi xuankan (Shanghai: Shanghai guji chubanshe, 1964). Lost works on Hainan are listed in Li Mo 李默, *Guangdong fangzhi yaolu* (Guangdongsheng difangzhi bianzuan weiyuanhui bangongshi, [1987]), especially pp. 433–5. On important Ming and Qing editions see also Wang Huijun 王會均, "Ming Qing 'Qiongzhou fuzhi' yanjiu," in *Hainan ji Nanhai xueshu yanjiuhui lunwenji*, ed. Guoli zhongyang tushuguan guanxun (Taibei: Guoli zhongyang tushuguan Taiwan fenguan, 1996), especially pp. 41–52.

3 Huang Zuo 黃佐, *Guangdong tongzhi*, 4 vols. (Hong Kong: Dadong tushu gongsi, 1977), now *GDTZ*.

4 See the contributions by Ralph Kauz, "Die Insel Hainan in persischen und arabischen Quellen," and Isabel Tavares Mourão, "L'île de Hainan à travers quelques récits portugais des XVIe et XVIIe siècles," in *Hainan*, ed. Claudine Salmon and Roderich Ptak, pp. 139–52 and 153–77; R. Ptak, "Hainan in the Letters by Cristovão Vieira and Vasco Calvo," in *D. João III e o Império. Actas do Congresso Internacional Comemorativo do seu Nascimento (Lisboa e Tomar, 4 a 8 de Junho de 2002)*, ed. Roberto Carneiro and Artur Teodoro de Matos (Lisbon: Centro de História de Além-Mar und Centro de Estudos dos Povos e Culturas de Expressão Portuguesa, 2004a), pp. 485–99.

5 See Nguyên Thê Anh's contribution "Hainan et les marchands hainanais dans les sources vietnamiennes," in *Hainan*, ed. Salmon and Ptak, pp. 179–94.

6 Edward H. Schafer, *Shore of Pearls* (Berkeley: University of California Press, 1970). One important specialized study is Eva Ehmke's *Das Hai-chu yu-lu als eine Beschreibung der Insel Hainan in der Ming-Zeit*, Mitteilungen der Gesellschaft für Natur- und Völkerkunde Ostasiens 115 (Hamburg, 1990). Early twentieth-century works include the well-known accounts by Stübel, Fenzel, and others.

7 For the routes, see, for example, Pierre-Yves Manguin, *Les Portugais sur les côtes du Việt-Nam et du Campa. Étude sur les routes maritimes et les relations commerciales, d'après les sources portugaises (XVIe, XVIIe, XVIIIe siècles)*, Publications de l'École française d'Extrême-Orient 81 (Paris: École française d'Extrême-Orient, 1972), especially the maps in appendix.

8 See, for example, R. Ptak, "Jottings on Chinese Sailing Routes to Southeast Asia: Especially on the Eastern Route in Ming Times," in *Portugal e a China. Conferências nos encontros de história luso-chinesa*, ed. Jorge M. dos Santos Alves. Lisbon: Fundação Oriente, 2001c, pp. 107–31.

9 See, for example, R. Ptak, "Die Paracel- und Spratly-Inseln in Sung-, Yüan- und frühen Ming-Texten: Ein maritimes Grenzgebiet?," in *China and Her Neighbours. Borders, Visions of the Other, Foreign Policy. 10th to 19th Century*, eds. Sabine Dabringhaus and R. Ptak, South China and Maritime Asia 6 (Wiesbaden: Harrassowitz Verlag, 1997), pp. 159–81.

10 Lu Wei 盧葦, "Lishi shang de Hainan zai guoneiwai maoyi zhong de diwei he zuoyong," *Guangdong shehui kexue* 22 (4/1989), p. 82; A. Schottenhammer, "Hainans politisch-ökonomische Anbindung," p. 60; Wang Xiangzhi 王象之, *Yudi jisheng*, Songdai dili shu shi zhong, 2 vols. (Taibei: Wenhai chubanshe, 1963), II, j. 124. More on the situation during the Song can be read in Atsushi Kōbata 小葉田淳, *Hainandao shi* (Chin. trans.; Taibei: Xuehai chubanshe, 1979), Chapter 2; and Yang Dechun 楊德春, *Hainandao gudai jianshi* (Changchun: Dongbei shifan daxue chubanshe, 1988), Chapter 2, 4.

11 F. Hirth and W. W. Rockhill, *Chau Ju-kua*, p. 178; Lu Wei, "Lishi shang de Hainan," p. 82; A. Schottenhammer, "Hainans politisch-ökonomische Anbindung," pp. 46–7;

Jacques Dars, "La marine chinoise du Xe siècle au XIVe siècle," *Études d'histoire maritime* 11 (Paris: Economica, 1992), p. 250.

12 See, for example, Chen Gaohua 陳高華 and Wu Tai 吳泰, *Song Yuan shiqi de haiwai maoyi* (Tianjin: Tianjin renmin chubanshe, 1981), Chapter 2 and 3; Paul Wheatley, "Geographical Notes on Some Commodities Involved in Sung Maritime Trade," *Journal of the Malayan Branch of the Royal Asiatic Society* 32, 2 (1959): 22ff.; *Haijiaoshi yanjiu* 13 (1/1988) is a special number dedicated to the *shibosi*. On Quanzhou the most recent Western monograph is A. Schottenhammer's *Quanzhou, Fujian, in der Song-Zeit (960–1279): Die Verknüpfung zwischen zentralstaatlicher Politik und regionaler wirtschaftlicher Entwicklung und deren Auswirkung auf den maritimen Handel* (Wiesbaden: Harrassowitz Verlag, 2002); see further, *The Emporium of the World: Maritime Quanzhou, 1000–1400*, ed. Angela Schottenhammer (Leiden: Brill, 2001a).

13 Lu Wei, "Lishi shang de Hainan," p. 83; A. Kōbata, *Hainandao shi*, pp. 50–1; A. Schottenhammer, "Hainans politisch-ökonomische Anbindung," pp. 12–14. Tolls being levied according to the size of ships (*geshuiqian* 格稅錢): This is reported in the *Zhufan zhi* (see F. Hirth and W. W. Rockhill, *Chau Ju-kua*, p. 178; more in *Zhufan zhi zhubu*, p. 467 n. 19).

14 See sources in n. 1. Also see A. Schottenhammer, "Hainans politisch-ökonomische Anbindung", pp. 48–54 (various products). For cloves, see, for example, R. Ptak, "China and the Trade in Cloves, *c.*960–1435," *Journal of the American Oriental Society* 113, 1 (1993): 1–13. Note: Han Zhenhua gives detailed comments on all imported commodities listed by Zhao Rugua. He believes *ding* in *dingxiang* is a scribal error for *deng* 等. See *Zhufan zhi zhubu*, pp. 459–64 n. 6 (especially p. 461). In earlier periods *dingxiang* may have referred to some type of lilac. See, for example, Edward H. Schafer, *The Golden Peaches of Samarkand. A Study of T'ang Exotics* (Berkeley: University of California Press, 1963), p. 171.

15 *Qiong tai zhi (QTZ)*, j. 9, 1a–b; A. Schottenhammer, "Hainans politisch-ökonomische Anbindung," pp. 54–5 (horses), 58 (salt); R. Ptak, "Hainans Außenbeziehungen während der frühen Ming-Zeit (Hongwu bis Hongzhi)," in *Hainan*, ed. Salmon and Ptak, pp. 107–8.

16 *QTZ*, j. 21, 19b; Xu Song 徐松 (comp.), *Song huiyao jigao*, 8 vols. (Beijing: Zhonghua shuju, 1957), VIII, *fanyi* 4/83 (p. 7755b); Li Jinming 李金明 and Liao Dake 廖大珂, *Zhongguo gudai haiwai maoyi shi*, Dongnanya wencong (Nanning: Guangxi renmin chubanshe, 1995), p. 67. Tribute delegations from Champa arriving in the Northern Song capital also asked for or received horses on several occasions. See, for example, Robert M. Hartwell, *Tribute Missions to China, 960–1126* (Philadelphia: author's edition, 1983), pp. 154–6, 159. Also see Hans Bielenstein, *Diplomacy and Trade in the Chinese World, 589–1276*, Handbook of Oriental Studies/Handbuch der Orientalistik, Section Four, China, vol. 18 (Leiden, Boston: Brill, 2005), especially pp. 41–8. Note: Zhao Rugua speaks of *xiao ma* in the Li area. Han Zhenhua, quoting a Qing work (*Nanyue biji*), thinks this term referred to *shanma*. See *Zhufan zhi zhubu*, p. 478 n. 52; Li Tiaoyuan 李調元, *Nanyue biji* (Hanhai, in Baibu congshu jicheng 37/11), III, j. 9, 1b–2a. For a brief discussion, leading to different conclusions, see R. Ptak, "Hainan and the Trade in Horses (Song to mid-Ming)," in *Pferde in Asien: Geschichte, Handel und Kultur. Horses in Asia: History, Trade and Culture*, eds. Bert G. Fragner, Ralph Kauz, Roderich Ptak, and Angela Schottenhammer, ser. Österreichische Akademie der Wissenschaften, Philosophisch-historische Klasse, Denkschriften 378 (Vienna: Verlag der Österreichischen Akademie der Wissenschaften, 2009), pp. 219–28.

17 Wang Dayuan 汪大淵, *Daoyi zhilüe jiaoshi*, in Zhongwai jiaotong shiji congkan, ed. Su Jiqing 蘇繼廎 (Beijing: Zhonghua shuju, 1981), pp. 93 (Xialaiwu 遐來勿), 123 (Suluoge 蘇洛鬲), 173 (Dudu'an 都督岸), 199 (Puben 蒲奔; all foregoing places: Hainan cotton); p. 114 (Luohu 羅斛; betel-nut). Diverse proposals have been made

concerning the identity of the places listed. Possibly they refer to the Klabat area on North Sulawesi, places in Siam (Luohu) and in Kalimantan.
18 F. Hirth and W. W. Rockhill, *Chau Ju-kua*, p. 185. Also *Zhufan zhi zhubu*, p. 479 n. 56. Furthermore Billy K. L. So, *Prosperity, Region and Institutions in Maritime China. The South Fukien Pattern, 946–1368*, Harvard East Asian Monographs (Cambridge, MA: Harvard University Press, 2000), pp. 96–7, 121. Note: Hainanese weaving techniques appear to have spread during the Yuan. See, for example, Hong Yongbin 洪用斌, "Yuandai de mianhua shengchan he mianfangye," *Zhongguo shehui jingjishi yanjiu* (3/1984), pp. 55–63.
19 A. Netolitzky, *Das Ling-wai tai-ta*, pp. 110–1, 113–4.
20 A. Schottenhammer, "Hainans politisch-ökonomische Anbindung," pp. 56–8. On Song coins and locally produced ceramics, see, for example, Dingan xian bowuguan ed. *Dingan xian wenwu zhi*, (Guangzhou: Zhongshan daxue chubanshe, 1987), p. 12 – I am grateful to Claudine Salmon for pointing out this source to me.
21 See, for example, Jitsuzô Kuwabara, "On P'u Shou-kêng ... a Man of the Western Regions ...," *Memoirs of the Research Department of the Toyo Bunko*, especially 7 (1935), pp. 4, 21–2 n. 18; A. Netolitzky, *Das Ling-wai tai-ta*, p. 37; Pierre-Yves Manguin, "Études Cam. II: L'introduction de l'Islam au Campa," *Bulletin de l'École française d'Extrême-Orient* 66 (1979), especially p. 259; Chen Dasheng and Claudine Salmon, "Rapport préliminaire sur la découverte de tombes musulmanes dans l'île de Hainan," *Archipel* 38 (1989): 75–106; Zhang Xiumin 張秀民, *Zhong Yue guanxishi lunwenji* (Taipei: Wenshizhe chubanshe, 1992), pp. 311ff. For summaries in traditional sources, see, for example, *QTZ*, j. 21, 19a–22a, Dai Xi 戴熺 and Ouyang Can 歐陽燦, *Qiongzhou fuzhi* (Wanli ed., 1617), j. 4, p. 134. I have been unable to consult *Guangdong Hainan Huizu yanjiu* (Guangzhou: Guangdong renmin chubanshe, 1982). Pang Keng-Fong has written several studies on Hainan's Muslims, mostly on contemporary issues. See, for example, "Being Hui, Huan-nang, and Utsat Simultaneously: Contextualizing History and Identities of the Austronesian-Speaking Hainan Muslims," in *Negotiating Ethnicities in China and Taiwan*, ed. Melissa J. Brown (Berkeley: Institute of East Asian Studies, 1996), pp. 183–207.
22 For example, *QTZ*, j. 21, 19b–20a; also see note 16, above.
23 See, for example, Lu Wei, "Lishi shang de Hainan," p. 83 (quoting j. 3 of the Wanli edition of *Qiongzhou fuzhi*); Zhang Xiumin, *Zhong Yue*, pp. 292, 308–9, 314–20, and sources there. Also see, for example, Zhang Xi 張嶲 et al. (comp.), *Yazhou zhi*, ed. Guo Moruo 郭沫若 (Guangzhou: Guangdong renmin chubanshe, 1983), j. 16, pp. 332, 336 (*fanfang* following the name Mai Qi 麥齊); map in *QTZ*, j. 1, 15b (*fanfang* near Yazhou).
24 For Danxian, see Zhang Xiumin, *Zhong Yue*, pp. 312–3. The Champa chapter in Tuo 脫脫, *Song shi*, 40 vols. (Beijing: Zhonghua shuju, 1977), XL, j. 489, p. 14080, and j. 1 and 2 of the Kangxi edition of *Danxian zhi* are quoted.
25 F. Hirth and W. W. Rockhill, *Chau Ju-kua*, pp. 179–82; Li Jinming and Liao Dake, *Zhongguo gudai haiwai maoyi shi*, p. 67. There was a famous spring near Jiyang and a temple in the Wan'an area. Useful details may be found in *Zhufan zhi zhubu*, p. 471 n. 27 and 28; p. 475 n. 42, and sources in n. 58, below. Zhou Hui 周輝 in his *Qing bo bie zhi* also refers to foreign merchants in the Jiyang area (quoted after Li and Liao). Another work, Lou Yao's 樓鑰 *Gongkui ji* (Juzhenshan congshu, in Baibu congshu 27/72), II, j. 3b, also gets frequently quoted; it indicates that ships had to stop in Hainan on the way from and to China.
26 On tribute shipments, see, for example, Hartwell, *Tribute Missions*, and Lin Tien-wai (Lin Tianwei 林天蔚), *Songdai xiangyao maoyi shigao* (Hong Kong: Zhongguo xueshe, 1960), pp. 174–208 (table).
27 Several essays on the *fanfang*, mostly found in the *Haijiaoshi yanjiu* journal, are quoted in Chang Pin-tsun (next note) and R. Ptak, "China's Medieval *fanfang* – A Model for Macau under the Ming?," *Anais de História de Além-Mar* 2 (2001): 47–71.

28 Chang Pin-tsun, "The Formation of a Maritime Convention in Minnan (Southern Fujian), c.900–1200," in *From the Mediterranean to the China Sea: Miscellaneous Notes*, ed. Claude Guillot, Denys Lombard and R. Ptak, South China and Maritime Asia 7 (Wiesbaden: Harrassowitz Verlag, 1999), especially pp. 148–50, 153.
29 Tang Kaijian 湯開建, "Yuandai dui Hainandao de kaifa yu jingying," *Ji'nan xuebao* 45 (4/1990), p. 132.
30 *QTZ*, j. 18, 2a; j. 19, 2a; Tang Kaijian, "Yuandai," p. 133.
31 *QTZ*, j. 21, 20a–22a (especially 21a); Tang Kaijian, "Yuandai," p. 133; Zhang Xiumin, *Zhong Yue*, p. 304.
32 Song Lian 宋濂, *Yuan shi*, 15 vols. (Beijing: Zhonghua shuju, 1976), I, j. 12, p. 257; XV, j. 209, p. 4647; also *QTZ*, j. 21, 21a; Tang Kaijian, "Yuandai," pp. 133–4.
33 Details in Tang Kaijian, "Yuandai," pp. 136–9.
34 Details in Tang Kaijian, "Yuandai," pp. 139–41.
35 For a detailed survey see Yu Changsen 喻常森, *Yuandai haiwai maoyi* (Xi'an: Xibei daxue chubanshe, 1994), especially Chapter 3. Yu also presents all important entries in the *Yuan dianzhang*, with explanations and comments (see pp. 50–81, there). Earlier studies on the *shibosi* structure under the Yuan include, for example, articles by Wang Guanzhuo 王冠倬 and Sun Wenxue 孫文學, both superseded by Yu Changsen. One difference between the Song and Yuan systems lay in the fact that import duties levied during the earlier period were calculated according to a ship's dimensions, while in the Yuan period they were based on the total value of the imported goods. See Yu Changsen, p. 52.
36 *Yuanshi*, II, j. 17, p. 374; j. 18, p. 389; VIII, j. 91, p. 2315; *QTZ*, j. 21, 22a; Yu Changsen, *Yuandai haiwai maoyi*, pp. 46–8 (for 1294 and 1308).
37 Details, for example, can be found in R. Ptak, "Südostasiens Meere nach chinesischen Quellen (Song und Yuan)," *Archipel* 56 (1998): 5–30, and "Chinesische Wahrnehmungen des Seeraumes bis zur Küste Ostafrikas, c.1000–1500," in *Der Indische Ozean. Das afro-asiatische Mittelmeer als Kultur- und Wirtschaftsraum*, eds. Dietmar Rothermund and Susanne Weigelin-Schwiedrzik, Edition Weltregionen 9 (Vienna: Verein für Geschichte und Sozialkunde, ProMedia, 2004), pp. 37–59.
38 Ralph Kauz, "Die Insel Hainan in persischen und arabischen Quellen", p. 152.
39 References are collected in Tang Kaijian, "Yuandai," p. 142.
40 *QTZ*, j. 9, 21a–25a. The *QTZ* also mentions diverse textiles (j. 21, 25b–26b) and other locally manufactured goods (j. 9, 29a–32b), some of which, I am sure, were sold abroad, possibly already during the Yuan. Another important reference to Hainanese products, or rather, Hainanese production technoloy, can be found, for example, in Tao Zongyi's 陶宗儀 *Nancun cho geng lu* 南村輟耕錄 (Beijing: Zhonghua shuju, 1959), j. 24, p. 297. The passage in question can be read as a case of "textile technology transfer" from Hainan to China. However, to what extent such artistic and technological traditions were spread from Hainan to other regions remains unknown.
41 Some Cham wares have been found in the Philippines. Many other wares of Indochinese origin have been excavated across islands in Southeast Asia. Literature includes, for example, the first two articles of the *Journal of East West Maritime Relations* 2 (1992) and Yoji Aoyagi, "Production and Trade of Champa Ceramics in the 15th Century," in *Commerce et Navigation en Asie du Sud-Est (XIVe-XIXe siècle)*, eds. Nguyên Thê Anh and Yoshiaki Ishizawa, *Recherches asiatiques* (Paris and Montreal: L'Harmattan, 1999), pp. 91–100. Cham links with the Philippines had many facets; possibly even including script transfer, as Geoff Wade has suggested in his "On the Possible Cham Origin of the Philippine Scripts," *Journal of Southeast Asian Studies* 24, 1 (1993): 44–87. Some of these contacts may have been via Hainan and Quanzhou.
42 On Hainan's new administration, see for example, *QTZ*, j. 2, 19a, 20b, 21b, 31a–b; j. 3; Zhang Tingyu 張廷玉 et al., *Ming shi*, 28 vols. (Beijing: Zhonghua shuju, 1974),

IV, j. 45, pp. 1145–7; Li Xian 李賢 et al. (comp.), *Da Ming yitong zhi*, 10 vols. (Taibei: Wenhai chubanshe, 1965), X, j. 82, 16a–17d (pp. 5049–51); Gu Zuyu 顧祖禹 (comp.), *Dushi fangyu jiyao*, 6 vols. (Beijing: Zhonghua shuju, 1955), V, j. 105; Ming Yi 明誼 (comp.), *Qiongzhou fuzhi*, in Zhongguo fangzhi congshu 47, 2 vols., ed. Zhang Yuesong 張岳松 (Taibei: Chengwen chubanshe, 1967; original ed. 1841), I, j. 1.

43 See, for example, Jiang Zuyuan 蔣祖緣 and Fang Zhiqin 方志欽 ed. *Jianming Guangdong shi* (Guangzhou: Guangdong renmin chubanshe, 1987), pp. 242–4; Li Jinming, "Shilun Mingdai haiwai chaogong maoyi de neirong yu shizhi," *Haijiaoshi yanjiu* 13 (1/1988): 175. On tribute trade and the *shibosi* in "primary" sources, see, for example, *GDTZ*, j. 66, 67aff. (pp. 1782ff); *Ming shi*, VII, j. 81, pp. 1980–2; Li Dongyang 李東陽 et al. (comp.), *Da Ming huidian*, 5 vols. (Taibei: Huawen shuju, 1964), III, j. 105ff.

44 See, for example, A. Kōbata, *Hainandao shi*, pp. 100ff.; Yang Dechun, *Hainandao gudai jianshi*, pp. 82–6; Lu Wei, "Mingdai Hainan de 'haidao', bingbei he haifang", *Ji'nan xuebao* 45 (4/1990), p. 107. For "primary" sources, see *QTZ*, j. 18; j. 20, 19a–b (ships), 21aff. (on the so-called *minzhuang* 民壯); j. 21, 10bff., or *Ming shi*, VIII, j. 90, pp. 2202, 2217 (Hainan *wei* 衛), 2218 (different battalions).

45 See, R. Ptak, "Hainans Außenbeziehungen," pp. 101–4. Some general ideas on categorizing *wokou* activities can be found in R. Ptak, "Piracy along the Coasts of Southern India and Ming-China: Comparative Notes on Two Sixteenth Century Cases," in *As relações entre a Índia portuguesa, a Ásia do Sueste e o Extremo Oriente. Actas do VI Seminário Internacional de História Indo-Portuguesa*, eds. Artur Teodoro de Matos and Luís Filipe F. Reis Thomaz (Macau and Lisbon, 1993), pp. 255–73.

46 On the Ming war in Vietnam, see for example, R. C. Majumdar, *Champa. History and Culture of an Indian Colonial Kingdom in the Far East, 2nd–16th Century A.D.* (rpt. Delhi: Gian Publishing House, 1985), pp. 129ff; J. K. Whitmore, *Vietnam, Hô Quy-ly and the Ming (1371–1421)* (New Haven: Yale University Press, 1985), who also refers to the studies by A. B. Woodside. See also Zheng Yongchang 鄭永常, "Ming Yongle nianjian (1407–1424) Zhongguo tongzhi xia de Annam," in *Zhongguo haiyang fazhanshi lunwenji*, vol. 5, ed. Zhang Bincun 張彬村 and Liu Shiji 劉石吉 (Taibei: Zhongyang yanjiuyuan, Zhongshan renwen shehui kexue yanjiusuo, 1993), pp. 61–109.

47 See, for example, *QTZ*, j. 18, 6bff.

48 See, for example, *MSL*, Xianzong, j. 92, pp. 1774–5; j. 136, pp. 2553–4; j. 219, pp. 3793–4; Geoff Wade, *The Ming Shi-lu (Veritable Records of the Ming Dynasty) as a Source for Southeast Asian History – 14th to 17th Centuries*, 7 vols. (PhD diss., University of Hong Kong, 1994), pp. 1647–9, 1668–9, 1725–7. Wade's English translation is now also available online at www.epress.nus.edu.sg/msl/.

49 See, for example, *QTZ*, j. 38, 8bff., j. 39 and 40 passim (officials at the *xian* level). Also see *Yazhou zhi*, j. 16, pp. 335ff.

50 One possible exception is a mission to Siam (1429), led by a eunuch surnamed Niu 牛, with Xiang Gui 項貴, a company commander stationed on Hainan, as military escort. See *QTZ*, j. 18, 6a; 19, 13b; 21, 22b. Also see Li Wenxuan 李文烜 and Zheng Wencai 鄭文彩 (comp.), *Qiongshan xianzhi*, Zhongguo fangzhi congshu, Huanan 166, 6 vols. (Taibei: Chengwen chubanshe, 1974; originally 1857), j. 11, 17a (p. 937). Note that the *Qian wen ji*, which gives an accurate itinerary of Zheng He's seventh voyage, does not mention Hainan; for translations see Paul Pelliot, "Les grands voyages maritimes chinois au début du XVe siècle," *T'oung Pao* 30 (1933): 305–11, and J. V. G. Mills trans. and ed., *Ma Huan: Ying-yai Sheng-lan. The Overall Survey of the Ocean's Shores [1433]* (Cambridge University Press, 1970), pp. 14–18. Nor does the famous Mao Kun map pay much attention to Hainan; in fact, the route from China to Southeast Asia by-passes the island; see, for example, *Xin bian Zheng He*

hanghai tuji, ed. Haijun haiyang cehui yanjiusuo, Dalian Haiyun xueyuan hanghaishi yanjiushi (Beijing: Renmin jiaotong chubanshe, 1988), pp. 40–3.
51 On Hainan's demography, see, for example, *QTZ*, j. 10, 4aff. Also see Wang Jiazhong 王家忠, "Mingdai Hainan renkou lun," *Zhongguo bianjiang shidi yanjiu* 28 (2/1998): 24–33. Other estimates can be found in Ehmke, *Das Hai-cha yu-lu*, table p. 212 (especially Wenchang).
52 *QTZ*, j. 21, 22b–23a. Details here in the following paragraphs and also in Ptak, "Hainans Außenbeziehungen," pp. 96–8.
53 In respect of Siam: The *MSL* – edition used in 133 vols. (Nangang: Zhongyang yanjiuyuan lishi yuyan yanjiusuo, 1966) – only refers to the 1397 envoy. See, for example, Geoff Wade, "The *Ming shi-lu* as a Source for Thai History – Fourteenth to Seventeenth Centuries," *Journal of Southeast Asian Studies* 31, 2 (2000): 283, 286 (appendices); Promboon Suebsaeng, *Sino-Siamese Tributary Relations, 1282–1853* (PhD diss., University of Wisconsin, 1971), Chapter II. Also see *QTZ*, j. 18, 6a, and 19, 18a (on Zhu Dewei 祝德威 in the context of the 1397 mission). Regarding the 1459 envoy: The *QTZ* refers to a Siamese envoy who had erected a shrine near Qiongshan (j. 24, 6a; also see the 1841 ed. of the *Qingzhou fuzhi*, j. 11 shang, 8b). The *MSL* also mentions a Thai envoy in the Chinese capital in 1462, possibly the same person. On the latter see Wade, *The Ming Shi-lu*, p. 1609 (on the envoy's name there: pp. 1449, 1469–73), and his *The Ming Shi-lu*, pp. 266, 284, 290. In respect of Champa: Identical dates for the first four envoys are seen in the *MSL*. The envoys from 1463 to 1504 are listed one year later in the *MSL* (probably because of the long distance from Hainan to the north). The 1518 envoy (*QTZ*) was probably identical with one listed for 1520 in the *MSL*. Generally, also see Hiroshi Watanabe, "An Index of Embassies and Tribute Missions from Islamic Countries to Ming China (1368–1644) as Recorded in the *Ming Shih-Lu*, Classified According to Geographic Area," *Memoirs of the Research Department of the Toyo Bunko* 33 (1975): 39 (327). Furthermore, sources in Wade, *The Ming Shi-lu*, p. 247. *Melaka*: The *MSL* lists an envoy for 1508; cf. Geoff Wade, "Melaka in Ming Dynasty Texts," *Journal of the Malayan Branch of the Royal Asiatic Society* 70, 1 (1997): 65. References to tribute envoys are of course also in *Ming shi*, XXVIII, j. 324, pp. 8383ff. and 8396ff., j. 325, pp. 8416ff., and in the 1857 ed. of *Qiongshan xianzhi*, j. 11, 17a (p. 937). It may be of interest to recall here that Qiu Jun 丘濬, one of Hainan's most distinguished literati, refers to relations with Melaka in his "Song Lin huangmen shi Manlajia guo xu". Finally, *MSL* entries on Sino-foreign tribute relations may also be found in certain other works, for example Li Guoxiang's 李國祥 et al., eds. *Ming shilu leizuan. Guangdong Hainan juan* (Wuhan: Wuhan chubanshe, 1993).
54 *MSL*, Taizu j. 88, pp. 1564–5; G. Wade, *The Ming Shi-lu*, pp. 47–8; *GDTZ*, j. 66, 46b–47a (pp. 1771d–1772a).
55 *MSL*, Yingzong, j. 317, p. 6608; G. Wade, *The Ming Shi-lu*, p. 1588.
56 *MSL*, Xianzong, j. 284, p. 4806, and j. 286, p. 4836; *QTZ*, j. 21, 23a; Zhang Xiumin, *Zhong Yue*, pp. 315–6; Wade, *The Ming Shi-lu*, pp. 1775–6, 1776–8, also p. 390. Occasionally Hainanese persons were employed in diplomacy vis-à-vis Annam and Champa. One such person is Li Shan 李珊. See *QTZ*, j. 38, 4b; *MSL*, Xianzong, j. 105, p. 2061; Wade, *The Ming Shi-lu*, pp. 1655–6; Lin Ying 林英 et al. (eds.), *Hainan mingren zhuanlüe* (Guangzhou: Guangdong lüyou chubanshe, 1993), II, pp. 22–4.
57 Zhang Xiumin, *Zhong Yue*, pp. 308–9, plus sources provided therein. Furthermore, *Yazhou zhi*, j. 16, p. 332. N.b.: The *QTZ*, j. 1, 15b, contains a map which shows a *fanfang* (foreign quarter near Yazhou). For this also see *Yazhou zhi*, j. 16, p. 336.
58 See, for example, *Qinding gujin tushu jicheng*, Fangyu huibian, Zhifang dian, ce 196, j. 1380, 52b, ed. Zhonghua shuju (under "Zhaoying miao" 照應廟); F. Hirth and W. W. Rockhill, *Chau Ju-kua*, pp. 181, 188 n. 28; *Qiongzhou fuzhi* (Wanli ed.), j. 4, p. 109; Kuwabara, "On P'u Shou-kêng," vol. 7 (1935), pp. 21–2; Zhang Xiumin, *Zhong Yue*, p. 314. Han Zhenhua, in *Zhufan zhi zhubu*, p. 475 n. 42, relates the Zhaoying

miao to the Bozhu 舶主 shrine of Song times. Also see, in *Gujin tushu jicheng*, references to Fancun 番村 and Fanpu 番浦; as well as Chen Dasheng and Claudine Salmon, "Rapport," p. 81, and J. Kuwabara (as above). Finally, see Ehmke, *Das Haicha yu-lu*, pp. 112–3 (*Gujin tushu jicheng* on foreigners).

59 See, for example, Zhang Xiumin, *Zhong Yue*, pp. 305ff. General information also in L. Carrington Goodrich and Fang Chaoying (eds.), *Dictionary of Ming Biography, 1368–1644*, 2 vols. (New York and London: Columbia University Press, 1976), I, pp. 474–9; Zhang Dexin 張德信 (ed.), *Ming shi Hai Rui zhuan jiaozhu* (Xi'an: Shaanxi renmin chubanshe, 1984).

60 See *GDTZ*, j. 66, 60b (p. 1778d). Early Ming Hainan was also in touch with Japan; see, for example, *QTZ*, j. 42, 21a–b.

61 See *MSL*, Xiaozong, j. 204, p. 3789; Wade, "Melaka in Ming Dynasty Texts," p. 65; Wade, *The Ming Shi-lu*, p. 1907.

62 *QTZ*, j. 21, 17a–b; A. Kōbata, *Hainandao shi*, p. 164.

63 See, for example, Atsushi Kōbata and Mitsugu Matsuda, *Ryukyuan Relations with Korea and South Sea Countries. An Annotated Translation of Documents in the Rekidai Hôan* (Kyoto, 1969), especially Chap. III (relations between Melaka and Ryukyu). The documents collected in this work indicate many Ryukyuan shipping disasters on the way to Southeast Asia. Furthermore, several persons named Cai are listed (p. 201); perhaps one of these persons was identical with Cai Bowu. For a statistical survey of the relations between Naha and Southeast Asian ports, see, for example, Chang Pin-tsun, *Chinese Maritime Trade: The Case of Sixteenth-Century Fu-chien (Fukien)* (PhD diss., Princeton University, 1983), pp. 353–4.

64 *MSL* Xiaozong, j. 104, p. 1901; Wade, *The Ming Shi-lu*, pp. 1835–6.

65 *MSL*, Taizu j. 155, p. 2413; Wade, *The Ming Shi-lu*, p. 88. Further cases, also involving Chinese vessels, in *MSL*, Yingzong, j. 326, pp. 6729–30; Xiaozong, j. 202, pp. 3766–7; Wade, pp. 1599–1600, 1906. Occasionally ships were also grounded on the Annam coast; see, for example, *MSL*, Xiaozong, j. 153, pp. 2704–5; Wade, pp. 1859–60.

66 Some references have been mentioned earlier. See, for example, for 1391: *QTZ*, j. 18, 9b, 12b–13a, 30a, 31b; j. 21, 14b; Yang Dechun, *Hainandao*, p. 83; early Hongzhi, *QTZ*, j. 18, 14b.

67 Details in Paola Calanca, "Aspects spécifiques de la piraterie à Hainan sous les Ming et au début des Qing," in *Hainan*, ed. Salmon and Ptak, especially pp. 113, 115–23. Atsushi Kōbata and Lu Wei distinguish between several periods of illegal activities. Details in A. Kōbata, *Hainandao shi*, pp. 164ff.; Lu Wei, "Mingdai Hainan de 'haidao'," pp. 103ff.

68 Most missions are listed in the *MSL*. Also see Li Guoxiang, *Ming shilu leizuan*, the Hainan section. See furthermore *GDTZ*, j. 68, especially 17aff. (pp. 1839ff.), and R. Ptak, "Hainan and the Trade in Horses."

69 Inner Asia, Southwest China, Korea and other maritime areas also sent horses. See, for example, Chang Pin-tsun, *Chinese Maritime Trade*, pp. 355–7, and R. Ptak, "Pferde auf See. Ein vergessener Aspekt des maritimen chinesischen Handels im frühen 15. Jahrhundert," *Journal of the Economic and Social History of the Orient* 34 (1990): 199–233, plus sources cited there.

70 Further details in Lu Wei, "Lishi shang de Hainan"; *QTZ*, j. 9, 21bff.; *Da Ming yitong zhi*, X, j. 82, 22a (p. 5061).

71 Examples in *MSL*, Taizu, j. 55, p. 1078; *QTZ*, j. 18, 5b–6a; j. 21, 12b. Also see Lu Wei, "Lishi shang de Hainan," pp. 81–2.

72 See, for example, *MSL*, Taizu, j. 115, pp. 1887–8; Taizong, j. 35, p. 617; *QTZ*, j. 18, 5b.

73 See Isabel Tavares Mourão, "L'île de Hainan." See also Charles R. Boxer, *The Great Ship from Amacon. Annals of Macao and the Old Japan Trade, 1555–1640* (Lisbon: Centro de Estudos Históricos Ultramarinos, 1959), pp. 25–6, 32–3.

74 See, for example, Manel Ollé, "La invención de China. Percepciones y estrategias filipinas respecto a China durante el siglo XVI," *South China and Maritime Asia* 9 (Wiesbaden: Harrassowitz Verlag, 2000), p. 149, and Manel Ollé, *Estrategias filipinas respecto a China: Alonso Sánchez y Domingo Salazar en la empresa de China (1581–1593)*, 2 vols. (PhD diss., Barcelona: Universitat Pompeu Fabra, 1998), I, p. 132.

3 China in India
Porcelain trade and attitudes to collecting in early Islamic India

John Guy

This chapter is concerned with the circulation of objects and imagery within the Asian trading system. It examines the Muslim courts of Sultanate India centred in Delhi in the fourteenth and fifteenth centuries, and the early Mughal courts of the sixteenth and seventeenth centuries which, along with other wealthy Muslim courts of West Asia, served as significant markets for the porcelain producers of southern China in the Yuan and early Ming periods (Figures. 3.1–3.3, 3.5). The Sultanate rulers of northern India were largely of Turkic-Mongol descent and shared with their successors, the Mughals, a common Mongol ancestry which linked them to the Timurid royal house of Ferghana.[1] In both cases they represented ethnic groups with close and long associations with the Central Asian trade routes that linked their world with both China and the Indian subcontinent.

Chinese glazed ceramics had travelled to West Asia since the middle Tang Dynasty via the overland camel routes of the Silk Road. In the early ninth century archaeological evidence begins to appear of ceramics travelling in commercial quantities by the sea routes of the Southern Sea, the Nanhai.[2] Thereafter the porcelain-producing regions of China were increasingly linked by merchant shipping to the Indian Ocean world of India, the Middle East, Africa and Europe.[3] The Asian markets were far from homogenous, differentiating quality and object type to specific niche markets. Even within known markets, the range of wares revealed levels of differentiation and specialization only alluded to in the written sources which describe this trade.

Early Chinese engagement with the Indian subcontinent

Among the earliest and most valuable sources in this respect are those provided by Chinese Buddhist pilgrims who left detailed accounts of their hazardous journeys to and from India. These describe the mechanics of travel in maritime Asia, predating the Arabic navigation literature which can be said to begin with Ibn Khurdadhbih's *Kitab al-Masalik*, around CE 850.[4] The Chinese Buddhist pilgrim Faxian's travels to India, in the first decade of the fifth century, provided one of the earliest accounts of the region. Having travelled overland via the Silk Road to northern India, he resided for two years at Tamralipti, eastern India's great international sea-port located in Bengal, transcribing the Buddhist sutras and

Figure 3.1 Chinese porcelain and other treasures being transported by cart, displayed and used; details of manuscript paintings preserved in the Istanbul Album, Aqqoyunlu Tabriz, later fifteenth century.

Source: Topkapi Saray Museum, Istanbul (H.2153).

Figure 3.2
Source: Topkapi Saray Museum, Istanbul (H.2153).

drawing pictures of images.[5] Indian merchant-ships then took him to Sri Lanka, which he described as rich in pearls and precious stones. At Anuradhapura, the capital of Sri Lanka and a centre of Buddhist learning, he studied and transcribed Buddhist texts unknown at that time in China. At Abhayagiri monastery, he saw a [Chinese] merchant presenting as his offering a fan of white silk.[6] The continuing presence of Chinese merchants in the region is confirmed by the seventh-century Pallava dynasty royal endowed temple of Vaikuntaperumal at their capital of Kanchipuram, which has sculptural reliefs depicting figures dressed in seemingly Chinese dress and carrying umbrellas, being received by the temple's patron, King Narasimhavarman II (r. 700–728). In the centuries immediately

Figure 3.3
Source: Topkapi Saray Museum, Istanbul (H.2153).

following, Chinese glazed ceramics began appearing in Sri Lanka, most notably at the capital Anuradhapura and its seaport Mantai, where ninth-century Hebei province glazed white and green-splashed wares, and Hunan province Changsha polychromed wares have been excavated.[7] Other centres of Buddhist wealth, as well as the ports servicing these centres, such as Mantai and Trincomalee, have yielded similar finds.[8] A recently identified shipwreck offshore from Nilaveli, north of Trincomalee, laden with early fourteenth-century Yuan celadon, confirms the ongoing demand for Chinese porcelain in the region and the veracity of the accounts by contemporary commentators such as Wang Dayuan (1349).[9]

Faxian continued his journey on an Indian merchantman from Sri Lanka to Srivijaya, and thence to southern China. The type of trading vessel used by Faxian is alluded to in the sixth-century *Liang sigong ji* 梁四公記 (Memoirs of the Liang Dynasty [502–556]): "A large junk of Funan which had sailed from western India arrived [in China] and offered for sale a rock-crystal mirror".[10] This "junk of Funan" was likely operated by Malay mariners based in Southeast Asia. A succession of Indian embassies are recorded being received in China, especially from south India in the late seventh and eighth centuries. The strength

Figure 3.4 Jar decorated with qilin, phoenixes and peonies in underglaze cobalt blue. Early Ming period, second-half fourteenth century, likely reign of Hongwu (1368–98). Ht. 48 cm. From the collection of William Cummins formed in India 1864–83.

Source: © The Trustees of the British Museum, London (O.A.1963.5–20.1).

of this relationship is witnessed by the construction of a temple by the Pallava ruler at Kanchipuram, Narasimhavarman II (Sri Narasimha Potavarman in the Chinese records). A Chinese source, the *Jiu Tang shu* 舊唐書, records that in 720 the Pallava king built a temple for the use of Chinese merchants visiting south India (probably at the port city of Mamallapuram) and requested that a

Figure 3.5 Turkic nobleman with cloud collar robe, being offered wine from a blue-and-white porcelain ewer; detail of a manuscript painting from the Istanbul Album, Aqqoyunlu Tabriz, later fifteenth century.

Source: Topkapi Saray Museum, Istanbul (H.2153).

dedicatory inscription be supplied from China, which was done, though no trace of either the temple or inscription is preserved.[11]

These accounts serve to underscore the long-established nature of Sino-Indian relations. It is only in the ninth century that glazed ceramics begin to feature prominently in this trade. This period marks the beginnings of the systematic export of Chinese ceramics on an industrial scale to Southeast Asia, India and the Middle East. White ware, plain and green-splashed white wares, Yue celadon, and polychromed Changsha wares dominate this early ceramic traffic. Examples excavated in the late Tang dynasty ports of southern China, notably Ningbo, Yangzhou, Hangzhou and Guangzhou, and at transshipment sites in Southeast Asia and South Asia, and habitation sites in the Middle East, confirm the path of their distribution.[12] The Isthmus of Kra on the Malay peninsula, Mantai in northern Sri Lanka, Brahmidabad in northwestern India, Bambhore in Pakistan and Siraf in the Persian Gulf, all bear witness to the popularity of this new trade in glazed ceramics.

The Arabic, Persian and Chinese sources

Whilst the Chinese records continue to provide a sketch-like impression of overseas trade, principally through the recording of foreign tribute missions, it is the Arabic and Persian sources which most enlarge our understanding of the reality of the ceramic trade from the ninth to twelfth centuries. These sources make clear that the *lingua franca* of seafarers was Arabic, and a favoured medium of exchange was the Caliphate gold dinar. This currency assumed international credibility from its introduction around 695 until the tenth and eleventh centuries, when it was progressively displaced by Chinese tin and copper coinage. The successive prevalence of these two currencies serves to illustrate the early dominance of the Arab world in Asian long-distance trade, and the subsequent arrival of the Chinese.

The *Akbar al-Sin wa'l-Hind* (*c.*851), itself a compilation of a number of earlier Arabic sources, gives the first full account of the India–China trade. It states that Koulam (Kollam, Quilon) in Kerala was the major Indian port for Chinese-trade ships serving the Persian Gulf, and that this trade was dominated by Arabs.[13] A recently excavated shipwreck in the Java Sea of an Arab dhow, still loaded with its cargo of in excess of 60,000 pieces of Chinese glazed ceramics, confirms the pattern.[14] The discovery of a Changsha bowl in the cargo with an inscribed date most probably equivalent to 826 makes clear that this Arab-dominated trade in Chinese ceramics was well underway by the second quarter of the ninth century.

It is not known where the early Sultanate courts of northern India sourced their collections of Chinese porcelain. Items may have been supplied to the Gujarati ports of western India, but to date there is no archaeological evidence to verify this. We do, however, have a reference in Zhao Rugua's *Zhufanzhi* (1225) to Gujarat, with its ancient port of Cambay, as a market for Chinese goods and an important source of cotton goods and textile dyes.[15] Malabar is expressly cited by Zhao Rugua as another market for Chinese porcelain, and it is recorded that such goods were reaching as far west as Zanzibar by this period. The *Zhufanzhi* makes clear that the sea-routes were now ascendant, advantaged by access to newly expanded and increasingly prosperous Asian markets. The growth in this sea trade in turn stimulated the expansion of ceramic production in southern China to an industrial scale, especially at kilns accessible via the river systems to the ports of coastal Zhejiang, Fujian and Guangdong.

The ascendant role of Arabs in this trade is confirmed by Mas'udi (956) who refers to the presence of Arab and Indian traders in south China in the mid-tenth century.[16] The volume of the Nanhai trade motivated the Chinese government in 971 to establish a post of Overseas Customs Officer at Guangzhou, expressly to regulate and tax this growing trade. Similar posts followed at other southern ports over the next century. The late tenth century also saw a rebellion by Tang troops who sacked a number of southern port cities, including Hangzhou and Guangzhou, causing temporary disruption to overseas trade. Many foreign merchants were massacred and others fled and settled at intermediate ports in the Nanhai, including Tonkin, Cham port-polities, and the Malay peninsula. "Kalah"

(Arabic), probably modern-day Kedah, features prominently in Arabic and Persian geographies of the period. From there they traded with China; others likely used Palembang as their base, the presumed location of the maritime entrepôt of Srivijaya.

One of the first comprehensive lists of Chinese trade goods that record the presence of ceramics is contained in the *Song shi* 宋史, which describes the late tenth to thirteenth centuries. It includes, among China's major exports, precious and base metals, glazed ceramics, and silks. Imports include cotton textiles (possibly from India), aromatics, rhinoceros horns, ivory, coral, amber, pearls, turtle shell, sappanwood (a dye source), rock crystal and semi-precious stones.[17] This trade proved highly profitable for the Song government and overseas trade was now actively encouraged. The most westerly point reached by Chinese vessels in the twelfth century appears to have been Quilon, on the Malabar coast of southwest India, the home of black pepper and long a terminus for West Asian trade goods, as recent excavations at Pattanam in Kerala have revealed.[18] Chinese vessels do not seem to have ventured beyond this point until the Zheng He voyages of the early fifteenth century.

The Chinese commentators identified five regions of economic importance in South Asia: Sri Lanka and southwest India, most importantly Malabar, and its ports of Quilon, Cochin and Calicut; western India, identified as Gujarat and Malwa, its hinterland; the northwest, including the region of the river Indus and Kashmir; the Coromandel coast in the southeast, and finally Bengal. Chinese understanding of Indian geography in this period appears to have still been largely informed by Arabic sources.

A new type of informant appears in the Song period, the commercial commentators (who nonetheless often held a government post). The *Lingwai Daida* 嶺外代答 (1178) was written by Zhou Qufei, a customs official based in Guangzhou. This work was drawn upon heavily by Zhao Rugua when he came to write his *Zhufanzhi* (1225) some fifty years later.[19] Zhao Rugua, who held a similar post in Quanzhou, provided the most detailed account known of the Southern Ocean trade, detailing the goods carried and the routes sailed. Both of these port cities were renowned for their large foreign merchant communities and these authors would have had access to first-hand informants, the merchants and mariners who sailed these routes. They undoubtedly provided different perspectives from those available in official sources. This new type of writing found its successor in the works of Wang Dayuan.[20] His *Daoyi zhilue* 島夷誌略 (1349) provided the clearest picture we have of China's trade with foreign countries at the time; this included a robust trade in Fujian ceramics to a variety of countries. Ma Huan's *Yingyai Shenglan* 瀛涯勝覽 (The Overall Survey of the Ocean's Shores, 1433), continued this trend, chronicling Zheng He's seven expeditions and the trading opportunities identified.[21]

Extensive information on sailing routes began to appear in Chinese sources of the Yuan period and this trend continued into the early Ming. The strongest evidence of a growing level of direct Chinese trade to India comes from these Chinese treatises, typically navigational texts. One of most detailed is the fifteenth-century anonymous *Shunfeng Xiangsong* 順風相送 (Fair Winds for Escort) of *c*.1430. It describes the routes both north-south and west-east, from Java to Japan, and from Timor to Hormuz. The two major routes, namely the Eastern Route and the Western Route, are comprehensively described.[22] The Western Route is summarized as follows: Guangzhou, down the coast of Vietnam, across the South China Sea to Pulau Tioman, then joining the Siam route to Melaka, thence to Samudra-Pasai (north Sumatra), across the Indian Ocean to one of three Indian destinations: Masulipatam, north to Bengal or south to Quilon. This is the main Chinese route to India and western Asia. The Eastern Route departs Quanzhou via Taiwan for Luzon, south via Mindoro, Mindanao and Sulu to Borneo and Halmahera for eastern Indonesia, especially the Moluccas (south Borneo and East Java were best reached by branch routes off the eastern Route, and link with the Siam–Mindanao route). A sixteenth-century source, the *Xiyang chaogong lu* 西洋朝貢典 (Records of the Tributary Countries in the Western Ocean) (1520) by Huang Xingzeng largely follows Ma Huan (1433), but adds descriptive sea-routes, including a route to Masulipatam, Bengal and Quilon.

The major destinations cited in these navigation gazetteers represent the centres of Asian maritime commerce in these periods. The historical veracity of these accounts can be confirmed by the concentrations of Chinese ceramics found at the places listed.[23] The most frequently cited destinations include the Ryukyus, Taiwan, the Philippines including Luzon, Palawan, Sulu, and Mindanao; Borneo including Brunei, Banjarmasin, Pontianak; Sulawesi, Java including Gresik, Tuban, Demak, Surabaya, Banten, Cirebon; Lombok, Timor, Siam, Pattani, Pulau Tioman, Melaka, Sumatra including Palembang, Pasai, Aceh and Barus; west to Sri Lanka (Beruwala), Calicut, and beyond to Aden and Hormuz. The majority of these places were visited at least once during Zheng He's seven monumental voyages despatched by emperor Yongle (1402–24) and continued by Xuande (1426–35), between 1405 and 1433.[24] Voyages I, II and III terminated at Calicut, whilst voyages IV, V and VI went as far west as Hormuz. On voyages V and VI some vessels also reached Aden and East Africa. These ambitious expeditions represented a high-point in Chinese imperial attitudes to the merits of international trade and influence. State interest dwindled thereafter and long-distance sailing beyond Southeast Asia became a rarity, with Melaka assuming a new importance as China's South Sea terminus. By the mid-fifteenth century increasingly large private vessels were being built for overseas trade, to service the massive movement of both goods and people.

Zhao Rugua's *Zhufanzhi* 諸蕃志 of 1225 provides the most comprehensive account of China's international maritime trade and the demand for her products in foreign lands in this period. Serving as the harbor master of Quanzhou, Zhao Rugua's informants were the merchants who frequented his port and the trade they conducted under his supervision. India features in his description of distant destinations. Speaking of Malabar, southern India, he observes that in this region there was demand for Chinese silks and porcelain, together with cloves, the latter being sourced from the Moluccas in eastern Indonesia: "Every year ships come to this country from San-fo-qi [Srivijaya]" and other places in Sumatra. Such vessels would undoubtedly have supplied the cloves, and probably the aromatics also cited. Chinese copper cash and gold and silver are also mentioned, the presumption being that they were now displacing the Arab Caliphate dinar as the dominant forms in monetary exchange.

Throughout the Song period we witness the expansion and consolidation of China's place in Asia's international sea trade. Nonetheless, the Arab-Persian world continued to play a significant role, as witnessed by the appointment of a Muslim to the post of Superintendent of Shipping at Quanzhou in 1270, the position held by Zhao Rugua some fifty years earlier. He shifted his loyalties to the ascending Yuan forces in 1276 and served as an advisor on overseas trade to the first Mongol emperor.[25] The Yuan conquest of south China was complete by 1281, and the Mongol administration immediately set about establishing its diplomatic links and expanding maritime trade. Bilingual inscriptions in Chinese and Tamil have been recorded from both Quanzhou and Guangzhou, a clear indication of the ongoing nature of China's foreign trade relations with southern India. The Guangzhou inscription records a Srivijayan mission arriving in China in 1281 to establish immediate links with the new Yuan administration;[26] the Quanzhou inscription records the dedication of a Hindu temple by a Tamil Shaiva community.[27]

The blue-and-white revolution

The Yuan period was marked by radical developments in high-fired ceramic technology. In the course of the first half of the fourteenth century the kilns at Jingdezhen, in northern Jiangxi Province, began to produce radically new types of porcelain. These wares differed in all major respects from what had gone before: form, design and colouring techniques all represented a dramatic break from the past. Yuan blue-and-white was in production in the second quarter of the fourteenth century, and after civil strife disrupted production, was revived in the early Ming, most notably in the Yongle (1403–24) and Xuande (1426–35) periods (Figures 3.30, 3.31, 3.33).

Unlike the monochrome wares that were the hallmark of the Song period, these newly devised shapes with complex painted underglaze cobalt blue decoration were first conceived for a foreign clientele, the Islamic markets of India and West Asia. Forms were in large part imitative of contemporary Islamic metalwork vessels, especially the engraved and inlaid brass wares of Mamluk Egypt and Iran.[28] Significant numbers of these innovative ceramics also found a ready market among the elites of Southeast Asia in a period when a proselytizing Islam was gaining widespread support in the region. A recently identified fragment of a Yuan covered jar (*guan*) with applied and beaded ogival cartouche decoration with underglaze cobalt blue and copper red was recovered from the Java Sea (Figure 3.6). This exceedingly rare masterpiece of Yuan porcelain is represented in China by an underglaze decorated jar (*guan*) from the hoard discovery at Baoding, Hebei Province (Figure 3.7).[29]

Figure 3.6 Fragment of a jar, Yuan polychrome and applied decoration in ogival cartouche, mid-fourteenth century. Recovered from the Java Sea, Indonesia.

Source: Private Collection, Jakarta. Photograph John Guy.

Excavations in recent decades at the official kilns at Zhushan, Jingdezhen and at the nearby Hutian kilns, in Jiangxi Province, have confirmed that the spectacular Yuan – and early Ming – porcelains discovered in India and West Asia were made in Jingdezhen (Figures 3.13, 3.30).[30] These finds also establish that the official kilns had an important commercial dimension to their activity in the Yuan as well as the early Ming period, and did not confine their output to the production of wares for court use alone. Further excavations elsewhere in China have revealed a growing number of examples of Yuan blue-and-white porcelain recovered from residential sites, hoards and tombs, establishing that these wares were quickly taken up by the Chinese elite, as witnessed by the Baoding hoard,

Figure 3.7 Yuan porcelain jar with underglaze copper red and cobalt blue and applied decoration. Jingdezhen, mid-fourteenth century, ht. 41.3 cm.

Source: Found Baoding. Hebei Provincial Museum.

and at residential sites at such remote outstations as Jininglu in Inner Mongolia.[31] The imperial and aristocratic interest in blue-and-white very probably led directly to the dwindling of supplies of the finest quality Jingdezhen blue-and-white porcelain being available for the export markets.

These wares required unprecedented advances in large-scale potting, the use of moulding, cobalt decorating and highly controlled firing conditions. This technology was mastered in the second quarter of the fourteenth-century,[32] and production continued undisturbed only until the collapse of social order at Jingdezhen in 1352, the result of peasant revolts. The David altar vases, dated to 1351, now displayed in the British Museum, represent the climax of this spectacularly fertile moment in China's extended ceramic history. The window of opportunity for the Middle Eastern and Indian elites to acquire these premier wares thus proved to be surprisingly narrow. Official production does not appear to have resumed on a significant scale until the restoration of order with the establishment of the Ming dynasty under emperor Hongwu in 1368, although civil order had been restored to the region well before that, and private kilns were likely active again. The Imperial Factory at Zhushan then became an important centre for blue-and-white production for the early Ming, continuing and extending the achievements of the Yuan.

China in India

To this point this chapter has been concerned with constructing the historical framework in which large quantities of high quality Chinese stonewares and porcelains came to circulate in Asia's maritime diaspora. I now wish to turn to the evidence, textual and archaeological, which illuminates our understanding of the patterns of consumption of Chinese ceramics in one of its most discriminating markets, South Asia. There is no evidence to suggest that the Indian subcontinent ever provided a mass market for Chinese ceramics in the way that Southeast Asia clearly did. Rather, the archaeological record points to the select consumption of high quality wares at a succession of Indian courts. It is not coincidental that these all belonged to foreign households of West and Central Asian origin who had established themselves as ruling dynasties in northern India. The taste that these rulers exhibited for collecting Chinese porcelain, along with jades of Central Asian and Chinese origin, would appear to have been the result of a shared cultural ancestry.[33]

They had a close and sustained experience of the Central Asian Silk route and the wondrous commodities that circulated along that trade road. They had an appetite for, amongst other things, the finest porcelain that China would permit to be traded beyond its borders. It was Yuan blue-and-white porcelain, and its early Ming successors that most attracted the ruling households of the Islamic world. These were luxury goods by any measure, in demand in the great Islamic courts of the day, including Delhi, Isfahan and Istanbul.

Sultanate India

The Mongol Yuan dynasty was contemporary with the Turki-Mongol Tughlaq Sultanate which ruled Delhi from 1320 to 1414. Both shared a common ancestry in Central Asia and it is arguably for this reason above others that their taste in the decorative arts found a meeting place in Chinese porcelain. Mughal taste for Chinese porcelain was similarly established in Central Asia, at their home of Ferghana on the Silk Route. Large numbers of Yuan blue-and-white sherds have been recovered at Karakorum and at the ruined city of Khara-Khoto, centres marking overland trade routes reopened by the Mongols.[34] Many are directly comparable to the finds from Sultanate Delhi to be discussed on pp. 61–8 (Figures 3.8, 3.9). The Mongols of Ferghana would have had access to these sources, as would the Timurid Sultanates of Delhi.

Timur (Tamerlane, 1336–1405), the great Mongol ruler, was – in common with other Central Asian rulers – infatuated with Chinese porcelain. His appreciation of this material was witnessed by the Spanish ambassador Ruy Gonzalez de Clavijo at the ruler's capital, Samarkand, in 1403–6. Clavijo described the use of Chinese porcelain during Timur's banqueting: "The slices of meat were placed in ... basins, some of gold, and some of silver [and] porcelain ... much esteemed and of very high price".[35] Such wares were highly prized and passed down from generation to generation, as reflected in illustrated editions of the lives of the Mughal emperors, notably the *Baburnama*, which chronicles the life

Figure 3.8 Porcelain bowl with underglaze cobalt blue design of a pair of ducks in aquatic landscape. Yuan period, second-quarter of the fourteenth century. Excavated at the Tughlaq Palace of Firuz Shah Kotla, Delhi. Archaeological Survey of India, New Delhi.

Figure 3.9 Porcelain bowl with lotus bloom scrolling and a band of lotus petal cartouches in underglaze cobalt blue. Yuan period, second-quarter of the fourteenth century. Excavated at the Tughlaq Palace of Firuz Shah Kotla, Delhi. Archaeological Survey of India, New Delhi.

of Timur's son Babur, who first established Mughal rule in north India, and the *Akbarnama*, the official chronicle of emperor Akbar, Babur's grandson. Both illustrated manuscript editions were commissioned by Akbar in the imperil scriptorium in the 1590s (Figures 3.10, 3.29).

A number of the finest examples of Chinese porcelain that survive from West Asian and Indian collections bear inscriptions establishing that they were inventoried as part of imperial households; in some cases, the porcelain's manufacture pre-date the owner inscriptions by more than 200 years, indicative of how prized these luxury goods were. Some display the use of copper rivets to carefully repair those broken in use, witness to the esteem with which they were held over successive generation of ownership.

Two contemporary sources, one Chinese, the other West Asian, refer to the Chinese ceramic trade into India in the first half of the fourteenth century. The

Figure 3.10 Celebrations in honour of the birth of Humayun in the Chahar Bagh of Kabul (1508), depicting the Mughal emperor Babur and couriers dining from blue-and-white and greenware dishes. Folio from an illustrated edition of the *Baburnama*, the life of emperor Babur, commissioned by his grandson, Akbar, *c.*1590.
Source: The British Library Board, London (Or.3714, folio 295r.).

Daoyi zhilue (1349) mentions large quantities of Chinese porcelain entering India.[36] This was precisely the quarter century when Jingdezhen was producing its unrivalled Yuan porcelains, and that such a specific market should be worthy of mention may underscore the economic importance that was attached to it.

The Islamic perspective is provided by the Moroccan traveller Ibn Battuta, whose first-hand knowledge of the sea-passages was unrivalled in his day. His travels, undertaken between 1324 and 1354, took him from his native Tangier to Mecca, India and China. He described the western Indian port of Kollam (Quilon, Kerala) as a major entrepôt receiving large Chinese ships built in Zaitūn (Quanzhou) and Guangzhou. The southern Chinese port of Quanzhou in Fujian had seemingly now surpassed Guangzhou as the preferred terminus for many long-distance traders. Battuta confirmed that it was "the first city we reached after our sea voyage", in 1341. He describes its port as "one of the largest in the world, recording 100 large junks and a multitude of smaller vessels, and the city "immense", boasting a Muslim quarter: "In one of the quarters of this city is the Muhammadan town [with] mosque, hospice and bazaar". Most critically for our purposes, he observed that porcelain "is manufactured only in the towns of Zaitūn and Sín-kalán", the identity of the latter being uncertain, but presumably one of the premier coastal port cities, perhaps Guangzhou (Canton). Battuta appears here to be assuming the place of manufacture is also that of sale. He appears to be describing Jingdezhen, the centre of the ceramic industry producing the unique blue-and-white porcelain so admired in the West. Battuta describes the process of preparing the body for true porcelain using kaolin, and observes that this produces the best quality. As Battuta undoubtedly never visited remote Jingdezhen, in Jiangxi Province, he presumably saw these porcelains in the markets of a great port city, and was (mis)informed as to where they were made. He continues that "the price of this porcelain is the same as, or even less than, that of ordinary pottery in our country" and that it was "exported to India and other countries, even reaching as far as our own lands in the West, and it is the finest of all."[37] He is most effusive in his praise of Sín-kalán: "Porcelain is manufactured there as well as Zaitūn. Its bazaars are first rank. One of the largest of these is the porcelain bazaar, from which porcelain is exported to all parts of China, to India, and to Yemen".[38]

Ibn Battuta's experiences of China enabled him to observe that at Quanzhou were "junks ready to sail for India [including] a junk belonging to an al-Malik az-Zahir, the ruler of Jawa [Sumatra], the crew of which were Muslims".[39] He recounts that they sailed direct to the western Indian ports of Quilon and Calicut. On his earlier sojourn at Calicut, Battuta had recorded seeing thirteen Chinese ships at the western Indian port of Calicut – India's main port for the China trade – "laden with porcelain and other goods".[40] Their cargoes were presumably then sold on to other merchants, depending on the intended market; some of the porcelain went north to Cambay, and hence to the Sultanate court at Delhi; other shipments went to vessels destined for the Islamic courts of West Asia, via the Persian Gulf and Red Sea ports. The discovery by amateur divers of high quality Yuan dynasty blue-and-white porcelain dishes at an unnamed shipwreck site in the Red Sea in the late 1990s signals this important trade axis.[41] Such a cargo was likely destined for Cairo and Istanbul.

Only one contemporary Chinese commentator was in a position to rival Ibn Battuta in the authority of his writings on this subject. Wang Dayuan, who seems to have been a merchant, published his descriptions of China's overseas trade in his *Daoyi zhilue* (A Brief Description of the Island Foreigners) in 1349, only eight years after Ibn Battuta visited China.[42] He provides a brief account of the peoples and customs of the ninety-nine countries he claims to have visited, and makes reference to the trade goods exchanged there. His is especially enlightening on the importance of China's porcelain trade and its markets. Chinese porcelain is listed as being in demand in forty-five of these countries, with eighteen expressing a preference for blue-and-white, and fifteen for greenwares (celadon). Of those expressing a preference for blue-and-white all belonged to the kingdoms of India and Saudi Arabia. Chinese ships traded to *Da Julan* (Kollam, Kerala) with porcelain, and the markets enroute demanded different grades of quality according to their means; ports in Bengal, Orissa and Calicut were named as markets for high quality wares, whilst "coarse bowls" were sold at Trincomalee in Sri Lanka. The importance of Trincomalee, and of Wang Dayuan's report, was demonstrated when a quantity of Yuan celadons were washed ashore at nearby Nilaveli, signalling the presence of a shipwreck offshore.[43] Trincomalee served as the port for the Chola-occupation administration of the Sri Lankan city of Polonnaruwa, where the Nilaveli shipwreck cargo was likely destined.

It is Ibn Battuta who described first-hand how Chinese porcelain was used and regarded by its new consumers in the courts of Sultanate India. Uniquely in his time, he recorded the consumption of Chinese porcelain at the courts of India. He spent time as a guest of Sultan Muhammad bin Tughlaq (r. 1325–51) at Tughlaqabad, the Delhi Sultanate capital, arriving there in 1334. His account of life at court includes reference to a large quantity of Chinese porcelain in use at receptions and dinners, and descriptions of the items employed. No traces of these wares have been found in excavations of the fort, suggesting that these highly prized utensils were transferred to nearby Firuz Shah Kotla, the fort built in 1351 by the sultan's son and successor, Firuz Shah Tughlaq (r. 1351–88), at the new city of Firozabad, in Delhi. There, some years later, they appear to have been intentionally broken, on the orders by the sultan himself. The *A'fif Tarikh-I-Firuzshahi*, the history of Muhammad bin Tughlaq and Firoz Shah Tughlaq's reigns, written by Ziyā' al-Dīn Baranī in 1357, confirms that the latter sultan grew increasingly conservative, leading to his order "that pictures of living things were no longer to be tolerated".[44] It would seem that his wishes were systematically carried out. The destruction of this imperial collection of Chinese porcelain, between the years 1351 and 1357, fits well into this historical moment when Islamic conservatism included the prohibition of the depiction of living creatures.

Subsequently, both these Tughlaq ruler's fort-palaces were sacked by Timur's invading army, as part of the 1398 Mongol campaign that led to the destruction of the last sultanate in Delhi, the Afghan Lodi. A chance find in the grounds of the Kotla Firoz Shah palace complex in 1961, revealed a spectacular group of over seventy-two identifiable pieces of fourteenth-century Chinese porcelain, re-assembled from a larger group of fragments. Sixty-seven Yuan Jingdezhen blue-and-white porcelains and five Longquan celadon are identifiable (Figures 3.8–3.9, 3.11–3.12, 3.14–3.15, 3.17–3.18, 3.20–3.28).[45] The find spot was likely in the immediate vicinity of the palace's royal kitchens, and all displayed signs of intentional breakage. The hoard, as best can be judged by the re-assembly of the fragmentary remains, consisted of forty-four blue-and-white dishes and plates, twenty-three bowls, and five celadon plates. Of these seventy-two pieces, a remarkable fifty-three carry inscriptions, "written" in the porcelain by drilling a series of holes to form the Arabic letters (Figure 3.12). The inscriptions are in Persian, written in *naskh* script. The majority state that they are the property of the royal kitchen (*matbah-e-khas*) or variation on this; some add the word *sad*, indicating the item was acceptable for use in the royal kitchen. Several have contemporary riveted repairs in which copper wire was employed to rejoin past breakages, indicating that these objects were highly valued and indicative of them having been in use for an extended period of time before their apparently intentional destruction. This is consistent with them being first employed at Tughlaqabad before their transfer to Firozabad, presumably in 1351. Whether the *naskh* inscriptions refer to the ownership of Muhammad bin Tughlaq or his

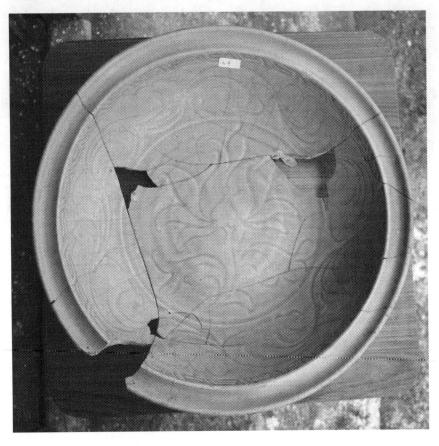

Figure 3.11 Celadon dish with incised lotus bloom and scrolls. Yuan period, c.1350. Excavated at the Tughlaq Palace of Firuz Shah Kotla, Delhi. Archaeological Survey of India, New Delhi.

successor, Firoz Shah Tughlaq, is not indicated, but given reference by the royal chronicler Baranī to a policy of iconoclasm at court sometime before 1357, the inscriptions can reasonably be assigned to the reign of Muhammad bin Tughlaq. His reign exactly corresponds with the high point of Yuan blue-and-white porcelain production at Jingdezhen, and indicates that these prestige objects were exported promptly to their intended markets, in this case only to be destroyed a few decades later.

The Delhi Sultanate collection, as witnessed by the Kotla Firoz Shah hoard, represents the largest collection of mid-fourteenth century Yuan porcelain known.

Fragmentary finds have also been reported from excavations at Lal Kot, another Sultanate palace complex in Delhi, in levels associated with coins of

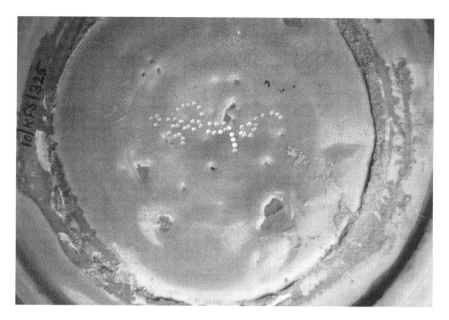

Figure 3.12 Detail of a celadon dish glazed base with drilled *naskh* script inscription *matbah-e khas*, 'royal kitchen'. Yuan period, c.1350. Excavated at the Tughlaq Palace of Firuz Shah Kotla, Delhi. Archaeological Survey of India, New Delhi.

Figure 3.13 Fragments of porcelain dishes with underglaze cobalt blue design, left with moulded monochrome cartouche, and right with cloud-collar lappet design. Yuan period, second-quarter of the fourteenth century excavated from Jingdezhen, Jiangxi (*After* Liu Xinyuan, 1999).

Figure 3.14 Detail of porcelain dish with reserved white-on-blue ground of four lappets ('cloud collar') design framing a central floral meander. Yuan period, second-quarter of the fourteenth century. Excavated at the Tughlaq Palace of Firuz Shah Kotla, Delhi. Archaeological Survey of India, New Delhi.

Figure 3.15 Porcelain dish with underglaze cobalt blue design of eight-petalled medallion and reserved white lotus scroll with five blooms in the cavetto, Yuan period, second-quarter of the fourteenth century. Excavated at the Tughlaq Palace of Firuz Shah Kotla, Delhi. Archaeological Survey of India, New Delhi.

Figure 3.16 Porcelain dish with underglaze cobalt blue design of a chrysanthemum surrounded sixteen auspicious motifs in lappets, reversed white moulded cavetto and wave pattern cusped rim. Yuan period, second-quarter of the fourteenth century.

Source: With permission of the Royal Ontario Museum, ROM, Toronto (2004.969.19).

Figure 3.17 Porcelain dish with underglaze cobalt blue design of six-petalled medallion reserved in white-on-blue, enclosing circle with textile grid pattern, six cartouches in cavetto. Yuan period, second-quarter of the fourteenth century. Excavated at the Tughlaq Palace of Firuz Shah Kotla, Delhi. Archaeological Survey of India, New Delhi.

Figure 3.18 Detail of porcelain dish with underglaze cobalt blue design of the auspicious Eight Buddhist Treasure in lotus petal cartouches imitative of metalwork (cf. Figure 3.19), with central medallion of a crane in flight, repeated in eight cartouches in cavetto. Yuan period, second-quarter of the 14th century. Excavated at the Tughlaq Palace of Firuz Shah Kotla, Delhi. Archaeological Survey of India, New Delhi.

Figure 3.19 Cup stand decorated with the Eight Buddhist Treasures, silver with repoussé decoration. Yuan period, fourteenth century. Diam. 15.6 cm.

Source: The Metropolitan Museum of Art, New York, Purchase, 2006 Benefit Fund (2007.187).

Figure 3.20 Detail of porcelain dish with underglaze cobalt blue design of eight paneled design with floral motifs reserved in white-on blue. Cusped edges imitative of metalwork. Yuan period, second-quarter of the fourteenth century. Excavated at the Tughlaq Palace of Firuz Shah Kotla, Delhi. Archaeological Survey of India, New Delhi.

Figure 3.21 Detail of porcelain dish with underglaze cobalt blue design of moulded peony bloom and floral meanders reserved in white-on-blue hatched ground. Yuan period, second-quarter of the fourteenth century. Excavated at the Tughlaq Palace of Firuz Shah Kotla, Delhi. Archaeological Survey of India, New Delhi.

Figure 3.22 Porcelain dish with underglaze cobalt blue design of two phoenix in flight amidst lotus and vines, repeated on the cavetto. Yuan period, second-quarter of the fourteenth century. Excavated at the Tughlaq Palace of Firuz Shah Kotla, Delhi. Archaeological Survey of India, New Delhi.

Firoz Shah Tughlaq's reign, suggesting that the presence of Chinese porcelain at the Delhi Sultanate courts was extensive.[46] These highly prized objects were very probably exhibited in a manner similar to that known to have been the practice in later Mughal palaces, where dedicated China Rooms (*Chinikhana*) were created with wall niches designed to display these high-value exotic objects. They were used on court occasions, and are visible in court paintings recording state audiences.

Others were kept in the royal kitchens for use during banqueting, as first observed by Ibn Battuta in the 1330s. At a conservative estimate of seventy-two items, this Yuan-period hoard significantly outnumbered any other known collection. Even the Ardabil Shrine porcelains donated by the Isfahan royal household, and the Topkapi Saray collection of Ottoman Istanbul, with which it may most directly be compared, do not rival the sheer scale of the Delhi Sultanate Yuan-assemblage. The extent of other major shrine collections, such as that donated by the pious and wealthy Safavid princess Mahin Banu Khanumas (1519–62) to the shrine of Ali al-Ridha, in Mashad, in north-eastern Iran, and subsequently looted and dispersed, will never be known.[47]

Figure 3.23 Porcelain dish with underglaze cobalt blue design of an aquatic bird in garden landscape, with melon, grapevine and plantain; terrace wall in foreground. Yuan period, second-quarter of the fourteenth century. Excavated at the Tughlaq Palace of Firuz Shah Kotla, Delhi. Archaeological Survey of India, New Delhi.

The Topkapi Saray Museum is the most extensive holding of Chinese ceramics preserved today that formed part of the China–Middle East trade; inventories exist from 1495.[48] A similar collection once existed in the Chihl Sutun, Isfahan. The Ardabil Shrine, in northern Iran once housed a treasury of such objects. This Shi'ite shrine is dedicated to Shaykh safi al-Din, the spiritual patriarch of the Safavid royal family. According to a contemporary source, in 1611 emperor Shah 'Abbas I (r. 1588–1629) presented the family shrine with a collection of 1,162 Chinese porcelains. When catalogued in 1956 some 805 remained, now housed in the Gulistan Museum, Tehran.[49] These imperial collections, together with the Delhi Sultanate collection, represent the largest corpus of fourteenth and fifteenth century Chinese porcelains preserved globally.[50] Since the reporting of these remarkable finds, excavations at Jingdezhen have established that Yuan wares of precisely this quality and type were the product of the official kilns.

Figure 3.24 Porcelain dish with underglaze cobalt blue design of garden landscape of plantain, melon and grapevine. Yuan period, second-quarter of the fourteenth century. Excavated at the Tughlaq Palace of Firuz Shah Kotla, Delhi. Archaeological Survey of India, New Delhi.

This passion for Chinese porcelain was shared by other Muslim rulers in the subcontinent, and the scale of their collecting was also impressive. When the Golconda minister Khajeh Jahan received his sultan in 1471, he "presented him with so many rich curiosities.... One hundred Faghfoori [Chinese] dishes and cups not to be seen but in the palaces of a few great princes".[51] Frequent diplomatic exchange with China had ensured a reliable supply of porcelain, which grew significantly in volume. The early Ming emperor Hongwu (r. 1368–98) sent embassies to the Coromandel Coast in 1369–70, offering opportunities for trade, as did the renowned voyages of Admiral Zheng He, which took place in the reign of emperor Yongle (1403–33).[52] In 1405, on his first voyage, Zheng He reached Calicut, carrying porcelain as one of the principal cargo items. He also visited Indian ports in Bengal, the Coromandel and Malabar coasts, and Gujarat on his voyages to the "Western Ocean". Porcelain was a regular feature of these trade missions.

Figure 3.25 Detail of Figure 3.24, plantain and grapes. Archaeological Survey of India, New Delhi.

Figure 3.26 Porcelain dish with underglaze cobalt blue design of a carp swimming amidst waterweed. Yuan period, second-quarter of the fourteenth century. Excavated at the Tughlaq Palace of Firuz Shah Kotla, Delhi. Archaeological Survey of India, New Delhi.

Figure 3.27 Detail of Figure 3.26, tonal modelling of fish and pooling of cobalt in waterweed visible. Archaeological Survey of India, New Delhi.

Figure 3.28 Detail of a porcelain dish with underglaze cobalt blue design of a mythical winged *qilin* amidst foliate landscape. Yuan period, second-quarter of the fourteenth century. Excavated at the Tughlaq Palace of Firuz Shah Kotla, Delhi. Archaeological Survey of India, New Delhi.

Figure 3.29 Akbar receiving the Iranian ambassador Sayyif Beg. Right-hand folio from a double-page composition, from the *Akbarnama*. Composition by La'l, painting by Ibrahim Kahar, Mughal, c.1586–89. Gouache on paper; 30.8 × 19.1 cm.

Source: Victoria and Albert Museum, London (IS. 2–1896, 27/117).

74   John Guy

Imperial taste

The successors to the Delhi Sultanate rulers, the Mughals, shared Muhammad bin Tughlaq's taste for fine Chinese porcelain. Timur's descendant Babur (r. 1526–30), founder of the Mughal empire, and his successors Humayan, Akbar, Jahangir and Shah Jahan, were all keen collectors of Chinese porcelain. The peripatetic lifestyle of the early Mughals does not appear to have dissuaded them from collecting and enjoying fine porcelain. The *Baburnama*, the official history of Babur's reign, recounts a series of misadventures involving porcelain, such as a pack animal carrying the royal kitchen's Chinese bowls being successfully rescued during a hasty strategic retreat. References abound to the collections and display of Chinese porcelain in the residences of the Mughal emperor and members of his nobility. The *Baburnama* provides the first description of a China Room, built by Babur's grandfather Ulugh Beg (1411–49) to display his Timurid jade and Chinese porcelain collections: "In the [same] garden he also built a four-doored hall, known as the *Chinikhana* because its *izara* are all of porcelain; he sent to China for the porcelain used in it".[53]

By the reign of Akbar (1556–1605) porcelain utensils were a regular feature of court life, as witnessed by contemporary paintings (Figure 3.29). The *Akbarnama*, which chronicles his early life, includes illustrated pages that depict palace interiors in which Chinese porcelain features prominently, both in use and for display. Following in the tradition of his forefathers Ulugh Beg and Babur, Akbar created rooms expressly for the display and enjoyment of the imperial Chinese porcelain collection. Abu'l Fazl, the emperor's official biographer, recorded that the Imperial Treasury contained "25 lakhs worth of the most elegant vessels of every kind of porcelain and coloured glass".[54] Little survives of these Mughal interiors, apart from bare niches at Agra Fort and Fatephur Sikri. Mughal and Iranian court miniatures reveal however that such displays were a regular feature of the finest palaces, where Chinese porcelain was proudly displayed alongside Syrian and Iranian glass and metal objects in vogue at the time. Such court tastes were widely emulated by ministers, regional governors and wealthy merchants, generating greater demand. According to Abul Fazl, author of the *Akbarnama*, an active overland trade was maintained with Kabul, as well as the regular sea trade via Surat, the leading port serving the Mughal capital. Kabul continued to hold its prominence as a market for luxuries such as Chinese ceramics into the early seventeenth century.

The emperor Jahangir (r. 1605–27) continued this passion for Chinese ceramics, acquiring antiquarian pieces of the highest quality, such as a superb wine ewer now archaeologically linked to the imperial kilns at Jingdezhen (Figures 3.31, 3.32).[55] According to his memoirs, *Tuzik-i-Jahangiri*, he received among his New Year gifts in 1612 "porcelain from China … and other valuable presents procured in Kabul".[56] This again reinforces the importance of regional demand for imperial quality Chinese porcelains within the western Asia-India sphere. Kabul was well connected to such wealthy Iranian markets as Shiraz and Isfahan, which served that region's demand for such objects. It is likely that

Figure 3.30 Wine ewers, monochrome white and underglaze cobalt blue. Early Ming – Yongle and Xuande periods – early fifteenth century. Excavated from the Zhushan Ming imperial kiln site, Jingdezhen, Jiangxi (*After* Liu Xinyuan, 1999).

Figure 3.31 Porcelain wine ewer with blue-and-white floral meander decoration. Xuande (1426–35), Jingdezhen. Inscribed and dated Shah Jahan AH 1038, equivalent to 1628.

Source: Courtesy Christies Images Limited.

Figure 3.32 Detail of cartouche of Figure 3.31, inscribed in Persian *nasta'liq* script.

Mughal India's ongoing demand for highest quality wares was principally satisfied by this route.

The *Tuzuk-i-Jahangiri* praises Jahangir for his expertise in Chinese ceramics. When the emperor was presented with gifts of porcelain, his diary distinguished two types, *Khata* from northern China and *Faghfuri* from other regions. Such was the level of knowledge of Chinese porcelain prevailing in India at the beginning of the seventeenth century. The prevailing connoisseurship at court ensured that only objects of the highest quality entered the imperial household, as witnessed by the small corpus of surviving inscribed examples. They are also known to have commanded very high prices. The English Ambassador of James I, Sir Thomas Roe, presented two China cups to Prince Khurrum (later Shah Jahan; r. 1628–58) when they met on 12 October 1617. He later observed that the emperor Shah Jahan valued porcelain highly and that among the gifts presented by the ruler of Bijapur were "Chinawares and one figure of christall which the king accepted more than that masse of wealth".[57] Roe despaired at the lavish gifts the Dutch trading company (VOC) representative presented at court: "a great present of Chinaware, sandalwood, parrots and cloves", commodities presumably sourced via Bantam, the VOC's Asian headquarters in west Java. Nor would Roe's modest gifts have made much impression when set beside the early Ming period blue-and-white dish with a design dominated by two lotus blooms, and a Xuande-period blue-and-white porcelain ewer, both of which entered Shah Jahan's collection in 1628, likely as gifts to mark his ascension to the throne (Figures 3.31–3.32).[58] A superb monochrome white ewer, the so-called "monk's hat" type believed to have inspired by Tibetan metalwork vessels, produced at Jingdezhen early in the reign of Yongle (r. 1402–24), was marked some 200 years later as belonging to the imperial collection of Shah

Jahan, when it was elegantly inscribed in Persian *naskh* script as the property of the Mughal emperor in the year 1643 (Figures 3.33, 3.34).[59]

A spectacular dish with grape and vine design further demonstrates the close relations between the premier Islamic courts of Mughal India, Safavid Iran and Ottoman Turkey (Figures 3.35–3.37). Where this dish was for the 100 years immediately following its manufacture is unrecorded, but a donative inscription indicates that by the second quarter of the sixteenth century it had entered the collection of the Mahin Banu Khanumas. A century later, in 1643, it was inventoried in Shah Jahan's imperial collection in Agra. Another grand blue-and-white porcelain dish with a leaping *qilin*, of mid-fourteenth century production, was inventoried as belonging to Shah Jahan in 1653, with a drilled inscription on the underside of the rim assigning it to the imperial household (Figures 3.38–3.39).

Figure 3.33 Monk's cap ewer of white monochrome, Yongle period (1402–24), Jingdezhen. Inscribed in *nasta'liq* script the property of Shah Jahan and dated AH 1052, equivalent to 1643.

Source: Aga Khan Museum, Toronto (AKM 966).

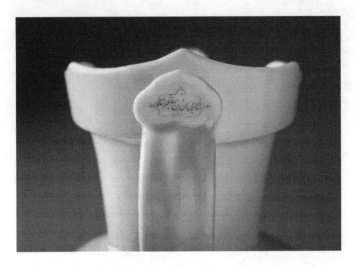

Figure 3.34 Detail of ogival cartouche of Figure 3.33, inscribed in Persian *nasta'liq* script.

Figure 3.35 Porcelain dish (so-called Mahin Banu dish), with underglaze cobalt blue grapes and vine design, Ming dynasty, Yongle (r. 1403–24). Jingdezhen, *c*.1420. Inscribed with a *vaqf* cartouche recording donation by (Princess) Mahin Banu to the Shrine of Ali al-Ridha, Mashad, Iran, and subsequently in *nasta'liq* script the property of Shah Jahan in AH 1053, equivalent to 1643.

Source: Photograph Courtesy of Sotheby's, Inc. © 2015.

Figure 3.36 Detail of Iranian ownership inscriptions of base of Figure 3.35. The Shah Jahan inscription appears on the foot exterior.

Figure 3.37 Detail of Shah Jahan inscription on the foot exterior of Figure 3.35.

Figure 3.38 Porcelain dish with blue-and-white *qilin* design, Yuan dynasty, Jingdezhen, mid-fourteenth century. Inscribed in *nasta'liq* script the property of Shah Jahan and dated AH 1063, equivalent to 1653.

Source: John D. Rockefeller 3rd Collection (1979.151). Courtesy of Asia Society, New York.

Figure 3.39 Detail of inscription of Figure 3.38, inscribed in Persian *nasta'liq* script.

A monochrome bowl which also entered Shah Jahan's collection in 1643 bears the religious endowment cartouche (*vaqf*) of Shah 'Abbas I of Iran, establishing that it had once formed part of the group of porcelains gifted to his family shrine at Ardabil in 1611. How it was dispersed from there to Mughal India is unrecorded, but as it had served as a religious donation it would have been inappropriate to subsequently be offered as a state gift. Thus, it likely formed a part of the private luxury trade. Such a provenance does much to establish the status of high-quality Chinese porcelain in the Muslim courts of West Asia and the Indian subcontinent, and their acceptability both as gifts between imperial households, and as elite commodities for private sale.

The combined collections of India and West Asia demonstrate the scale and quality of Yuan porcelain expressly produced for export to some of the wealthiest clients in medieval Asia. The Sultanate collection of Yuan porcelains discovered in Delhi was one of the earliest and grandest to be assembled, but it was not unique. However, unlike its compatriot collections in other courts of the Muslim world, its destruction in the later fourteenth century, ensured that it remained together, albeit in a fragmentary state. Its rival collections were gifted, plundered and traded over the ensuing centuries, so our understanding of their original grandeur is much diminished. The Tughlaq palace finds of Kotler Firoz Shah, Delhi, provide a unique window on the fourteenth-century collecting habits and tastes of the Muslim world.

Notes

1 Of the five Delhi Sultanate dynasties, only the last, the Lodi, were not Turkic-Mongol, but rather of Afghan origin.
2 John Guy, "Early Ninth-century Chinese Export Ceramics and the Persian Gulf Connection: The Belitung Shipwreck Evidence", in *Chine – Mediterranee, Routes et échanges de la Céramique jusqu'au XVIe Siècle, TAOCI*, Revue annuelle de la Société française d'Étude de la Céramique orientale, vol. 4, 2006: 9–20; John Guy, "The Phanom Surin Shipwreck, a Pahlavi Inscription, and their Significance for the History of Early Lower Central Thailand", *Journal of the Siam Society*, vol. 105, 2017: 179–96; John Guy, "Shipwrecks in Southeast Asia: Southern China's Maritime Trade and the Emerging Role of Arab Merchants in Late First Millennium Indian Ocean Exchange", in Angela Schottenhammer (ed.), *Exchange, Transfer, and Human Movement Across the Indian Ocean World*, London, Palgrave Macmillan, 2019, pp. 121–61.
3 John Guy, "Rare and Strange Goods: International Trade in Ninth-Century Asia", in Regina Krahl, John Guy *et al.* (eds.), *Shipwrecked. Tang Treasures and Monsoon Winds* (Washington D.C.: Sackler Gallery, 2010): 19–28.
4 G.R. Tibbetts, *Arabic Navigation in the Indian Ocean Before the Coming of the Portuguese* (London: Royal Asiatic Society, 1981), 2.
5 Li Rongxi, "The Journey of the Eminent Monk Faxian", in BDK English Tripitaka, *Lives of Great Monks and Nuns* (Berkeley, Numata Center, 2002), 203.
6 Li Rongxi, "Journey of the Eminent Monk Faxian", 204.
7 John Guy, *Oriental Trade Ceramics in South East Asia: Ninth to Sixteenth Centuries* (Singapore: Oxford University Press, 1986); and for the Mantai excavations, see John Carswell, Siran Deraniyagala, and Alan Graham, *Mantai. City by the Sea* (Colombo: Archaeological Department of Sri Lanka (Aichwald: Linden Soft Verlag, 2013), Chapter 12.

8. John Carswell, "China and Islam: A Survey of the Coast of India and Ceylon", *TOCS*, vol. 42 (1977–78): 24–69. See also Noboru Karashima, "Trade relations between South India and China during the 13th and 14th centuries", *Journal of East-West Relations*, vol. 1 (1989): 59–81.
9. For the Nilaveli shipwreck, see J. Carswell, *Blue and White. Chinese Porcelain Around the World* (London: British Museum Press, 2000), 174. For Wang Dayuan, see W.W. Rockhill, "Notes on the Relations and Trade of China with the Eastern Archipelago and the Coast of the Indian Ocean During the Fourteenth Century", *Tu'ong Pao*, vol. 15 (1914): 419–47; vol. 16, (1915): 61–159, 236–71, 374–92.
10. K.A.N. Sastri, *Foreign Notices of South India. From Megasthenes to Ma Huan*, (Madras: University of Madras, 1939); Chapter X.
11. Sastri, *Foreign Notices of South India*: Chapter XVI.
12. S. Adhyatman, *Notes on Green Wares Found in Indonesia* (Jakarta: Ceramic Society of Indonesia, 1983); Guy, *Oriental Trade Ceramics*; and John Guy, "Early Ninth Century Chinese Export Ceramics and the Persian Gulf Connection: The Belitung Shipwreck Evidence", in *Chine-Méditerranée Routes et échanges de la céramique avant le XVIe siècle*, *TAOCI*, vol. 4 (2006): 9–20.
13. Jean Sauvaget, *Aḫbār aṣ-Ṣīn wa l-Hind. Relation de la Chine et de l'Inde rédigée en 851* (Paris: Belles Lettres, 1948).
14. John Guy, "Early Asian Ceramic Trade and the Belitung ('Tang') Cargo", *Transactions of the Oriental Ceramic Society*, vol. 66 (2001–2): 13–27.
15. F. Hirth, and W.W. Rockhill, *Chau Ju-kua* [Zhao Rugua], *His Work on the Chinese and Arab Trade in the Twelfth and Thirteenth Centuries, Entitled Chu-fan-chï* (St Petersburg: Imperial Academy of Sciences, 1911) (rep. Taipei 1967), 88, 92.
16. G.R. Tibbetts, *A Study of the Arabic Texts Concerning Materials on South-East Asia* (London: Royal Asiatic Society,1979), 37. Tibbetts, *A Study of the Arabic Texts*, 37.
17. Hirth and Rockhill, *Chau Ju-kua*. See also Paul Wheatley, "Geographical Notes on Some Commodities Involved in Sung Maritime Trade", *Journal of the Malaysian Branch of the Royal Asiatic Society*, vol. XXXII, pt. 2, (1959): 1–140; and Grace Wong, *A Comment on the Tributary Trade between China and Southeast Asia*, Southeast Asian Ceramic Society Transactions no. 7 (1979).
18. P.J. Cherian and J. Menon, *Unearthing Pattanam. Histories, Cultures, Crossings* (New Delhi: National Museum, and Kerala Council for Historical Research, 2014).
19. Hirth and Rockhill, *Chau Ju-kua*.
20. Roderich Ptak, "Images of Maritime Asia in Two Yuan Texts: *Daoyi zhilue* and *Yiyu zhi*", *Journal of Song-Yuan Studies*, vol. 25 (1995): 47–75.
21. Ma Huan, *Ying-yai Sheng-lan (The Overall Survey of the Ocean's Shores, 1433)*, trans. by J.V. Mills (Cambridge: Hakluyt Society, 1970).
22. J.V. Mills, "Chinese Navigators in Insulinde about A.D. 1500", *Archipel* 18 (1979): 69–93.
23. John Guy, *Ceramic Excavation Sites in South-East Asia. A Preliminary Gazetteer* (Adelaide: University of Adelaide, 1987).
24. Ma Huan, *Ying-yai Sheng-lan*.
25. B. Gray, "The Export of Chinese Porcelain to India", *Transactions of the Oriental Ceramic Society*, vol. 36 (1964–66): 31–7.
26. Lo Hsiang Lin, "Islam in Canton in the Sung Period. Some Fragmentary Records", in F.S. Drake (ed.), *Symposium on Historical, Archaeological and Linguistic Studies on Southern China, South-East Asia and the Hong Kong Region*, Hong Kong University, 1967: 176–9.
27. John Guy, "Tamil Merchant Guilds and the Quanzhou Trade" in Angela Schottenhammer (ed.), *The Emporium of the World. Maritime Quanzhou, 1000–1400* (Leiden: Brill, 2001): 283–317.
28. Compare J. Allen, *Islamic Metalwork. The Nuhad Es-Said Collection* (London: Sothebys, 1982).

29 Published in James C.Y. Watt (ed.), *The World of Khubilai Khan. Chinese Art in the Yuan Dynasty* (New Haven: Metropolitan Museum of Art/Yale University Press 2011), 284–5.
30 Liu Xinyuan, "Imperial Export Porcelain from Late Yuan to Early Ming", *Oriental Art*, vol. XLV, no. 3 (1999): 48–54, and Huang Wei and Huang Qinghua, "Yuan qinghua ciqi zaoqi leixing de xin faxian – cong shizheng jiaodu lun Yuan qinghua ciqi de qiyuan" [New discoveries of Yuan blue-and-white ceramic types – an evidentiary investigation into the origin of Yuan blue-and-white porcelain], *Wenwu*, 2012, no. 11: 79–88.
31 Chen Yongzhi (ed.), *Porcelain Unearthed from Jininglu Ancient City Site in Inner Mongolia* (Inner Mongolia Institute of Cultural Relics and Archaeology, 2004).
32 The 1323 date of the Sinan shipwreck, a Chinese vessel laden with a mixed cargo of high quality Chinese porcelain (but without any blue-and-white) destined for the Japanese market, is taken as the clearest indication that blue-and-white was not yet in commercial production by this date. For the Sinan cargo, see Chung Yang-mo, *Cultural Relics Found off the Sinan Coast* (Seoul: National Museum of Art, 1977).
33 Robert Skelton, "The Shah Jahan Cup", *Victoria and Albert Museum Bulletin*, vol. II, no. 3, July 1966: 109–10.
34 E. Lubo-Lesnichenko, "The Blue-and-White Porcelain of Yuan Period from Khara-Khoto", *International Symposium on Ancient Chinese Trade Ceramics: Collected Papers* (Taipei: National Museum of History, 1994).
35 G. le Strange (trans.), *Clavijo. Embassy to Tamberlane. 1403–1406* (London: George Routledge and Sons, 1928), 224.
36 Gray, "The Export of Chinese Porcelain to India".
37 H.A.R. Gibb (transl.), *Ibn Battuta. Travels in Asia and Africa 1325–1354* (London: Routledge Kegan Paul, 1929): 282–3.
38 Gibb, *Ibn Battuta*, 289.
39 Gibb, *Ibn Battuta*, 301. For the debate surrounding the identification of "Jawa", see Arlo Griffiths, "The Problem of the Ancient Name Java and the Role of Satyavarman in Southeast Asian International Relations Around the Turn of the Ninth Century CE", *Archipel*, 85 (2013): 43–81.
40 Gibb, *Ibn Battuta*, 235.
41 J. Carswell, *Blue and White. Chinese Porcelain Around the World*, London, British Museum Press, 2000.
42 Rockhill, "Notes on the relations and trade of China".
43 J. Carswell, *Blue and White. Chinese Porcelain Around the World* (London: British Museum Press, 2000), 110 and 174.
44 S. Digby, "The Literary Evidence for Painting in the Delhi Sultanate", *Bulletin of the American Academy of Banares* I, i (1967): 47–58, 50.
45 The Kotla Firuzshah hoard was first described by E. Smart, "Fourteenth Century Chinese Porcelain from a Tughlaq Palace in Delhi", *Transactions of the Oriental Ceramic Society*, vol. 41 (1975–77): 199–230. See also B.R. Mani, *Delhi – Threshold of the Orient (Studies in Archaeological Investigations)* (New Delhi: Archaeological Survey of India, 1997).
46 B.R. Mani, *Delhi – Threshold of the Orient (Studies in Archaeological Investigations)* (New Delhi: Archaeological Survey of India, 1997).
47 A. Soudavar, "A Chinese Dish from the Lost Endowment of Princess Sultanum (925–69/1519–62)", in Kambiz Eslami (ed.), *Iran and Iranian Studies in Honor of Iraj Afshar*, Princeton, 1998: 125–34.
48 Regina Krahl, *Chinese Ceramics from the Topkapi Saray Museum, Istanbul, A Complete Catalogue*, ed. by J. Ayers, 3 vols. (London: Sotheby's, 1986).
49 J.A. Pope, *Chinese Porcelain from the Ardebil Shrine* (Washington: Freer, 1956) (2nd edn 1981).
50 Topkai Saray. See J.A. Pope, *Fourteenth Century Blue and White, A Group of Chinese Porcelain in the Topkapi Sarayi Muzesi, Istanbul* (Washington: Freer, 1952)

(revised edn 1970); and T. Misugi, *Chinese Porcelain Collections in the Near East, Topkapi and Ardebil*, 3 vols. (Hong Kong: University of Hong Kong Press, 1981).
51 E.H. Hunt, "Old Hyderabad China", *Journal of the Hyderabad Archaeological Society* (January 1916): 48–87. See 73. The bulk of the Chinese porcelain preserved today in the Nizam's Salar Jung Museum, and in the State Archaeology Museum, Hyderabad, are Ming period and later.
52 Ma Huan, *Ying-yai Sheng-lan* and Haraprasad Ray, "The South East Asian Connection in Sino-Indian Trade", in R. Scott and J. Guy (eds.), *South East Asia and China: Art, Interaction and Commerce*, Percival David Foundation of Chinese Art Colloquies on Art and Archaeology, no. 17 (London: University of London, 1995): 41–54.
53 A.S. Beveridge (trans.), *The Baburnama in English*, 2 vols (London: Luzac, 1922), vol I, 80. For Ulugh Beg's famous Timurid jade collection, see Robert Skelton, "The Shah Jahan Cup", *Victoria and Albert Museum Bulletin*, vol. II, no. 3 (July 1966): 109–10.
54 A. Aziz, *The Imperial Treasury of the Indian Mughals* (Delhi: Cosmo Publications, 1972), 404.
55 Liu Xinyuan, "Imperial Export Porcelain from Late Yuan to Early Ming", *Oriental Art*, vol. XLV, no. 3 (1999): 48–54.
56 A. Rogers (trans.) and H. Beveridge (ed.), *The Tuzuk-i-Jahangiri or Memoirs of Jahangir From the First to the Twelfth Year of his Reign* (London: Royal Asiatic Society, 1909–14).
57 W. Foster, *Early Travels in India, 1583–1619* (Oxford: Oxford University Press, 1921), 99.
58 The dish is now housed at Wallington House, Northumberland, England, inventoried to Shah Jahan's household in 1628.
59 An inferior quality example, of smaller scale but with its lid intact, is in the Capital Museum, Beijing; published in Watt, *The World of Khubilai Khan*, figure 298.

Part II
Political interactions in the maritime realm and overland

4 Ming China and Southeast Asia in the fifteenth century

Geoff Wade

Introduction

In early fourteenth-century China, the Yuan regime experienced a decline in both political power and military strength. This situation provided an opportunity and incentive for power-seeking or simply self-protection by other political players. The highly-militarized state of Chinese society in this age determined that warfare between Yuan loyalists, local self-defence leaders, smugglers, and sectarian rebels marked much of the succeeding decades. By the 1350s, rival rebellions had resulted in the "China" which the Yuan rulers had controlled being divided into diverse polities which warred against each other. A rebel leader known as Zhu Yuanzhang was eventually able to secure control over increasingly large areas and establish a new Chinese state, which he named Great Ming (大明). With the establishment of his capital at Nanjing in 1368, Zhu began a dynasty whose power was to extend until 1644.[1] Even after the establishment of the capital, however, the Ming forces still needed to engage in huge battles against competitors. One such battle which involved Ming forces fighting against the Yuan loyalist Kökö Temür in 1370 saw 85,000 of the latter's troops and 15,000 of his cavalry horses being captured. However, by that time, the Ming forces had already captured the Yuan capital of Dadu, renaming it Beiping, or Northern Peace, and the consolidation of the new state was well in train.

Ming concerns with the Mongols whom they drove from China was to influence much of both domestic and foreign policy over the following centuries, and was also to result in some dithering by the Ming founder over the final location of his capital.[2] After establishing his capital at Nanjing, naming his heir and his empress, creating six ministries and appointing his major administrative officials, he issued a new Ming law code, all of which provided the foundations for the new dynasty. During the 1370s, Zhu Yuanzhang expanded the structure of the Ming government and, partly due to a growing paranoia, established an increasingly large contingent of palace eunuchs to act as his trusted advisers and counter-balances to the civil administration. This administrative apparatus which he created was to remain essentially in place for the remainder of the dynasty. It was this imperial and administrative structure which was to initiate and implement both the domestic and foreign policies of the Ming for the next 280 years.

Ming foreign policies and Southeast Asia

As reflected in both official and non-official Chinese texts, the Ming rulers saw themselves, or at least depicted themselves, as being divinely sanctioned by Heaven to rule China and those beyond, extending to "all under Heaven". This required that they "enfeoff" rulers of surrounding polities, who were then expected to submit regular "tribute" to the Great Ming. It was this understanding that was to provide the rhetorical and ritual bases of much of the Ming's relations with polities beyond its immediate administrative control.[3]

That not all rulers of Southeast Asian polities agreed with this perception of their position vis-à-vis China is obvious, even from the Chinese texts. In the middle of the fifteenth century, for example, Krung Phra Nakhon Sri Ayudhya, the ruler of Ayudhya refused to accord with the Ming envoy's demands to bow to the north in respect to the Ming emperor and the Chinese envoy to Ayudhya was "secluded" and subsequently died.[4] However, despite such instances, achieving recognition from the Ming court appears to have been important for some rulers and did play an obvious role in the polities and economies of Southeast Asia during this period. The Ming acted as a counterbalance to other hegemons such as Majapahit, and provided polities with both access to a "tribute"-trade relationship with China, and an alternative security system. Participation in this system is overtly accepted in the Vietnamese annals, where it is noted, for example, that the Đại Việt ruler "sought enfeoffment" (求封) from the Ming in 1457.[5]

Ming relations with Southeast Asia have already been subject to some scholarly attention,[6] and on the basis of these works, there are a few generalities which can be dealt with first. It needs to be stated at the outset that there was frequent exchange of envoys between Ming China and the polities of Southeast Asia. One of the first acts of the Ming rulers on coming to power was to send officials to other polities to announce the new reign. Ming envoys were also sent to these polities for a range of other functions including "enfeoffments", or to offer sacrifices on the deaths of rulers. These envoys were usually supervising secretaries (給事中) from the various Offices of Scrutiny (六科). A few examples will suffice to show (at least the stated) functions of some of these missions.

1 Offering sacrifices for deceased ruler of Champa 1452.[7]
2 Offering sacrifices for deceased ruler of Siam and enfeoffing son in 1453.[8]
3 Enfeoffing ruler of Malacca in 1459.[9]
4 Enfeoffing ruler of Annam in 1460.[10]
5 Enfeoffing ruler of Champa in 1478.[11]

Another major element of Ming-Southeast Asian interactions was the "tribute" missions from the Southeast Asian polities, which are widely recognized as having had a strong trade element. These have been the subject of a range of articles and an excellent index exists which can be used to track the incoming missions to the Ming of at least the Islamic polities of Southeast Asia for much of the fifteenth century.[12] The lack of attention given to these missions in this chapter is a function of the amount of research already conducted on them rather than an indicator of their relative importance.

Even if one is sceptical of the degree to which Chinese texts reflect what was happening in Southeast Asia in the fifteenth century, or even if one considers that the "enfeoffments" and "tribute relations" of which the Ming texts wrote were no more than exchanges of diplomatic niceties between polities, we can still say, with much certainty, that the Ming was heavily involved in Southeast Asia throughout the century.

In examining the effects that the Ming had on what we now know as Southeast Asia in the fifteenth century, it is perhaps first necessary to look at what policies were pursued in respect of the region by the successive Ming rulers. A chronological study of these policies constitutes the first part of this chapter, and it is followed by an attempt to synthesize the individual policies and activities into a more coherent account of how the Ming state and its agents affected Southeast Asia through that century.

Southeast Asia-related policies of Ming Taizu (1368–98)

Early in his reign, Zhu Yuanzhang, the first Ming emperor, provided instructions as injunctions to later generations. These dictums included advice to the Chief Military Commission as to which countries posed a threat to the Ming polity and those which did not. He stated that those to the north were dangerous, while those to the south did not constitute a threat, and were not to be subject to unwarranted attack.[13] Yet, either despite this, or as a result of it, it was the polities to the south of the Ming which were to suffer the greatest effects of Ming expansion over the following century.

Invasions of Yunnan polities

In 1369, not long after Zhu Yuanzhang founded his new dynasty, he sent proclamations for the instruction of "the countries of Yunnan and Japan". (雲南日本等國).[14] This early recognition of Yunnan as a "country" which lay beyond the Ming was to change very soon thereafter. By 1380, Yunnan was considered to have been China's territory since the Han dynasty,[15] and 250,000 troops were deployed in an attack on the polity, taking Dali, Lijiang and Jinchi in 1382. Thereby, the Ming founder took control of the major urban centres of the northwestern part of what is today Yunnan, including several Tai areas.

By 1387, Ming Taizu had extended the aspirations of his enterprise and, in preparation for an attack on the Baiyi (Möng Mao) polity to the south of his earlier conquests, a military officer was sent to Sichuan to buy 10,000 ploughing cattle. These were to be used to plough the fields necessary to feed the troops on the likely long-term expedition. Under the commander Mu Ying, the Ming forces attacked the Baiyi with firearms, taking a claimed 30,000 heads.[16] Si

Lunfa, the ruler of the polity, was subsequently dunned for all the costs of the military expedition against him, as a *quid pro quo* for recognizing him as ruler of the Baiyi![17] When Dao Ganmeng rebelled against Si Lunfa in 1397, the Chinese state gave sanctuary to the fleeing ruler, sent troops against Dao Ganmeng and restored Si Lunfa, extracting vast tracts of land from him for the assistance rendered to him.[18] The Ming state also broke down his former territory into the polities of Luchuan, Mengyang, Mubang, Mengding, Lujiang, Ganyai, Dahou and Wan Dian, all under separate rulers.[19] This was the beginning of a policy of divide-and-rule which was to be pursued throughout the Ming, and which had such profound effects on the upland Tai polities.

The "native offices" of Yunnan

The new polities which were "created" (or recognized) in Yunnan under the first Ming ruler were known to the Ming as "native offices" (*tusi* – 土司), as they were, initially, usually left under the control of the hereditary rulers. It was through these rulers that the Ming exerted control and engaged in economic expropriation involving tribute demands and other levies. Cheli (Chiang Hung), a Tai polity which was an antecedent of Sipsong Panna, was recognized as a "native office" in 1384 with the original ruler as the "native official". In 1385, the Ming established the Yinyuan Luobi Dian Chief's Office in Yuanjiang prefecture, Yunnan (near the Red River). This Tai polity had a "circulating official" Chief and a native-official deputy chief. The circulating official was a part of the formal Ming bureaucracy while the deputy chief was undoubtedly part of the hereditary leadership family.[20] Here, then, we see the beginnings of the process by which formerly Southeast Asian polities were gradually absorbed into the Chinese state.

Economic exploitation of Yunnan

In the process by which they were gradually absorbed by the Ming, these polities were subjected to a wide range of tribute demands, labour levies and other claims, including troop provision. As an example, in the case of the Tai Mao polity of Luchuan/Pingmian, the Ming court demanded 15,000 horses, 500 elephants and 30,000 cattle from the ruler Si Lunfa in 1397.[21] Subsequently, large silver demands (silver in lieu of labour) were levied on Luchuan. An annual amount of 6,900 *liang*[22] of silver was initially set and subsequently it was almost tripled to 18,000 *liang*. When it was realized that this was impossible to meet, the levy was reduced to the original amount.[23] Diverse other levies were applied to the other polities and enforced through the use or threat of military force.

Tribute/trade

The Hongwu reign was marked by frequent sending of Chinese envoys to foreign polities and the court's reception of envoys from the maritime polities of

Annam, Champa, Cambodia, Siam, Cochin, San Foqi, Java, Japan, Ryukyu, Brunei, and Korea. They were apparently drawn to China by the trade concessions available to tribute envoys and the rewards given to the rulers who submitted "tribute".[24] However, the trade-diplomacy machine was also apparently utilized by some within the Ming administrative structure to exercise influence and control. It was the failure to report the arrival of an envoy from Champa that led to Hu Weiyong (胡惟庸), the Ming prime minister from 1377 to 1380, being subject to intense investigation and subsequently execution on charges of treason.[25] The possible involvement of Hu Weiyong in a wider range of unofficial links with the polities of Southeast Asia has already been discussed by Wolters,[26] and need not be reiterated here. Suffice it to say that members of the Ming bureaucracy were likely already heavily involved in Southeast Asian maritime politics by the 1390s.

Maritime prohibitions

In the early 1370s, the coastal people in China were forbidden to cross the oceans other than on official missions.[27] Fujian military officials who had privately sent people across the seas to engage in trade were punished not long thereafter.[28] The prohibition was restated in 1381[29] and 1384[30] and an imperial command "strictly prohibiting people from having contact with foreign *fan*"[31] was promulgated in 1390.[32] The frequency of these prohibitions suggests that they were not very effective, and the reason given for the imperial command was that "at this time in Guangdong/Guangxi, Zhejiang and Fujian, there were foolish people who did not know of this [the prohibitions] and frequently engaged in private trade with foreign *fan*". In 1394, it was recorded that previously there had been restrictions imposed on foreign traders coming to China and only Ryukyu, Cambodia and Siam were allowed to come and offer tribute. At this time, ordinary people in China were prohibited from using any *fan* goods or *fan* aromatics.[33] The prohibition on going abroad to trade privately was reiterated in 1397.[34] Whether these prohibitions actually affected maritime trade between southern China and Southeast Asia is something which is not immediately apparent from the Ming texts, and perhaps through further archaeological research it will be possible to piece together the ebbs and flows in maritime trade between China and Southeast Asia during this period.

Southeast Asia-related policies of Ming Chengzu (1403–24)

Knowledge of the reign of Ming Taizu's successor, the Jianwen emperor (1399–1402), has been almost entirely lost to us as a result of the civil war and *coup d'état* launched by his uncle Zhu Di. In the aftermath, Zhu Di tried to eliminate all evidence of his nephew's reign from the historical record. As such, the links between Ming China and Southeast Asia in this crucial period must remain in the realm of conjecture.

The period of Yongle, as Zhu Di was to name his reign, is however, very well-documented and it is this period in which many of the most dramatic Ming interactions with Southeast Asia occurred.

Like his father, after coming to power, Zhu Di ordered the Ministry of Rites to send "instructions" to foreign polities requiring them to bring tribute to court.[35] In the same year, he also established Maritime Trade Supervisorates in the provinces of Zhejang, Fujian and Guangdong, in order to control the sea trade with all foreign polities.[36] In 1405, it was ordered that hostels be established under each of the above-noted provinces to look after the foreign envoys who would come from abroad.[37] It was already apparent at this early stage of the reign that the Yongle Emperor was planning to have much to do with maritime Asia.

At the same time, the new emperor was also anxious to advertise the cultural superiorities of the Ming to the rest of the known world and, to this end, he distributed 10,000 copies of *Biographies of Exemplary Women* (烈女傳) to various non-Chinese polities for their moral instruction.[38] Whether any motifs from this Chinese text have appeared in Southeast Asian literature has not yet, it appears, been studied. Court calendars were also distributed to Southeast Asian polities by the Ministry of Rites.[39] A number of major military expeditions into Southeast Asia were to also mark the Yongle reign.

The invasion of Đại Việt

In 1406, in an effort to increase Ming influence and power in Đại Việt – the polity which was known to the Ming as Annan (安南) – the Yongle emperor attempted to send a puppet ruler named Chen Tian-ping (Trần Thiên Bình) into that polity.[40] Trần Thiên Bình was killed as he proceeded into the country.

This killing by the Vietnamese aspirant became the immediate pretext for Yongle to launch an invasion of the polity,[41] but this move had obviously been planned well before the event. In that same year of 1406, two huge Chinese armies were sent along two routes, via Yunnan and Guangxi, into Đại Việt. The subsequent campaigns and military actions have already been dealt with in some detail in several works, including John Whitmore's *Vietnam, Hồ Quý Ly, and the Ming (1371–1421)*. Chinese forces claimed seven million of the Vietnamese killed in this initial campaign to take the polity.[42] In 1407, Jiaozhi[43] became Ming China's fourteenth province, and remained so until 1428, when the Ming were forced by the Vietnamese to withdraw. However, this 21-year period was one of almost incessant fighting.

As soon as the Ming forces had taken control of the polity, the changes began. In the first year, 7,600 tradesman and artisans (including gun founders) captured in Đại Việt were sent to the Ming capital at today's Nanjing.[44] This stripping of some of the most skilled members of the society would undoubtedly have had extensive social effects on Vietnamese society. Subsequently, more Chinese and non-Chinese troops were brought into the region to maintain some semblance of control, and a wide range of new organs of civil administration were established. By 1408, Jiaozhi had 41 subprefectures, and 208 counties,[45] all being administered in a Chinese mode, but many staffed by Vietnamese. In a claimed effort to further inculcate Chinese ways, Confucian schools were established and Chinese persons were appointed to teach in them.⁴⁶ Regardless of how much political hegemony was subsequently thrown off in the late 1420s, when the Ming were driven out, the administrative legacy of the Chinese occupation must have had a major and wide-ranging impact on the societies of the polity.

The year 1407 also saw a new Maritime Trade Supervisorate (市舶提舉司) being established at Yuntun City in Jiaozhi, while two further such offices were established at Xinping (新平) and Shunhua (順化) in 1408. Thus, within two years, three maritime trade supervisorates had been created in this new province, the same number as existed in the rest of China. This was a clear indication of the desire of the Ming to control maritime trade to the south and exploit the economic advantage of such control.⁴⁷ Other economic exploitation of the new province involved grain taxes, annual levies of lacquer, sapan wood, kingfisher feathers, fans and aromatics, and the imposition of monopolies on trade in gold, silver, salt, iron and fish. In addition, eunuchs were sent to Jiaozhi with the task of treasure-collecting for the Emperor, but an equal amount of treasure collection appears to have been done for themselves. The rapaciousness of the eunuchs, at least as depicted in Ming accounts, was such that even the emperors intervened on some appointments. The Hongxi Emperor objected to the re-sending of the eunuch Ma Qi to Jiaozhi, when he attempted to have himself reappointed to control the gold, silver, aromatics and pearls of the region in 1424.⁴⁸

By 1414, the Ming were sufficiently well entrenched in the north of Đại Việt to allow a push further south, establishing four further subprefectures in a region south of Jiaozhi which had formerly been administered by Champa.⁴⁹ The role which the Chinese occupation of Đại Việt and beyond during this period played in the later southward expansion of the Vietnamese state and eventual destruction of the Cham polity should not be ignored.

But the levies and demands made on the new province by the Ming meant that even its capacity to feed itself suffered. While thousands of "native troops" from nine guards in Jiaozhi were also being employed on military farms in 1426, it was still insufficient to feed the people and the forces, and on numerous occasions in the 1420s, it was necessary to arrange transport of grain from Guangdong and Guangxi into Jiaozhi.⁵⁰ Such deficiencies would have had profound effects on social structure and social stability in the region, compounded by the intermittent warfare and the attempted imposition of Chinese norms. The range of colonial policies which the Ming pursued⁵¹ undoubtedly had wide-ranging effects both on the society at the time as well as the future development of the Vietnamese state.

Invasion of Yunnan polities under Yongle

Prior to Yongle's invasion of the Vietnamese polity in 1406, he engaged himself in further expansion into the polities of Yunnan. By 1403, the Ming had established new military guards on the distant border, with two Independent Battalions being established at Tengchong and Yongchang directly under the Yunnan

Regional Military Commission.⁵² These were to be the bases from which the subsequent further occupation and control of the Tai regions was to be pursued. In the same year, new Chief's Offices (長官司) were established in Yunnan, at Zhele Dian, Dahou, Ganyai, Wan Dian and Lujiang,⁵³ and in 1406 a further four Chief's Offices were established under Ningyuan Guard in what is today Sip Song Chau Tai in Vietnam.⁵⁴ The two major Tai polities of Mubang (Hsenwi) and Mengyang in areas which are today northern Burma, were "recognised" as Military and Civilian Pacification Superintendencies by the Ming in 1404.⁵⁵ When the various Tai polities did not accord with what the new Ming emperor required, military actions were launched against them. In 1405, for example, the senior Chinese representative in Yunnan, Mu Sheng, launched an attack on Babai (Lanna).⁵⁶

After some sort of recognition or acceptance of the superior position of the Ming court, Chinese clerks or registry managers were appointed to the "native offices" to "assist" the traditional ruler, and ensure that Ming interests were served. Chinese clerks were appointed to carry out Chinese language duties in the various native offices of Yunnan in 1404,⁵⁷ while similar circulating-official clerk positions (to be filled by Chinese) were established in seven Chief's Offices in Yunnan in 1406.⁵⁸

The "native office" polities were then subject to demands in terms of gold/silver in lieu of labour (差發銀/金), administered by the Ministry of Revenue,⁵⁹ and also required to provide troops to assist in further Ming campaigns. Mubang, for example, was required to send its troops against Babai (Lanna) in 1406.⁶⁰ This pattern of exploitation continued through the reign.

The voyages by Zheng He and other eunuchs

The despatch of various eunuch-led maritime missions to the "Western Ocean" (maritime Southeast Asia west of Borneo and the Indian Ocean), as well as other lesser-known missions to the Eastern Ocean (today's Philippines, Borneo and Eastern Indonesia) was the third of the three prongs of southern expansion pursued by the Yongle Emperor. The most widely-known of these envoys was Zheng He, otherwise known as "San-bao", or "Three Treasures", and it is around this eunuch that many of the legends relating to the voyages are centred. Other eunuch commanders included Wang Guitong and Hou Xian. Eunuch envoys such as Zhang Qian were responsible for voyages to the polities in the Eastern Ocean – Boni, Pangasinan, Sulu and Luzon – and for bringing their envoys and rulers to China.

The eunuch-led missions were, like Yongle's expansions into Yunnan and occupation of Đại Việt, intended to create legitimacy for the usurping emperor, display the might of the Ming, bring known polities to demonstrated submission to the Ming and collect treasures for the Court.⁶¹ To achieve these aims, the maritime forces needed to be both huge and powerful. Ship-building began almost as soon as the Yongle emperor assumed power. In 1405, just after Zheng He departed on his first expedition, Zhejiang and other regional military commissions were ordered to build 1,180 ocean-going ships.⁶² By 1408, the task was assigned to a central ministry and the Ministry of Works was ordered to build 48 "treasure-ships" (寶船).⁶³

The size and number of ships which accompanied the eunuch commanders on the voyages to Southeast Asia and beyond has long been an issue of debate. However, it seems likely that some of the ships were more than 250 feet long.⁶⁴ Mills suggests that "it seems reasonable to conclude that Cheng Ho's [Zheng He's] largest ships were probably about three hundred feet long and about one hundred and fifty feet broad, and displaced about three thousand one hundred tons".⁶⁵ The ships were capable of carrying cavalry and some served as water tankers. Fleets ranged from 50 to more than 100 ships and remained away for up to two years. A sixteenth-century Chinese account suggests that 27,500 persons accompanied the largest missions to the Western Ocean.⁶⁶ The point here is not to dwell on the technical aspects of the fleets, but simply to note that they were huge armadas, larger than any other fleets which existed in the world at that time. These fleets died only slowly. An "Imperial force for Voyages to Barbarian lands" (下番官軍) still existed and was being used for voyages at least to Champa as late as 1453.⁶⁷

To enable these great fleets to sail through the Indian Ocean to Africa, it was necessary to create staging posts and garrisons in what is today Southeast Asia. These were established at the port city of Malacca and at the northern end of the Straits of Malacca next to Samudera. The Straits of Malacca were probably more vital in the fifteenth century, when international linkages were entirely dependent on shipping, than they are today, and controlling this waterway was an essential first step in controlling the region. It was also thus that the Ming assisted the growth of the new polity of Malacca, so that its own base could be protected. The links between Malacca and the Ming thereby remained intimate for much of the fifteenth century. The degree to which the development of the port city of Malacca was a product of Ming policies in Southeast Asia in the early fifteenth century, needs to be further investigated.

The military aspect of these voyages needs underlining, in part because of the stress placed on these missions in current PRC scholarship as "voyages of friendship". A large proportion of the members of the missions were military personnel, and in a *Ming shilu* reference of 1427, there is reference to "10,000 crack troops who had formerly been sent to the Western Ocean",⁶⁸ suggesting that a large proportion of the members of these fleets were highly trained military men. It is obvious that such a force would have played a major threatening role, useful in encouraging recalcitrant foreign rulers to travel to the Ming court. However, there were other times when more than military threat was required and the history of the Zheng He voyages is replete with violence as the eunuch commanders tried to implement the Ming emperor's demands. Major military actions included:

Attack on the Old Port pacification superintendency (1407)

By the early fifteenth century, Old Port (or 舊港) near Palembang in Sumatra, had apparently long been home to a large number of Chinese persons. After it came to Ming notice in 1405, the local leader Liang Daoming travelled to China. In 1407, Zheng He returned from his first major mission abroad, bringing with him a "pirate" Chen Zuyi captured at Old Port, for reportedly having "feigned surrender but secretly plotted to attack the Imperial army".[69] The Ming fleet reported 5,000 persons killed, with ten ships burnt and seven captured in the battle. Later in the same year, the Ming recognized the polity of Old Port. However, because of the large numbers of Chinese, both ex-military personnel and civilians, from Guangdong and Fujian who lived there, it was deemed not to be a country. Rather, it was recognized as a "pacification superintendency" (宣慰使司), a term which was commonly used to refer to polities ruled by non-Chinese on the Chinese borders. The person appointed as the Superintendent, Shi Jinqing, was more than likely someone appointed by Zheng He as the local ruler to represent the Ming state.[70] During the Yongle reign, Malacca sought the territory of Old Port,[71] possibly because of the Malaccan ruler's origins in Sumatra, or else because it was deemed a threat. Either way, the fact that the request was made to the Ming suggests something of Ming control over the polity. Contemporary Chinese references to this polity end in 1430, implying that its fortunes were tied to the continuance of the Ming presence in Southeast Asia, which further suggests that the rulers were indeed agents of the Ming state.

Violence in Java (1407)

In 1407, Zheng He's troops went ashore in Java, on which was situated the polity of Majapahit, one of the Ming's major competitors for regional hegemony in maritime Southeast Asia. In an ensuing battle, some 170 of the Ming forces were killed. The Chinese records suggests that the Chinese troops "went ashore to trade", "where the Eastern king had ruled", which suggests Chinese involvement, intentional or otherwise, in a Javanese civil war. In response, the Ming dunned the Western king of Java (presumably the ruler of Majapahit) for compensation.

> Immediately pay 60,000 *liang*[72] of gold in compensation for their lives and to atone for your crime.... Fail to comply and there will be no option but to despatch an army to punish your crime. What happened in Annam can serve as an example.[73]

The threatening reference is to the Ming invasion of Annam noted above. The methods of the later European colonial armies in Asia, demanding compensation following their own military adventures, might be seen as useful comparative examples of such imperial opportunism.

Threats to Burma (1409)

In the early years of his reign, while vying with Ava-Burma for influence in Yunnan, Yongle was particularly concerned about the polity of Mubang (Hsenwi). When the Mubang envoy came to the Ming court in 1409, reportedly complaining about Na-luo-ta,[74] the Ava-Burma ruler, the response by Yongle included the following:

> Na-luo-ta, with his petty piece of land, is double-hearted and is acting wrongly. I have long known of this. The reason that I have not sent troops there is that I am concerned that good people will be hurt. I have already sent people with instructions requiring him to change his ways and start anew. If he does not reform, I will order the generals to despatch the army. The troops will attack from the ocean route and you can arrange to have your native cavalry attack overland. The despicable fellow will not be equal to that.[75]

This reference to a maritime force was to the Western Ocean ships of the eunuch commander, Zheng He, who together with Wang Jinghong and Hou Xian, had been commanded to proceed on another mission to the Western Ocean. This threat by the Ming emperor underlines the militaristic and intimidating nature of the maritime voyages.

Attack on Sri Lanka (1411)

Perhaps the event most telling as to the nature of the eunuch-led maritime voyages was the military invasion of Sri Lanka, the capture of a ruler and his carrying back to the Ming court in modern Nanjing in 1411. This occurred during the return voyage of a mission led by Zheng He which had taken the Ming forces to the west coast of the Indian subcontinent, including Quilon, Cochin and Calicut. According to the Ming texts, on the outward voyage, the Sri Lankan ruler Ya-lie-ku-nai-er (Alagakkonara)[76] had been "insulting and disrespectful", which meant obviously that he did not recognize the pre-eminence of the Ming and its envoys. He was also depicted as a local tyrant who "enticed" Zheng He back to the island, so that he could rob them. This, according to the official Ming history, is what gave rise to the hostilities by which Zheng He invaded the royal city, captured the king, destroyed his military and carried the king and his family members back to the court.[77] As was the case in similar scenarios in Yunnan, the Ming appointed a puppet ruler to replace the abductee, presumably tasked with acting in ways beneficial to the Ming.[78] The Chinese troops who returned from the expedition to Sri Lanka were rewarded in the same manner and at similar levels to those forces which invaded Đại Việt in 1406, suggesting similar aims of the forces.[79]

Attack and capture of Su-gan-la of Samudera (1415)

A further example of the aims and methods of the maritime missions is seen in 1415, when Su-gan-la, the reported "leader of the Samuderan bandits" was taken to China from Sumatra by Zheng He. According to the *Ming shilu*, Su-gan-la (Iskander?) was plotting to kill the local ruler Zainuli Abidin and seize the throne, and was angered that the Chinese envoys did not recognize him as ruler and confer presents upon him. He thus led his forces against those of the Ming, but was defeated and fled to Lambri. He was there captured together with his wife and children, and shipped to China for punishment.[80] While the events which did occur in 1414 and 1415 remain obscure,[81] it is certain that Zheng He and his forces inserted themselves in a civil war in northern Sumatra, supported the side which was not hostile to the Ming and engaged in warfare against the other. Again, we see an instance of the maritime expedition acting mainly as a military force in an attempt to impose a *pax Ming* on what we now know as Southeast Asia and the Indian Ocean.

The examples above suggest that the maritime forces sent abroad in the first third of the fifteenth century were intended to achieve the recognition of Ming pre-eminence among all the polities of the known maritime world. Those who would not recognize this supremacy of the Ming were subjected to military force. This is not to say that all polities needed military coercion. The economic benefits flowing from "tribute missions" suggests that some would likely have gladly sent tribute and personally travelled to the Ming court.

However, the number of Southeast Asian rulers travelling to China with the Zheng He missions suggests that coercion must have been an important element. There are very few other examples of rulers visiting other polities within Southeast Asia in this period, suggesting that some great pressure must have been imposed on them to encourage them to journey to the Ming court, and thereby demonstrate their subordinate status before the Chinese emperor.

Southeast Asia-related policies of Ming Xuanzong (1426–35)

The reign of the Emperor Xuanzong was marked by the decision to maintain the Ming capital in Beijing,[82] rather than return it to Nanjing, possibly prompted by a fairly quiet northern border. The movement of the Ming capital north did, it is proposed, move the interest and attention of the Ming state further away from the maritime realm of Southeast Asia. Charles Hucker opined that the emperor Xuanzong had "no ambitions for expansionist adventures or dramatic new enterprises. Rather, he was inclined toward tightening up the governmental mechanism and perhaps above all alleviating distress among the people".[83] He attempted to regularize fiscal administration, and yet he revived the eunuch-led maritime voyages, which had been ended by his predecessor the Renzong emperor,[84] and which perhaps suggests that these missions were intended as seekers of further revenue sources.

Đại Việt

To the south, the major problem remained that of Jiaozhi, the occupied Đại Việt, inherited from his predecessors. It was this emperor Xuanzong who decided to end the Ming involvement in Vietnam, when it became clear that the Ming could neither sustain the military expenditure, nor suppress the militant opposition they faced. With this decision by the Ming state, the Vietnamese general Lê Lợ'i sent his representatives to the court in 1427 to negotiate a new relationship between the Vietnamese and the Ming.[85] In the protracted negotiations which ensued over the following years, the Vietnamese denied that they had detained any Chinese persons or their weapons, claiming that all the Chinese officials and troops had been sent back.[86] The term Annam was revived as a formal Chinese name for the polity, but it was to be some years, before the Ming recognized the "country" status of Đại Việt.

Eunuch-led voyages revived

During this reign, the eunuch-led maritime voyages were revived, with Zheng He leading a voyage to the East Coast of Africa in 1431–33.[87] For a fairly detailed description of this mission, including itinerary and dates at which foreign ports were reached, see the extract from Zhu Yunming's *Qian-wen-ji*, translated by Mills.[88]

Yunnan policies

In Yunnan, Chinese administrative control was extended during this reign, with police offices being established at the major passes in Tengchong and Weiyuan in 1433.[89] A former military administration – the Yongchang battalion – was changed into Lujiang Subprefecture, a civil office under the Yunnan Provincial Administration Commission, as Chinese control was consolidated. In the same year, the Ming "established" the Dong-tang Chief's Office, within Burmese territory, as an attempt to split the territory and power of the Ava-Burma polity.[90] Other "native offices" were also "established" (i.e recognized by the Ming), including the Niuwu Chief's Office in Hani/Akha territory.[91] Likewise, postal relay stations were established to aid in the Ming court's communications with its military and civilian administrations in the area.[92]

As was required of the rulers of the maritime polities in Southeast Asia by the gunboats of the Zheng He missions, so was the sending embassies of submission to the Ming court required of the polities which comprised the greater Yunnan. These missions to the Ming capital were likewise coordinated by eunuch officials sent to these polities. In 1433, the eunuch Yun Xian brought to the Court envoys from the Yunnan polities of Mubang, Luchuan/Pingmian, Ava-Burma, Mengding, Jingdong and Wusa, Weiyuan, Guangyi, Zhenkang, Wan Dian, Nan Dian, Dahou and Tengchong, as well as Lujiang, Ganyai, Chashan, Wa Dian, and Menglian.[93] These polities constituted the majority of the Tai and Burman polities north of Ayudhya and west of Laos.

Southeast Asia-related policies of Ming Yingzong and Ming Daizong (1436–64)

The three reigns noted above are conflated in the *Ming shilu* record under the temple name Yingzong, given that the two reigns of the emperor Yingzong were punctuated by the reign of Ming Daizong, as a result of the former being temporarily captured by the Mongols in a campaign in 1449.[94] That event underlines how important the northern border was in the thinking of the Ming in this period, but that did not prevent the state from engaging in activities which were to have profound effects on mainland Southeast Asia. It was the Yunnan border which was to see the most intense Ming–Southeast Asian interaction during these 28 years.

Military attacks on "Yunnan" polities

The three major attacks against the Tai Mao polity known to the Chinese as Luchuan,[95] extending from 1438 to 1445, have been essentially neglected in the studies of Southeast Asian history. However, they were some of the most important events in the history of fifteenth-century Southeast Asia, resulting in the fragmentation of one of its largest polities.

The Tai Mao political leader Si Renfa had, during the 1430s, made attempts to recover territory formerly subject to his father Si Lunfa, but which had been atomized by earlier Ming policies. He had gained control over Ganyai, Nan Dian, Tengchong, Lujiang and Jinchi by 1438, when the Court sent generals to assist the local commander Mu Sheng against him.[96] While the Chinese forces claimed initial success, a further 50,000 troops from all over southern China were mobilized in 1439 for the first major Luchuan expedition.[97] By 1440, it was being claimed that 120,000 troops would be needed if victory was to be achieved against Si Renfa,[98] suggesting something of the power of the Möng Mao polity at that time. In 1441, the Ming court ordered another expedition, led by the generals Jiang Gui and Wang Ji.[99] Wang Ji was to claim the taking of 50,000 heads at Shang Jiang on the Salween River within the first year, and claimed that his forces had taken and destroyed Luchuan in 1442, but that Si Renfa had escaped.[100] In August 1442, a further expedition was launched against Luchuan,[101] and both Wang Ji and Jiang Gui were recalled to lead it. The year 1444 saw the destruction of Luchuan, the power base of Si Renfa, the killing of Si Renfa, and the establishment by the Ming of Longchuan Pacification commission (apparently the first use of the term pacification commission 宣撫司 in Chinese history) to partially replace Luchuan. A former Luchuan chieftain Gong Xiang, who had gone over to the Ming was then appointed as pacification Commissioner.[102] More details of these military expeditions are provided by Liew.[103]

A further major Ming military expedition which was to greatly affect the upland Southeast Asian polities was that launched in 1448 to capture Si Jifa, a son of Si Renfa. At a date equivalent to April/May 1448, Imperial instructions were issued to Wang Ji requiring him to capture Si Jifa and the chieftains of Mengyang.[104] The surrounding polities of Ava-Burma, Mubang, Nan Dian, Ganyai and Longchuan were also required to provide troops for deployment against Si Jifa.[105] The imperial orders sent to Wang Ji presaged the disruption which such an expedition would have wrought in the region.

> He [Si Jifa] may flee into Ava-Burma's territory and be concealed by the people there. If so, capture persons as the situation demands, so that the *yi* people will know fear and the Great Army will not have been sent in vain.[106]

While Wang Ji reported success in his attack on Si Jifa's stockade,[107] later accounts tell of how Wang Ji had sought personal advantages from the "native officials" and how in fact he had been defeated by Si Jifa.[108]

Again in 1454, Chinese forces were despatched, this time against Si Kenfa and others in Mengyang, who had established their own regime in competition with the Ming appointee.[109]

Economic exploitation in Yunnan

Increased control over non-Chinese polities in the Yunnan region gave the Ming greater opportunity to impose economic demands, both to boost state revenue and to pay for the huge expense of mounting the military expeditions noted above. This obviously had deep-going effects on the societies controlled by the persons recognized by the Ming. In 1447, even the Yunnan administrative commissioner Li Guan was concerned about the effects of the exploitative policies which the Ming imposed either directly or indirectly, and noted that:

> native officials have been appointed without adequate investigation and they have been pressed for payment of gold and silver in lieu of labour. The *yi* people have been stirred up and this has resulted in them cherishing anger and feuding with and killing each other.... It is requested that all previously agreed payments of gold and silver be cancelled and that they only be required to bring local products to the court at fixed intervals.[110]

We read also, in 1449, of how Ming officials and military personnel based at Jinchi in Yunnan were lending money to non-Chinese persons, drawing them into the money economy and then taking field produce and children in payment for the debts.[111] Further direct exploitation is seen in a reference of 1458, which noted that land surrounding Tengchong, the major Chinese outpost in the region, was forcibly appropriated by Chinese officials, and the people were divided into farming families subject to tax levies. This resulted in many people fleeing from the region.[112] We can see here aspects of the colonial processes by which formerly non-Chinese polities were turned into Chinese spheres.

Achieving a balance between economically exploiting the newly conquered or incorporated areas in Yunnan and trying to maintain social stability and thereby control in those areas was something the Ming and its agents constantly debated over. Despite claims that social stability was at risk in Yunnan in the 1440s due to the levies, the Ministry of Revenue refused to reduce any of the gold and silver payments required, claiming that "they are an old system dating from the Hongwu reign, and it is difficult to abolish them".[113] The degree to which these newly incorporated polities were seen as revenue sources is underlined by events in the 1460s when lack of gold in the central treasuries resulted in Yunnan silver levies being converted into gold demands. Only after a Yunnan official advised that there was no gold to be had in Yunnan was this policy reversed.[114]

The gold, silver and horse demands which the Ming state imposed on the Tai polities of Yunnan and beyond not only depleted the polities, but also left them open to imposition of other demands by the Ming. In the 1440s for example, Mubang (Hsenwi, Theinni) deployed its forces to assist the Chinese forces arrayed against Si Renfa in exchange for the cancelling of an outstanding debt to the Chinese state (which had been unilaterally imposed by the Ming) of 14,000 *liang* of silver. In 1448, the gold, silver, rice, paper money, cowries and horses owed in lieu of labour by eight prefectures in Yunnan, plus Jinchi, Tengchong, Ganyai, Nan Dian, Longchuan, Cheli, Mengyang, Mubang, Mengding, Menggen, Weiyuan, Wan Dian, Zhenkang and Dahou, being mainly Tai polities stretching right across Indochina, were all cancelled in reward for their military assistance in destroying the power of the Möng Mao polity of Luchuan.[115]

Southeast Asia-related policies of Ming Xianzong (1465–87)

The Chenghua reign saw the Ming state heavily involved in military activities on various borders. In the north, the Great Wall was extended for 600 miles in Shaanxi to defend against the Mongols, while there were major military expeditions into Jurchen territory between 1465 and 1479. To the south, there were massive military expeditions between 1465 and 1472 against Yao polities in what are today Guangdong and Guangxi, and these saw some of the bloodiest battles of the century.[116] These expeditions broke the back of many of these traditional polities in a similar way to which the expeditions against Yunnan in the 1440s destroyed polities and societies there.

Yunnan policies

During this reign, in the Yunnan region there were attempts to assimilate the political leaders of the non-Chinese peoples into the orthopraxy which some say defines Chineseness, by sending the heirs of the "native offices" to study at Confucian schools. The Xianzong emperor spoke of this in 1481, instructing the Yunnan grand coordinator as follows:

> You are to instruct all of the native officials to send their due heirs to study, as the grand coordinator and ministry suggested. In this way, the habit of the

man and the *mo*[117] of struggling for succession will gradually die out and the civilizing influences of Chinese propriety and righteousness will reach to the distance.[118]

The economic exploitation of the polities of the Yunnan region, and in fact all regions to the south of the Ming during this reign is apparent from a memorial submitted to the emperor in 1476 by Shang Lu, the Minister of Personnel. He noted that:

> In recent years, Guangdong, Yunnan and other places have offered in tribute wonderful and rare plants, exotic birds and strange animals, pearls, precious stones and utensils of gold and silver. These goods do not come from the persons who offer them, but are invariably taken from the people. If they cannot be taken from the people, they are obtained from native offices and the *yi* people. To offer one item in tribute involves trouble ten times its value.

Shang Lu went on to note that Yunnan was particularly close to Annam,[119] and that the polities were particularly prone to rebellion, implying the possibility of Annam being able to gain the allegiance of polities in the region as a result of the exploitation visited upon them by the existing Ming systems.[120]

Đại Việt

Đại Việt was a polity of particular concern to the Ming during the Chenghua reign. A memorial submitted to the court in 1481 by the Minister of War Chen Yue outlined the key concerns:

> The country of Annam is secluded in the South-west, 10,000 *li* away, and it borders Yunnan and Guangxi/Guangdong. During the Yongle reign (1403–24), the Imperial army subdued it and its land was divided into sub-prefectures and countries. Subsequently, the defence officials lost control, and it again sank into its former ways. Now it has again turned to evil, and through force, it has to the east swallowed up Champa and to the west annexed Laos. It has brought destruction to Babai, sent false Imperial orders to the Cheli Pacification Superintendency (Chiang Hung) and killed envoys from Melaka. We cannot but concern ourselves with this. A few years ago, some border people returned from Annam and claimed that those in that country intended to attack Yunnan, and they only desisted after being reproved by the king's mother.... The envoys from Champa have also said that Annam has prepared 3,000 warships and intends to attack Hainan. We must make preparations for this.[121]

In the same year, three senior ministers urged that the Cham ruler, living in exile, be given support against Đại Việt, and that the latter be required to leave the Cham territory which it had occupied.¹²² The aim was obviously to give Đại Việt concerns on its southern border, to reduce the threat it could pose to China. The Xianzong emperor was, however, not enthused about getting the Ming involved in another war to the south, and issued nothing but a letter of warning addressed to the Vietnamese ruler.

Further concerns about Đại Việt were apparent from a memorial submitted by the Ministry of Revenue in 1482, urging prohibition against the smuggling of copper from Yunnan into Annam, which "assist Jiaozhi in the manufacture of its weapons."¹²³ These weapons were presumably firearms. Sun Laichen has written extensively on the importance of firearms for the Vietnamese state in its expansion southwards, westwards and northwards during the fifteenth century, with this technology, he suggests, having been provided through the Ming occupation of the polity in the early part of the century.¹²⁴

Private maritime trade with Southeast Asia

In a *Ming shilu* account dated to the equivalent of 4 January 1485, we read:

> As 37 large ships which had been in communication with the *fan* had anchored in the jurisdiction of Chaozhou Prefecture in Guangdong, the Assistant Commissioner responsible for defence against Japanese pirates Yao Ying, the Maritime Route Inspector and Surveillance Vice Commissioner Zhao Hong and the general maritime circuit Assistant Commissioner Weng Yan led the troops in pursuit of those on these ships and took 85 heads.¹²⁵

The fact that a private fleet of 37 large ships was trading out of Chaozhou, almost certainly to Southeast Asia, suggests that at least in this period of the fifteenth century, and despite official prohibitions, private Chinese maritime trade with the region was still buoyant, even if the consequences of capture were sometimes quite drastic for those so involved.

Southeast Asia-related policies of Ming Xiaozong (1488–1505)

The Hongzhi reign, noted for the growth of the eunuch bureaucracy, also saw the Ming engaged in renewed military activities to the south in Guizhou and Hainan and to the west in and around Turkestan. However, the Ming was still somewhat involved with Southeast Asia.

Yunnan policies

The attempts by the Chinese state to bring the Tai polities of Yunnan more firmly under the Ming yoke continued in the last decades of the fifteenth century. In the 1490s, we see Chinese forces being despatched, together with Mengyang forces, against Si Die of Mengmi.¹²⁶ Then again, in the early 1500s, ministers were urging a military expedition against Si Lu of Mengyang.¹²⁷

To assist in maintenance of order and in revenue procurement, in 1489, the Ministry or Revenue urged conferral of surnames on *man* and *yi* of Yunnan. The proposal was approved by the emperor, and it is supposed that some sort of Chinese surname allocation programme did go ahead in this period.

Maritime trade with Southeast Asia

In 1493, Min Gui, the supreme commander of Guangdong/Guangxi memorialized to the court in Beijing, noting:

> In the coastal areas of Guangdong, many people are privately dealing with those who come on the *fan* ships. The ships come in an unbroken stream and, without waiting for the examination of their tally slips, [those on the] *fan* ships start selling their merchandise. The government forces responsible for guarding against the Japanese pirates have made reports about the growing power and disorderliness of the traders....

The Ministry of Rites in the Chinese capital responded, claiming:

> According to Gui's memorial, the problem lies with the great number of *fan* ships and the hardship brought to the offices. According to this ministry, since the first year of the Hongzhi reign (1488/89), the only *fan* ships which have brought tribute missions through Guangdong have been one from Champa and one from Siam. Because the prohibition against the private ships (私船) has been relaxed, they have proliferated, while because the prohibition against *fan* ships has been strictly enforced, they have not been coming....[128]

We thus see, in the late fifteenth century, a movement away from the formal, regulated tribute trade system toward one which, while perhaps not formally "allowing" private shipping, at least tolerated it. The trade with Southeast Asia engaged in by those of the southern provinces seems to have been increasingly ignored by the administration in Beijing.

Southeast Asia-related policies of Ming Wuzong (1506–21)

The Zhengde reign was marked by the dominance of a eunuch named Liu Jin, who managed to achieve the resignation of most of the grand secretaries in 1506. By 1507 he had gained control of imperial administration in the capital and in the provinces. Liu was also in charge of revenue-raising programmes and these were increasingly important as imperial expenditure soared on construction of new palaces and other facilities. Harsh levies were instituted throughout the country, including the newly incorporated Yunnan polities. Concerns in the foreign affairs realm were essentially those related to the north and west, although it was also during this reign that the Portuguese first arrived in southern China.

Yunnan

As Ming administration extended further into the "native offices" of Yunnan during the early sixteenth century, a revenue raising system was instituted among the "native officials" in 1507. This involved the sale of official headwear and belts for silver.[129] These funds then used to pay for military rations and further extension of Chinese administration into these areas. Thereby the Ming state managed to have the local rulers fund their own demise.

General relations with Southeast Asian polities

By the end of the fifteenth century and the early sixteenth century, it was apparent that the Ming court and its central administrators were losing interest in the area we know today as Southeast Asia. A few examples of this will suffice. In 1515, when requested to provide an envoy from the Ming capital to Annam to accompany the son of the Duanqing Prince (端慶王), the Ministry of War opined "We should not do things for the distant *yi* if it means annoyance for China".[130] This contrasts markedly with the rhetoric at the beginning of the century, when the Ming rulers had greater *pax Ming* aspirations. Likewise, when the Portuguese invaded Malacca and the Malaccan ruler and supporters fled, there was little interest on the part of the Ming officials or emperor to involve themselves in the violence occurring well to the south of the country.[131]

There was an associated decline in the importance of the Translator's Institute (四夷舘), an agency heavily involved in Ming relations with foreign polities. In the mid-1460s, the Institute had 154 translation officials and students,[132] but by 1490, it was noted that: "Recently, all of the departments have lacked officials. There are no instructors to provide training and no young men to engage in study".[133] This suggests the degree of neglect, to where even the basic infrastructure for external relations was being allowed to run down.

Maritime trade

As has been noted above, by the end of the fifteenth century, there was increasing evidence of private maritime traders operating out of Southern China into the area we now know as maritime Southeast Asia. We read in 1501, for example, of people from Jiangxi Province who had sailed to Java to trade.[134] That the tribute system was also beginning to see difficulties is suggested by a memorial of 1530 criticizing both the decline in the formal tribute system and proposals to further open trade to the Portuguese. It advocated the firm policing of the tribute system and prohibition of private trading ships.[135]

Overview of Ming policies affecting Southeast Asia

We can condense the range of policies noted above as having been pursued in respect of Southeast Asia by the successive Ming emperors to a number of themes.

Political expansion by the Ming

In 1534, a Chinese Vice Minister Xu Wen noted in a memorial that: "Guangdong/Guangxi and Yunnan/Guizhou were the areas beyond the frontiers in ancient times".[136] How these areas had become part of China was not further addressed, as all Xu Wen wanted to explain was why a large number of non-Chinese people lived in these regions.

The Ming dynasty provides a useful era through which to examine the processes by which a Chinese state absorbed areas previously beyond its administrative control. The fifteenth and sixteenth centuries were periods of great expansion by the Ming state and provide diverse sources on the various processes by which that expansion occurred. The invasion and occupation of Đại Việt, for example, has been detailed above, and its obvious aim in expanding the scope of the Ming empire needs little further comment here.

However, the Yunnan experiences provide different examples of expansion. As exampled elsewhere in this chapter, when polities were brought to submission by the Ming through military expeditions, or threats thereof, and turned into "native offices" (土司), it often happened that "registry managers" (經歷都事), "registry clerks" (經歷知事) or "clerks" (吏目) from the Chinese bureaucracy were appointed by the Ming to "assist" the traditional rulers in their administration. In 1404, registry manager and registry clerk positions were created for the mainly Tai polities of Mubang, Mengyang, Luchuan/Pingmian, Laos, Ava-Burma, Babai/Dadian, Mengding and Weiyuan.[137] Over time, some of these polities underwent a process known in Chinese as "*gaitu guiliu*" (改土歸流), by which the Ming (and later the Qing dynasty), on various pretexts, replaced the hereditary family rulers with officials from the bureaucracy, thereby changing a formerly autonomous or semi-autonomous polity into a part of the Chinese empire.

The first half of the fifteenth century saw quite an expansion of the Chinese administration in "Yunnan",[138] spurred in some way by the efforts of the Möng Mao ruler Si Renfa to recover his polity's territory which had been previously taken by the Ming. The Ming, responding to what it saw as a new Nanzhao (南詔), made great efforts to expand its own influence in the region, appointing "chiefs" as "pacification commissioners", while local commanders were given titles as police officers, either in anticipation of or reward for achievements against Si Renfa and his forces.[139]

Efforts by the Ming to expand its control in the *dong* (洞/峒)[140] areas which straddled the region north of Vietnamese control and south of the Ming-administered areas continued throughout the Ming. By the first half of the fifteenth century, the *dong* rulers had been recognized by the Ming and poll taxes had been instituted. The efforts to incorporate them into the Chinese state continue today.

The policies pursued by the Ming in Đại Việt and some areas of Yunnan over the fifteenth century suggest that the process by which the Ming state expanded into new areas can be summarized as follows: (1) Validation of a military action was sought out or created; (2) A military expedition was launched; (3) Assistance of some local leaders was gained; (4) Intimidation by slaughter was conducted;[141] (5) The existing leaders were killed or removed elsewise; (6) Orders were issued locally advising the moral rectitude of the military action and noting that it was conducted to free the people from their evil rulers or other predicament; (7) Chinese bureaucrats were appointed as either registry managers or more broadly in the larger polities; (8) Military guards and civil administrative offices were established; (9) Grain and labour levies were instituted, and monopolies over salt, gold and silver were instituted, or else it was demanded that such be provided to the state in lieu of labour; (10) Useful human resources were stripped;[142] (11) Further opportunities for territorial gain were sought out. Some of the specific ways in which this affected the Southeast Asian polities during the fifteenth century are detailed below.

"Employing Yi to attack Yi" (以夷攻夷)

In reference to a proposed Chinese military advance into Ava-Burma in the 1440s, the Chinese administration noted that the Imperial army could not penetrate deeply into Burma due to environmental conditions and the difficulty of maintaining supply routes.[143] It was in response to such restrictions that, like imperial powers through history, the Ming made wide use of the military forces of non-Chinese polities over which it exercised control or influence. In their efforts to incorporate the polities of Yunnan, it was more convenient (but not always more successful) to use local forces rather than mobilize and move forces from Chinese areas.

The history of Yunnan in the late fourteenth and throughout the fifteenth century is replete with examples of such. In 1389, Si Lunfa of the Baiyi (Möng Mao polity) was ordered by the Ming to pursue and capture "rebels" in Yunnan.[144] Two years later, the Hongwu emperor employed the troops of Babai (Lanna) to attack the Baiyi.[145] When the Ming intended to attack Ava-Burma in 1409, Mubang was ordered to prepare its troops for an overland attack, while the Ming forces were to attack from the sea.[146] Mubang (Hsenwi) was a frequent pawn in the Ming-Burma machinations, as it lay between the two and was subject to demands by both polities.

In the expedition against Luchuan in the 1430s, imperial orders were sent to the generals noting: "Using *yi* to attack *yi* was a fine method used by the ancients. You are to employ it." It was thus that, in 1438, the Ming accepted "offers" by Mubang and Dahou to deploy 100,000 of their troops against Luchuan.[147] Subsequently, in 1440, the polities of Mubang, Ava-Burma, Cheli, Babai/Dadian, Weiyuan and Shi Dian were ordered to combine their forces and lead them against Si Renfa of Luchuan,[148] while the polities of Weiyuan and Shunning were also offered rewards for military assistance provided.[149]

Again in 1447, when Su Jifa had grown in power in Mengyang, the Ming ordered Ava-Burma and Mubang to provide troops for an attack on Mengyang.[150] Subsequent reports indicated that 100,000 Mubang and Ava-Burma troops were involved in razing Si Jifa's stockades on Mt Guiku to the west of the Irrawaddy. The use of "native troops" by the Ming continued unabated into the sixteenth century and beyond.

Divide and rule

"When there is contention between the *yi* and the *di*,[151] it benefits China". So wrote Chen Yongbin, the grand coordinator of Yunnan in the first decade of the seventeenth century. But this perception has been part of China political thought for millennia, and it certainly conditioned the policies of the Ming state in the fifteenth century.

The aim of "divide-and-rule" was achieved in various ways. The major method was to break down major polities into smaller units, thereby making them rivals of each other and less of a threat to the Chinese state. This is what occurred in the late fourteenth century, when after assisting Si Lunfa to recover control over his polity of Luchuan/Pingmian (Möng Mao), the Ming rulers divided its territory into Luchuan, Mengyang, Mubang, Mengding, Lujiang, Ganyai, Dahou and Wan Dian, all under separate rulers.[152] The validation was: "The states surrounding Luchuan have, since ancient times until now all had their own rulers. They have never been united".[153] The concerns of the Chinese bureaucracy are also seen in a memorial submitted by the official Liu Qiu in 1443, during planning for an expedition against Luchuan. He noted that after an expedition against Luchuan:

> Ava-Burma will push for rewards for its achievements and will seek the division of Luchuan's land between itself and Mubang. If they are not given it, they will harbour resentment, while if they are given it, these *yi* areas will grow by half in terms of territory and population. Their power will grow and later it will not be possible to control them. While eliminating one Luchuan, we will be creating two further Luchuans.[154]

Further examples are numerous. An attempt by the Ming to divide the power of major entities to the south was seen in 1404 with efforts to divide Babai/Dadian (Lanna) into Babai/Dadian (likely Chiang Mai) and Babai/Zhennai (Chiang Rai).[155] This was eventually unsuccessful, despite a Chinese-sponsored attack on Lanna.[156] The Menglian Chief's Office was another example.[157] In 1409, Zhenkang Subprefecture was created to reduce the territory of Wan Dian,[158] while a similar attempt by the Ming state to split the Tai polity of Cheli (the later Sipsong Panna, centred on Chiang Hung) into Cheli and Cheli/Jingan in 1421, so as to reduce its power and allow the appointment of a Chinese registrar and military commissioner in the latter, was successful, but only for a decade.[159] In 1406, the Menglian Chief's Office was established as a means of reducing the power of the Tai polity of Mengding.[160] The establishment, by the Ming, of the Mengmian Chief's Office in Jingdong (Kengtung), in today's Shan States, also resulted in a weakening of the latter's power.

As an extension of the divide-and-rule policy, the Ming often supported alternate rulers to those in power. Gong Xiang of the Tai polity of Luchuan was supported in the 1440s as a way of breaking down the power of Si Renfa, and was then given a ruling position in the newly created polity of Longchuan. Later in the century, Zhao Sai, the younger brother of Si Jifa (the son of Si Renfa), ruler of the polity of Mengyang, was employed in the Ming's Embroidered-Uniform Guard, in the hope that he could eventually be used against his brother.[161]

More extreme examples were seen in the maritime realm, particularly in the cases of Old Port/Palembang and Sri Lanka, where the rulers were removed and replaced. These have been detailed above under the section relating to the Yongle reign.

The Ming efforts to fragment the power of the Tai polities in wider "Yunnan", which were always supported by the implicit or explicit threat of the use of military force, continued through the dynasty. Promises were also used, but rarely fulfilled. When, after the military defeat of Luchuan in the 1440s, Mubang (Hsenwi) sought that part of Luchuan territory which it had been promised by the Ming prior to the battle, the Ming administration fearing that this would increase the power of Mubang, advised that persons in the areas of Mengsa, Mingying and Mengmeng within this territory had already sought the establishment of their own offices and thus no land could be assigned to it.[162] Again, in the 1490s, with the defeat of Si Lu and the capture of the territory of Manmo (Bhamo), the Ming "established" the new office of Manmo, rather than give it to either of the claimants (Mengmi or Mubang), which had been instrumental in its capture.[163]

Maritime policies and tribute/trade

In order to try to ensure a state monopoly over maritime trade, the Ming rulers issued repeated prohibitions against private maritime trade. The various prohibitions issued during the late fourteenth century are detailed under the Hongwu reign above. The frequency of the issue of such notices implies that they were, if not ignored, at least looked on lightly by the populace. The effects which the eunuch-led missions in the first third of the fifteenth century had on private trade has never been truly assessed, but that they stimulated later private maritime links with Southeast Asia is unquestioned. In 1435, along with the ending of the eunuch-led voyages, efforts were again (or still) being made to prevent non-state agents from travelling overseas. In that year, at the beginning of the Zhengtong reign, the Ministry of Revenue urged that seaports be guarded to ensure that coastal people did not engage in overseas activities.[164]

Whether these prohibitions actually affected maritime trade between southern China and Southeast Asia is something which is not immediately apparent from the Ming texts, and it is perhaps only through further archaeological research that it will be possible to piece together, through material evidence, the ebbs and flows in maritime trade between China and Southeast Asia during this century.

There is little effort in the Chinese official record to hide the essentially mercantile nature of the tribute/trade system in this period. Three maritime trade supervisorates were established to handle trading goods – both state goods and those belonging to envoys. Some of the trade exchanges are detailed in the Ming texts. In 1425, for instance, Arya Huang Fu-xin, an overseas Chinese envoy from Java,[165] was provided with 159,050 *ding* of paper money in "reward". Given the huge size of the reward, it is likely that this was payment for trade goods.[166] Private trade by the tribute envoys was also condoned. It was specifically recorded in 1427 that a Javanese envoy named Arya Xu-li-man[167] and others had offered tribute on their own behalf and were rewarded in compensation for its value.[168] In a particularly telling incident in 1447, an envoy from Siam haggled with the Ming officials over the price of the "bowl-stone" (perhaps nephrite) he had brought to China. He requested that he be compensated at 250 *guan* of paper money per *jin*, but was only given 50 *guan* and told not to bring any more.[169]

But the benefits of the tribute/trade system were obviously great to those travelling to China, or so it is suggested by the number of occasions on which the Ming issued orders requiring the tribute envoys to only come at the stipulated frequency.[170] In 1443, Guangdong officials complained that envoys from Java arrived too frequently and made excessive demands on the local officials.[171] By 1453, the large Javanese missions had been so demanding that orders were issued requiring them to send only a chief envoy, deputy envoy and a few attendants to the Court.[172] But, this was not something which only the Javanese saw as beneficial. In 1478, for example, the envoys of Annam were prohibited from bringing large quantities of private trade goods to China.[173] By 1501, new regulations allowed foreign tribute envoys to trade for only five days with merchants from two counties near Beijing, who reportedly had no idea what the Southeast Asians wanted. Following official representations, this decision was reversed.[174] That the arrangement was instituted in the first place suggests that the tribute/trade system was not seen as a particularly important economic aspect for the Ming rulers by the early sixteenth century.

By 1510, the tribute and trade systems had apparently diverged somewhat from each other, for in addition to regular tribute missions, a new category of "ocean-going" merchant (ships) (泛海商客) appeared in reports from the coastal provinces.[175] As a corollary of this development, proportional taxes (抽分) were levied on these trading ships. A new maritime situation thus emerged, particularly in terms of Chinese merchants and others travelling abroad. By 1514, a report from Guangdong was noting:

> Recently, the administration has been permitted to levy proportional taxes [on ships and cargoes] and there has been open trade. This has resulted in thousands of evil persons building huge ships, privately purchasing arms, engaging in evil activities upon the sea, illicitly linking up with the various *yi* and bringing great harm to the area.[176]

This situation of open trade was in marked contrast to the maritime prohibitions[177] which had barred such trade for most of the fifteenth century, and this change would obviously have given new impetus to private trade between Southeast Asia and the ports of southern China. However, the social problems it brought to the coastal areas resulted in the local officials submitting repeated memorials against such trade, and urging that trade be limited to tribute missions.[178] This resulted in the issuing in 1524 of new regulations curbing private trade by Chinese with "the *fan* and the *yi*",[179] and the closing down of the Chinese maritime trade supervisorates, while in 1530, the dismantling of large ocean-going ships was ordered.[180]

It was also in this "window" between the end of the fifteenth century and 1524 that the Portuguese first arrived in southern China, having previously invaded and occupied Malacca. This arrival was momentous in terms of the eventual links which Chinese commerce was to develop thorough it.[181]

This booming of private trade in the early sixteenth century also suggests that the shift which Hamashita[182] sees occurring under the Qing, whereby, as a result of opposition to its tribute/trade policies, the Chinese state was "compelled to shift from the role of monopolistic trade-merchant to that of tax collector", was already taking place at the end of the fifteenth century and at the beginning of the sixteenth century.

Economic exploitation

As has been suggested in the chronological studies above, the economic and other demands imposed on the border polities and colonies by the Ming were adjusted apparently to ensure that enough of the accumulation of the area was drawn off so as to inhibit the rise of too powerful a local regime, but not so great an amount as to induce rebellion among the people of that polity. The "newly attached" polities were seen as providers of gold, silver and other valuables, of pearls, of precious stones, of horses and of labour, military and otherwise.

Apart from this systemic state exploitation in terms of silver levies, troop demands and so forth, the Yunnan polities, like the maritime countries and Đại Việt, had to deal with appropriations by court-appointed eunuchs. On occasions, their excesses even upset the central administration. In 1429, for example, two eunuchs Yun Xian (雲僊) and Xu Liang (徐亮) were recalled from Yunnan, where they had been sent as envoys because "these persons were constantly disposed to envious hatred and they both induced the local officials to engage in feuding and killing, and had them hinder and obstruct the other envoy".[183] In the late 1420s, the eunuch Ma Qi (馬騏) was accused of having maltreated the people in Jiaozhi, thereby inducing rebellion and aiding the rise of Lê Lọ'i.[184] The withdrawal of the "gold and silver payment expediting eunuchs" (催辦金銀內官) from Mubang (Hsenwi) in the mid-1430s[185] (at the same time as the eunuch-led voyages were being closed down) seems to indicate that up until that time the administration had centrally appointed officials governing the collection of silver and gold in the border colonies. The pull-back was, however, only temporary. The phenomena of intense exploitation by eunuch agents of the state appears to have continued through the century, with the regional inspector of Yunnan submitting a memorial in 1499 accusing Ji Qing (吉慶), the eunuch grand defender of Jinchi, of instituting excessive levies, causing *yi* people to flee, maintaining a private army, selling off trained troops and generally acting in avaricious and improper ways.[186] Again in the early sixteenth century, Sun An (孫安), the eunuch director of Jinchi/Tengchong, the major distant Chinese outpost in Yunnan, was ordered to "collect strange and wonderful objects, gold, silver, pearls and other things".[187] The accounts of extra-systemic economic exploitation by eunuchs continued into the sixteenth century.

Despite the regional variations, it is possible to observe a clear Ming policy of economic exploitation of frontier polities involving a progressive intensification of demands. After initial contacts through war or threats, the Ming state required large indemnities or other payments. This was subsequently systematized, following Chinese appointment or recognition of the local ruler, into a regular payment of gold or silver "in lieu of labour" (差發金/銀). At the same time, people of the region were drawn into the Chinese economy. When this process had proceeded sufficiently, poll or household taxes and commercial taxes were levied. The aim of this process was to reduce the economic independence of the local ruler of the polity and provide the economic means by which the Chinese state could meet the costs of increasing its own administration in these areas. Thereby, the formerly independent polity became a part of the Chinese state. During the fifteenth century, we see the Ming pursuing these policies among the polities it defeated or brought to submission by threats in Yunnan and those temporarily gained in Đại Việt.

Policies inducing human movement

As in some other colonial enterprises, the extension of Chinese administration into Yunnan and into Vietnam was accompanied by the inflow of Chinese persons into areas previously not occupied by the Chinese. Sometimes the movement was involuntary, such as in 1439, when Chinese criminals who were unable to redeem their sentences through rice payment, were moved into areas of Yunnan.[188]

Other state policies which encouraged movement of Chinese people into newly conquered areas included the establishment of state farms (屯田) and military farms (軍田). One of the limiting elements for further expansion by the Ming state was the availability of grain to feed, initially, troops and later, officials and settlers. Military farms and state farms were thus established to provide this grain. In 1426, during the latter years of the Ming occupation of Đại Việt, at least 8,000 "native troops" (土軍) from nine guards in Jiaozhi were being employed on military farms.[189] While the opening of such farms in Yunnan was in evidence throughout the dynasty, the 1490s saw a marked upsurge under the new military commander.[190] Even at the end of the sixteenth century, the Ming were planning further southward movement, with it being noted that "when the six *zhao* (referring to the six pacification superintendencies) are brought to peace, Baxiong Pass will be breached and thousands of *li* of land will be opened up with 10,000 *mu* of state farms.[191]

Associated with the extension of the range of Chinese administration and of areas settled by Chinese people was another practice, the so-called *kaizhong*

(開中) system.[192] This system involved selling state-monopoly salt to merchants for grain which the merchants were required to transport to areas where border troops were stationed. The system was instituted in Yunnan during the Hongwu reign (1368–98) in order to feed the Ming forces sent to occupy the region. In the 1420s, with the Ming occupation of Vietnam, the merchants preferred to sell their grain to the forces in Vietnam, rather than continue to supply Yunnan.[193] In the 1430s, the system was strongly revived in Dali and Jinchi in Yunnan to supply the forces to be used against Si Renfa of Luchuan. It was still being used in 1445 to feed the persons building the walled city at Tengchong, the new Chinese outpost in Yunnan.[194] A proposed expedition against Si Die of the Tai polity of Mengmi (Möngmit) in 1493 again induced the reintroduction of the system in the same area.[195]

The system played a major role in extending the Chinese administration, first by feeding troops who were engaged in military activities aimed at expanding the Ming state, and second by the fact that many merchants, rather than transporting the grain over vast distances, set up their own farms with their imported farm labourers in the border areas to grow locally the grain which they would sell for state salt. It also promoted Chinese settlement of these areas, as when the *kaizhong* system was no longer in force, the farms and the labourers would usually remain, and subsequently these areas settled by Chinese persons would come under the control of the Chinese administration.[196]

The growth in the number of Chinese people residing in maritime Southeast Asia during the fifteenth century was a result of both state and non-state factors. We read of members of a Chinese mission fleeing while in Cambodia in 1404,[197] and there is no reason to assume that among the tens of thousands of soldiers and sailors who accompanied the eunuch-led missions to Southeast Asia, there were not those who fled, were shipwrecked or who just remained at the ports where the ships called. However, as suggested above, there was also much Chinese private trade with maritime Southeast Asia through the fifteenth century as well as reports of large Chinese communities at Palembang in Sumatra, at Tuban and Gerisik in Java, and in Malacca and Ayudhya, some of which communities likely derived from such trade either in the fifteenth century or earlier.[198]

Overall effects of Ming policies towards Southeast Asia in the fifteenth century

To conclude this chapter, a few short comments are perhaps necessary on the specific areas where Ming policies affected fifteenth-century Southeast Asia. These are, rather than anything like analyses of the effects of the Ming on the region, simply notes on where further research in this sphere might be concentrated.

Changes in Southeast Asian political topography – Yunnan

As detailed in the sections above, the Ming push into the Tai polities of "Yunnan", and the divide-and-rule policies pursued throughout the fifteenth century, obviously played a major role in the atomization of Tai power. The breaking down of the Möng Mao polity in the late fourteenth century and again in the middle of the fifteenth century interrupted the rise of a polity which may have played a role similar to Sukhothai or Lan-Xang for the upland Tai polities.[199] The beginnings of the transformations of a large number of Southeast Asian[200] upland polities into Chinese administrative units was one of the major characteristics marking the history of Southeast Asia in the fifteenth century. This gradual reduction and dismantling of huge Tai polities such as the Möng Mao polity undoubtedly greatly changed the course of mainland Southeast Asian history. The "what-ifs" of history are infinite, but the destruction of one of the great Tai polities and the absorption of the territory and people into the Chinese state certainly wrought a new political and social structure in Indochina south of the Yangtze.

Changes in Southeast Asian political topography – Vietnam and Champa

The Ming invasion and occupation of Đại Việt had profound effects on Mainland Southeast Asia. By expanding the borders of their new province of Jiaozhi, particularly to the south, during their quarter century of control, the Ming left the Đại Việt which resurged in the late 1420s with a larger polity than it comprised formerly. The new technologies, new administrative measures and other factors introduced by the Ming invasion also contributed to the capacity of Lê Vietnam to expand its border over the following century, allowing it to destroy the Cham polity and incorporate both Cham and Lao territories.

Changes in Southeast Asian political topography – Malacca and Samudera

The control which the Ming exercised over the Straits of Malacca through their bases at either end of the Straits during the first third of the fifteenth century also had great effects on the political topography of the region. The support provided by the Ming to Malacca, underlined by the repeated visits to China by the Malaccan rulers, was almost certainly a *quid pro quo* for allowing the Ming to establish their base there. There seems to be general agreement among scholars that the rapid rise of Malacca in the fifteenth century was in part due to its close links with the Ming.

The Ming relationship with Samudra is much less clear from the sources, but the facts that the Ming had a major base on an island just off the Samudran coast, that the Samudran envoys often came to the court with those of Malacca and that the Ming forces appear to have fought a war to support Zainuli Abidin, the Samudran ruler, suggest that Ming support was also very important for the maintenance of that polity at least during the first third of the fifteenth century.

Changes in Southeast Asian political topography – decline of Majapahit's influence

The emergence of the Ming as a major political player in the maritime Southeast Asian world at the beginning of the fifteenth century appears to have had great effects on the capacity of Majapahit to continue its command of its far-flung empire.[201] Compounded by the division of Java and the civil war which marked the beginning of the fifteenth century on the island,[202] the Ming presence undoubtedly affected Javanese influence in Sumatra, the Malay Peninsula, Brunei and what is today the southern Philippines.

Changes in Southeast Asian economic topography – new economic networks

The policies pursued by the Ming state which affected Southeast Asia economically either directly or indirectly during the fifteenth century can be divided into a number of spheres:

The Ming maintained a booming nominally "imperial monopoly trade"[203] relationship during the fifteenth century with the major Southeast Asian polities/economies of Annam, Cambodia, Champa, Java, Malacca, Palembang, Samudera and Siam,[204] as well as with a host of smaller polities/economies. In addition, the eunuch-led voyages during the first third of the century (as well as the non-state players who were obviously continuing to trade from China to Southeast Asia, and vice-versa through much of the fifteenth century), meant that the Southeast Asian, Indian and Middle Eastern goods required by China must have been procured in larger quantities during this century. In 1390, for example, 171,000 *jin* (more than 100 tonnes)[205] of aromatics were delivered to the Chinese capital by the envoy from Siam.[206] The effects which the monopoly trading demands of the Southeast Asian rulers had on domestic procurement patterns, collection areas and economic systems is something which might also be further examined. The obtaining of Chinese porcelain, silks and coinage by the Southeast Asian rulers through this trade would also have likely aided their capacity to maintain local economic networks beneficial to themselves.

Changes in Southeast Asian economic topography – rise of new trade ports

The apparent increase in maritime trade during the century also appears to have induced the rise of new ports. Malacca, as a major entrepôt polity has already been mentioned above. Reid[207] has also written on the rise of new port-polities as a result of a "trade take-off around 1400" and growth in trade during the beginnings of his "Age of Commerce", and the increased urbanization which subsequently occurred in these port cities. The rise of the northern Javanese ports is a particularly noticeable aspect of this trend.[208] The decline of Majapahit was obviously a factor in this, but the Chinese voyagers seem also to have played a

Ming China and Southeast Asia 117

part in the emergence of Demak, Japara, Gresik and Cirebon. These new polities and the shipping routes which connected them also produced new regional trading networks among both the Chinese[209] and the Southeast Asians. It might be said that the fifteenth century produced the first East Asian[210] trading system.

Changes in Southeast Asian economic topography – new mediums of exchange?

Copper cash rewards/payments were provided to some of the Southeast Asian envoys/merchants who travelled to the Ming court. It appears that the eunuch-led missions to the region also carried such rewards. Reid makes a strong claim that "Chinese copper cash, and local coins modelled on them, were the basic lubricant for the increasing commercialization of the region after 1400".[211] This is supported by research which indicates that from about 1300, inscriptions in Java cease to mention Javanese weights and measures and refer only to *picis*, the Javanese word for cash. This supports a thesis that it was late Song commercial operators or those who accompanied the Yuan invasions which introduced the coins to Java. Other uses of Chinese copper coins, or those modelled on the Chinese, are seen in the Philippines and Vietnam, the latter most certainly deriving from the Chinese model. Reid also cites early European travellers who noted that Chinese coins were the basic coinage in use in Brunei, Sumbawa, and Maluku by the early sixteenth century.[212] The interactions during the fifteenth century appear to have consolidated the connections between the Southeast Asian and Chinese economies.

Changes in Southeast Asian technological topography – shipbuilding

The technological influence of the Ming Chinese on fifteenth-century Southeast Asia has been cited in at least three major areas. The first was shipbuilding. Southeast Asian and Chinese shipbuilding traditions have been detailed by Manguin[213] and Needham[214] respectively, while Manguin has also looked at the cross-influences between the Southeast Asian and Chinese shipbuilding traditions, and posits a hybrid South China Sea junk.[215] Reid has examined the role of hybrid shipbuilding in the broader scope of Sino-Javanese shipping.[216] It seems however, given the present state of research and evidence, that the degree to which Chinese maritime technology, including shipbuilding, affected Southeast Asian traditions in the fifteenth century can only be assessed through further discoveries of excavation of shipwrecks of the period.

Changes in Southeast Asian technological topography – firearms

One of the most original recent theses of Chinese influence on Southeast Asia during the fifteenth century is that of Sun Laichen, who has suggested that the Ming greatly affected Southeast Asian history through its introduction of firearms.[217] He concludes that "the founding of the Ming dynasty in 1368 started the 'military revolution' not only in Chinese but also world history in the early modern period". These weapons were certainly used in the Ming wars against the Vietnamese and the Tai polities in the fifteenth century and were particularly effective against the elephants which the Tai relied upon. Sun sees a significant transfer of Chinese military technology (and specifically firearms) to the Vietnamese in the early Ming, particularly through the Ming occupation of the Viet polity. Subsequently, he suggests, the Vietnamese used this new technology to mount major military expeditions in the 1470s, into Champa, and then across through the Tai heartlands as far as the Irrawaddy. This sphere promises great potential for further research on the effects of Chinese technology on Southeast Asia in the fifteenth century.

Changes in Southeast Asian technological topography – ceramics manufacture

Chinese ceramics have been major trade products into Southeast Asia for well over a millennium. The obvious appeal of Chinese ceramics to the rulers and markets of Southeast Asia both before and during the early Ming, obviously gave rise to imitators within the region. The Si Satchanalai and Sukothai celadons of the fourteenth and fifteenth centuries appear to have benefited from Chinese ceramic technologies, as did the Vietnamese wares of the fourteenth and fifteenth centuries.[218] There exists vast potential for further research on the specific innovations which did take place in the Southeast Asian ceramic traditions, their origins and period of introduction, and whether there was any influx of Chinese potters into Southeast Asia.

Changes in Southeast Asian cultural topography – Vietnam

Many parts of Southeast Asia were culturally very different at the end of the fifteenth century from what they were at the beginning of that period, and in the changes which did take place over that century, Ming China appears to have been a major influence. During the Ming occupation of Đại Việt in the first quarter of the century, for example, the Ming introduced a wide range of practices which would have changed society in diverse ways. John Whitmore has already discussed some of these.[219] The establishment of Confucian schools, as well as geomancy schools and medical schools in the Ming colony, would certainly have had some impact on the population. However, it was the overall Ming administrative structure and procedures which existed for these 20 years, along with the presence of a huge number of Chinese persons which would have had most effect in changing society. Whether all of the Ming policies, such as that proposed during the occupation that Vietnamese should adopt Chinese mourning customs,[220] actually had a long-lasting effect on the society is an issue which needs to be subject to much further study.

Likewise, the destruction of the carriers of Vietnamese culture which occurred under the Ming administration, such as the burning of Vietnamese books,[221] needs to be further examined, as do the consequences of the removal of many of the skilled artisans and other personnel from Đại Việt into China,²²² which undoubtedly had major repercussions on Vietnamese society.

The new bureaucratic and other government systems which were introduced into Đại Việt following the withdrawal of the Ming can also be said to have been, in some ways, products of the Ming, if only by the fact that the invasion and subsequent destruction forced the Vietnamese to create new systems post-Ming withdrawal.²²³

Changes in Southeast Asian cultural topography – Yunnan

In the same way that the influx of Chinese administration and Chinese persons changed the cultural milieu of Đại Việt in the early fifteenth century, so they must have greatly affected the peoples of the Yunnan polities who, either suddenly or gradually, were subject to the cultural norms of Chinese societies and polities. Non-Chinese persons in Yunnan were assigned Chinese surnames by the Taizu emperor in 1383,²²⁴ and this was part of a long process of acculturation during the Ming by which Sinicization of the indigenous populations proceeded, in both active and passive modes.

There was constant pressure on newly colonized peoples in Yunnan to accord with certain Chinese cultural practices. As in Vietnam, these were instilled through the establishment of Confucian schools, mainly for the indigenous elite. A school was established at Jingdong Guard in 1446,²²⁵ and by 1510, Confucian schools had also been established in the Yunnan outposts of Jinchi and Tengchong. A proposal in 1481 that the heirs to "native-official" posts in Yunnan be sent to Confucian schools in nearby prefectures so that their own cultures could be replaced by Chinese values, while emerging more from frontier security considerations than any "desire to civilize", still undoubtedly had effects, especially in terms of Chinese literacy among the peoples of Yunnan. There is little research on how the processes of Sinicization proceeded among the peoples of the Yunnan polities and this is also an area where much research remains to be done.

Changes in Southeast Asian cultural topography – maritime Southeast Asia

To what degree did the Chinese maritime traders, the Ming envoys and the people who accompanied them on their voyages to Southeast Asia have an impact on cultural practices in the local societies? Did the sending of didactic texts and guides to [Chinese] behaviour, as happened frequently during the early reigns, particularly with *Biographies of Exemplary Women* (烈女傳), really have any effect on the Southeast Asia societies? Claudine Salmon has studied the influence of Chinese literature on the literatures of societies surrounding China from the seventeenth century,²²⁶ but further studies on earlier literature and possible connections with Chinese texts likely to have been distributed in Southeast Asia by Ming agents might prove worthwhile.

Certainly, the use of Chinese languages would have increased in the major port cities of the region, particularly when the huge eunuch-led armadas were in town. The adoption of Chinese terms for a vast range of food and other daily products into most of the major languages of the archipelago likely began or, at least, expanded during the early fifteenth century. Kong Yuanzhi has done much work on identifying Chinese lexical items borrowed into Malay and Indonesian.[227] However, determining the periods during which such borrowings were made is nigh impossible.

The rise of hybrid Sino-Southeast Asian societies as a result of fairly large-scale migration of Chinese persons to Southeast Asia in or around the fifteenth century, with hybrid food, hybrid language and hybrid cultural expression has been discussed elsewhere by Reid.[228] Even the ships and crews which had to remain at Southeast Asian ports to await the monsoon winds, or to provide security for polities and/or Chinese ships and supplies would have been both culturally influential and influenced.

The role of the Zheng He voyages and Chinese Muslims more generally as being carriers of Islam throughout Southeast Asia is a topic which has continued to attract attention. Many of the members of the eunuch commanders' retinues were Muslims and their voyages to the Middle East of many appear to have also included the *hajj*. The Parlindungan/Poortman text,[229] which appears to be derived at least in part from Chinese local accounts in Java, claims that there was a network of Chinese Hanafi Muslims throughout Southeast Asia in the fifteenth century, and that this network, which had derived from the Zheng He voyages, established the first Islamic communities in Palembang, Sambas and in many ports along the north coast of Java. It seems wise to concur with Reid's opinion that "More systematic work needs to be done, however, before it can be accepted as a credible source for the fifteenth century".[230]

The Zheng He voyages also left Southeast Asia with another religious legacy. Throughout the region, particularly among Chinese communities, there still circulate various legends and beliefs about Zheng He, Wang Jinghong and other eunuchs. Temples have also been erected to worship San-bao-gong, the honorific name for Zheng He. Kong Yuanzhi has done much work on the temples, legends and beliefs relating to Zheng He in Southeast Asia.[231]

It appears that Chinese weights and measures also had some impact in the archipelago during the fifteenth century. In 1404, an envoy from Siam to the Ming court requested that Chinese "weights and measures be conferred upon them".[232] Is there any evidence of changes in Southeast Asian metrological standards during the fifteenth century? This is difficult to assess, but at least by the middle of the sixteenth century, in a Portuguese text of 1554, we read that "In Malacca the weight used for gold, musk, &c., the *cate*, contains 20 *taels*, each tael 16 *mazes*, each maz 20 cumduryns; also 1 paual 4 mazes, each maz 4 *cupongs*; each cupong 5 cumduryns".[233] The "cate" and "tael" are the Malay terms for the Chinese *jin* (斤) and *liang* (兩) respectively. While it cannot be categorically stated that these units were introduced to Southeast Asia during the fifteenth century, it seems likely that they were at least introduced to Malacca in that century.

Can it thus be said that the fifteenth century constituted the first major wave of Sinicization of Southeast Asia?[234] Given that the way in which the term "Southeast Asia" has been used within this article, as reference to "non-China" that lay to the south of the Chinese polities, this claim cannot be made, as the non-Chinese areas south of the Yangzi were subject to many waves of Sinicization over the preceding millennium. However, it does seem that the degree of Chinese influence within Southeast Asia did expand in the fifteenth century, so perhaps it will suffice just to claim, in conclusion, that the fifteenth century saw the first major wave of Sinicization of maritime Southeast Asia.

Notes

1 For more detailed accounts of the demise of the Yuan dynasty and the founding of the Ming, see F.W. Mote, *Imperial China 900–1800* (Cambridge Mass.: Harvard University Press, 1999), pp. 517–83; and also F.W. Mote, "The Rise of the Ming Dynasty 1330–1367" in *Cambridge History of China* (Cambridge: Cambridge University Press, 1998), Vol. 7, pp. 11–15.

2 Zhu Yuanzhang had inspected Kaifeng, the former Song capital, and his birthplace of Fengyang (Haozhou), as well as the Han and Tang capitals of Xi'an, as his potential capitals. He did, however, subsequently decide to remain at Yingtian (the modern Nanjing), possibly because of its distance from the Mongol heartlands.

3 For some broad-ranging studies of imperial China's foreign relations, see the essays within J.K. Fairbank (ed.), *The Chinese World Order: Traditional China's Foreign Relations* (Cambridge, Mass.: Harvard University Press,1968); Morris Rossabi (ed.) *China Among Equals: the Middle Kingdom and Its Neighbors 10th–14th Centuries* (Los Angeles: University of California Press, 1983); and Mark Mancall (ed.), *China at the Center: 300 Years of Foreign Policy* (Transformation of Modern China series) (NewYork: Free Press, 1984).

4 *Ming Xianzong shilu*, juan 229.4a and *Wuzong shilu*, juan 2.19a.

5 Chen Ching-ho, 陳荊和 （編校） 校合本 <大越史記全書> (3 本), (*Đại Việt sử ký toàn thư*) (Tokyo: 1985–86. See pp. 635 and 641).

6 The works of Wang Gungwu, J.V.G. Mills, Oliver Wolters, Roderich Ptak and Sun Laichen are notable in this area, and include: Wang Gungwu's "The Opening of Relations Between China and Malacca" in J.S. Bastin and R. Roolvink (eds.) *Malayan and Indonesian Studies: Essays Presented to Sir Richard Winstedt* (Oxford: Clarendon Press, 1964), 87–104; "Early Ming Relations with Southeast Asia: A Background Essay", in Fairbank, *The Chinese World* Order; 48–55; "The First Three Rulers of Malacca" in *Journal of the Royal Asiatic Society Malaysian Branch*, Vol. 41 (1968): 11–22; and "China and Southeast Asia 1402–24" in J. Chen and N. Tarling (ed.) *Social History of China and Southeast Asia* (Cambridge: Cambridge University Press, 1970), 375–402: J.V.G. Mills' *Ma Huan,Ying-yai Sheng-lan, "The Overall Survey of the Ocean's Shores" [1433]*, (Cambridge: Cambridge University Press for the Hakluyt Society, Extra Series No. XLII, 1970); and "Chinese Navigators in Insulinde about A.D.1500" in *Archipel* 18 (1979): 69–93; Oliver Wolters' *The Fall or Srivijaya in Malay History* (Ithaca: Cornell University Press, 1970); Roderich Ptak's essays collected in *China and the Asian Seas: Trade, Travel, and Visions of the Other (1400–1750)*, (Collected Studies, 638), (Farnham: Ashgate, 1998) and *China's Seaborne Trade With South and Southeast Asia 1200–1750*, (Collected Studies, 640), (Farnham: Ashgate, 1999); and *Fei Hsin, Hsing-ch'a sheng-lan: The Overall Survey of the Star Raft*, translated by J.V.G. Mills; revised, annotated and edited by Roderich Ptak (Wiesbaden: Harrassowitz Verlag, 1996):

and Sun Laichen's *Chinese Military Technology and Dai Viet: c.1390–1497* in Nhung Tuyết Trần and Anthony Reid (eds.), *Viet Nam: Borderless Histories* (Madison, Wisconsin: University of Wisconsin Press, 2006); "Military Technology Transfers from Ming China and the Emergence of Northern Mainland Southeast Asia (*c.1390–1527*)" in *Journal of Southeast Asian Studies* Volume 34: 3 (October 2003): 495–517; and *Chinese Military Technology and Dai Viet: c.1390–1497*, Asia Research Institute Online Working Paper No. 11 (September 2003), www.ari.nus. edu.sg/docs/wps/wps03_011.pdf.
7 *Yingzong shilu*, juan 218.1a.
8 *Yingzong shilu*, juan 225.11a–b.
9 *Yingzong shilu*, juan 306.5a–b.
10 *Yingzong shilu*, juan 306.5a–b.
11 *Xianzong shilu*, juan 181.2a–b.
12 Watanabe Hiroshi, "An Index of Embassies and Tribute Missions from Islamic Countries to Ming China (1368–1466) as Recorded in the *Ming Shih-lu*, Classified According to Geographic Area" in *Memoirs of the Research Department of the Toyo Bunko*, No. 33 (1975): 285–347.
13 *Taizu shilu*, juan 68.4a–b.
14 *Taizu shilu*, juan 39.1b. Another reference to Yunnan as a country can be found at *Taizu shilu*, juan 53.9a–b.
15 *Taizu shilu*, juan 138.5a–b.
16 *Taizu shilu*, juan 189.14b–16a.
17 *Taizu shilu*, juan 198.2a–b.
18 *Taizu shilu*, juan 255.2a–b and 255.8a–b.
19 *Taizong shilu*, juan 15.2a and 16.3a.
20 *Taizu shilu*, juan 172.5b.
21 *Taizu shilu*, juan 190.3b.
22 A Chinese unit of weight, often referred to as a "Chinese ounce". During the Ming, it averaged 37 grams.
23 *Taizong shilu*, juan 17.6a.
24 In 1384, it was stated that the accompanying goods brought by tribute envoys were not to be taxed. See *Taizu shilu*, juan 158.5b.
25 The failure to advise the Emperor of the arrival of the Cham envoys in 1379 was apparently the act which sparked investigations of Hu Weiyong and colleagues. This led to his jailing and eventual death, and the killing of a further reportedly 15,000 other individuals. For further details, see Chan Hok-lam's account of Hu Weiyong in L. Carrington Goodrich and Chaoying Fang's *Dictionary of Ming Biography* (New York: Columbia University Press, 1976), 638–41. See also Frederick W. Mote and Denis Twitchett, *The Cambridge History of China – Volume 7: The Ming Dynasty 1368–1644 Part* 1, 155, 162–4.
26 O.W. Wolters, *The Fall of Srivijaya in Malay History* (Ithaca: Cornell University, 1970), 68–70.
27 *Taizu shilu*, juan 70.3b.
28 *Taizu shilu*, juan 70.7a–b.
29 *Taizu shilu*, juan 139.7a.
30 *Taizu shilu*, juan 159.4b.
31 A generic term for foreigners, often used to refer to those who came from the maritime realm.
32 *Taizu shilu*, juan 205.4a.
33 *Taizu shilu*, juan 231.2a–b.
34 *Taizu shilu*, juan 252.2b.
35 *Taizong shilu*, juan 12B.7a.
36 *Taizong shilu*, juan 22.3a–b.
37 *Taizong shilu*, juan 46.1a.

38 *Taizong shilu*, juan 34.3a.
39 *Taizong shilu*, juan 185.1a.
40 *Taizong shilu*, juan 52.6a–7a.
41 But in the same year, we have the Emperor claiming: "Annam is secluded in a cranny in the ocean. Since ancient times, it has been an administrative division (郡縣) of China". (*Taizong shilu*, juan 58.1a).
42 *Taizong shilu*, juan 68.3b–7a.
43 The occupied Đại Việt.
44 *Taizong shilu*, juan 71.6a.
45 *Taizong shilu*, juan 80.3b–4a.
46 *Xuanzong shilu*, juan 3.12b–13a.
47 The importance of Vietnamese maritime trade in this period is underlined in Momoki Shiro, "Đại Việt and the South China Sea Trade: From the 10th to the 15th Century", in *Crossroads*, Vol. 12, No. 1 (1999): 1–34.
48 *Renzong shilu*, juan 4A.5b–6a.
49 *Taizong shilu*, juan 149.4b–5a.
50 *Taizong shilu*, juan 250.6b and *Xuanzong shilu*, juan 24.8a.
51 For further discussion on the colonial nature of the Chinese invasion and occupation of Đại Việt in the fifteenth century, see Geoff Wade, "Ming Colonial Armies in 15th-Century Southeast Asia" in Karl A. Hack and Tobias Rettig (ed.), *Colonial Armies in Southeast Asia* (London: RoutledgeCurzon, 2004).
52 *Taizong shilu*, juan 23.4b.
53 *Taizong shilu*, juan 16.3a.
54 *Taizong shilu*, juan 53.2b.
55 *Taizong shilu*, juan 32.1a.
56 *Taizong shilu*, juan 49.1a–b.
57 *Taizong shilu*, juan 35.2b.
58 *Taizong shilu*, juan 55.1b.
59 See, for example, *Taizong shilu*, 17.6a.
60 *Taizong shilu*, juan 57.2a–b.
61 The eunuchs sent to Jiaozhi (the occupied Đại Việt) and to Yunnan by the Ming emperors were also engaged in the collection of precious stones, gold and pearls. A later reference from 1459 suggests that the obtaining of gold was a major task of the eunuch-led voyages. See *Yingzong shilu*, juan 307.3b.
62 *Taizong shilu*, juan 43.3b.
63 *Taizong shilu*, juan 279.1a.
64 The claims that some of Zheng He's ships were 450 feet in length have generally been regarded as nautically impossible. For some literature relating to the debate over the size of Zheng He's ships, see Robert Finlay, "The Treasure Ships of Zheng He: Chinese Maritime Imperialism in the Age of Discovery", *Terrae Incognitae*, 23 (1991): 1–12, p. 3, note 11.
65 Mills, *Ma Huan: Ying-yai Sheng-lan*, 31.
66 Mills, *Ma Huan: Ying-yai Sheng-lan*, 15.
67 *Yingzong shilu*, juan 231.15a.
68 *Xuanzong shilu*, juan 26.2a.
69 *Taizong shilu*, juan 71.1a.
70 *Taizong shilu*, juan 71.5a.
71 *Taizong shilu*, juan 143.1b.
72 A Chinese unit of weight, often referred to as a "Chinese ounce". During the Ming, it averaged 37 grams.
73 *Taizong shilu*, juan 71.6a–b.
74 The phonetics suggest Nawrahta, but this name does not accord with existing lists of Burman rulers.
75 *Taizong shilu*, juan 94.5b.

76 Possibly Vira Alakesvara (Alagakkonara), the chief minister under Bhuvanekabahu V (r. 1372–1408). See Chandra Richard de Silva, *Sri Lanka: A History* (New Delhi: Vikas Publishing House, 1987), 94–5.
77 *Taizong shilu*, juan 116.2a–b.
78 *Taizong shilu*, juan 130.1b–2a.
79 *Taizong shilu*, juan 118.4a.
80 *Taizong shilu*, juan 168.1a–b.
81 For a likely romantic account of the origins of Su-gan-la, see the account of Samudera in *Yingyai sheng*lan. This has been translated in J.V.G. Mills' *Ma Huan: Yingyai Sheng-lan*, pp. 116–17.
82 Formally designated as the capital by the Yongle emperor in 1420.
83 Charles O. Hucker. "Entry on Chu Chan-chi" in L. Carrington Goodrich and Chaoying Fang, *Dictionary of Ming Biography* (New York: Columbia University Press, 1976), pp. 279–89.
84 Reigned 1424–25.
85 *Xuanzong shilu*, juan 32.9b–10b.
86 *Xuanzong shilu*, juan 64.4a–5b.
87 The orders by which he was sent are contained in *Xuanzong shilu*, juan 67.3b–4a.
88 Mills, *Ma Huan:Ying-yai Sheng-lan*, pp. 14–19.
89 *Xuanzong shilu*, juan 106.2a–b, 106.5a and 106.7b.
90 *Xuanzong shilu*, juan 106.7a–b.
91 *Xuanzong shilu*, juan 106.7b.
92 *Xuanzong shilu*, juan 106.8a.
93 *Xuanzong shilu*, juan 106.8b.
94 For details of the campaign and the capture of the emperor, see Mote and Twitchett, *Cambridge History of China the Ming Dynasty, Part* 1, 319–25.
95 Located in what is today western Yunnan and northern Myanmar.
96 *Yingzong shilu*, juan 44.7b.
97 *Yingzong shilu*, juan 51.7a–b.
98 *Yingzong shilu*, juan 73.11b–12a.
99 *Yingzong shilu*, juan 75.6a.
100 *Yingzong shilu*, juan 86.6a–7b and 88.8a–9b.
101 *Yingzong shilu*, juan 94.7b.
102 *Yingzong shilu*, juan 127.1b.
103 Liew Foon Ming: "The Luchuan–Pingmian Campaigns (1436–1449) in the Light of Official Chinese Historiography", in *Oriens Extremus* 39:2 (1996): 162–203.
104 The polity known in Shan as Möng Yang or Möng Kawng and in Burmese as Mohnyin or Mogaung.
105 *Yingzong shilu*, juan 164.5a–6a.
106 *Yingzong shilu*, juan 164.5a–6a.
107 *Yingzong shilu*, juan 175.8b.
108 *Yingzong shilu*, juan 179.7b–8a.
109 *Yingzong shilu*, juan 241.4b–5a.
110 *Yingzong shilu*, juan 156.1a.
111 *Yingzong shilu*, juan 150.3a.
112 *Yingzong shilu*, juan 298.5a.
113 *Yingzong shilu*, juan 156.1a.
114 *Yingzong shilu*, juan 335.1b.
115 *Yingzong shilu*, juan 189.3b.
116 See Mote and Twitchett, *Cambridge History of China, The Ming Dynasty, Part* 1, 377–84 for details of some of the Ming wars against peoples to the south.
117 *Man* (蠻) and *mo* (貊) were generic, disparaging terms of reference for non-Chinese people.
118 *Xianzong shilu*, juan 212.6a–b.

119 Đại Việt.
120 *Xianzong shilu*, juan 155.7b–9b.
121 *Xianzong shilu*, juan 219.5a–b.
122 *Xianzong shilu*, juan 219.6a–7b.
123 *Xianzong shilu*, juan 220.2a–3a.
124 See, for example, Sun Laichen, "Chinese Military Technology and Dai Viet".
125 *Xianzong shilu*, juan 259.5b.
126 *Xiaozong shilu*, juan 148.6b–9a.
127 *Xiaozong shilu*, juan 167.4b–5b.
128 *Xiaozong shilu*, juan 73.3a–b.
129 *Wuzong shilu*, juan 25.1a.
130 *Wuzong shilu*, juan 124.3a.
131 *Shizong shilu*, juan 4.27b.
132 *Xianzong shilu*, juan 39.10a–b.
133 *Xiaozong shilu*, juan 35.4a–5a.
134 *Xiaozong shilu*, juan 172.3a–b.
135 *Shizong shilu*, juan 118.2b–3a.
136 *Shizong shilu*, juan 169.1a–2b.
137 *Taizong shilu*, juan 35.2b. Interesting comparisons could be drawn with the system of Residents and Advisers whom the British appointed in colonial India and the Malay states some four and a half centuries later.
138 The term Yunnan seems to have had a broad meaning during the Ming, encompassing any polity to the south of the region controlled by the authorities in Kunming. In this sense, it was used much like the term "the West" was used in the European expansion across the North American continent.
139 See, for example *Yingzong shilu*, juan 57.5b where, in August 1439, 8,364 persons were rewarded or appointed to posts for their achievements in the campaign against Si Renfa at Lujiang. In addition to promotions for Chinese people involved, the non-Chinese Chiefs of Chief's Offices were promoted to Pacification Officers, while Local Commanders were promoted to Police Officers.
140 The term *dong* appears to be a Tai (Zhuang or Dong) term meaning the catchment area of a watercourse. It was widely used throughout areas which are today part of southern China as a territorial/administrative designation. Within the last century, the term was still being used in the New Territories of Hong Kong. See James Hayes, "The Pattern of Life in the New Territories in 1998", *Journal of the Hong Kong Branch of the Royal Asiatic Society*, New Series, Vol. 2 (1962): 75–102.
141 In their victory memorial to the throne, the Ming commanders who had captured Đại Việt claimed that seven million of the Vietnamese forces had been killed. See *Taizong shilu*, juan 68.3b–7a. Even allowing for the rhetoric, other reports of the Ming invasion suggest huge mortality on both sides.
142 In 1407, 7,700 tradesmen and artisans, including gun-founders, were forcibly transported from Annam to the Ming capital at modern Nanjing. (*Taizong shilu*, juan 71.6a).
143 *Yingzong shilu*, juan 103.2a.
144 *Taizong shilu*, juan 198.2a–b.
145 *Taizu shilu*, juan 210.3a.
146 *Taizong shilu*, juan 94.5a–b.
147 *Yingzong shilu*, juan 46.9b.
148 *Yingzong shilu*, juan 76.4b.
149 *Yingzong shilu*, juan 81.5b–6a.
150 *Yingzong shilu*, juan 152.2b–3a.
151 Both *yi* (夷) and *di* (狄) are disparaging generic terms for non-Chinese peoples.
152 *Taizong shilu*, juan 15.2a and 16.3a.
153 *Taizu shilu*, juan 244.2b–4a.

154 *Yingzong shilu*, juan 105.2b–3a.
155 *Taizong shilu*, juan 31.5a–b.
156 *Taizong shilu*, juan 49.1a–b.
157 *Taizong shilu*, juan 53.3a.
158 *Taizong shilu*, juan 94.3b–4a.
159 *Taizong shilu*, juan 233.4b and 235.1b–2a.
160 *Taizong shilu*, juan 53.3a.
161 *Yingzong shilu*, juan 154.7a.
162 *Yingzong shilu*, juan 150.7a–8a.
163 *Xiaozong shilu*, juan 195.3a–4a.
164 *Yingzong shilu*, juan 7.8a.
165 It was common for "Chinese" persons who resided in the polities of Southeast Asia to be involved in the tribute/trade system which linked those polities with the Ming. Their language abilities, cultural knowledge and, likely, business links, ensured that they were more efficient than those without this acumen. It is thus probable that the Ming tribute/trade system helped promote the emergence or the strengthening of Chinese trade networks throughout the archipelago. See also Chan Hok-lam, "The 'Chinese Barbarian Officials' in the Foreign Tribute Missions to China During the Ming Dynasty", *Journal of the American Oriental Society*, Vol. 88 (1968): 411–18.
166 *Renzong shilu*, juan 10.1a. There seems to be no record of Chinese paper money circulating in Southeast Asia, and it is likely that such rewards were converted into other trade goods before the tribute envoys left China.
167 Probably Arya Suleiman.
168 *Xuanzong shilu*, juan 33.5a.
169 *Yingzong shilu*, juan 157.8a–b.
170 Generally once every three years.
171 *Yingzong shilu*, juan 106.8a–b.
172 *Yingzong shilu*, juan 234.3b.
173 *Xianzong shilu*, juan 176.5a–b.
174 *Xiaozong shilu*, juan 170.5b–6a.
175 *Wuzong shilu*, juan 65.8b–9a.
176 *Wuzong shilu*, juan 113.2a.
177 Noted above and also detailed in Bodo Wiethoff, *Die chinesische Seeverbotspolitik und der private Überseehandel von 1368 bis 1567* (Hamburg: Gesellschaft für Natur- und Völkerkunde Ostasiens, 1963); and Chang Tseng-hsin, *Maritime Activities on the Southeast Coast of China in the Latter Part of the Ming Dynasty* (明季東南中國的海上活動), Vol. 1 (Taipei: Dongwu daxue zhongguo xueshu zhuzuo jiangzhu weiyuanhui, 1988), 3–16.
178 See for example *Wuzong shilu*, juan 113.2a of 1514; *Wuzong shilu*, juan 123.4b of 1515; *Wuzong shilu*, juan 149.9a-b of 1517; and *Shizong shilu*, juan 2.14b of 1521.
179 *Shizong shilu*, juan 38.4b–5a.
180 *Shizong shilu*, juan 108.7a.
181 For further details, see Chang Tseng-hsin 張增信, *Mingji dongnan Zhongguo de haishang huodong* 明季東南中國的海上活動 (Maritime Activities on the Southeast Coast of China in the Latter Part of the Ming Dynasty). Vol. 1 (Taipei: Sili dongwu daxue zhongguo xueshu zhuzuo jiangzhu weiyuanhui, 1988); and Jin Guoping's various articles in his *Zhong-Pu guanxi shidi kaozheng* (中葡關係史地考證) (Macau: Macau Foundation, 2000).
182 Hamashita Takeshi, "The Tribute Trade System and Modern Asia", *Memoirs of the Research Department of the Toyo Bunko*, No. 46 (1988): 7–23. See page 23.
183 *Xuanzong shilu*, juan 52.9b.
184 *Xuanzong shilu*, juan 57.7b–8a.
185 *Yingzong shilu*, juan 2.12a.
186 *Xiaozong shilu*, juan 153.10b–11b.

187 *Wuzong shilu*, juan 33.3b.
188 *Yingzong shilu*, juan 64.5b–6a.
189 *Xuanzong shilu*, juan 17.11b–12a.
190 *Xiaozong shilu*, juan 48.2a.
191 *Shenzong shilu*, juan 338.4b–5a.
192 One of the most detailed studies of the *kaizhong* system during the Ming dynasty is "Mingdai de kaizhongfa" 明代的開中法 [The Kaizhong System during the Ming Dynasty], in *Zhongguo wenhua yanjiusuo xuebao* 中國文化研究所學報, Hong Kong, 4, 2 (1972): 371–493.
193 *Xuanzong shilu*, juan 7.9a–b.
194 *Yingzong shilu*, juan 131.8b–9a.
195 *Xiaozong shilu*, juan 80.1a–b.
196 For a far more detailed and systematic study of the migration of Chinese people into previously non-Chinese areas of this region, see James Z. Lee, *The Political Economy of a Frontier: Southwest China, 1250–1850* (Cambridge, Mass.: Harvard University Press, 2002) and particularly Chapter 4 – Immigration.
197 *Taizong shilu*, juan 34.1a–b.
198 See, for example, Chang Pin-tsun, "The First Chinese Diaspora in Southeast Asia" in Roderich Ptak and Dietmar Rothermund (ed.), *Emporia, Commodities and Entrepreneurs in Asian Maritime Trade, c.1400–1750* (Stuttgart: Franz Steiner Verlag, 1991), pp. 37–52.
199 The reasons for the alleged dearth of a large-scale Tai empire have been addressed in Nick Tapp, "A New Stage in Tai Regional Studies: The Challenge of Local Histories" in Andrew Turton (ed.), *Civility and Savagery: Social Identity in Tai States* (Richmond, Surrey: Curzon Press, 2000), 351–9; and in Craig Reynolds, "Review article: Tai-land and its others" in *South East Asia Research*, 11 (2003): 114–30.
200 For what constituted mainland Southeast Asia, the generic definition being applied here is "that which is not China", in the diverse ways in which this can be construed.
201 C.C. Berg has, however, questioned whether the listing of Nusantaran dependencies of Majapahit noted in the *Nagrakertagama* had any historical basis at all. See D.G.E. Hall, *A History of South-East Asia*, third edition (London: Macmillan, 1970), 86–7.
202 See Slamet Muljana, *A Story of Majapahit* (Singapore: Singapore University Press, 1976), 192. Further details are available in the *Pararaton*. See I Gusti Putu Phalgunadi, *The Pararaton: A Study of the Southeast Asia Chronicle* (New Delhi: Sundeep Prakashan, 1996), 131–3.
203 Often obscured under the "tribute system" rubric.
204 For details of missions to China from these polities in the period we are examining, see Chang Pin-tsun, "The First Chinese Diaspora in Southeast Asia" in Ptak and Rothermund (ed.), *Emporia, Commodities and Entrepreneurs in Asian Maritime Trade, c.1400–1750* (reprinted in Felipe Fernández-Armesto, *The Global Opportunity*, Volume 1 of *An Expanding World* series (Aldershot: Variorum, 1995). A listing of such missions can be seen on p. 28. Further details of the missions to and from China by these polities during the first quarter of the century can be found in Wang Gungwu, "China and Southeast Asia 1402–24" in Wang Gungwu, *Community and Nation: China, Southeast Asia and Australia* (Sydney: ASAA in conjunction with Allen and Unwin, 1992), 119 and 123.
205 For details of the shipment of aromatics throughout the region, but mainly in later periods, see the chapters on cloves and pepper in David Bulbeck, Anthony Reid, Lay Cheng Tan and Yiqi Wu (comp.), *Southeast Asian Exports since the 14th Century: Cloves, Pepper, Coffee and Sugar* (Singapore: ISEAS, 1998).
206 *Taizong shilu*, juan 201.1b.
207 Anthony Reid, *Southeast Asia in the Age of Commerce, 1450–1680. Volume Two: Expansion and Crisis*, (New Haven: Yale University Press, 1995), 10–15 and "The City and Its Commerce", 62–131.

208 For the background to which, see Anthony Reid, "The Rise and Fall of Sino-Javanese Shipping", in Anthony Reid, *Charting the Shape of Early Modern Southeast Asia* (Singapore: ISEAS, 2000), 56–84. See particularly "Chinese and the Rise of *Pasisir* Muslim States", 66–9.
209 For the growth of the Hokkien network, see the various works by James Chin Kong, particularly his doctoral thesis, "Merchants and other sojourners: the Hokkiens overseas, 1570–1760", University of Hong Kong, 1998.
210 Used in its current broad sense, which includes both Southeast Asia and North Asia.
211 Reid, *Southeast Asia in the Age of Commerce*, Volume Two, 95.
212 Ibid. 96–7.
213 See, for example, Pierre-Yves Manguin, "The Southeast Asian Ship: An Historical Approach", *Journal of Southeast Asian Studies*, XI: 2 (1980): 266–276; and his "The Vanishing *Jong*: Insular Southeast Asian Fleets in Trade and War (Fifteenth to Seventeenth Centuries)", in Anthony Reid (ed.) *Southeast Asia in the Early Modern Era: Trade, Power and Belief* (Ithaca: Cornell University Press, 1993), pp. 197–213.
214 Joseph Needham, *Science and Civilization in China, Vol. 4, No. 3 – Civil Engineering and Nautics*, (Cambridge: Cambridge University Press, 1971).
215 P.-Y. Manguin, "Relationships and Cross-influences between Southeast Asian and Chinese Shipbuilding Traditions", *SPAFA Final Report on Maritime Shipping and Trade Networks in Southeast Asia*, 1984.
216 Reid, "The Rise and Fall of Sino-Javanese Shipping" in Anthony Reid (ed.), *Charting the Shape of Early Modern Southeast Asia* (Chiang Mai: Silkworm Books, 1999), 56–84.
217 See Sun Laichen "Chinese Military Technology and Dai Viet: *c.*1390–1497", in Nhung Tuyết Trần and Anthony Reid, eds., *Viet Nam: Borderless Histories* (Madison, Wisconsin: University of Wisconsin Press, 2004).
218 See Roxanna M. Brown, *The Ceramics of South-East Asia, their Dating and Identification* (Kuala Lumpur: Oxford University Press, 1977); John Guy, *Ceramic Traditions of South-East Asia* (Singapore: Oxford University Press, 1989); and Dick Richards, *South-East Asian Ceramics: Thai, Vietnamese, and Khmer, from the Collection of the Art Gallery of South Australia* (Kuala Lumpur: Oxford University Press, 1995). For an excellently illustrated collection of the Chinese blue-and-white wares and their Vietnamese equivalents, see Larry Gotuaco, Rita C. Tan and Allison I. Diem, *Chinese and Vietnamese Blue and White Wares Found in the Philippines* (Manila, Bookmark Inc., 1997).
219 See John Whitmore, *Vietnam, Hồ Quý Ly, and the Ming (1371–1421)* (New Haven: Yale University Press, 1985).
220 *Taizong shilu*, juan 214.1b.
221 For which see Alexander Ong's various recent articles.
222 In 1407, 7,700 tradesmen and artisans, including gun-founders, were sent from Annam to the Ming capital at modern Nanjing (*Taizong shilu*, juan 71.6a). Zhang Xiu-min also details the architects and other prominent persons who were taken off to China by the Ming and subsequently served the Chinese state. See Zhang Xuemin 張秀民, *Zhong Yue guanxishi lunwenji* 中越關係史論文集 [Collected Studies on the History of Sino-Vietnamese Relations] (Taipei: Wenshizhe chubanshe, 1992), particularly pp. 45–74, 75–114 and 199–234.
223 For details of the processes of administrative, economic and artistic restoration following the end of the Ming occupation of Vietnam, see Lê Thành Khôi, *Histoire du Viêt Nam des Origines à 1858* (Paris: Sudestasie, 1992), 219–24.
224 *Taizu shilu*, juan 152.4a.
225 *Yingzong shilu*, juan 140.7a.
226 Claudine Salmon, *Literary Migrations, Traditional Chinese Fiction in Asia (17–20th Centuries)* (Beijing: International Culture Publishing Corporation, 1987).
227 See Kong Yuanzhi 孔遠志, "Zhongguo yindunixiya wenhua jiaoliu" 中國印度尼西

亞文化交流 (Beijing: Beijing daxue chubanshe, 1999). The listing of borrowed lexical items can be seen on pp. 128–56.
228 See Reid, "Rise and Fall of Sino-Javanese Shipping".
229 For which see H.J. de Graaf and Th. G. Th. Pigeaud (edited by M.C. Ricklefs), *Chinese Muslims in Java in the 15th and 16th Centuries* (Melbourne: Monash Papers on Southeast Asia, 1984).
230 Reid, "The Rise and Fall of Sino-Javanese Shipping", 68.
231 See Kong Yuanzhi, *Muslim Tionghoa Cheng Ho, Misteri Perjalanan Muhibah di Nusantara Pustaka* (Jakarta: Populer Obor, 2000).
232 *Taizong shilu*, juan 34.3a.
233 Henry Yule and A.C. Burnell, *Hobson Jobson: Glossary of Colloquial Anglo-Indian Words & Phrases, & of Kindred Terms Etymological, Historical, Geographical & Discursive*, new edition edited by William Crooke, Fourth edition (Delhi: Munshiram Manoharlal Publishers, 1984). See entry for "Candareen", p. 155.
234 Chang Pin-tsun speaks of diaspora rather than Sinicization in his article "The First Chinese Diaspora in Southeast Asia" in Ptak and Rothermund, *Emporia, Commodities and Entrepreneurs*.

5 The Portuguese occupation of Malacca in 1511 and China's response

Liao Dake

Before the arrival of Western colonists in the East, "the tributary system was the medium of diplomacy, the tool of China's foreign relations"[1] and also the main form of relations between China and Southeast Asian nations. Following the establishment of the Ming Dynasty, an international order began to emerge in Southeast Asia, which was based on the tributary system and centred on China. However, in the early sixteenth century, the Portuguese invaded Southeast Asia and occupied Malacca, which was then a tributary of China. These events resulted in drastic changes to the international order in Southeast Asia and radically shook the so-called "China-and-Barbarians Order". Confronted with such a turbulent situation, the highest rulers of the Ming administration remained ignorant and unaware of the world situation and made improper responses and decisions, which inevitably resulted in Malacca's doom. The fall of Malacca marked the turning point in the relationship between China and Southeast Asia. Thereafter, China lost its previous prestige in Southeast Asia, and the influence of the Ming state in Southeast Asia waned steadily, making it difficult to sustain tributary relations. China thereby began its history of backwardness and humiliating defeats.

The origins of the tributary system

China's tributary relationships date back to the Shang Dynasty. Ancient records indicate that the Shang Dynasty issued the "Universal Tribute Decree" soon after it was established. However, the so-called "four barbarians" at that time mainly referred to inhabitants of the minority groups on the peripheries of the empire. After the Shang was overthrown by the Zhou, the new dynasty combined the patriarchal clan system based on blood ties and the regime by implementing a massive enfeoffment system in which clansmen, allies and descendants of the Shang were granted titles as feudal vassals. Thus, this system of patriarchal enfeoffment integrated enfeoffed states into a common polity, and the rule of the Zhou Dynasty was maintained. Under this patriarchal feudalism, the emperor of the Zhou Dynasty was the "Son of Heaven", the supreme leader of the world and the common master of all under Heaven, whereas vassal states had lesser leaders. They were subordinate, and were required to come for regular audiences with the Zhou emperor, to offer tribute of money, valuables and native products, and to provide troops and labour in the service of the emperor on a regular basis. Feudal princes meeting with the emperor were assigned different terms for different seasons and occasions in the *Zhou Rituals*, a classical work of ritual in ancient China – "it is called 'having an audience' (*chao*) in the spring, 'appearing at court' (*gong*) in the summer, and 'presenting themselves before the emperor' (*jin*)". In pre-Qin historic annals, "*chao*" referred to liegemen presenting themselves before the emperor and "*gong*" meant underlings presenting tribute to the master, which reflected the superior–subordinate relationship between the emperor and feudal vassals – the overlord–vassal relationship. Following the establishment of the Qin Dynasty, the two words "*chao*" and "*gong*" were used in combination to mean "tribute".

Following the establishment of the Qin and Han Dynasties, the ruling class abolished the system of enfeoffment, and instead established a centralised system of prefectures and counties in areas under the direct control and jurisdiction of the regime, and initiated a uniform taxation system. Thereafter, the tributary system lost its previous role and purpose and was confined to areas inhabited by minority groups where chiefs of minority local regimes accepted the conferral of titles of nobility from the emperor, acknowledged allegiance to the central government and presented tribute. It can be affirmed that the Han Dynasty should be credited for the extension of this means of ruling domestic minority groups to foreign relations and for its subsequent institutionalisation. Han rulers considered all visits by all polities in neighbouring and faraway lands and regions to be "tribute missions". Visiting foreign diplomatic envoys typically brought with them some specialty products from their countries as gifts to the court, no matter what the purpose of their visit. These, however, constituted "tribute" in the eyes of China's feudal rulers, who, in line with normal practice, would then grant noble titles and offer some gifts in return. As the contacts between China and foreign nations increased, "barbarians from all sides came to pay tribute; although they were occasionally disobedient, diplomats from these barbarians states continued to stream in".[2] The tributary system thus began to emerge in the foreign relations realm.

The tributary exchanges between China and other countries date back to the Han Dynasty. Emperor Wudi of the Han Dynasty, who was a man of great talent and bold vision, was the first to include foreign countries in the tributary system. He kept a close watch on foreign nations and embarked on many inspection tours travelling by sea.

> Whenever the emperor cruised out on the sea, he was always accompanied by foreigners. They passed through big cities with large populations, generously bestowing money and silk to display the wealth and abundance of the Han Dynasty; wrestling and amusing dramas were performed and monsters were displayed, attracting huge crowds of local people. Money and gifts were bestowed, sumptuous banquets were provided, and foreign guests were shocked by the abundance of storehouses and vastness of the Han Dynasty.[3]

Emperor Wudi also sent envoys to foreign countries to establish tributary relations with them. The *History of the Han Dynasty* notes of the country of Huangzhi (黄支), likely located on the southeast coast of the Indian subcontinent: "The state has a vast territory, a huge population, and many exotic materials, and has been paying tribute since the time of Emperor Wudi of the Han Dynasty".[4] At that time, countries and regions in Southeast Asia that paid tribute to the Han Dynasty included Yuechang 越裳 (possibly located in the Indochinese Peninsula),[5] Ye-diao 叶调 (located in Java or Sumatra), the Shan country 掸国 (in what now is Burma), and Jiu-bu-shi 究不事 (possibly in what is today Cambodia).[6] Following on from the Han, the subsequent Chinese rulers basically followed the Han system as the model for establishing a "tributary" relationship with countries in Southeast Asia and they conducted a wide variety of exchanges with those countries within the framework of the "tributary" system.

Theoretically, the core of the so-called "tributary" relationship was the emperor's governance of the world and containment of "barbarians", which involved the combination of notions of universal dominance and supreme imperial power. This was recorded in the *Spring and Autumn Annals* through the concepts of "the Heavenly Kingdom being supreme", "barbarians being different from the Han" and "barbarians presenting tribute to the Han", with their corresponding feudal hierarchical and ethnic notions, which were then extended and applied to the field of foreign relations. The tributary system covered politics (such as presenting oneself before the emperor, and being granted noble titles), ceremonial rituals (such as offering congratulations and expressing gratitude for the favour of the emperor), diplomacy (cementing relations with rulers of minor polities by marrying daughters of the imperial family to them, establishing diplomatic relations, and sending envoys), military matters (assisting with troops and requesting the deployment of troops), economic issues (barter, trade and tribute), and culture (such as literary pursuits and cultural emulation). Chinese feudal rulers hoped that the tributary relations with foreign nations would help them to "influence and educate" the barbarians in moral standards and codes of conduct, but they did not attempt to exercise administrative governance over these foreign countries or try to interfere in their internal affairs. This international order with Asian characteristics was the so-called "China-and-barbarians order" or "China's traditional world order".[7] However, up until the Song Dynasty, with regard to the tributary system, China followed the principle that "all are welcome to come and free to go", as recorded in *The History of the Song Dynasty*. Tributary relations were thus established on a voluntary basis rather than being imposed on other countries by the large power that was China, and therefore were not a relationship of dependency.[8] The so-called "Heavenly Kingdom" and "superior power" were nothing but the complacent rhetoric of the Chinese feudal rulers, and the "tributary" activities were simply a form of friendly contacts between China and overseas nations which had come into existence under specific historical conditions. This was to change with the Ming.

The emergence during the early Ming Dynasty of an international order in Southeast Asia with China as the core

After Zhu Yuanzhang, the founding emperor of the Ming Dynasty, overthrew the Yuan Dynasty and founded the Ming, he altered the tradition of previous imperial courts. Immediately after he ascended the throne, he set about soliciting tribute from foreign countries.

During the first year of the Hongwu reign (1368), the emperor dispatched the district magistrate Yi Ji to deliver an imperial edict to Annam.[9] During the second year of the Hongwu reign (1369), the emperor "sent envoys to issue imperial decrees to Japan, Champa, Java, and the Western Ocean countries".[10] During the third year of the Hongwu reign (1370), envoys were again sent to overseas countries, such as Annam, Korea, Champa, the Colas, Java, Siam, Srivijaya, Brunei, and Cambodia. It is said that during Zhu Yuanzhang's reign "the envoys despatched to neighbours reached 36 nations and heard about a further 31 nations, each having different customs. They found that there were 18 big countries and 149 small ones abroad".[11] The envoys' travel covered all major countries and regions in Southeast Asia. Such actions were fully indicative of the emperor's eagerness for tribute from overseas countries.

Emperor Taizu actively sought tribute from foreign countries. On the one hand, he desired that "all nations under heaven and on earth would pledge allegiance to China" so as to establish his legitimacy. On the other hand and more importantly, "out of his admiration and remembrance of the great eras of the Han, Tang and Song Dynasties as well as his hatred of Mongol rule",[12] the emperor believed that the relationship between China and neighbouring countries should be one with "China occupying the centre to restrain the barbarians and barbarians residing outside to serve China".[13] Following the restoration of Chinese legitimacy, the emperor was naturally interested in renewing the influence of Chinese civilisation on foreign countries and he sought to establish his ideal international order based on the traditional tributary system. During the first year of the Hongwu reign (1368), Emperor Taizu issued an imperial edict to Annam, which noted that:

> Previous emperors have treated all nations under the sun as equals regardless of their distance; therefore, China enjoys stability, as do neighbouring countries. I didn't deliberately seek the subjugation of your nation. After the Yuan rule was plunged into confusion, the whole nation was in chaos caused by the war for 17 years, making it hard to maintain contact with foreign countries located far away. I have established a new dynasty in Jiangsu, overpowered all other competitors, brought stability to China, and received support from the people. I am now the master of China; the new country that I have founded is named the Great Ming and my reign is called Hongwu. Not long ago, I sent troops to conquer the Yuan capital – Beijing. The entire country has now been unified and legitimate rule has been restored. I hope that we can live in harmony with each other and enjoy the

blessings of peace and tranquillity. Chiefs and commanders of your nations may not be aware of the new situation in China; therefore, this edict is hereby issued so that all of you can have an understanding of the new circumstances.[14]

During the second year of the Hongwu reign (1369), an imperial edict issued to Java read:

Rulers since ancient times have embraced all nations on the earth and under the sun. Nations, whether far or near, as long as they involve human beings, are all in pursuit of the stability of the nation and a happy life for their people. However, China must absolutely be stable so that all other nations will submit themselves to China.[15]

The wording was clearly indicative of Emperor Taizu's desire to create an international order centred on China. To achieve his ambitious goals, Emperor Taizu initiated a series of measures as a supplement to the implementation of his foreign policies:

1. Tributary trade was adopted as the only channel for Sino-foreign trade exchanges. Emperor Taizu was fully aware that "overseas countries offering tribute are actually doing so in the hope of gaining some profits".[16] In order to exact tribute from overseas countries, the emperor decreed that "countries sending ships with tribute will be allowed to trade with China, and non-tribute-paying countries will be barred from doing business with China".[17] At the same time, he imposed a ban on private maritime trade and prohibited private Chinese citizens from engaging in overseas trade. Overseas countries that defied this decree were punished and their tribute was rejected. Thus, by taking advantage of the desire of overseas countries for Chinese goods, the Ming court successfully manipulated economic measures to force overseas countries into its tributary system. The use of foreign trade as a tool for achieving diplomatic goals was actually an invention of Emperor Taizu.

2. The system of *kanhe* (verification seals) was implemented. "The so-called *kanhe* refers to a documentary proof bearing the official seal". "In the 16th year of the Hongwu reign, Siam became the first nation to receive *kanhe*, a system which was soon extended to other countries".[18] As it was difficult to verify the identity of tribute-paying barbarians, the Ministry of Rites created *kanhe* records, which were then issued to 59 places including Siam, Champa and Ryukyu. Nations which intended to pay tribute were awarded *kanhe*, which was verified by the respective administrative commissions against their records, and allowed to proceed to the capital.[19] The system of *kanhe* was designed to verify the authenticity of tribute-paying diplomats and to block civilians from engaging in unauthorised foreign trade, thereby ensuring the efficient functioning of the tributary system.

3   The Ming court exacted tribute from weaker nations by taking advantage of its status as a powerful nation. As described in the preceding paragraphs, voluntary submission was traditionally supposed to be the principle behind the tributary relationship between overseas countries and China. Emperor Taizu abolished this tradition in the process of restoring tributary relations. For example, during the third year of the Hongwu emperor, Ming officials Zhang Jingzhi and Chen Zhi embarked on a diplomatic mission to Brunei to encourage the king into paying tribute. However, the king of Brunei said, "Our land is barren and our people are poor; we have nothing valuable to present to the emperor; this is the only reason why we have not paid tribute to China". Chen Zhi replied, "The emperor owns the four seas and is extremely wealthy. What else does he desire? The submission of your country as a vassal state to China and nothing else". Thus, the king of Brunei was forced into the tributary system.[20]

Following his enthronement, Emperor Yongle, who believed that "the emperor resides in the centre and holds the reins of all other nations and all things under the sun",[21] inherited his late father's foreign policies and increased efforts to solicit tribute from foreign countries, in the hope of building a tributary system "attracting tribute from ten thousand nations". The *History of the Ming Dynasty* notes:

> After Emperor Chengzu [Yongle] defeated all his rivals and unified the country, he intended to ensure that foreign nations succumb to the superior Ming Dynasty, and thus sent envoys to foreign nations to demand tribute. Countries in the western region, big and small alike, gave their allegiance to Ming China and vied with one another in presenting treasures to China. Envoys dispatched by Emperor Chengzu reached the farthest places in the north and the sea in the south; eastward and westward. The envoys arrived at places where the sun rises and sets. Any place accessible by ship or carriage was visited.[22]

For overseas countries, Emperor Yongle ordered Zheng He (Cheng Ho) to undertake seven voyages to the Indian Ocean and the Western Pacific, which tremendously solidified the tributary system. Thanks to the great efforts of Emperor Yongle, the overseas countries:

> prepared specialty products, exotic animals and rare birds, and sent envoys to deliver the gifts to the Chinese capital by travelling in Zheng He's "treasure fleets".[23] Endless streams of incoming envoys from abroad resulted in the spectacular phenomenon of "tribute-paying envoys from different countries filling the roads"[24] and "envoys carrying gifts and valuable jades jostling with each other in a crowd".[25]

Thereby, the tributary relationship between China and Southeast Asian countries was brought to a peak. It should be noted that the tributary system created during the reigns of Hongwu and Yongle was not simply a duplication or expansion of that in the previous dynasty. The new tributary system had undergone some substantial transformations.

First, the Ming court's push for the tributary system was based on national strength and relied heavily on its military might as an inducement. By the early fifteenth century, the Ming state, after 30-plus years of painstaking efforts, had significantly improved its national strength and possessed sufficient resources to realise its grand overseas ambitions. "As military might is a clear yardstick of the prestige of a nation",[26] the Ming state built a strong navy as a powerful tool to implement its foreign policies.[27] Emperor Chengzu sent Zheng He to command a naval force to explore the West Ocean and cruise through the waters of Southeast Asia and the Indian Ocean. These wondrous voyages were aimed at "displaying China's military might and showing off China's prosperity to foreign countries"[28] and thereby exacting tribute from overseas and establishing a new political order in Southeast Asia. In the places Zheng He visited, he "announced imperial edicts and rewarded the king, presented lavish gifts and provided local chiefs with appropriate official caps and robes".[29] Zheng He also "captured overseas kings who were irreverent or attempted to hinder his display of Ming might and killed anyone who resisted with military force or tried to loot".[30] It was with this powerful naval force that Zheng He successfully established a formidable presence abroad, captured the Sumatran Chinese Chen Zuyi, toppled the Sri Lankan ruler Yalierkunaier 亚烈苦奈儿, captured Suganla 苏干剌 in Sumatra, and forced the Western King of Java Dumaban 都马板 into "paying tribute once every year or every other year, or several times every year".[31] To ensure a long-term "display of military might overseas", the Ming court made an unprecedented move to prop up the kingdom of Malacca. Malacca had been a small fishing village and a dependency of Siam. During the third year of the reign of Emperor Yongle (1405), the Malaccan ruler Parameswara 拜里迷苏剌 visited the Ming court and had the title of King of Malacca conferred upon him by Emperor Yongle; he was offered military aid and "provided with sea-going vessels to be brought home for the defence of his land"[32] to ensure that "there was no intrusion from Siam".[33] Malacca thus became independent of Siam. During Zheng He's voyages, a huge number of troops were stationed there, and Malacca was built into a naval base.

When Chinese "treasure fleets" arrived at Malacca, barriers and fences were erected like city walls, watch towers were built over the doors on the four sides, and patrols carrying alarm bells were posted at night. A second fence was built within the stockade, turning it into a small city; storehouses were also constructed to store money and grain. Home-going vessels gathered here and were loaded with foreign goods and started their voyage back home around mid-May when the southern wind was blowing.[34]

It was indeed the maritime superiority of the Ming that "compelled overseas barbarian countries to submit themselves to the power and prestige of the Son of

Heaven and encouraged tribute-paying envoys from everywhere".[35] The tributary system of Southeast Asia was thus solidified. In other words, the tributary system of the Ming dynasty was not built on a peaceful and voluntary basis, but rather was based on military dominance and even warfare in some cases.

Second, a suzerain-dependency relationship with a certain amount of binding force had emerged between China and various other polities. The suzerain status of the Ming as a "Superior Nation with a Heavenly Dynasty" was not merely an expression of self-importance, but was a status unequivocally recognised by overseas countries. Although this sort of relationship between China and Southeast Asian nations was not a typical suzerain-dependency relationship in the strict sense of the term, such relations had already taken on the basic characteristics of a suzerain-dependency relationship. That is to say major countries in Southeast Asia, including Annam, Champa, Siam, Cambodia, Laos, Srivijaya, Sumatra, Java, Brunei, Sulu and Malacca, recognised China as the suzerain, and kings of these nations would accept the conferral of titles, seals and robes from the Ming court and offer regular tribute of treasures as well as fulfil other obligations.[36] During the seventeenth year of the reign of Hongwu, for example, the Ming court sent "Yang Pan, an instructor in the Directorate of Education, as well as other officials, to Annam to request grain to supplement military supplies in Yunnan". In response to the imperial edict, Cheng Wei, king of Annam, immediately provided 5,000 *dan* of grain.[37] The Ming court also extended this rule further abroad. During the reign of Emperor Yongle, Naluota, the ruler of Burma, remarked that despite their remote location, the Burmese were much pleased to hear the news of the visit of the emperor's envoy and were willing to acknowledge allegiance to the emperor. They also begged for the conferral of official robes and a seal so that they could benefit from the emperor's heavenly prestige and could offer tribute every year.[38]

Emperor Yongle therefore established the Burma Pacification Commission (缅甸宣慰使司).[39] Places beyond the Ming state where the Ming established pacification commissions included Palembang, Laos, Mubang and Luchuan/Pingmian. The establishment of these pacification commissions further solidified the status of the Ming court as a suzerain. Manarejiana, the ruler of Brunei, who himself brought tribute to the Ming court, supposedly stated that he travelled a long distance with his wife and children to China and encountered no threat during his voyage on the high seas because all people under heaven have submitted themselves to the rule of the Chinese emperor. Such remarks were a true indication of the reality of the relationship between Southeast Asian nations and the Ming state.

Third, the Ming court served as the highest arbitrator in the international affairs of Southeast Asia. As the Ming court was the de facto suzerain in Southeast Asia and was responsible for "maintaining peace among all nations"[40] and providing mediation in disputes between dependencies, the court was actively involved in the international affairs of Southeast Asia to maintain stability in this region and keep the tributary system in motion. During the reign of Hongwu, the Ming court sent envoys seven times to Southeast Asia to mediate territorial disputes and other disputes between countries. During the first year of the reign of Emperor Yongle (1403), Champa sent an envoy to complain of attacks by Annam. In response, Emperor Yongle admonished the king of Annam noting that:

> your two countries inherited your land from your ancestors and are both subjects of the emperor. How can you engage in transgression of your neighbouring country simply because you're stronger? Evil acts will bring disasters and this has been a lesson since ancient times. Since your transgression happened before my admonishment, I will talk no more about it. From now on, you are required to defend your own country, provide rest and relaxation to your people, discontinue your aggression and restore the friendly relations between your two nations.[41]

This admonishment compelled the Annam ruler to apologise for his aggression. During the third year of the Yongle reign (1405), Java bullied the weaker Brunei into offering to Java annual tribute and Brunei complained to the Ming court. Emperor Yongle ordered Java to stop extracting tribute from Brunei.[42] During the seventeenth year of the Yongle reign (1419), in response to Siam's aggression against Malacca, the emperor again sent an envoy who brought the following message to the king of Siam:

> For a long time, I have been much pleased by the king's gestures of respect toward China, the service you provide as a smaller nation to China as a stronger country, and the fulfilment of your obligation to pay tribute. When the Malaccan king Iskandar Shah ascended the throne, he was able to realise his father's unfulfilled wishes by travelling with his wife to China to present tribute to the Ming court. His sincere respect for a big nation is the same as yours.... Moreover, Malacca has become a dependency of China, and is therefore a subject of the Ming court. If you had had any grudge against the ruler, you should have complained to the Ming court and should not have launched a war against him. Your aggression is disrespectful to the Ming court.[43]

Upon receiving this message, Siam withdrew its troops and the independence of Malacca was restored. Although the Ming court might not have been successful in all its attempts to mediate, its policy of active intervention did ensure its role as the highest arbitrator in Southeast Asian affairs.

In short, following Zheng He's wondrous voyages, through its display of military might and intervention in the international affairs of Southeast Asia, the Ming court, for the first time in Chinese history, successfully established an international order in Southeast Asia which was centred on China. "Beginning around the 15th century, in terms of its foreign policies, China had established an informal ruling relationship with the tributary system as the core; internally, the trade relationship called tributary trade had also emerged".[44]

After Emperor Yongle, the Ming rulers turned away from the sea and adopted conservative policies. Although the tributary system was on the wane and "the barbarians complained of tough navigational conditions in the south and east seas and tribute-paying envoys became less frequent",[45] the Ming court was generally able to maintain the basic pattern of the tributary system.

The Portuguese occupation of Malacca

From the mid-fifteenth century, European society underwent tremendous transformation and capitalist productive relations began to emerge, resulting in a strong desire by Western European countries to explore new sea routes to the East. The Portuguese were the first to journey by sea to the East. As early as 1488, a Portuguese linguist, soldier, spy and diplomat named Pêro da Covilhã, on the orders of the Portuguese king, boarded an Arabian vessel and, arriving in India, visited Calicut.[46] A decade later, Vasco da Gama commanded a fleet which arrived at the Malabar Coast in India where he heard something about the Chinese. He learnt from Indians that the Chinese people, who had long braids and no beard except for a little moustache, came there every two years; their fleet consisted of more than 20 vessels, all of which were large four-masted ships. As to whom they really were and from where they came, the Indians had no idea.[47]

In 1509, Diogo Lopes de Sequeira led a fleet of six warships which arrived at Malacca on 11 September. Anchored at Malacca, there were only three ships belonging to the Chinese.

> The Chinese reside in the easternmost country we have ever known, which was referred to by ancient geographers as "the land of Synas". They live in a northernmost place; they wear clothes made of fabric and use other stuff, just as we do. When they saw the equipment of our ships, although they had been warned by the Muslims that we were suspicious people, they immediately got a totally different impression of us. A proof of the impression is that their ships securely and unsuspectingly started ferrying around us and stayed very close to us.[48]
>
> They sailed towards the ship of the commander [Sequeira], who warmly received them, and played music and fired gun salutes ... they talked about many things and inquired each other about their kings and things in their kingdoms.... They talked for quite a while. The Chinese captain invited the commander and his captains to a dinner on their ship some other day; the commander gladly accepted their invitation.[49]

This was the first intrusion of the Portuguese into China's tributary system and also the first direct contact of the Portuguese with the Chinese. In July 1511, Afonso de Albuquerque, the Portuguese viceroy in India, led a massive fleet to Malacca. He saw Chinese vessels on the sea and talked with them. He enjoyed talking with them. Since rumours had it that the Chinese emperor was very powerful, his territory was vast, his government was massive, and the nation was full of wealth, Albuquerque was able to judge the authenticity of such rumours from the words, attitudes and behaviour of the Chinese merchants.[50]

When Albuquerque ordered the burning of vessels of the Gujaratis, he spared other foreign ships anchored at the port of Malacca, including five Chinese vessels. For this reason, Chinese merchants "offered their sailors and ships to help him in the fight". Albuquerque declined this offer, but used their sampans to transport his men onto the shore.[51] In August, the Portuguese attacked and occupied Malacca. The Malaccan Sultan Mahmud Shah fled to Johor and Bintan Island to continue his resistance against the Portuguese.

The Portuguese occupation of Malacca "not only allowed Albuquerque to solidify his status as the master of the Indian Ocean, but also opened the door to his expansion in the Pacific".[52] The Portuguese continued to sail northwards. In 1513, Jorge Álvares arrived at Tunmen Island in the estuary of the Pearl River of Guangdong on board a Chinese ship. He erected stone columns engraved with armorial bearings on that island. Jorge Álvares was the first Portuguese person to arrive in China. Thereafter, more Portuguese arrived in the coastal areas of Guangdong, directly knocking on the door to ancient China. Some of the Portuguese even reached the Fujian and Zhejiang coasts where they engaged in trading and raiding activities.

China's response to the Portuguese occupation of Malacca

The Portuguese occupation of Malacca constituted a major event in the international relations of Southeast Asia, and also marked a turning point in the relationship between China and Southeast Asia. Ever since the reign of Emperor Yongle, Malacca had been a key link in the tributary system built by the Ming dynasty, which was due to not only its status as the most important protectorate of the Ming state, but also its strategic geographical location that straddled the navigation route between the East and West. Malacca therefore occupied a central position in the Southeast Asian tributary system.

The Portuguese fully recognised the importance of Malacca. Afonso de Albuquerque decided to take Malacca, believing that "it is a major seaport of the entire world, attracting the Moors (Muslims) to search for spice here, especially the Moors from Cairo and Mecca; it is also a gateway to the strait for all people moving eastwards",[53] and that "its importance lies not only in its status as a commercial centre in the Orient, but also in its role as a link between China and the countries in South Asia and Southeast Asia".[54] Tomé Pires, a Portuguese envoy, also held that:

> Without doubt, Malacca is so important and so lucrative that in my mind it is unmatched all over the world ... whoever is Lord of Malacca has his hand on the throat of Venice. As far as from Malacca, and from Malacca to China, and from China to Moluccas, and from Moluccas to Java, and from Java to Malacca and Sumatra, goods will all be controlled by us.[55]

Whoever controlled Malacca could thus dominate the international affairs of Southeast Asia. Therefore, the fall of Malacca signified that the original tributary system was disrupted and the international order in Southeast Asia with China as the core was dealt a heavy blow.

Faced with such an abrupt change, how did China respond? Ming rulers, ranging from the emperor to local civil and military governors, were mostly corrupt, ignorant, stagnant, and out of the "surging tides that sweep across the world", and had no idea of what was going on outside China, nor did they make any efforts to understand the outside world. It is not surprising that for an extended period of time, Ming rulers had no knowledge of the Portuguese occupation of Malacca. Six years after the fall of Malacca, the Portuguese government sent Fernão Peres de Andrade to escort Tomé Pires on a diplomatic mission to China to establish trade links. Tomé Pires and his entourage arrived in Canton in 1517; local Guangdong officials had never heard about Portugal until the Portuguese arrived, and were still ignorant of the Portuguese occupation of Malacca, continuing to act in a proud manner and accepting the offered "tribute" as usual.

Therefore, Tomé Pires and his entourage were received with great courtesy by Governor Chen Jin and local generals, who "failed to locate the nation of Portugal in the Encyclopaedia of the Great Ming Dynasty and decided that they should stay in the post house and not continue their journey until instructions were received from the imperial court".[56] However, Tomé Pires managed to obtain permission to go on to Beijing by bribing Jiang Bin, an official at court who was good at ingratiating himself with Emperor Wuzong. According to the Portuguese, on their way north, Tomé Pires and his entourage received an audience with Emperor Wuzong in Nanjing during his inspection tour of the city. Members of the Portuguese diplomatic mission recalled that:

> The Emperor bestowed favours upon us. He was pleased to see us, and played chess with Tomé Pires, sometimes in our presence. He also ordered us to attend all key banquets; thus, we have seen him three times so far. He even boarded our vessel and ordered all cases be taken out and instructed us to put on clothes that he thought looked best. Moreover, he bestowed gifts upon Tomé Pires and told us to continue our journey to Beijing before sending us away. He gave orders to provide us with China's best boats and goods, and as mentioned before, sent us off with grace.[57]

Upon the arrival of the Portuguese mission in Beijing, Jiang Bin recommended Khoja Hassan 火者亚三 to Emperor Wuzong, who, as a fun-loving person, was amused by the way Khoja Hassan talked and "delighted in imitating his language occasionally"[58] and even "romped with him", regarding diplomacy as a trifling matter.

It was not until the fifteenth year of the Zhengde reign (1520) when the ruler of Malacca sent an envoy to request assistance that the Ming court became aware of the occupation of the port. As recorded in the *Veritable Records of the Ming Dynasty*:

The overseas Portugal had heretofore failed to establish diplomatic relations with China, and in recent years had devoured Malacca, expelled its king, and sent an envoy to bring tribute to Beijing and request the conferral of titles ... Malacca had also sent in a petition for assistance, but the court had not taken any action. At this time, the Investigating Commissioner Qiu Daolong remarked, "Malacca is a tributary state under the Ming Dynasty, but Portugal annexed it and attempted to secure the status of a tributary state from us by presenting tribute. Portugal's occupation of Malacca is morally wrong and its tribute should be rejected and our stance on this issue must be made crystal-clear to them. Portugal should not be allowed to present tribute until the territory of Malacca is returned. If Portugal refuses to mend its ways, although this barbarian is militarily powerful, we should call on all other barbarian states to respond to this aggression".

The imperial Censor He Ao advised that "the Portuguese are known for aggressiveness and guile" and that "all barbarian vessels and barbarian residents in Macau should be expelled; private association with the Portuguese must be banned and defences must be strengthened". The Ministry of Rites suggested that:

> It would be better to wait until the Malaccan envoy arrives and then ask the translator to interrogate the Portuguese envoy over the reason for its aggression against another country and disturbance of the land, and seek the advice of the Emperor to deal with the issue. Guangdong local patrolling and defence officials failed to provide effective defence and therefore the garrison patrol officer should be ordered to arrest and interrogate these officials; from now on, measures should be toughened to impose a strict ban. Barbarians staying in courier stations should be prohibited from making personal contacts or engaging in trade; barbarians coming to China during a non-tribute year should be driven away and no taxes should be levied. Wu Tingju set the precedent and should be removed from office and investigated by the Ministry of Revenue and Population. All officials should be ordered to implement these measures.[59]

During the fifteenth year of the Zhengde reign (1520), Malacca sent in its first petition for assistance, seeking "the Emperor to instruct all kings to send troops to help the Malaccan ruler to regain his nation".[60] The Ming court at first turned a deaf ear to the request and did not take any action. It was not until Qiu Daolong and He Ao presented memorials to the throne that the emperor decided to expel the Portuguese and to punish some local officials in Guangdong. The imperial edict, however, was a mere scrap of paper. Emperor Wuzong continued to be fooled by Khoja Hassan 火者亞三 and romped with him and provided the Portuguese with protection. Before Emperor Wuzong died in the sixteenth year of the Zhengde reign, an imperial decree was issued requiring that "the Portuguese bringing tribute should be rewarded before their return".[61]

The Portuguese occupation of Malacca   143

The Portuguese writer Afonso de Albuquerque (Albuquerque's son) also wrote about Malacca's sending of an envoy to China. He wrote to the effect that following the fall of Malacca:

> The king fled to Pahang, and realizing that his disaster was irreversible, he decided to send an envoy to meet with China's emperor and seek his assistance in restoring his lost city. In order to secure support, he reminded the Chinese emperor that the king of Malacca had maintained a long-standing friendship with the king of China and was subordinate to the king of China as a vassal. To accentuate the sincerity of the sending of the envoy, the king of Malacca sent his most-trusted uncle Tuao Nacem Mudaliar (recorded in the *Ming Veritable Records* as Wei Xiying) as the envoy to China ... Tuao Nacem Mudaliar and his wife, accompanied by some Moors and his retainers, boarded a ship and travelled to Canton. The Cantonese authorities immediately reported their arrival to the King. As the journey had been delayed for over two months, the King sent an imperial decree to the governor to allow the envoy and his entourage to proceed to Beijing and provide them with everything they needed for their journey to the capital. Upon the receipt of this favourable reply, the envoy set off to the court immediately.... When he arrived at the court, he was warmly received by the officials; and a couple of days later, he had an audience with the King. As a gesture of respect, the envoy lay prostrate before the King as the Chinese did and requested him to help his king.... The Malaccan envoy told the Chinese emperor that after he was toppled, the king of Malacca fled to the Pahang Kingdom and waited there in the hope that the Chinese emperor would grant his request for help and send troops and fleets to restore his territory and to revenge the insult which the captain of the Portuguese king had inflicted on him. Although he had learnt about the incident from Chinese people who had returned from Malacca, the Chinese emperor seemed very glad to listen to the account of the envoy and inquired particularly about Albuquerque and the Portuguese: who were they, what their combat tactics were ... However, the emperor actually was unwilling to promise to help the King of Malacca, because his intention and wish were to maintain friendly relationship with the king of the Portuguese and Albuquerque and he wanted to send somebody to visit him, because he knew a lot about Albuquerque and understood that he had treated Chinese people well at the port of Malacca, and hoped to open trade with him there. Another incident that heavily influenced the Chinese emperor's determination to adopt such a policy was the complaints of Chinese people that the king of Malacca had imposed a high duty on their goods.... The envoy stayed at the court for a very long time but failed to fulfil his mission. During his stay, his wife died. A few days later, the emperor gave him a reply through his officials, declining his request for help and explaining that the main reason was that he was fighting the Tartars (Mongols).[62]

The Malaccan envoy failed to achieve what he wished and also died later in China. Although there exist some differences between the Chinese and Portuguese accounts, there is one aspect in common, that is, that Emperor Wuzong, the ruler of the Ming dynasty, was reluctant to help the Malaccan ruler to recover his nation and instead aimed to maintain friendly relations with the Portuguese.

In the third month of the sixteenth year of the Zhengde reign (1521), Emperor Wuzong died and was succeeded in the fourth month by Emperor Shizong, who executed Jiang Bin and Khoja Hassan, signalling a change in the attitude of the Ming court towards the Portuguese. In the sixth month of the same year, the Malaccan ruler sent another envoy to the Ming court in the hope of obtaining its support. The Ming court warmly received the Malaccan envoy and "generously rewarded the envoy and sent some gifts to the king's concubine in return, according to relevant regulations".[63] According to Portuguese records, the Malaccan envoy, called Tuao Mafame [Tuan Mohammad], brought a letter to the Chinese emperor which read:

> The Portuguese, bold bandits, led many troops to Malacca, occupied the place and caused much damage; they killed many people and looted the city; some people were held captive while the rest were put under the rule of the Portuguese. The King of Malacca was therefore saddened and worried. He fled with great fear to Bentao with the seal awarded by the king of China and has stayed there ever since. Meanwhile, his supporters and relatives fled to other places. The Portuguese envoy in the Chinese land is fake and not real; he has come to China's land in disguise. To obtain the favour of the Chinese emperor, the king of Malacca presents tribute in grief, requesting help and troops so that he can return to his land.[64]

The pleading of the Malaccan envoy prompted the Ming court to put assistance to Malacca on its agenda.

> At that time, Guangdong reported again that ocean vessels claiming to be from Portugal were bringing in clothing and grain to the envoy, and suggested levying taxes on the goods according to relevant regulations. The matter was referred to the Ministry of Rites, which replied: "Portugal is not a tributary state and has the audacity to intrude into our neighbouring country. In gross violation of laws and precedents, Portugal is attempting to bring in goods to openly trade here under the disguise of providing supplies; the Portuguese mind is incomprehensible; the Portuguese have stayed here for many days and appear to be on watch for something. It's advisable that the garrison patrol officer be ordered to expel them and bar them from entering Chinese territory.... As to the matter of Malacca's request for help, the Ministry of War should be consulted." Shortly afterwards, the Ministry of War advised that Portugal should be condemned and ordered to return the land of Malacca. The emperor should also call on all other barbarian states to rescue Malacca to show sympathy for its suffering. Some sea patrol and

defence officers failed to report the barbarian incident and should be arrested and questioned. All these suggestions were accepted by the emperor.[65]

It was thus that the Portuguese diplomatic mission was expelled in May 1521 and left Beijing for Guangdong, where they were imprisoned. In Guangdong, the Chinese authorities and the Portuguese diplomatic mission negotiated over the issue of Malacca. The Ming government condemned the Portuguese occupation of Malacca, a tributary state of China, and demanded its return. The *History of the Ming* recorded that:

> The Portuguese were powerful and dispatched troops to invade Malacca. The king of Malacca went into exile and sent an envoy to request help from China. After he ascended the throne, Emperor Shizong condemned the Portuguese and demanded the return of the occupied land. The emperor called on neighbouring countries such as Siam to rescue Malacca, but no one responded, and Malacca was devoured.[66]

Chinese historical records do not elaborate on the negotiations between China and Portugal, but the Portuguese sources provide some details.

> Viera, a member of Tome Pires's diplomatic mission, wrote in his letter: Upon our arrival in Guangdong, we were brought to the administration commissioner, who put us in a few jail cells.... During this period of time, they ordered Tome Pires and his entourage be brought to the judicial officials; the Malays were also brought in. They said that their king ordered our king to return the occupied lands of Malacca to the Malays. Tome Pires replied that he was not here for this issue, he was not in a position to talk about it, and that he knew no more about it. The Chinese king ordered letters to be sent to the governor of Guangdong, telling him not to receive any Portuguese envoy. The letter from the Portuguese king was burned. His envoy and entourage were questioned on how they took over Malacca and were forbidden to leave. They were ordered to write a letter to the Portuguese king to inform him of this incident and to let his mandarins know about this incident soon, and to return Malacca to the so-called Malaccan king. If the Portuguese king intended to return Malacca and its people to the Malaccan king and the Malacca king recovered the land, then the envoy would be allowed to leave. If the Portuguese refused to return Malacca to its king, some other measures might be considered....[67]

The Chinese mandarins discussed this with one another for a while and then ordered the envoy of the Portuguese king to write a letter, which was given to Tuao Alemancet, the envoy of the Malaccan king, who was to bring it to Malacca and deliver it to the Portuguese king from there, asking him to return the land and the people in his hands, which he had grabbed; the letter was also expected to be sent to Tuao Mafame. Also, the Portuguese envoy was ordered to send a letter to the Chinese king, in the vein of the letter written to the Malaccan king, to inform the Chinese king of the intention of Portugal to return the land and people of Malacca. And, if the Portuguese king wouldn't return the land of Malacca to its king and wouldn't send a letter to express his intention to return the land, then his envoy wouldn't be allowed to leave, and other measures might be considered. In the jail, Guangdong officials ordered a Chinese letter to be translated into the Portuguese language and made into three copies, with one to the king of their nation, one to the governor and one to the Malaccan captain; the letter was also delivered to the judicial officials on 1 October 1522.

The mandarins ordered the Malaccan envoy to take the letters and carry them to Malacca; according to the message he carried, his nation was to be returned. The envoy was reluctant, saying that in Malacca he would be beheaded for the few letters, and that if permitted, he would buy a small ship and ask half of his people about the whereabouts of the king, because he was not aware of where the king was, and if possible, he would bring a letter. He was permitted to leave on a small ship with 15 Malays and a few Chinese, on the last day of May 1523. He arrived at Patani 北大年. Then he sent the news to the Malaccan king and returned to Guangdong on 5 September. Chinese who sailed the ship all stayed at Patani, unwilling to return to China. The letter of the envoy was to the following effect:

> The Malaccan king is in Bentao, surrounded by the Portuguese and living in poverty and despair, praying day and night to be rescued by the king of his master nation China; however, if no rescue can be rendered, vassals should be sent in to help and food supplies should be ordered, and so on.[68]

The records kept by the Portuguese were basically consistent with the *History of the Ming Dynasty*, both accounts stating that the requests of the Ming court were rejected by the Portuguese envoy, who was consequently detained by the Ming until the Portuguese promised to return the occupied Malacca. Following the failure of China's negotiations with Portugal, the Ming government sent an envoy to Siam, requesting it to dispatch troops to rescue Malacca, but such a request failed to achieve any response; and the fate of Malacca seemed sealed.

Why did China, then the primary nation in Asia which had awed overseas nations into fearful subservience with the expeditions of its formidable navy not long before, appear so flaccid and impotent in its dealing with Portugal, a small nation in Western Europe, and why did it fail to adopt any effective measures to reverse the fate of its own protectorate?

First of all, since the mid-Ming Dynasty, the power of the Ming empire had been on the wane, plagued as it was by internal troubles and foreign aggression. Domestic politics was in chaos and the ruling class was corrupt; social contradictions were acute and peasant uprisings were frequent. Meanwhile, in the north, the Oyrats and Tartars emerged and were marauding into the outlying areas of the Ming state. The Ming's miserable defeat in 1449 at Tumu signified the decline of its military power; in the west, in 1514 the Islamic Turfan occupied Hami, a frontier town of strategic importance, posing another serious threat to the Ming Dynasty. On the South and East coasts, Japanese pirates continued to pillage the maritime areas.[69] All of the above suggests that the Ming empire was stuck in the depths of crisis by the early sixteenth century. In terms of its foreign policies and strategies, the Ming rulers were forced to switch from offence and advance to defence and retreat and they turned away from the seas to their interior front lines in the north and northwest.[70] Under these circumstances, the Ming court was preoccupied with domestic troubles and foreign aggression. While the spirit was willing the capacity to act was weak – even if the Ming Empire had been willing to rescue Malacca from subjugation, it could not afford the deployment of troops overseas. Without significant military strength, it was virtually impossible for China to maintain its standing in the international order of Southeast Asia.

Second, there were intrinsic defects and inertia in China's traditional political and cultural structures. China's traditional emphasis on agriculture and the suppression of commerce had a direct bearing on the foreign policies of the Ming ruling class. Overseas expansion would not improve the national economy or the livelihood of the populace and was incompatible with the governance principle that "the only way to govern a country is to regard ample food supplies as the fundamental requirement". Emperor Taizu reiterated that "when the people have ample clothing and food, a country will be prosperous and peaceful. This is the top priority of state governance and the foundation of a nation",[71] and that "for barbarian countries, even if their lands are taken, their people will not be obedient without an adequate supply of food".[72] Although during the Hongwu and Yongle reigns, the Ming administration was avid in its seafaring, the primary purpose of such activities was to display Chinese power, extend its traditional tributary system overseas and build an ideal international order where the emperor was the "common master of all under Heaven", in the ways that Emperor Shihuang of the Qin and Emperor Wudi of the Han had been. The overseas expeditions of the Ming court were not aimed at "subjugation"[73] or obtaining profits from building an overseas colonial system. On the surface, the overseas expeditions of the early Ming state constituted a breaking of the constraints of "tradition". However, the Ming administration was fundamentally a feudal dictatorship built on a natural economy; the guiding principles of its foreign policies were the traditional notions of "differences between China and the barbarians" and were therefore passive in nature, and followed the model of the traditional tributary system in practice. Although the Ming court successfully built an international order in Southeast Asia centred on China, this sort of new order could only be maintained on the basis of national might and was uncompetitive without the support of naval prowess and a colonial system. When confronted with the strong challenge of the Western European colonial forces, the Ming administration was unable to respond.

Furthermore, ever since the Song Dynasty, Neo-Confucianism had been the orthodoxy dominating the intellectual and cultural realms in China. As the official philosophy, Neo-Confucianism carried on Confucian orthodoxy and took the maintenance of the centralised feudal system as the heavenly principle and ultimate guideline. An important part of Confucian thought in the Song Dynasty was the loyalty advocated by Confucius and Mencius and the emphasis on defence against barbarians. Neo-Confucianism was obsessed with the notions of "differences between China and the barbarians" and was tinted with ultra-nationalism, which was characterised by self-centredness and disparagement of barbarians. Neo-Confucianism hindered the formation of an open mind with which the Chinese people could take the initiative in learning about the outside world, understanding the world, and benefiting from other advanced cultures. Instead, it gave rise to a narrow mindedness, conservatism, contentment with the status quo and indiscriminate rejection of anything foreign. In the early years of the Ming Dynasty, as a result of the rule of the Mongols during the previous dynasty, the orthodox position of Neo-Confucianism had been weakened and its restraining effect on the ideas of the people reduced, making it possible for the ruler to adopt aggressive and ambitious foreign policies. However, with the increased stability of the feudal order, the ruling class spared no efforts in advocating Neo-Confucianism. After Emperor Yongle ascended the throne, Neo-Confucianism dominated the intellectual and cultural fields, putting the entire society in the shackles of orthodox morals and ethics and binding people's notions of economic values to the land, which eventually resulted in the formation of an ideology that followed the beaten track, preferred agriculture over commerce, and favoured the land over the sea. Even the international order which had China as the core, and which was established during the initial stage of the Ming Dynasty, failed to alter the world outlook of the egoistic feudal ruling class. Instead, it served to prolong the inveterate concept of a "Heavenly court" and egoism, making the Ming court unable and unwilling to understand the world situation and to keep abreast of the times.

The manifestation of such a mentality in the enactment and implementation of foreign policies was that, following the Yongle reign, the Ming rulers switched to foreign policies of passive defence. Emperor Xuanzong claims that "Barbarians are different from us, and are therefore disobedient and rebellious; it is vital to guard against them ... to prevent them from becoming a source of trouble for China", and that "to rein in barbarians, defence is of foremost importance".[74] Thus, the obsession with defence against "barbarians" permeated China's foreign policies. Shortly after his enthronement, the Ming emperor Renzong adopted the suggestions of Xia Yuanji, former minister of the Ministry of Revenue and Population, and halted all seafaring activities.[75] During the reign of Emperor Chenghua, "a court favourite tried to remind the emperor of the stories of the earlier reign of Emperor Yongle, and suggested the resumption of Zheng He's voyages and the retrieval of Zheng He's seafaring logs"; however, Liu Daxia, as well as some other court officials, argued that the westward voyages were "bad politics", and had the logs destroyed to "pluck out the evil by its roots". Thus, the idea of resuming the seaward expeditions died away.[76] Following Emperor Yingzong's restoration, the emperor attempted to imitate Emperor Yongle by sending envoys to visit nations in the Western Ocean.

The Portuguese occupation of Malacca 149

However, such attempts ran into fierce opposition from court officials; and consequently, the idea of resuming marine expeditions had to be abandoned.[77] As a result of the prevailing mentality of passive defence, it was no wonder that the ruling clique of the Ming took such a passive stance when Malacca pleaded for help at the time of Portuguese occupation.

Third, the foreign policies of the Ming administration were poorly conceived. For a long time, in order to build and maintain its suzerain status, the Ming had implemented a foreign policy of containing powerful nations and supporting weaker countries. For example, the Ming supported Champa in its resistance to Annam; propped up and protected Malacca, a vassal state of Siam, in its attempts to seek independence; stopped Java from invading Brunei; and dispatched envoys to mediate in the warfare between the Möng Mao Tai polity and Burma. Although the Ming played an effective role in inhibiting the territorial ambitions of some Southeast Asian nations and maintaining the tributary system, such foreign policies failed to ease the tension among Southeast Asian nations. Siam remained hostile to the independent Malacca, while Annam didn't genuinely accept the Ming Dynasty's "edict for reconciliation" with Champa. Following the reign of Emperor Yongle, the national strength of the Ming Dynasty declined steadily. The Ming withdrew its forces from Annam at the end of the second year of the Xuande reign (1427), marking the beginning of its retreat from Southeast Asia. From then on, the Ming administration was no longer able to provide effective protection to its elaborate tributary system. Even under such circumstances, the Ming once again mistakenly used its suzerain status to instruct Siam, a long-standing rival of Malacca, to send troops to assist Malacca; this was tantamount to "asking a tiger for its skin", because the king of Siam felt that "Albuquerque was doing him a favour by punishing the place like this".[78] And, inevitably, the consequence was that "no one responded and Malacca was devoured".[79]

On the other hand, the Portuguese boasted a formidable military might and attached great importance to diplomatic activities, and strove for colonial expansion through an apt combination of military might and diplomatic initiatives. Before the general offensive against Malacca, Albuquerque sent the Malay-fluent Duarte Fernandez to visit Siam by boarding the ship of some Chinese merchants. Fernandez brought a letter from Albuquerque to Siam, in which Albuquerque informed the king of Siam of what would happen in Malacca and claimed that he would drive Muslims out and welcome Siamese people to go to Malacca, and that the Portuguese king had learned that the Siam king practised Hinduism rather than Islam and was willing to maintain a peaceful and friendly relationship with him. Albuquerque also promised to ensure the safety of the Siamese people and merchant vessels which came to Malacca for trade. Additionally, Albuquerque sent the Siamese king a generous quantity of gold and jewellery as gifts.[80] Upon his arrival at the palace in Siam, Fernandez followed the rituals of Hinduism in saluting the king, and displayed outstanding diplomatic skills in his conversation with him, and was therefore warmly received. The Siamese king later sent an envoy to travel with Fernandez to Malacca with a letter for the Portuguese king as well as gifts in return, including

150 *Liao Dake*

a bell studded with rubies, a gold crown and a double-edged sword. In his letter, the king expressed his desire to establish friendly relations with the Portuguese because the Portuguese were opposed to Muslims and hoped that the Portuguese would help him to seek revenge on the Malaccan king.[81] As a result of the instigation and wooing, there existed "an apparently friendly atmosphere between Siam and Portugal".[82] Consequently, Siam did not interfere in the Portuguese occupation of Malacca.

The implications of the Portuguese occupation of Malacca for the relationship between China and Southeast Asia

The Portuguese occupation of Malacca had profound implications for the history of Southeast Asia and the relationship between Southeast Asia and China. First of all, it disrupted the tributary system of the Ming Dynasty and undermined the international order of Southeast Asia which had China as its core. The Portuguese occupation of Malacca not only damaged China's prestige and status among Southeast Asian nations, but also helped the Portuguese to control the key strategic marine strait in Southeast Asia and blocked the route of the tributary states to China, resulting in a rapid deterioration in the tributary relations between China and Southeast Asia. A Chinese history noted that:

> After the fall of Malacca to Portugal, Malacca was totally different in its behaviour and merchant vessels had become rare with most of them sailing directly to Sumatra; however, Malacca is located right on the route and cannot be avoided; therefore, many vessels have been intercepted by the Portuguese and the sea route has virtually been broken.[83]

Further, the Portuguese colonists used Malacca as a base for aggression against China; the Ming thus came under direct threat from the Portuguese and its tributary system was further undermined. During the twelfth year of the Zhengde reign (1517), the Portuguese, under the pretext of "paying tribute", pillaged coastal areas of Guangdong Province and occupied some islands off the coast.[84] In order to fend off the invaders, the Ming government beefed up its coastal defences and ordered the closure of ports in Guangdong Province; therefore, "tribute-paying states came rarely".[85] Although the Ming attempted to restore the tributary system after a few years, its prestige had "dropped remarkably"[86] and Southeast Asian nations halted their tribute to the Ming court. Only three countries maintained their tributary relationship with the Ming court, that is, Annam, Champa and Siam; however, even these countries paid tribute less frequently. The *Veritable Records of the Ming* indicated that during the 45-year reign of Emperor Jiajing, of the Southeast Asian countries, Siam paid tribute only twice. Thus, the tributary relationship between the Ming court and Southeast Asian nations had basically come to its end.

Second, the Portuguese occupation of Malacca resulted in a closed-door policy by the Ming government. The fall of Malacca led to an increased sense of

The Portuguese occupation of Malacca   151

insecurity and alertness against "external barbarians",[87] and marked a U-turn in the foreign policy of the Ming court towards conservatism; while the "maritime ban" which had been relaxed in the initial years of the Zhengde reign was re-tightened. The Ming court ordered that:

> From now on, overseas countries bringing scheduled tribute to the court must also pay taxes according to relevant regulations; if they do not show their verification tally slips when they are here and fail to bring their tribute goods on time, they should be rejected.[88]

Thus, the Ming court adopted the extreme measure of total rejection in its overseas contacts, which eventually led to the closed-door policy of completely banning "barbarian vessels" in the reign of Emperor Jiajing.[89] Tributary trade between China and Southeast Asian nations virtually halted and the civilian maritime trade received a severe setback, resulting in a rapid diminishing of China's previous superiority in the handicraft industry, commerce and shipbuilding industry. From then on, China's status as an advanced power of the world steadily declined, eventually plunging China into an awkward situation of backwardness and defeat.

Third, the Portuguese occupation of Malacca fundamentally altered the pattern of international relations in Southeast Asia and it helped to establish Portugal's status as a maritime power in Southeast Asia. The fall of Malacca to Portugal posed a threat to the security of Southeast Asian nations and put the international navigation and trade in Southeast Asia in the hands of the Portuguese, compelling China's existing tributary states to halt their submission of tribute to the Ming court and to instead recognise the supremacy of Portugal. Within the first few years, Pahang, Kampar and Indragiri became tributary states of Portugal, while Minangkabau, Aru, Pase and Pegu became its friendly vassal states. In addition, Maluku, Grisek in Java, Tuban, Sidayu, Sunda and Brunei all pledged allegiance to the Portuguese".[90] This shook the Ming tributary system to its roots.

The Portuguese used Malacca as a stepping stone to occupy Ternate in the Moluccas and Macao in China and monopolised the maritime trade in East Asia and between Asia and Europe for over a century. Dutch and Spanish colonists followed hot on the heels of the Portuguese. The arrival of the Western colonists thus fundamentally changed the existing international situation in Southeast Asia, and the Southeast Asian countries, in their divided and backward state, were unable to organise an effective resistance against the invasion of Western colonists. Meanwhile, with the retreat of the Ming forces, there was no power to help Southeast Asia to fend off the aggression of the West; as a matter of fact, the international order which had China as its core had crumbled. After that, Chinese forces in Southeast Asia were mainly civilian maritime fleets, which put up long-term resistance against the penetration of Western colonial forces. Although China's civilian maritime trading forces at the time still enjoyed a strong superiority in number and in certain areas:

Through the lack of support from the state, the nature of such forces and of maritime trade in the West Pacific, the superiority turned into inferiority, and the formerly dominating independent force deteriorated into a subsidiary force subject to the control of others and began its descent.[91]

From then on, Southeast Asia was reduced from part of China's sphere of influence to that of the Western colonists.

Notes

1 J. K. Fairbank, *Trade and Diplomacy on the China Coast*, vol. 1 (Cambridge University Press, 1953), p. 30.
2 Fan Ye 范曄, *Hou Han shu* 後漢書 [*History of the Later Han*] (Beijing: Zhonghua shuju, 1973), p. 2810.
3 Sima Guang 司馬光, *Zizhi tongjian* 資治通鑒 [*Comprehensive Mirror of History for Aid in Government*] (Beijing: Zhonghua shuju, 1956), p. 696.
4 *Han shu* 漢書 [*History of the Han Dynasty*], juan 28, *Annals of Geography* (Zhonghua shuju, 1975), p. 1671.
5 *History of the Han Dynasty*, juan 99, *Biography of Wang Mang*, p. 4047.
6 *History of the Later Han Dynasty*, juan 86, *Biographies of Southern and Southeastern Barbarians*, pp. 2837, 2851.
7 John King Fairbank, "The Chinese World Order" (Chinese translation) in Tao Wenzhao (comp.), Lin Hai *et al*. (trans.) *Works of Fei Zhengqing* [John King Fairbank] (Tianjin: Tianjin People's Publishing House, 1992).
8 *History of the Song Dynasty*, juan 485, Foreign Countries I (Beijing: Zhonghua shuju, 1977 edition), p. 13981.
9 *Veritable Records of Ming Emperor Taizu*, juan 37, *12th Month of the 1st Year of the Reign of Emperor Hongwu* (Shanghai Ancient Literature Press, 1983), p. 750.
10 *Veritable Records of Ming Emperor Taizu*, juan 38, *1st Month of 2nd Year of the Reign of Emperor Hongwu*, p. 775.
11 *Veritable Records of Ming Emperor Taizu*, juan 243, *12th Month of 28th Year of the Reign of Emperor Hongwu*, pp. 3534–5.
12 J. K. Fairbank and E. O. Reischauer, *China: Tradition and Transformation* [Chinese translation] (Nanjing: Jiangsu People's Publishing House), 1996, p. 179.
13 *Veritable Records of Ming Emperor Taizu*, juan 26, *10th Month of 28th Year of the Reign of Emperor Hongwu*, pp. 3534–5.
14 *Veritable Records of Ming Emperor Taizu*, juan 37, *12th Month of 1st Year of the Reign of Emperor Hongwu*, pp. 750–1.
15 *History of the Ming Dynasty*, juan 324, *Account of Java* (Zhonghua Book Company, 1974), p. 8402.
16 *Veritable Records of Ming Emperor Taizu*, juan 134, *10th Month of 13th Year of the Reign of Emperor Hongwu*, p. 2125.
17 Wang Qi, *Xu wenxian tongkao*, juan 31, *Complete Library in the Four Branches of Literature*, juan 185 (Qilu Book Agency, 1995), pp. 617–8.
18 Li Dongyang 李東陽, *et al*., *Da Ming huidian* 大明會典 [*Compilation of State Regulations of the Great Ming Dynasty*], juan 108, *Normative Practices of the Tributary System* (Taipei: Shinwenfeng Print Co., 1976), p. 1620.
19 Zheng Shungong 鄭舜功, *Riben Yijian* 日本一鉴, juan 7.
20 Yan Congjian, *Records of Foreign States*, juan 8 (Beijing: Zhonghua Book Company, 1993), p. 302.
21 *Veritable Records of Ming Emperor Taizu*, juan 24, *10th Month of 1st Year of the Reign of Emperor Yongle* (Shanghai Ancient Literature Press, 1983), p. 435.

22 *History of the Ming Dynasty*, juan 332, Account *of Kuncheng* (坤城), p. 8625.
23 Gong Zhen 鞏珍: *Chronicles of States in the Western Ocean* 西洋番國志, Preface (Zhonghua shuju, 1961), p. 12.
24 *Veritable Records of Ming Emperor Taizong*, juan 236, *4th Month of the 19th Year of the Reign of Emperor Yongle*, p. 2265.
25 He Qiaoyuan 何喬遠, *Min shancang* 名山藏, *Anectotal History of the Ming Dynasty* (Nanjing: Jiangsu Guangling Ancient Literature Engraving and Mimeograph Agency, 1993), p. 6041.
26 Hans J. Morgenthau, *Politics among Nations: The Struggle for Power and Peace* [Chinese translation] (Beijing: Commercial Press, 1993), p. 113.
27 Lo Jung-pang, "The Decline of the Early Ming Navy", *Zheng He Studies*, 3rd Issue, 1998, p. 52.
28 *History of the Ming Dynasty*, juan 304, *Biography of Zheng He*, p. 7766.
29 Ma Huan, *Yingyai Shenglan (Wonderful Views of the Ocean's Shores): Calicut State* (Shanghai: Commercial Press, 1935), pp. 42–3.
30 *Stele Recording Contacts with Foreign Countries in the Celestial Imperial Concubine Palace in Liujiagang, Loudong*, 天妃宮石刻通番事蹟記. See Zheng Hesheng, Zheng Yijun (eds.) *Collection Records on Zheng He's Voyages to the Western Ocean*, Volume 1 (Qilu shushe, 1980), p. 40.
31 *History of the Ming Dynasty*, juan 324, *Account of Java*, p. 8403.
32 Ma Huan, *Yingyai Shenglan: Manlajia guo* (Triumphant Visions of the Ocean Shores: Account of the Country of Malacca), p. 22.
33 Mao Ruizheng 茅瑞徵, *Huangming xiangxulu* 皇明象胥錄, juan 5 (Peiping: National Peiping Library, 1937), p. 1.
34 Ma Huan, *Yingyai Shenglan: Account of the Country of Malacca*, p. 25.
35 *History of the Ming Dynasty*, juan 326, *Account of Ceylon*, p. 8844.
36 When the Portuguese arrived in Southeast Asia, they believed that Southeast Asian countries were dependent states of China. Pires classified China's dependent states into two groups: those which paid tribute to the Chinese king, such as Champa, Annam, Ryukyu and Japan; and those which presented gifts but were not obliged to pay tribute to the Chinese king, such as Java, Siam, Pasai and Malacca. Kings of these countries dispatched envoys every five or ten years to China with China-granted seals and credentials and presented their countries' best goods to the Chinese king (cf. Armando Cortesão, *The Suma Oriental of Tomé Pires*, vol. 1 (London: Hakluyt Society, 1944), p. 18.
37 *Veritable Records of Ming Emperor Taizong*, juan 163, *7th Month of 17th Year of Emperor Yongle*, p. 2527.
38 *Veritable Records of Ming Emperor Taizong*, juan 24, *10th Month of 1st Year of Emperor Yongle*, p. 439.
39 The pacification commissions constituted a mechanism employed by the Ming court to rule areas where it could not institute formal administration. The Court did not interfere with their internal affairs; however, incoming pacification commissioners had to report to the Court, be appointed by the Court and fulfil regular tribute payment obligations.
40 *Veritable Records of Ming Emperor Taizong*, juan 28, *2nd Month of the 2nd Year of Emperor Yongle*, p. 510.
41 *Veritable Records of Ming Emperor Taizong*, juan 22, *8th Month of the 1st Year of Emperor Yongle*, p. 408.
42 *History of the Ming Dynasty*, juan 325, *Account of Brunei*, pp. 8412–3.
43 *Veritable Records of Ming Emperor Taizong*, juan 217, *10th Month of the 17th Year of Emperor Yongle*, pp. 2161–2.
44 Hamashita Takeshi, *Early Modern China's International Turning Points – The Tribute Trade System and Early Modern Asia* (Beijing: Chinese Social Sciences Press of Social Sciences, 1999), p. 60.

45 He Qiaoyuan, *Mingshan cang*, p. 6041.
46 K. M. Panikkar, *Asia and Western Dominance: A Survey of the Vasco da Gama Epoch of Asian History*, p. 24.
47 E. G. Ravenstein, *A Journal of the First Voyage of Vasco da Gama, 1497–1499* (London: Hakluyt Society, 1898), p. 131.
48 C. R. Boxer, "Notes on Chinese Abroad in the Late Ming and Early Manchu Periods. Compiled from Contemporary European Sources, 1500–1750", *T'ien Hsia Monthly*, IX (5) (December 1939): 449.
49 Anonymous, "Chronicles of the Portuguese Discovery and Conquest of India", *Culture Journal, Macau*, Issue 31 (1997): 27.
50 C. R. Boxer, "Notes on Chinese Abroad in the Late Ming and Early Manchu Periods", p. 218–268.
51 d'Albuquerque, *The Commentaries of Great Alfonso Dalboquerque, Second Viceroy of India* (London: Hakluyt Society, 1875–84), vol. III, pp. 97–8.
52 Panikkar, *Asia and Western Dominance*, p. 50.
53 D'Albuquerque, *The Commentaries of Great Afonso D'Alboquerque, Second Viceroy of India*, p. 100.
54 K. M. Panikkar, *Asia and Western Dominance: A Survey of the Vasco da Gama Epoch of Asian History*, p. 49.
55 Armando Cortesão, *The Suma Oriental of Tome Pires*, vol. II (London: Hakluyt Society, 1944), pp. 285, 287.
56 Gu Yingxiang 顧應祥, *Jingxuzhai xiyinlu* 靜虛齋惜陰錄 juan 12, *Complete Library of the Four Branches of Literature*, juan 84, pp. 207–8.
57 Zhang Haipeng, *et al.*, *Collection of Materials on the History of Sino-Portuguese Relations* (Chengdu: Sichuan People's Publishing House, 1999), p. 191.
58 He Qiaoyuan 何喬遠, *Mingshan cang* 名山藏, p. 6216.
59 *Veritable Records of Ming Emperor Wuzong*, juan 194, *12th Month of the 15th Year of the reign of Zhengde* (Shanghai Ancient Literature Press, 1983), pp. 3630–1.
60 *Veritable Records of Ming Emperor Shizong*, juan 4, *7th Month of the 16th Year of the Reign of Zhengde* (Shanghai Ancient Literature Press, 1983), p. 208.
61 *Veritable Records of Ming Emperor Wuzong*, juan 197, *3rd Month of the 16th Year of the Reign of Zhengde*, p. 3682.
62 D'Albuquerque, *The Commentaries of Great Afonso Dalboquerque, Second Viceroy of India*, pp. 131–4.
63 *Veritable Records of Ming Emperor Shizong*, juan 3, *6th Month of the 16th Year of the reign of Zhengde*, p. 143.
64 Zhang Haipeng, *et al.*, *Collection of Materials on the History of the Sino-Portuguese Relationship*, pp. 166–7.
65 *Veritable Records of Ming Emperor Shizong*, juan 4, *7th Month of the 16th Year of the Reign of Zhengde*, p. 208.
66 *History of the Ming Dynasty*, juan 325, *Account of Malacca*, p. 8419.
67 Zhang Haipeng, *et al.*, *Collection of Records on the History of the Sino-Portuguese Relationship*, p. 162.
68 Zhang Haipeng, *et al.*, *Collection of Records on the History of the Sino-Portuguese Relationship*, p. 167.
69 Qian Wei 錢薇, "Yu dangdao chuwo yi" (與當道處倭議 On Dealing with the Japanese Pirates), in Chen Zilong 陳子龍 et al. compil. *Ming jingshi wenbian* 明經世文編, juan 214 (Zhonghua shuju, 1962), pp. 2234–8.
70 Cf. Lo Jung-pang, "The Decline of the Early Ming Navy", Translated by Chen Xiyu, *Zheng He Studies*, 3rd Issue (1998): pp. 52–61.
71 *Veritable Records of the Ming Dynasty*, Appendix, *Treasured Instructions of Emperor Taizu* (Shanghai Ancient Literature Press, 1983), p. 31.
72 *Veritable Records of Ming Emperor Taizu*, juan 68, *9th Month of the 4th Year of the Reign of Hongwu*, p. 1277.

73 *Veritable Records of Ming Emperor Taizu*, juan 38, *12th Month of the 1st Year of the Reign of Hongwu*, p. 750.
74 *Veritable Records of Ming Emperor Xuanzong*, juan 38, *2nd Month of the 2nd Year of the Reign of Xuande* (Shanghai Ancient Literature Press, 1983), pp. 591–2.
75 *History of the Ming Dynasty*, juan 149, *Biography of Xia Yuanji*, p. 4153.
76 Yan Congjian, *An Account of Foreign States*, juan 8 (Beijing: Zhonghua Book Company, 1993), p. 307.
77 *History of the Ming Dynasty*, *Biography of Zhan Shao*, pp. 4458–9.
78 Henri Cordier, "L'arrivee des portugais en Chine", *T'oung Pao*, XII (1911): 508.
79 *History of the Ming Dynasty*, juan 325, *Account of Malacca*, p. 8419.
80 D'Albuquerque, *The Commentaries of Great Afonso Dalboquerque, Second Viceroy of India*, pp. 113–14.
81 D' Albuquerque, *The Commentaries of Great Afonso Dalboquerque, Second Viceroy of India*, pp. 154–5.
82 Charles Edward Nowell, *A History of Portugal* (Chinese translation) (Jiangsu People's Publishing House, 1974), p. 133.
83 *History of the Ming Dynasty*, juan 325, *Account of Malacca*, p. 8419.
84 Cf. Dai Yixuan, *Annotation of the History of the Ming Dynasty, Account of Portugal* (China Press of Social Sciences, 1984), pp. 3–9.
85 Gu Yanwu, *Tianxia Junguo Libing Shu*, juan 120, *Overseas Countries*, p. 5 (Edition: 27th year of the reign of Emperor Guangxu).
86 *History of the Ming Dynasty*, juan 325, *Account of Brunei*, p. 8415.
87 Wan Ming, *Zhongguo rongru shijie de bulu: Ming yu Qing qianqi haiwai zhengce bijiao yanjiu* 中國融入世界的步履：明與清前期海外政策比較研究 (China's Integration into the World: A Comparative Studies on the of Overseas Policies in Ming and Early Qing). Beijing: Shehui kexue wenxian chubanshe, 2000, p. 198.
88 *Veritable Records of Ming Shizong*, juan 4, *7th Month of the 16th Year of the Reign of Zhengde*, p. 208.
89 Huang Zuo, *Complete Works by Mr. Huang Taiquan*, juan 20, *Dai Xunfu Tong shibo shu*, woodblock edition, dated 21st year of the Kangxi reign.
90 Armando Cortesão, *The Suma Oriental of Tomé Pires*, vol. II, pp. 282–3.
91 Yang Hanqiu, "Shiwu zhi shiqi shiji zhongye zhongxi hanghai maoyi shili de xingshuai 十五至十七世紀中葉中西航海貿易勢力的興衰" (The Rise and Fall of the Sino-Western Seafaring and Trading Forces from the 15th to the mid-17th Centuries). Beijing: *Lishi yanjiu* 歷史研究 5 (1982): 93–105. Wang Gungwu, "Sojourning: The Chinese Experience in Southeast Asia", in *Sojourners and Settlers: Histories of Southeast Asia and the Chinese*, ed. Anthony Reid (Sydney: Allen and Unwin, 1996), pp. 1–14.

6 The Chinese factor in the shaping of Nguyễn rule in Southern Vietnam during the seventeenth and eighteenth centuries[1]

Danny Wong Tze Ken

The Nguyễn family's rule over southern Vietnam during the seventeenth and eighteenth centuries was an important historical period in the history of Southeast Asia. The Nguyễn began its expansion in 1558 with a provincial military governorship in Thuận Hóa, in the then southern-most reaches of Vietnamese territory. By its end in 1776, Nguyễn rule had extended beyond Thuận Hóa by incorporating the regions of Quảng Nam, Phú Yên, the former Champa kingdom of Panduranga (Bình Thuận and Khánh Hòa), and the Mekong Delta, including Hà Tiên. In the process, the Nguyễn destroyed the remnants of the declining kingdom of Champa, and wrested most of the Mekong Delta from a much-weakened Khmer kingdom.

Many factors have been mentioned as having contributed to the development of Nguyễn rule in southern Vietnam. Among these was the military capability of the Nguyễn which included its superior cannons and elephant forces.[2] The Nguyễn's pragmatism in promoting external trade by inviting foreign traders to the various ports in southern Vietnam also contributed to their prosperity and enabled the Nguyễn to consolidate their rule over southern Vietnam.[3] The weaknesses of their southern neighbours, Champa and Cambodia, facilitated the Nguyễn's territorial expansion to the south.[4]

Another factor that contributed to the shaping of Nguyễn rule in southern Vietnam was the role of the Chinese, an aspect which is the focus of this chapter. This subject is by no means a new one, having been examined and written on by other scholars in the field including Chen Chingho, the pioneer in this subject who contributed works that paved the way for future research.[5] There is also Nguyễn The Anh's overview study on the Chinese factor in the history of the Vietnamese southward movement.[6] In his survey on the contribution of Nguyễn rule to Vietnamese history, Yang Baoyun also devoted a section to the Nguyễn's dealings with China.[7] In her path-breaking work, Li Tana also examined the Chinese factor in the social and economic transformations during Nguyễn rule in southern Vietnam.[8] The most recent study on the Chinese connection with Nguyễn rule is Liam C. Kelley's examination of the Mạc family of Hà Tiên.[9]

Much attention has been given to the role of the Chinese in helping to advance the Nguyễn interests in southern Vietnam through territorial expansion and trade. Others have examined the role of the Mạc family in acquiring Hà Tiên. This chapter, however, will draw attention to another aspect of the Chinese factor in the shaping of Nguyễn rule in southern Vietnam: it will look into the Nguyễn Lords' relations with China. It will first focus on the dimension of government-to-government relations, to be followed by an examination of the religious and cultural linkages.

In 1558 Nguyễn Hoàng, the patriarch of the Nguyễn family, one of the families contending for power in the Lê Court (Lê Dynasty, 1428–1788), was sent to garrison the province of Thuận Hóa. In 1570 he added the adjacent province of Quảng Nam to his seat of rule. After Nguyễn Hoàng's death, his successor, Nguyễn Phúc Nguyên (r. 1613–1635), decided to break with the Lê Court. This decision thrust the Nguyễn family into armed conflict with the Trịnh family which was controlling the Lê Court. The Nguyễn family continued to rule the southern part of Vietnam until it was defeated by the Trịnh army in 1776. By then the Nguyễn family had extended its rule over much of present-day southern Vietnam at the expense of the kingdom of Champa and the Khmer-controlled Mekong. It is in this context that the Nguyễn's connection with China and the Chinese will be considered.

Government-to-government relations

Given the circumstances of Nguyễn rule in southern Vietnam, where it was considered a renegade entity by the Lê Court (Le Dynasty, r. 1428–1788), no official government-to-government relations should have taken place between Nguyễn southern Vietnam and China, at least in the strictest sense. Nonetheless, such relations did exist, and came mainly through two channels. The first was through the Nguyễn Lords' initiatives to cultivate a form of quasi intergovernmental relations with China. The second, from the Chinese response to the Nguyễn Lords' initiatives.

In the first instance, the Nguyễn Lords looked to China as a source of authority and legitimation. This was in view of the development of the Nguyễn from a mere provincial governor to a de facto independent political ruler. The break between the Nguyễn and the Trịnh-controlled Lê Court in 1627 was the turning point for Nguyễn rule in southern Vietnam. That year, Nguyễn Phúc Nguyên (r. 1613–1635), the second Lord, refused to send the tax receipts of the Thuận Hóa and Quảng Nam provinces, which were under his charge, to the Lê government. This prompted punitive action from the Lê Court that was under the influence of the Trịnh family, the main rival of the Nguyễn family.[10] In the civil war that ensued from 1627 to 1672, neither party was able to overcome the other. A deadlock was reached and the two sides remained separated from one another.

For the Nguyễn Lords in the south, the war of 1627–1672 and the following years saw southern Vietnam physically and culturally severed from the centre of Vietnamese culture and authority. Given the enmity of the Trịnh family, any attempts by the Nguyễn Lords to elevate their position in the Lê Court would have been impossible. This separation allowed Nguyễn southern Vietnam to move away from the former constraints of loyalty to the Lê Court to become a quasi-independent entity.

Under such circumstances, successive Nguyễn Lords began efforts aimed at enhancing and consolidating the family's rule over southern Vietnam. The opportunity to break away from the Lê Court came after the status quo of 1672 was reached. With the removal of the military threat from the Trịnh, the Nguyễn Lords were able to concentrate on state-building and territorial expansion.

By the turn of the eighteenth century, the Nguyễn Lords' efforts had resulted in the doubling of the size of its original holdings of Thuận Hóa and Quảng Nam by incorporating new regions under their control. The Nguyễn expansion to the south began with the war against Champa during the second half of the seventeenth century, and the subsequent incorporation of the remnants of this Hindu-Malay kingdom under Nguyễn rule in 1693. The annexation of the Khmer-dominated Mekong Delta during the eighteenth century saw the Nguyễn's influence expanding further to the south.[11] While the Nguyễn's population remained smaller than that of the Trịnh's in the north,[12] the land was rich in natural resources. The economic position of the Nguyễn Lords improved after the move to promote international trade. This placed the Nguyễn Lords more or less in the same league as the Trịnh, and inevitably prompted Nguyễn Hoàng's successors to seek a remedy to this unequal position between the two families.

However, with the Lê Court effectively beyond the reach of the Nguyễn family, China became the natural choice when the question of political legitimation arose. The first attempt to elevate the Nguyễn Lords' status was through the attempt to obtain recognition from China. In 1702, Nguyễn Phúc Chu (r. 1691–1725) sent a delegation to the Qing Court, seeking recognition and admission to the Chinese tributary arrangements. Nguyễn Phúc Chu was said to have been influenced by the Chinese Buddhist monk Da Shan's[13] suggestion that the Nguyễn seek recognition from China as a means of enhancing the status and power of their rule.[14]

The mission was led by two of Da Shan's followers, Hoang Chen, a former student at the Chinese National Academy (Guo Zijian), and Xing Che, a Buddhist monk; both were natives of Guangdong. They went to Guangdong on board a Siamese 'secondary' tribute vessel that had earlier drifted into the Nguyễn port of Hội An.[15] The mission carried an impressive list of goods to be presented as tribute to the Manchu Court. These included two elephant tusks with a combined weight of 350 catties; one catty and 13 taels of gold; flowery rattan (50 pieces); and precious stones (5 catties four taels).[16] Nguyễn Phúc Chu also made a presentation of 50,000 *liang* of silver to the governor of Guangdong and Guangxi (commonly known as the Two Guang), possibly as an inducement to facilitate the tribute mission's admission.[17]

Both the *Đại Nam Thức Lục Tiền Biên* (hereafter *Tiền Biên*) and the *Phủ Biên Tạp Lục* (Miscellaneous Records of the Frontiers) reported that the mission was rejected by the governor of the Two Guang. The reason given was that the

Chinese acknowledged the Nguyễn as subjects of the Lê Dynasty. Any attempt to admit the Nguyễn into the Chinese tributary system would have contravened China–Lê relations. However, later Nguyễn historians who compiled the *Tiền Biên* tried to explain the Chinese decision in terms of their apprehension that if granted recognition, the Guangnan Guo (Nguyễn southern Vietnam, known in Chinese as the kingdom of Quảng Nam) would supersede the authority of the Lê government.[18]

By requesting political recognition from China, Nguyễn Phúc Chu was not only acknowledging the Chinese system of tributary relations; his action was also in some way reinforcing the traditional manner in which the Vietnamese elite perceived China, and how they perceived that relations between China and Vietnam should be conducted. The step confirmed China's unique position as the source of authority in the hearts of the Vietnamese literati and political elite. By gaining recognition from China, the Nguyễn family would have by-passed the Lê Court in elevating its position vis-à-vis the Trịnh.

While compiling the *Phủ Biên Tạp Lục*, Lê Quý Dôn collected materials from the family of Nguyễn Quang Tiền,[19] the man responsible for drafting the Nguyễn letter to the Qing Court in 1702. In the letter to the governor of the Two Guang in 1702, Nguyễn Phúc Chu stated his reasons for seeking admission to tributary relations; among these he mentioned that he was fulfilling the intentions of his forebears to expand the Nguyễn Lords' territories. He also explained that it was only with his growing strength that he was ready to pay homage to the Chinese Court. In addition, he highlighted his tutelage under the Chinese monk Da Shan.[20]

China's refusal in 1702 to grant recognition to the Nguyễn's overlord position in southern Vietnam did not mean the end of official contact between the two. Most of the subsequent meetings took place through the initiatives of the Vietnamese. In 1724, when Yang Ling, the governor of the Two Guang, died, Nguyễn Phúc Chu sent his condolences to the family. He also sent 100 taels of gold to the governor's family.[21] Though the *Tiền Biên* is silent on this event, it is likely that, despite the rejection in 1702, Nguyễn Phúc Chu remained in contact with the governor of the Two Guang, possibly with the hope of cultivating closer relations to facilitate later attempts to seek admission to the tributary arrangements and trade relations. Judging from the personal contact maintained by Nguyễn Phúc Chu with the governor of the Two Guang, it is conceivable that similar relations were also maintained by his successors. Indeed, Lê Quý Dôn, the compiler of the *Phủ Biên Tạp Lục*, even commented that Thuận Hóa maintained regular correspondence with the governor of Guangdong.[22] However, the Nguyễn Lords made no further attempts to seek similar recognition from the Qing Court.

One aspect that requires further investigation is the hidden agenda of Nguyễn Phúc Chu's tribute mission of 1702. Official recognition aside, a more tangible or even pressing aspect of the Nguyễn's needs would have been permission to trade officially with China. Until 1702 the Chinese who went to trade in Nguyễn southern Vietnam were private traders, many of them operating out of China.[23]

As Nguyễn Phúc Chu's mission is not mentioned in any Chinese source, it is difficult to ascertain what actually transpired when the mission arrived at Guangzhou. It is likely that by the time of Nguyễn Phúc Chu's delegation's arrival at Guangdong, the Chinese official expected by Da Shan to facilitate the Nguyễn delegation's admission had been transferred from his post.[24] That same year also saw Da Shan falling from grace. He was arrested under the allegation of being a corrupt monk who had enriched himself through overseas trade. It is possible that Da Shan was being returned to his hometown in chains when the Nguyễn delegation arrived.[25]

It is worthwhile to determine how the Chinese viewed the Nguyễn. In one of the earliest official records of a transaction between the Nguyễn and the Chinese authorities in 1669, the Chinese referred to Nguyễn southern Vietnam as Guangnan Guo (Kingdom of Guangnan or Quảng Nam). On that occasion a trading ship from Guangnan Guo arrived at Guangzhou carrying Liu Sifu, a Chinese military officer with the rank of Dushu (Brigade Vice-Commander) and fourth rank in the official hierarchy, who had drifted out to sea and landed at Quảng Nam. The Nguyễn repatriated him and took the opportunity to trade in Guangdong.[26] The Nguyễn delegation was led by Zhao Wenbin, a Chinese person who had lived abroad for many years. The Nguyễn were commended by the Chinese officials. However, the trading goods were confiscated as China was still enforcing the ban on overseas trade and travel, and any attempt to send goods to China outside the tribute year would not be accepted. In this case the Chinese were likely to be conscious of Nguyễn southern Vietnam's status. However, it was not so on other occasions.

In commenting on the origin of Nguyễn rule in southern Vietnam, the *Qing Shi* shows that it was unaware of the rivalry between the Trịnh and the Nguyễn family, "The Lê Emperor sent the Nguyễn Lord to govern Xun Hoa (Thuận Hóa). He was given the title of the King of Guangnan."[27] When outlining the various territories in Vietnam, the *Qing Shi* mentioned how the two provinces of Guangnan (Quảng Nam) and Xunhua (Thuận Hóa) were originally the Nguyễn's holdings.[28] Such little information, albeit distorted, on Nguyễn southern Vietnam demonstrates two points: that the Qing Court had always regarded the Nguyễn as under the sovereignty of the Lê, as indicated in the reply cited in the Vietnamese accounts; and second, that the Chinese government was simply ignorant of the actual status of Nguyễn rule in southern Vietnam.

When Nguyễn Phúc Khoat (r. 1738–1765) unilaterally declared himself as Vương (king), he did not repeat Nguyễn Phúc Chu's attempt to obtain recognition from China. Nevertheless, government-to-government relations between Nguyễn southern Vietnam and China continued, albeit for rather special circumstances – the repatriation of criminals and those persons shipwrecked.

In 1747 some Chinese from Fujian including a person called Lý Văn Quang (Li Wenguang) were causing trouble at Gia Định in the Mekong Delta.[29] According to the *Tiền Biên*, Li was a trader who had turned to plundering activities. He styled himself as the King of Đong Phố in Gia Định, and led a force of about 300 men to attack the garrison at Tran Bien.[30] Pierre Poivre, who was critical of the Chinese presence in southern Vietnam, considered Li Wenguang's venture as a major threat that could throw the Nguyễn kingdom into political turmoil and instability.[31] Li Wenguang was, however, defeated and was repatriated to China with 57 other Chinese prisoners. Along with the prisoners, Nguyễn Phúc Khoát also despatched gifts, which included: eaglewood (five catties), sharks fin (30 catties), sea cucumber (30 catties), black pepper (30 catties), bamboo (20 sticks) and flowery rattan (20 sticks).[32] Even though the gifts were inexpensive, the gesture was important in cultivating a long-term relationship with the relevant authorities in China.

Chinese sources, however, provide a slightly different version of the Li Wenguang affair. According to the *Qing Shi*:

> In 1754, Li Wenguang who was a native of Guangdong was in league with the local chieftain, Nguyễn, and was creating trouble at Đong Nại and other places. Li was arrested by the local military forces and was kept in prison.[33]

In 1757 Li was sent back to Fujian with 16 others. In his report to the emperor, the governor of Fujian reported that even though Li Wenguang was arrested earlier, the primitive nature of An Nan (southern Vietnam) made it difficult for them to carry out justice. Hence, Li Wenguang was repatriated.[34] The date is different from that provided by the *Tiền Biên* – 1747. The *Qing Shi* cited Guangdong as the place of origin for Li Wenguang, whereas the *Tiền Biên* mentioned Fujian.[35]

In his dealings with China, Nguyễn Phúc Khoát adopted a similar practice to Nguyễn Phúc Chu in the use of the lower rank held by the successive Lords under the Lê system. Nguyễn Phúc Khoát even adopted a much lower rank of Ty Mu – provincial commissioner of Thuận Hóa-Quảng Nam and all places in An Nam.[36]

To the Chinese, however, the Nguyễn gestures meant little. In many instances the Chinese were confused with the actual situation in Vietnam, especially with the two Vietnamese entities of Trịnh and the Nguyễn. Nonetheless, in most cases the Chinese, even though they did not officially recognise the Nguyễn as a separate entity, had a name for Nguyễn's southern Vietnam, Guangnan Guo (Kingdom of Quảng Nam).

The Chinese Court's confusion over the actual status of the Nguyễn rule in southern Vietnam is also reflected in another incident reported in the *Bang Giao Luc*. In 1718 the governor of the Two Guang confiscated two boats from Thuận Hóa, carrying a total of 26 people. During the process of repatriation, the Governor sent the crews to the Lê Court. The letter was also addressed to the Lê Emperor.[37] This transaction suggests that the Chinese probably did not know that the Nguyễn were no longer represented at the Lê Court, and that Thuận Hóa had become a separate polity.

The Nguyễn Lords' relations with China during the reign of the last three Lords were rather similar to those under the preceding lords. Relations at the official level were negligible. From the Nguyễn sources, for instance, any level of contact with China would warrant a mention. Even trivial matters such as the 1754 repatriation of ship crews from Qingzhou in China received a mention in the *Tiền Biên*. That year, the Chinese authorities at Qingzhou sent back a group of explorers from Quảng Ngãi who had been gathering sea produce at the Hòang Sa Archipelago (Paracel Islands), but had drifted into Chinese territory. The explorers were from the village of An Vinh in the Binh Som district.[38] The exploration of the Paracels was their designated labour tribute to the Nguyễn Lordship.

The initiatives of the individual Nguyễn Lords had very little bearing in effecting a change in the Chinese outlook on Nguyễn southern Vietnam. The Chinese official reaction was basically non-engagement. It is obvious that the vague Chinese perception of Nguyễn rule over southern Vietnam remained unaltered in this case as they only recognised the Lê Court at Thăng Long.

On the other hand, despite gaining few tangible results from their transactions with the Qing, the Nguyễn family did not let up in their attempts to win favour with the Chinese government. The Nguyễn Lords continued to look to the Chinese court as the essential alternative, if not the ultimate, source of authority for the legitimation of Nguyễn rule in southern Vietnam.

The Chinese link in religious development

Apart from being a source of political legitimation, China was in a unique position as the source of spiritual and cultural inspiration for Nguyễn rule. This was especially so in the case of the shift towards Buddhism. During the early stage of their rule over southern Vietnam, the Nguyễn Lords practised the veneration of localised deities and spirits. Many temples of this nature were indeed set up under their patronage; and chief among these were the Thiên Mụ temple, Quốc Am Pagoda, and Bảo Quốc Pagoda, all near Phu Xuân. Most of these temples were built during the administration of the early Nguyễn Lords when few elements of Buddhism could be detected. Buddhism only became important in the late seventeenth century when Nguyễn Phúc Trăn (r. 1687–1691), a pious Buddhist, took the initiative to promote the religion by inviting Buddhist monks from China.

Buddhism in Vietnam had suffered greatly under the Lê Dynasty. The Hong Đức Code of Law (*c.*1475), promulgated by Lê Thánh Tông (r. 1460–1497), omitted Buddhism from the social institution of the Vietnamese people, considering it to be a harmful influence best erased from Vietnamese society. But the situation began to change during the late seventeenth and early eighteenth centuries. Wearied by civil wars, the population began to crave for spiritual solace, which allowed Buddhism to make a comeback.[39] In the south, the Nguyễn Lords also craved spiritual solace, which allowed Buddhism to develop and flourish under their patronage.[40] This helped to attract many learned Buddhist clergy and scholars to the Nguyễn domains, including some from China.

Over many years, Chinese Buddhist monks had been going to Vietnam to impart Buddhist teachings to the Vietnamese. One of the earliest Buddhist monks who arrived in the Nguyễn domain was Chuyet Chuyet who left China with some of his disciples in 1630. They first arrived in Đồng Nại at the Mekong Delta before moving to Champa.[41] Shortly afterwards he left for the north, presumably after the outbreak of hostilities between the Nguyễn and the Trịnh.

During the second half of the seventeenth century, following the fall of the Ming Dynasty in China, many Chinese monks, refusing to live under the new Qing regime, left for Vietnam. Among the first of these Chinese Buddhist monks who served the Nguyễn was the abbot Tạ Nguyên Thiều (Xie Yuan Shao). A native of Chaozhou in Guangdong, he first went to Qui Ninh in 1665.[42] During his stay in southern Vietnam he built three temples – the pagoda of Thap My To, the Quốc An pagoda and the Phu Đong pagoda – all near Phu Xuân (present-day Huế). Nguyễn Phúc Trăn also asked him to invite a learned monk from southern China and to purchase religious tools and texts.[43]

By the time of monk Da Shan's arrival in 1695,[44] Nguyễn Phúc Trăn had died. His son, Nguyễn Phúc Chu (r. 1691–1725) took on the efforts to promote Buddhism. These moves in the area of religion and culture were made possible since the Nguyễn–Trịnh open warfare had ceased in 1672.

Among the many Chinese who arrived and stayed in Nguyễn southern Vietnam, none had more profound influence upon the development of religion and culture of the Nguyễn rule than the monk Da Shan. For a man who spent only one and a half years in the Nguyễn domain, Da Shan's influence on various aspects of the Nguyễn rule was substantial, especially in taking the first step towards the legitimating of their de facto rule in southern Vietnam.

Da Shan, a native of Zhejiang in central China, was known to be a learned man, well-versed in politics, astronomy, painting and verse.[45] Before travelling to southern Vietnam, Da Shan was the abbot of the Zhangshou temple in Guangzhou. He was recommended to Nguyễn Phúc Trăn by the Chinese monk Tạ Nguyên Thiều. Apparently, it took three invitations to get Da Shan to go to Vietnam. The third, coming in late 1694, touched Da Shan, who was impressed by the sincerity of Nguyễn Phúc Chu who had succeeded Nguyễn Phúc Trăn.[46]

Da Shan departed from Guangzhou in 1695 and on arrival was installed at a temple near Phu Xuân. Judging from the accounts in Da Shan's memoir, *Hai Wai Ji Shi* (*HWJS*) and the *Đại Nam Liệt Truyện Tiền Biên*, Nguyễn Phúc Chu was very fond of Da Shan, and was frequently in his company.[47] Nguyễn Phúc Chu's immediate family and many other nobles were also known to be disciples very devoted to Da Shan.

Da Shan stayed in Nguyễn southern Vietnam from 1695 till mid-1696. The significance of his presence in the Nguyễn court has to be seen from two angles: as a spiritual advisor and as a political counsellor to Nguyễn Phúc Chu. As a renowned abbot, Da Shan naturally had to play the role of a teacher. This he did with distinction. Da Shan also conducted lessons for all the Buddhist monks from Thuận Hóa and Quảng Nam. In carrying out this task, Da Shan helped to institute some sense of discipline and learning among the Buddhist monastic orders in southern Vietnam.

Da Shan's presence also strengthened Nguyễn Phúc Chu's personal faith in Buddhism. Nguyễn Phúc Chu became a frequent visitor to the monk's residence, and they spent a great deal of time together, sometimes engaging in discussion until late in the night. Nguyễn Phúc Chu also took part in several sessions of fasting and religious ceremonies conducted by Da Shan, some lasting for two weeks.[48] In the *HWJS* there are several letters written by Da Shan to royal nobles containing his discourse on the teaching of Buddhism. These were valuable as the indigenous Vietnamese Buddhist monks at that time seemed unable to provide such teaching.

It could be argued that the revival of Buddhism and its emergence as the dominant religion in southern Vietnam was the result of the work of Da Shan,[49] through the patronage of Nguyễn Phúc Chu, who was known as the most devoted Buddhist among all the Nguyễn Lords. Many monks, including those from China, had thus far failed to exert the kind of influence that Da Shan had on Nguyễn Phúc Chu and his family in relation to their Buddhist faith.

Nguyễn rule also benefited from Da Shan's counsel on politics and governance. Barely 20 days after his arrival, Da Shan began to provide counsel to Nguyễn Phúc Chu on four matters relating to governance.

First, Da Shan counselled Nguyễn Phúc Chu to seek official recognition from China. This, according to Da Shan, was paramount to the security and prestige of Nguyễn southern Vietnam.[50] This advice was to have a profound effect on the thinking of Nguyễn Phúc Chu and subsequent Nguyễn Lords, especially on the way they perceived their position in relation to the Trịnh. This culminated in the 1702 mission sent by Nguyễn Phúc Chu to Guangdong seeking recognition. Even though the request was denied, it marked the beginning of a de facto secession from the Lê Emperor in the north. This later culminated in the 1744 unilateral proclamation of Nguyễn Phúc Khoat as king (Vương).

Second, during the very short time that he had spent in Thuận Hóa and Quảng Nam, Da Shan noticed how the Nguyễn Lord had placed military concerns over civilian affairs. He had also taken note of the concentration of armed forces in the Quảng Bình province and that the corvee and military service demands the Nguyễn Lords imposed on its population had become a burden.[51] For Da Shan, such relics of the 1627–1672 wars should have been dismantled and restructured to allow the soldiers to return home periodically to be with their families.[52] This advice was heeded by Nguyễn Phúc Chu, who later introduced a series of reforms in the Nguyễn armed forces and relaxed the harsh rules of corvee and military service. In 1708 Nguyễn Phúc Chu reformed his army and, subsequently, the navy.[53] New corvee and taxation regulations were also introduced for the 1707 census. Even though the new regulations did not actually represent a significant relaxation in the corvee system, it did provide many provisions for a large number of the population to be exempted from corvee.[54]

Third, Da Shan also pointed out to Nguyễn Phúc Chu the need for the Nguyễn domain to be governed by well-qualified persons who should not be concentrating on military affairs. He urged the setting up of places of learning to cultivate Confucian culture. According to him, it was only through such measures that Nguyen southern Vietnam would be known as a civilised kingdom.[55] This was a very important observation by Da Shan. When Nguyễn Phúc Chu came to power in 1691 the Nguyễn had effectively broken with the north for more than 64 years. During that period, Nguyễn officialdom experienced a significant change in composition because, by then, there were none who had sat for public examinations under the Lê administration. The war had prevented the Nguyễn from recruiting sufficient and able personnel into its service, with perhaps the occasional man of talent from the north coming to enter the Nguyen's service. Nguyễn Phúc Tần (r. 1648–1687) had recognised the negative impact on the administration of the lack of qualified personnel and in 1667 the first public examination and selection of officials in the Nguyễn domain were organised.[56] Nguyễn Phúc Chu conducted similar examinations in 1694, but only to select those who knew the Chinese language to fill the positions of official in charge of rites and provincial administration.[57]

Da Shan's advice only served to strengthen the belief in the need to source talented men for the Nguyễn administration. Almost immediately after being advised by Da Shan, Nguyễn Phúc Chu instituted a public examination in 1695 and selected a larger pool of successful candidates to fill the positions of secretary/district magistrates, advisors/teacher, rites officials, and provincial administrative officials.[58] In the eighth month of the same year, Nguyễn Phúc Chu called for an in-house promotion exercise for the secretaries and officials of the Tam Ty system (provincial administration). The examinations conducted by the Nguyễn Lords were not as elaborate as those held under the Lê Dynasty. Nonetheless, they helped to identify more learned people to serve the state and help the Nguyễn to sustain their rule in southern Vietnam.

On 24 April 1696 Da Shan put forward to Nguyễn Phúc Chu the need for the ruler to delegate responsibility and establish a proper chain of command in the state. Da Shan was obviously horrified that Nguyễn Phúc Chu had personally taken part in the supervision of a fire-fighting effort to put out a fire in the main garrison camp, an act Da Shan thought was unnecessary and had put the Nguyễn Lord in danger.[59] For this, Da Shan asked Nguyễn Phúc Chu to institute a system of chain of command based on the system practised by the Chinese court and garrison.[60] The system would serve as a mechanism to limit the Nguyễn Lords' personal involvement in trivial matters that could be handled by others, thereby sheltering them from taking unnecessary personal risks.

Before Da Shan's departure from southern Vietnam, Nguyễn Phúc Chu had asked Da Shan to grant him the knowledge of good governance. Da Shan responded by introducing an 18-article public service code of conduct based on the social ethics of the Chinese, and had them put up in both the Court and public places in order to educate the people.[61] At the suggestion of Da Shan, Nguyễn Phúc Chu also instituted a system of public complaints, modelled after that practised in China. In this localised Nguyễn system, 24 plaques were put up, each engraved with a specific complaint. The plaques were placed at the entrances of all magistrate courts; a complaint was instituted with the relevant plaque being presented in the court.[62]

Da Shan's host, Nguyễn Phúc Chu, was obviously impressed and appreciated what Da Shan had done for the Nguyễn state. His devotion towards Da Shan was quite genuine, to the extent of believing that the presence of Da Shan was the major cause of the prosperity and well-being of the Nguyễn domain. In his first farewell to the monk,[63] Nguyễn Phúc Chu commented that the number of ships coming to Hội An had increased from 6–7 to 16–17 ships in 1695. As if Da Shan was invested with some special power, Nguyễn Phúc Chu also expressed his willingness to obey whatever instructions Da Shan cared to give.[64]

The extent of Da Shan's influence on Nguyễn Phúc Chu and on the Nguyễn regime was enormous, as demonstrated by the case of Liu Qing. During his stay in Hội An, Da Shan recommended Liu Qing to Nguyễn Phúc Chu for the position of customs officer in charge of Western ships. He did so on the advice of another mandarin. Liu Qing was a Chinese descended from the remnants of the Ming army who had settled in southern Vietnam. Nguyễn Phúc Chu took Da Shan's advice and appointed Liu Qing to the position. Liu was asked to pay 10,000 taels of silver as commission; this he obtained through extortion from the traders. When Da Shan heard of these acts, he asked that Liu Qing be sacked. Such was the extent of Da Shan's influence on Nguyễn Phúc Chu that he entertained this request.[65]

Da Shan finally left the Nguyễn domain in June 1696. Two ships were needed to take back Da Shan and his followers and all the gifts given to them by the grateful Nguyễn family and the many devotees. Included in the cargo were exotic Vietnamese produce such as bird's nests, honey and sandalwood as well as garments, textiles, silver, gold and money. Nguyễn Phúc Chu also gave 5,000 taels of gold for the rebuilding of Zhangshou temple, Da Shan's home temple, along with precious eaglewood as the building material.[66] The story of Da Shan after his return to China, however, was a tragic one. He died a prisoner, accused of being a corrupt monk.

The influence of Da Shan over Nguyễn Phúc Chu and his successors can be seen from the new-found confidence they demonstrated. Following the advice of Da Shan, the Nguyễn aspired to be regarded as equal to the Trịnh Lords in the north. Da Shan's advice on governance and administration was institutionalised, and became a permanent feature of the Nguyen's public administration in southern Vietnam. More importantly, it is obvious that Da Shan had addressed Nguyễn Phúc Chu as king (Vương) throughout his stay in southern Vietnam. He also used the corresponding terms when referring to Nguyễn Phúc Chu's immediate family members, according them with titles such as queen, queen mother, brother of king and son-in-law of king. It is not clear if Da Shan had any other agenda in doing so, but it is clear that what he did was merely to acknowledge the de facto situation of the Nguyễn Lords as the rulers of a separate and independent kingdom. This was consistent with his calls to Nguyễn Phúc Chu to seek recognition from China. The effect of Da Shan's actions can be seen in the way Nguyễn Phúc Chu addressed himself as Đại Viet Quốc Vương, Nguyễn Phúc Chu (Nguyễn Phúc Chu, the King of Đại Viet) when he wrote to Da Shan in 1696.[67] All this definitely contributed to nurturing the idea of an independent polity.

In 1714 Nguyễn Phúc Chu sent another mission to China, for the purpose of purchasing Buddhist scriptures and commentaries. The mission purchased more than 1,000 copies of texts and subsequently deposited them at the Thiên Mụ

Pagoda.[68] This development again demonstrated China's role as the source of the Nguyễn Lords' spiritual inspiration and knowledge. Nonetheless, this point requires some degree of qualification, especially in relation to the Nguyễn–Trịnh rivalry which had prevented any possibility of the flow of cultural exchanges with the north.

Apart from Da Shan, other Chinese monks were living in Nguyễn southern Vietnam at that time. Among them was Jue Linh, a native of Guangdong who was the 35th Master of the Linh Thu Buddhist sect. Jue Linh had first arrived at Đong Pho, in Đong Nại. He later went to Phu Xuân and served in the Phi Văn Pagoda.[69] Further, either being influenced and led by their ruler, who was a devoted Buddhist, or simply trying to please him, the Vietnamese who served in the court also devoted much attention to the study of Buddhist teachings. On occasion, a crowd of as many as 600 gathered to listen to Da Shan's teaching.[70]

In his letter to the Governor of the Two Guang in 1702, Nguyễn Phúc Chu stated that he and his ancestors were Buddhists.[71] This statement was the first time a Nguyễn Lord had identified with an established religion. The Nguyễn Lords before Nguyễn Phúc Chu had concentrated on building and developing localised deities and spirits. The growing importance of Buddhism among the southern Vietnamese under the Nguyễn Lords definitely had its roots in the role played by the respective Chinese Buddhist monks, especially Da Shan who was able to gain the patronage of Nguyễn Phúc Chu in promoting the Buddhist religion in southern Vietnam during the late seventeenth century.

Chinese in the court and administration

To the Vietnamese living under the Nguyễn Lords, China was also seen as the source of knowledge. In this regard, the Vietnamese in Quảng Nam, for instance, were reported to be willing to pay high prices for books imported from China via the port of Hội An. The seventeenth-century account, *Dongxiyang Kao*, remarked, "The local people are fond of (Chinese) books. Each time [the Chinese junks arrived], they competed to purchase the books at high prices".[72] This phenomenon clearly demonstrated how the closing of the northern borders with Lê–Trịnh had deprived the population of their traditional cultural ties, which prompted the Nguyễn Lords' Vietnam to rely on China as the alternative source for knowledge.

Nguyễn southern Vietnam's craving for all things Chinese was also noticed by Da Shan who related in his memoirs the enthusiasm among the Vietnamese to emulate the "Han Feng" ("Chinese Wind", meaning Chinese trends). Da Shan was continually asked about current practices in China.[73]

One of the more important contributions of the Nguyễn regime to the demographic development of Vietnam was their policy of allowing large numbers of Chinese refugees to resettle in their domains after the fall of the Ming Dynasty in 1644. This resulted in a significantly large number of Chinese in the south. These Chinese refugees included soldiers, merchants, men of literary learning, artisans, physicians and Buddhist monks.

Apart from the cultural effects of the presence of the Chinese, the Nguyễn Lords had their own reasons for accepting these political refugees. First, the Nguyễn Lords were hoping to utilise, if not absorb, some of the literati who had arrived in southern Vietnam. Second, the Nguyễn were hoping that the presence of large numbers of Chinese might help to attract more Chinese to trade in the various ports in the Nguyễn domain. In this regard the presence of the Chinese in the various southern Vietnamese ports produced the desired results.

Among some of the earliest Chinese refugees who arrived in the Nguyễn domain in the mid-seventeenth century were men of learning. The Nguyễn Lords looked upon their presence with great interest. By then the Nguyễn regime was facing a dire need to fill the literati void created by the demise of earlier men of learning who had served the earlier Nguyễn Lords. The problem was compounded by the severing of intellectual and cultural ties with the north since 1627 which had barred learned men in the north from entering the south.

Zhu Shunsui (1600–1682), a Ming scholar from Jiangnan who, because of his loyalty towards the Ming Dynasty, refused to serve the Manchu, was among the early arrivals in the Nguyễn domain and left us with an account of his stay. Between 1646 and 1656, Zhu went to Hội An six times, with the purpose of garnering support for the Ming cause in China. His presence became known to Nguyễn Phúc Tần, who wished to obtain Zhu's services. Zhu rejected Nguyễn Phúc Tần's offer of positions, though he did not object to helping Nguyễn Phúc Tần carry out some secret business in Japan.[74]

In 1657 Zhu was seized by Nguyễn soldiers at Hội An, and was asked to submit to the authority of the Nguyễn Lord. He refused and was interned at Dinh Cát, the former Nguyễn centre of administration. There he was compelled to help the Nguyễn Lords write official letters to the Trịnh and China. He was also asked to serve in other capacities, for example, explaining certain Chinese terms used in letters that were received. However, Zhu remained adamant in his position regarding service to the Nguyễn Lords. When confronted, he pleaded loyalty to the Ming as his reason for refusing to pledge loyalty to Nguyễn Phúc Tần.[75]

Zhu's undying loyalty to Ming China was not peculiar to him. Many were probably unable to accept the Nguyễn's assumption of the role of an independent ruler. Despite its de facto status, Nguyễn southern Vietnam was basically a renegade entity. In response to the treatment received at the hands of the Nguyễn Lords, Zhu Shunsui held a very negative impression of Nguyễn rule: "It is a small country but it is arrogant. Its studies are superficial and mediocre. It has little talent, and its rivalry is like that of Yelang...."[76]

Such perceptions, however, changed with the passage of time, and varied from person to person. Others were more receptive and willing to serve the so-called 'renegade' Nguyễn regime. One such person was Wei Jiuguan, a native of Fuzhou in Fujian. Wei, who also refused to serve the Manchu state, went to Nguyễn southern Vietnam during the time of Nguyễn Phúc Tần. Apparently, he still harboured a desire to help to revive the Ming Dynasty. While Wei did not officially serve the Nguyễn, he undertook several commercial missions to Japan for the Nguyễn. From his correspondence with Nguyễn Phúc Trăn, who was then yet to succeed his father, it is clear that Wei was involved in helping the Nguyen to obtain Japanese goods as well as attempting to obtain arms and ammunition from that country. Wei was trusted by the Nguyễn Lords who entrusted him, at times, with large sums of money that often amounted to 5,000 taels of silver.[77] However, Wei did not stay on in Nguyễn southern Vietnam. Sensing the futility of reviving the Ming Dynasty, Wei and his sons settled in Japan.

Another case of Chinese willing to work for the Nguyễn was the family of Trần Hung, a second-generation Chinese of the settlement of Minh Hương Xã in Thừa Thiên, Thuận Hóa. Hung was the second son of Trần Dương Thuận, a merchant from Zhangzhou in Fujian, who had arrived in Vietnam in the 1670s. Hung's mother was a Vietnamese. According to the Trần family register, Hung, who was also known as Minh Chính Công, was a physician of Chinese medicine. He befriended and served Nguyễn Phúc Chu for more than 10 years.[78] It is not known if Hung continued to serve the Nguyễn Court after the death of Nguyễn Phúc Chu in 1725, but after Hung's death in 1730, his son, who was also a doctor, moved his practice to Vuon Rau (in present-day Ba Die in Saigon).

The family register of Trần Hung provides interesting information on the spouses of several women born in the family who married Chinese or Chinese descendants, some of whom were in the service of the Nguyễn Lords. They included Hoàng Đại Tan, who was the Nội-lương-y-ty (Court physician). He married Trần Thị Lan, the fourth daughter of Trần Tôn. Another was Truong-Thien Du, a Noi Vien Thị-hau (member of the Inner Office of the Imperial Academy), who married Trần Thị Hiep, the second daughter of Trần Vy. The third daughter of Trần Vy, Trần Thị Hien, married Ngo Triu Don, eldest son of Nội Các Đại Học Sĩ, Chieu Thanh Hầu (Member of the Learned Inner Cabinet). Trần Vy's fourth daughter married Ngo Trieu Hao Thị Du, the second son of Chieu Thanh Hầu, who was himself a Minh Hương resident in Thánh Hà, Thừa Thiên.[79]

It is evident that successive Nguyễn Lords after Nguyễn Phúc Tần placed many Chinese in the inner Court circle, mainly to serve in the civil administration, as well as Court physicians. This reflected the lack of learned Vietnamese in southern Vietnam to serve in the various administrative positions. Even though there had been efforts by various Nguyễn Lords after Nguyễn Phúc Tần to introduce public examinations to recruit learned Vietnamese to serve in the Court and at provincial levels, the results were wanting. In addition, the utilisation of Chinese even in the inner Court demonstrated the Nguyễn Lords' sense of pragmatism. The Nguyễn Lords could recruit well-trained scholars from among the ranks of the Chinese scholar refugees without having to source others through the rudimentary public examinations they had organised since the mid-seventeenth century.

Concluding remarks

Nguyễn rule, especially during the transitional period of 1672–1720, owed much to the cultural and religious contribution of the Chinese refugees who had flocked to southern Vietnam. This is evident in the manner in which religious personnel were venerated and their teachings followed. The Nguyễn administration also made use of Chinese scholars who had drifted into their domain as scribes and administrators, filling a gap due to the demise of Vietnamese scholars and to the cultural barriers between the south and the north created by the Nguyễn–Trịnh hostilities.

It is thus clear that Chinese links were important factors that shaped the nature of the Nguyễn rule in southern Vietnam during the seventeenth and eighteenth centuries. This chapter has highlighted two aspects of the Chinese factor in the shaping of Nguyễn rule in southern Vietnam: the government-to-government relations and the religious and cultural links. These two factors, though less noticeable than other aspects, such as the Chinese role in the Nguyễn Lords' territorial expansion to the south and the contribution of the Chinese to the trade of southern Vietnam, were nevertheless significant.

It can be argued that the government-to-government relations had contributed in reinforcing the Nguyễn Lords' sense of independence vis-à-vis the Lê Court. Even though government-to-government relations were kept to a minimum by the Chinese government's stand regarding its official relations with the Lê Court, initiatives from the respective Nguyễn Lords ensured that such relations existed. For the Nguyễn Lords, China remained the ultimate source of legitimacy for its position vis-à-vis the Lê Court, and hence its rule in southern Vietnam. Though the Nguyễn initiatives, including the attempt to gain official recognition from the Chinese, were not reciprocated by the Chinese, the Nguyễn did not abandon their attempts to win favour with the Chinese government.

The Nguyễn Lords gained more tangible results from their Chinese links in the development of the Buddhist religion and culture. With the exodus of Chinese Buddhist monks and scholars after the fall of the Ming Dynasty, Nguyễn southern Vietnam benefited from the knowledge and skill of these men. The role of Chinese monk Da Shan was especially important in bringing about the emergence of Buddhism as the dominant religion in southern Vietnam. More importantly, it was through his suggestion that the Nguyễn Lords made an attempt to obtain recognition from China for their rule in southern Vietnam. Though the attempt failed, it nevertheless helped make the Nguyễn aware of their actual position as the de facto ruler of southern Vietnam.

Other suggestions from Da Shan also helped to strengthen the administrative apparatus of the Nguyễn regime in southern Vietnam. This was further enhanced by the presence of Chinese scholars such as Zhu Shunsui and other skilled personnel such as the Trần [Chen] family, who helped to improve the quality of Nguyễn rule in southern Vietnam.

Notes

1 The writer would like to thank Dr. Loh Wei Leng of the Department of History, University of Malaya, for her valuable comments on this chapter.
2 See Li Tana, *Nguyễn Cochinchina: Southern Vietnam During the Seventeenth and Eighteenth Centuries*, Ithaca: Cornell University, Southeast Asian Program, 1998,

pp. 41–46; L. Cadiere, "Les Elephants Royaux", *Bulletin des Amis de Vieux Hue*, Vol. 9, No. 1, 1922: 41–102.

3 See Nguyễn Thanh Nha, *Tableau Economique du Vietnam aux XVIIe et XVIIIe siecles*, Paris: editions Cujas, 1870; Thành Thế Vỷ, *Ngoài Thương Việt-Nam: Hồi Thế Kỷ XVII, XVIII và đầu XIX*, Hanoi: Sử Học, 1961.

4 See Paul Boudet, "La Conquete de la Cochinchine par les Nguyễn et le Rôle des Émigrés Chinois", *Bulletin d'École Française d'Extrême-Orient*, Vol. 42, 1942: 115–132.

5 Chen Chingho, "The Minh Hương Village and Thanh Hà Pho in Thừa Thiên (Central Viet-Nam)", *The New Asia Journal*, Vol. 4, No. 1, August 1959: 305–329; "Shiqi ba shiji Huian zhi Tangrenjie ji qi Shangye [The Chinese Town of Hoi An and its Trade During the 17th and 18th Centuries]" *Xinya Xuebao [New Asia Journal]*, Vol. 3, No. 1, Hong Kong, 1960: 273–332; "Hexianzhen Yezhen Moshi Jiapu Zhishi [Notes on the Genealogy of the Mac Family from Hà Tiên]", *Wenshizhe Xuebao (Bulletin of the College of Arts of Taiwan National University)*, No. 7, 1956: 77–140.

6 Nguyễn Thế Anh, "L'Immigration Chinoise et la Colonisation du Delta du Mékong", *The Vietnam Review*, No. 1, Autumn–Winter 1996, pp. 154–177.

7 See Yang Baoyun, *Contribution a l'histoire de la Principaute des Nguyễn au Vietnam Meridional, 1600–1775*, Geneve: editions Olizane, 1992, pp. 156–174.

8 Li Tana, *Nguyễn Cochinchina*, pp. 68–71.

9 Liam C. Kelley, "Thoughts on a Chinese Diaspora: The Case of the Macs of Hà Tiên", *Crossroads*, Vol. 14, No. 1, 2000, pp. 71–98.

10 For studies on the genesis of Nguyễn rule, see Keith Taylor, "Nguyen Hoang (1525–1613) and the Beginning of Viet Nam's Southward Expansion", in Anthony Reid (ed.), *Southeast Asia in the Early Modern Era: Trade, Power and Belief*, Ithaca: Cornell University Press, 1993, pp. 42–65; Nola Cooke, "Regionalism and the Nature of Nguyễn Rule in Seventeenth Century Đàng Trong (Cochinchina)", *Journal of Southeast Asian Studies*, Vol. 29, No. 1, March 1998, pp. 122–161.

11 Nguyễn The Anh, "Le Nam Tiến dans les texts Vietnamiens", in P. B. Lafont (ed.), *Les frontièrs du Viet Nam*, Paris: L'Harmattan, 1993, pp. 121–127; from the Cambodian point of view, see Mak Phoeun, *Histoire du Cambodge, de la fin du XVIe siecle au debut du XVIIIe*, Paris: Ecole Francaise d'Extreme-Orient, 1995, Chapters IV–X.

12 At the close of the seventeenth century, the Nguyen's population is estimated to have been about one million compared to five million in the north. See Li Tana, *Nguyễn Cochinchina*, Ithaca: Cornell University Southeast Asia Program, 1998, pp. 159–160.

13 For a biography of Tich Da Shan, see *Đại Nam Liệt Truyện Tiền Biên* (hereafter DNLTTB), Vol. 5: 24–25. See also Jiang Boqin, *Qingchu Lingnan, Chanxue Shi Yanjiu Chubian: Shilian Da Xian Yu Aomen Chanshi, (Thach Liem Da Shan and the Development of Zen in Macau)* Shanghai: Xuelin Chubanshe, 1999.

14 This was also acknowledged by Da Shan in his *Haiwai Jishi* (hereafter *HWSJ*), Vol. 2.

15 *Đại Nam Thức Lục Tiền Biên* (hereafter, *Tiền Biên*), Vol. 7: 20. The Siamese secondary tribute ship was most likely to have been manned by Chinese seamen as it was common for the Siamese and other Southeast Asian nations to commission a seagoing Chinese vessel to travel to China. This is highlighted by Yoneo Ishii in his *The Junk Trade from Southeast Asia, Translation from the Tosen Fusetsu-gaki, 1674–1723*, Singapore: Institute of Southeast Asian Studies and Research School of Pacific and Asian Studies, Australian National University, 1998, pp. 2–3 and 18–21; see also Jennifer Wayne Cushman, *Fields from the Sea: Chinese Junk Trade with Siam During the Late Eighteenth-century and Early Nineteenth-century*, Ithaca: Cornell University Southeast Asia Program, 1993, pp. 2–3.

16 *Tiền Biên*, Vol. 7: 20. The *Phủ Biên Tạp Lục (Miscellaneous Records of the Pacification of the Frontiers* hereafter *PBTL*) differs slightly from the *Tiền Biên* regarding the contents of the tribute. In addition to the items listed in the *Tiền Biên*, the *PBTL* list

includes two pieces of sapan wood, three pairs of song birds, and one pair of "lightning" bronze bracelets, see *PBTL*, Vol. 5: 27.
17 *PBTL*, Vol. 5: 27.
18 *Tiền Biên*, Vol. 7: 20.
19 Nguyễn Quang Tiền was a native of Thừa Thiên in Quảng Diền (Thuần Hóa). Known as a talented man, Quang Tien entered the Nguyễn service during Nguyễn Phúc Chu's reign. He was responsible for drafting the letter to seek admission to the Chinese tribute system in 1702. He was also one of the few talented people identified by Lê Quý Dôn. See *DNLTTB*, Vol. 5: 31–32 and *PBTL*, Vol. 5: 11.
20 *PBTL*, Vol. 5: 28.
21 *PBTL*, Vol. 5: 29–30.
22 *PBTL*, Vol. 5: 27.
23 See, for instance, Yoneo Ishii, *The Junk Trade from Southeast Asia*, p. 3; see also Chen Chingho, "Shiqi ba shiji Huian zhi Tangrenjie jiqi Shangye [The Chinese Town of Hoi An and its Trade During the 17th and 18th Centuries]" *Xinya Xuebao (New Asia Journal)*, Vol. 3, No. 1, Hong Kong, 1960: 273–332.
24 In *HWJS* Nguyễn Phúc Chu asked Da Shan to pave the way at Guangzhou to facilitate the sending of the tribute delegation, see *HWJS*, Vol. 3: 2–3.
25 This idea was expressed by Jiang Boqin in *Qing Chu Lingnan Chanxue Shi Yanjiu Chubian: Shilian Daxian Yu Aomen Chanshi*, p. 415.
26 *Huang Zhao Wenxian Tongkao*, Vol. 33.
27 *Qing Shi Gao Jiaozhu*, Vol. 534; *Lie Zhuan*, Vol. 314: 2097.
28 *Qing Shi Gao Jiaozhu*, Vol. 534; *Lie Zhuan*, Vol. 314: 12098.
29 See *Qing Shi Gao Jiaozhu*, Vol. 534; *Lie Zhuan*, Vol. 314: 12096.
30 *Tiền Biên*, Vol. 10: 13–14; see also *Gia Định Thành Thông Chí*, Vol. 2: 8–9.
31 Pierre Poivre, "Description de la Cochinchine (1749–1759)", *Revue d'Extreme-Orient*, T. III, 1887, p. 107.
32 *PBTL*, Vol 5: 30.
33 *Qing Shi Gao Jiaozhu*, Vol. 534; *Lie Zhuan*, Vol. 314: 12096.
34 *Qing Shi Gao Jiaozhu*, Vol. 534; *Lie Zhuan*, Vol. 314: 12096.
35 See *Qing Shi Gao Jiaozhu*, Vol. 534; *Lie Zhuan*, Vol. 314: 12096. See also *Qing Chao Wen Xian Tong Kao*, Vol. 296, as cited in Yang Baoyun, *Contribution a l'Histoire de la Principaute des Nguyễn*, p. 160 and see also *Tiền Biên*, Vol. 10: 13–14.
36 *PBTL*, Vol. 5: 30.
37 *Bang Giao Luc*, Vol. 1, as cited in Yang Baoyun, *Contribution a l'Histoire de la Principaute des Nguyễn* p. 161.
38 *Tiền Biên*, Vol. 10: 24.
39 Minh Chi, Ha Van Tan and Nguyễn Tai Thu, *Buddhism in Vietnam*, Hanoi: The Gioi Publishers, 1993, p. 148.
40 Nguyễn Long, *Viet Nam Phat Giao Su Luon, Tap 2*, Hanoi: Nha Xuat Ban Van Hoc, 1992, p. 184.
41 Minh Chi, Ha Van Tan and Nguyễn Tai Thu, *Buddhism in Vietnam*, p. 150.
42 For a biography of Tạ Nguyên Thiều, see *DNLTTB*, Vol. 6; see also *Đại Nam Nhất Thống Chí* (Geographical Gazetteer of Dai Nam): Thừa Thiên, p. 79.
43 *DNLTTB*, Vol. 6: 23.
44 For biography of Da Shan, see *DNLTTB*, Vol. 6: 24–25. The *Liet Truyen Tiền Biên*'s portrayal of Da Shan was full of praise for his contribution to Nguyễn rule compared to the portrayals in the Chinese sources, see Chen Chingho (ed.), *Shiqi Shiji Guangnan zhi xin Shiliao* (New Sources on Seventeenth Century Guangnan), Taipei: Zhonghua Chong Shu, 1960, pp. 5–15.
45 For some examples of Da Shan's painting, see, *Qingchu Lingnan Chanxue Shi Yanjiu Chubian, Shilian Daxian Yu Aomen Chanshi*.
46 *Hai Wai Ji Shi* (hereafter *HWJS*), Vol. 1: 1. See also "Report of Ship No. 36 from Guangnan, Vol. 22, 1695" in *Kai-Hentai*, Vol. 2, Tokyo: Toyo Buno, 1958–1960):

1744. According to the report, the two Nguyen envoys, Chen Tianguan and Wu Ziguan, were both Chinese.
47 *HWJS*, Vol. 1: 32.
48 *HWJS*, Vol. 2: 1 and 2: 22–23.
49 Minh Chi, Ha Van Tan and Nguyễn Tai Thu, *Buddhism in Vietnam*, p. 165.
50 *HWJS*, Vol. 1: 34.
51 *HWJS*, Vol. 1: 35.
52 *HWJS*, Vol. 1: 35b–36b.
53 For instance, Nguyễn Phúc Chu ordered the establishment of military flags for his navy, and was constantly conducting manoeuvres to keep his army in good shape. *Tiền Biên*, Vol. 7: 17.
54 *Tiền Biên*, Vol. 8: 1–3.
55 *HWJS*, Vol. 1: 35.
56 *Tiền Biên*, Vol. 5: 3.
57 *Tiền Biên*, Vol. 7: 8.
58 *Tiền Biên*, Vol. 7: 10.
59 *HWJS*, Vol. 2: 31. The incident, however, was recorded slightly different in the *DNLTTB*, Vol. 6: 25.
60 *HWJS*, Vol. 2: 32.
61 *HWJS*, Vol. 2: 32–33.
62 *HWJS*, Vol. 2: 32.
63 Da Shan's first departure was on the first day of the seventh month of 1695, but he only went as far as Hội An, where he was taken ill. He then decided to stay on until 1696.
64 "Nguyễn Phúc Chu's letter to Da Shan", as cited in Chen Chingho, *Shiqi Shiji Guangnan zhi xin Shiliao* (New Sources on Seventeenth Century Guangnan), pp. 24–25.
65 *HWJS*, Vol. 5: 2.
66 Chen Chingho, *Shiqi Shiji Guangnan zhi xin Shiliao* (New Sources on Seventeenth Century Guangnan), p. 26.
67 *HWJS*, Preface, p. 6.
68 *Tiền Biên*, Vol. 8: 18.
69 *DNLTTB*, Vol. 6: 26.
70 *HWJS*, Vol. 2: 1.
71 *PBTL*, Vol. 5: 27.
72 *Dongxiyang Kao*, Vol. 1: 19, see also Chen Chingho, *Historical Notes on Hoi-An (Faifo)*, Carbondale: Center for Vietnamese Studies, Southern Illinois University, 1974, p. 20.
73 *Hai Wai Ji Shi*, Vol. 1: 20.
74 Salmon, Claudine. "Regards de Quelques voyaguers Chinois sur le Vietnam du XVIIe Siecle." In *Asia Maritima: Images et réalité Bilder und Wirklichkeit, 1200–1800*, eds. Denys Lombard and Roderich Ptak, South China and Maritime Asia 1. Wiesbaden: Harrassowitz Verlag, 1994, p. 126.
75 Zhu Shunsui, *Annan Congyi Jishi*, p. 303 and 305–306.
76 Yelang, a small state which existed in the region of Guizhou during the Han Dynasty whose king was regarded to be presumptuous. See Zhu Shunsui, *Annan Gongyi Jishi*, p. 315.
77 "Nguyen Phuc Tran to Wei Jiuguan", 11 August 1673 as cited in *Ming Do Su*, Vol. 7: 95. *Ming Do Su* is a private manuscript kept by the Le family, now part of the manuscript collection of the Institute of History at Hanoi, MSS No. 285.
78 See the family register of the Tran family in Chen Chingho (ed.), *A Brief Study of the Trần Family Register, A Ming Refugee Family in Minh-Huong-Xa Thua-Thien (Central Vietnam)*, Southeast Asian Studies Section, New Asia Research Institute, Chinese University of Hong Kong, Hong Kong, 1964, p. 46.
79 Ibid., p. 15.

7 King Taksin and China

Siam-Chinese relations during the Thonburi period as seen from Chinese sources

James K. Chin

King Taksin, a well-known figure in the history of Thailand, has been for some time the subject of considerable reassessment by historians, despite the fact that he remained prominent on the historical stage for only 15 years. Much has been written about Taksin's merits and faults in his efforts to unify Siam. The Thonburi period is very important both in Thai history and in examining the history of the relations between Thailand and China. Given the fact that Taksin was half Chinese, one might have expected that the relationship between Siam under Taksin's rule and China would have been more friendly and intimate than that during the Ayutthaya period. What the Chinese historical sources suggest to us, however, is a situation which is entirely the reverse. As a matter of fact, King Taksin was initially on very bad terms with the Qing court and, despite efforts, he failed to win, in his lifetime, the recognition from China that he craved. Why was the Chinese court reluctant to recognize and support Taksin's regime? How did Taksin manage gradually to improve relations with China? And what were the motives behind the China-oriented foreign policy formulated by Taksin? This study will try to provide answers to these questions by examining the relationship between Taksin and the Chinese court from 1768 to 1782, mainly on the basis of information gleaned from the Chinese sources.

The early years

Taksin was born in 1734 at Ayutthaya, where his Chinese father, Zheng Yong (鄭鏞), who had married a Thai woman named Nok-iang, was earning his living as a tax-farmer for gambling houses. Taksin was adopted by Chao Phraya Chakri, the Samuha Nayok (Chief Minister) during King Boromakot's reign, when he was a boy. He grew up fully bilingual, and besides Chinese and Thai in which he was fluent, he studied Vietnamese and one of the Indian languages.[1] By the time of the Burmese invasions, he was the governor of Tak near Kamphaeng Phet with the rank of Phraya, and was thus known as Phraya Tak. With his troops he was engaged in the defence of Ayutthaya, but when he became aware that the capital was incapable of withstanding the Burmese attack, he fled Ayutthaya with his followers before the Burmese conquest.[2] When Ayutthaya was captured by the Burmese on 28 April 1767, Taksin was already in control of both Rayong and Chonburi. In June, he secured Chonthaburi and conquered Trat shortly afterwards. By October 1767, Taksin had established his power over a large territory outside of Burmese control.³ In October 1767, his armies took the port of Thonburi on the west bank of the Chaophraya River, and he established his headquarters there. Two months later, with the support of his fellow-countrymen (the Teochews), and his officials and soldiers, Taksin declared himself the king of Thonburi.⁴ According to the Qing archives, as soon as he set up his capital at Thonburi, Taksin sent Chen Mei (陳美), a Teochew Chinese merchant engaged in the trade between Siam and China, to Guangdong in China. Chen Mei reached Guangzhou (Canton) by junk in early August 1768, carrying with him three letters, one for the Chinese emperor, Qianlong (乾隆), one for Li Shiyao (李侍堯), the Governor-General of Guangdong and Guangxi, and one for the Viceroy of Guangdong. In these letters, Taksin reported to the Chinese government that the city of Ayutthaya had been sacked by the Burmese forces, and that the old dynasty had been ended. He also gave an account of how he had led the Siamese troops in defeating the Burmese forces in Siam, and how the people of Siam had consequently enthroned him as their new king. At the same time, Taksin complained that the unsubdued local leaders and governors of three principalities, that is, Fu-si-lu (扶世祿 Phitsanulok), Lu-kun (祿坤 Nakhon Si Thammarat) and Gao-lie (高烈 Khorat), still defied his authority in Siam, and he was thus requesting the Celestial Court to grant him investiture and recognition.⁵

It was in this manner that Taksin's name first appeared in the Chinese imperial record. For some reason, in the memorial presented to the Qianlong emperor by Li Shiyao in early September 1768 Taksin's name was given as Gan Enchi (甘恩敕), which may represent a Chinese alias, a Thai name or a Thai official title. Despite the fact that Taksin was actually half Chinese and that he had already acceded to the Siamese throne, the Chinese court refused to recognize his claim to the throne and rejected his request for investiture. In his imperial order of 29 September 1768, the Qianlong emperor noted:

> Gan Enchi was originally a humble person in China. He sailed far across the sea and became a chieftain of the *yi* (夷 barbarians). He served the king of the country of Siam as a minister. Now in that place [Siam] the country has been destroyed and the king has died, and Gan Enchi has dared to take advantage of the disorder. He has forgotten the kindness shown to him by the deceased king and not sought to install the king's descendants in order to revive the country and carry out retribution. Rather, he has sought to establish himself as ruler and wildly requested Imperial enfeoffment, so that he has the authority to lord over others. This is truly outrageous.⁶

The emperor not only ordered Li Shiyao to return to Chen Mei the letters written by Taksin, but also commanded the Council of State (軍機處) to draft and send to Taksin a strong letter of rebuff in the name of the Governor-General. The rejection letter, which clearly reflected the Chinese court's haughty attitude towards Taksin, stated that:

You sent Chen Mei to come to Guangdong to deliver your letters, seeking orders of enfeoffment from the Heavenly Court. This is truly improper. The kings of Siam, although far across the sea, have for generations respectfully offered tribute. The Emperors were pleased with their respectful obedience, and conferred rewards and enfeoffment upon them. Now, after repeated attacks and plunder by the Burmese (Lit: the tattooed-body barbarians), the country has been destroyed and the King has been killed. You were one of his chieftains, and served him as his minister. When you saw that your ruler had been killed, you should have become more loyal, and tried to restore the state, and avenge the attack. After the destruction of the country, the people of Siam fled from the fighting and could not sustain their lives. The situation was certainly difficult to reverse. You should have tried to assist the descendants of your ruler in reviving the country, so that the family line of your deceased king could be continued. If you had done this, would not all of the officials and chieftains of Siam have lauded and admired your assistance and loyalty? Then, when the rightful heir had inherited the throne, and you memorialized advice to this effect to the Heavenly Court, naturally your achievements would have been admired; and when the Emperor had heard of them, he would have been very pleased. However, it has been heard that after you had eliminated and achieved victory over the tattooed-body Mons and the Burmese, you went into the mountains to obtain elephant tusks and rhinoceros horns and provided these things to meet the needs of the refugees. This shows that you are a man of skills and talent. Now, Zhao Wangji (詔王吉) who is the elder brother of your ruler, and Zhao Cui (詔萃) as well as Zhao Shichang (詔世昌), who are grandsons of the ruler, are all in hiding within the territory [Siam?]. You did not seek to join with your numerous chieftains in establishing and assisting them, actions whereby you would have achieved everlasting fame. Rather, you took advantage of the chaos to violently establish yourself. You wildly sought enfeoffment and you appropriated the title of king. You violated your place and your status, ignored propriety, and turned your back on grace. What is more evil than this? If you examine yourself, can you feel at ease? You were originally an ordinary person from China, and you must be familiar with the principles of righteousness. You must also know that many rebellious ministers and bandits have taken the traditional values of China as an excuse for their actions. Now, let us consider your situation. You are putting pressure on the three administrations of Silu, Lukun and Gaolie, because you wish to control their territories. If they join forces and take up arms against you, their actions will be right and proper, while your actions will be in violation of propriety and principles. The Way of Heaven is to assist those who follow the principles and to bring harm to those who violate them. It is very clear who will be victorious and who will be defeated. Do you wish to bring destruction upon yourself? The great emperor, in soothing the Yi (夷 barbarian) and the Xia (夏 Chinese) uses benevolence to educate them and righteousness to correct them. He provides an example for the myriad lands. The situation you have described is a gross violation of the law. I cannot report this to the Emperor, so I am returning your letters to Chen Mei to take back. My post is responsible for border defence, and I have the duty to make known the Court's virtue. I commiserate with your benightedness and confusion, and am thus especially issuing these instructions for your enlightenment. If you repent and change your ways, show loyalty to your ruler, and manifest the Court's will to restore the broken line, you will forever enjoy the limitless blessed protection of the Emperor. Do not persist in your erroneous actions! This is so instructed.[7]

The statements above explicitly show that the traditional Chinese concept of legitimacy in respect of the succession of rules was the primary reason why the Chinese Emperor took this negative position. However, there was another factor which contributed to the strong rebuff by the Qing court. From the memorial of Li Shiyao to the court, we know that, at virtually the same time as Chen Mei was arriving in Guangzhou with Taksin's letters, an official named Lin Yi (林義), who had been sent by Mo Shilin (莫士麟), (a powerful Chinese leader in Ha-tien, Southern Vietnam, who had emigrated from Leizhou Prefecture, Guangdong), also arrived at the Governor-General's office. He was accompanied by the interpreter, Mo Yuangao (莫元高), and the guards Shi Ning (史寧) and Huang Yang (黃揚). After presenting maps of Siam and other countries in Southeast Asia, the embassy sent by Mo reported to the Chinese government that Zhao Cui (Chau Chai?) and Zhao Shi-hang (Chau Sisang?), who were grandsons of King Ekathat (Suriyamarin), had already taken refuge in Ha-tien from the fighting in Siam. We further learn from the *Genealogy of the Mo Family in the Towns of Ha-tien and Ye* (河仙鎮葉鎮莫氏家譜), that at this time Mo Shilin also had his eye on hegemony in Siam, and intended to vie for supremacy with Taksin by escorting the princes of Siam home and then providing them with supplies by which to achieve the unification of Siam.[8] Being a member of the Chinese literati, Mo Shilin of course well understood the Confucian ideas about legitimate succession, and was quite sure that the Qing court would prefer that the princes of the Ayutthaya dynasty be restored to the throne in order to uphold this traditional doctrine. It is therefore not strange that Mo's embassy provided an account of Taksin's family background to Li Shiyao, which emphasized the lowly position of Taksin in Siam. In view of the fact that during the 1760s the Chinese government had been gathering its information on Siam mainly through the polity ruled by the Mo family at Ha-tien, and that what the Mo embassies reported was therefore usually trusted by the Qing court, there is little doubt the Mo's belittlement of the importance of Taksin was to some degree a factor in the negative attitude adopted by the Chinese government towards Taksin's first envoy. Mo Shilin's aim in sending the embassy to China was thus achieved. His own envoys received a warm welcome in Guangzhou, and they returned with imperial presents of satin and a letter of citation from the Qianlong emperor, while Taksin's request was flatly rejected.

Another important point which needs to be noted is that the Chinese government was anxious at that time to cooperate with Siam in launching a pincer attack on the Burmese. The conflict between China and Burma had begun earlier, at the end of 1762, when the Burmese made a surprise attack on the Gengma (耿馬) area and Maolong (茂隆) silver mining zone in Yunnan.[9] In 1765, the Sino-Burmese war had finally erupted. The Manchu armies, however, suffered successive defeats due to tropical diseases, such as pernicious malaria, which caused the death of a large number of troops. It is interesting thus to note in the Qing sources that soon afterwards, in May 1767, about one month after the fall of Ayutthaya, Yang Yingju (楊應琚), the Governor-General of Yunnan and Guizhou, proposed an unusual plan, suggesting that the Qing court despatch 50,000 soldiers to launch a pincer attack on the Burmese troops in coordination with the Siamese forces. This proposal was, however, condemned by the emperor as "absolutely ridiculous".[10] Despite its rejection of Yang's proposal, the Qing court was still much concerned with the situation in Siam and watched attentively the development of the war between Burma and Siam. On 12 July 1767, the Qianlong emperor even sent an imperial decree to Li Shiyao in Guangzhou, ordering him to inform the king of Siam of the date the Manchu armies proposed to attack the Burmese, and of the expectation of the Qing court that the Siamese forces would assist in pursuing and capturing the Burmese chieftains who might, it was believed, flee into Siam after the attack by the Manchu troops. Moreover, the emperor instructed Li Shiyao to collect navigational information, such as the nautical distance from Guangdong to Siam, the anchorages and polities along the coast of the Indochinese Peninsula, as well as journey times, in case of need. The important diplomatic note, however, never reached the Siamese court in Ayutthaya. Just as Li Shiyao's courier, the Brigade Commander Xu Quan (許全) was preparing to depart, the mission from Ayutthaya which had left China for Siam several weeks previously returned to Guangzhou. There they relayed the news, which they had heard on their way home, of the downfall of Ayutthaya at the hands of the Burmese and the death of King Ekathat. In other words, only at the end of July 1768, more than 15 months after the fall of Ayutthaya, was the Chinese court aware of the event. Consequently, the imperial letter and presents bestowed upon King Ekathat were returned to the Qing court, and Xu Quan was despatched to Siam to investigate the situation there.[11] Nevertheless, the emperor made a confidential decision on 13 August 1768 that, in order to assist in the unification of Siam and to drive the Burmese out of Siam, the Chinese government would send a naval force to Siam to attack the Burmese troops as soon as the kingdom of Siam asked China for help.[12] In short, for the purpose of winning the war with Burma, the Qing court at this time anxiously desired that the princes of Ayutthaya, rather than Taksin, the illegitimate successor to the Ayutthaya dynasty, would appeal for China's assistance.

It is probable that his initial diplomatic failure discouraged Taksin, or that he was preoccupied with the enterprise of expelling the Burmese and subjugating other independent local rulers at home, as well as otherwise consolidating the kingdom. For whatever reason, during the following three years, no further missions from Thonburi were sent to China. The Chinese government, on the other hand, was still much concerned with the situation in Siam. In November 1768, Cheng Zhe (程轍), an Assistant Brigade Commander (守備) who had been captured by the Burmese, sent a message from Ava to the Chinese emperor noting that the collapsing kingdom of Siam wanted to recover its lost power. Upon receiving the message, the emperor ordered Li Shiyao to swiftly despatch somebody to Ha-tien to determine from Mo Shilin the actual situation in Siam.[13] To this end, the Brigade Vice Commander, Zheng Rui (鄭瑞), was sent aboard a Chinese merchant junk to Ha-tien in December. Seven months later, it appears that the Chinese investigator had still not returned to China and it was not known what had happened to him, as on 22 July 1769, the Qianlong emperor again enquired of his Grand Ministers of State as to who exactly held real power, who was in control of Siam, and whether or not the Chinese government had received any further letter from Taksin.[14] Consequently, another investigator, the Brigade Commander Cai Han (蔡漢), was sent by Li Shiyao to Ha-tien in early August 1769, with the mission of instructing Mo Shilin to capture the Burmese army deserters. By an unexpected turn of events, after Cai Han arrived in Ha-tien, Mo Shilin suggested that orders should also be sent to Taksin. Cai Han subsequently without authorization transmitted an official note to Taksin which required that he also pursue and capture the Burmese deserters.[15] On 15 August 1769, the emperor received Li Shiyao's memorial based on Zheng Rui's investigation report of the situation in Siam. It was only at this time that the Qing court realized that Taksin actually had control of Siam, and that the descendants of the Ayutthaya court had no hope of being restored to the throne.[16] In response to this new situation in Siam, the Chinese government had no choice but to adjust its diplomatic policy in respect of Siam, and to gradually change its cold attitude towards Taksin. At the same time, as a result of the information collected by Zheng Rui and subsequently Cai Han at Ha-tien, the Qing court became aware of the fact that Taksin at Thonburi and Mo Shilin at Ha-tien were preparing to wage war on each other, and that Mo was continually seeking to sow dissension between China and Siam. As a result, the reports from Mo Shilin were increasingly distrusted by the Qing court.[17]

In September 1769, Mo Shilin despatched 50,000 soldiers under the command of Chen Wenfang (陳文方) to attack Chanthaburi, which was Taksin's major stronghold in Siam, with the intention of challenging Taksin's supremacy. The raid proved to be completely unsuccessful, and two months later, Chen Wenfang led the remnants of the routed army back to Ha-tien, having suffered a loss of more than 30,000 soldiers.[18] Shortly afterwards, Mo Shilin forwarded a petition to the Chinese government in which he asked China to help him by ordering the Burmese forces to attack Taksin in coordination with his own forces. Times, however, had changed. The Qing court had already modified its policies in respect of both Taksin and Mo Shilin, and therefore in his reply, the emperor neither endorsed Mo's attack on Taksin nor agreed to order the Burmese to invade Siam. The emperor sought to remain neutral in the struggle between Taksin and Mo Shilin. It is interesting to note that, from this time onwards, in its official documents the Chinese government used the name Pi-ya-xin (丕雅新

Phraya Sin) rather than Gan Enchi to refer to Taksin.[19] This was one of the manifestations of change in the Chinese government's attitude towards Taksin.

The apogee

If the period from 1768 to 1770 can be seen as a difficult period for Taksin, then the years after 1771 saw the gradual improvement of relations between Taksin and China. Perhaps Taksin was informed of the new policy adopted on the Chinese side, but in any case, he took the chance to send a second mission to China in August 1771 with the intention of reviving, on his own initiative, the previous cordial relations between the two countries. On the pretext of responding to the call from the Qing court which was transmitted by Cai Han two years previously, the mission from Thonburi brought with them, among other presents, 12 Burmese captives, male and female, including a Burmese army chieftain named Xie-du-yan-da (瀉都燕達), and asked the Chinese government to allow Taksin's government to send tribute to the court.[20] When he received the news of the arrival in Guangzhou of another mission from Taksin, the Qianlong emperor immediately sent Li Shiyao instructions on how to treat Taksin's mission. It appears that the emperor was afraid that the Governor-General may not have fully comprehended the new policy towards Taksin. The emperor's instructions read:

> Now, Phraya Sin has indicated his reverence for the Imperial orders, and he knows how to respect the ministers of the Heavenly Court. Thus, there is no need to completely ignore him. Cutting him off would be too excessive an action.[21]

Two months later, after the Qing court confirmed that the person forwarded by Taksin was indeed a Burmese chieftain, it demonstrated an amicable attitude towards Taksin, and on 24 November 1771, the emperor set forth an explanation for the changes in Chinese policy towards Taksin:

> The maritime barbarians on the distant borders do not understand propriety and righteousness. Changes in ruling families and struggles for power are frequent occurrences. In the country of Annam, for example, we have seen the Chen (陳 Trần), Mo (莫 Mạc) and Li (黎 Lê) dynasties revolving as rulers. So, this is not just the case in Siam. When the Burmese bandits attacked Siam, Phraya Sin in the name of revenge, just acted as the situation demanded. He did not openly seize power. Further, when he found out that a senior minister in China had issued instructions, he respectfully obeyed the orders, and sent troops to attack Chiang Mai (青霾). Among those he captured was a chieftain of the Burmese bandits. There is certainly no doubt that he has avenged the attack by the Burmese barbarians. He has repeatedly requested enfeoffment and sought Imperial grace, and he knows how to respect the Heavenly Court. Thus, there is no need to adhere to the opinions

of the past, and cutting him off would be too excessive an action. As to the details of his becoming the ruler, we do not need to be too strict about his status, or to investigate the situation too fully. Phraya Sin has only just initiated his rule, and because his power is limited, he has sought someone he can rely on. If China continues to reject and refuse him, he may become frightened and transfer his allegiance to the Burmese bandits. This would not be a good strategy.[22]

Consequently, the emperor sent orders to Li Shiyao requiring that if in the future Taksin sent missions to request investiture from China or present tribute, he should submit a memorial to Beijing (Peking), and the Qing court would accede to Taksin's request.

Presumably, Taksin was encouraged by the good response from the Chinese side, as he pursued a more active China-oriented foreign policy thenceforth. In July 1772, subsequent to his attack on and conquest of Ha-tien in 1771, Taksin despatched a mission to send back to Guangzhou Chen Junqin (陳俊卿), and Liang Shangxuan (梁上選) together with 33 Chinese farmers, who were sojourners in Ha-tien from Haifeng County (海豐縣), Guangdong, and who had been captured by the Siamese troops.[23] Three years later, 19 Chinese captives who belonged to the Yunnan provincial forces were rescued by Taksin's armies when the latter seized Tavoy, and were sent back to Guangzhou by Chen Wansheng (陳萬勝), a Chinese merchant of Thonburi.[24] In 1776, Taksin managed to help and send back to China three Chinese merchants from Yunnan who had been caught up in the chaos of war.[25] A further group of Burmese captives was sent under escort to China from Thonburi in the following year.[26] Having realized that Taksin had become the most powerful ruler in Siam, and that he was sincerely seeking to establish formal relations with China, the Qing court decided to further improve its relations with him. As a result, from August 1772 the name of Taksin recorded in Chinese official documents was further changed from Pi-ya-xin (Phraya Sin) to Zheng Zhao (鄭昭), which meant the king (昭) whose surname is "Zheng".[27] The transition in the name by which the Chinese court referred to Taksin, from "Xianluo Guo Yimu Gan Enchi" (暹羅國夷目甘恩敕 i.e. the barbarian chieftain Gan En-chi of the Kingdom of Siam) to Pi-ya-xin, and then from Pi-ya-xin to Zheng Zhao, explicitly reflected that the position of Taksin in the view of the Chinese government was steadily rising, and that the improvement of the relations between Siam under Taksin's rule and China was undergoing a long and complex process.

In an attempt to show the amicable sentiments towards Taksin, the Qing court made an exception by allowing Taksin's mission to purchase some military materials in Guangdong. In 1775, the Chinese merchant, Chen Wansheng, who had been sent by Taksin, bought 50 piculs of saltpetre and 500 iron cooking pans in Guangdong. Under the laws of the Qing court, it was normally prohibited to export these items. Another Chinese merchant, Mo Guangyi (莫廣億), purchased 100 piculs of saltpetre on behalf of Taksin in the following year.[28] On 14 August 1777, the emperor sent instructions to Yang Jingsu (楊景素) the newly appointed

Governor-General of Guangdong and Guangxi,[29] reminding him to keep the door open to Taksin's government, if they wanted to buy more saltpetre or other necessities.[30]

In 1775, Taksin's troops encircled and captured the Burmese stronghold at Chiang Mai, and all of the Burmese forces retreated from Siam during the following year on account of the death of the Burmese king. After consolidating the whole kingdom, Taksin now had the time and ability to develop the domestic economy and to expand foreign connections. In July 1777, he despatched three envoys to China. In his letter to Yang Jingsu, Taksin explained that since the fall of Ayutthaya, Siam had not presented tribute to the Chinese emperor, and that he wished to offer tribute according to the usual practices. It was thus that he had sent his envoys with an official letter to China, and he hoped that the Governor-General could transmit his wish to the court in Beijing. After he received Yang Jingsu's memorial on the mission sent by Taksin, the emperor ordered the Grand Ministers of State to draft a letter in reply in the name of the Governor-General. This letter, dated 25 August 1777, states:

> This spring when Governor-General Li was transferred to the post of Governor-General of Yunnan and Guizhou, he advised me that you had taken revenge on the bandits who killed the former ruler of Siam. As a result, the people promoted you, and because there were no descendants of the Zhao (Chao) family line, you managed the affairs of the country. You have inclined in heart towards the Heavenly Court, and repeatedly demonstrated your loyalty. It is thus appropriate that you be rewarded and encouraged. In future if you have further requests, we will consider them in accordance with the situation. Since I took up this post, I have dealt with all matters in accordance with previous precedents. Your request to offer tribute can now be approved. When your tribute goods arrive in Chinese territory, your memorial will be forwarded to the Court. As to your statement that you need to borrow the Court's majesty in order to accord with the people's hopes, it appears that you are seeking enfeoffment, but dare not express this openly. I cannot really forward such an ambiguous statement to the Court. If you sincerely prepare the tribute, send an envoy to respectfully present it, clearly detail how the people of the country have earnestly promoted you and how there are no descendants of the Chao line, and submit a request for enfeoffment, I will transmit your memorial to the Emperor. Only after you respectfully receive the Emperor's grace, will your legitimacy as king be confirmed.[31]

There is little doubt that shortly after Taksin received this positive response from China, he began preparing a large-scale mission with the object of establishing formal diplomatic relations with China. In May 1781, a large Siamese diplomatic mission comprising 11 vessels and headed by Phraya Sundhon Aphai was despatched to China.[32] The fleet which was fully loaded with a cargo of elephant tusks, sapan wood, ebony, red-wood, rhinoceros horns and garcinia etc. arrived in Guangdong between June and July, at the same time as Ba Yansan (巴延三) replaced Gui Lin as the Governor-General of Guangdong and Guangxi. According to the memorial of Ba Yansan and Li Hu (李湖), prior to the arrival of the Siamese mission in Guangdong, two Siamese tribute vessels had already reached Nanhai County (南海縣), Guangdong in June, and they carried with them two official letters intended for the Governor-General from Taksin. In one of the letters, Taksin informed the Governor-General that he was sending envoys to present elephants and various other local products of Siam in tribute, and he requested the provincial authorities to report to the emperor the impending arrival of the tribute mission. At the end of this letter, however, Taksin also requested the Guangdong government to issue trading licences to Siamese junks allowing them to trade to Xiamen (厦門 Amoy) and Ningbo (寧波), and sought the assistance of the Governor-General to secure for the Siamese merchants a Chinese pilot to guide the Siamese junks to Japan. Because the kingdom of Siam had just been consolidated, Taksin added, the royal treasury was empty, and the Siamese government had no money for the construction of Thonburi city, the new capital. It only had the local products of Siam to trade, and therefore, he wished to send Siamese junks to trade with the merchants in Fujian and Zhejiang (浙江), as well as those in Japan. Aside from the requests set forth in the above letter, Taksin, in the other letter, sought from the Qing court permission to present "supplementary tribute" (貢外之貢) and purchase some copper items such as copper plate and copper stoves.[33] In February 1782, under the escort of Guangdong provincial officials, the Siamese mission arrived in Beijing. However, the envoy Phraya Sundhon Aphai died of illness on his way to Beijing, and a funeral was arranged by the host government in accordance with the Qing court rites.[34] After presenting the credentials of Siam to the Qianlong emperor, the mission received a warm welcome and enjoyed state banquets for several days at the Shangao Shuichang (山高水長) Hall.[35] In July 1782, the Siamese mission headed by deputy envoy, Luang Phijaya Saneha, set out to return to Thonburi with the imperial gifts. However, they were to arrive too late for Taksin to see with his own eyes that which he had sought for more than 14 years. In early April 1782, King Taksin, was deposed and executed, and naturally, the story of relations between Siam and China during the Taksin period came to an end.

Factors related to Taksin's China-oriented foreign policy

During his reign in Thonburi, Taksin sent seven missions to China seeking recognition from the Qing court. Why did Taksin plan and pursue such a China-oriented foreign policy? Can it be said that Siam under Taksin's rule really wanted to be one of the vassal states of the Qing court? There is now enough evidence to suggest that diverse factors led to the China-oriented foreign policy adopted by Taksin. Factors of particular importance to Taksin's China-oriented mentality included, in my opinion, his family background and the relationships within which he was brought up and engaged in his enterprise. According to the

Chinese sources, Taksin's ancestors migrated to Chaozhou (Teochew) from Putian (莆田), Fujian province, during the Song Dynasty, and his father was an impoverished farmer who lived in Huafu Village (華富村), Chenghai County (澄海縣), and probably migrated to Ayutthaya with other fellow-countymen who were engaged in the flourishing rice trade between Siam and China during the 1720s.[36] The overseas Chinese who sojourned or settled in Siam were mostly Teochews and Hokkiens, both of whom belong to the Southern Fujian dialect group. Because Taksin's father belonged to this group, it was these people who gave energetic support to him during his attempts to gain and consolidate power in Siam. According to Kromphra' Damrong Ratchanuphap, when Taksin withdrew from Ayutthaya in January 1767 with more than 500 soldiers, many of his followers were Chinese. In addition, the direction in which Taksin and his troops fled may have been influenced by their ethnic background, as pointed out by B.J. Terwiel.[37] Rather than moving north or eastward, they fled in a southeasterly direction, towards the region of Chanthaburi where there was a leading entrepôt due to its strategic position, good commercial facilities and closer links to China. It was also a traditional place of settlement of Chinese in Siam. This was one of the major factors that led Taksin to move towards Chanthaburi, as he hoped to obtain the necessary assistance from the Chinese there, both in terms of finances and manpower. The Chinese merchants in Ayutthaya and Chanthaburi in fact provided a great amount of the funds, foodstuffs, goods, and even the fleets needed for the warfare that enabled Taksin to take control of Siam. Undoubtedly, Taksin's foreign policy was influenced to a certain degree by those ethnic Chinese officials and merchants around him, for most of them had diverse ties with China, and they often sought assistance from their homeland when facing desperate situations. In turn, Taksin's pro-China policies and the favour he showed to Chinese of his own speech group doubtless attracted many more Chinese to Siam.

Another element which should not be overlooked is the fact that, after setting up the new regime in Thonburi, Taksin faced a strong challenge from several regional leaders or governors who regarded his accession to the throne as illegitimate. For fear of losing the throne to his rivals, and in order to ensure his newly established bureaucracy as well as his own authority, King Taksin was extremely anxious to obtain Chinese recognition, even though such recognition rarely had any effect on succession to the throne.

We must also take into consideration the military and political situations in the Indochinese peninsula at that time. Burma, during the reign of King Alaungpaya, was at the height of power and splendor, and the Burmese were extending their realm by expanding into Siamese and Laotian territories, and even the border area between Burma and China. This situation, however, inevitably led to the Burmese becoming a common enemy of both countries. That is to say, it was at war with Siam in the south and involved in conflict with the Chinese in the north. This eventually resulted in Siam and China assisting each other against the Burmese forces. It is reasonable to assume that Taksin thoroughly understood the situation in the peninsula, and was fairly confident that because of this situation, the Chinese government would sooner or later recognize his Siamese regime. It is thus that he repeatedly sent Burmese captives to Guangzhou to demonstrate his stand and to earnestly request Chinese assistance.

A more important element, nevertheless, was the economic factor. With the object of winning the war with the Burmese and consolidating Siam, Taksin desired to trade the local products of Siam and Southeast Asia for the strategic materials produced in China and urgently needed in Siam, such as saltpetre, iron and copper. However, under the tribute system of the Qing empire, any foreign country which wanted to trade with China had to present its tribute through the traditional tribute trade channel. Taksin, of course, knew this well, and that is why he formulated his China-oriented foreign policy and despatched Chinese merchants or envoys to Guangzhou time and again to seek resumption of the previous tribute–trade relations. It is however, misleading and unrealistic to believe that Taksin really wanted Siam to be a vassal state of the Chinese empire. What Taksin wanted and was actually interested in was the revenue derived predominantly, if not exclusively, from the tribute trade with China, and the capacity to obtain large quantities of construction materials for building the new capital in Thonburi. Aside from this, Taksin hoped that with the help of the Chinese government, as well as the trade networks of Chinese merchants in southeastern China, the Siamese junks would be able to sail as far as the ports in Fujian and Zhejiang, and even to the ports of Japan, thereby extending the Siamese long-distance maritime trade to Northeast Asia. It is obvious that Taksin was quite familiar with the mentalities of the Chinese government and the emperor, and his efforts to bring his regime within the Chinese tribute system were aimed at securing profits which would help to provide the financial security essential for his political security. In other words, the Chinese recognition requested by Taksin was only a political formality confirming his existing position as a reigning king and a prerequisite for economic privileges. As it happened, what Taksin emphasized in his later requests was not the conferral of the title of king, but recognition and permission to engage in tribute trade. This may explain why he showed little interest when the Qing court decided to confer on him the title of "King" in 1777,[38] for he had already secured his throne, and no longer needed the power and influence of China to consolidate his position.

Last but not least, it should be recognized that the historical relations between Siam and China had been very close since the thirteenth century. During the Ayutthaya period, the Siamese government despatched missions frequently to China, thereby becoming one of the intimate contacts of China in Southeast Asia. Having such a solid foundation laid by the Ayutthaya court, Taksin, who was quite familiar with the advantages of tribute trade, naturally sought to continue such relations with China.

Concluding remarks

With the goals of consolidating his new regime in Thonburi, and of developing the economy of Siam, Taksin spent more than 14 years and endured much humiliation in seeking recognition from China and permission to participate in the Chinese tribute trade. However, the development of the relations between Siam and China during this period was influenced by two aspects of antagonistic contention in the Indochinese peninsula. One aspect which connected Siam and China together through common interests was the wars between Siam and Burma and between China and Burma. This was undoubtedly a major factor in Siam–Chinese relations over this period. The other element was the conflict between Taksin and Mo Shilin, with both persons obviously scrambling for supremacy in Siam. Nevertheless, with the increase in China's understanding of Taksin and Mo Shilin as well as Taksin's conquest of the Mo polity in Ha-tien, this element disappeared as a factor influencing the relationship between Siam and China. What is particularly important is that Taksin defeated the Burmese and established his supremacy in Siam without any assistance from the Chinese. Only after seeing what had happened in Siam, did the Chinese government change its diplomatic policy towards the Siamese court in Thonburi. In short, Taksin paid a high price for his efforts to establish official relations with China. Although he did not receive the formal recognition from China before his death, he provided a strong base for the establishment of diplomatic relations between the subsequent Bangkok dynasty and China.

Notes

1 William G. Skinner, *Chinese Society in Thailand: An Analytical History*, Ithaca and New York: Cornell University Press, 1957, pp. 20, 387–388; Rong Syamananda, *A History of Thailand*, Bangkok: Chulalongkorn University Press, 1973, p. 93.
2 W.A.R. Wood, *A History of Siam*, Bangkok: The Siam Barnakich Press, 1933, p. 248.
3 M. Turpin, *History of the Kingdom of Siam*, Translated by B.O. Cartwright (Bangkok: American Presbyterian Mission Press, 1908), pp. 167–179; Ronald Bishop Smith, *Siam or the History of the Thais from 1569 A.D. to 1824 A.D.* (Bethesda, Maryland: Decatur Press, 1967), p. 102.
4 David K. Wyatt, *Thailand, A Short History* (Yale University Press, New Haven, 1982), pp. 140–141.
5 "Memorial of the Governor-General Li Shiyao", *Shiliao xunkan* (史料旬刊 Historical materials, published every ten days), National Palace Museum, Beijing, 1930–31, No. 30, pp. 104b–107a.
6 *Qianlong chao donghualu* (乾隆朝東華錄 Imperial records from the Dong-hua Hall, Qianlong reign. Hereafter *QLCDHL*), 1911, Beijing, juan 68.
7 *Da Qing gaozong chunhuangdi shilu* (大清高宗純皇帝實錄 Veritable records of the Qianlong Emperor. Hereafter *DQGZCHDSL*), Beijing reprint, 1986. Juan 817.
8 Chen Chingho, "Hexianzhen Yezhen Moshi Jiapu Zhushi" (陳荊和:"河仙鎮鄚鎮鄚氏家譜注釋 Notes on the Genealogy of the Mac Family in the Towns of Hà Tiên and Ye), *Wenshizhe xuebao* (文史哲學報 Journal of Literature, History and Philosophy), Taipei: Taiwan University, Vol. 7, pp. 100–101.
9 *DQGZCHDSL*, juan 752.
10 *DQGZCHDSL*, juan 783.
11 "Despatch of the Board of Rites", *Ming-Qing Shi-liao: Geng-bian* (明清史料：庚編 Historical materials of the Ming and Qing Periods: Series G. Hereafter *MQSLGB*), Taipei, 1960, Book VI, 538; "Li Shiyao's memorial", Gongzhong dang Qianlong chao zouzhe (宮中檔乾隆朝奏摺 Secret palace memorials of the Qian-long reign.

Hereafter *GZDQLCZZ*), National Palace Museum, Taipei, 1983, juan 27, pp. 691–692; juan 31, pp. 470–471.
12 *DQGZCHDSL*, juan 814.
13 *GZDQLCZZ*, juan 32, juan 361–362; *DQGZCHDSL*, juan 820.
14 *DQGZCHDSL*, juan 837.
15 *DQGZCHDSL*, juan 891.
16 *DQGZCHDSL*, juan 838; *QLCDHL*, juan 70.
17 *QLCDHL*, juan 72.
18 Chen Chingho, "Hexianzhen yezhen moshi jiapu zhushi", Ibid, pp. 104–105.
19 *DQGZCHDSL*, juan 864.
20 *QLCDHL*, juan 74.
21 *DQGZCHDSL*, juan 891.
22 *DQGZCHDSL*, juan 895.
23 *MQSLGB*, Book VI.539.
24 *DQGZCHDSL*, juan 990.
25 *DQGZCHDSL*, juan 1022.
26 Qinchuan jushi (琴川居士) compil. "The memorial of Li Shiyao", in *Huangqing zouyi* (皇清奏議 Memorials of the Qing Dynasty), Taipei,1967, juan 62, pp. 25–30.
27 *QLCDHL*, juan 76.
28 *QLCDHL*, Vol. 84.
29 Probably due to a misunderstanding of the Qing archives, Dr Sarasin Viraphol in his *Tribute and Profit: Sino-Siamese Trade, 1652–1852*, which was published in 1977, made some mistakes. On p. 313, note 14, for example, he mistakes Chen Junqing and Liang Shangxuan as the heads of an embassy in 1772 sent by Taksin, as well as erroneously considering Yang Jingsu to be a Chinese merchant who led Taksin's embassy to China in 1777.
30 *DQGZCHDSL*, Vol. 1036.
31 *DQGZCHDSL*, juan 1037.
32 It is not clear why Dr Sarasin Viraphol in his book (pp. 145–152) notes the sending of this large mission and the deposing of Taksin as occurring one year earlier.
33 "The memorial of Ba Yan-an and Li Hu on 27 July 1781", Junjichu lufu zouzhe, Waijiaolei; Taiguo (軍機處錄副奏摺，外交類：泰國 Copies of memorials during the Qing period kept in the Council of State, Diplomatic documents: Thailand. Unpublished). Beijing, First Historical Archives.
34 *DQGZCHDSL*, juan 1152; *GZDQLCZZ*, juan 50, p. 283.
35 *MQSLGB*, Book VI, p. 540; Qingchao Wenxian Tongkao (清朝文獻通考 Encyclopaedia of the historical records of the Qing dynasty), Shanghai, 1936, juan 297.
36 Si-shi-er-mei-ju-shi, Zheng Zhao Zhuan (四十二梅居士："鄭昭傳" Biography of Chao Taksin), *Shan Hu Fortnightly* (珊瑚半月刊), Vol. 3, No. 2, August, 1939; Zheng Changshi, Hanjiang jianwenlu (鄭昌時：《韓江見聞錄》[Things seen and heard in the Hanjiang area], 1824.
37 B.J. Terwiel, *A History of Modern Thailand, 1767–1942* (Brisbane: University of Queensland Press, 1983), pp. 38, 66.
38 *DQGZCHDSL*, juan 1065.

8 Upland peoples and the 1729 Qing annexation of the Tai polity of Sipsong Panna, Yunnan
Disintegration from the periphery[1]

Christian Daniels

From the thirteenth to twentieth centuries many Tai (Dai) polities flourished and declined in the vast poly-ethnic region that extends from Assam (India), to Southern Yunnan, and across the Shan States of Myanmar (Burma), the northern parts of Thailand and Laos to Lai Châu in Vietnam. The Japanese linguist Shintani Tadahiko 新谷忠彦 tried to capture the strains of linguistic and cultural coherence that ran through this ethnically diverse region by naming it the Tai (Dai) Cultural Area (TCA).[2] Shintani's concept is founded on the predominant position of the Tai language and culture in this region, and it emphasised the gentle unifying force exerted by Tai polities. This concept allows us to straddle present-day national boundaries, and interpret these polities as sharing similar political and social characteristics that moulded the area into a loosely-connected whole. If we accept Tai polities as sharing common characteristics and traits, then historical events in the TCA can be understood as inter-linked, rather than as a motley collection of sporadic unrelated happenings. Recent studies that transcend national borders have stressed the vibrant interaction between Tai polities, as well as the contribution by large polities such as Lanna to the formation of modern nation-states like Thailand.[3]

The seventeenth and eighteenth centuries marked a period of reorganisation for Tai polities. This era followed the watershed of the sixteenth century when the large Tai polities, which had flourished since the thirteenth and fourteenth centuries, fell under the sway of the Burmese court, and when the Ming court eliminated the last vestiges of the older large Mon-Khmer polities in southwestern Yunnan, which probably predated the rise of Tai polities.[4] For their rulers, adjustment to the realities of Burmese domination and increasing interference from the newly-founded Qing dynasty became major issues during the seventeenth and eighteenth centuries. The in-migration of Han males into the peripheral parts of Tai polities during the eighteenth and nineteenth centuries further complicated matters by swelling upland populations, which increased pressure on land and food resources.[5] The revolt analysed in this chapter erupted in 1727 in the uplands of the Sipsong Panna polity in southern Yunnan. During the same century Han migrants flocked into Western Hunan and ensuing resistance from indigenous Miao brought military conflict with the Qing in 1703, 1728–1730 and 1797–1800.[6] The revolt by upland peoples in Sipsong Panna was therefore by no means unique, but rather a common response by peoples to changed political, social and economic conditions at the peripheries of areas under direct administration by the Qing in southwest China and mainland Southeast Asia.

During the reign of the Yongzheng emperor (1723–1735) the Qing court tightened up on what it perceived as misbehaviour by Native Officials and Native Administrators. This shift in policy emerged while Gao Qizhuo 高其倬, a bordered yellow banner man, served as Governor-general of Yunnan and Guizhou between 1722 and 1725, and reached its apex with his successor the aggressive administrator E' ertai 鄂爾泰 (1680–1745), a bordered blue Manchu banner man. Enjoying the full confidence and deep trust of the emperor, he was originally sent to the southwest to pacify a Miao rebellion in Guizhou,[7] and it was his appointment to the post of Governor-general of Yunnan and Guizhou sometime between 25 October and 23 November 1726 (tenth month Yongzheng 4) that heralded the beginning of tougher treatment for Tai rulers and other non-Han leaders who could not measure up to standards set down by the Qing court. E'ertai took punitive action against recalcitrant Tai rulers in southern Yunnan, and even incorporated some of their polities into regular administrative units under direct Qing rule. These notorious measures are known under the rubric *gaitu guiliu* 改土歸流, a term literally meaning abolishing Native Officials and placing their domains under direct administration by regular imperial official bureaucrats, known as circulating officials (*liuguan* 流官). The Ming dynasty employed similar measures for eliminating Native Officials, and the Yongzheng emperor's endorsement of *gaitu guiliu* policies merely continued the centuries-old process of extending direct administration to non-Han political regimes. The Yongzheng emperor did not specifically target Tai rulers for disempowerment; he implemented *gaitu guiliu* measures widely over an assortment of ethnic groups. Many Native Officials and Native Administrators resisted with force in protest against what they regarded as unreasonable violations of their sovereignty, and E'ertai often had to resort to military action.[8]

Gaitu guiliu measures had grave consequences for non-Han polities. Sometimes they resulted in the dismantlement of large polities, and/or their reorganisation into smaller polities, but they did not necessarily lead to full incorporation into the Chinese state. For instance, after the elimination of the belligerent polity of Mäng² Maaw² (Kausambi) in 1454 by the so-called "three expeditions against Luchuan 三征麓川", the Ming court recognised the impracticality of establishing regular administrative control, and split Mäng² Maaw² territory into smaller polities, appointing pro-Ming Tai rulers to administer as Native Officials.[9] During the 1720s, when the Qing began to assert tighter bureaucratic control over Southern Yunnan, it replaced some smaller Tai polities with regular imperial officials. Even the large polity of Sipsong Panna did not get off unscathed, although it had hitherto remained relatively free from serious interference by the Chinese state. In 1729, E'ertai annexed a part of its territory with the intention of transferring it to control by imperial bureaucrats. Sipsong Panna had been a vassal of both the Burmese and the Chinese courts since the sixteenth century, and this action by E'ertai ended up orientating it more strongly than ever towards China. As I shall show, the annexation did not succeed, and Tai rulers continued to administer most of the annexed territory, but it was significant as it launched the polity on the path towards full absorption into the Chinese state, a long journey that did not end until the 1950s.

Why did the Qing annex a part of the Sipsong Panna polity? Was it solely due to misgovernment of the uplands as claimed by E'ertai, or was it due to internal factors in the polity as well? In this chapter, I will use memorials written by contemporary Qing administrators who reported in detail on local conditions. By clarifying the reasons that led to the annexation of 1729, I hope to throw some light on broader issues, especially the role played by upland ethnic groups within Tai polities and the common historical process of the incorporation of Tai polities into nation states during the twentieth century. As shall become evident in due course, it was violence by upland ethnic groups that precipitated the annexation of Sipsong Panna. In the past, ethnologists have emphasised the dichotomy between lowland and upland ethnic groups in Tai polities, while historians have focused on the dominant lowland Tai ethnic group. This article aims to draw attention to the importance of upland peoples to Tai polities, and demonstrate how unrest in the uplands could lead to the downfall of polities.

Tai polities and the Chinese state

Tai political organisation is renowned for its hierarchical structure with a major division between royalty/aristocrats (lords) and commoners (subjects). At the apex of aristocratic society stood the *caw phā* (*caw fā*) or supreme lord, who presided over the entire polity as paramount leader. Polities usually consisted of multiple political units known as *mäng* (*muang*), or principalities, each of which was administered by a hereditary prince called *caw mäng*, who owed feudatory allegiance to the paramount leader. Hereditary princes levied corvée labour and taxes on the populace within their domains, and also requisitioned males for military service in times of war. Paramount leaders, who simultaneously maintained their own *mäng*, governed the entire polity through the constituent hereditary princes (*caw mäng*) and a body of bureaucrats with clearly defined responsibilities. So, in effect, the Sipsong Panna polity amounted to the sum total of *mäng* principalities owing feudatory allegiance to its paramount leader.

Tai polities were poly-ethnic states that included Mon-Khmer, Tibeto-Burman, Yao/Miao and Karenic-speaking ethnic groups. The Tai mainly lived in the basins, while the others dwelt on the surrounding hills. The basic social relationship between lord and subject overrode ethnicity. Katō Kumiko 加藤久美子 has demonstrated the varying degrees of bondage in the lord/subject relationships among the Tai Lü (Lue) of the Sipsong Panna polity during the first half of the twentieth century. She classified lowland commoners into two main groups, the Tai Mäng ([free] people of the *mäng*) and the Kun Hän Caw (people of the Prince's House), and showed how the hereditary princes (*caw mäng*) utilised the latter, who were more subordinate to them than the relatively independent and autonomous former group, to clear wasteland and cultivate their own personal estates on the lowlands.[10] Rulers organised upland ethnic groups into administrative units named *khwën*.[11] For them, political assimilation, especially the absorption of subjects into their corvée labour-based *mäng* principalities, was a more pressing issue than cultural assimilation.

The economic foundation of each *mäng* principality rested on wet rice agriculture within the basins. Though Tai rulers claimed sovereignty over and administered all ethnic groups within their domains, regardless of whether they resided in the basins or on the hills, they extracted most of their revenue and manpower needs from Tai wet rice agriculturalists because lowland societies produced greater surpluses than did upland ones. This is not to say that rulers ignored non-Tai upland peoples. Quite to the contrary, they often relied on upland products as commodities in long-distance trade, and, as we shall see, some upland groups displayed strong ties of allegiance to Tai rulers. In many parts of the TCA, rulers probably actively engaged in the caravan trade of local products, such as salt, minerals and forest products, in order to augment their personal wealth.[12]

In the new political environment of the seventeenth and eighteenth centuries, both the Burmese and Chinese courts strove to intensify their authority over Tai polities. One major difference between Burmese and Chinese policies lay in their systems of control. After the Burmese conquest of the Shan Plateau, northern Thailand and northern Laos during the later half of the sixteenth century, most of the Tai rulers in the TCA became vassals of the Burmese throne, and in many cases this tributary relationship persisted until the nineteenth century. Although Burmese courts sent governors (*myowun*) to oversee Tai rulers and stationed troops in the occupied areas, generally they did not attempt to abolish and completely integrate Tai polities into the Burman state as regular administrative units. The Qing state, however, exhibited an entirely different attitude.

This historical process is related to the broader issue of how non-Han areas became part of China. As more Han people migrated overland towards Southeast Asia, the imperial state gradually extended bureaucratic administration over areas on the autonomous southern periphery until the final fixture of international borders by the People's Republic of China. Recent research has focused on clarifying the assimilation of indigenous communities. Studies of the Song and Qing periods differentiate between the actions of the migrants and the state,[13] and scholars have demonstrated that the two did not always work in unison due to a conflict of interest between them. Stevan Harrell has advanced the idea of civilising projects to explain how Confucianism and Christianity subordinated peripheral peoples.[14] Kikuchi Hideaki 菊地秀明 has identified the adoption of five Han institutions that promoted the assimilation of the Zhuang 壯族 in Guangxi 廣西 from the sixteenth century. These included: (1) the establishment of Guangdong 廣東-style lineage organisations; (2) the construction of ancestral shrines (*citing* 祠堂); (3) the introduction of Han burial customs; (4) the use of the examination system to gain entrance to the ranks of the Han elite; and (5) the adoption of Han-style economic activities and strategies.[15] This scholarship emphasises the diversity in the ways and means by which the Qing state incorporated indigenous peoples into regular administration.

The political organisation of non-Han ethnic groups distributed from Southwest China through to the TCA varied greatly. Groups like the Yao 瑤 and Miao 苗 generally had no leaders, though communities did elect competent men to mediate affairs according to their own autonomous rules and regulations. Sometimes, especially in times of crisis, villages leagued together to form alliances and acted in accordance with consensual contracts made at conferences.[16] Since the position of mediators was not hereditary, their authority remained limited, and never constituted a stable unified political force. This situation stood in sharp contrast to that of Tai and Yi (Luoluo 猓玀) ethnic groups whose hierarchical societies had strong social and political structures. The hereditary leaders who headed Tai polities exercised coercive power through a lord–subject relationship, and this aspect distinguished them from the consensual politics of Yao and Miao groups in which elected mediators wielded no effective authority. Chinese and Burmese dynasties found it convenient to negotiate with Tai polities in the TCA because they were well organised as political systems, and their rulers possessed the right to rule their own subjects.[17]

In order to maintain political stability on its southwestern periphery the Qing state adhered to the Yuan and Ming practices of utilising indigenous regimes as local administrative organs. It achieved this end by awarding designations to indigenous leaders who recognised the Chinese emperor as their overlord. These official titles carried a rank, and recipients were called Native Officials (*tuguan* 土官) and Native Administrators (*tusi* 土司) depending on whether they came under the jurisdiction of the Board of Rites (*Libu* 禮部) or the Board of War (*Bingbu* 兵部); such appointments bore great significance for the Chinese state because they affirmed the subordination of indigenous leaders within the imperial administrative hierarchy. The actual scope of power commanded by indigenous leaders varied in size from confederations of *mäng* principalities, as was the case with the Tai, to headmen of a single village, a more common situation for upland swidden agriculturalists. The ranks of titles conferred generally accorded with the strength and importance of leaders and their regimes.

From the viewpoint of Tai rulers these titles acknowledged their positions as sovereigns. The emperor appointed them to exercise authority over their own polities, and issued Native Officials and Native Administrations with letters patent, credentials and seals as proof of appointment. In return for ritual subordination, the court expected them to present tribute at prescribed times, and to assist the imperial army in times of need. Otherwise, they retained the freedom to rule their own subjects according to past custom. However, failure to comply with rules, regulations and prescribed codes of behaviour laid down by the court could lead to elimination, and even full incorporation into the regular Chinese administrative system. The abolition of Native Officials and Native Administrators therefore, to a large extent depended on how strictly the court wished to enforce its rules and regulations.

Sipsong Panna during the 1720s and 1730s

Sipsong Panna remained relatively free from outside interference prior to the Burmese conquest of 1563. As mentioned earlier, the polity comprised a confederation of *mäng* principalities, each with their own hereditary prince (*caw mäng*). The principality of Ceng Hung seems to have retained its position as the foremost *mäng* throughout the entire history of the Sipsong Panna polity, and Tai chronicles traced its foundation to the late twelfth century. The hereditary prince of this principality, who simultaneously served as the paramount leader of the whole polity, was known by a number of titles, which included the terms *caw phā, caw phën tin* (Lord of the Territory) and so forth. The Ming and Qing courts conferred the rank of Cheli Xuanweishi (車里宣慰使 The Cheli Pacification Commissioner) on him. Katō Kumiko, who made full use of Tai sources in her study, has identified the 1720s and 1730s as a turning point in the history of the Sipsong Panna polity, and as the period when Chinese influence began to supersede that of the Burmese.[18]

According to Katō, prior to the 1720s the Burmese exerted stronger influence on the internal organisation of the polity than the Chinese. As evidence she pointed out that Sipsong Panna (meaning 12 *panna*) as a name for the whole polity, first appeared in Tai sources after the Burmese conquest of 1563. She wrote that the Tai instituted the 12 *panna* as units to collect tribute for delivery to the Burmese King when a Burmese princess betrothed to the paramount leader Caw Ing Mäng (reigned *c*.1569–1598) returned to visit her father. Grabowsky demonstrated on the basis of empirical evidence that the term *panna* was the basic administrative unit between *mäng (muang)* and village (*ban*) level in the Lan Na polity.[19] It was a unit originally associated with wet rice cultivation, and was used for the recruitment of manpower for public projects and military service from the thirteenth century onwards, and may even date back to the eleventh century in the principality of Phayao. This administrative unit was introduced from Lan Na to Sipsong Panna Polity centuries before the re-organisation into 12 *panna* in 1570,[20] so it cannot be cited as evidence for Burmese influence on the internal organisation of the polity. Six of the *panna* were located on the east bank of the Mekong River, while the other six lay on the west bank after 1570, and the Burmese king ratified the authority of the paramount ruler in 1583.

Katō also drew attention to the depopulation of Sipsong Panna by the Burmese court as chastisement for their dispatching an army to aid the neighbouring Tai polity of Khemarattha (Tay: Ceng Tung or Kengtung) which was at war with Burma in 1616. The Burmese expelled the paramount leader of Sipsong Panna, and the hereditary prince of the influential Mäng Cë principality to Ava, and deported most of the lowland populace on the west bank of the Mekong to Ava with them as well. This left the west bank desolated, and apparently the area still remained under-populated in 1728. In short, before the 1720s, Burma loomed larger than China as a real threat to the sovereignty of Sipsong Panna.

During the 1720s the situation altered. In 1729 E'ertai annexed the six *panna* east of the Mekong belonging to Sipsong Panna and placed them under the jurisdiction of Pu'er Prefecture 普洱府. These six *panna* included Mäng La (Simao 思茅), Mäng Hin (Puteng 普藤), Ceng Tung (Zhengdong 整董), Mäng U (Mäng Wu 猛烏), Six Great Tea Mountains 六大茶山 and Mäng Ham (Ganlan Ba 橄欖壩). Hasegawa Kiyoshi 長谷川清, who studied this incident earlier than Katō, argued that the annexation signalled the onset of more intensified political intervention by the Qing in the affairs of government in Sipsong Panna. He identified the following measures as indicators of their intent to establish firmer control:[21]

1. The Qing court established regular administrative units to govern Sipsong Panna, its former territories and adjacent areas to its north. The Qing created Pu'er Prefecture in 1729 (Yongzheng 7) and built an earthen-walled city at Simao 思茅 for the Sub-prefectural Magistrate (Tongpan 通判). It placed the five principalities of Mäng Hin (Puteng 普藤), Mäng Bang (Meng Wang 猛旺), Ceng Tung (Zhengdong 整董), Mäng U (Meng Wu 猛烏) and Mäng U Nä (Wude 烏得), all of which formerly belonged to Sipsong Panna, under the jurisdiction of Ning'er county 寧洱縣 when authorities transferred the seat of Pu'er prefecture there in 1735 (Yongzheng 13). In the same year they appointed a Simao Sub-Prefectural Magistrate (Simao Tongzhi 思茅同知) to administer nine *mäng* and the headman of one mountain area. The list included the principalities of Ceng Hung (Cheli 車里), Mäng La Tay (Liushun 六順), Mäng Ban (Yibang 倚邦), I Ngu (Yiwu 易武), Mäng La (Meng La 猛獵), Mäng Cë (Meng Zhe 猛遮), Mäng Ngaat (Meng A 猛阿), Mäng Long (Meng Long 猛籠), Mäng Ham (Ganlan Ba 橄欖壩) and the Headman of Youle (Youle Tumu 攸樂土目).
2. The Qing issued administrative titles to a total of 11 hereditary princes (*caw mäng*) within the polity who owed allegiance to the paramount leader. Qing bureaucrats thus came to exercise authority over individual *mäng* principalities within the polity, whereas previously they only negotiated with the paramount leader.
3. Qing bureaucrats imposed taxes on individual *mäng* principalities. These taxes included the grain tax (*qiuliang mi* 秋糧米), labour service tax commuted into silver (*tiaoding yin* 條丁銀) and a surcharge tax (*huohao yin* 火耗銀). The *Mäng* on the east bank of the Mekong River paid a larger percentage of the total than those on the west bank.

According to Katō, these measures upset the internal balance of power within the polity. She argued that the Qing policy of issuing titles to hereditary princes (*caw mäng*) feudatory subjects of the paramount leader eroded the authority of the paramount leader vis-à-vis the hereditary princes and elevated the position of Mäng Cë, the largest and most powerful *mäng* on the west bank of the Mekong and a potential rival to the paramount leader at Ceng Hung (景洪). Katō empirically demonstrated that the Qing paid Mäng Cë a 16 tael 兩 annuity for assistance rendered in the suppression of the "revolt" of Mäng Ham in 1727, and that they assigned Mäng Cë the highest-ranking administrative title of all *mäng* on the west bank apart from the paramount leader. Katō also surmised that the commutation of taxes to silver was made possible by an increased circulation of silver in Sipsong Panna after the opening of silver mines in neighbouring Mäng Lëm sometime before 1709.[22] Even though control exercised by Qing bureaucrats over the Tai populace remained nominal, particularly on the west bank, these events undoubtedly put the polity and its leaders under closer imperial surveillance. After 1729 external threats from the Qing exacerbated existing rifts among the contending hereditary princes of the polity.

It took the Chinese a long time to establish direct bureaucratic control over the Sipsong Panna polity. They did not succeed in eliminating the paramount leader and the hereditary princes until the first half of the 1950s, and the 1729 *gaitu guiliu* merely marked the first abortive attempt to absorb this polity into China. The second attempt occurred in 1913 when Ke Shuxun 柯樹勳 (1857–1925) set up the Pusi Yanbian Xingzheng Zongju (普思沿邊行政總局 General Administrative Office of the Pu'er and Simao Border), and unsuccessfully tried to directly administer the indigenous population. The reasons Ke Shuxun gave for his failure to abolish the government of the paramount leader (that is the Cheli Pacification Commission) are most illuminating:[23]

1   The Yunnan provincial government lacked sufficient funds to implement regular administration.
2   The rulers of the polity and their subjects simply refused to acknowledge Chinese authority.
3   The paramount leader suggested postponing *gaitu guiliu* and introducing the same system used by the British in neighbouring Cengtung (Kengtung) instead. According to his scheme, Tai rulers would retain control over the internal affairs of their polity, while the Chinese government would handle foreign affairs.
4   The huge cultural gap between the ethnic groups in Sipsong Panna and the Han hindered direct administration by Chinese bureaucrats. Tai concepts of governance differed greatly, and language difficulties obstructed their execution of public affairs. Rulers in Sipsong Panna issued all of their directives and orders in the Tai Lü language and script. Their subjects did not comprehend the Chinese language, and the communication barrier forced Chinese administrators to work through the medium of Tai rulers; their instructions had to be translated into Tai Lü to be understood. Ke Shuxun proposed education (the establishment of schools) and intermarriage as methods for narrowing the gap.

In short, it was the hierarchical nature of Tai society reinforced by strong bonds of allegiance between rulers and their subjects that impeded direct governance by Chinese bureaucrats. The reality of the 1913 situation revealed that the inhabitants of Sipsong Panna had not adopted many Han Chinese norms and ways in the 184 years since 1729. Although the *gaitu guiliu* of 1729, and subsequent events, had serious implications for power politics within Sipsong

Panna, no significant success had been achieved in terms of either political, or cultural, assimilation to Han society in Yunnan by 1913.

The reasons for the annexation

The *gaitu guiliu* of 1729 meant loss of territory for Sipsong Panna. The military might of the Qing made it difficult for the paramount ruler to refuse their demands; he was their vassal, and the Qing had already eliminated two Tai polities to his north in 1725 and 1727. The current of the times was too strong to row against, so he had no alternative but to acquiesce.

For E'ertai, intervention in the affairs of Sipsong Panna derived from a very real concern about unrest on the autonomous periphery. Maintenance of peace and order figured as the major reason for extending firmer bureaucratic control over this polity. In his memorial entitled "Qing she Pu'er Zhen shu (請設普洱鎮疏 Reasons for requesting the establishment of the Pu'er Garrison)", E'ertai explained the annexation of Sipsong Panna territory east of the Mekong in the following terms:

> Originally the twelve *panna* of Cheli and the Tea Mountains all came under the jurisdiction of the Pacification Commission. The native administrator, Dao Jinbao 刀金寶 [Taw Kin Paw, the incumbent Pacification Commissioner], has requested the establishment of imperial bureaucrats because he is unable to contain the reckless and violent behaviour of the barbarians subordinate to him (*shuyi* 屬夷). In reality this will benefit the area. The six *panna* of Mäng La (Simao), Mäng Hin (Puteng), Ceng Tung (Zhengdong), Mäng U (Mäng Wu), Six Great Tea Mountains, and Mäng Ham (Ganlan Ba) should be placed under the administration of regular imperial bureaucrats, while the remaining six *panna* lying outside [west] of the [Mekong] river should still remain under the governance of the Pacification Commission, the boundary clearly demarcated and registers compiled and sent to the Ministry.[24]

> 車茶十二版納、原俱隸宣慰司管轄。該土司刀金寶自以不能兼顧、以致屬夷肆橫，拟請分設流官，實於地方有裨，應將思茅、普藤、整董、猛烏、六大茶山及橄欖壩六版納歸流管轄、其餘江外六版納、仍隸宣慰司經管、劃清界址、造冊達部。

Irrespective of whether the request by the paramount leader of Sipsong Panna was fact or fiction, this statement warrants comment because it demonstrated how E'ertai legitimised his own action. To E'ertai, the ruler of Sipsong Panna had proved unfit to govern his own domain, and therefore, *ipso facto*, the Qing was justified in annexing it. Here, he may have been echoing the opinions of military officials. The Yunnan Provincial Military Commander 雲南提督, Hao Yulin 郝玉麟, who led an expedition to Mäng Ham, remarked in a memorial to the throne dated 28 May 1728 (20/04/Yongzheng 6); "In reality Dao Jinbao [Taw Kin Paw] is unable to attend to administration 刀金寶實在不能兼顧管

理".²⁵ In other words, it was the incompetence of the paramount leader "to contain the reckless and violent behaviour of the barbarians subordinate to him" that lay at the heart of the matter. According to this logic, the need for stability justified the establishment of direct bureaucratic administration if the paramount leader proved inept. The unrest derived from conflict, which initially broke out in the Tea Mountains, and then embroiled Mäng Ham (Ganlan Ba), a powerful *mäng* in the Sipsong Panna confederation.

The 1727 "revolt" of Mäng Ham

The so-called "revolt" started out as a rampage against Han migrants who came to purchase tea in the mountains under the administration of Mäng Ham. A late eighteenth-century source stated that the six Tea Mountains measured "eight hundred li in circumference" and listed their names; Youle 攸樂, Gedeng 革登, Yibang 倚邦, Mangji 莽技, Manduan 蠻嵩 (or Manzhuan 蠻嵩) and Mansa 慢撒.²⁶ Sino-Tibetan-speaking ethnic groups occupied these uplands, and though Tai rulers could not govern them as tightly as the lowlands due to the nature of the terrain, all inhabitants owed fealty to the Sipsong Panna hereditary princes.

The *Dian Yun Linian Zhuan* (滇雲歷年傳 A Chronological Record of [Events] in Yunnan), prefaced by its compiler Ni Tui 倪蛻 in 1737 (Qianlong 2) but not printed until 1826 (Daoguang 46) recorded the origin of the disturbance. It began when a Woni (窩泥 a sub-group of the Hani 哈尼族 under the present PRC ethnic classification) man named Mabupeng 麻布朋 from Mangzhi 莽芝 (probably the same tea mountain as Mangji above) murdered an itinerant Jiangxi merchant who had sexual relations with his wife. Mabupeng cut off the merchant's pigtail and displayed it as a warning to other Han sojourners (Ni 1992, pp. 595–596). This incident must have broken out prior to 26 and 27 May 1727 (06 and 07/04/Yongzheng 5), for the Woni killed at least 37 Han people on these two days.²⁷ Though Taw Kin Paw (Dao Jinbao 刀金寶), the paramount leader who concurrently held office as the Pacification Commissioner between 1724 and 1729, ordered the hereditary prince of Mäng Ham, Dao Zhengyan 刀正彦, to suppress the uprising, his handling of the affair angered E'ertai. According to E'ertai, Dao Zhengyan pleaded on behalf of the Woni offenders, claiming that they rioted because "many of the tea merchants and numerous peddlers lent money to the Woni at exorbitant rates of interest which constantly harmed them 茶商眾客多以重利滾滾砌窩泥". To make matters worse, instead of taking firm steps to stop the violence, Phyā Ku 叭枯 and the other officials despatched by Dao Zhengyan only aggravated the problem by inciting the recalcitrant Woni to burn villages in Mäng Ban (Yibang 倚邦) and block roads. News that the Woni had killed 17 Qing soldiers with crossbows further deepened E'ertai's mistrust in the Tai polity leaders, and so he took the matter into his own hands and dispatched 3,000 troops to pacify the area.²⁸ The Qing army quelled the Woni, and captured Dao Zhengyan in the domain of Mäng Lā (Meng La 猛獵) on 12 April 1728 (04/03 Yongzheng 6) after reaching Mäng Ham in the lowlands beside the Mekong River (*GZDYZ*, 10:174.). Dao was sent to Kunming and executed along with Mabupeng.²⁹

Qing officials asserted that Dao Zhengyan perpetrated the disturbances by the Woni. According to their allegations, he instigated the uprising as a part of a larger premeditated plan to usurp the position of Pacification Commissioner from his nephew Taw Kin Paw.[30] After his execution, angered and confused Tai subjects of Dao Zhengyan took up arms. Together with Theravada monks they burned the house of a Han sojourner in Mäng Ham on the night of 26 August 1728 (21/07/Yongzheng 6). The situation only worsened after Qiu Mingyang 邱名揚, the Assistant Regional Commander of the Puwei Brigade 普威營參將, killed 20 to 30 members of an armed Tai party numbering some several hundred bent on avenging the death of their lord Dao Zhengyan on 29 August (24/07/Yongzheng 6). Qiu beheaded 12 captives and publicly displayed their heads as a warning, but this only caused the unrest to spread to places outside Mäng Ham. On 14 September (11/08/Yongzheng 6), Qing soldiers defeated a contingent of 200 to 300 at I Ngu (Yiwu 易武), and on 21 September (18/08/Yongzheng 6), Qiu Mingyang received word that Tai from Mäng Cë (猛遮) and Mäng Long (猛籠) were approaching along separate routes at the incitement of Dao sympathisers.[31] Later, society was unsettled further when Li Axian 李阿先, a local non-Han leader, burned Qing army barracks sometime between 29 March and 17 April 1729 (third month of Yongzheng 7) in retaliation for bullying by soldiers. Whole villages in Mäng Ham fled south into present-day Laos out of fright.

This train of events forced Hao Yulin 郝玉麟, the Yunnan Provincial Military Commander 雲南提督, to abandon brute force and adopt a pacification policy in order to repopulate the area. He began by restoring confidence in the authority of the paramount leader Taw Kin Paw who had taken refuge in Mäng Cë. Hao recalled Taw back to his throne at Ceng Hung, absolved him of responsibility for the revolt, and lavishly bestowed silver, gowns and hats on him at their meeting on 1 January 1729 (02/12/Yongzheng 6). This ostentatious display of support by the Qing for the paramount leader and his regime proved effective, and between 29 January and 27 February 1729 (first month Yongzheng 7) Hao had already managed to repatriate 8,100 people or 1,600-plus households.[32] In the end, a total of 12,300-plus households, totalling about 20,000 to 30,000 men and women, were returned to their homes. The Yongzheng emperor promoted Hao Yulin to be Governor-general of the Liang Guang 兩廣總督 in appreciation for his skilful handling of the whole affair.[33]

Despite success in the pacification of Mäng Ham, the Qing did not initiate direct administration over the six annexed *panna*. They permitted the paramount leader to continue to govern all 12 *panna* as before on the condition that he paid taxes in silver to officials in Pu'er prefecture.[34] The high casualty rates from an epidemic that raged during the 1728 campaign, and the death of practically all the men later sent to construct a walled city at Mäng Ham from disease must have greatly influenced this decision.[35] Here we see no evidence of plans by the Qing for implementing direct administration, and in reality the so-called annexation of 1729 turned out to be nominal, even though, as Katō Kumiko has shown, it altered the balance of power between hereditary princes.

The endless frontier and intractable uplanders

Now let us turn to the issue of why the Qing chose to meddle in the internal affairs of Sipsong Panna in the first place. In this section I shall argue that unrest by disconcerted upland people, or at least what the Qing court perceived as rebellious behaviour on their part, can be identified as one of the long-term causes for Qing interference in Tai polities. Constant outlaw behaviour for over 50 years prior to the 1720s by non-Han groups, who Chinese sources christened "the outlaws (literally wild bandits) of Lukui Mountain 魯魁山野賊", cannot be overlooked when considering Qing motives. Before proceeding any further let us confirm two facts.

First, the annexation of 1729 did not take place in isolation from contemporary events occurring in adjacent Tai polities lying north of Sipsong Panna. The Qing had recently eliminated the Tai rulers of Weiyuan Native Subprefecture 威遠州土知州 in 1725 (Yongzheng 3) and Zhenyuan Native Prefecture 鎮沅府土知府 in 1727 (Yongzheng 5) because of their collusion with the outlaws of Lukui. The replacement of the Zhenyuan Native Prefectural Magistrate, Dao Han 刀瀚, by an imperial bureaucrat named Liu Hongdu 劉宏度 led to further turmoil. Misgovernment by Liu caused serious dissatisfaction, and precipitated a multi-ethnic uprising by Tai, Hani, Lahu, Yi and Han peoples; the Qing army soon captured and executed the leaders Dao Ruzen 刀如珍, and five others.[36] In the case of Zhenyuan, alignment of upland and lowland peoples in a protest movement against the new administration stood out as a salient feature.

Second, in times of crisis the outlaws of Lukui depended on protection from Tai rulers. For this purpose, they maintained strong ties with the rulers of Tai polities over a large tract of land east of the Mekong river which extended south from Xinping 新平, through Zhenyuan 鎮沅, Jinggu 景谷, and into the Tea Mountains of Sipsong Panna.

The trouble spot, Lukui Mountain, formed a part of the Ailao mountain range, which runs along the borders of Xinping County. Situated at the edge of the Han Chinese world, it constituted an uncertain zone between land under the jurisdiction of imperial bureaucrats and territory governed by non-Han native administrators, and had been a hotbed of agitation since the late sixteenth century. Cai Yurong 蔡毓榮 (?–1699), a Han white banner man (漢軍正白旗人) who served as the Governor-general of Yunnan and Guizhou from 1682 to 1686, drew attention to its strategic position:

> Lukui is located in the middle of the myriad mountains, and overlaps with the borders of Xinping County, Xi'e County, Menghua, Yuanjiang, Jingdong and Chuxiong [Prefectures]. It stretches far and wide, and has deep forests and thick ravines. The bandits can enter the areas of Xinping, Xinhua, Yuanjiang, Yimen, Ejia, Nan'an and Jingdong all of which lie on the inside, and abscond into the areas of Sipsong Panna (Cheli), Pu'er, Cengtung [Kengtung], Zhenyuan, Mäng Mën (Meng Mian 猛緬: Lincang county 臨滄縣), and Vietnam (Jiaozhi 交阯) which lie on the outside. For

this reason, it is very difficult to guard against them, and it is also not easy to suppress them.³⁷

魯魁在萬山之中，跨連新嶍蒙元景楚之界，綿亙廣遠，林深箐密，其內則新平，新化，元江，易門，石十咢嘉，南安，景東一帶地方，賊皆可入，其外則車里，普洱，孟艮，鎮沅，猛緬，交阯一帶地方，賊皆可出。故防之甚難，而剿之亦不易也。

From their lairs at Lukui the outlaws could easily raid the areas under regular imperial administration to the north, east and west of the mountain, and escape into areas controlled by non-Han leaders in the south where imperial bureaucrats could not apprehend them. To the Chinese officials this frontier must have appeared as endless, for outlaws crossed it and simply vanished into thin air, always returning to their old haunts once the storm had abated.

Outlaw utilisation of the periphery to evade elimination by the Chinese state can be documented from the late sixteenth century. In a memorial to the throne dated 20 November 1624 (10/10/Tianqi 4), Min Hongxue 閔洪學, the Grand Coordinator 巡撫 of Yunnan, reported the pacification by the Ming army of the Lukui outlaws who resisted for a whole year between late 1623 to 1624. The disturbances started with a raid on the area around the Baoxiu market 寶秀街 in Shiping Sub-prefecture 石屏州 on 27 November 1623 (06/10 intercalary month/ Tianqi 3) by 600-plus men from Xinping County. In view of its significance for eighteenth century events, I cite it in full:

Xinping County was the former haunt of the Dingju 丁苴 and Baigai 白改 [barbarians].³⁸ Its mountains are deep and obstructive, its barbarians are fierce and rude, and it is their custom to menace and kill for their livelihood. It is as if Heaven has created another world, congenitally outside the pale of civilisation. After the great army succeeded in suppressing them in the 19th year of Wanli [1591], the county seat was established for the first time and [administration] got under way, but they repeatedly rebelled and submitted. A count shows that there have been five military operations over the past thirty years, and this is the sixth one.

When I arrived in Yunnan in January 1623 (twelfth month Tianqi 2), the barbarian stockades in the Xi'e 嶍峨 area suffered from their poison. I sent Lu Chonggong 祿崇功, the Native Official of this county, home from the provincial capital with troops to remedy the situation, but the bandits fled, going within the border of Shiping again. Baoxiu [in Shiping sub-prefecture] requested emergency help, so I ordered Long Zaitian 龍在田, the Native Official of this sub-prefecture, back home from Qujing 曲靖 with troops to rescue them, but they escaped again. Since the bandits could not have their own way in Xi'e 嶍峨 and Shiping, they put up a show of force by stubbornly resisting with vigilant hostility using precipitous mountains as a stronghold. When I heard that Xinping and Xinhua had raised the alarm, I realised that we had no alternative but to smash the bandits as the situation had become volatile. Therefore, I assembled several thousand Han and native (漢土) [troops], summoned the Brigade Commander Li Sizhong 李思忠 and the sub-prefect Cao Yujun 曹育俊, and entrusted them with the task of exterminating the bandits. As soon as the bandits got word that imperial troops were coming, those in Yuanjiang 元江 and Zhele 者樂 crossed the river *en masse*, while others in Xinping and Xinhua hid in the ravines. Our troops caught them off their guard, captured and beheaded 110 of them. At this time, our army had gained some momentum, while the vigour of the bandits had slightly waned. By assessing the advantages, planning for expediency and deploying troops appropriately, we could have defeated the enemy without having to call up reinforcements; punitive action would have compelled the resistors to comply of their own will. But the strategy amounted to nothing more than this, and after by chance achieving a small victory that failed to inflict serious damage on the enemy, our troops withdrew which only caused the trouble to flare up again. This was the fault of Cao Yujun and Li Sizhong.

I assembled more soldiers and horses, and put them under the leadership of the Brigade Commander Liu Chongli 劉崇禮、with the Vice Commissioner Hu Qizao 胡其慥 superintending. I gave them a stratagem for extermination and pacification, and made them pledge the following; they must eradicate the root of the unrest by extermination; they must instil a change of heart in the bandits by pacification; they should strive to bring an end to the main trouble by resolving all causes of discord; never again rely on military action; and should never speak of withdrawing troops [until they achieved success]. They fully comprehended, and the campaign ended within about 100 days.

Although the number of ears cut off from captives did not reach 300, these figures do not include the countless number of bodies of those who hung themselves from trees, lay dead in the gullies and those who drowned in the rivers. Their rambling homeless spirits all have been summoned and placated. Command Posts (*shao* 哨) have been established at each of the strategic villages that they occupied in order to administer them separately, and our defences, like tight fitting dog's teeth, have no interstices. After the thorough handling this time there should be no more trouble for several tens of years to come.[39]

新平縣者、故丁苴、白改巢穴也。其山峩阻、其夷獞玀、其俗以摽殺為生涯。若天生化外、另一世界。自萬曆十九年、大兵剿洗之後開設縣治、始就樊籠、然屢附屢叛。屈指三十年間、用兵者五、至於今而六矣。方臣等天啟二年十二月入境、嶍峩一帶夷寨正被其毒、臣等發該縣土官祿崇功、自省城統兵歸救、而賊遯去、復流入石屏界中。寶秀告急、又發該州土官龍在田、自曲靖統兵歸救、而又遯去。於是不得志於嶍峩石屏、耽耽之虎、負嵎而逞矣。新平、新化並以警來聞、臣等以賊氛炎炎不容不撲、故集漢土數千、檄遊擊李思忠、通判曹育俊、屬以剿處之事。賊聞官兵之來、元江者樂之賊相率渡江。二新之

> 賊各避匿入箐。我兵以其間掩賊不備、所俘斬亦百十人。當是之時、
> 我軍聲稍張、賊勢稍戢。使能度利規便、可兵兵之、不亦招而下之、
> 則有所處分、反側自帖。乃計不出此、俛得小捷を得、不痛不癢。引
> 師輒還、致煩再舉、此亦曹育俊、李思忠之過也。
>
> 及臣等添集士馬、統以遊擊劉崇禮、監以副使胡其愼、授以剿撫
> 方畧、與之約剿必剗根、撫必革心、務一了百了、役不再藉。非是者、
> 兵不得言撤、而道將果一一領畧、凡百之日而竣厥役焉。雖俘馘不滿
> 三百、然投繯於樹者、捐瘠於壑者、葬於江魚之腹者、纍纍藉藉不在
> 此數。其鼠匿之遊魂、又悉招致而安揷之。其盤錯之險郵、又各置哨
> 分轄而犬牙以制之。此番徹底料理之後、或可數十年無事矣。

This long passage is significant on two accounts. First, it demonstrated that even after implementing Chinese administration in the newly founded Xinping county, Ming officials failed to maintain Han style law and order for rebellions occurred once every five years on the average. The Ming dynasty had to set up 12 Command Posts to guard against further incursions.[40] Second, it revealed the prototype pattern of outlaw behaviour that eventually precipitated trouble in Weiyuan, Zhenyuan, and Sipsong Panna. Let us examine the second point in more detail.

After Ming troops pacified Xi'e, the bandits immediately fled to Shiping, and when the troops followed them there, they slipped away to Xinping and Xinhua. The bandits from Xi'e and Shiping crossed the Yuan River, while those from Xinping and Xinhua fled into the wilderness. Ming officials failed to eradicate them for two reasons. First, outlaws always had access to a refuge, and second, once imperial troops withdrew, they were able to immediately return to their old haunts. Below, I show that they used the same stratagem again during the 1720s.

As shown in Table 8.1, outlaw groups in the Lukui mountain area created incessant turmoil between the 1670s and 1720s. The incorporation of the four outlaw leaders Yang Zongzhou 楊宗周, Pu Weishan 普為善, Fang Conghua 方從化 and Li Shangyi 李尚義 (all Yi 彝族 ethnic people) into the Qing administrative system in 1672 (Kangxi 11) was done in response to their pillaging in the previous year; and by issuing official titles the Qing attempted to gain some measure of control over them. These appointments were made a year before Wu Sangui 吳三桂 (1612–1678), the general who had exercised civil and military control over Yunnan since the conquest of 1659, rebelled and declared himself emperor of a new dynasty, the Zhou 周, the first year of which was 1674. All four Yi outlaw leaders retained their titles during the rebel Zhou dynasty and, after it collapsed, the Qing re-issued the titles in 1682. Fan Chengxun 范承勳 (?–1714), who succeeded Cai Yurong as the Governor-general of Yunnan and Guizhou, ratified their positions in the official hierarchy by assigning fresh seals and new titles (see Table 8.1) between 3 January and 1 February 1688 (twelfth month Kangxi 26).

What factors enabled outlaw activities to prevail for over 50 years? Ritual subordination by outlaw leaders in response to shifts in Chinese political authority obviously played an important role. Another factor was their exaction of

Table 8.1 Activities of the outlaws of Lukui Mountain, 1671–1724

Date	Outlaw activities
2 November – 30 November 1671 (Tenth Month Kangxi 10)	Le Ang 勒昂 (also known as Yang Zongzhou 楊宗周) led over 300 men to pillage villages in Nan'an Sub-prefecture 南安州 in Chuxiong prefecture 楚雄府.[1]
After 1672 (Kangxi 11)	Wu Sangui appointed Le Ang 勒昂 (Yang Zongzhou 楊宗周) as commandant (shoubei 守備) and as vice general (fujiang 副將) of Zhongshun Brigade 忠順營 in Xinping 新平 and Xinhua 新化. Wu Sangui also appointed the headmen Pu Weishan 普爲善, Fang Congua 方從化 and Li Shangyi 李尚義 as brigade vice commanders (dusi 都司).[2]
1681 (Kangxi 20)	When Qing forces first entered Yunnan in the second lunar month the outlaws plundered widely, but when they reached Yunnan Prefecture, Yang Zongzhou, Pu Weishan, Fang Conghua and Li Shangyi surrendered and handed over their seals to Qing officials. The Qing dynasty appointed Yang Zongzhou as native vice general (tu fujiang 土副將) of Xinping 新平 and Xinhua 新化 and Pu Weishan and the others as native brigade vice commanders (tu dusi 都司).[3]
1687 (Kangxi 26)	The Governor-general of Yunnan and Guizhou, Fan Chengxun 范承勳, despatched officials to soothe the four leaders of the outlaws. They appointed Yang Zongzhou as native vice magistrate (tu xiancheng 土縣丞) of Xinping county and invested each of the other three, Pu Weishan, Fang Conghua and Li Shangyi with the title native police chief (tu xunjian 土巡檢).[4]
1690 (Kangxi 29) to 1691 (Kangxi 30)	Between 1–30 November 1690 (tenth month Kangxi 29), Li Shangyi assembled several thousand local ethnic people, solicited protection money (suobao 索保) and plundered. He committed suicide somewhere between 29 January –27 February (first lunar month) of the following year, and the hereditary position of the Li family as native police chief of Yangwu ba 陽武垻 in Xinping county was abolished. Thereafter there was direct administration by imperial bureaucrats.[5]
21 November – 20 December 1699 (Tenth lunar month Kangxi 38)	Bandit leader Li Juba 李什壩 and Laosan 老三 of the Woni 倭泥 (Hani) extorted protection money (baojing qian 保境錢) at two villages Zhalong 札籠 and Bangma 邦馬 in Jingdong prefecture 景東府.[6]
8 November 1723 (11/10/ Yongzheng 1)	Fang Jingming 方景明 and Pu Youcai 普有才 gathered people and besieged the prefectural city of Yuanjiang 元江府城 where the Luo 倮 (Yi 彝) leader Shi Heshang 施和尚 against whom they harboured a deep-seated grudge had taken refuge. Unable to defend the city, circumstances forced the vice general (fujiang 副將) Wu Kaiqi 吳開祈 to drive Shi Heshang, his family members and dependents out of the city walls, and some were cruelly murdered while others were taken as captives. Fang Jingming later surrendered to the Qing army, but Pu Youcai escaped.[7]
24 February – 24 March 1724 (Second month Yongzheng 2)	Pu Youcai assembled a group of Luo barbarians 倮夷 and plundered the tea mountains under the jurisdiction of Sipsong Panna. The Qing army captured one concubine and one daughter of Pu Youcai, but failed to apprehend him.[8]

Notes
1 1691 Yunnan Tongzhi (雲南通志) juan 卷 29 Ywen 藝文 3, 36b and Ni Tui 倪蛻, Dian Yun Linian Zhuan 滇雲歷年傳 p. 528.
2 1691 Yunnan Tongzhi, juan 29 Ywen 3: 37a.
3 1691 Yunnan Tongzhi, juan 29 Ywen 3: 37b–38a.
4 1691 Yunnan Tongzhi, juan 29 Ywen 3: 69a–70a and Ni Tui Dian Yun Linian Zhuan, p. 540.
5 Ni Tui, Dian Yun Linian Zhuan, p. 548.
6 Ni Tui, Dian Yun Linian Zhuan, p. 552.
7 Ni Tui, Dian Yun Linian Zhuan, p. 573.
8 GZDYZ, 2: 497–499 and Ni Tui, Dian Yun Linian Zhuan, p. 575.

money from the local populace. Since the Qing state regarded this as a criminal offence, they had to be careful. The annulment of the hereditary native police chief (*tu xunjian* 土巡檢) title of Li Shang 李尚義 in 1691 (Kangxi 30) illustrates how extortion and looting led to punishment (see Table 8.1). Outlaw leaders depended on these activities for their income, so they were not inclined to relinquish them and reconcile themselves to poverty.

During the early 1680s, Cai Yurong 蔡毓榮 (?–1699) described the Lukui outlaws as a menace to the whole of Yunnan. According to Cai, Wu Sangui's issuing of administrative titles (see Table 8.1) in return for annual payments of leather and helmet silver (*pikui yinliang* 皮盔銀兩), in reality sanctioned their imposition of private levies:

> The bandits freely go out to the four quarters, and issue each village with one piece of engraved wood. They collect protection silver (*baotou yin* 保頭銀), which varies in amounts from over ten taels to twenty or thirty taels, and are insatiable in their demands for pigs, sheep, fowls and rice wine. Any slight failure to satisfy them, leads to arbitrary plundering and killing. As a result, destitute and homeless people, along with those in the vicinity of the wild bandits, gladly join their ranks as robbers. For as long as eight years [the bandits] have enlisted even larger numbers of displaced people, and 80% to 90% of the villages and estates in all the prefectures, sub-prefectures, and counties in Yunnan comply with their extortions.[41]

> 縱賊四出，每村給一木刻，派定保頭銀十數兩， 二， 三十兩不等，豬羊雞酒，索取無厭，稍有不遂，劫殺隨之。於是， 流離之民暨相近野賊之民樂於附賊為盜。八年之久，招集亡命愈多，全滇各府州縣村莊聽其索保者十之八，九。

Although no sources corroborate whether the outlaws ever collected imposts from as large a part of Yunnan as Cai claimed, their leaders patently understood that Wu Sangui had granted them license to tax farm the local population. They assumed that the administrative titles issued by the Qing in 1681 sanctioned their continued collection of imposts from people within their spheres of influence. Qing officials portrayed Yi outlaw leaders as rapacious strongmen, defining their imposts as protection money *(baotou qian* 保頭錢), but in reality such appropriations may have constituted the economic foundations of their regimes.

For their own safety the Yi outlaws forged close and intricate relationships with non-Han leaders lying to their south. In a secret memorial to the throne dated 11 May 1724 (19/04 Yongzheng 2), Gao Qizhuo 高其倬, the Governor-general of Yunnan and Guizhou, identified such associations as one of the main reasons for not being able to apprehend them:

> Ailao mountain is encircled on three sides by battalions and posts of each sub-prefecture and county, but the south-western side adjoins the territory of Weiyuan Native Sub-Prefecture, Zhenyuan Native Prefecture and the

Pacification Commission of Cheli [Sipsong Panna]. Weiyuan is therefore a most strategic place, and in times of peace, the bandits enter into marital relations, assume father/sons relationships or swear oaths as brothers with the native administrators, their children and headmen. As soon as trouble breaks out, imperial troops attack the bandits from three sides, but they escape in the direction of the native administrators. The native administrators either hide and conceal them, or allow them to pass without hindrance to places in the miasma ridden lands beyond the border, which makes it difficult for government troops to sally out and arrest them. Governors-general and Grand Coordinators also are prone to be afraid of punishing them out of fear of prolonging the affair; they offer amnesties, exempting them from punishment as a temporary measure, thereby acknowledging the current situation. As a result these fugitives take the opportunity of the amnesties to return to Qing-administered territory (內地) again and harm the people as before. It is precisely because no one has been willing to directly investigate the situation thoroughly in the past that we have been left with a legacy of disaster now.[42]

哀牢一山、各州縣營汛環其三面、其西南一面、則係威遠土州、鎮沅土府及車里宣慰司之地。而威遠尤當衝要。賊人無事之時、與土司及其子弟頭人皆結婚姻、或拜爲父子、或盟爲兄弟、一經有事、官兵三面進攻、賊即從土司一面迯出、土司即行護庇藏匿、或縱出境外煙瘴之地、令官兵難以前往查捕。督撫亦徃徃以曠日持久、恐干处分、姑以免罪招安。且了目前之局、而此輩借此一招復歸內地仍前害民。皆因從前不肯直窮到底、是以貽串至今。

Gao Qizhuo identified topography, intermarriage with Tai aristocracy and amnesties as the three main factors enabling the persistence of illegal activities. Yi outlaw leaders and their followers entered into marital and fictive family relationships with Tai hereditary princes and their officials whose polities lay on the escape routes to lands outside the sphere of Qing influence in present-day northern Burma and northern Laos. Since Tai native officials would not arrest them, Qing bureaucrats were compelled to resort to pardons. In his memorial Gao also reported that during the 1723 disturbances by the outlaws of Lukui, the Weiyuan Native Sub-prefecture, Zhenyuan Native Prefecture and the Pacification Commission of Cheli [the paramount leader of Sipsong Panna] ignored orders to apprehend the fugitives and intentionally allowed them to escape. He also testified that Dao Guanghuan 刀光煥, the Native Sub-prefectural Magistrate of Weiyuan, and the incumbent Tai hereditary prince of Mäng Wo, had sheltered the elusive Pu Youcai 普有才 (see Table 8.1), with whom he maintained a fictive father/son relationship.[43] As punishment, the Qing court exiled Dao Guanghuan to Jiangxi and put his territory under direct administration, renaming it the Weiyuan Independent Sub-prefecture 威遠直隷廳.

It was in this way that the cruel murder of Shi Heshang 施和尚 in 1723 (see Table 8.1), an event which triggered the train of events in the first place, had serious repercussions on Tai polities. The accommodation of Yi outlaws by Tai rulers encouraged the Qing authorities to tighten control over what to them seemed like a sprawling endless frontier. Maintenance of law and order therefore had already turned into a major issue for the administration of Tai affairs before E'ertai began to grapple with disturbances in the Tea Mountains of Sipsong Panna.

Han traders and the money economy

Economic transactions between Han traders and Sino-Tibetan speakers caused discord in the uplands. Han traders in constant search for commodities saleable on regional and empire-wide markets, such as tea and salt, introduced market economy practises that did not resonate with traditional upland lifestyles. Dao Zhengyan, the deposed hereditary prince of Mäng Ham, pointed to usurious money-lending as the prime reason for the outbreak of violence by the Woni on 26 May and 27 May 1727; he reported, "many of the tea merchants and numerous peddlers lent money to the Woni at exorbitant rates of interest 茶商衆客多以重利滾滾砌窩泥".[44] By the 1720s, if not earlier, the purchase and sale of goods and services by Han sojourners had surpassed the level of mere barter, and this incident, which triggered the unrest leading to the annexation of 1729, reflected the amount of tension generated by the money economy.

The massacre of 37 Han, including one woman, by 70 Woni over two days bespoke deep-seated grievances against the Han. E'ertai mentioned the names of 19 victims in a memorial, so it is certain that the Woni personally knew many of them (see Table 8.2). Six came from Yunnan, three hailed from HuGuang (present-day Hunan and Hubei) and two from Jiangxi. The fatalities included one woman, the wife of Xiao Laowu 蕭老五 from HuGuang, which showed that some Han women accompanied their husbands. The murder of a bronzesmith, Li Chongwen 黎崇文, revealed that artisans as well as tea buyers visited the tea-growing uplands. That large numbers of adult Han males from various walks of life traded there during the 1720s can be corroborated by the existence of a territorial god shrine (Tuzhu Miao 土主廟) in Mangzhi 莽芝 (see Table 8.2). The plundering of two horses, 11 loads (duo 馱) of tea and 11 saddles after murdering a muleteer (趕馬的) named Wang 王 from Western Yunnan (Yixi 迤西), reflected Woni dissatisfaction over transaction practises.[45] Resentment against unfair treatment at the hands of Han traders ran so deep that in wreaking their revenge the Woni targeted any Han person they came across.

As a remedial measure, E'ertai set up a General Tea Store (zongchadian 總茶店) at Simao managed by the Sub-prefectural Magistrate (tongpan 通判) in 1729 (Yongzheng 7). Ni Tui 倪蛻 commented:

> It has been long-standing practise for tea produced in the six great mountains to be [purchased] by merchants resident there, who advance [money] and collect [tea leaves] (zuofang shoufa 坐放收發); each merchant sells it at Pu'er where taxes are paid and transhipment takes place. Now that the

Table 8.2 Han migrants massacred by Woni, 26/27 May 1727 (06 and 07/04/sixth Yongzheng 5)

Number murdered	Name of deceased	Native place	Details and place of murder
1	surname: Wang 王	Jiangxi 江西	Probably killed at Mangzhi Small Village 莽芝小寨.
1	surname: Li 李	Jingdong 景東	Probably killed at Mangzhi Small Village.
1	surname: Chen 陳	Shiping 石屏	Probably killed at Mangzhi Small Village.
1	surname: Zhang 張	Yixi 迤西	Unknown
1	Zhao Xianhan 趙先翰	Unknown	He was killed at the front gate to the territorial god shrine (Tuzhu Miao 土主廟).
2	Xiao Laowu 蕭老五 and his wife	HuGuang 湖廣	He was killed on the Xiaoman Brick road 小蠻磚路. His remains were buried.
1	Liu Kezhang 劉客長	Unknown	Unknown
1	Li Erge 李二哥	Unknown	Unknown
1	Feng Dajia 馮大價	Shiping 石屏	Unknown
1	Lao Yan 老閻	Unknown	Unknown
14	Unknown	Unknown	Unknown
1	Li Chongwen 黎崇文	Unknown	He was a bronze smith (銅匠), and was killed while travelling in the Manke 慢棵 area.
1	Yao Hongshu 姚泓樹	HuGuang 湖廣	He was chased to a restaurant (jiufang 酒房) in Meng Lun 猛崙 and murdered.
1	Fan Laoguan 范老官	Unknown	He was chased to a restaurant (jiufang 酒房) in Meng Lun 猛崙 and murdered.
1	Zhang Huguang 張湖廣	Unknown	He was chased to a restaurant (jiufang 酒房) in Meng Lun 猛崙 and murdered.
1	Liu Shaoxian 劉烈光	Dali 大理	He was chased to a restaurant (jiufang 酒房) in Meng Lun 猛崙 and murdered.
2	Unknown	Unknown	They were chased to a restaurant (jiufang 酒房) in Meng Lun 猛崙 and murdered.
1	Yang Feilu 楊飛祿	Jiangxi 江西	Heavily wounded, he hung himself at Small Village 小寨.
1	Su Laosan 穌老三	Unknown	After being wounded, he came to hide in a Small Village 小寨 but died within a few days.
1	Unknown	Unknown	Chased by the outlaws from Manlin 慢林. He died of poison from arrows after arriving at Small Village 小寨.
1	Liu Jiangxi 劉江西	Unknown	Unknown
1	Surname: Wang 王	Yixi 迤西	A muleteer (趕馬的) who was chased to the banks of the Xiyaozi River 細腰子河 and killed there.

Source: National Palace Museum. Ed., *Gongzhongdang Yongzhengchao Zouzhe* (宮中檔雍正朝奏摺 Secret Palace Memorials of the Yongzheng Period: Qing Documents at the National Palace Museum). Taibei: National Palace Museum Press, 1977–1980, 9: 287–288.

merchants have caused trouble by practising usury, the establishment of a General Tea Store to monopolise the economic rights has been discussed. Thereupon the Sub-prefectural Magistrate, Zhu Xiu 朱繡, has proposed expelling all merchants both old and new, and sending back in wooden neck-collars those who stay or re-enter. Tea-producing households have been ordered to transport all of their tea to the General Tea Store 總茶店 where they receive its worth. People are punished for buying and selling it privately, and they find it particularly intolerable if inspections are strict. Also, [previously] since the merchants and the peddlers gave the price first and collected the tea later, so [the tea-producing households] benefitted from the accommodation of the loan. In the trade between the officials and the people, contingencies cannot be met.

Furthermore, some places in the Tea Mountains are situated several tens of *li* from Simao 思茅 while others lie over 1,000 *li* away. People who live close bear the hardships of keeping watch for delivery and collection, their labour service imposts and expenses are extremely numerous, and it is difficult for them to avoid [being cheated by officials who] tamper with the steelyards to get more tea for less money. As a result, they are only paid the price for fifty *jin* out of one hundred *jin* [of tea]. Distant households spend a month coming and going, and only bring small amounts of tea. With the malpractices mentioned above, how are they able to not return empty-handed?

The common people depend solely on tea for their livelihood. They do not regard it as an asset, but as a burden, not to speak of the demands from civil officials to submit tea as imperial tribute, and the coercion from military officials for interest payments [on loans]. They have no alternative but to sever the roots [of the tea trees] and denude the mountains.⁴⁶

六大山茶產、向係商民在彼地坐放收發、各販於普洱上納稅課轉行、由來久矣。至是、以商民盤剝生事、議設總茶店以籠其利權。於是通判朱繡上議、將新舊商民悉行驅逐、逗留復入者俱枷責押回。其茶、令茶戶盡數運至總店、領給價值、私相買賣者罪之。稽查嚴密、民甚難堪。又商販先價後茶、通融得濟。官民交易、緩急不通。且茶山之於思茅、自數十里至千餘里不止。近者且有交收守候之苦、人役使費繁多。輕戥重秤、又所難免。然則百觔之價、得半而止矣。若夫遠戶、經月往來、小貨零星無幾、加以如前弊孔、能不空手而歸。小民生生之計、只有此茶。不以為資、又以為累。何況文官責之以貢茶、武官挾之以生息、則其截其根、赭其山、是亦事之出於莫可如何者也。

Upland ethnic groups detested the government monopoly. Though it liberated them from exploitation by Han traders, at the same time it deprived them of the benefit of short-term loans to tide them over until the harvest. It also imposed new burdens such as the transportation of tea to Simao which, coupled with exactions by local officials, made it unprofitable for them to grow tea any more. They rebelled out of frustration, and their rebellion raged over an area wider than in 1727–1728. It extended from the Tea Mountains in the south to Xinping and Yuanjiang in the north, and it lasted for two years, from roughly 24 May 1732 (fifth intercalary lunar month, Yongzheng 10) until 1–29 July 1734 (sixth month, Yongzheng 12). Upland peoples even severed the roots of tea trees and denuded the mountains in protest. The scale of the rebellion can be gauged from the figures available for the period up to 14 April – 13 May 1733 (third month Yongzheng 11) by which time the Qing army had already beheaded and captured over 3,600 people and repatriated over 42,600 non-Han men and women.[47] Woni (窩泥 Hani), Kucong (苦蔥 a branch of the Lahu) and Puman (蒲蠻 Mon-Khmer speakers) participated in disturbances at Youle Tea Mountain. They chopped down tea trees and filled in salt wells out of desperation after the death of their lord, Dao Xingguo 刀興國, a Tai aristocrat appointed as a native squad leader (*tu bazong* 土把總) who rebelled against Qing authorities in a futile attempt to protect upland people under his charge.[48] Their hostile action testified to the widespread dissatisfaction with the tea monopoly among upland people.

Though the term General Tea Store (*zongchadian* 總茶店) does not appear in any contemporary sources other than the *Dian Yun Linian Zhuan*, the existence of the monopoly system can be corroborated from a memorial by Yin Jishan 尹繼善 (a Manchu Yellow bordered Bannerman), the Governor-general of Yunnan, Guizhou and Guangxi. Written to propose measures for strengthening administrative control of southern Yunnan after the suppression of this rebellion in 1732–1734, the memorial included a provision entitled:

> Severe punishment should be stipulated for abuses by officials who privately trade in tea and for harassment by soldiers and errand-runners who enter the mountains (*guanyuan fanmai sicha bingyi rushan raolei zhi bi yi yan ding chufen ye* 官員販賣私茶、兵役入山擾累之弊、宜嚴定處分也).

It reported the burdens of harsh exactions by civil and military local officials in no uncertain terms (Shi; 1817, 8:4 *yiwen*, *Chou zhuo Pu Si Yuan Xin Shanhou Shiyi Shu* (籌酌普思元新善後事宜疏):

> The Tea Mountain area of Simao is infertile and does not produce rice. The barbarian people are destitute, and solely rely on tea leaves for their subsistence. Regrettably, between the second and third lunar months both civil and military officials despatch soldiers and errand-runners into the mountains to collect tea every year; they abuse people at will, force them to part with [tea] at low prices, and then sell it far and wide [themselves], while randomly requisitioning people to work as porters to transport it along the way. In the upshot, the source of the people's daily sustenance has turned into a target for profit-making by officials, soldiers, and errand-runners, and the barbarian people suffer great hardship on account of it. Formerly, the Governor-General E'ertai, with imperial approval, prohibited soldiers and errand-runners from entering the mountains. We have to strictly prohibit

private tea trading by officials again, but we will not be able to eradicate the harmful practises unless we stipulate severe punishment.

思茅茶山地方瘠薄、不產米穀、夷人窮苦、惟藉茶葉養生、無如文武各員每歲二、三月閒卽差兵役入山採取、任意作踐短價強買、四處販賣、濫派人夫沿途運。是小民養命之源、竟成官員兵役射利之藪。夷民甚為受累。前經陞任督臣鄂爾泰題明、禁止兵役不許入山。臣等又將官販私茶嚴行查禁、但不嚴定處分弊累不能永除。

This passage reveals beyond doubt the real situation after 1729; first it shows that private tea trading by officials seriously damaged the livelihood of upland peoples, and second it indicates that on their annual trips soldiers and errand-runners obtained and transported tea by coercion. Yin Jishan demanded the tightening of regulations concerning private tea trading by civil and military officials precisely because of deepened upland dissatisfaction over the disregard for the prohibitions laid down by E'ertai, earlier.

That officials maintained a monopoly along the lines of the General Tea Store described above is also verified by the absence of any remarks concerning Han traders; Yin Jishan only mentioned officials, soldiers and errand-runners involved in tea transactions with upland peoples. He reasoned that unfair practices by officials would naturally disappear with a full ban on private tea trading thereby eradicating the cause of the trouble. The Qing clearly maintained the tea monopoly until the end of the Yongzheng period at least.

Though no source recorded when the monopoly started, judging from its principal purpose of mitigating upland dissatisfaction a highly probable date would be about 1729 (Yongzheng 7), the year of annexation. Until the outbreak of the "Revolt of Mäng Ham" in 1727, Han traders perambulated the mountains buying tea, but, as already mentioned Dao Zhengyan reported, their usurious money-lending activities inflicted great hardship on the growers. The "advancing of [money] and collection [of tea leaves]" must refer to some type of putting out system in which Han merchants advanced, or lent funds, to growers at exceptionally high rates of interest. The statement in the *Dian Yun Linian Zhuan* cited above showed that Qing officials discussed "the establishment of a General Tea Store to monopolise the economic rights" because "the merchant people have caused trouble by practising usury" lends credence to the idea that government regulation of the trade began in 1729.

The government monopoly must have been abolished well before the late eighteenth century when the numbers of Han sojourners in the Tea Mountains had swelled. A long-term resident of Yunnan, Tan Cui 檀萃 (1724–1801), wrote:

Several ten thousand people have entered the [six tea] mountains to grow tea. The tea buyers make purchases and transport it away to various places. One may well say that [the scene] of them always crowding the roads resembles a great [transportation train of] cash and grain tax 入山作茶者數十萬人、茶客收買於各處、每盈路可謂大錢糧矣。[49]

In 1786 (Qianlong 51) shifts in Qing policy concerning the procurement of tribute tea (*gongcha* 貢茶) for imperial consumption led to the legalisation of tea-growing by Han within the Tai polity of I Ngu (Yiwu 易武), the main cultivation area within the Sipsong Panna polity east of the Mekong river. With Qing approval, the hereditary ruler surnamed Wu 伍 who concurrently served as a native squad leader, permitted Han to buy land and grow tea in Mansa 漫撒 in return for taking responsibility for tax collection, including all duties related to tribute tea. The ratification of these measures by the paramount ruler of Sipsong Panna in 1789 (Qianlong 54) set firmer foundations for Han migration to the tea hills,[50] and enabled merchants to establish stable control over tea production and trade during the nineteenth century.

During the first half of the twentieth century, Han-owned tea companies, in cooperation with hereditary Tai princes, undertook tea processing and collection in Sipsong Panna. In Mäng Hāy (Menghai 猛海), the centre of tea production on the west bank of the Mekong river, tea companies procured tea leaves by subletting land rented from Tai villagers to tea-growing tenants. They also gathered leaves from swidden cultivators through the brokerage of upland village headmen with official rank in the Tai political system. In I Ngu, tea companies obtained land through intermarriage with local Tai aristocrats.[51] During the 1720s, the Han traders did not command as strong a foothold in the Tea Hills as they had by the close of the eighteenth century. There is no evidence for major landholdings by Han for growing tea, or large merchant houses this early. At this time traders procured tea by perambulating the mountains; they lodged in the houses of tea growers, appraising the condition of the crop, and advancing money.

Anthropologists recognise that the exchange of goods is inseparable from social methods of exchange. Though we have no precise knowledge of exchange customs in Woni (Hani) society at this time, we may assume that any type of gift exchange that they practised differed from trade exchange as known to the Han. While tea-growing had begun to draw the Woni into the Chinese market economy, the hostilities of 1727 clearly demonstrated that in their cross-cultural transactions the Han and Woni had not yet reached a common understanding about methods of exchange; both groups held different ideas of what money signified. Invoking ideas espoused by Richard White about Native American-European relations, Giersch (2000 and 2006) has suggested that the market in the Yunnan/Burma border area functioned as a middle ground in the eighteenth century. The case of the Tea Mountains testified that the "middle ground" was not easily founded, and if formed was accompanied by incessant violence, particularly when Han traders moved into isolated swidden agriculturalist societies. This point becomes even more poignant if we consider the fact that the failure of the Woni to adjust to Han methods of exchange embroiled the Tai rulers of Sipsong Panna in a violent struggle with Qing bureaucrats. Conflict over economic transactions between migrants and indigenes greatly affected the fortunes of Tai polities.

Sources recorded the role of Tai leaders as spokesmen for upland subjects on many occasions. We have witnessed how Dao Zhengyan articulated Woni grievances, reporting to E'ertai, that the cause of the disturbance lay in usury by Han traders. According to the *Dian Yun Linian Zhuan*, it was the refusal of Qing officials to listen to the passionate pleas of the aristocrat Dao Xingguo on behalf of his upland subjects that triggered a large-scale rebellion which had its origins in the siege of Simao City between 22 June and 21 July 1732 (intercalary fifth month/Yongzheng 10). Dao Xingguo was the son of the head of Simao (思茅土目) Dao Mengpin 刀猛品, and had been appointed a native squad leader (*tu bazong* 土把總) for distinguished service in assisting the Qing army in the Mäng Ham campaigns of 1728.[52] Up until this time he had been pro-Qing, cooperating in exacting levies from upland dwellers, but when Tong Shiyin 佟世蔭, the Prefect of Pu'er Prefecture, prepared a tax collecting expedition into the uplands between 26 March and 24 April 1732 (third lunar month/Yongzheng 10) Dao made an emotive appeal for deferment on the grounds of impoverishment in the uplands. "Removing his hat and kowtowing (免冠頓首)" Dao pleaded:

> The influence of the moral teaching of the Governor-general has exhausted the resources of the people, and it is as if they are unable to make ends meet. Please wait until next year for the taxes. By way of custom the barbarian people are unwilling to sell their sons and daughters, and now with tea under management by officials they no longer have any means of borrowing. They can only offer cattle and swine at the most.[53]
>
> 總督風行草偃、民力已竭、似未能連奉後車、請待之明年。夷人例不肯賣鬻兒女、茶又歸官、借貸路絕。惟牲牛圈豕以爲貢獻之地耳。

Tong Shiyin rejected his petition and aired his displeasure towards Dao Xingguo. Even the clerks humiliated him, throwing away his hat and kicking the chair from underneath him. Dao Xingguo,

> went into a great rage, tore off his ceremonial dress and declared, "Death is the only way out. Why do I have to put up with such treatment" (興國乃大怒、褫其補服曰、死耳。烏用此為。),

and left, after which Dao "called his followers together and swore an oath of alliance (號眾而盟)",[54] Reports cited in memorials mentioned that he led his Kucong followers (*xiangxia zhi ren* 項下之人), one account referred to them as tenants (*dianhu* 佃戶), to besiege Simao.[55] At that time the Kucong had begun to worship a Burmese monk (*mianseng* 緬僧) as a supernatural being (*shenxian* 神仙) at a place named Bats Cave on the Manba river 蠻壩河蝙蝠洞.[56] Lahu historians have stressed that Dao Xingguo pledged an alliance with the Kucong in his uprising.[57] The lord–subject relationship obliged Tai rulers to act as articulators for their subjects, but outright rejection by Qing officials of appeals on their behalf only drove desperate upland dwellers closer to unfurling the banner of revolt.

In his entreaty that "by way of custom the barbarian people are unwilling to sell their sons and daughters", the Tai ruler revealed deep acquaintance with economic practises in Han society. Chen Wuzhi 陳武志 (2015) in his recent quantitative study of bride-price in eighteenth- and nineteenth-century China argued that men sold their wives and concubines as instruments of risk insurance. Though strictly speaking such sales were illegal, they were taking place and a bride-price market had emerged. Chen hypothesised that in the absence of a viable financial market, Han men used women as insurance assets to trade for other resources, specifically to insure against natural disasters, debt and other risks. The reluctance of Kucong men to sell their daughters attested that, unlike contemporary Han, they neither followed this practice, nor shared the notion of women as assets that could be liquidated to pay debts when families came under threat. This episode also highlighted the different levels of monetisation and attitudes to debt in the two societies.

The tea trade of the 1720s marked the first attempt by Han traders to draw the uplands of the Sipsong Panna polity into the money economy of China. Han traders found little to attract them in lowland areas, the core of the polity where the hierarchical structure of Tai society was reinforced by strong bonds of allegiance between rulers and villagers. The prevalence of malaria and epidemic diseases also acted as deterrents. Rather they chose the periphery of the polity, a place where Tai administrative control remained lax and they could wield a freer hand. Historians have overlooked the importance of upland peripheries to the maintenance of Tai polities, but the case of the 1729 annexation clearly demonstrated how vital they were to the welfare of Sipsong Panna as a whole.[58] Unrest in the hills led to the incorporation of some peripheral territories into the newly founded Pu'er Prefecture, and almost caused the alienation of the six *panna* at the core. Interaction between Han traders and upland peoples had inaugurated a process of slow disintegration from the periphery.

Conclusion

Hasegawa and Katō portrayed the events of 1727 to 1729 as aggression by the Qing state. Neither of them analysed the intricacy of the causes, and merely emphasised the outcome; firmer control gained by the Qing over the Tai polity. Since Sipsong Panna now lies within Yunnan province, one might assume that it was destined to become directly administered by China, and that Qing interference merely marked the first step on that path. But this study demonstrates that state intervention was not predestined; it followed closely in the footsteps of Han traders in the uplands of Sipsong Panna. The Qing court carefully monitored Tai ruler's handling of trouble arising between Han and upland peoples, and took quick action against what it deemed to be misgovernment in 1725 and 1727–1728. The driving force behind Qing aggression came not from grand designs for territorial enlargement, but from the perceived need to establish norms of law, order and government that accorded with Chinese sensibilities. Qing officials became so adamant about pursuing this ideal that they sometimes ignored considerations of economic cost that had deterred officials from taking firm action in the past.

The accession of the Yongzheng emperor to the throne spelt the end of lenient policies towards non-Han leaders. The sudden crackdown by the Qing on how native officials governed their own domains caught Tai rulers off guard. The paramount ruler of Sipsong Panna failed to adjust swiftly to the mutating political and economic circumstances of the 1720s. The money economy brought into the uplands by Han traders and the resultant increase in trade exchange caused hill peoples great hardship. Qing officials no longer turned a blind eye to violence in upland areas, whether under the jurisdiction of Tai rulers, or other ethnic leaders. They refused to sanction solutions, such as the issue of administrative titles to accommodate recalcitrant upland outlaws that Wu Sangui and Fan Chengxun employed during the 1670s and 1680s. The political environment had altered, and Yongzheng's policy was more rigid, and less pliant, than that of the Kangxi emperor.

The Yongzheng emperor trumpeted a fresh vision of law and order in Yunnan; he demanded the complete eradication of upland outlaws, and would not tolerate ritual subordination any longer. Tai rulers failed to understand that increased trading by the Han had created problems that they could not manage effectively within the confines of the lord–vassal relationship. The incidents leading up to the 1729 annexation testified to the divergent concepts of social order embraced by the Qing court and the Tai rulers. Dao Zhengyan and E'ertai stood divided on how to settle conflicts between Han and non-Han ethnic groups. Tai rulers correctly identified the real cause of the violence as deriving from the economic activities of Han traders, and they attempted to resolve the problem through negotiation and by siding with their grievant, non-Han subjects. In contrast, E'ertai had little time for any ethnic group that disrupted social order whatever the cause, and resorted to military force when inept native officials and administrators failed to remedy the situation. The new administrative policy required Tai rulers to manipulate upland peoples in a way acceptable to the Yongzheng emperor, and at the same time ensure the safety of Han as well as non-Han inhabitants; if they proved unfit by not being capable of establishing firm control over upland areas, then the Qing annexed their territory. The writing was on the wall, but the Tai rulers failed to notice.

From the perspective of upland peoples, Tai rulers proved ineffective as articulators. By failing to prevent Qing troops from killing their subjects the paramount leader of Sipsong Panna had violated the unspoken agreement that Tai rulers should always put the interests of their subjects over those of external powers, using every means possible to shield them from outside harm. Violence by Qing troops in the uplands and direct administration of the hill tracts underlined the waning power and authority of Tai rulers. This, in turn, weakened the traditional bonds of fealty felt by upland vassals towards their Tai overlords. This change in the lord–vassal relationship among upland ethnic groups under the jurisdiction of Weiyuan Native Sub-prefecture, Zhenyuan Native Prefecture and the Sipsong Panna polity gradually became salient from 1725.

Scott (2009) has drawn sorely needed scholarly attention to upland societies. In the past, historians generally shied away from this endeavour for two reasons.

First, pre-occupation with writing national histories, underpinned by a great deal of sheer prejudice, has encouraged historians to ignore them. The assumption that upland peoples could not possibly have contributed to the formation and administration of Tai polities in any significant way has dominated scholarship. Second, the dearth of source materials written by hill peoples themselves, and scanty accounts of them in Tai chronicles have also acted as deterrents. Recent scholarship has empirically demonstrated through cases studies from northern Laos and Dehong in Yunnan that upland ethnic groups participated in the foundation and administration of Tai polities.[59] Evidence pieced together from scattered sources presented in this study draws attention to a hitherto little noticed change in the internal workings of post-eighteenth century Tai polities; the weakening of the lord–vassal relationship between rulers and their upland subjects.

Debilitated bonds with indigenous upland peoples made it harder for Tai rulers to meet the new challenges posed by the sudden burgeoning of Han populations in the uplands of southern Yunnan and northern Burma during the eighteenth and nineteenth centuries. Han migrants expanded commercial cotton and tea cultivation, and engaged in mining, and these new mutative politico-economic conditions exacerbated conflicts between upland and lowland in this area.[60] According to Kataoka Tatsuki (2013), a new ideology for the articulation of ethnic consciousness, the ideology of a stateless people, was generated among one upland ethnic group, the Lahu 拉祜, within this milieu. He points out that the Lahu came to embrace the notion of statelessness in response to their incorporation into the Chinese state. Outside pressure fostered the concepts of state and kingship amongst the Lahu, and caused them to build their own autonomous upland polity headed by "Buddha kings *(fu jaw maw)*" which lasted from the late eighteenth century until the late nineteenth century. The Lahu first appeared in Chinese sources as the Kucong (subjects of Dao Xingguo) and Luohei 猓黑 during the Yongzheng period. Their first Buddha King began rebelling against the lowland Tai rulers of Mäng Lëm and Mäng Mäng in 1799. They built their tiny polities in the upland peripheries of Tai territory, far removed from Qing administration, but later became embroiled in a violent struggle against the authority of both in order to uphold their independence. This attempt at polity-building by a hill people occurred in the context of weakened ties between Tai rulers and their upland subjects, and as this study has demonstrated, the portents of change in upland/lowland relations originated early during the 1720s and the 1730s.

Notes

1 This is an English translation of my article published in Japanese entitled: "Yōsei 7 nen Shinchō ni yoru Shipusonpanna Ohkoku no chokkatsuchika ni tsuite: Tai kei minzoku Ohkoku wo yurugasu sanchimin ni kansuru ichi kōsatsu" 雍正七年清朝によるシプソンパンナー王国の直轄地化について―タイ系民族王国を揺るがす山地民に関する一考察 [The annexation of Sipsong Panna by the Qing Dynasty in 1729: An examination of hill peoples who rocked the foundations of a Tai kingdom], *Tōyōshi Kenkyū* 東洋史研究 62 (4) (2004): 694–728. I have updated and augmented

the text with brief discussions of, and references to, selected studies published since 2004, without changing the conclusions in the original article.
2 Shintani (1988), pp. 2–18. Except for some well-known terms such as Tai, the romanisation of Tai words in this article follows the Shintani system which is outlined in Shintani Tadahiko (2000).
3 Examples include Grabowsky (1999); Giersch (2001); Katō (2000); Daniels (2000a); Iijima (2001).
4 Daniels (2000a).
5 See Takeuchi (2003), pp. 4–7; Giersch (2006), pp. 133–135; Nomoto and Nishikawa (2008), pp. 15–34; and Takeuchi (2010), pp. 117–143.
6 Sutton (2003).
7 For the relationship between the Yongzheng emperor and E'ertai see Miyazaki (1991), pp. 93–96. For the administration of Yunnan by E'ertai, see Kambe (1990).
8 Kambe (1990), p. 124 described E'ertai's administration of Yunnan as "the starting point of a new struggle for minority peoples".
9 In actual fact, there were four punitive campaigns, see Liew Foon Ming (1996), pp. 162–203. For an outline of the splintering of Tai power see Daniels (2006), pp. 26–33.
10 Katō (2000), pp. 68–146.
11 Katō (1997), p. 4.
12 Katō (1997), pp. 11–13 and Katō (2001).
13 Von Glahn (1987); Shepherd (1993); and Millward (1998).
14 Harrell (1995).
15 Kikuchi (1998), *Honbun Hen*, vol. 2, pp. 127–137.
16 Takeuchi (1982), pp. 26–56; Takeuchi (1987), pp. 53–54; Liu (1934), pp. 89–101.
17 Daniels (1999), pp. 12–32.
18 The account below is based on Katō (2000), pp. 30–47.
19 Grabowsky (2005), pp. 19–30.
20 Grabowsky (2005), p. 29.
21 Hasegawa (1982), pp. 132–136. Hasegawa mainly relied on the 1851 *Pu'er Fu Zhi* and other nineteenth century sources for his evidence.
22 Katō (2000), pp. 45–47; Katō (1997), pp. 10–13.
23 Daniels (2000b), pp. 63–69.
24 *Yuanjiang Zhigao*, 22: 1b–2a.
25 GZDYZ, 10: 295.
26 Tan (1804), 11:3a.
27 GZDYZ, 9:286–288; and Table 8.2 in this article.
28 GZDYZ, 9:288.
29 Ni (1992), p. 596.
30 Sun Hongben 孫弘本 related the following incident which occurred before the disturbances. On 6 February 1727 (16/01 Yongzheng 5) when a large crowd of Panna headman, Tai and 1,000 Woni assembled to venerate Dao Zhengyan as the ruler of Cheli (Ceng Hung), he refused to accept the seal and letters patent of office that the Pacification Commissioner Taw Kin Paw offered him; acceptance would have given him some claim to official recognition as the paramount leader of Sipsong Panna. Dao Zhengyan, who sat on a platform raised higher than that of Taw Kin Paw, reputedly said, "I do not want the seal and letters patent (*yinxin* 印信). I will administer our barbarian people, you go and handle the Han people", see GZDYZ, 10:293–294.
31 GZDYZ, 11:246–247.
32 GZDYZ, 12:315–316.
33 Ni (1992), pp. 600–601.
34 Ni (1992), p. 601. For a study of the introduction of the silver tax system and how it influenced the power politics of Sipsong Panna see Katō (1997), pp. 6–13.

35 *GZDYZ*, 11:909–910, *GZDYZ*, 12:23 and *GZDYZ*, 12:315 all reported that over half of the soldiers contracted an epidemic disease (*shiyi* 時疫 either cholera, dysentery or typhus) which raged from 4 September to 30 November 1728 (eighth–tenth month Yongzheng 6), and which even claimed the life of Sun Hongben 孫弘本, the Regional Commander of Lin'an and Yuanjiang 臨沅總兵官. Ni (1992), p. 601 recorded that almost all men sent to build a wall city at Mäng Ham died of *yanzhang* (煙瘴, either endemic malaria or schistosomiasis), and that over 1,000 personnel died in the construction of a walled city at Youle 攸樂 in the Tea Mountains before it was abandoned. For the history of epidemics in eighteenth-century Yunnan, see Benedict (1996), pp. 18–20.
36 *GZDYZ*, 8:184–185 and Ni (1992), p. 593.
37 Cai Yurong (1691), *juan* 29, *yiwen* 藝文 3:36a.
38 According to the *Dianzhi*, p. 56, Xinping county 新平縣 originally came under the jurisdiction of Xi'e county 嶍峨縣, but it was "later occupied by the Dingju and Baigai barbarian bandits, and converted into a county for the first time after pacification in Wanli 19 (1591) 後為丁苴、白改夷賊所拠、萬曆十九年討平之、始改為縣。".
39 Min (1626), 5:60b–62a, "Xinping Jiaozei Baojie Shu" 新平剿賊報捷書. A digest of this memorial appears in the *Xizong Shilu*, 2492–2496.
40 Ni (1992), pp. 484.
41 Cai (1691), juan 29, *yiwen* 藝文 3, 37a–37b.
42 *GZDYZ*, 2: 498–499.
43 *GZDYZ*, 2:499.
44 *GZDYZ*, 9:288.
45 *GZDYZ*, 9:288.
46 Ni (1992), p. 602.
47 *GZDYZ*, 21:308.
48 Ni (1992), p. 623. A similar passage appears in the *Pu'er Fuzhi* 13. Ni Tui recorded Dao Xingguo as a Native Battalion Commander of the Tea Mountains (茶山土千戶), but I follow the *GZDYZ*, 20:112, which gives his official title as Native Squad Leader (土把總). *GZDYZ*, 20:112 reported that the Kucong were tenants of Dao Xingguo. A memorial by Gao Qizhuo dated the twenty-second day of the ninth lunar month 1732 (Yongzheng 10) recorded the situation on the twenty-first day of the eighth lunar, "All of the Woni, Kucong and Puman have already rebelled, only the Baiyi [Tai] are still waiting to see what happens", see *GZDYZ*, 20:568.
49 Tan (1804), 11/3a.
50 Takeuchi (2010), pp. 119–129; Nishikawa (2015), p. 173.
51 Hill (1998), pp. 73–86.
52 *GZDYZ*, 20:67.
53 Ni (1992), p. 621.
54 Ni (1992), p. 621.
55 *GZDYZ*, 20:99. See *GZDYZ*, 20:112 for the Kucong as tenants of Dao Xingguo. *GZDYZ*, 20:116 mentioned that the Kucong had assembled in the Manba 蠻壩 district where Dao San 刀三 a relative of Dao Xingguo resided.
56 *GZDYZ*, 20:98; *GZDYZ*, 20:112.
57 Lahuzu Jianshi Bianxiezu (1986), p. 32.
58 For a case study of the importance of upland peoples to the political stability of Tai polities, see Daniels (2013), pp. 133–170.
59 Badenoch and Tomita (2013); Daniels (2013).
60 For population movements see Nomoto and Nishikawa (2008) and Nishikawa (2015); for commercial crops see Takeuchi (2010); for changes in trade see Giersch (2011).

Part III
Chinese commerce in Southeast Asia

9 The rise of Chinese mercantile power in maritime Southeast Asia c.1400–1700

Chang Pin-tsun

In a distinguished lecture on government, Mancur Olson pointed out a pitfall of economic rationality: it tends to overlook what is the most obvious to everyone, just like a rational stroller tends to overlook the big bills lying on the sidewalk.[1] The same pitfall sometimes may be found in historical rationality, which, by focusing entirely on the positive elements, often ignores the side-effects of some seemingly negative elements. Looking from the vantage point of Chinese economic power in Southeast Asia today, this chapter tries to search for the "big bills" in relation to its origin, which have been long ignored in the study of Chinese maritime history. One big bill comes instantly to my attention: the unintended consequences of Ming maritime policy and the trade monopoly of the Dutch United East India Company (VOC). Benefitted by historical hindsight, we are now able to credit these phenomena with their positive effects and see them as the most critical contributory elements in the foundation of Chinese mercantile dominance in maritime Southeast Asia. These effects have been largely ignored or inadequately dealt with. Suffice it to say that they were chiefly responsible for the displacement of South and West Asians by the Chinese in the competition for commercial interests in this region. The displacement process took place over a period of about three centuries, roughly from 1400 to 1700.

The following discussion is arranged in four sections. Section one introduces the superiority of South and West Asians' commercial power in Southeast Asia up to the end of Yuan dynasty (1276–1367). Section two discusses the functions of Ming maritime policy in bringing about the power shift in Chinese favour. The third section shows how the commercial interests of South and West Asians were almost completely eliminated in maritime Southeast Asia primarily as a result of the trade monopoly of the VOC. The fourth and final section is a brief conclusion.

The period of mercantile dominance by South and West Asians

The South and West Asians in Southeast Asia referred to here were diverse groups of traders including Indians from South Asia, Persians, Arabs, and other smaller groups like Armenians and Jews from West Asia. Their mercantile dominance in Southeast Asia began before the Christian era and lasted until the time of our concern.[2] In view of its millennial continuity, its phasing-out in the three centuries from 1400 to 1700 was a very dramatic historical break indeed.

To gain an overall idea of their "mercantile dominance", let us begin with a simplified trade model. Three economies, China, India, and Southeast Asia, are engaged in direct bilateral trade. Their exports are marked by "–" and imports are marked by "+". China exports silks and imports spices. India exports cotton piece goods and imports both silks and spices. Southeast Asia exports spices and imports both silks and cotton textiles. Assuming all trade is balanced, the model commodities flows will end up with something like in the following table.

The values represented by the numbers in the Table mask an unrealistic assumption: zero transaction cost. In the real world this cost exists in all market exchanges and is reflected in the price difference between the origin and destination of any particular commodity. In this example of external trade between three economies, the transaction costs will be mostly absorbed by shipping and marketing services plus the risk premium therein. Assuming all the commodity prices at the port of origin are double at the destination port, we will arrive at a result shown in the following box.

Transaction costs were very high in a pre-modern world like maritime East Asia in the period of our concern. A doubling of commodity price between provenance and destination ports was quite reasonable.[3] If we, for simplicity, count out the earnings accruing to the investors, it is conceivable that the 100 per cent price rise all went to cover the cost of shipping and marketing.[4] Table 9.2 tells us that this cost amounts to 11 value units, equal to the total of original values.

This example is given to impress readers with the economic weight taken on by the service sector of shipping and marketing. Half of the total value units fell into the grip of those servicing in shipping and marketing. By inference we may conclude that whoever controlled this service sector, dominated the mercantile economy. Historically South and West Asians dominated the business of shipping and marketing in Sino-Southeast Asian trade until the late fourteenth century.

Before the nineteenth century, China was the largest economy in East Asia, and likewise India was the largest economy across South and West Asia. Each of these two economies was closely tied to Southeast Asia not merely because

Table 9.1 Trade model: China, Southeast Asia and India

Product	China	Southeast Asia	India
Silks	–2	+1	+1
Spices	+2	–5	+3
Cottons	0	+4	–4

Table 9.2 Trade model with transaction cost: China, Southeast Asia and India

Product	China	Southeast Asia	India
Silks	−2	+2	+2
Spices	+4	−5	+6
Cottons	0	+8	−4

of geographical proximity, but primarily because of the unique natural endowments Southeast Asia had in terms of the production of spices. India itself produced the more ordinary spice of pepper on the Malabar coast, and Ceylon supplied cinnamon, but for such finer spices as cloves, nutmeg and mace, India had to rely upon imports from Southeast Asia. In fact, the whole world had to rely upon it as they could be grown only in the Spice Islands of Southeast Asia.[5] The production of pepper in India was more expensive and by the seventeenth century, India even had to import Southeast Asian pepper for home consumption.[6] As for China, all spices including pepper had to be imported from Southeast Asia. It was primarily through the palatal pleasure deriving from these tropical spices that Southeast Asia lured both India and China into significant economic exchanges. From these exchanges all parties benefitted with absolute advantages which were absent in a closed economy. Sino-Southeast Asian or Indo-Southeast Asian trade, in whatever forms it might have taken, was an economic "must" dictated by different natural endowments in these three economies.

Trade relationships between South Asia and Southeast Asia began in prehistoric times. There is no reason to suppose that those who carried out the trade came from just one side; instead scanty records hint that both regions seemed to have supplied maritime traders for a long time. Entering the Christian era, however, this trade increasingly came under the control of Indian merchants. The spread of Indian cultures is generally believed to have followed the Indian traders. The so-called "Indianization" in Southeast Asia, whether in the form of Hinduism or Buddhism, took place in such a sweeping way that it completely dwarfed the "Sinicization" visible only in today's Vietnam. It is no exaggeration to say that before the introduction of Islam in northwestern Sumatra in the thirteenth century and its subsequent rapid spread, in terms of foreign cultural imports, the whole of Southeast Asia was almost totally shrouded in Indian culture.[7]

The spread of Indian culture far and wide in Southeast Asia indicates that Indian traders had travelled far and wide in this region from ancient times. Indeed, they were the first alien group of people to assume mercantile power there. The Islamic proselytizers, like their Hindu predecessors, followed traders to Southeast Asia. These Muslim traders primarily consisted of Indian converts, though Persians and Arabs were also active among them. The Islamization of maritime Southeast Asia therefore saw the continuation of Indian commercial power, despite the fact that West Asians began to share part of it from the thirteenth century onwards. To be more general, from the perspective of the Indian Ocean the mercantile interests in Southeast Asia were firmly in the grip of the South and West Asians, of whom the Indians were the most active.

Looking at East Asian waters we find a similar dominance by these traders. This is not only demonstrated by the limited scope of Sinicization. The control of shipping and marketing in Sino-Southeast Asian maritime trade provides more direct and telling evidence.

Though maritime Southeast Asians seem to have come to trade in China earlier than the South and West Asians, they were soon overwhelmed by the latter at least by the seventh century. Between 700 and 1000 CE, the Indians, Persians, and Arabs nearly completely displaced the Southeast Asians in handling the mercantile services of Sino-Southeast Asian trade. They criss-crossed the South China Sea, engaging in profitable country trade. Starting from the late seventh century some of them were even found to have taken up residence in various Chinese ports, apparently in coordination with their travelling countrymen to handle the export and import business in China. As for the Chinese they remained passive receivers on the coast. They did not venture to trade to the South Seas themselves until the latter half of the eleventh century.[8]

It seems that Chinese junks began to sail to Korea and Japan for commercial purposes earlier than to the South Seas. At least the Fujianese were recorded to have traded there since the early eleventh century.[9] This can be explained by the market conditions at that time. The South and West Asian traders had a firm grip on the marketing business in Southeast Asia, but they had no control over it in Northeast Asia.[10] Therefore when Chinese were able to build and sail their junks overseas, they first went to Korea and Japan where external trade was open and easier to enter. These Chinese traders, according to Ts'ao Yung-ho, seem to have resold spices and other tropical products brought to China by the South and West Asians, in addition to popular Chinese goods such as silks and porcelains.[11]

Just how much the Chinese had learned from the West and South Asians in the field of shipping and marketing, is hard to determine.[12] It is apparent, however, that after centuries of observation on the shore and in business dealings with foreigners at ports of calls, the Chinese had slowly accumulated practical knowledge in relation to maritime exploration in Southeast Asia. It is quite plausible that some Chinese would have travelled overseas on the trading ships of the West and South Asians, acquiring practical experience by serving as apprentices on the ships. This is especially natural if we take into account the fact that quite a few West and South Asians had resided in China for a long time and had married Chinese women, thereby producing hybrid offspring to succeed them in running Sino-Southeast Asian trade. They would send out their children as trade agents on board their countrymen's ships if necessary. It is probable that these half-Chinese traders were the harbingers of Chinese participation in the Sino-Southeast Asian maritime trade.

It is generally held that Chinese maritime foreign trade was in its full bloom from the eleventh to the fourteenth century. During this period Chinese government was most enthusiastic in promoting this trade, and Chinese private traders called at the greatest number of ports in the South Seas and the Indian Ocean. While there is no quibble to be raised over the truth of Chinese spectacular achievements in overseas trade during these three centuries, it must be noted that exactly in the same period the South and West Asians were the most active at various Chinese ports, indicating an impressive surge of their mercantile interests in maritime Asia as a whole and in Sino-Southeast Asia in particular.[13] In fact their firmly entrenched interests in maritime Asia were not shaken at all by Chinese participation in shipping and marketing services. The range and scale of maritime trade in the South Seas and the Indian Ocean were then greatly enlarged, to the extent that Chinese entry was a net plus for it, rather than a substitution factor. With the special privileges extended by the Mongols, the South and West Asians had actually expanded their commercial interests in China to the greatest extent during the Yuan dynasty.[14] In retrospect we may conclude that, during these three centuries, for the first time Chinese were able to share the profits derived from mercantile services in maritime foreign trade, which were previously monopolized by the South and West Asians. However, Chinese traders were, at this time, but a minor player in this trade.

This situation was completely altered from the end of the fourteenth century. Private traders from South and West Asia stopped coming to China, and residential foreigners very soon disappeared entirely from Chinese ports. The South and West Asians continued to carry out maritime trade in Southeast Asia, but their business was now limited to the periphery of the Indian Ocean. Their communities were still found in Southeast Asia, holding on to their traditional service of marketing for their seafaring countrymen when they arrived at the Southeast Asian ports. By the late seventeenth century, however, except in today's Burma and Thailand, the South and West Asians had almost totally disappeared from the maritime scene in Southeast Asia, and their communities in this region faded away too. They were not to come back to maritime Southeast Asia in significant numbers until the nineteenth century, and they never appeared again as an impressive group on China's shores until after Hong Kong was colonized by the British in 1842. Despite their return, they no longer had the dominant commercial interests once enjoyed by their ancestors for about a millennium in Southeast Asia.

The account above outlines South and West Asians' remarkable success in the maritime trade of Southeast Asia and beyond, and its abrupt interruption. Their mercantile power in Southeast Asia was partially eclipsed from the late fourteenth to the early seventeenth century; it was almost completely displaced at the close of that century. Its decline and fall was closely related to the implementation of Ming maritime policy and the intrusion of European maritime powers, especially the Dutch VOC, in Asian waters.

Ming maritime policy

Ming maritime policy comprised two elements: maritime prohibitions and tribute trade. Through maritime prohibitions the Ming regime suppressed all private maritime foreign trade; through tribute trade it monopolized most Sino-foreign economic exchanges via the sea routes. This maritime policy was implemented at the inception of the Ming dynasty (1368–1644). It was later relaxed a little in 1567, when the seaport of Yuegang, renamed Haicheng, of Zhangzhou prefecture in Fujian province, was opened for Chinese private maritime traders to sail out to overseas countries except Japan. Perhaps the permission by Chinese local authorities for the Portuguese to lease Macao in Guangdong province in 1557 can be viewed as another relaxation, though it was not formally sanctioned by the court. Save for these modifications, Ming maritime policy as designed by the dynastic founding emperor, remained valid in principle, though the effectiveness of its enforcement varied greatly over time.[15] With regards to Sino-foreign economic exchanges, enforcement was what mattered, not the policy embodied in the Ming code.

Generally speaking, Ming maritime prohibition was very effective in the half century of 1380–1430. Though it was announced one year before the dynastic foundation, the ambitious founding emperor was not able to implement it effectively until his control over Southeast China was consolidated and a system of coastal garrisons was set up in the mid-1380s.[16] This system, by which he was able to create a "Maritime Great Wall", provided effective policing along the coast to seal off China from overseas countries.[17] Cracks in this "Maritime Great Wall" began to appear in the 1430s, and they widened as time drew on. Cracks were not made by pirates; they were made primarily by smugglers. They appeared at a time when the Ming government took actions to reduce the scale of tribute trade after the 1430s.

In terms of state security, the aspect of tribute trade was no less important than maritime prohibition. Absolute advantage existed in external trade, and this advantage was to be tapped in one way or another, officially or privately. Historically, Chinese governments had allowed both state and private trade to operate, but the Ming regime decided to close the private channel and leave open only the official one. This was the channel of tribute trade.

Under the Ming tribute trade arrangements foreigners were allowed to enter China in the name of paying tribute to the Chinese emperor, thus recognizing his overlordship.[18] Commodity exchanges took place in two ways. The overseas tributary missions presented part of their cargoes as tribute gifts to the emperor, who in return would grant them a reward consisting of coveted Chinese goods. For the rest of the cargoes the foreigners were permitted to sell them to Chinese civilians at the port of call and the imperial capital. Meanwhile Chinese goods could be purchased at these two places too. All transactions had to be done within a designated period under the government's close supervision. These two aspects of goods exchange constituted the main content of the tribute trade in China.

There was a third element in the arrangement of Ming tribute trade, that is, the transactions done overseas by Chinese envoy missions dispatched by the Chinese emperor. Prior to the end of the Xuande reign (1426–1435) these missions were frequently sent out by the Ming court to invite tributary payments from the overlords of overseas states or to carry out the ceremony of their investiture. The peak of Chinese envoy dispatches came with the seven voyages of Zheng He between 1405 and 1433. Leading a tremendous fleet, he invited a great number of overseas states to send tributary missions to China, and engaged in official trading overseas on a large scale. His purchase of pepper alone, according to T'ien Ju-k'ang, was so enormous that from then on this spice was turned from a luxury item into an item of common consumption in China.[19]

The goods exchanges carried out by overseas tributary missions in China and by Chinese envoy missions overseas represented the whole range of Ming tribute trade, which was envisioned by the Ming rulers to constitute the entirety of Chinese foreign economic exchanges. Admittedly this tribute trade system functioned most smoothly from the Yongle reign (1403–24) to the end of the Xuande reign in 1435. It so functioned because it was then open enough to allow for much private trade to be conducted in disguise under official tribute trade, in China as well as in overseas countries.[20] In order to sustain tribute trade on such a large scale, the Ming court had to shoulder very heavy financial burdens, particularly from its generous treatment of foreign missions and cargoes, as well as the expenses of the expeditionary fleets. No wonder this trade was dramatically scaled down from the 1430s when the imperial purse shrank, and the non-economic purposes of such relations were no longer a matter of imperial concern.[21]

Tribute trade existed throughout the era of imperial China. In comparison with the tribute trade of other dynasties one extraordinary feature stood out in the Ming system: total monopoly of Sino-foreign trade by the government. While tribute trade at other times was generally a supplement to private trade in the whole Sino-foreign resources exchange, during the Ming it was the totality of this exchange. Ming tribute trade thus marked a total suppression of private trade, for which a policy of maritime prohibition was in place.

As indicated above, the commercial interests of West and South Asians in China peaked during the Mongol Yuan period. It is inconceivable that their interests would have evaporated abruptly had there not been a dynastic change that brought about not only the end of their privileges, but also the death knell of their businesses. The death knell was tolled by the Ming maritime policy, which in Chinese maritime history was an utter aberration. On the one hand, maritime prohibition implemented by the Ming government cut off completely their connections with fellow countrymen overseas. The total suppression of private trade meant not only that they could not sail out of China, but also that their countrymen could not come to China either. On the other hand, the arrangement of tribute trade made it an imperative for the Southeast Asians to institute direct contact with the Chinese. If any foreigners were needed by the tributary missions, they could not be persons other than Chinese. And indeed, Chinese were found to assume the active role of intermediaries from then on, a role that previously had been played primarily by the South and West Asians in Sino-foreign maritime trade.[22]

The identity of South and West Asians in China saw another threat, beyond the loss of maritime trade opportunities during the Ming. This was the Ming policy of forced naturalization which was a direct challenge to their identity. In 1372 the founding emperor ordered that henceforth foreigners, like the Mongols staying in China, were allowed to marry only Chinese and were not permitted to marry among themselves.[23] With this imperial order effectively enforced, the South and West Asians in China virtually disappeared in a few decades.

The Ming maritime policy, with its two components, thus made it possible for the Chinese to monopolize for the first time the service of shipping and marketing in Sino-foreign resource exchange, the scale of which was the greatest in East Asian maritime trade. Concomitant with this monopoly, Chinese communities in overseas countries began to spring up, heralding their "diaspora" in Southeast Asia.[24] These communities took over the functions long performed by the West and South Asian communities in servicing the Chinese junk trade in Southeast Asia. The details provided in Table 9.3 are indicative of their growth.

The table brings together all the information we currently have from the Chinese sources concerning Chinese communities in maritime Southeast Asia. Prior to the thirteenth century, no Chinese communities are known to have existed in Southeast Asia. In the fourteenth century they appeared in two places, but records about them are very short and simple. In contrast Chinese sources in the fifteenth century, which all came from the experiences of Zheng He's voyages, describe nine Chinese communities in considerable detail. Excluding the vague references to communities in Malacca and Siam, we still find that seven Chinese communities in maritime Southeast Asia had come into existence by the first half of the fifteenth century, some of them being as large as several

Table 9.3 Chinese communities in Southeast Asia thirteenth – early seventeenth century

Source (date)	Chinese communities mentioned
Zhenla Fengtuji[25] (1225)	Cambodia
Daoyi Zhilue[26] (1351)	Cambodia, Gelam islet
Xiyang Fanguozhi[27] (1434)	Tuban, Geresik, Surabaya, Majapahit, Palembang, Siam
Xingcha Shenglan[28] (1436)	Gelam, Palembang, Malacca, Cambodia
Yingyai Shenglan[29] (1451)	Tuban, Geresik, Surabaya, Majapahit, Palembang, Gelam, Siam
Dongxiyang Kao[30] (1618)	Siam (Nakhon), Sunda Kelapa, Cambodia, Pattani, Kelantan, Palembang, Malacca, Djambi, Molucca islands, Luzon

thousand people.[31] The last text in the table records 10 places with Chinese communities in the early seventeenth century. In fact, by then Chinese people were being recorded by the Europeans almost wherever they sailed in maritime Southeast Asia.[32]

Thus, in the fifteenth and sixteenth century, and subsequently, many Chinese took up residence in Southeast Asia, side by side with the South and West Asians. Chinese sojourning traders, as well as their South and West Asian counterparts, thronged to the various seaports across Southeast Asia where international trade thrived. From the 1430s two distinct spheres of commercial interest had discernibly come into being, with Malacca marking the point of division.[33] Just as the Chinese junks stopped sailing west of Malacca, South and West Asian ships seldom went to the east of it. When the Ming tribute trade declined after the mid-fifteenth century, with maritime prohibitions still in force, private trade in the form of smuggling began to fill the vacuum. Though international elements like the Portuguese and the Japanese also contributed to this clandestine trade in China and elsewhere, it was Chinese people who constituted the backbone of the smugglers. Chinese mercantile dominance in Southeast Asia thus continued without interruption. The power of Chinese smugglers immediately came to light once the Ming government legalized private trade at Haicheng port in 1567; 100 permits were immediately issued to 100 Chinese junks trading overseas each year. In 1589 the Haicheng authorities tried to reduce the number of permits to 88 a year, but they soon abandoned this change following objections by merchants. In 1593, 110 permits were issued, and this number remained unchanged throughout the Ming Dynasty. In addition to this number, many ships sailed overseas without legal permits. For example, in 1593 when an official pardon was given to unlicensed ships trading and staying overseas, 24 of them returned for registration.[34]

Thus, we see that Ming maritime policies helped bring about the rise of Chinese mercantile power in Southeast Asia. By denying foreigners access to the Chinese market, it changed the rules of the game in favour of Chinese merchants and, accordingly, to the detriment of the businesses run by South and West Asians. Chinese mercantile power thus began to emerge in Southeast Asia, side by side with that of the South and West Asians who still dominated the trade in the maritime world of the Indian Ocean. A division of commercial interests between these two groups of traders subsequently appeared in Southeast Asia in the fifteenth and sixteenth centuries.

In the following century the South and West Asians finally gave up their mercantile interests almost completely in Southeast Asia. They certainly did not give them up voluntarily; rather, they were forced out of the maritime trade between Southeast Asia and India and West Asia, by the European maritime powers.

The trade monopoly by the Dutch United East India Company (VOC)

When the European ships began to sail to Asia following the sea route discovered by Vasco Da Gama in 1498, South and West Asian traders had already yielded to the Chinese their mercantile interests in East Asian waters. As they still commanded trade in the Indian Ocean, they continued to hold on to many commercial interests in Southeast Asia, as did the Chinese there. With the arrival of European ships, their interests were increasingly threatened and, in the end, were mostly lost to the Europeans. Among the European maritime powers responsible for the decline and demise of the commercial interests of the South and West Asians in Southeast Asia, three deserve our special attention: the Portuguese, the Dutch, and the English. It was the Dutch who were to prove to be the worst threat.

Europeans engaged in two kinds of maritime trade in Asia: Europe–Asia trade, and intra-Asia country trade (port-to-port trade within Asia). The asymmetry of market demand between Europe and Asia resulting from Europe's heavy reliance upon imports from Asia and its inability to offer desirable exports for Asia in return, compelled Europeans to resort to the following two solutions: export of precious metals, and country trade within Asia. Starting from the early sixteenth century the Portuguese had procured gold from Africa to buy spices and other Asian products for European consumption. The discovery of American silver in the 1540s and its massive production from the 1560s was a timely relief for their international liquidity constraints, especially in Europe–Asia trade.[35] European ships bound for the East Indies carried silver to pay for their return cargoes purchased in Asia. This seems to have become a matter of routine in the late sixteenth century. However, due to the growing demand for precious metals within Europe itself and the increasing popularity of mercantilism in European political circles, silver exports from Europe become more and more difficult from the mid-seventeenth century. In fact, European silver exports were never, even from the beginning, sufficient to pay for their return cargoes. Profit deriving from the country trade within Asia was the alternative means for maritime Europeans to create an even greater trade imbalance with the Asians. This sort of profit was so important that, as early as 1623, the Governor General of the Dutch VOC in Batavia had suggested to Amsterdam the possibility of solely using these profits to buy their return cargoes without shipping out precious metals from the Netherlands.[36] It is in this profit from the Europeans' country trade that we can find the information concerning the displacement of the mercantile interests of South and West Asians by the Europeans in maritime Southeast Asia.

After retreating from the East Asian waters in the early fifteenth century, South and West Asian traders concentrated their trading activities in the Indian Ocean. The most profitable businesses, then under their control, were shipping and marketing between India and maritime Southeast Asia. The cotton textiles produced in many places of coastal India had been widely used for centuries in the Indian Ocean world, particularly in Southeast Asia. Unlike Chinese silks and porcelains which were essentially for elite consumption, Indian cotton piece goods commanded a very popular market and therefore were most welcome in bartering for the spices and other tropical products in maritime Southeast Asia. Spices were then distributed, via many rounds of transaction, in India, Persia, the Arab world, and even Europe via the Mediterranean maritime traders like the Venetians. Indians, and later on Muslim traders from South and West Asia, had long dominated the economic exchanges between India and Southeast Asia through the control of shipping and marketing. In view of their early and long-lasting predominance in the Indian Ocean and Southeast Asia, their control of shipping and marketing in Sino-Southeast Asian maritime trade from the late seventh to the late fourteenth century was merely a logical consequence.

The dominance of the South and West Asians in Indo-Southeast trade was not challenged until the sixteenth century. From then on they were challenged first by the Portuguese, and then by northwest Europeans from various countries. The Dutch proved to be the most powerful rival who finally inflicted the fatal blow upon them.[37]

Two events marked the first disruption of South and West Asian commercial dominance in the Indian Ocean by the Portuguese: the fall of Goa to the Portuguese in 1510 and of Malacca in 1511. In Goa the Portuguese set up their *Estado da India*, or state of India, which was to serve in the next three centuries as the nerve centre for the whole Portuguese maritime empire from east of the Cape of Good Hope to Nagasaki in Japan. The traditional country trade from India to Persia and West Asia began to be impacted as the Portuguese government in Goa, after occupying Hormuz in 1515, tried to block the connections between the maritime and caravan trade routes through which Asian products were supplied to Europe. As is well known this connection made possible an active international market in the Levant and the mercantile dominance by Venice in the Mediterranean world. Although the Portuguese effort did not succeed, the blocking of this trade was later achieved in 1622 when the Portuguese base of Hormuz was seized by the English.[38] But the fall of Malacca into Portuguese hands had a more direct and much greater impact on Indo-Southeast Asian trade. For over a century Malacca had been the greatest entrepôt in maritime Asia to where traders from all corners of maritime Asia thronged to exchange their commodities. Among these traders, the South and West Asians were the foremost group, after which came the Chinese. In addition to Chinese goods, Indian cotton textiles and Southeast Asian spices were the most valuable commodities in Malacca.[39] Portuguese occupation of the city disrupted the regular trade there, forcing Asian traders to seek other ports in which to conduct their business. Though the Portuguese made great effort to restore its trading functions, Malacca was never to resume its former prosperity. Several ports in Sumatra, Java, and the Malay Peninsula emerged to take over the trade lost by Malacca, but none of them was able to replace it. It was not until the rise of Batavia under the Dutch in 1619 that we find an emporium able to grow into a new distribution centre in maritime Southeast Asia.

The Portuguese at first attempted to monopolize the Euro-Asian trade as well as the Indo-Southeast Asian trade, but they failed on both counts. Constrained by military and financial capacities, they soon had to abandon the plan for a trade monopoly and, by the mid-sixteenth century, the Portuguese *Estado da India* had lapsed into more of a redistributive system than a commercial organization, deriving its revenues increasingly from selling protection rather than from trading. Niels Steensgaard (1973) has characterized it as follows:

> *Estado da India* was a dynamic system, but the innovations were kept within the pattern of redistribution and the profit was consumed in a seigneurial way of life or reinvested in redistributive enterprises, not in productive or productive-increasing enterprises. The Portuguese were tax-gatherers and *Estado da India* was a redistributive institution.[40]

This view of the *Estado da India* very closely accords with that advanced by van Leur. Although recent research has attacked his views on the basis of more comprehensive material, I do not find any evidence has been produced that would shake his fundamental assertion:

> ... the commercial and economic forms of the Portuguese colonial regime were the same as those of Asian trade and Asian authority: a trade relatively small in volume conducted by the government as a private enterprise, and all further exercise of authority existing only to ensure the financial, fiscal exploitation of trade, shipping and port traffic, with higher officials and religious dignitaries recruited from the Portuguese aristocracy....

He further noted: "The Portuguese colonial regime, then, did not introduce a single new element into the commerce of Southern Asia".

As a mere participant among the many Asian trading groups in the Indian Ocean, the Portuguese did not bring about radical changes in the Asian trading world. They were content to enjoy the income deriving from the tax revenues of the ports under their control and from selling passes of safe conduct in the Indian Ocean, thereby allowing the maritime trade there to go on in its traditional way. As a participant, the Portuguese came to share with the South and West Asians the carrying and marketing business of Indo-Southeast Asian trade, squeezing to some degree the scope of commercial interests of South and West Asians in Southeast Asia. The squeezing effect was limited though, as their trade volume was small. Meanwhile Portuguese commercial interests had stretched too far and too wide in Asia, to be effectively maintained by their limited human resources.[41] Save for a few strategic trading sites like Hormuz, Goa and Malacca, where the Portuguese domination was effectively present, trade in Asia went on largely unaffected. By just paying a tax for free passage, an Indian ship could sail and trade as freely as before. With regard to Indo-Southeast Asian trade, the Portuguese had to compete with traditional Asian traders on relatively equal terms in open market operations. Of course, the Portuguese government in India was never an efficient economic organization either.

The northwestern Europeans appearing in the late sixteenth century were very different from the Portuguese in their vision of Asian trade. In contrast to the Iberian conquest empire overseas, the northwestern Europeans came to Asia solely in pursuit of a maritime trading empire. Grouping themselves under

The rise of Chinese mercantile power 233

various private companies they began to show up in Asian waters in the 1590s. After a few years of experimentation two important chartered companies emerged at the beginning of the seventeenth century: the English East India Company (1600, EIC), and the Dutch United East India Company (1602, VOC).[42] These companies were completely oriented to commercial profit, which they achieved, with their military and financial might, through exercising quasi-monopolistic regulation of supply and prices "within the limits determined by marginal rates of substitution".[43] That is, by adjusting the quantity mix and price mix of various spices and other tropical products the companies were able to accomplish their target profits in spite of the fluctuations of supply and demand. Characterized by an institutional arrangement that could sensitively respond to cost-benefit accounting, they internalized protection costs and increased market transparency as much as they could, effectively linking maritime Asia to the world market in an unprecedented way.[44]

Domestically these companies were chartered to monopolize the trade of their home country with the Asian world. Externally they had to compete in the Euro-Asiatic as well as the intra-Asian trade. Unlike the EIC, which was content with an open international market for European participants, the Dutch VOC with an initial capital of more than ten times that of the EIC, was more earnest in pursuing a policy of trade monopoly in maritime Asia. This it pursued chiefly through the control of production and distribution; whereby the VOC was the single buyer and the only seller. In the country trade between India and Southeast Asia, the Dutch VOC from the very beginning tried not only to monopolize the purchase and sale of spices from Southeast Asia; it also tried to monopolize the export of cotton piece goods from India to Southeast Asia. Political divisions and financial weakness in both India and Southeast Asia opened the way for the Dutch VOC's success.[45]

In the early half of the seventeenth century competition from the EIC and other European companies was able to thwart Dutch ambition of monopoly in maritime Asia. But with the Dutch occupation of the Spice Islands and the fall of Banten into their hands in 1682, the VOC's monopoly of finer spices, which were most demanded in India and Europe, was virtually achieved.[46] By blocking South and West Asians from buying spices in Southeast Asia and by controlling the stable supply of cotton textiles in India, the VOC finally again succeeded in monopolizing the export of Indian cotton textiles to maritime Southeast Asia. The traditional role of South and West Asians in servicing the Indo-Southeast Asian trade was thereby totally wiped out by the success of the Dutch monopoly. Their long-lasting commercial interests in this region accordingly died away quickly, leaving Chinese as the only intermediaries to cooperate with European interests represented by the Dutch VOC, to carry out international trade in Southeast Asia. Anthony Reid has the following observation:

> Indian and West Asian traders were among those lost out in the crisis period. Turks, Persians and Arabs virtually ceased traveling 'below the winds' with the collapse of spice route from Aceh to the Red Sea in the first

two decades of the seventeenth century. Gujaratis continued to bring their cloth to Aceh until about 1700, though in much reduced numbers after the Dutch onslaught on Aceh's tin and pepper resources in the 1650s. Chulia Muslims from Coromandel coast of Tamil Nadu were the only major group of Asians from 'above the winds' who continued to trade into the eighteenth century, and they too were losing out to European traders during that period.[47]

In addition to the "push" created by the Dutch VOC, Indian maritime traders were increasingly attracted by the "pull" arising from a rapidly-expanding market demand for Indian textiles in Europe and America in the seventeenth century. This new demand was so huge that economic gains from it were somehow able to offset the loss of the traditional trade they were then suffering in maritime Southeast Asia. Many of them quickly shifted their resources to the less risky and very lucrative business of supplying European companies with Indian textiles.[48] In this way this new demand hastened the retreat of the Indians' commercial interests in maritime Southeast Asia. Having abandoned trading to Banten after 1682, the EIC totally dropped its business in maritime Southeast Asia, leaving a comfortable VOC monopoly there for over a century. It began to concentrate much of its business on exporting Indian textiles to England, from whence a considerable part was re-exported to Europe and America by other companies. While the VOC purchased Indian textiles mainly as an intra-Asiatic country trade item in maritime Southeast Asia, the EIC collected these products primarily to supply its home market and beyond. In terms of this "pull" effect, the EIC was more important as England and British America began to consume the greatest quantity of exported Indian textiles after the mid-seventeenth century.

Unlike the Indians or West Asians, the Chinese continued to have competitive advantage over foreigners in China's overseas trade, as foreigners were still banned from China until 1684. Even after four Chinese ports were opened in 1684, foreigners were not allowed to take up permanent residence in China but had to depart the port of call when trade was completed. Chinese ports were opened mainly for Chinese merchants to trade overseas, not for foreigners to come to. Therefore, except for Macao, no European factories or trading bases, much less settlements, were established in Chinese ports. This arrangement made Chinese traders indispensable intermediaries to the Europeans trading to China.[49] After the South and West Asians withdrew from maritime Southeast Asia in the late seventeenth century, Chinese further expanded their market networks which not only serviced Sino-Southeast Asian trade, but facilitated the VOC's monopoly of Indo-Southeast Asian trade as well.[50]

Conclusion

This chapter traces the origin of Chinese mercantile power in maritime Southeast Asia over the period from 1400 to 1700. The argument in it is simple. Thanks to the retreat of South and West Asian commercial interests, the Chinese began to take on the role of trading intermediaries in Southeast Asia, shipping and marketing being their most important businesses. Between 1400 and 1600, the South and West Asians were displaced by the Chinese in conducting Sino-Southeast Asian trade. Between 1600 and 1700 they were again displaced by the Dutch and other Europeans in servicing the Indo-Southeast Asian trade. Their displacement in these two bilateral trades, which constituted the lion's share of the maritime trade in Southeast Asia, marked the end of the long-lasting dominance of South and West Asian mercantile interests in this region and the beginning of Chinese dominance in their place.

Two elements were most responsible for the phasing out of South and West Asians mercantile power in maritime Southeast Asia. These were the Ming maritime policy and the Dutch VOC monopoly. Ming maritime policy consisted of two components: maritime prohibition and tribute trade. Maritime prohibition completely ruined their trading bases in China and obviated their role as intermediaries in Sino-Southeast Asian trade. Tribute trade gave Chinese people total control over shipping and marketing in Chinese maritime foreign trade. These two components combined to force South and West Asians out of the trading business between China and maritime Southeast Asia (or even the whole maritime East Asia), thereby paving the way for the rise of Chinese mercantile power in this region.

The Dutch VOC was the only European trading empire that successfully enforced a monopoly of trade between many parts of maritime Southeast Asia and India in the seventeenth century. Through this monopoly, South and West Asians were, in this century, again driven out of most of the shipping and marketing services for the Indo-Southeast Asian maritime trade. Their mercantile power in maritime Southeast Asia was thus nearly entirely eliminated. Due to the importance of the China trade, which was controlled by the Chinese traders, and the impossibility of operating local marketing by themselves within maritime Southeast Asia, the Dutch had to rely upon Chinese people, both permanent residents and seafaring sojourners, to help carry out their monopoly trade to India and Europe. The stage was thus set for Chinese mercantile dominance in this region.

Ming maritime policy was restrictive to all private traders, Chinese and foreigners alike. It closed the Chinese market to South and West Asians for the first time in Chinese history. The Dutch VOC monopoly was restrictive to South and West Asians, but relatively open to Chinese traders. It closed the maritime Southeast Asian market to the South and West Asians for the first time in Southeast Asian history too. Just as the Ming maritime policy was devised to maximize the political gains of state security, the monopoly policy was pursued by the Dutch to maximize the commercial profit deriving from an assured market. They were not designed to help Chinese private traders, but in the end they both turned out to help establish the foundation of Chinese mercantile dominance in maritime Southeast Asia, essentially at the expense of the commercial interests of South and West Asians. In view of its historical significance and present relevance, the unintended consequence of these two elements reviewed here should not have been long overlooked. The pity is that it has been overlooked as a false bill all the time, until this moment when we picked it up from the sidewalk.[51]

Notes

1 Mancur Olson, "Big Bills Left on the Sidewalk: Why Some Nations are Rich, and Others Poor?", *Journal of Economic Perspectives*, 10.2 (1996): 3–24.
2 Kenneth R. Hall, "Economic History of Early Southeast Asia", in *The Cambridge History of Southeast Asia*, vol. 1, ed. Nicholas Tarling (Cambridge: Cambridge University Press, 1992), pp. 183–275.
3 At the end of the fifteenth century, for the Bengali textiles exported to Malacca, "profits of 200% to 300% were not infrequent"; and for the pepper exported from Malacca to China, "very large profits were made, as a *quintal* of pepper which was bought for 4 *cruzados* could be sold in China for 15 or 16 *cruzados*". See M. A. P. Meilink-Roelofsz, *Asian Trade and European Influence in the Indonesian Archipelago between 1500 and about 1630* (The Hague: Martinus Nijhoff, 1962), pp. 68 and 76. In 1621 the Dutch VOC recorded a gross profit in the home market of 320 per cent for the Chinese silks exported from Jacatra, and 325 per cent for those exported from Formosa. See Kristof Glamann, *Dutch-Asiatic Trade, 1620–1740* (The Hague: Martinus Nijhoff, 1958), p. 114.
4 In contrast to our example here, Billy So assumes a 100 per cent net return on investment, counting out the operating cost (shipping and marketing for example) that should also be reflected in the price difference. See his significant book: *Prosperity, Region, and Institutions in Maritime China: The South Fukien Pattern, 946–1368* (Cambridge, MA: Harvard University Press, 2000), p. 213, Table 9.1.
5 Prior to 1770 when the Dutch monopoly was broken, the production of cloves was concentrated in the Molucca islands (Ternate, Tidore, Makian, Motir Bacan), Ambon, and Seram. Until the eighteenth century, nutmeg and mace were produced only in the cluster of tiny islands collectively known as Banda. For details see Anthony Reid, *Southeast Asia in the Age of Commerce, 1450–1680: Volume 2, Expansion and Crisis* (New Haven: Yale University Press, 1993a), p. 4.
6 Ibid., p. 9.
7 For a brief and useful account, see Lynda N. Shaffer, *Maritime Southeast Asia to 1500* (New York: M. E. Sharp, 1996).
8 Wang Gungwu gives a very good account of the Chinese passive role and the domination of Sino-Southeast Asian trade by South and West Asians in "The Nanhai Trade: A Study of the Early History of Chinese Trade in the South China Sea", *Journal of the Malayan Branch of the Royal Asiatic Society*, 31.2 (1958): 113–5. Also see K. N. Chaudhuri, *Trade and Civilization in the Indian Ocean: An Economic History from the Rise of Islam to 1750* (Cambridge: Cambridge University Press, 1985), pp. 49–53; Billy So, *Prosperity, Region, and Institutions in Maritime China: The South Fukien Pattern, 946–1368* (Cambridge, MA: Harvard University Press, 2000), pp. 11–26.
9 Shiba Yoshinobu, *Sōdai Shōgyōshi Kenkyū* [*Commercial Activities during the Sung Dynasty*] (Tokyo: Kazama shoten, 1969), pp. 430–4.
10 In *Prosperity, Region, and Institutions*, pp. 225–6, Billy So has pointed out the risk cost Chinese merchants took on when entering Southeast Asian markets then under the monopoly of South and West Asians.
11 Ts'ao Yung-ho, "Zhongguo Haiyang Shihua" [A Discourse on Chinese Maritime History], in his book *Zhongguo Haiyangshi Lunji* (*Collected Essays on Chinese Maritime History*) (Taipei: Lianjing Press, 2000b), pp. 46–7.

12 Wang Gungwu, "The Nanhai Trade", pp. 112–16; and Billy So, *Prosperity, Region, and Institutions*, pp. 216–26, have speculated the Chinese learned from South and West Asians ideas and practices in relation to maritime trade.
13 Billy So, *Prosperity, Region, and Institutions*, pp. 27–127; Hugh Clark, "Muslims and Hindus in the Culture and Morphology of Quanzhou from the Tenth to the Thirteenth Century", *Journal of World History* 6, 1 (1995): 49–74.
14 The South and West Asians were politically ranked above the Chinese but next to the Mongols; the Mongols never took part in maritime foreign trade though. See Chen Gaohua, "Yuandai de Haiwai Maoyi (Foreign Maritime Trade in Yuan Dynasty)", in his book *Yuanshi Yanjiu Lungao (Collected Essays on Yuan History)* (Beijing: Zhonghua shuju, 1991), pp. 99–112.
15 A very good account of Ming maritime trade based on the tribute trade system is provided by Roderich Ptak, "Ming Maritime Trade to Southeast Asia, 1368–1567: Visions of a System", in *From the Mediterranean to the China Sea*, eds. Claude Guillot, Denys Lombard and Roderich Ptak; with the assistance of Richard Teschke (Wiesbaden, Germany: Harrassowitz Verlag, 1998), pp. 157–91.
16 Ts'ao Yung-ho, "Shilun Ming Taizu de Haiyang Jiaotong Zhengce" [On the Maritime Policy of Emperor Taizu], in his book *Zhongguo Haiyangshi Lunji*, pp. 187–8.
17 Mao Yuanyi, *Wubei Zhi [A Treaty of Military Defense]*, 1624 ed., vol. 223, p. 2a; Charles Hucker, "Hu Tsung-hsien's Campaign against Hsu Hai, 1556", in *Chinese Ways in Warfare*, ed. John K. Fairbank (Cambridge, MA: Harvard University Press, 1974), p. 275.
18 Roderich Ptak, "Ming Maritime Trade to Southeast Asia", pp. 157–91; Wang Gungwu, "Early Ming Relations with Southeast Asia: A Background Essay", in *The Chinese World Order*, ed. John K. Fairbank (Cambridge, MA: Harvard University Press, 1968a), pp. 35–62.
19 T'ien Ju-k'ang, "Cheng He's Voyages and the Distribution of Pepper in China", *The Journal of the Royal Asiatic Society of Great Britain and Ireland* no. 2 (1981): 186–97.
20 In Anthony Reid, *Southeast Asia in the Age of Commerce*, pp. 10–2, Reid expresses the opinion that Chinese market demand created by tribute trade in this period triggered a trade take-off in Southeast Asia.
21 Wang Gungwu on the other hand holds Confucianism most responsible for the change. He says:

> The maritime power as exhibited during those 65 years or so should not be seen as the natural outcome of Chinese political or economic history which was arrested by unprogressive Confucian bureaucracy but as an exceptional phenomenon which lasted as long as the emperors Hung-wu (1368–98) and Yung-lo (1402–24) were alive and which fizzled out once the traditional state was permitted to regain its equilibrium.
>
> (p. 127)

See his essay, Wang Gungwu, "Public and Private Overseas Trade in Chinese History", in *China and the Chinese Overseas* (Singapore: Time Academic Press, 1991), pp. 117–29.
22 The story of Chinese intermediaries serving in the foreign tributary missions are best documented in the case of the Ryukyuan kingdom, which has been well-studied by Atsushi Kōbata, *Chūsei Nantō Tsūkō Bōekishi no Kenkyū (Studies on the History of Trade and Communication in the Southern Islands)* (Tokyo: Nihon Hyōronsha, 1939).
23 Shen Shixing, comp. *Da Ming Huidian (Collected Statutes of the Ming)*, rep. of 1587 ed. (Taipei: Xinwenfeng Publisher, Taipei, 1976), vol. 20, p. 21a.
24 Wang Gungwu, "Merchants without Empire: The Hokkien Sojourning Communities", in *The Rise of Merchant Empires*, ed. James D. Tracy (Cambridge: Cambridge

University Press, 1990), pp. 409–21; Chang Pin-tsun, "The First Chinese Diaspora in Southeast Asia in the Fifteenth Century", in *Emporia, Commodities and Entrepreneurs in Asian Maritime Trade, c.1400–1750*, eds. Roderich Ptak and Dietmar Rothermund (Stuttgart, Germany: Franz Steiner Verlag, 1991), pp. 13–28. For a concise explanation of diaspora, see J. L. Heilbron, "In Diaspora", in *The Chinese Diaspora: Selected Essays*, ed. Wang Ling-chi and Wang Gungwu (Singapore: Times Academic Press, 1998), pp. xii–xiv.

25 Zhou Daguan 周達觀, *Zhenla Fengtuji* 真臘風土記, annotated by Xia Nai 夏鼐 (Beijing: Zhonghua shuju, 1981), p. 147.

26 Wang Dayuan汪大淵, *Daoyi Zhilue* 島夷誌略, annotated by Su Jiqing 蘇繼廎 (Beijing: Zhonghua shuju, 1981), pp. 69–71, 248.

27 Gong Zhen 鞏珍, *Xiyang Fanguozhi* 西洋番國志, annotated by Xiang Da 向達 (Beijing: Zhonghua shuju, 1961), pp. 4–6, 8, 11–13. Records here largely repeat what is found in *Yingyai Shenglan*.

28 Fei Xin 費信, *Xingcha Shenglan* 星槎勝覽, annotated by Feng Chengjun 馮承鈞 (Taipei: Commercial Press, 1970), Part I, pp. 9–10, 18, 20, and Part II, p. 1. It notes that Chinese descendants could be found at Malacca, but does not say if a Chinese community existed there (p. 20).

29 Ma Huan 馬歡, *Yingyai Shenglan* 瀛涯勝覽, annotated by Feng Chengjun 馮承鈞 (Taipei: Commercial Press, 1970) pp. 8–11, 16–17, 19. This source does not explicitly mention the existence of a Chinese community in Siam, but hints at it (p. 19). For the exact locations of these places, see J. V. G. Mills, *Ying-yai Sheng-lan: The Overall Survey of the Ocean's Shore*, White Lotus reprint of the 1970 ed. by Hakluyt Society (Bangkok, Thailand: White Lotus Press, 1997), Appendix 1, pp. 185–235.

30 Zhang Xie 張燮, *Dongxiyang Kao* 東西洋考 (Beijing: Zhonghua shuju, 1981), pp. 33, 44, 48, 55, 57–59, 62, 65, 67, 70, 89–95, 101.

31 Both Ptak and Wang Gungwu speculate that many of these Chinese emigrants were Sinicized Chinese Muslims forced out of China by the Ming policy. See Wang Gungwu, "Merchants without Empire", p. 405; and R. Ptak, "Merchant and Maximization: Notes on Chinese and Portuguese Entrepreneurship in Maritime Asia, c.1350–1600", in *Maritime Asia: Profit Maximization, Ethics and Trade Structure*, ed. Karl A. Sprengard and Roderich Ptak (Wiesbaden, Germany: Harrassowitz Verlag, 1994), pp. 29–35. Also see Anthony Reid, "The Rise and Fall of Sino-Javanese Shipping", in his book *Charting the Shape of Early Modern Southeast Asia* (Chiang Mai, Thailand: Silkworm Books, 1999), pp. 56–84.

32 Rajeswary Ampalavanar Brown describes the Chinese at that time in Southeast Asia as "omnipresent", in *Capital and Entrepreneurship in Southeast Asia* (New York: St. Martin's Press, 1994), p. 17.

33 M. A. P. Meilink-Roelofsz, *Asian Trade and European Influence in the Indonesian Archipelago between 1500 and about 1630* (The Hague: Martinus Nijhoff, 1962), pp. 27–88.

34 In 1593, save for 10 permits for trading in Taiwan, all were given to ships trading to Southeast Asia. See Zhang Xie 張燮, *Dongxiyang Kao* 東西洋考 (Beijing: Zhonghua Bookstore, 1981), pp. 132–3; Xu Fuyuan 許孚遠, *Jinghetang Ji* 敬和堂集, 1594 ed., 8 juan, pp. 10a–b.

35 Harry E. Cross, "South American Bullion Production and Export 1550–1750", in *Precious Metals in the Later Medieval and Early Modern Worlds*, ed. J. F. Richards (North Carolina: Carolina Academic Press, 1983), pp. 397–423.

36 Om Prakash, "Restrictive Trade Regimes: VOC and Asian Spice Trade in the Seventeenth Century", in *Emporia, Commodities and Entrepreneurs in Asian Maritime Trade*, eds. R. Ptak and D. Rothermund (Stuttgart: Franz Steiner Verlag, 1991), p. 120. See also Holden Furber, *Rival Empires of Trade in the Orient, 1600–1800* (Minneapolis: University of Minnesota Press, 1976), p. 36.

37 M. A. P. Meilink-Roelofsz, *Asian Trade and European Influence*, pp. 117–294. Portuguese influence is well summarized in K. N. Chaudhuri, *Trade and Civilization in the India Ocean*, pp. 63–79.
38 Niels Steensgaard, *The Asian Trade Revolution of the Seventeenth Century* (Chicago: The University of Chicago Press, 1973).
39 M. A. P. Meilink-Roelofsz, *Asian Trade and European Influence*, pp. 27–88.
40 Niels Steensgaard, *The Asian Trade Revolution*, pp. 85–6. J. C. van Leur further asserted that it was the Dutch and the English that heralded a new era in Asian commerce. See J. C. van Leur, *Indonesian Trade and Society: Essays in Asian Economic and Social History* (The Hague: W. van Hoeve, 1955), pp. 118–19. I thank Kuo-tung Chen for reminding me of van Leur's pioneering work.
41 C. R. Boxer, *The Portuguese Seaborne Empire* (London: Hutchinson & Co. Ltd., 1969), pp. 51–63.
42 There were other European East India Companies of lesser significance engaging in Indo-Southeast Asian country trade at that time, among which the Danish company which began in 1616 and the French company formed in 1654 were the main ones to be reckoned with. See Holden Furber, *Rival Empires of Trade in the Orient, 1600–1800* (Minneapolis: University of Minnesota Press, 1976), pp. 79–124; Stephan Diller, "The Participation of the Danish Trading Companies in Euro-Asiatic and Intra-Asiatic Trade", in *From the Mediterranean to the China Sea*, pp. 215–32.
43 Niels Steensgaard, *The Asian Trade Revolution*, p. 152.
44 K. N. Chaudhuri, *The Trading World of Asia*, p. 7.
45 Jurrien van Goor, "A Hybrid State: The Dutch Economic and Political Network in Asia", in *From the Mediterranean to the China Sea*, pp. 193–214; S. Arasaratnam, "Merchants of Coromandel in Trade and Entrepreneurship *circa* 1650–1700", in *Emporia, Commodities and Entrepreneurs in Asian Maritime*, pp. 37–51; Holden Furber, *Rival Empires of Trade in the Orient*, pp. 79–124.
46 Reid (1993, 23–4) points out that the Dutch VOC established a monopoly over the nutmeg and mace of Banda in 1621, and a monopoly of the Moluccan clove in about 1650. Banten, however, remained an emporium for international spice trade until it succumbed to the Dutch army in 1682. And in the 1680s the Dutch had become de facto ruler of Ceylon and achieved the control of cinnamon trade there, thereby completing the monopoly of all finer spices in Asia. See Jurrien van Goor, "A Hybrid State", p. 207.
47 Nicholas Tarling, ed., *The Cambridge History of Southeast Asia* (Cambridge: Cambridge University Press, 1992), vol. 1, p. 494. See also Om Prakash, "Restrictive Trade Regimes", pp. 107–26.
48 K. N. Chaudhuri, *The Trading World of Asia and the English East India Company, 1660–1760* (Cambridge: Cambridge University Press, 1978), pp. 10–15 and 237–312. S. Arasaratnam, "Merchants of Coromandel", pp. 37–51.
49 Jennifer Cushman has noticed the significance of "the exclusive access to Chinese ports other than Canton enjoyed by junks" in the survival of Sino-Siamese junk trade into the nineteenth century. See J. Cushman, *Fields from the Sea: Chinese Junk Trade with Siam during the Late Eighteenth-century and Early Nineteenth-century* (PhD diss., Cornell University, 1975), pp. 188–9.
50 The best account is given by Leonard Blussé, *Strange Company: Chinese Settlers, Mestizo Women and the Dutch in VOC Batavia* (Dordrecht, the Netherlands: Foris Publications, 1986), pp. 35–155. Also see Melink-Roelofsz, *Asian Trade and European Influence*, pp. 236–46. For a discussion of the economic complementarity between VOC and Chinese merchants in the East Indies, see Chang Pin-tsun, "Dutch VOC and the Rise of Chinese Mercantile Power in Maritime Southeast Asia in the Seventeenth Century", *Journal of the South Seas Society*, 56 (2002): 88–97.
51 In fact the VOC's positive contribution to Chinese mercantile power has been noticed by scholars like Reid (1992, 494) and Blussé, who in an interesting essay reaches the

following conclusion: "Western expansion of power meant paving the way for Chinese expansion of trade". See his essay L. Blusse, "In Praise of Commodities: An Essay on the Crosscultural Trade in Edible Bird's-Nests", in *Emporia, Commodities and Entrepreneurs in Asian Maritime Trade*, p. 334. However, neither scholar has paid attention to the significance of the retreat of the South and West Asians in the face of European competition.

10 Chinese traders in the Malay archipelago, 1680–1795

M. Radin Fernando

The Chinese undoubtedly played a significant role in generating economic growth in Southeast Asia in the nineteenth and twentieth centuries.[1] Their contribution to economic growth and development in the region prior to 1820, however, is less conspicuous, despite the fact that Chinese persons had been arriving in the region in increasing numbers for several hundred years.[2] There is no shortage of contemporary historical records which contain a great deal of information on the Chinese communities in Southeast Asia before 1800. The vast repositories of European trading companies and various local Chinese institutions such as social and economic associations contain a large amount of fascinating information on the rise and expansion of Chinese populations in the region, *albeit* scattered and interspersed with information on various other matters, and in most cases are yet to be explored.[3] This chapter presents preliminary results of a study of Chinese mercantile activities in the Malay Archipelago from the 1620s through to 1800 based on some unique contemporary records.

The Melaka harbour-master's list of ship movements was an important set of papers located at the bottom of a large amount of papers the officials of the United East India Company or the *Verenigde Oostindische Compagnie* (*VOC*) in Melaka dispatched to the Company's headquarters in Batavia every year and included in the documents Batavia sent to the Company's directors – the *Heeren XVII* – in Amsterdam. These documents received little attention in Batavia, much less in Amsterdam, because they contained information on day-to-day administration with which the upper echelons of the Company's administration had little time or inclination to involve themselves, unless required. The series of shipping lists for Melaka begins in 1677 and ends in 1792, with some minor gaps up to 1743 and with a major gap from 1743 to 1760. A typical entry in the harbour-master's record provides the date a ship arrived and left the port of Melaka, the name of the skipper, his ethnicity and place of residence, the type of ship, its dimension and number of the crew, the place of origin, destination, details of the cargo and information about previous visits to and from Melaka. For much of the first half of the eighteenth century, we also have information on the affiliations between skippers and ship owners. The data in the harbour-master's records are ideal for a serial study of the vicissitudes in regional commerce from the late seventeenth to the end of the eighteenth century.[4]

In addition to a corpus of over 6,000 individual records of traders, each record containing up to 40 variables of information, which provides a continuous narrative of commercial activities of the Chinese across the Malay Archipelago contained in the shipping lists, sporadic but more intricate details of Chinese commercial activities can also be found in numerous records of a legal character buried in the local archives of the Melaka *comptoir*.[5] The last wills and notorial papers recording business transactions, court cases of disputes over property including money and the records of borrowing money provide a rich array of information with which to study Chinese mercantile activities in Melaka. It will take a long time for any assiduous student to sift through this bulk of information and weave a narrative of Chinese mercantile activities at that time. This chapter argues that, in order to understand the magnitude and character of Chinese mercantile activities we need to locate them in the broad context of institutional development underlying all economic activities.[6]

A lively regional trade which linked port-polities stretching from the western tip of the Malay Archipelago to the South China Sea was a major factor of economic growth in the region after 1400. The vicissitudes of regional trade in which diverse groups of local and foreign merchants were involved to varying degrees are not so clear and the significance of regional commerce in domestic economic growth is often ignored by scholars who are dazzled by the growing long-distance trade between Europe and China across the Greater Indian Ocean. There is a general perception that regional commerce was economically insignificant, because it was conducted on a small scale and oriented towards the material needs of local people, while also being a feeder-service to the long-distance trade. The assertive measures adopted by the VOC, furthermore, aimed at gaining full control over both regional and long-distance trade in local products are believed to have dealt a detrimental blow to regional trade after 1620.[7]

There was indeed a great deal of change in regional commerce as a result of the operations of the VOC, among which re-direction of the junk trade to Batavia, the centre of all Dutch commercial activity in the region after 1619, was perhaps significant for its widespread repercussions on trade in many local ports.[8] But neither the occupation of various ports in the archipelago nor the treaties the VOC concluded with local rulers actually provided the Company with full control over regional trade in the archipelago. It remained largely outside the control of the VOC, because the Dutch had neither desire nor the means to control it once it became clear that anything resembling full control over regional commerce was simply beyond the Company's resources. There was plenty of room for local traders to operate, as seen from the example of Chinese traders who were perhaps highly skilled in adapting to new situations within the VOC regime of regional commerce and make a noteworthy contribution to domestic economic growth in the seventeenth and eighteenth centuries.

Years of adjustment, 1620–1680

By 1620, a considerable number of Chinese were scattered in the port-polities across the Malay Archipelago. Batavia was perhaps the most bustling port-city and there a large number of Chinese were concentrated in response to the lucrative business opportunities.[9] There were, however, Chinese traders at the ports of Banten, Cirebon, Semarang, Jepara and Surabaya, Melaka, Aceh and Patani, which were the other most important centres of commerce in the western part of the region. This commercial arch encompassing the western parts of the archipelago provided room for trade on varying scales as revealed by the size and composition of cargo conveyed by Chinese traders in the troubled years leading up to the consolidation of Dutch control over the Straits of Melaka in 1641.[10]

There were also settlements of Chinese traders in Sumatra, Siam, Burma and Vietnam, but it is extremely difficult to provide even a well-informed guess as to the scale of mercantile activities of Chinese in those areas at this time. The scale of commercial activities of Chinese outside Melaka, Kedah and the port-cities in Sumatra appears to have been rather small and remained so for some time to come. While Batavia seems to have attracted a large number of Chinese, not necessarily only as traders, other port-cities also began to attract more Chinese traders once Melaka came under Dutch control and trade across the Straits of Melaka became safer and better regulated. The new masters of Melaka welcomed Chinese as a group of people who would promote its economic prosperity through their own communal administrative institutions. This institutional framework of community administration proved highly conducive to the business activities of the Chinese in Melaka.

The Melaka harbour was open to all traffic without hindrance and it was governed more or less along the lines of administration laid down in the course of the fifteenth century.[11] The office of *syahbandar*, revived after a period of disuse under Portuguese rule, began to control a smooth flow of traffic at the cost of a tax of 10 per cent of the value of the cargo.[12] Local traders were free to conduct trade in commodities outside the Company's monopoly on spices and tin, and any local trader who paid the tolls and obtained passes could proceed to other ports in the archipelago. The institutionalization of port administration and trade regime within the pass system, introduced in order to maintain some control of traffic within the Dutch sphere of influence, appears to have encouraged the Chinese traders to test the limits of freedom allowed by new laws. The VOC authorities in Batavia were firmly against Melaka becoming a terminus for the junk trade with China, a policy which remained effective until the end of the eighteenth century, and allowed only a few junks to travel directly between Amoy and Melaka. The long-arch of Amoy–Melaka trade is argued to have been the life-line of trade and commerce within the archipelago before the 1620s and the diversion of Chinese junks from Amoy to Batavia is believed to have severely reduced indigenous – and Chinese – trade between South China and Southeast Asia, particularly the insular region.[13] This view requires a careful revision, for the Chinese traders settled at local port-cities, together with their

Malay counterparts, asserted a major role in regional commerce which had only a tenuous link with the junk trade between Amoy and Melaka.[14]

Melaka had a modest population in the late seventeenth century, when as much as half of the population was Chinese. They had begun moving to Melaka on a regular basis immediately after the Dutch captured the town in 1641. The Dutch encouraged the Chinese to come to Melaka in order to revive it as a centre of commerce, much against the set policy of the VOC, which forbade Melaka to make any effort to challenge Batavia's supremacy as the centre of all commercial activity in the archipelago.[15] This policy was, however, formulated in order to foster the long-distance trade with China, hence the prohibition of Chinese junks visiting any port other than Batavia, and did not encompass what was considered to be purely regional trade within the archipelago itself. Thus, Melaka's Chinese population, most of whom comprised traders, rose in number and emerged as a major group of traders engaged in a lively competition with their Malay counterparts.

The majority of Chinese lived in the inner suburb on the northern strand, where most residential quarters had been located since the early sixteenth century. A large number of Chinese also lived around the Bukit Cina area, another place where the Chinese had lived since the fifteenth century. There was apparently little change in this spatial distribution of Chinese population in Melaka until well into the early nineteenth century (see Table 10.1).

Chinese commercial activities were concentrated near the harbour. There were two markets near the port. One was located at the end of the First Cross Street, virtually on the bank of the river, which facilitated all traffic. There was another market behind the temple devoted to the Goddess of Mercy, which also served as the seat of the Captain of Chinese who administered all affairs of the local Chinese community.

We may now enter the world of Chinese merchants who crowded the tollgate, the narrow streets and the markets of Melaka in a flurry of activity of buying and selling, conducting business deals and preparing for the next journey.

The pattern of Chinese trading

It is perhaps necessary to begin the discussion with a brief sketch of Chinese commercial networks encompassing the western part of the archipelago. Melaka

Table 10.1 Spatial distribution of Chinese Population in Melaka, 1677

Area	Men	Women	Children	Slaves (men)	Slaves (women)	Slaves (children)
North Coast	94	113	117	48	90	51
Beyond north coast	11	6	7	10	7	9
Bukit Cina	22	21	35	35	34	0
Total	127	140	159	93	131	60

Source: VOC 1330, letter, Governor of Melaka to Batavia, 22 November 1677, NAN.

was evidently the centre of regional commerce despite the efforts of the Dutch East India Company to concentrate all trade in Batavia. The Chinese traders were numerically the second largest group of traders to operate in the commercial network with Melaka as its epicentre (Figure 10.1).

There was a rapid rise in the number of Chinese traders operating through Melaka in the first half of the eighteenth century, which was partly a result of the internecine conflicts among the Malays on both sides of the Straits of Melaka. The curve dips suddenly at one point and oscillates several times after 1760 due to the stiff competition between the Chinese and Malay traders, who made a bold effort to carve out a larger share of the booming regional trade for themselves. Like other groups of traders, the Chinese were engaged in circulating the commodities produced in different areas and goods brought from outside.

The port of domicile, or base of operation, played a significant role in traders' success or failure, for their ability to procure credit and capital as well as commodities was entirely based on their links with the local merchant community. This was particularly important for the Chinese traders, who had extensive communal ties strengthened by clan relationships. It seems that most traders remained steadfastly bound to a particular base of operation, suggesting a strong relationship with their friends and relatives, who provided them with capital and other facilities such as boats and crewmen as well as business partners in commercial activities.

A detailed analysis of shipping movements by the home base of the captain provides a clear picture of the vicissitudes in Chinese mercantile activities across the archipelago (Table 10.2a and Table 10.2b). From the early 1680s to the early 1740s, most Chinese traders were located in the Malay Peninsula with Melaka as their *locus primus*, in Java with Batavia and Semarang their main domiciles, and in Siam. There were some significant changes in this pattern in the second half of the eighteenth century: the number of Chinese

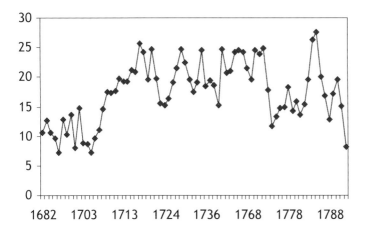

Figure 10.1 The proportion of Chinese traders of all traders, 1682–1792.

Table 10.2a Base of operation of Chinese traders, 1682–1742

Base	1682	1698	1700	1715	1720	1725	1730	1735	1742
Ujung Salang								3	3
Patani	1								
Kedah									
Pulau Pinang									
Perak	2								
Melaka	13	2	13	31	24	12	26	27	35
Linggi				1	1				1
Johor		4	11	1	15				
Riau	1			20	18	18	4		6
Terengganu						1			
Malay Peninsula	17	6	24	53	58	31	30	30	45
Aceh	1								
Batu Bara							1		1
Asahan									4
Bengkalis	1								
Jambi									
Palembang		2		2					4
Sumatra	2	2		2			1		9
Batavia	10	9	9	10	14	17	22	32	1
Cirebon	4	10	3		11	5	2	4	1
Pekalongan		2		10					
Semarang	2	15	9	9	17	17	32	25	2
Jepara	3	9	6		1		2		
Surabaya		4		1	1			2	
Sumanap		1							
Java	19	50	27	30	44	39	58	63	4
Makassar		1							
Borneo					1		1		
Pegu									
Siam	1			17	10	27	3	5	
Cambodia				2		2			9
Mainland	1			19	10	29	3	5	9
Amoy				1					2
Other Places	3	2		1	3	3		2	1
The rest of the archipelago	5	3		40	23	61	7	12	21

traders based in Java declined considerably and Semarang usurped the place of honour as the preferred base of Chinese traders in Java. This was obviously due to the cataclysmic events in Batavia in 1740, which decimated Batavia's Chinese population and sent the Chinese packing for less hostile areas in Java and in the Malay Peninsula.[16] It seems that Melaka became a preferable place of domicile for the Chinese, perhaps a little less profitable compared with Batavia but nonetheless more agreeable given its reputation as an old Chinese settlement. The reasons for the falling number of Chinese traders visiting Melaka from the mainland ports is less clear. It suggests a more isolationist policy on the part of indigenous rulers, but an effort to re-orient trade towards

Table 10.2b Base of operation of Chinese traders, 1761–1792

Base	1761	1765	1770	1775	1780	1785	1792
Ujung Salang							
Patani							
Kedah	6	2	4	8		9	7
Pulau Pinang							4
Apung					2		
Perak	1					2	
Melaka	35	79	95	14	67	107	12
Linggi							
Selangor			3	3	2		
Johor							
Riau	1		2	1	6	22	5
Terengganu							
Panny						1	
Malay Peninsula	43	81	104	26	77	141	28
Aceh							
Batu Bara			3	2	1	5	
Bukit Batu		3					
Asahan	1						
Rokan					2	1	
Siak		2	3	38	4	39	14
Bengkalis							
Jambi							
Palembang		1	1				
Padang			3				
Sumatra	1	6	10	40	7	45	14
Batavia	4	2	6	2	2	3	
Cirebon	6	6	5	6	8	1	
Pekalongan				2			
Semarang	4	4	11	8	13	9	2
Jepara			1	7	2	1	
Surabaya	1		4		4		1
Sumanap							
Java	15	12	27	25	29	14	3
Makassar							
Borneo							
Pegu			2				
Siam	1	10	1		4	4	
Cambodia		2	2				
Amoy		6				2	
Cancouw			9	4	2		
Other Places	1		1	1			
The rest of the archipelago	2	18	15	5	6	6	
Total	61	117	156	96	119	206	45

alternative ports and the increased use of European ships for business appear to be more likely explanations.

The Chinese traders were more mobile than Malay or European traders. The movement of Chinese traders can be ascertained by looking at the port of origin and destination of a given trader or a ship. This information is very difficult to present in tabular or graphic form and it is perhaps sufficient to state broad patterns. Chinese traders based in Melaka, for instance, conducted their business in Perak, Jepara and Cirebon. Traders based in Semarang conducted business between Aceh, Batavia and Jepara, which must have kept them away from the base port for much of the year. Some traders confined their business activities within a reasonably narrow sphere – for instance, between Padang, Riau and Terenganu – perhaps in order to stay close to their base of operation. This practice apparently became popular among the Chinese traders after 1750, perhaps signifying a shift towards putting roots in a particular place as a part of the process of assimilation into the local community, which gathered momentum in the late eighteenth century.

There was very little traffic conducted by the Chinese between South China and the other port-cities in the Malay Archipelago, although the junk trade between South China and Batavia continued and even increased between 1680 and 1750, noticeably slackening thereafter.[17] There is further evidence of waning interest of Chinese settled in various parts of the Malay Archipelago in conducting long-distance trade with South China. The Chinese and Japanese sources clearly suggest a sharp decline in Chinese junks arriving at Nagasaki from Southeast Asian ports after 1700.[18] This state of affairs suggests that the long-distance trade between Amoy and Melaka, or any other major harbour in the archipelago, no longer exercised a strong influence on regional commerce. It is also clear that Chinese mercantile activities were flexible across the archipelago, because the frequency of voyages between numerous port-cities and Melaka varied over time as dictated by the needs of local markets as well as the circumstances which affect all commercial activities. While the magnitude of Chinese trading activities between different port-cities varied from time to time, the overall degree of Chinese commercial activities rose, attesting to the industry and business acumen of Chinese engaged in commerce across the archipelago.

The period from 1780 to 1820 was both politically and economically turbulent for the inhabitants of the archipelago. The old economic regime dominated by trade between China and Europe under the aegis of multi-national trading companies was coming to an end as industrialization gradually began to spread across Europe transforming its mercantile economy towards an industrial economy. It was the political dimension of this economic transformation in the disguise of intense conflicts between the Dutch and the British which gave the local population a sense of changing times. They were forced to realign their contacts and re-orient towards a new economic order whose dawn was heralded by the foundation of Singapore at the centre of new sea-lanes linking China and Europe. The profound economic implications of this shift in centres of economic activity were not lost on the local people. Most local traders operating in the

Straits with Melaka as their base immediately shifted themselves to Singapore whose spectacular growth within a decade transformed it into a hub of regional commerce with a pronounced Chinese community representation.[19] The magnitude of Chinese commercial activities between 1790 and 1820 is difficult to gauge precisely as the data by ethnic categories are not available. The impressionistic evidence is quite clear as to a sudden rise in the fortunes of Chinese in their new abode of prosperity, with its enhanced institutional advantages conducive to commercial activity across the archipelago.

Scale of commercial operations

The Chinese traders often conducted trade in groups of varying sizes in order to overcome the difficulties in procuring capital and other resources, with different members of the group or association apparently taking turns in leading the group in business trips.[20] This explains the overwhelmingly large number of traders who appear in the harbour-master's lists only once, although the number of traders operating on a given trade route or between a given number of port-cities remained more or less constant, or at least without substantial fluctuations that cannot be explained by other factors. It was a fair method of sharing the risks as well as rewards equally among all members of the group, for the *nakhoda* of a ship received a double portion of profits of the voyage according to the customary rules.[21]

There were four main categories of Chinese traders operating over a vast regional network of commerce centred on Melaka (See Table 10.3). First, we find a large number of small traders operating with small boats carrying small cargoes. They made one or two trips a year and never reappeared. For instance,

Table 10.3 Examples of merchant voyaging 1682–1742

Name	Base	Period of activity	Trade route
Bieko	Melaka	1697–1727	Melaka–Kedah–Asahan–Riau–Terengganu
Chieakon	Melaka	1726–1729	Melaka–Siantang–Terengganu–Borneo
Gouwko	Melaka	1715–1721	Melaka–Riau
Haijko	Melaka	1697–1714	Melaka–Riau
Hianko	Melaka	1715–1721	Melaka–Siam–Riau–Linggi
Kitko	Melaka	1714–1717	Melaka–Siantan–Asahan–Riau
Liensaij	Melaka	1715–1719	Melaka–Riau–Batavia
Lim Moeijko	Melaka	1728–1730	Melaka–Benkalis
Nio Saijko	Melaka	1728–1729	Melaka–Kedah
Peksoe	Melaka	1709–1714	Melaka–Siam–Dili–Asahan–Riau–Batavia
Phoeanko	Melaka	1712–1722	Melaka–Perak–Kedah–Ujungsalang
Santonko	Melaka	1717–1724	Melaka–Aceh
Soekietko	Melaka	1733, 1741	Melaka–Asahan–Kalang
Than Oeijko	Melaka	1733–1735	Melaka–Kedah
Thianko	Melaka	1701, 1720	Melaka–Langkawi, Terengganu
Thaijko	Melaka	1716–1718	Melaka–Johor–Terengganu
Tjongko	Melaka	1713–1721	Melaka–Siam–Linngi

Bie Ongko made three trips in 1764 and then disappeared from the records. He left Melaka for Bukitbatu on 12 July 1764, returned on 22 September and left for Siak on 12 October. Traders like Bie Ongko usually operated on one route linking two ports or markets. Representative figures for trips per trader are provided in Table 10.4.

Second, we find some small traders who reappear once again long after their first appearance. Thus, Thianko made his first appearance on the route connecting Melaka and Langkawi in 1701; he reappeared 19 years later in 1720, when he arrived in Melaka from Terengganu. This would seem to suggest that a trader would move out of a route if he found better opportunities on another route or at another port. Another plausible explanation is, as mentioned above, that traders operating as a group took turns in directing voyages.

Third, we find many traders operating on a trade route for several years and then disappearing from the records. For instance, Hianko, a trader based in Melaka, operated on a route that extended over a wide area from Siam to Riau-Lingga between 1715 and 1721. Hianko made only one trip to Siam and probably decided it was not worthwhile to go there again; thereafter he operated between Melaka and Riau. Thus, finding a profitable route was a matter of trial and error and most traders remained fixed on a route for several years once they had found a suitable market.

Table 10.4 Examples of merchant voyaging 1760–1792

Name	Base	Period of activity	Trade route
Baba Houw	Melaka	1765–1768	Melaka–Asahan–Batubara
Bing	Melaka	1773	Melaka–Siak
Bok Hanko	Melaka	1766	Melaka–Aceh–Batavia
Gan Lotjong	Melaka	1761–1770	Melaka–Batubara–Selangor
Hoeat [Hoewat]	Melaka	1767–1773	Melaka–Bukitbatu–Siak
Kaij	Melaka	1767–1775	Melaka–Siak–Bukitbatu
Khe Tho	Melaka	1766–1770	Melaka–Siak
Lim Hoeseng	Semarang	1771–1775	Melaka–Semarang
Oein Lanko	Melaka	1767–1768	Melaka–Siak
Oein Janko	Melaka	1769–1772	Melaka–Siak
Oein Pauw	Melaka	1770–1771	Melaka–Siak
Ong Engsiong	Melaka	1761–1769	Melaka–Batavia
Piauw Joeko	Melaka	1769–1770	Melaka–Siak
Poetjouw	Melaka	1766–1767	Melaka–Batubara–Selangor
Que Siang	Melaka	1767	Melaka–Siak
Sin	Melaka	1766–1772	Melaka–Siak
Tan Kongi	Melaka	1767–1769	Melaka–Semarang
Tan Paiko	Melaka	1761–1772	Melaka–Siak–Kampar
Tan Siong	Melaka	1763–1767	Melaka–Batubara–Asahan–Riau–Siam
Tan Tiauko	Cirebon	1765–1790	Melaka–Cirebon
Tan Hak	Melaka	1765–1773	Melaka–Siak
Tan Hakko	Melaka	1765–1771	Melaka–Siak
Thin Houw	Melaka	1771–1772	Melaka–Siak

Fourth, we find a large number of traders who operated on a fixed route over a long period. A notable example of this category of traders who was based in Melaka is Bieko. On his first visit to Melaka on 25 June 1697, he reported that he was based in Batavia. It seems that he shifted to Melaka a few years later and, between 1712 and 1727, Bieko was active over a long arch encompassing lucrative markets such as Kedah, Asahan, Riau and Terengganu. Another noteworthy merchant was Puchouw, who was active for just over a decade from 1766 to 1767 and conducted a brisk trade between Melaka, Batu Bahara and Selangor. It is reasonable to conclude that traders who operated on one route over a long period were leading members of the merchant community and had access to the resources to conduct business on a large scale. They procured funds, as we shall see below, to gather commodities, equip the ships and conduct business through numerous methods including loans, mortgage and joint-partnerships with other merchants.

There was a certain correlation between the type of vessel used by a trader and his circuit of operation and the resources at his disposal. The most popular vessels were *baluk*, *shallop*, *konting* or *gonting*, *pancalang* and *ruku* among a wide range of boats (Table 10.6). The vessels which the traders used were often determined by the distances travelled and the range and amount of goods conveyed, and sometimes by the base of the traders. Traders from Batavia, for instance, usually employed large boats such as *shallop*, *konting* and *wankang*, because they could carry a large amount of goods. Traders from Amoy always employed a junk capable of carrying a very large cargo. Those who covered a short distance from Siak to Melaka or from Johor to Melaka could use several kinds of small boats depending on the size of the cargo. The traders who lived in Melaka used a wide range of boats to suit their journeys to near or distant ports and to cater for cargoes of varying sizes.

Table 10.5 Number of trips per trader

Year	Number of trips								
	1	2	3	4	5	6	7	8	9
1682	25	8	1	1					
1698	34	9		1					
1700	28	7	3						
1715	41	17	3	2			1		
1720	53	5	2						
1730	34	18	5	1	1				
1742	34	13	1	1					
1761	31	12	2	4					
1765	49	19	3	2					1
1770	75	18	4	2	1	2	1		
1780	37	18	2	2	2	1	1		1
1791	36	14	6		1				

Table 10.6 Types of vessels used in particular years

Vessel	1682	1698	1700	1715	1720	1730	1742	1761	1765	1770	1780	1791
Baluk	1	1	1	9	25	12	11	23	40	75	61	25
Banting							1	3	4	9	3	2
Bark	3										11	
Brigantyn								2	2	7	18	
Chialup	19	36	13	18	25	42	6	15	21	22	5	
Conting	9	15	19	52	43	30	16	3		3		
Giljoen	1											
Hoeker										3		
Jacht	1		2									
Jagoan			4									
Junk	4			5			4	1	8			7
Kakap									7	4	1	2
Kiel							4					
Kits								1	2			
Lambu	3	1	2	1	2							
Meroe				11	2		5		14			
Pancalang				5	3	7	17	10	2	6	4	15
Panjajap								1		1		2
Perau					8							
Peraumayang								1	3	5	9	
Roekoe			10	5	10	2	3					
Sampan		1								8	3	1
Sloep		1										
Wankang		5							4	17	6	
Other		1	1		1				1			1
Total	47	56	51	107	118	93	67	61	116	155	119	54

However, the correlation between the type of ships used and the distance and size of the cargo cannot be precisely defined in view of the diversity of business practices discussed above. Those on board a vessel assisted in sailing, but they could also be business partners who shared a compartment in the hull where their cargo was stored. Sometimes a trader singly or in partnership with one or more other traders hired a ship and accompanied his cargo. The harbour-master's records provide information on the nature of the crew, whether it consisted of slaves, Chinese, Malay or Christians and whether there were any passengers on board. The slaves were obviously deck-hands but some crewmen are very likely to have been traders travelling with their cargo. Therefore, a simple correlation between the kind of ship and the distance travelled or crew size cannot be established. It is, nevertheless, possible to discern some general rules. The *baluk* was a small boat which carried a small cargo and a few men while a *shallop* was a larger vessel which sailed with six to 32 men on board and with a large cargo over a long distance. Another ship that shared the same characteristics was a *konting* and both kinds of ship were popular with the traders travelling between Javanese ports and Melaka. The junk was indeed a large vessel which, depending on the size of the cargo carried, could have weighed from 30 to hundreds of *lasts* (a *last* is equivalent to 4,000 lbs) and sailed with up to 60 men as was observed in the case of a single junk which travelled between Amoy and Melaka regularly almost every year with a very large cargo.

Wheels of commerce

The harbour-master's list prior to 1750 provides information of the ownership of ships where the *nakhoda* himself did not own it and stated his affiliations with other persons. We may reasonably assume that the *nakhoda* himself was the owner of his ship if no such information is given. A few examples of *nakhodas* working for others will give us a feeling for the way Chinese traders procured resources to conduct business.

There were several Chinese *nakhodas* conducting business on behalf of fellow Chinese of higher social standing such as the captain of Chinese. For instance, in the 1680s, Lijgwaka, a resident of Melaka, operated a *shallop* owned by Sisia, the Captain of Chinese in Melaka.[22] The Captain of Chinese in Batavia also once sent one of his minders, Khaijko, with a *shallop* carrying a cargo from Semarang in 1698.[23] Some Chinese traders had illustrious patrons as shown by the example of Siocko, a Chinese resident in Siam, whose patron was none other than the king of Siam.[24] This kind of affiliations with noblemen disappeared altogether after 1740, a development perhaps indicative of both the Chinese and Malay traders becoming independent from the feudal political order.

Occasionally we meet a Chinese trader hiring a boat or working for a leading merchant outside his ethnic group. Qiu Liem, for instance, worked for David Boelen, the Governor of Melaka from 1758 to 1764, and for Malik Fasula, a leading Muslim merchant in Melaka. Some leading merchants too engaged someone to conduct their business for them. In 1761, for instance, Oei Loko, a merchant in Melaka, had engaged Chan Thoko as his man of business while Chan Theko, another merchant in Melaka, engaged Chan Thianko as his man of business. It is just possible that some leading merchants had quite a few servants in their service and dispatched one of them as his man of business.

Many Chinese were able to gather resources to conduct business on their own, always assuming that our records do not mention any affiliation or partnership simply because there was none to report on the basis of information supplied by the traders themselves. One may assume, nevertheless, that Chinese traders usually formed business partnerships with one or more fellow Chinese who supplied funds to buy or hire a boat, to engage a crew and to buy the commodities being transported. This is more than likely in the case of Chinese traders who did not operate on a regular basis and disappear from the records after one or two trips abroad.

Only a handful of Chinese traders hired ships. In 1698, for instance, out of 55 traders only seven traders made use of boats that belonged to another person. Soequa, a trader based in Jepara, came to Melaka on a *shallop* that belonged to Oei Pinko, the captain of Chinese in Jepara. Khaiko, a trader in Batavia, came to Melaka on a *shallop* that belonged to Quekanqua, the Captain of Chinese in

Batavia. These cases, and other similar examples for the first half of the eighteenth century, suggest that these traders were probably operating on behalf of their patrons. The influential members of the Chinese community, such as the Captains of Chinese in Jepara, Semarang, Batavia and Melaka, were prominent merchants who engaged others to conduct business on their behalf.

The wide range of ships used by Chinese traders implies a scale of commercial activity, which ranged from occasional ventures to large-scale commercial operations involving a considerable amount of resources and many individuals. The shipping list unfortunately does not provide much information about the nature of mercantile organizations and their operation. There are no Chinese sources comparable to those on the Hong merchants in Canton, which have enabled historians to reconstruct a fascinating picture of the world of commerce in Canton in the late eighteenth and early nineteenth centuries.[25] The Chinese merchants operating in the Malay Archipelago have not left their ledgers, diaries or legal documents of the kind carefully preserved by merchants in Europe such as Francesco Datini, which yield a comprehensive account of mercantile operations in the age of commerce.[26] Occasionally we find a document describing mercantile activities of a merchant such as Hovhannes, an Armenian merchant operating between Isfahan and Tibet, and we can catch a glimpse of the intricate details of the world of commerce in Asia.[27] The only known documentary evidence relating to the operations of Chinese merchants in Melaka is found in legal documents such as deeds, bottomery bonds and court cases involving Chinese merchants after 1760. The shipping list nevertheless provides a certain amount of evidence to formulate tentative observations on the character of Chinese mercantile operations.

Being domiciled in one place for a long time apparently brought substantial advantages to the Chinese traders in conducting business. The institutional advantages of having a fixed base of operation is evident from the examples of traders who conducted medium or large-scale operations using the boats borrowed or rented from prominent merchants in their base port-city. The vast majority of Chinese traders had their own boats or rented them, but a fair number of traders who conducted business on a large scale over a long period used ships which belonged to a businessman with resources. For instance, Bauko, a trader in Batavia, who conducted several trips to Melaka in 1699, used a *shallop* which belonged to Que Pinko, the Captain of Chinese in Batavia. In 1718, Bieko, a trader in Melaka with eight partners in trade, travelled between Melaka and Terengganu in a *pancalang* that belonged to a fellow Chinese, Liersay, in Melaka. Lim Chenko in Batavia borrowed or rented a *shallop* from a fellow Chinese, Oei Loanko, in his home town to conduct business for several years from 1716 to 1730. Some Chinese traders such as Chin Koei Kwa, who was based in Siam, had illustrious patrons from whom to borrow or rent boats; in 1714–1715, Koei Kwa travelled between Siam and Melaka in a large junk of 60 *last* which belonged to none less than the *phrakhlang* (treasurer) of Siam. Small Chinese traders operating alone or in groups appear to have rented or borrowed boats from leading Chinese merchants, who often held the position of the Captain of

Chinese in Batavia and Semarang, both cities in Java with a substantial Chinese population connected by all kinds of relationships. During the second half of the eighteenth century Chinese traders apparently availed themselves of links with their kinsmen as well as outsiders to procure or rent boats. Leading members of the Dutch community in Melaka and other port-cities, who were engaged in a lucrative private business to supplement their meagre income from the Company, invested their money in ships and rented them out to reliable traders. Such transactions involving large sums of money – boats were costly to build and maintain – were most likely to have been properly documented, but unfortunately not all of them have survived the passage of time, depriving historians an opportunity to ascertain the full cross-cultural character of the commercial world in the archipelago.

A fairly large number of Chinese traders who had been well-established in their home ports were able to enjoy the patronage of noblemen and even kings, attesting to the prevailing mercantile spirit across ethnic boundaries in the world of commerce. There were many Chinese traders who operated as "servants" of Malay kings and noblemen from the 1680s through to the 1740s, when the Malay noblemen appear to have played a prominent role in regional commerce. The Bendahara of Johor, Tun Abdul Jalil, was a popular master of many Chinese traders. The noblemen such as the *bendahara* of Johor employed many traders as his agents, among whom we find a few Chinese. In 1698, for instance, we find Saiko, and in 1715, we find Lien Sainko and Peksoe, all travelling back and forth between Riau and Melaka conducting business on behalf of the *bendahara* of Johor.[28] Another Chinese trader affiliated with a nobleman was Hoeiko, who was a servant of the *Raja Muda* of Johor.[29] Some Chinese had already assimilated themselves into the local Malay society in the process of being a servant of noblemen. Thus, we find *encik* Poo, who was a servant of *pangeran* Samujaja in Palembang, conducting business on behalf of his master.[30]

Some Chinese traders ingratiated themselves to the Malay noblemen and procured letters from them ensuring them a degree of latitude in dealing with the Dutch custom officials who were always looking for avenues to raise the port dues. The port officials of Melaka invariably respected the letters of patronage issued by the noblemen of Johor and waived the port dues and, perhaps more importantly, issued passes allowing the traders who carried the letters unhindered passage through the Straits of Melaka. The Malay noblemen who granted such letters of patronage probably exacted a fee or availed themselves at the services of Chinese traders in conducting business.

The patronage of noblemen was conspicuous well into the 1730s. The absence of patrons thereafter does not necessarily mean that noblemen disassociated themselves from mercantile activity. It is indeed true that frequent political conflicts disrupted mercantile activity in the Malay kingdoms, notably in the Malay Peninsula, in the first half of the eighteenth century. But trade was essential to secure and strengthen political power in Malay polities and the Malay noblemen as a class persevered with trading amidst political conflicts. They had good reasons to engage more Chinese as intermediaries in conducting business, but we have no regular records of this in the second half of the eighteenth century. There was, however, another factor which needs to be taken into account in explaining the noticeable decline in the number of noblemen supporting traders, both Chinese and Malay, after 1740. Many traders probably felt secure enough and had access to resources to conduct business without resorting to the patronage of lords as local trade gathered momentum in the second half of the eighteenth century.

An important element in securing patronage, partners in business, capital and other resources to conduct trade was family relationships contracted through marriage into local Chinese or Malay families. Marriage proved a convenient and secure means for Chinese sojourners of identifying with the local population, and as the number of Chinese arriving from South Fukien rose after 1680, marriage alliances with local women was probably the most secure way of beginning a successful career in the new homeland.[31] The process of assimilation into the local society appears to have been going on for quite some time in certain parts of the archipelago such as Java, where the Chinese began to settle down at the very beginning of the resurgence in trade with China in the fifteenth century, as evinced by numerous Chinese traders who had described themselves as *peranakan* Chinese and adopted impressive Javanese names. There was, for instance, Kartadiwangsa from Cirebon (1713–1717) and *ingebai* Sutawitana (1695–1696) from Cirebon who were servants of Sultan Sepoh. Many more Chinese, however, adopted less grandiose but endearing Muslim Malay names such as Abdul Rahman, Nordin, Dul and Jamal while others settled for common Malay names such as Banjang, Tenga, Karanda, Kalar, Manak and Hamat. Some *peranakan* Chinese preferred to use the prefix *baba* suggesting a degree of indigenization. Many indigenized Chinese traders had formal links with a patron and borrowed or rented boats from a prominent person attesting to the extent to which indigenization facilitated commercial activities in a society where social relationships proved highly beneficial economically.

It is widely assumed that all commercial activities in the archipelago were conducted according to the rules laid down in the famous maritime code of Melaka, a set of rules widely used with minor variations across the region in the sixteenth century. But it is misleading to extrapolate business practices of traders from a prescriptive text and consider them valid for the following centuries as well. The old code of maritime laws is likely to have been adhered to in general terms, but the scale of commercial operations had changed considerably, and the rapid growth of commercial activities brought about further changes in all aspects of commercial transactions. The business practices as they evolved amidst a flurry of commercial activity probably combined elements of both Chinese and European norms alongside the old regulations of Melaka.

As mentioned, there were some small Chinese traders conducting business on behalf of a leading member of the Chinese community such as the Captain of Chinese after 1620, but most small traders were free men operating in partnership with others or on their own using funds procured from numerous sources. It is difficult to determine just how many small Chinese traders formed partnerships with others, for the shipping list does not provide any clue on this matter. One piece of evidence relevant in this context is the crew, which often consisted of slaves or hired men, who could not have been partners as was the case with the large Chinese junks arriving in *Nanyang* from Amoy.[32] The shipping list carefully notes the presence of passengers if any, which was a rare occurrence, so it is conceivable that most small Chinese traders were not involved in partnerships with others. The kinds of boats used by small Chinese traders also seem to suggest that often they could operate without such partnerships, which were essential if the operation was conducted on a medium or large scale. The small traders, nevertheless, appear to have relied on others to procure commodities on credit, when a cargo of more than two or three commodities in large quantities was involved.

Small Chinese traders appear to have conducted business mostly with their own resources well into the mid-eighteenth century. Only a handful of traders worked for another person or hired a ship from another person. The ship was perhaps the most important item in terms of cost and next came the crew, which had to be hired, and finally the commodities, which could be procured on credit or on the basis of an arrangement to share profits with the producers or intermediaries who dealt with the producers. The small traders were able to gather much in the way of funds or resources as shown by many examples. For instance, in early June 1682, Inko or Imko, a trader from Batavia, arrived in Melaka on a *shallop* with a crew of 23 men and a cargo that comprised of 12 *koyang* of rice, 13 *pikul* of sugar, one *pikul* of clove and two bales of cinnamon – the last two commodities probably purchased from the VOC stores in Batavia. The fact that most small traders carried a cargo of agricultural products such as rice, sugar and tamarind, all originating from the areas adjacent to Batavia, would seem to suggest a network of intermediaries in the hinterlands supporting traders in coastal towns.[33]

There were numerous economic institutions such as cooperatives (*hang*), collectives (*hui*) and credit pools (*yinhui*) in addition to the brotherhoods (*kongsi*) utilized by the Chinese in conducting business. They all played a role in the world of commerce, but, as noted, documentary evidence of commercial activities of Chinese organizations before the mid-eighteenth century is difficult to find. The existence and operation of traditional Chinese business institutions are captured in the local administrative papers of maritime cities such as Melaka and Batavia with a large Chinese population.

The basic institutional structures which facilitated Chinese business activities across the archipelago were clan or kinship networks further strengthened by common origins in Southern Fukien as well as familial relationships through marriage. The kinship network helped traders to obtain credit, either in the form of money or commodities, for a specific business venture or regular business over a period of time. The Captains of Chinese in port-cities apparently had a close-knit business network incorporating many fellow countrymen. For instance, the famous philanthropist Captain of Chinese in Melaka in the late eighteenth century, Chua Su Cheong, and his kinsman, Chua Tagoan, who was the Captain of Chinese in Semarang, provided credit to fellow Chinese traders.

On one occasion, Chua Su Cheong received a sum of 600 Spanish *reals* from Longenus, a Malay trader in Linggi, as a repayment of debt he owed to Chua Tagoan, which Chua Su Cheong directed to his kinsmen.[34] A good example of clan members joined in a business partnership is provided by a notorial contract signed by Tan Tiapko, Tan Kinko, Tan Hube and Koe Chuako, as co-debtors of Bernard Hoeynk van Panendrecht, a Dutchman who worked in the Comptoir in Melaka and supplied the four traders with a large amount of rice estimated at 6,527 *rijksdaalders*. The rice came from a friend and business co-partner of Papendrecht, Martinus Leonardus Gaaswijck, Resident of Juana – a rice-growing region on the northeast coast of Java – and the four Chinese traders pledged their property as security until the debt was repaid with interest.[35]

Kinsmen also provided a useful service as intermediaries on behalf of absent relatives as seen from a notorial document signed by Tan Hapko, an inhabitant of Melaka, to the effect that he has been appointed by Tan Tinko, who was a kinsmen and co-traveller to China unfortunate enough to be murdered while in China, to sort out his business transaction in Melaka. Tan Hapko nominated two of his friends, Lin Kanko and Kan Panko, in Melaka to act on his behalf and attend to the matters.[36] Another example of a business transaction based on kinship is reflected in a notorial act registered by Khoo Binko in Melaka together with his younger brother in China, Khoo Choanko, acknowledging the responsibility for managing the property of Khoo Chuko, their eldest brother who had recently passed away. The two younger brothers undertook to administer the property of their eldest brother, valued at 14,000 *reals*, and provide the profits and interests from trading to support the two widows of their dead brother – one widow was in China – and his surviving two daughters until they came of age.[37] There must have been many more similar business arrangements involving Chinese who had a natural propensity to make the best use of resources through the formal and informal institutions based on kinship and friendship.

Perhaps it is not surprising that most arrangements of that kind were never recorded legally except where large sums of money were involved, or the participants were at home in following modern legal customs. When Chinese traders sought funds for commercial activity beyond their own community, however, the transaction was meticulously recorded and registered as is shown by many notarial documents. The officials of the Dutch East India Company across the archipelago were foremost among the money lenders to Chinese traders who were well-known to them by domicile or through their acquaintances. Lending money for commercial ventures was probably the most secure way open to the Company officials, who earned a meagre income but had the grand ambition of striking it rich with ease in Asia. The Dutchmen who failed to contract lucrative marriages sought redress in money lending for trading purposes and through other commercial ventures in which Chinese often played an important role due to their trustworthiness and business acumen.[38]

The Chinese traders increasingly felt the need to cultivate cross-cultural alliances in order to survive and prosper in a highly competitive world of commerce in the eighteenth century as shown by numerous deeds of partnerships and bonds of credit registered in Melaka. In the early 1700s, small and medium Chinese traders appear to have made use of access to credit and funds on a larger scale as shown by the size of ship and crew and the cargo. There was also a noteworthy change in Chinese mercantile activities after 1750. With the upsurge in the long-distance trade between Europe and China after 1740, Melaka once again became a popular port of call for an increasing number of European ships on their way to and from China.[39] This state of affairs stimulated commercial activity in Melaka considerably as the local market became a supplier of commodities for the China trade. The Chinese traders emerged as the leading group of traders surpassing their Malay peers by 1770.

The increased volume of traffic required commercial activities on a large scale, which in its turn required greater access to the funds and resources offered by the Chinese as well as European institutions such as the Chamber of Orphans in Melaka, which lent money to creditworthy inhabitants on a regular basis, in the second half of the eighteenth century.[40]

The resurgence in both local and regional commerce appears to have provided an impetus for Chinese traders to make more frequent use of their formal and informal institutions to raise capital and conduct trade. The regular visit to Melaka of a large junk from Amoy, which was all that survived of a larger contingent of junks that visited Melaka and other regional port-cities before the VOC imposed stringent restrictions diverting all junk trade to Batavia, was probably based on a major business institution of Chinese merchants for offshore mercantile activities. The cargo of the Amoy junk in the early 1700s included nearly 30 types of products, which surely implies a business venture played for high stakes that involved a large sum of money including the cost of hiring the ship and the involvement of several traders in partnership as was customary in such overseas trading voyages. However, it must be admitted that it is difficult to ascertain whether this arrangement involved a cooperative (*hang*) or a collective (*hui*) or was simply a trading voyage undertaken by one affluent merchant at his own expense. It is equally difficult to determine just how many Chinese traders conducting business on a medium or large scale and on fixed trade routes within the archipelago utilized such customary business practices. They are believed to have come into existence as early as in the seventeenth century.[41] Living in closed quarters as they did in many maritime cities, the Chinese were arguably well situated to replicate in their new abodes all kinds of business institutions which prevailed in South China, in order to succeed in earning the means of livelihood and gather a fortune to go back home. The number of traders conducting business on a medium or large scale was greater after 1750, so it is reasonable to assume that the cooperatives and collectives became more popular as commercial institutions in order to cope with the increased demand for resources. It is no coincidence that the most famous of all Chinese economic institutions in the archipelago, *kongsi*, also later emerged as a force to be reckoned with.

The developments in Chinese commercial activities briefly discussed above no doubt raise many questions about the nature of Chinese entrepreneurship. The sheer multitude of small traders should not blind us to the fact that this was a particular form of commercial activity that involved a large number of operators in business partnerships of all kinds, some peculiar to the Chinese. There were various categories of traders, who conducted business at different levels involving varying amounts of resources and for different stakes.[42] The dynamics of Chinese commercial activities and the role they played in regional economic growth can thus only be revealed by a scrupulous examination of contemporary detailed records such as the shipping lists and legal papers.

Conclusion

There is little doubt that the Chinese traders operating across commercial networks in Southeast Asia at this time played a vital role in generating economic growth. With Melaka as the epicentre of the mercantile network, the Chinese traders conducted a brisk trade in domestic products between major markets in the archipelago and, after 1740 or so, as a feeder trade to the long-distance trade between Europe and China. While Melaka was the preferred base for most Chinese traders, some other ports too attracted an increasing number of Chinese traders in the eighteenth century. In view of the rising tide of commercial activity involving Chinese traders and others, it is difficult to agree with the conventional wisdom, and even some revisionist views, which claim that the regional Southeast Asian economy derived its momentum from the long-distance trade. The regional economy had its own rhythm, which reacted to the dynamics of long-distance trade but certainly was not entirely dependent on it.

The regional economy is often overlooked in favour of the flamboyant long-distance trade, which many scholars believe to have been the catalyst of economic growth in the region in the age of commerce. The function of domestic economic activities in maintaining economic growth in recent years amidst the collapse of world economic order should make us aware of the danger of arriving at a conclusion only partially correct. The Chinese traders were a highly valuable group of people who sustained the regional economies in times of prosperity and in times of hardship during the early modern period.

Notes

1 Carl A. Trocki, *Prince of Pirates: the Temenggongs and the Development of Johore and Singapore 1784–1885* (Singapore: Singapore University Press, 1979), Wong Lin-Ken, *The Malayan Tin Industry to 1914* (Tucson: University of Arizona Press, 1965) and John H. Drabble, *An Economic History of Malaysia, c.1800–1990* (London: Macmillan, 2000).

2 There is a substantial literature on the origins and spread of the Chinese diaspora in Southeast Asia; Wang Gungwu, *China and the Chinese Overseas* (Singapore: Times Academic Press, 1991a), Wang Gungwu, *The Nanhai Trade: The Early History of Chinese Trade in the South China Sea* (Singapore: Times Academic Press, 1998), Wang Gungwu, *Community and Nation* (Kuala Lumpur and Sydney, Heinemann, 1981), Ng Chin-keong, *Trade and Society. The Amoy Network on the China Coast, 1683–1735* (Singapore: National University Press, 1893), Leonard Blussé, *Strange company: Chinese settlers, mestizo women and the Dutch in VOC Batavia*

(Dordrecht-Holland: Foris, 1986); R. Ptak and D. Rothermund (eds.), *Emporia, Commodities and Entrepreneurs in Asian Maritime Trade, c.1400–1750* (Stuttgart: Franz Steiner Verlag, 1991) and James Chin Kong, *Merchants and Other Soujourners: The Hokkiens Overseas, 1570–1760*, unpublished Ph.D. thesis, University of Hong Kong, 1998.

3   For instance, information on economic activities contained in various inscriptions and tombstones in Malaysia is vast and has not received the attention it deserves. See Wolfgang Franke and Chen Tieh Fan (eds.), *Chinese Epigraphic Materials in Malaysia*, 3 vols. (Kuala Lumpur: University of Malaya Press, 1982–1987). The archives of Chinese *kongsi* are another fascinating source of information, to judge by materials contained in the recently published documents from Batavia's Gong Guan. See Leonard Blussé and Chen Menghong (eds.), *The Archives of the Kong Koan of Batavia* (Leiden: Leiden University Press, 2003).

4   It is difficult to provide a comprehensive list of the Melaka harbour-master's lists consulted in writing this chapter. They are mostly noted in the index of the series of documents entitled *Overgekomen Brieven en Papieren*, which contains all the papers Batavia sent to Amsterdam, and which are now located in the national archives of the Netherlands. The harbour-master's list is not always continuous and comprises of segments scattered in the papers Melaka sent to Batavia. Where particular examples from the Melaka harbour-master's list are presented, they are produced from the shipping list for the year concerned. When looking for a shipping list, or any other documents, for a given year, it should be borne in mind that it took one year or more for the papers from Batavia to arrive in Amsterdam. Thus, the documents for 1700 are usually found in the *Overgekomen Brieven en Papieren* for 1701.

5   A detailed study of the entire archives of the VOC comptoir of Melaka can be found in M.R. Fernando, "The Lost Archives of Melaka: Is It Really Lost?", *Journal of the Malaysian Branch of Royal Asiatic Society*, vol. 78, pt. 1, 2005, pp. 1–36. The extant papers of the archives of the Melaka *comptoir* are listed in I.A. Baxter, "Dutch Records from Malacca in the India Office Records", *Journal of the Malaysian Branch of the Royal Asiatic Society*, vol. 56, pt. 2, 1983, pp. 105–133.

6   The role of institutions, both formal and informal, in economic growth and change as expounded by Douglass North is useful in broadening our understanding of Chinese mercantile activities. See Douglass C. North, *Institutions, Institutional Change, and Economic Performance* (Cambridge: Cambridge University Press, 1991). North's analytical paradigm has been applied to examine the economic developments in South Fukien by Billy K.L. So in his *Prosperity, Region, and Institutions in Maritime China: The South Fukien Pattern, 946–1368* (Cambridge, Mass.: Harvard University Press, 2000).

7   A. Reid, *Southeast Asia in the Age of Commerce*, vol. 2, *Expansion and Crisis*, pp. 273–281. Victor Lieberman points out the importance of domestic economic activities in regional economic growth in his critique of Reid's study; "An Age of Commerce in Southeast Asia? Problems of Regional Coherence: A Review Article", *Journal of Asian Studies*, vol. 54, no. 3, 1995, pp. 796–807.

8   L. Blussé, "No Boats to China. The Dutch East India Company and the Changing Pattern of the China Sea Trade, 1635–1690", *Modern Asian Studies*, vol. 30, no. 1, 1996, pp. 51–76.

9   The best study of Chinese economic activities in Batavia in the seventeenth century is L. Blussé, *Strange Company: Chinese Settlers, Mestizo Women and the Dutch in VOC Batavia* (Dordrecht: Foris, 1988).

10 This conclusion is based on information contained in numerous letters written by Jan Pieterzoon Coen to his superiors, the *Heeren XVII* or the directors of the VOC; H.T. Colenbrander (ed.), *Jan Pietersz. Coen. Bescheiden omtrent zijn bedrijf in Indie* vol. 1 ('s Gravenhage: Nijhoff, 1919), pp. 33, 62, 77–78, 82, 87, 99, 114–116, 118–119 and 137–138.

11 The code of maritime laws of Melaka provides a detailed description of rules governing all commercial activities as they evolved in the course of the fifteenth century and remained operative not only in Melaka but in other port-polities of the archipelago in the sixteenth century; R. Winstedt and P.E. De Josselin De Jong, "The Maritime Laws of Melaka", *Journal of the Malayan Branch of the Royal Asiatic Society*, vol. 29, pt. 3, 1956, pp. 22–59.
12 VOC 1141, p. 212r, letter from Johan van Twist, Governor of Melaka, to the Governor-General and his Council in Batavia, 17 December 1642, National Archives of the Netherlands (hereafter NAN). The port dues of Melaka more than doubled between 1641 and 1677; VOC 1331, p. 248r, letter from the Governor-General and his Council in Batavia to the Heeren XVII, 13 February 1679, NAN.
13 For a discussion of the vicissitudes in junk trade, see A. Reid, "The Unthreatening Alternative: Chinese Shipping in Southeast Asia, 1567–1842", *Review of Malaysian And Indonesian Affairs*, vol. 27, nos. 1–2, 1993b, pp. 13–32 and L. Blussé, "No Boats to China. The Dutch East India Company and the Changing Pattern of the China Sea Trade, 1635–1690", *Modern Asian Studies*, vol. 30, no. 1, 1996, pp. 51–76.
14 M.R. Fernando, "Early Settlers in the Land of Promise; Chinese Traders in the Malay Archipelago in the Seventeenth and Eighteenth Centuries" in Wang Gungwu and Ng Chin-keong (eds.), *Maritime China in Transition 1750–1850* (Wiesbaden: Harrassowitz Verlag, 2004), pp. 227–244.
15 The Chinese played a key role in the proposed plan to revive Melaka after 1640; VOC 1136, p. 592v, Letter from Governor of Melaka to Batavia, 13 July 1641, NAN.
16 The classic study of the massacre of Chinese and the events leading up to it is J. Th. Vermeulen, *De Chinezen te Batavia en de Troebelen van 1740* (Leiden: E. Ijdo, 1938). The subject is also dealt with in W. Remmelink, *The Chinese War and the Collapse of the Javanese State, 1725–1743* (Leiden: KILTV, 1994).
17 Blussé, *Strange Company*, p. 123.
18 A. Reid, "The Unthreatening Alternative: Chinese Shipping in Southeast Asia, 1567–1842", p. 19.
19 This development is evident from the rapid concentration of regional commerce in Singapore; Wong Lin-Ken, "The Trade of Singapore, 1819–69", *Journal of the Malayan Branch of the Royal* Asiatic Society, vol. 33, pt. 4, 1960, pp. 278–290.
20 These principles of operation in trading ventures, especially in export trade, among the traders and merchants in South Fukien region are explained at length in Billy K.L. So, *Prosperity, Region and Institutions in Maritime China*, pp. 208–217 and Shiba Yoshinobu, *Commerce and Society in Sung China* (Michigan: University of Michigan, 1970), pp. 26–44.
21 R. Winstedt and P.E. De Josselin De Jong, "The Maritime Laws of Melaka", pp. 53–54.
22 Lijgwaka arrived in Melaka from Aceh on 15 October 1681 and left for Tonkin on 20 June 1682 on a *shallop* with a crew of 16 men carrying a large cargo including 200 *pikul* of saltpetre.
23 Khaijko arrived in Melaka on 16 April 1698.
24 Siocko arrived in Melaka on a junk from Siam on 3 July 1682.
25 Louis Dermigny, *La Chine et l'Occident: le commerce à Canton au XVIIIe siècle, 1719–1833*, 3 vols. (Paris: S.E.V.P.E.N., 1964) and Weng Eang Cheong, *Hong Merchants of Canton* (Surrey: Curzon, 1997).
26 Iris Origo, *The Merchant of Prato* (Harmondsworth: Penguin, 1963).
27 F. Braudel, *The Wheels of Commerce* (London: Collins, 1982), pp. 122–123.
28 Saiko came to Melaka on 30 August 1698 and left on 1 September 1698. Lien Sainko left Melaka on 30 March 1715; he had arrived in Melaka the year before. Peksoe arrived on 5 February 1715 and left on 16 February 1715.
29 Hoeijko arrived on 30 March 1715 and left on 20 April 1715.
30 *Encik* Poo arrived in Melaka on 19 June 1698.

31 For a detailed account of the scale of Chinese migration and the circumstances that fostered this in the late seventeenth and early eighteenth centuries, see Ng Chin-Keong, *Trade and Society: The Amoy Network on the China Coast 1683–1735* (Singapore: Singapore University Press, 1983).
32 Every year at least one large junk with a full cargo arrived in Melaka from Amoy. This operation may well have been conducted according to the business practices of Chinese merchants in Amoy. The building of a junk involved many people who joined in partnership. The cargo belonged to a number of merchants who were on board the ship; L. Blusse, *The Strange Company*, pp. 106–110.
33 The Chinese intermediaries were a notorious phenomenon in Java in the seventeenth and eighteenth centuries. See D.H. Burger, *Het Ontsluiting van Java's Binnenland voor het Wereldverkeer* (Wageningen: H. Veenman 1939), pp. 7, 9, 15–22.
34 This transaction, dated 11 September 1798, is recorded in R/9/22/21, pp. 295–296, The British Library.
35 This transaction, dated 6 July 1786, is recorded in R/9/19/22, no. 96, The British Library.
36 This transaction dated 4 July 1792 is recorded in R/9/22/11 p. 1689, The British Library.
37 This transaction dated 26 April 1793 is recorded in R/9/22/12, pp. 158r–159v, The British Library.
38 The habit of Dutchmen in Asia to contract lucrative marriages in order to become rich is examined at length in the context of a fascinating story involving a rich heiress, Cornelia van Neijenrode, a Japanese lady born to a Dutchmen, and Bitter, a high-ranking Dutch jurist in Batavia. See L. Blusse, *The Bitter Bonds: A Colonial Divorce Drama of the Seventeenth Century* (Princeton: Markus Wiener, 1997).
39 This phenomenon is discussed at some length in A. Reid, ed., *The Last Stand of Asian Autonomies* (London: Macmillan 1997), pp. 57–82.
40 The records of funds lent by the management of the Orphan Chamber are found in R/9/8, R/9/9 and R/9/10, The British Library.
41 James Chin Kong, *Merchants and Other Soujourners: The Hokkiens Overseas, 1570–1760*, p. 217. The writer does not provide any evidence supporting this view except that in Batavia Chinese were concentrated in specific areas where presumably they could easily form formal and informal associations.
42 This is clearly shown in the context of India. See Ashin Das Gupta, "Changing Faces of the Maritime Merchant" in R. Ptak and D. Rothermund (eds.), *Emporia, Commodities and Entrepreneurship in Asian Maritime Trade, c.1400–1750*, pp. 353–371. See also K.S. Matthew, "Kwaja Shams-ud-din Giloni: A Sixteenth Century Entrepreneur in Portuguese India" in R. Ptak and D. Rothermund (eds.), *Emporia, Commodities and Entrepreneurship in Asian Maritime Trade, c.1400–1750*, pp. 363–372.

11 *Cang hai sang tian* (沧海桑田)
Chinese communities in the Mekong delta in the eighteenth century

Li Tana

In this chapter I intend to explore some puzzling questions concerning Chinese communities in southern Vietnam. I believe that these questions are important in outlining a history of the Chinese in Vietnam, and for achieving a basic understanding of the nature of these communities. A common weakness of most existing scholarship on the topic of "the Chinese in Vietnam", is the attempts to explain "Vietnam" and the "Chinese" in isolated terms.[1]

This chapter tries to put Vietnam and particularly the eighteenth-century Mekong delta back into the larger world of Southeast Asia, and examine the topic in a more horizontal rather than vertical dimension. Many historical questions emerge from this approach. The first puzzle is, of all the Southeast Asian countries, Vietnam is the only country that shares a border with China as well as ten centuries of colonisation. This is surely "the best road to Rome", favourable to Chinese immigration in every respect. Yet, as compared with other Southeast Asian countries, the number of Chinese in Vietnam has been remarkably limited, even before 1975. In 1960, for example, there were 800,000 Chinese in South Vietnam, which was 85 per cent of the Chinese population in all Indochina. This number however was only one-third of the number of Chinese in Thailand or in Indonesia.[2] The Chinese accounted for only 5.6 per cent of the total population in South Vietnam, compared to the 37 per cent of Chinese in the Federation of Malaya.[3]

The economic influence of the Chinese in Vietnam was equally limited, if we take remittances to China as an indicator. Chinese remittances from Vietnam accounted for less than 5 per cent of the HK$108 million sent back to China via Hong Kong in 1930.[4] (see Table 11.1)

The figures above suggest two characteristics about the Chinese in southern Vietnam. First, they were smaller communities than those in most Southeast Asian countries and, second, in general they were economically weaker than their counterparts in other parts of Southeast Asia.

This leads to my second question: was this always the case? All data available for the seventeenth century seems to indicate that it was a totally different story for the Chinese in southern Vietnam, for up until that time southern Vietnam was one of the most popular destinations for the Chinese moving to Southeast Asia.

When the Dutch took Melaka in 1641, for example, the Chinese population there was reported to be something in excess of 400,[9] while in 1642 in Hội An

Table 11.1 Remittances from Southeast Asia to China (via Hong Kong) in 1930

From	Amount (HK$ m)	% of total	% of Chinese in polity population
Straits Settlements	42	38.7	34[5]
Dutch East Indies	29	26.7	2[6]
Siam	20	18.4	12.2[7]
Philippines	12.5	11.5	1.86
Indochina	5	4.6	3.6[8]

there were about "four to five thousand or more indolent Chinese" residing there.[10] This was more than ten times the number of Chinese persons in Melaka. According to the French ambassador to Ayutthaya, in the Siamese capital in the mid-seventeenth century there were 3,000 to 4,000 Chinese.[11] This was a similar number to the Chinese population of Hội An in the same period.[12]

A curtain dropped in the eighteenth century, however, and we lack data for the Chinese populations of both Cochinchina and Siam. The sketchy information we do have suggests that there was definitely a rise in Chinese migration to both areas in this period. In 1782, for example, about 10,000 Chinese were massacred in the Biên Hoà area, and in the 1760s, an army of 2,000 Chinese soldiers was helping to fight the Burmese in Ayutthaya.[13]

When the curtain lifts at the end of the eighteenth century following the interruption caused by political turmoil in Siam and Vietnam, and data becomes available again, the differences between the Chinese populations in the two countries are striking. Crawfurd estimated the Chinese population of Saigon in 1822 as 2,000–3,000,[14] and that of Bangkok as 31,000, ten times larger. This also suggests that the Chinese population of Saigon in 1822 was smaller than that of Hội An in the mid-seventeenth century, while Bangkok's Chinese population had grown to ten times that of seventeenth-century Ayutthaya. The Chinese population throughout southern Vietnam probably reached 30,000–40,000 in the early nineteenth century,[15] while that of Siam was 440,000, again ten times or more greater than that of southern Vietnam.[16]

It is clear that something significant happened between the seventeenth and early nineteenth centuries. Historical sources on the experiences which shaped the size of the Chinese population and the patterns of Chinese communities in southern Vietnam have been lost and some crucial data is missing. The following discussion represents a preliminary effort to trace and reconstruct the lost history of Chinese migration over this particular time and place.

The 1750s: a peak in Chinese immigration?

To begin the search, I am using some newly published clan genealogies from Fujian, hoping that the information at micro-level can remedy the absent information of Chinese population movement at macro-level. All relevant data seems to point to a remarkable rise in Chinese migration to the Mekong delta, Cancao (Hà Tiên) and Cambodia in the 1740s–50s. For example, eight persons from four generations of the Huang clan from Anhai district, born between 1720 and 1749, went to "Cambodia" Bến Nghé [located in modern Ho Chi Minh City], and most had died in Bến Nghé between 1753 and 1777.[17]

Persons from six generations of the Cai clan settled and died in Nanyang from the seventeenth to the mid-twentieth century. Members of two out of six generations migrated to Đồng Nai in the eighteenth century.[18] Two brothers of the Xiao clan also went to Đồng Nai in the same period. Both were born in the 1720s and died in Đồng Nai in 1764 and 1771 respectively.[19] The genealogy of the Xu clan from Jinjiang district confirms this eighteenth century migration to the Mekong delta and Cambodia. While only one of the eleventh generation who was born in 1730 died in Đồng Nai, six people of the thirteenth generation died either in Saigon or Cancao, mostly in the eighteenth century.[20] Even those who had developed ties in other parts of Southeast Asia turned to the Mekong delta in the eighteenth century. The Ke family from Anhai district, for instance, saw the father die in Batavia in 1726, and his son (born in 1713) and grandson (born in 1738) die in the Đồng Nai massacre in 1776.[21]

All of the above suggests that the mid-eighteenth century was a key period in Hokkien migration to the Mekong delta area. Some materials from the Qing archives verify that this was also a popular destination for Cantonese during this period. The Li Wenguang rebellion of 1746, for example, saw a Cantonese person Li Wenguang revolting against the *Nguyễn* in Biên Hòa with his 300 followers, most likely all Cantonese.[22]

If the eighteenth century was indeed a Chinese century, as Anthony Reid suggests,[23] then the period from the 1750s to the 1760s seems to have been crucial for Chinese trade and migration to the Mekong delta. Rice exports began to rise, and it seems that Bassac (today's Sóc Trăng) and Cancao (Hà Tiên) tended to become one trading destination. According to Paul van Dyke, of the 37 Canton junks sailing annually between Canton and Southeast Asia in the 1760s, 85–90 per cent traded to this area.[24]

This trend may have started in the 1730s, when there was a setback in Chinese shipping to Ayutthaya, due to a higher taxation on trade being imposed by the Ayutthaya court. The VOC recorded that the Chinese junks thus turned to other destinations such as Cambodia, especially the Bantei Meas or Cancao areas, where a lively trade developed.[25] The trend increased when political turmoil broke out in Siam in the 1760s. As Siam's rice production was affected, China had to seek rice from elsewhere. From that time on, rice from the Mekong delta became important to the China market. Sarasin Viraphol has observed, "Annam and Cambodia were mentioned more frequently than Siam",[26] and both these place names may have referred to the Mekong delta. This perhaps means that, in the China market, rice from the Mekong delta more or less filled the gap left by the dearth of Siamese rice between the 1760s and the 1770s.[27] An increasing number of Chinese migrants to the Mekong delta balanced this trade. This population flow was of course only one branch of the Chinese rush to Southeast

Asia in the mid-eighteenth century, particularly to the coastal areas of southern Vietnam, Cambodia, Siam and the Malay Peninsula – the Chinese Water Frontier of Southeast Asia.[28]

Parallel to the Chinese immigration to this part of Southeast Asia, there was a remarkable internal migration of Chinese within this Southeast Asian water frontier. The massacre of 10,000 Chinese in Batavia in 1740 and expulsion of the non-Catholic Chinese in the Philippines in 1755 (reinforced in 1766)[29] certainly helped in redirecting population movement. Barbara Andaya points out that some of the Chinese miners who arrived in Bangka in the mid-eighteenth century may have fled from Batavia after 1740, or derived from the overseas Chinese communities in Siam, Cambodia, and Vietnam.[30] Some other evidence suggests further Chinese population movement within the region, as "when the local people failed to deliver enough tin to Palembang, new labourers came from Siam and Cochinchina".[31]

This population movement and Chinese offshore production[32] most likely operated within the same regional trade system. Numerous Chinese settlements were established along the Southeast Asian water frontier in the eighteenth century. By the mid-1750s there were about 4,000 Chinese on Bangka working in 17 new tin-mining settlements and producing 73,000 piculs of tin annually.[33] Terengganu was also a popular destination; half of its population comprised Chinese settlers engaged in the cultivation of pepper, in gold mining, or in coastal traffic.[34]

The decisive characteristic of these Chinese settlements was that they emerged within a relatively short period of time and thus were not well-integrated into the local societies. As offshore production Chinese settlements, they were never self-sustaining economic entities. They had to live on rice brought to them from elsewhere, and their products were not produced for the local markets.[35]

The implication of this for the Mekong delta was that, right from the beginning, rice from the Mekong delta was produced for trading with both the water frontier, and the China market. It is likely that the water frontier region to the south was the earliest market for the Mekong delta. This world of multiple Chinese autonomous ports and settlements provided a perfect environment for the peddlers. To service these ports there must have been hundreds or thousands of intermediaries working in the trade network.

This also means that the new Chinese settlements in the eighteenth-century Mekong delta were markedly different from the previous generations of Chinese in central and northern Vietnam, where they gradually assimilated into the local societies. The sudden rush of a relatively large Chinese population compared to the thin local population in the frontier areas, with their livelihood directly linked to overseas markets, made these new settlements much more autonomous than all previous settlements.[36] This attribute foreshadowed the Li Wenguang rebellion in 1746, the distinctive Chinese armies on both sides of the civil war, and the massacre of 10,000 Chinese in Saigon in 1782.

Fluctuations in Hokkien migration to Vietnam can be seen from the Quanzhou genealogies. Of the 200 genealogies that include 10,000 people going overseas (the majority can only be identified as leaving to "Nanyang" or "*guo fan*") between the fifteenth and twentieth centuries, there were 263 men who either migrated to or had been born in southern Vietnam. Breaking the group into five bands based on their arrival period, we can construct the following table:

Table 11.2 Period of arrival of Hokkien persons in Southern Vietnam

Period	Number	%
Pre-eighteenth century	8	3.04
Eighteenth century	65	24.71
1800–1840	8	3.04
1841–1865	49	18.63
1865–early twentieth century	133	50.57
Total	263	100

Source: *Quanzhou pudie huaqiao shiliao yu yanjiu* [A Collection of Overseas Chinese Clan Genealogies and Research from Quanzhou].

The occupations of the Chinese in the eighteenth-century Mekong delta

What were the economic activities of the Chinese in the Mekong delta? No sources give specific information about this, but since the proportion of the Chinese was high against the total population of the eighteenth-century south, most of them were likely engaged in growing cash crops or shipbuilding rather than commerce. One source seems to clearly associate salt-making with the Chinese. According to *Gia Định thông chí*, the manufacture of a special red salt and trading was done by the Chinese.

> They weave areca leaves into sacks, each containing 5–6 *can* (2.5–3 kg) of salt, and 40 bags would make one Khmer "*xe*" [a measure of about 100–120 kg]. This trade is very profitable when the salt is sold in Cambodia.[37]

Another trade that the Chinese engaged in was sugarcane planting in the Biên Hòa area. Biên Hòa was the area that grew most of the sugarcane in southern Vietnam.[38] The sugar refining industry was also in the hands of the Chinese.[39] As Crawfurd observed, "Down to the present day they are the sole manufacturers, not only in the archipelago, but in the Philippines, Cochin-China and Siam".[40] It was said that there had been many sugar mills in the Biên Hòa area in the early nineteenth century and most likely prior to it, and that the good quality white sugar, praised by the Western merchants of the time, was from Biên Hòa.[41] It was not accidental that the areas growing sugarcane in Cochinchina in 1810 were concentrated in the Biên Hòa, Mỹ Tho and Hà Tiên areas, all previously heavily settled by the Chinese.[42] It is also well-known that the Chinese grew pepper in the Hà Tiên area.

Betel nut was one of the major items traded with Cambodia.[43] In fact betel nut was one of the most important Mekong delta export products during the eighteenth century. A Macau ship, for example, reportedly carried several thousand piculs of betel nuts back to Macau in 1798.[44] There seems to have been certain connections between the Chinese and the famous Vườn Trầu (Betel Nut Gardens) near today's Ho Chi Minh City. In 1731, for example, an ethnic Chinese army, led by Chen Shangchuan's son Chen Dading (Trần Đại Định in Vietnamese) defeated a Lao rebel army led by Sotot in Vườn Trầu.[45] Half a century later, the ethnic Chinese army of Hoà Nghĩa again ambushed the Tây Sơn army around Vườn Trầu and killed the Tây Sơn general Phạm Ngàn. This led immediately to the Tây Sơn's massacre of 10,000 Chinese in 1782.

Ship-building was a Chinese specialty in southern Vietnam. The confession made by Li Wenguang – who is mentioned above – to Qing officers in 1756 mentions that he went to Huế in 1744 with some friends to trade Chinese medicine, but soon they were sent to Đồng Nai to do logging and ship-building for the Nguyễn lord.[46] One of the newly discovered Minh Hương materials from Vĩnh Long lists the names of 31 heads of this Chinese community from 1783 to 1847, and describes certain tasks carried out by each of them. Among the duties of the Chinese were tailoring robes for the officers, and ship-building and repairing.

A major puzzle regarding the history of the Chinese in Vietnam is why southern Vietnam under the Nguyễn, which was the most open and tolerant regimes towards the Chinese throughout Vietnamese history, was also the place which experienced the worst massacre of the Chinese in all of the autonomous states in early modern Southeast Asia. What brought such confrontation and hatred? My preliminary research seems to indicate that this was intimately tied with the ethnic composition of Cochinchinese society in the Mekong delta. A careful reading of the Nguyễn chronicles of the 1770s and 1780s suggests an extremely high percentage of Chinese in the Nguyễn army and an overwhelming manipulation by the Chinese in the politics of the period. All this points to one direction, that the Chinese were by no means minorities in the eighteenth-century Mekong delta, and that the ethnic Chinese army was most likely the major force that the Nguyễn relied on during the 1770s and early 1780s. In other words, the Chinese were more likely soldiers or potential soldiers of the Nguyễn, than business rivals of the Vietnamese merchant class, as some scholars suggest.

The Saigon massacre

The *Gia Định Thông Chí* contains the following account of events in southern Vietnam in March 1782:

> March (1782): The Tây Sơn bandit Nguyễn Văn Nhạc invaded Gia Định by land and sea.... The Tây Sơn general Phạm Ngàn was killed. Hearing this news Nhạc was furious and vented his anger on the Chinese, as the Hoà Nghĩa army [which participated in the battle] were all Chinese. He ordered that all the Chinese be killed, whether they were long-time residents or newcomers, soldiers or merchants. More than 10,000 people were killed. Bodies

were scattered from Ngưu Tân to Saigon, some of them were thrown into the river and there were so many of them that the bodies stopped the river from flowing. For two to three months no one dared to eat fish or prawns in the river. Every family threw away goods that might associate them with the Chinese. Things like silk fabrics, tea, Chinese medicine, joss sticks and paper were scattered everywhere on the roads but no one dared to take them.[47]

The impact of this massacre was clearly felt. According to the same source, "The following year (1783), one *cân* (500 grams) of coarse tea cost as much as eight *quan*, and a single needle cost one hundred cash. Everything was as dear as this. People suffered".[48] Eight *quan* of Đàng Trong currency in the late 1770s was the equivalent of about four taels of silver.[49] This would have been sufficient to buy about 25 kilograms of the best tea in Canton in 1775.[50]

It is reasonable to assume that many Chinese fled rather than be massacred. The description of the Đồng Nai *dai pho* (great market) in Biên Hoà clearly indicates that this had been a densely-populated China town:

The houses were made of brick and their walls were painted. Row upon row of houses of varying heights were shining along the river and against the sun. The houses stretched for five *li* (1 *li* = 500 metres) and extended along three main streets. The main streets running north-south were paved with white stones and the east-west main streets with *đá ong* (a stone-like building material produced in southern Vietnam). The minor streets were paved with blue-ish bricks, the whole town was ringed with stones. The merchants and traders gathered here, the ocean junks and river boats anchored and queued here one after the other. As it was such a big metropolis this place saw the concentration of rich merchants, and such a situation was not seen anywhere else.... When the Tây Sơn bandits came in 1776, they dismantled the houses and took away bricks and stones, together with goods and treasures and shipped them back to Quy Nhơn, and this place was left in ruins. Since the Restoration [i.e. Ánh's recapturing of Saigon in 1788] there has been a recovery of population, but was not one tenth of a hundred or a thousand.[51]

There is critical information here about the size of the China town in Biên Hoà in the 1770s which "stretched for five *li*", while the Saigon of the 1820s was recorded by the same source as having extended for only three *li*.[52] In other words, eighteenth-century Biên Hoà was considerably larger than early nineteenth-century Saigon, which was at that time the major political and economic centre of the Mekong delta.

The description of Mỹ Tho equally suggests that it was also a populous area, that the town was covered with richly ornamented brick houses, big pavilions and huge temples. All kinds of ships and boats from the ocean or from the rivers came and left like shuttles waving fabrics. It was a big town, prosperous and

Chinese communities in the Mekong delta 271

lively. When the Tây Sơn bandits rose, this place became a battlefield, and everything was burnt down. Although it recovered somewhat from 1788 and people began to return to it, the size of the population was not half as dense as it was formerly.[53]

This seemed to be similar to Batavia in the same period. This is how Blussé describes Batavia: "Around 1780 the most respectable neighbourhoods of Batavia had already changed into caverns and ruins – by then there was no trace left of the prosperity and bloom that this capital still enjoyed only 25 years ago".[54] Also like Batavia, the most important reason for the decay of Biên Hoà and Mỹ Tho was the departure of the Chinese population. The collapse of Cancao must have been even more dramatic than that of the two areas above. All these factors considered, it is more than likely that the eighteenth-century Chinese population in the Mekong delta and Cancao area was as dense as that of the Menan Chao Phraya plain in Siam during the same period.

The flight of the major merchants

The damage to the business environment of the Mekong delta was even more serious. The *Gia Định thông chí* compared the trade environments in Biên Hoà before and after the 1782 massacre:

> When ships anchored and merchants settled they would give the list of their cargoes to the local merchants, who would check and repackage the items so that both the better and inferior goods could be sold. [If] the merchant wanted certain local cargoes, he would sign a contract with the agents so the latter could buy the goods on his behalf. It was very convenient both for the merchants abroad and the local agents, and the accounts were always kept as clear as should be. While the purchasing was going on, the merchant needed do nothing but go to the theatres and enjoy himself. The drinking water was clean and ships were well looked after. When the monsoon came and it was time to sail back, the merchant would leave with the fully-loaded ship....
>
> Now, when the junks come [to Biên Hoà], the merchants have to do retail trade themselves and at the same time collect local products, both at extreme pain. This was because there are no longer prominent local merchants to serve as agents for them. What is more, [as there are no more prominent merchants] swindlers would pretend to be rich merchants buying the cargoes but disappearing as soon as they got the goods. If the loss was minor the merchants could go without pursuing the issue but if it was a major one, the involved merchants had to stay for the winter and search for the swindlers themselves. This made trade increasingly difficult for the merchants overseas.[55]

It is clear from the account above that overseas trade in Biên Hoà in the pre-Tây Sơn period was operated within a credit system. That is, the local merchant would obtain the goods on credit from the importer, then sell the goods before the date of due payment, while using his position to buy products from the locals.[56] The local leading merchants played a crucial role in this community dominated by trade, and were the engines of such a community. It was thus disastrous for Biên Hoà when there were no "prominent merchants" left to organise trade and attract credit, or to finance and transport settlers, and thereby hold the society together. This was why the *Gia Định thông chí* sounds so bitter about the departure of the big merchants, in a community which had revolved around networks, contracts and special "trust" relations. The out-migration of the big merchants from the Mekong delta had the most damaging long-term effect on the overseas trade of the Mekong delta, as well as its local trade, which was no doubt hindered by the restricted overseas trade.

The lack of major merchants further contributed to the scattering of the Chinese population and made the communities more fluid than ever. The Chinese population in a Minh Hương village in Vĩnh Long province serves as an example: it was established in 1783, suggesting the founding role of some survivors from the 1782 massacre in Saigon. Yet, while right after its establishment the number of taxpayers was 88, this number began to drop each year to nil within five years, in 1787 and 1788. There was then a sudden upsurge of population in 1789, indicating the impact of in-migration, but then the population disappeared again in 1795 and once again in 1797. The real value of this snapshot is the way it details and highlights the fluidity of the Chinese population in the Mekong delta during this period.[57]

This fluidity of the Chinese in southern Vietnam, however, was not a blind population movement, as almost all of the movement was towards the south. A relatively large number of Chinese fleeing from southern Vietnam settled in Terengganu in the Malay peninsula. According to a story from a family surnamed Lim, whose ancestor Lim Eng Huat (林永发) was to become the Kapitan Cina of the Chinese community in Terengganu, their ancestors had lived in Annam but fled from it when there was chaos there in 1773. They fled in sampans and eventually came to Terengganu. The group was large, all male except for three females. They brought food and valuables with them, two of the women also tied pure gold leaves to their legs with ragged cotton fabrics, as if they were crippled. This was done in case they met pirates at sea.[58]

Another Kapitan Cina of Terengganu, Kow Geok Seng (高玉成), also came from Annam, and his family genealogy records are even more precise, noting that the family moved from Hatien.[59] Both accounts seem to suggest that the migration was well-organised by people with means, suggesting the migration of major merchants and their followers. It was these factors that enabled Kow and Lim to quickly rise to a leading position in the Chinese community in Terengganu, and there is a good basis to speculate that those who migrated from Vietnam formed a considerable percentage of the community and the power base of the Kow and Lim families. While the Kow family contributed three Kapitans Cina to Terengganu, the Lim family monopolised the position of Low Tiev (老爹 or Jurubahasa, or 雷珍兰 in the Dutch East Indies). In fact, the very title

Low Tiev (老爹) might also have been brought from the Chinese community in Vietnam. The leading Chinese figures in seventeenth and eighteenth-century Hoi An were also called Low Tiev (老爹).[60]

Qingho she (Thanh Hà village), the China town in Huế, saw a most dramatic drop in its population in the late eighteenth century. Its 792 registered taxpayers in 1789 were reduced to a mere 60 in the space of six years.[61] Interestingly, the name *Qingho she* reappeared in the inscriptions of Chinese temples in nineteenth-century Penang. It was among the top donors to the Chinese Town Hall in 1886.[62] Earlier evidence of the *Qingho she*'s involvement with the Fukien community in Penang was its donation to the *Ch'ing-yun yen* temple or the *She-miao* (Snake Temple) in 1880, which "had been the office of the Fukien community for several decades". *Qingho she* was the second largest supporter, donating $600.[63] Anyone who is familiar with Chinese epigraphic material will know that extremely few Chinese groups in Nanyang called themselves a "village" (*she* 社). Most of them were called "*kongsi* 公司" "*hao* 號" "*tang* 堂", or simply company names. The *Qingho she* is the only exception in thousands of inscriptions which called itself a "*she*", similar to *Qingho she*, which was a distinctive designation used by the Chinese communities in seventeenth- and eighteenth-century Cochinchina. There thus appears to be concrete connections between the *Qingho she* in Hue and that in nineteenth-century Penang. It is likely that these persons left Huế in large junks and in great numbers and thus were able to maintain their old name and even the structure of the Huế community. With numerous followers and capital brought with them, the heads of the previous communities (most often major merchants themselves), would easily become the leaders of the new communities they settled in. Both of the examples above seem to indicate this. Such migrants joined the major rush of the Chinese of the late eighteenth century to the Malay Peninsula, southern Siam and the Chao Phraya plain, which were to become major centres of growth in Southeast Asia in the early nineteenth century.

Conclusion

The discussion above suggests that when we speak of "the Chinese in Vietnam" we are talking about different communities in different periods. Between the late eighteenth and early nineteenth centuries there must have been several instances of rebuilding such communities. Those who fled from the destruction of Biên Hoà in 1776 moved to Saigon (today's Chợ Lớn), only to suffer a massacre in 1782. The Chợ Lớn China town had recovered some shape when Crawfurd visited it in 1822, but suffered another major blow by Minh Mạng in 1834, during the Lê Văn Khôi rebellion. Each incident was accompanied by the destruction of the community and out-migration of some Chinese, most of whom went to Siam and the Malay Peninsula. It could be suggested that most of the Chinese in Cochinchina whom the French first met in 1862 were likely first-generation migrants from China, rather than the descendants of the Chinese in the Mekong delta in the seventeenth and eighteenth centuries. The repeated shaping and reshaping of the Chinese communities in southern Vietnam thus has to be seen as one of the most remarkable characteristics of the Chinese in Vietnam.[64]

In closing this chapter I cannot help but recall a Chinese saying, *Cang hai sang tian* ("The seas changes into mulberry fields and mulberry fields into seas"). The rise and fall of the Chinese communities in the eighteenth-century Mekong delta do resemble such changes. But building such a picture requires a vision beyond the current scope of human geography, and certainly beyond the current nationalist boundaries. It is therefore important to see how intimately the Chinese community in the Mekong delta was tied to the Chinese water frontier of Southeast Asia, and what an important part it constituted. Only through such a context will the many dimensions be brought out – dimensions that were part of the history of the eighteenth-century Mekong delta, but which were lost in the new frames of time and space of nationalist historiography. On a higher level, it was perhaps this pre-nation-state world of shifting and multiple alliances that provided the context for the creation of the modern nation-states of Southeast Asia.

Notes

1 This was until the appearance of a most enlightening work by Christopher Goscha, *Thailand and the Southeast Asian Networks of the Vietnamese Revolution* (Richmond: Curzon, 1999).
2 Victor Purcell, *The Chinese in Southeast Asia* (London: Oxford University Press, 1965), p. 167.
3 Ibid, p. 3.
4 Charles F. Remer, *Foreign Investment in China* (New York, 1931), p. 185, cited in Purcell, *The Chinese in Southeast Asia*, p. 200, fn. 25. I accept that these remittances are only indicative, as the majority of recorded remittance were made by Chinese labourers rather than by merchants, that is, by the poor rather than the rich.
5 Purcell, *The Chinese in Southeast Asia*, p. 223.
6 Ibid, p. 386.
7 G. William Skinner, *Chinese Society in Thailand* (Ithaca: Cornell University Press, 1957), p. 183.
8 Purcell, *The Chinese in Southeast Asia*, p. 173. This figure is based on the percentages of Chinese in Cochinchina and Cambodia in 1937. Remittances to Swatow in 1912 confirm the same trend:

Table A11.1 Percentages of Chinese in Cochinchina and Cambodia in 1937

From	Amount (million yuan)	%	Chinese population 1912
Singapore & Penang	12.5	51	369,843 (20%)
Siam	10	41	1,264,744 (69%)
Annam	2	8	200,000 (11%)

From *Qiaohui liutong zhi yanjiu* [A Study of the Remittances of the Overseas Chinese], p. 125.

The figures for the Chinese populations in 1912 are taken from G. Hicks (ed.), *Overseas Chinese Remittances from Southeast Asia 1910–1940* (Singapore: Select Books, 1993), p. 4.

9 Balthasar Bort, trans. M. J. Bremner, "Report of Governor Balthasar Bort on Malacca, 1678", *Journal of the Malayan Branch of the Royal Asiatic Society*, 5,1 (1927): pp. 39–44.
10 Li Tana and Anthony Reid, eds., *Southern Vietnam under the Nguyen* (Singapore: EHSEAP, ANU/ASEAN Economic Research Unit, ISEAS, 1993), p. 31.
11 Skinner, *Chinese Society in Thailand*, p. 13.
12 These population figures correspond to the Chinese trade from Cochinchina and from Siam: the total number of the Chinese junks that arrived at Nagasaki from Cochinchina between 1647 and 1720 was 203, while from Siam was 138. See Li Tana, *Nguyễn Cochinchina* (Ithaca: SEAP, 1998), p. 68.
13 And robbing the palace when it suited them. See Dhiravat Na Pombejra, "Administrative and Military Roles of the Chinese in Siam during an Age of Turmoil, circa 1760–1782", in *Maritime China in Transition 1750–1850*, ed. Wang Gungwu and Ng Chin-keong (Wiesbaden: Harrassowitz Verlag, 2004), pp. 335–55.
14 See John Crawfurd, *Journal of an Embassy to the Courts of Siam and Cochin China* (Singapore: Oxford University Press, 1967), p. 214.
15 An official Vietnamese source gives 20,241 Minh Hương Chinese in Quảng Nam alone in 1805. *Châu Bản*, vol. 1, *Triều Gia Long* (the files of the Gia Long reign) kept in the National Archives no. 1, Hanoi. Crawfurd estimated the Chinese population in Saigon in 1822 to be 2,000–3,000. See John Crawfurd, *Journal of an Embassy*, p. 214.
16 Crawfurd, *Journal of an Embassy*, p. 450.
17 First generation of Huang family: Huang Tingfu was born in 1720 and died in 1777, while his brother was born in 1726 and died in 1753. A cousin was born in 1735 and died at Bến Nghé. Another cousin was born in 1737 and died in 1769. Second generation: Huang Tingfu's first son was born in 1748, and his second son was born in 1749, and both died at Bến Nghé. Third generation Qiashe was born in 1749, and died in 1800. Fourth generation: Qiashe's son was born in 1795 at Bến Nghé. See *Quanzhou pudie huaqiao shiliao yu yanjiu* [*A Collection of Clan Genealogies from Quanzhou*] (Beijing: Zhongguo huaqiao chubanshe, 1994), vol. 2, p. 685.
18 This family seemed to have moved first to Hội An first, then from there to Đồng Nai. *Quanzhou pudie*, vol. 2, pp. 738–9.
19 Ibid., vol. 2, p. 749.
20 Ibid., vol. 2, pp. 796–7.
21 Ibid., vol. 2, pp. 693–4.
22 *Secret Palace Memorials of the Ch'ien-lung Period: Ch'ing Documents at the National Palace Museum* (Taipei: National Palace Museum, 1983), no. 15 (August 1756–December 1756), pp. 485–6. The Vietnamese chronicles mistook Li for a Hokkien. See *Tiền Biên*, vol. 10, p. 140.
23 Anthony Reid, "Introduction", in Anthony Reid (ed.) *The Last Stand of Asian Autonomies* (London and New York: MacMillan and St. Martin's Press, 1997), pp. 11–4.
24 Paul Van Dyke, "The Canton-Vietnam Junk Trade in the 1760s and 1770s: Some Preliminary Observations from the Dutch, Danish, and Swedish Records", paper for the International Workshop "Commercial Vietnam: Trade and the Chinese in the 19th Century South", Ho Chi Minh City, December 1999, chart 5.
25 Archives VOC 2534, Daily register Ayutthaya 1740–1741, pp. 153–4 (3 May 1740), cited in Remco Raben *et al.* (ed.) *In the King's Trail: An 18th century Dutch Journey to the Buddha's Footprint* (Bangkok: Royal Netherlands Embassy, 1997), p. 69.
26 Sarasin Viraphol, *Tribute and Profit: Sino-Siamese Trade, 1652–1853* (Cambridge, Mass.: Council on East Asian Studies, Harvard University, 1977), pp. 105–6.
27 During this period Đàng Trong [Southern Vietnam] sometimes supplied rice to Siam. One Thai source said that when Taksin ascended the throne, rice was so scarce that he had to send vessels to ship it from as far away as Pontemeas (Cancao, or Hà Tiên) for sale in Thonburi. Ibid., pp. 107–8. Siamese rice importation to Guangdong was not mentioned again until the 1780s.

28 See Nola Cooke and Li Tana (ed.), *Water Frontier: Commerce and the Chinese in the Lower Mekong Region, 1750–1880* (Lanham: Rowman and Littlefield, 2004); Li Tana, "The Eighteenth-Century Mekong Delta and its World of Water Frontier", in Nhung Tuyet Tran and Anthony Reid (ed.), *Viet Nam: Borderless Histories* (Madison: University of Wisconsin Press, 2006), pp. 147–62. See also Geoff Wade, "The Southern Chinese Borders in History", in Grant Evans, Christopher Hutton, and Kuah Khun Eng (ed.), *Where China Meets Southeast Asia: Social and Cultural Change in the Border Regions* (Bangkok: White Lotus and Singapore: The Institute of Southeast Asian Studies, 2000), pp. 28–50.
29 Anthony Reid, "Introduction", in *Last Stand of Asian Autonomies*, p. 11.
30 Barbara Andaya, *To Live as Brothers*: *Southeast Sumatra in the 17th and 18th Centuries* (Honolulu: University of Hawaii Press, 1993), p. 189.
31 Mary S. Heidhues, *Bangka Tin and Mentok Pepper: Chinese Settlement on an Indonesian Island* (Singapore: Institute of Southeast Asian Studies, 1992), p. 10.
32 The term "Amoy network" was employed by Ng Chin-keong. See his *Trade and Society: The Amoy Network on the China Coast 1683–1735* (Singapore: Singapore University Press, 1983). See also Carl Trocki, "Chinese Pioneering in Eighteenth-Century Southeast Asia", in Reid (ed.) *The Last Stand of Asian Autonomies*, p. 87.
33 Barbara Andaya, *To Live as Brothers*, pp. 190–1.
34 Leonard Blussé, "Chinese Century: The Eighteenth Century in the China Sea Region", *Archipel*, 58 (1999): 123.
35 Carl Trocki, "Chinese Pioneering", pp. 83–101.
36 Carl Trocki, "Chinese Pioneering", p. 91.
37 Trình Hoài Đức, *Gia Định thông chí* [Gia Dinh gazetteer] (Saigon: Phủ Quốc vụ khanh đặc trách văn hoá, 1972), vol. 3, p. 7b.
38 Nguyễn Đình Đầu, *Nghiên cứu địa bà triều Nguyễn: Biên Hòa* [Cadastral registers study of Nguyen dynasty: Bien Hoa] (Hochiminh City: Hochiminh City Publishing House, 1994), p. 129.
39 The technique of sugar refining in Cochinchina was undoubtedly Chinese, according to Christian Daniels. See Joseph Needham, *Science and Civilisation in China*, vol. 6 (Cambridge University Press, 1996), pp. 432–4. I am grateful to Professor Daniels for his advice.
40 Crawfurd, *Journal of an Embassy*, p. 410.
41 Nguyễn Đình Đầu, *Nghiên cứu địa* bà, pp. 129–30.
42 Trình Hoài Đức, *Gia Định thông chí*, vol. 5, pp. 4a–7a. The Chinese who fled from Cochinchina to Terengganu were said to have also engaged in sugarcane planting.
43 Sơn Nam, *Đồng bằng sông Cửu Long* [*The Mekong Delta*], (Ho Chi Minh City: Ho Chi Minh City Press, 1993), p. 36.
44 *Colecção de Documentos Sinicos do IAN/TT Referentes a Macau durante a dinastia Qing (A Collection of the Qing Archives on Macau, held in Torre do Tombo [Portugal])*, (Macau: Macau Foundation, 1999), vol. 1, p. 247.
45 Trình Hoài Đức (Zheng Huaide), "Gia Định thông chí: Thành trì chí*"*, *in Lingnan zhi guai deng shi liao san zhong* [Three primary Vietnamese sources of *Lĩnh Nam trích quái*, *Gia định thông chí* and *Hà Tiên trấn diệp trấn Mạc thị gia phả*], eds. Dai Kelai and Yang Baoyun (Zhengzhou: Zhongzhou guji Press, 1991), p. 209. See also Chen Chingho, "Qingchu Zheng Cheng Gong bu zhi yi zhi nan qi" [The migration of the Cheng partisans to South Vietnam in the early Qing], *Hsin Ya Hsueh Pao*, 8 (August 1968): p. 473.
46 *Secret Palace Memorials of the Ch'ien-lung Period: Ch'ing Documents at the National Palace Museum* (Taipei: National Palace Museum, 1983), no. 15 (August 1756–December 1756), pp. 485–6.
47 Trình Hoài Đức, *Gia Định thông chí*, p. 78.
48 Ibid., p. 78.
49 Li and Reid, *Southern Vietnam under the Nguyen*, p. 137.

50 Hosea B. Morse, *The Chronicles of the East India Company Trading to China, 1635–1834*, vol. 1 (Clarendon: Oxford University Press, 1926), Chinese translation, p. 325.
51 Chen Chingho, "Zheng Huaide zhuan Jiading Tongzhi chengchi zhi zhushi" [Annotations on the Gia Định gazetteer: On towns], in *Nanyang xuebao*, 12, 2 (1956): 24.
52 Ibid., p. 17.
53 Chen Chingho, op. cit., p. 27.
54 Leonard Blussé, *Strange Company: Chinese Settlers, Mestizo Women and the Dutch in VOC Batavia* (Dordrecht: Foris Publications, 1986), p. 33.
55 Chen Chingho, op. cit., p. 18.
56 M. R. Fernando and David Bulbeck, eds., *Chinese Economic Activity in Netherlands India* (Canberra/Singapore: ECHOSEA, ANU/Institute of Southeast Asian Studies, 1992), p. 145.
57 This fluidity was perhaps typical of the eighteenth-century Southeast Asian water frontier area. For example, because of the Burmese raids on Junkceylon (Thalang, later Phuket), between 1784 and 1824 the population dropped to 6,000, a quarter or a fifth of what it was before, and output of tin ore fell from 500 tons per year to a mere 20 tons. Gerolamo E. Gerini, *Old Phuket: Historical Retrospect of Junkceylon Island* (reprinted from the *Journal of the Siam Society*, Bangkok: The Siam Society, 1986), p. 98.
58 Huang Yao, *Xingma huaren zhi* [*History of the Chinese in Malaysia and Singapore*], (Hong Kong: Ming Jian Press, n.a.), p. 12. For a list of the Chinese kapitans in Terengganu, see "Carta masa sejarah kesultanan Terengganu", in *Seminar Darul Iman 2001: Persejarahan Terengganu sehingga abad ke-18*, 13–14 October 2001, Muzium Negeri Terengganu, p. 47.
59 Family genealogy of Kow Geok Seng. My thanks to Wong Yee Tuan for sharing this valuable source with me.
60 Chen Chingho, *Historical Notes on Hoi-An (Faifo)* (Carbondale: Center for Vietnamese Studies, Southern Illinois University, 1973), p. 45; Chen copied a tablet in the Minh Huong temple which recorded 10 老爷 (Low Tiev), but a few manuscripts of the Minh Huong clearly called them 老爹 (Low Tiev).
61 Chen Chingho, "Chengtian mingxiangshe yu qinghepu" [The Minh Hương Village and Thanh Hà Pho in Thừa Thiên (Central Viet-Nam)], *Xinya xuebao* [*New Asia Journal*], 4, 1, p. 319.
62 Wolfgang Franke and Chen Tieh Fan, *Chinese Epigraphic Material in Malaysia* (Kuala Lumpur: University of Malaya Press, 1985), vol. II, p. 801. Thanh Hà (the Chinese village in Huế) could be rendered in different ways: Qing Ho (Thanh Hà), Qing Ho (Thanh Hoà; see Malaysian inscriptions), or Qing Xia (Thanh Hạ; see Quanzhou family genealogies, vol. 2, p. 694).
63 Franke and Chen, *Chinese Epigraphic Material in Malaysia*, p. 580.
64 The 1930s depression saw the survival of only one in every four rice merchants, while nine out of every ten of those engaged in the sale of hardware and fabrics failed. As some French scholars observed in the 1930s: "The fact must be faced that a whole generation of Asiatic merchants is on the way to replacing those who have disappeared". Charles Robequain, James Russell Andrus, and Katrine R. C. Greene, *The Economic Development of French Indo-China*, trans. Isabel Ward (London and New York: Oxford University Press, 1944), p. 43; also see Virginia Thompson, *French Indo-China* (New York: Macmillan, 1937), p. 127.

Part IV

China–Southeast Asian interactions during the age of European imperialism

12 Shifting categorisations of Chinese migrants in Burma in the nineteenth and twentieth centuries[1]

Michael W. Charney

Introduction

As Prasenjit Duara explained in his analysis of Chinese histories during the first half of the twentieth century, there is a tension between local, regional, and state-centred historical narratives that should be identified and kept in mind when one studies a country's history.[2] The prevailing historiography on pre-independence Burma, however, continues to focus on either local or "national" history without attempting to clarify the relationship between the two. While some ethnic groups, such as the Karen and the Kachin, have attracted scholarly attention, the history of many other groups, such as the Chinese community in Burma, remains largely ignored. This is starting to change, specifically for Burma's postwar history, and to a far lesser extent for the many centuries during which there was migration from China into Burma prior to the Second World War. Hokkien, Cantonese, Hakka, Teochew, and other migrants from China (especially the Southeastern maritime provinces) to Burma have been viewed in most of the secondary literature as Chinese nationals, rather than as different ethnic or sub-ethnic groups of Burma. This inability to separate the Chinese in Burma and their history from the nation-state paradigm generally continues.[3]

This chapter is concerned chiefly with Burmese and European accounts rather than the Chinese sources because the latter have received thorough attention from scholars well-versed in the Chinese-language literature.[4] With a few exceptions,[5] this literature tells us little of the day-to-day experiences of Chinese residents in most of Burma during this period (with the exception of northeastern Burma). Despite the limitations of state documentation and state-centred historical narratives (the nature of the majority of available Chinese sources), they are still accepted as the necessary basis for an authoritative historical narrative of the Chinese in Burma. It will be one contention of this chapter that this reliance upon state documentation has led to a misunderstanding of the "Chinese" identity and place in Burmese history for the last several centuries.

Chinese migrants in precolonial Burma: an indigenous state-centred perspective

The Kingdom of Burma's historical relationship with the Empire of China was framed by China's long-standing tribute system. The Chinese tribute system governed the Celestial Empire's relationship with the small states along the rim of the middle kingdom. Yearly royal tribute missions were sent from Southeast Asian courts to the Chinese capital and regalia and imperial charters granting sovereignty to Southeast Asian rulers were provided in return. Failure to pay tribute, or the usurpation of the throne of a local ruler tributary to China sometimes led to an imperial punitive mission. Over the course of the thirteenth to late eighteenth centuries, Chinese armies invaded Burma on many occasions for similar reasons.[6] The long-standing importance of the tribute system gave the Burmese and Chinese an intimacy that Europeans lacked in their relationships with the Burmese court during a later period. When Michael Symes visited the Burmese court in 1795, a Chinese imperial mission arrived in that court on the same day and Symes was told by the Burmese that their relationship with the Chinese was much more cordial than that with the English.[7] Diplomatic ties between Chinese and Burma were so regular and intimate, some Burmese officials were able to converse with the Chinese envoys in Chinese.[8]

The tribute system and China–Burma state relations also had a major impact on Burmese perceptions of Chinese migrants in Burma. One side of the Burmese state-centred perspective was that Chinese migrants consisted of one homogenous migrant group. The "Burma" state-centred view, for example, was that the Chinese were subjects of the Emperor of China, with a single and united political identity. This view holds that the Chinese were a single people, called "Tayoub" by the Burmese, or at least could be identified as such. This perspective is to be found in texts composed in the Burmese court or based upon Burmese royal court records.[9] One of the few exceptions is an early modern text from western Burma, far away from the Irrawaddy Valley, which included nine Chinese "peoples" in its listing of the 101 races of mankind, but did not specify to which nine groups it referred to.[10] This account, however, was not integrated into Irrawaddy Valley traditions until the conquest of Arakan by Burma in 1784/1785; until then, and for some time afterwards, Irrawaddy Valley or "Burmese" perceptions were simply of the Chinese as one ethnically undifferentiated people.

One reason for the Burmese state-centred perspective of the Chinese as one group is that the Burmese court probably saw identities in terms of political relationships. These relationships were reflected in several ways. First, the subjects of the Chinese empire were all Chinese, perhaps in much the same way that political affiliations helped determine whether one was "Burman" or "Mon" in mid- to late-eighteenth century Burma.[11] Second, the Burmese court and its ministers were regularly visited by Chinese embassies and, in wartime, Burmese warriors and commanders fought Chinese armies and commanders. All Chinese state relations with Burma were overland, between Yunnan and northeastern

Burma, the same quarter that saw all of the warfare between the Chinese Empire and the Kingdom of Burma. Hence, the Burmese traditionally viewed the Chinese as an inland people and not a people emanating from the maritime world. This was partly demonstrated by the placement of Chinese war captives. While captured European sailors and soldiers were deported far away from the sea and into Upper Burma,[12] Chinese captives were often sent to Lower Burma, in the opposite direction. Many of the Chinese in Rangoon at the time of the outbreak of the Anglo-Burmese War, for example, appear to have been war captive deportees, being placed at Rangoon "to work, and to increase the population".[13] Similarly, Chinese were settled at Bassein where they were "made to manufacture gunpowder and fireworks".[14] Symes held a different view and claimed that in the late eighteenth century, Chinese captives were settled around the royal capital in Upper Burma.[15] Until more information becomes available, I tentatively suggest that Symes mistook as captives Chinese migrants, both skilled laborers and free traders, connected with the Yunnan caravans, a view supported by other accounts of this community around the royal capital.[16] In any event, the general Burmese approach to Chinese war captives reflected a concern indicated in early modern Burmese texts of the dangers of Chinese expansion into the Irrawaddy Valley. These texts claim that even during the times before the foundation of Pagan, buffers were needed between the Irrawaddy Valley kingdom of Tagaung and the Chinese: "The King of Tagaung ... placed fifty-seven villages to the east and west of the Salween river as obstacles to the Tayoub [Chinese] ...".[17]

For the pre-colonial period, Burmese historiography has been dependent upon the state-centred historical perspective. The available Burmese accounts are also generally court-centred, consisting of royal chronicles based upon materials in royal libraries, royal orders (*amein-daw*), and local official reports (*sit-tàns*). These documents and historical narratives focus almost exclusively, in regard to the Chinese, upon state-to-state relations. Furthermore, Burmese-language histories prior to the twentieth century rarely shed light on the activities of Chinese immigrants in Burma, indicating a general absence of interest in Chinese immigrants themselves (save only for when they were involved in events related to state activities). The revised chronicle sponsored by King Mindon (r. 1853–1878), the *Duti-ya Maha-ya-zawin-daw-gyì*, for example, includes information on a Chinese revenue-farmer in Tenasserim only because he was mentioned in an interrogation of a Vietnamese envoy who had landed in Penang en route to Burma and had relied on the revenue-farmer's services in getting to the Burmese court.[18] The Burmese court perspective on the Chinese of Lower and Upper Burma, both local and non-local, as forming one "Tayoub" or "Chinese" group also had a great impact on colonial and post-colonial historiography, as historians of Burma have depended upon these written materials as important indigenous sources.

The early colonial perspective

In the early days of British interaction with Burma, just prior to the extension of British rule to two of Burma's maritime provinces (Arakan and Tenasserim) in 1826, the British also viewed the Chinese in Burma as representatives of Chinese trade and economic connections in Upper Burma. British traders were chiefly concerned with how to gain access to the overland trade with China.[19] The British accounts of the Chinese in Burma in the late eighteenth and early nineteenth centuries were thus chiefly concerned with the role of Chinese merchants in Burma, their imports and exports, and how they carried on the trade.[20] Michael Symes in 1795[21] and Hiram Cox in 1796–1798[22] may have disagreed on the nature of the Burmese court, but they agreed on the rich potential of Burmese overland trade connections with China. These and later accounts by Henry Gouger[23] and John Laird[24] created an early basis for the British framing of the Chinese relationship with Burma.

These accounts chiefly sought to answer the most important questions of British officials and commercial interests: what products did the Chinese buy and sell, how frequently, how many merchants were involved, what routes did they take, and, implicitly, how could one tap this resource and gain overland access to the Chinese market? The interrogation of Henry Gouger before John Crawfurd at the close of the First Anglo-Burmese War (1824–1826), for example, reveals Crawfurd's (and that of the EIC authorities) deep and almost exclusive interest in the intermediary merchant role played by the Chinese on the Yunnan border, not in Lower Burma. Crawfurd drilled Gouger on his knowledge of the Chinese trade with Burma: "What articles do Chinese import, and what do they export ... What description of tea is generally imported by the Chinese ... What is the quality and quantity of the cotton exported by the Chinese?".[25] As with Gouger, John Laird was also asked about Burma's trade with China: "Do you know anything of the trade carried on between the northern parts of the Burman dominions and China?".[26] Although some British surveys of Upper Burma's trade during 1826 provided additional information on the activities of Chinese living in Upper Burma, this information also focused exclusively upon their commercial activities. Gouger's and Laird's image of the Chinese trader, for example, was of a small merchant, one of hundreds who came in the yearly caravans.[27] At the same, other interests in gaining access to China, such as the spread of the Gospel by Baptist missionaries such as Adoniram Judson, also helped to reinforce the European focus on Burma's overland connections with China.[28]

Beginning in the latter part of the 1820s, however, British documents on Tenasserim indicate an emerging attention to dialect divisions among the local Chinese of Lower Burma, much as the British perceived Chinese communities in the Straits. The British view of the Chinese in the Straits tended to reflect more of a local perspective toward the Chinese in the area. The censuses for Chinese in the Straits Settlements, including Penang, Singapore, Melaka, and Province Wellesley, for example, usually included a major chart breaking up the Chinese into different Chinese "tribes". These tribes also included the "Baba Chinese", referring to the children of Chinese who had intermarried with Malays. First-hand accounts also reveal the critical place of Chinese dialect divisions in external perceptions of the Chinese in the Straits Settlements. These perceptions pervade the contemporaneous documents, from the Straits Settlements Records to the Hearings in 1867 regarding the Penang Riots of the same year, and beyond.[29] These were not the simple observations of foreigners who mistook what they saw. The well-known 1848 account of the Chinese in Singapore by Siah U Chin, for example, indicated the same kinds of divisions, also referring to the Chinese groups as "tribes". After referring to six chief "tribes", including the Hokkien, the Baba, the Teochew, the Guangdong, the Khe, and the Hainanese, he explains, "[e]ach individual tribe speaks the dialect of that tribe".[30] It is likely the case that the early British colonial perceptions of different Chinese "tribes" in Tenasserim came from the Chinese migrants themselves. Many of these migrants played with different identities: relying on Guangdong, Hokkien, Teochew, or other sub-Chinese identities among other Chinese while portraying themselves as Chinese to Europeans and others.

If this was the case, however, why did British perceptions change over the course of the nineteenth century, very noticeably from the 1830s? Differences between colonial perspectives on the Chinese in Burma between the 1820s and early 1840s cannot be simply explained by the existence of different colonial administrative groups. Until 1843, the principal colonial administrators in Tenasserim were drawn from a generation of British colonial officials who had cut their teeth in Penang in the context of Straits Settlements society. The First Commissioner of Tenasserim (1826–1833), Anthony de la Combe Maingy, had first served as Superintendent of Province Wellesley, and the Second Commissioner (1833–1843), Edmund Augustus Blundell, had been Administrative Officer and Collector of Customs at Penang before coming to Tenasserim.[31] This first generation of colonial administrators likely carried their impressions of the Chinese in the Straits into Tenasserim in the early decades of British administration. Perceptions changed within the 1826 to 1843 period, so a better answer is needed.

British perspectives of the Chinese in Burma appear to have been adjusted due to the need for Chinese settlement in British Tenasserim. In the 1820s and early 1830s, British views of the Chinese in Tenasserim were influenced more heavily by local economic concerns. With low population reserves, its landscape historically ravaged by war, and an economy poorly suited for growing world markets, British authorities entertained doubts as to whether Tenasserim would ever pay for itself.[32] There was even some consideration of handing Tenasserim back to the Burmese.[33] This economic context appears to have exerted a strong influence on British perceptions of the Chinese in the area. Colonial documents and perspectives, for example, saw the Chinese as a possible, if short-term, solution to Tenasserim's economic woes:

> The temporary employment of Chinese workmen as the most ready and expert might indeed be convenient at present[,] but temporary convenience

> would be dearly purchased ... [in] depend[ence] on expensive foreign labour instead of the cheaper work of our own natural subject.[34]
>
> (Maingy, 1826, 38)

At first, it also looked like new developments involving Chinese immigrants to Burma would help the development of a strong economy in British-held areas of Lower Burma. For many Chinese, particularly the Chinese of Penang, the extension of British control into Lower Burma during the First Anglo-Burmese War (1824–1826) represented an unprecedented economic opportunity. At issue were the old Burmese royal restrictions on trade, and British regiments occupying Rangoon and other key Lower Burmese towns opened up new trade possibilities. Most of the immediate opportunities, however, were directly linked to the British regiments themselves, as British soldiers, unused to life in Burma, were good customers for familiar foods and wares. After the British had occupied Rangoon for some time (c.1825), Captain F.B. Doveton recalled:

> ... a most refreshing cup of tea and a most delicious piece of bread fell to my share. This luxury had just been introduced into Rangoon, through the agency of some enterprising Chinese, if I remember rightly, to whom, by the way, we were indebted for many of the supplies and comforts that latterly flowed in upon us so abundantly. Some thousands of Chinese were, after a time, located in the town, having come mostly from Penang. These brought over with them, in their junks, pigs, poultry, vegetables and tea and sugar, in abundance. The pork-butchers in particular, carried on a most flourishing trade, there being ever a great demand for pork chops and sausages; and many of these gentry, doubtless, amassed considerable sums, as they well deserved, by their industry and enterprise, in the exercise of which attributes, as far at least as relates to commerce, the Chinese have no superiors.[35]

This episode bodes misleadingly well for the activities of the Chinese of Penang in Lower Burma, especially in Rangoon. It was to be a short-lived development, however, as the British withdrew from the Lower Burma delta at the close of the First Anglo-Burmese War. When Burmese rule was re-extended over Rangoon, the Chinese community suffered as a result.[36]

It also appeared that Tenasserim would benefit from problems suffered by the Chinese in Rangoon, brought about by the return of Burmese rule to central Lower Burma after the Treaty of Yandabo (1826). The Burmese who returned after the British withdrawal took out their anger on the Chinese for several reasons. First, when the Burmese had first evacuated the city, some Chinese in the city had engaged in looting and hoarding:

> [The Chinese there] were amongst the greatest rogues in existence. Plunder being prohibited to the British forces, the Chinese carried off every thing in the Burmans' absence. Their houses were full of all kinds of commodities, and I believe they were the only people who had abundance.[37]

Second, the Chinese had carried on business as usual when Mon rebels briefly held the town after the British had evacuated. Those Chinese who remained when the Burmese won back the city did not fare well:

> [A]mong the prisoners there were some Chinese, who were sold by the captors on the spot to the highest bidder. These had not served the Talains [Mons] nor were they taken in arms. They had not, however, quitted the suburbs where their dwellings were, when the Burmans returned to the stockade, which was considered suspicious, and thus, was an offence which merited punishment.[38]

Further, the Mon rebellion had left the Chinese quarter of Rangoon in ruins.[39] Indeed, under these circumstances, many Chinese immigrants in Lower Burma fled to neighbouring British-held areas such as Tenasserim.[40]

British rule was also extended to Tenasserim at a time when economic growth in the Straits spurred the large-scale immigration of Southeastern Chinese and this migration pushed northward into Burma. Viewed from the vantage point of local historical narratives and local perspectives, there was a continuity of Chinese migration from Southeast China around the Straits and into Lower Burma, merging Coastal Burma and the Straits together into a single zone for the Chinese.[41] This flow of Chinese migrants into Lower Burma from the Straits helped to dramatically increase the presence of specifically Southeastern Chinese. By the 1830s, Chinese merchants had moved as far up the coast as Akyab in western Burma.[42] As one observer noted in 1901:

> The Chinese used to come to Bamaw from Yunnan by way of Momeit, which was the route followed both by trade and by invading armies, at the terminus of which Chinese have been settled for long. But they have not spread in Burma from that centre. The peaceable invasion of Chinese comes by way of Canton [Guangdong], Singapore, and the Burmese ports.[43]

Teochew, Hokkien, Guangdong, Hakka, and other migrant groups settled throughout Lower Burma as part of this "peaceable invasion". The earlier years of this immigration of Overseas Chinese into Lower Burma (as opposed to the Overland Chinese in Upper Burma) and its role in the emergence of the "Chinese of Burma", however, has only recently received greater consideration in the literature.[44]

Early British administrators used the Chinese communities in Tenasserim in two ways. On the one hand, Anthony de la Combe de Maingy and others retained hopes that Tenasserim would be prosperous once Chinese immigration into the area had begun. British documents from Tenasserim during this period, especially those lamenting Tenasserim's poor economic performance, suggest that the arrival of Chinese in Tenasserim was either begun under British rule, would eventually begin under British rule, or was as yet insufficient to keep the economy going. In 1826, for example, Maingy wrote to the Governor of Prince of Wales Island explaining why he had failed to begin exporting significant supplies of tin:

> My expectations respecting the produce of the Tin Mines have not been realized owing to the want of Chinese laborers, and the few that have been employed, having suffered from Fever are unwilling to return to the Mines until the setting in of the N.E. Monsoon.[45]

This is in sharp contrast, however, to the non-British sources (and even some British ones) that indicate a long-term and significant Chinese role in Tenasserim's maritime economy. In an earlier publication,[46] I discussed the Cochin-Chinese embassy of 1821–1822 to Burma that was sent by a provincial Vietnamese governor who hoped to gain access to Tenasserim's esculent birds' nests so that he could sell them in China where they were in high demand and he would make a great profit. Nothing came of the mission, aside from a few exchanges back and forth between Burma and Vietnam. Certainly, nothing was resolved by 1824 when a follow-up Vietnamese mission was given a free ride to Rangoon aboard British warships on their way to invade Lower Burma. This episode is important to us here because the return mission to Vietnam in 1822 included, in addition to Burmese ministers, a British *Shah Bandar* of Rangoon, in Burmese employ, and a Chinese merchant of Penang who controlled the Tenasserim esculent birds' nest farm in the name of the King of Burma. In the contemporary documents of this event, the British documents emphasise the supposedly pivotal role played by the Englishman, but make no reference at all to the presence of the Chinese merchant. The Burmese and the Vietnamese documents, however, do mention this Chinese merchant and the Burmese sources explicitly state that he was Chinese. Similarly, the Burmese and Vietnamese accounts make no mention of the Englishman. Thus, for unclear reasons, the British ignored the intermediary role of the Chinese in the Burmese and Vietnamese relationship, in contrast to indigenous sources.

This episode is also important because it indicates a phenomenon that is gradually being pieced together from indigenous and some European sources: the Chinese, especially those with connections to Penang, had played a critical role in the Southeastern Burmese economy long before, and during, the opening years of British rule in Tenasserim. Ultimately, some of the early monopolies farmed out in Tavoy (such as those for opium and gambling) were taken under the colonial state's direct management due to disagreements between Maingy and the Chinese of Tavoy.[47]

On the other hand, and in contradictory fashion, these same British colonial officials blamed the Chinese for all their failures in Tenasserim during the same period. At the same time that British administrators pointed to the absence of Chinese in Tenasserim, some British officials – sometimes the same officials – blamed Tenasserim's problems on a Chinese community that suddenly did exist in Tenasserim. In other words, when the British were focused upon Tenasserim itself, in the hopes of developing Tenasserim's colonial economy, they stressed the local context, in which the Chinese were a convenient scapegoat for the failures of these same colonial officials. Maingy, for example, focused attention on local Chinese in the context of the sale of birds' nests, opium, and gambling farms. Maingy spread the word that the local Chinese had grouped together in order to drive down prices and improve the terms of sale. Maingy, of course, adopted various strategies to try to improve the British position in these sales and the management of the farms but generally failed.[48] As Maingy explained in 1826:

> I regret to report that the same combination that prevailed among the Chinese farmers during your stay here has continued and that I have found it impossible to rent the farms upon the system you directed to be pursued, that of dividing each farm into a certain number of shares and licenses. Several attempts have been made to dispose of the two that remain unsold but not a bidder for them was to be found excepting at rates I would not listen to ... Lieutenant Briggs states the combination among the Chinese at Mergui as being even greater than it is here ... [T]he Propensity to combination, exclusion of others and spirit of monopoly which characterizes the Chinese must therefore be guarded against at the outset....[49]

Even when evidence of Chinese syndicates was not available, Maingy still found ways to point his finger directly at the Chinese for the economic failures of the colony. As Maingy reported in 1833: "One cause of this failure is, I think, [is] to be attributed to the circumstances of none but poor and insolvent Chinese having hitherto engaged in working the tin mines".[50]

There is thus a connection between the importance of the locality and the locally relevant historical narratives of the British during this period and their perceptions of the local Chinese in Burma. As the example of Maingy discussed above indicates, British authorities shifted between local and non-local perspectives when it suited their economic interests and, in terms of the Chinese in Tenasserim, moved back and forth between silence and accusations when it was convenient to do so. British colonial administrators in Tenasserim viewed the Chinese, whether or not the Chinese were actually there, as the key to a potential economic miracle in Tenasserim or as a scapegoat for colonial failures. With lenses focused upon the Chinese communities in coastal Burma, at least during this moment, their heterogeneity became visible to colonial officials as the local narrative became relevant to the state-centred one.

British accounts of the Chinese in Tenasserim during this period read very much like British documents on the Chinese in Penang and Singapore. In Maingy's report of 22 October 1825, for example, he explained that he had postponed selling off the esculent bird's nest farm in the Tavoy islands out of suspicion of the eagerness of the Guangdong Chinese from Rangoon to buy it, apparently having some reason to distrust the Guangdong over other Chinese dialect groups. Maingy, of course, referred to them, as did British colonial administrators of the period in the Straits, not as Guangdong but as Macao

Chinese.⁵¹ Part of the reason may have been that Maingy wanted to avoid intergroup conflict between the Chinese so early in his administration of the province, even before political stability or economic viability had been assured. As Maingy explained, regarding the farm for esculent bird's nests in the Tavoy islands and the Mergui islands: "It has been the custom not to dispose of the farms separately and the Chinese here, being all of the same tribe, no competition for them has taken place ...".⁵² Apparently, all of the Chinese in this case were Hokkien, one of the two chief Chinese dialect groups in Lower Burma, as suggested by Maingy's fear that selling one farm to the Guangdong would have stirred things up. Maingy also hints here how relevant dialect groups were for colonial administrators concerned with Tenasserim per se, as both the functioning of the farms and keeping domestic peace required taking into account dialect affiliations and treating such matters with delicacy.

In short, after the First Anglo-Burmese War (1824–1826), British colonial administrators were saddled with a large colony of little obvious economic value that was only important for strategic reasons. Being unprofitable, the British were concerned that it would be an excessive drain on their resources.⁵³ Thus, economically, the British were specifically interested for many years in making the colony self-sufficient. As a result, local colonial officials in Tenasserim were chiefly concerned with the locality. In this context, divisions among the Chinese became very visible to colonial officials because these divisions were relevant to the state's prospects for building up Tenasserim's economy. Thus, for this period, the local narrative was emphasised in British documents.

In the 1830s, British perceptions of the Chinese began to change again. In the face of Tenasserim's poor economic outlook, an idea gradually emerged in the minds of the British administrators of Lower Burma that Southwest China was their saving economic connection for their new Province of Tenasserim. Since, as mentioned, early British attempts to develop the economy failed, in the 1830s, a series of missions was sponsored to help link up the colony with the Chinese caravan trade coming out of Yunnan. The first of these exploratory missions was that of a certain Dr. Richardson who made two long journeys from Moulmein, one in 1829–1830 and another in 1834, up to the Shan states in the hopes of contacting Chinese caravans moving through the area and attempting to divert them in the future to Tenasserim. Richardson related his sentiments in his diary made en route in early 1830:

> A Chinese who is here ... is to start to-morrow for Zimmay, to bring up some of the principal Chinese traders said to have arrived there, and I have strong hopes, from the enterprizing character of the Chinese, they may be induced to visit the [Tenasserim] coast.⁵⁴

The missions did not become important enough to publicise until the Second British Commissioner for Tenasserim, Edmund Augustus Blundell, had the diaries and journals from Richardson's journeys published in the *Journal of the*

Shifting categorisations of Chinese migrants 291

Royal Asiatic Society of Bengal in 1836. Even then, however, they had not yet been a success:

> It is expected that a portion of this caravan will this year extend their journey to Maulamyne, and hopes are entertained that this will lead to annual visits in increasing numbers, and the opening of an important overland trade between China and our possessions on the Tenasserim coast.[55]

It should be stressed that at this time, exploiting resources from or expanding into the areas visited by Richardson north of Tenasserim were not important for local British administrators. Blundell's comments, for example, imply a lack of any interest in the area between China and Tenasserim itself on the part of the colonial administration of Tenasserim: "[t]he trade of the country [visited by Richardson] is unimportant".[56] What was important was how to get commerce going between Chinese markets and Tenasserim and thus stimulate economic growth. A small number of Chinese merchants from the north did travel to Tenasserim in 1836, an event that helped to convince the British that they needed to redouble their efforts. Thus, in 1836–1837, another mission was sent out, this time under Lieutenant T.E. MacLeod, Assistant Commissioner of the Tenasserim Provinces. Unlike Richardson's missions, MacLeod pushed up past the Shan states and up to the border of the Kingdom of Burma with China. As MacLeod excitedly reported the prospects of opening up increased trade:

> These [Chinese] merchants informed me that they were most anxious to carry on a brisk trade with our provinces, and that the market was most satisfactory, but that the road travelled by those who visited us in 1836 was such as to render it impracticable for them to come visit by it. This objection I am happy to say can be easily overcome by their taking the road travelled by me on my return here from Zumue.[57]

From this point on, British colonial perceptions of the Chinese in Burma and the Straits underwent a slow but dramatic bifurcation. While British colonial officials in Penang and Singapore continued to stress fragmented Chinese communities in their colonies, British colonial officials in Burma moved away from early discourse on the fragmented Chinese tribes of Lower Burma. In part, this was because the British administrators in Tenasserim were now looking for a non-local solution to Tenasserim's economic problems and their attention moved away from local perspectives. As their view broadened, their attention no longer concentrated on the internal divisions of the Chinese in Tenasserim who, in British colonial eyes, had together failed to save Tenasserim economically, and instead British colonial officials focused on developing connections that linked China and its markets to Tenasserim. There was thus a strong incentive to see local Chinese in an overall "Chinese" context.

Early British historiography on Burma was strongly committed to Chinese-Burmese relations to the neglect of other aspects of Burmese history. The interest here is unmistakable as no full-fledged British historiography on Burma emerged until the 1860s, with the publication of Arthur Phayre's historical surveys, which together formed the basis for his classic 1883 study. Henry Burney, for example, translated large extracts from the Burmese royal chronicles that dealt with the history of China–Burma relations, and these were published in the *Journal of the Asiatic Society of Bengal* in the late 1830s.[58] British perceptions of and historiography on the Chinese in Burma, then, was at first a continuation of, or perhaps paralleled, that of the Burman court. Just as Burma's state documentation and royally sponsored chronicles focused on state relations between Burma and China, British state documentation of and historiography on the Chinese in Burma focused on their single national identity, due to considerations of the importance of China in the interests of British Burma. Contemporary colonial views clearly tied Chinese immigration to the northeastern border with China:

> [T]he Empress of India and the Emperor of China are firm friends and allies. The Government of the Queen is anxious to do what may be possible to make Burma a pleasant home for Chinese settlers and the Viceroy of India has summoned from China an officer of experience in the China consular service, who knows the Chinese language. This gentleman is now on his way to Mandalay, and he will make it his business to ascertain and to remedy any difficulties or disabilities under which Chinese settlers here, at Bhamo, at Myingyan, or elsewhere, may be laboring.[59]

Colonial historiography on Burma thus tended to view Chinese migration into Burma as emanating from the northeast, out of Yunnan, and portrayed Chinese migrants there as forming a homogenous "Chinese" ethnic group. This view is to be found in Arthur Phayre,[60] G.E. Harvey,[61] and even the revisionist Burmese historian Maung Htin Aung.[62] Post-war British historiography on Burma, as well, has done little to challenge these colonial impressions. I would suggest that the central importance of trade with China in the minds of nineteenth-century British administrators and commercial interests in Burma led to their focus on the Chinese in Upper Burma in their historical narratives, to the total exclusion of Chinese in Lower Burma.

The middle colonial perspective

In the latter part of the nineteenth century, the British wanted to establish a base from which to exploit the trade potential of western China. This was built upon what Warren Walsh calls the "Yunnan Myth", beginning in the 1860s. According to this myth, which, over the course of four decades, came to encompass four other Southwest Chinese provinces in addition to Yunnan, Southwest China was a region of immense wealth only waiting to be exploited by the British or the French, pushing north out of Burma and Indochina respectively.[63] After serious exploration during this period, by the end of the nineteenth century, however, this hope never materialised.⁶⁴ While current, however, this myth exerted a strong influence on local British and French colonial officials.

It should also be noted that this transition in British policy followed the British acquisition of the remainder of Lower Burma in 1852 as a result of the Second Anglo-Burmese War (1852–1853). British attention to Burma and within Burma shifted away from Tenasserim specifically and focused more upon the Irrawaddy Deltaic portion of Lower Burma surrounding Rangoon.⁶⁵ Lower Burma became relevant to broader British colonial interests in part as a potential conduit for opening up Yunnan to British commercial penetration.⁶⁶ As mentioned above, this view was strengthened although not caused by the fact that the upper levels of the colonial administration in Burma had, from the 1840s, shifted away from administrators with experience in the Straits Settlements to administrative officers who had spent the earlier years of their careers in Bengal.

The perception of China in India was very different from that held in Tenasserim. For one thing, British possessions in India did not depend upon bringing caravans down to connect them with China. For another thing, the British in India had from an earlier date considered gaining an outlet for Indian goods in China through Yunnan. As Dr. C. Williams explained in his 1864 "Memorandum on the Question of British Trade with Western China via Burma":

> At the time of first turning my thoughts to a career in Burmah, and especially in Upper Burmah, one of the prospects most distinctly in my view, was that of the old route to China by the Irrawaddy being re-opened and made available to British commerce....⁶⁷

This hope was short-lived among the British colonial administration in Bengal, as earlier surveys with this development in mind had already taken place. These included the 1848 exploratory mission sent out from Calcutta to Yunnan with the intention of "showing the great commercial and political importance of the Burmese town of Bhanmo, on the Upper Irawady, and the practicability of a direct trade overland between Calcutta and China".⁶⁸ It should be noted that in most of these accounts, and in the two examples just mentioned of British interest in connecting India to China through Burma, no reference to Tenasserim was made, and there was also no reference to any Chinese migrant resident in coastal Burma.

In any event, the Yunnan myth was important for overall British policy towards China in the late nineteenth century, but also pivotal for British perceptions of the Chinese community in Burma. The emergence of large-scale rice exports via maritime routes from the 1850s produced a boom economy in British Burma that should have shifted British attention away from the Chinese caravans coming out of Yunnan.⁶⁹ Due to the Yunnan myth, however, British interest in Burma's overland connections with Southwestern China was rekindled. Thus, the focus on China of British colonial interests in Lower Burma continued throughout the remainder of the nineteenth century.

The transition from the focus on bringing Chinese caravans down to Tenasserim to the goal of gaining access to Yunnan for the sake of exploiting Yunnan's local resources can be dated to the early 1860s. One of the first major policy statements on the subject was Dr. C. Williams' 1864 memorandum. As a result, for nearly 70 years, from the very beginning of British interest in bringing Chinese caravans to Tenasserim in the 1830s, through the evolution of the Yunnan Myth, and up until the late nineteenth century, British officials and commercial interests remained uninterested in local perceptions of identities or identifications among the Chinese settlers in Lower Burma.

It was only when the British were interested in using the Chinese of Lower Burma to fit into overall British economic strategies regarding China that attention was refocused upon Chinese immigrants in Lower Burma. At this time, however, the Chinese in Burma were considered as one Chinese people. Differences among the Chinese were ignored either as unimportant or incompatible with British economic interests in Southwestern China. When the Chinese became critical to colonial economic interests, they entered the state-centred historical narrative not as a heterogeneous and local community; but instead as a singular community connected to China. As I have tried to indicate, there was no single "Chinese" identification across time. Rather different colonial representations of the "Chinese" co-existed, interacted, and, most importantly, contradicted each other at different times in different contexts. I have tried to show that British identification and essentialising of the Chinese changed in tandem with shifting British economic interests in the region, and in relation to developments within China that affected British economic interests.

A late nineteenth-century British study approached this issue by analysing Chinese-language materials for what they had to say about the China–Burma relationship. Edward H. Parker's *Burma with Special Reference to Her Relations to China* (1893), which appeared a decade after the publication of Phayre's magnum opus, *The History of Burma* (1883), summarised and organised information from Chinese texts on China's relations with Burma. Parker's study became almost a handbook for British officials and historians interested in Burma and this book – or a *précis* on Chinese–Burmese relations, also composed by Parker – is, until today, cited in the bibliographies of all significant histories of Burma as *the* standard reference for the history of the Chinese in Burma.[70] Relying upon the Chinese state-centred perspective affirmed perceptions developing within the ranks of the British colonial authorities in Burma. However, there was little British interest in the local Chinese community in Burma itself.

Late colonial perspectives

As British Burma entered the late 1890s, prevailing state-centred perspectives were contested by popular impressions of the Chinese in Burma. These perceptions appear to have existed from the beginning, but as local histories tend to be integrated into state-centred narratives only when they are relevant to the state, they remained local and unnoticed by colonial authorities. There are a number of reasons why this change should have occurred at this time. First, the Chinese population in Burma increased dramatically from the 1890s to the 1930s and their importance in commercial activities and their urban concentration, especially in Rangoon and Mandalay, made them much more visible to the British and to growing numbers of Burmese.

Second, the Chinese migrant population had achieved the critical mass necessary to launch Chinese-language newspapers, form larger numbers of associations and clubs,[71] and to participate in the print literature of the region. The Chinese also engaged in a range of new professional occupations, such as dentistry.[72] More importantly, Chinese merchants also came to dominate opium monopolies,[73] and were well represented among liquor licensees.[74]

Chinese also represented "the other side" of licensed operations; when many Chinese attempted to circumvent opium monopoly limits on distribution, or to operate illegal liquor stalls, they became the subject of frequent newspaper reports on crime among the "Chinese".[75] Conversely, it was also Chinese residents of Rangoon who took a significant stand against the spread of the "poison" of opium.[76]

The Chinese were, in fact, becoming more real, diverse, and, above all, local. As a result, a tension emerged in late colonial British historiography on Burma. This tension was between those scholars who continued to view the Chinese as foreigners, temporary sojourners, much like the British colonials themselves, and those who saw the Chinese as local actors in Burmese history. The former view was certainly reflected in early twentieth-century British historiography on Burma. The best example is the colonial historian B.R. Pearn's magnum opus, the *History of Rangoon*, which is so detailed and large that historians of Southeast Asia have frequently treated it as a primary source. Despite the incredible importance of Chinese merchants and Chinatown in the history of Rangoon, there is only scant reference to the Chinese population of the city.[77] Although important in local narratives, and Pearn was writing not from the perspective of Rangoon, but rather from the British colonial perspective on the place of Rangoon in Burma, the Chinese in Rangoon appear to have been considered as irrelevant to the overall state-centred historical narrative.

At the same time, the traditional British view which emphasised the historical relationship between the Burmese and Chinese courts, continued. The Chinese invasion of Burma in the late thirteenth century probably received more attention in the late colonial historiography than any other single event involving the Chinese in Burma, at least for the pre-1940 period.[78] A second area of chief interest regarding the Chinese in Burma was the series of Chinese invasions of Upper Burma in the eighteenth century, all of which were defeated by Burmese armies.[79]

As the Chinese communities in Burma grew, prospered, and became more sedentary, the self-promotion of special cultural activities, the construction of community-specific temples, and the establishment of dialect associations made more obvious the "Chinese view" of themselves. Dialects, as opposed to standard Mandarin, remained dominant;[80] even the leading Sino-Burmese colonial administrator of the late nineteenth century, Taw Sein Ko, had to be sent at government expense to Peking to learn "Chinese [Mandarin]".[81] Further, when Chinese nationalists came to Burma to promote their cause of a unified Chinese Republic and a single Chinese nation they were met solely by their dialect-speaking counterparts in Rangoon.[82] Even today, the Chinese in Rangoon see themselves in ways similar – both in the present and in the past – to those of the Chinese communities in Penang and Singapore, divided into associations and with diverse origins in Southeastern China. Further, among the Chinese in Rangoon, some have connections with the Chinese of Yunnan. The centre of Chinatown, for example, is still essentially divided into two blocks, the Guangdong and the Hokkien sides of the street.[83] Dialect associations still form the basic bodies for community functions, and, aside from the Chinese Chamber of Commerce, no blanket Chinese organisation exists for Chinese community-wide activities or interaction (personal interview, 1999).

Two other recent explorations of Chinese society in Burma have found that the oral histories of the Chinese in Burma and their present-day perspectives are very similar to those prevalent among the Chinese in the former Straits. Mya Than, in an article on the Chinese in the 1990s, has offered the first publication as far as I am aware that has drawn attention to and specified external and internal differences in Chinese identities and identifications in Burma as being highly relevant aspects of the Chinese community in Rangoon.[84] But his purpose in the article was to discuss contemporary data about and the economic roles of the Chinese in Burma and not to interrogate their identities and identifications, discuss their origins, or put them into a broader and dynamic historical context. Jocelyn Co Thein has also found similar divisions in her research on the same community.[85] However, as her work is focused upon the 1967 anti-Chinese riots in Rangoon and this Chinese community in the 1980s and 1990s, her interests were focused on contemporary continuities rather than differences in the historiography.

Despite developments that have promoted a national Chinese identity overseas since the 1910s, including the 1911 Revolution, the Second World War, the establishment of the People's Republic of China (PRC) and the Cultural Revolution, this internal view of Chinese difference remains strong among the Chinese in Burma today. According to one septuagenarian Chinese resident who had lived his entire life in Burma, prior to the Second World War, the Chinese in Rangoon, who had no problems inter-marrying with Burmans, Karens, and Mons, would not marry across dialect lines among the Chinese.[86]

This perspective of diverse Chinese communities, rather than a single Chinese national identity, also emerges in the Burmese local-centred narrative. The average Burmese did not come into contact with Chinese embassies or even Chinese armies on a regular basis. Few Burmese likely ever went to any major Chinese city prior to the nineteenth century. At the same time, many average Burmese lived in close proximity to Chinese communities, interacted with them, and did notice that Chinese were not a uniform group but were of diverse identities. Unlike the state-centred narrative then, local narratives and popular impressions saw a much more heterogeneous Chinese population. We know, for example, that locally derived information from the early seventeenth century, that was incorporated into some of the state-centred narratives, assigned non-Chinese identifications to certain groups from China. One example is an account of late sixteenth-century Toungoo about the situation of Muslim Panthey traders that was later included in the early eighteenth-century chronicle, the *Maha-ya-zawin-gyì*.[87] In addition to such written evidence, popular oral traditions divide the Chinese of Burma into different groups. However, these distinctions appear to be based more on occupational than on dialect distinctions per se. Burmese popular traditions see two chief groups of Chinese in Burma: (1) The "short-sleeves" referring to carpenters and coolies, almost always of Guangdong origin and (2) the "long-sleeves", referring to merchants and moneylenders, almost always of Hokkien origin.[88] As these two occupational groups lived in divided blocks of Rangoon from the nineteenth century, they were seen as forming two different Chinese communities; not specifically Hokkien and Guangdong, perhaps, but the division among the Chinese migrants was clearly perceived.

Other self-perceptions among the Chinese are always in the making. The Chinese in Rangoon, for example, have begun to see themselves, Guangdong, Hokkien and otherwise, as a single migrant Chinese group characterised by sub-ethnic diversity, a poor and peaceful group, separate from the Chinese communities in Mandalay and elsewhere in Upper Burma, whom they view as rich and criminal.[89] Another interviewee also saw a similar divide, but couched it in different terms, splitting the Chinese into "noodle shop" (local) Chinese and "diplomat" (PRC) Chinese.[90] Likewise, the Second World War and the PRC's emergence did more than bond the Chinese together as "Chinese", as it also created a new division along political lines. Perceptions of the Chinese in Burma as "White Chinese" and those of the PRC as "Red Chinese", as just one example, are commonly voiced by the Chinese in Burma today.[91]

Conclusion

In sum, the historiography on the Chinese in Burma has, since the 1820s, relied heavily on three different but mutually reinforcing state-centred historical narratives (British, Burmese, and Chinese) to the neglect of local historical narratives, particularly those of the Chinese migrants themselves or of local Burmese. The reliance of historians upon textual sources at the centre, the use of state documents and the maintenance of state interests, has played a significant role in influencing the ways in which the Chinese in Burma have been perceived, both in the past and in the present. These sources do not provide a balanced representation of local and non-local perspectives, but rather represented the shifting focus of colonial administrators as their interests changed. When we consider the Chinese in Burma, the impressions locked into colonial and Burmese state documentation need to be challenged. We should also take into consideration not just sources reflective of British colonial interests or the impressions of the Burmese royal courts, the external views, but also local perspectives, the internal view, of the Chinese in Burma themselves.

In short, when researchers have depended upon either British or Burmese state-centred documents and historical narratives, they get a picture of a homogeneous Chinese national community in Burma. Researchers who focus on local source materials and local historical narratives have found a different picture of the Chinese in Burma, one that emphasises the heterogeneous nature of the Chinese community, or, more accurately, the co-existence of different Chinese communities in Burma. There is thus a tension between the Burmese and the British state-centred approaches, or the external view of the Chinese in Burma, and the local approach of recent researchers, who take into consideration internal views of the Chinese themselves.

General British approaches to the Chinese in Burma appear to have changed several times throughout colonial rule. At several key junctures, British colonial interests shifted their emphases between local and non-local perspectives. In some cases, this agreed with Burmese indigenous historiography, whilst in other cases it did not. But whether in agreement or not, it must be recognised that the tensions between local and non-local perspectives in Burma had an enormous impact upon the perceptions of the Chinese as reflected in colonial and postcolonial historiography in Burma. To generalise, I suggest that this may be one answer or at least part of the answer needed to explain the different perceptions of the Chinese in Burma and the Straits in colonial and post-colonial historiography.

Notes

1 The author has benefited considerably from conversations with Hong Liu, Takeshi Hamashita, Laichen Sun, James Chin Kong, and Atsuko Naono concerning the Overseas Chinese in Burma.
2 Prasenjit Duara, *Rescuing History from the Nation: Questioning Narratives of Modern China* (Chicago: The University of Chicago Press, 1995).
3 Some work on altering our view of the Chinese in Burma has recently been forthcoming by Yi Li, who views the community in part in their broader British and China contexts. See her *Chinese in Burma: A Migrant Community in a Multiethnic State* (New York: Palgrave Macmillan, 2017).
4 For a survey of this literature, see Edouard Huber, "La fin de la dynastie de Pagan", *Bulletin de l'École française d'Extrême-Orient* 9 (1909): 663–80; Janice Stargardt, "Burma's Economic and Diplomatic Relations with India and China from Early Medieval Sources", *Journal of the Economic and Social History of the Orient* 14 (1971): 38–62; and Sun Laichen, "Chinese Historical Sources on Burma: A Bibliography of Primary and Secondary Works", *Journal of Burma Studies* 2 (1997): 1–116.
5 For example, see Zhu Mengzhen. c.1584. "Xinan yi fengtuji [Descriptions of the Customs and Geography of the Southwestern Natives]", Unpublished translation by Sun Laichen provided to the author.
6 See, for example, Michael Symes, *An Account of an Embassy to the Kingdom of Ava* (London: Nicol & Wright, 1800), pp. 68–71.
7 Symes, *An Account of an Embassy to the Kingdom of Ava*, pp. 221, 294–5.
8 Symes, *An Account of an Embassy to the Kingdom of Ava*, p. 295.
9 See, for example, Ù Kala c.1730. *Maha-ya-zawin-gyì*. 3 vols (Rangoon: Hanthawaddy Press, 1960); *Hman-nàn Maha-ya-zawin-daw-gyì*. 4 vols. (Mandalay: Royal Press, 1883); and Ù Tin, *Kòn-baung-zet Maha-ya-zawin-daw-gyì*, 3 vols. (Rangoon: Hanthawaddy Press, 1968).

10 "Rakhine Mìn-raza-grì Arei-daw Sadan" [Palm-leaf manuscript, number 1632] AMs [1775, copied in 1784], National Library, Ministry of Culture, Yangon, Union of Myanmar. See folio 34a.
11 Victor B. Lieberman, 1978. "Ethnic Politics in Eighteenth-Century Burma", *Modern Asian Studies* 12.3 (1978): 455–82. See p. 457.
12 Father Manoel da Fonseca, "Father Manoel da Fonseca, S.J., in Ava (Burma) (1613–1652)", *Journal of the Asiatic Society of Bengal* (New Series) 5 (1835): 19–48. See pp. 28, 37–9.
13 Henry Lister Maw, *Memoir of the Early Operations of the Burmese War: Addressed to the Editor of the United Service Journal* (London: Smith, Elder, 1832). See p. 88.
14 John Crawfurd, *Journal of an Embassy from the Governor-General of India to the Court of Ava, in the Year 1827*. 2nd edn. 2 vols. (London: K. Bentley, 1834). See p. 421.
15 Symes, *An Account of an Embassy to the Kingdom of Ava*, p. 71.
16 Crawfurd, *Journal of an Embassy*, pp. 471–2.
17 "Rakhine Mìn-raza-grì Arei-daw Sadan", folio 4b.
18 "Duti-ya Maha-ya-zawin-daw-gyì" (Mandalay: 1919), p. 26; Than Tun (ed.), *The Royal Order of Burma, A.D. 1598–1885* (Kyoto: Kyoto University Center for Southeast Asian Studies, 1988), Vol. 8, pp. 384–5; Michael W. Charney, "Chinese Business in Penang and Tenasserim (Burma) in the 1820s: A Glimpse from a Vietnamese Travelogue", *Journal of the South Seas Society* 55 (2002a): 48–60.
19 Bertie Reginald Pearn, *A History of Rangoon* (Rangoon: Baptist Mission Press, 1939), p. 39.
20 Henry Gouger, "Deposition" (1826) in Horace Hayman Wilson *Documents Illustrative of the Burmese War with an Introductory Sketch of the Events of the War and an Appendix* (Calcutta: Government Gazette Press, 1827). See pp. 219–22.
21 Symes, *An Account of an Embassy to the Kingdom of Ava*.
22 Hiram Cox, 1821, *Journal of a Residence in the Burman Empire* (London: Colburn, 1821).
23 Gouger, "Deposition", pp. 219–20.
24 John Laird, "Deposition" (1826), in Horace Hayman Wilson, *Documents Illustrative of the Burmese War with an Introductory Sketch of the Events of the War and an Appendix* (Calcutta: Government Gazette Press, 1827), pp. 223–29.
25 Gouger, "Deposition", p. 222.
26 Laird, "Deposition", p. 226.
27 Gouger, "Deposition", p. 223 and Laird, "Deposition", p. 227.
28 Adoniram Judson, *A Memoir of the Life and Letters of the Rev. Adoniram Judson, D. D.* Compiled by Francis Wayland (Boston: Philips, Sampson & Company, 1853). See Vol II, pp. 98–100.
29 Related by Wang Gungwu in the discussion following my talk "The External and Internal Sides of Chinese-ness: Colonial Historiography and the 'Overseas Chinese' in Burma", delivered at the East Asian Institute, National University of Singapore on 29 September 2000.
30 Siah U Chin, "The Chinese in Singapore: General Sketch of the Numbers, Tribes and Avocations of the Chinese in Singapore", *Journal of the Indian Archipelago* 2 (1848), p. 283.
31 Jatswan Singh, "The Origins of British Burma: Arakan and Tenasserim, 1826–1852". M.A. Thesis, University of Malaya, 1992. See pp. 246–7.
32 William Cavendish Bentinck, *The Correspondence of Lord William Cavendish Bentinck: Governor-General of India 1828–1835*. Edited and with an introduction by C.H. Philips (Oxford: Oxford University Press, 1977). See Vol. I, pp. 164–5.
33 *Rangoon Gazette and Weekly Budget*, 18 February 1887, p. 17.
34 A.D. Maingy, "Report by Mr. A.D. Maingy on the Provinces of Mergui and Tavoy (1826)" Straits Settlements Records, L-16 (Penang: Mergui and Tavoy). Reports by Commissioners. Vol. I. Singapore National Archives. Singapore.

35 F.B. Doveton, *Reminiscences of the Burmese War in 1824–5–6* (London: Allan and Co., 1852) (Originally published in the *Asiatic Journal*), London, 1852. See pp. 227–8.
36 Crawfurd, *Journal of an Embassy*, 339.
37 Maw, *Memoir of the Early Operations*, pp. 88–9.
38 Crawfurd, *Journal of an Embassy*, Vol 2, p. 41.
39 Crawfurd, *Journal of an Embassy*, Vol 2, p. 39; Bertie Reginald Pearn, *A History of Rangoon* (Rangoon: Baptist Mission Press, 1939), pp. 133, 156.
40 Crawfurd, *Journal of an Embassy*, p. 345.
41 Michael W. Charney, "Problematics and Paradigms in Historicizing the Overseas Chinese in the Nineteenth- and Twentieth-century Straits and Burma", *Journal of the South Seas Society* 54 (1999): 93–106. See p. 101.
42 Howard Malcom, *Travels in the Burman Empire* (Edinburgh: William and Robert Chambers, 1840), p. 118; and Henry Harper Spry, "A Three Weeks Sail in Search of Health", *Journal of the Asiatic Society of Bengal* (1841): 143–8. See p. 144.
43 Max Ferrars and Bertha Ferrars, *Burma* (London: Sampson Low, Marston and Company, 1901), p. 156.
44 Charney, "Problematics and Paradigms" and Michal W. Charney, "The External and Internal Sides of Chinese-ness: Colonial Historiography and the 'Overseas Chinese' in Burma", Seminar presented at the East Asian Institute, NUS, Singapore, 29 September 2000.
45 Government of India, *Selected Correspondence of Letters Issued From and Received in the Office of the Commissioner Tenasserim Division for the Years 1825–26 to 1842–43* (Rangoon: Superintendent, Government Printing and Stationery, Burma, 1928), p. 43.
46 Michael W. Charney, "Chinese Business in Penang and Tenasserim (Burma) in the 1820s: A Glimpse from a Vietnamese Travelogue", *Journal of the South Seas Society* 55 (2002a): 48–60.
47 Maingy, "Report by Mr. A.D. Maingy", p. 37.
48 Government of India, *Selected Correspondence of Letters Issued From and Received in the Office of the Commissioner Tenasserim Division*, pp. 28–37.
49 Maingy, "Report by Mr. A.D. Maingy", pp. 37–8.
50 Government of India, *Selected Correspondence of Letters Issued From and Received in the Office of the Commissioner Tenasserim Division*, p. 104.
51 Government of India, *Selected Correspondence of Letters Issued From and Received in the Office of the Commissioner Tenasserim Division*, p. 29.
52 Maingy, "Report by Mr. A.D. Maingy", p. 28.
53 Bentinck, *The Correspondence of Lord William Cavendish Bentinck*, pp. 164–5.
54 D. Richardson, "An Account of some of the Petty States Lying North of the Tenasserim Provinces, Drawn up From the Journal and Reports of Dr. Richardson, Esq., Surgeon of the Commissioner of the Tenasserim Provinces," *Journal of the Royal Asiatic Society of Bengal* 5 (October 1836): 601–625; 5 (November 1836): 668–707. See p. 619.
55 Richardson, "An Account of some of the Petty States", p. 604.
56 Richardson, "An Account of some of the Petty States", p. 604.
57 T.E. MacLeod, "Abstract Journal of an Expedition to Kiang Hung on the Chinese Frontier. Starting from Moulmein on the 13th December, 1836", *Journal of the Asiatic Society of Bengal* 6 (December 1837): 989–1005. See p. 992.
58 Henry Burney, "Some Account of the Wars Between Burmah and China. Together with the Journals and Routes of Three Different Embassies Sent to Peking by the King of Ava: Taken from Burmese Documents", *Journal of the Asiatic Society of Bengal* 6 (1837): 542–59.
59 *Rangoon Gazette and Weekly Budget*. 4 March 1887, p. 2.
60 Arthur P. Phayre, *A History of Burma including Burma Proper, Pegu, Taungu, Tenasserim, and Arakan: From the Earliest Times to the End of the First War with British India* (London: Trübner, 1883).

61 G.E. Harvey, *History of Burma: From the Earliest Times to 10 March 1824 the Beginning of the English Conquest* (London: Longmans, Green, 1925).
62 Maung Htin Aung, *A History of Burma* (New York: University of Columbia Press, 1967).
63 Warren Walsh, "The Yunnan Myth", *Far Eastern Quarterly* 2.3 (May 1943): 272–85. See p. 273.
64 Walsh, "Yunnan Myth", pp. 284–5; *Rangoon Gazette and Weekly Budget*, 7 December 1895, p. 6.
65 Thaung Blackmore, "British Quest for China Trade by the Routes across Burma (1826–1876)". In F.S. Drake and Wolfram Eberhard (eds.). *Symposium on Historical Archaeological and Linguistic Studies on Southern China, South-East Asia and the Hong Kong Region: Papers Presented at Meetings held in September 1961 as part of the Golden Jubilee Congress of the University of Hong Kong* (Hong Kong: Hong Kong University Press, 1968): 180–90. See pp. 181–2.
66 Walsh, "Yunnan Myth", p. 273; *Rangoon Gazette and Weekly Budget*, 28 August 1888, p. 12.
67 C. Williams, "Memorandum on the Question of British Trade with Western China via Burmah." *Journal of the Asiatic Society of Bengal* 33 (1864): 407–33. See p. 407.
68 Baron Otto Des Granges, "Short Survey of the Countries Between Bengal and China, Showing the Great Commercial and Political Importance of the Burmese Town of Bhanmo, on the Upper Irawady, and the Practicability of a Direct Trade Overland Between Calcutta and China", *Journal of the Asiatic Society of Bengal* 17 (1848): 132–7. See p. 132.
69 Laird, "Deposition", p. 227.
70 Harvey, *History of Burma*, p. 383.
71 *Rangoon Gazette and Weekly Budget*, 14 December 1895, p. 13; 29 February 1896, p. 11; 17 July 1896, p. 7.
72 *Rangoon Gazette and Weekly Budget*, 6 January 1894, p. 12.
73 See for example, *Rangoon Gazette and Weekly Budget*, 24 March 1894, p. 2; and 5 June 1896, p. 7.
74 *Rangoon Gazette and Weekly Budget*, 14 December 1895, p. 13; and 14 March 1896, p. 5.
75 See, for example, *Rangoon Gazette and Weekly Budget*, 6 January 1894, p. 9; 3 November 1894, p. 10; 17 November 1894, p. 11; 19 January 1894, p. 11; 30 March 1895, p. 1; 24 May 1895, p. 13; 29 May 1896, p. 2; 7 August 1896, p. 12; 14 November 1896, p. 10.
76 *Rangoon Gazette and Weekly Budget*, 22 September 1894, p. 7.
77 Pearn, *A History of Rangoon*, pp. 53, 188, 195, 291.
78 For this literature see Huber, *La fin de la dynastie de Pagan*, pp. 648–55, 659–80.
79 G.H. Luce, "Chinese Invasions of Burma in the 18th Century", *Journal of the Burma Research Society* 15.2 (1925): 115–28; W.L. Barretto, "Maha Thiha Thura: The Saviour of Burma from the Chinese Invasion (Which Lasted From 1765 to 1769)", in W.L. Barretto, *Heroes of Burma: A Compilation of Lectures* (Rangoon: Burma Union Press, 1930), pp. 38–54; Victor Lieberman, *Burmese Administrative Cycles: Anarchy and Conquest, c.1580–1760* (Princeton, New Jersey: Princeton University Press,1986), pp. 224, 226–7, 247, 269).
80 *Rangoon Gazette and Weekly Budget*, 7 August 1896, p. 2.
81 Taw Sein Ko, *Burmese Sketches*, 2 vols. (Rangoon: British Burma Press, 1920b), Vol. 2, p. 220.
82 For example, see Chen Yi-sein, "The Chinese Revolution of 1911 and the Chinese in Burma", *Journal of Southeast Asian Researches* 2 (1966c): 95–102, p. 95.
83 Jocelyn Co Thein, "The Resilience of an Immigrant Community: The Chinese-Burmans in Twentieth-Century Rangoon Chinatown". Unpublished B.A. thesis, Department of East Asian Languages and Civilizations. Harvard College, Cambridge, Massachusetts, 1997, p. 15.

84 Mya Than, "The Chinese in Myanmar", In Leo Suryadinata (ed.), *Ethnic Chinese as Southeast Asians* (Singapore: Institute of Southeast Asian Studies, 1997): 115–57.
85 Jocelyn Co Thein, "The Resilience of an Immigrant Community".
86 Other evidence suggests that this was generally the case, although we do know of exceptions, as in the case of Aw Boon Par, a Hakka, who married a Guangdong woman in Rangoon.
87 Ù Kala, *Maha-ya-zawin-gyì*.
88 Mya Than, "The Chinese in Myanmar", p. 117; *Rangoon Gazette and Weekly Budget*, 2 July 1889, p. 21.
89 Personal interview, 1999.
90 Personal interview, 2000.
91 Personal interviews, 1999 and 2000.

13 Revenue farming and the Chinese economy of colonial Southeast Asia

Carl A. Trocki

In this chapter I examine an attempt by a syndicate of Straits Chinese to monopolise a number of opium farms in other parts of Southeast Asia and Hong Kong.[1] In particular, I would like to focus on the long-term resilience of the Straits-born Chinese in Singapore and Malaya during the nineteenth century.

One of the striking things about the social and economic history of Singapore has been the shifting balance between different groups of Chinese. In particular, I have been interested in the relationship between what might be called the more assimilated groups of Chinese such as the Straits Chinese or the so-called Babas and the newer arrivals, sometimes known as *sinkeh*s or "new guests" in Malaya and Singapore, or as "totoks" in Indonesia. The history of their participation in revenue farming in Singapore is instructive.

The Straits Chinese in Singapore

In the initial years of Singapore's existence, the leading Chinese figures in the colony's economic life were the Straits Chinese. In most cases, they belonged to Chinese families that had been settled in the Straits for one or perhaps as many as two or even three generations. When Singapore was founded, it immediately became a magnet for ambitious Chinese settlers from Penang, Melaka, Riau and even Java. In particular, the Melaka Chinese seem to have been the most prominent, and initially the most important and influential groups. They came from established local families, they often had access to capital, and they already possessed some local knowledge. Many of them spoke some English, having grown up in Melaka which had been under British rule since 1795, and some were even acquainted with Singapore's European founders including Thomas S. Raffles and Major William Farquhar.

These connections gave them an edge when it came to gaining government contracts for much of the construction work to be done in the new colony as well as in procuring concessions such as the revenue farms. The European rulers were most inclined to work with those whom they already knew and may have already come to trust, or at least, to depend upon. With their capital and local expertise, they were also useful to European merchants. Thus, they came to act as compradores or as independent middlemen linking Europeans to the "natives".

Possession of this middle ground, both socially and economically gave them many advantages from which they carved a dedicated niche for themselves in the colonial market place. The colonial economy has been described as a kind of chain made up of many links or segments. From the European end, it began with the European merchant, himself a middleman for more distant interests in India or in the metropole. Such a man would have access to capital, usually in the form of trade goods, delivered to him on credit from his distant collaborators. Since the trading world of Asia was largely opaque to him, he prospered by lending his goods to a trustworthy Chinese middleman, usually Baba or Straits Chinese. Such individuals as Tan Tock Seng, Whampoa, Tan Che Sang, Choa Chong Long and Kiong Kong Tuan were some of the key figures of this group who were identified later by Song Ong Siang in his book about the Chinese in Singapore.[2]

The British administrators too, facing a similarly opaque population of unknowable Asians found it useful to likewise rely on this same group of individuals to assist them in collecting taxes. Since they acted in a quasi-official capacity, they had to be trustworthy individuals and they had to possess capital, or at least have the means of gathering some together. Thus, the first generation of revenue farmers in Singapore were Straits-born Chinese such as Tay Han Long, Cheang Sam Teo and Kiong Kong Tuan. However wealthy they may have been at the start; ownership of the revenue farms, particularly the opium farms, placed them among the wealthiest and most powerful men in the colony.

The other factor that made the Babas important to both European merchants and administrators was their ability to work with both the Southeast Asians, that is, the Malays, Bugis and other traders of the Archipelago, and the newly-arriving Chinese – the small traders, the labourers and craftsmen who came to work in the town, and the agriculturalists and miners who came through Singapore on their way to the jungles of Singapore's hinterland. These were the individuals with whom trade goods were exchanged in order to fill the orders of their European partners. The newly arrived Chinese labourers offered the most fertile field for exploitation. The mines and plantations in which they worked provided important commodities, valuable, not only for the China trade, but also for export to Europe and the west. Their products included tin, gold, pepper, gambier, tapioca, sugar and later on, rubber. Ultimately rubber and tin became the most valuable Malayan exports, remaining so until the 1970s. These labourers were also the major consumers of opium, thus providing the tax base for the colonial and other states that hosted them.

In order to access these workers and their products, it was necessary for the Straits Chinese middlemen to develop downward linkages into the world of the "newly arrived" *sinkehs*. They had to establish relationships with smaller merchants who had their own links to the plantation owners and mine bosses. The creation of these links posed certain challenges as well as opportunities. Among the challenges were the language and culture gaps. Although both the Babas and the newcomers were "Chinese", so far as Europeans were concerned, there was often little sense of solidarity among them, or even among the *sinkeh* themselves.

In terms of sub-ethnicities, most of the Babas were said to be of Fujian backgrounds, usually known as "Hokkien" in Singapore, but this was not always the case. Clearly, some were Teochew from around Swatow (Shantou), or Hakka (Ke-jia) from other parts of Guangdong, some were Cantonese from the Guangzhou area and there were smaller groups of others. Because there were few Chinese women available, the male ancestors of the Baba families had married locally-born women, either Malay or of some other Southeast Asian background. As a result, they were highly indigenised. Linguistically, they often spoke a mixture of Malay and Hokkien at home. Their wives tended to be culturally closer to their Malayan mothers, usually dressing in baju and kebaya (traditional Malay-style clothing), chewing betel nut and cooking food that often owed more to Southeast Asian tastes than to Chinese. Home life tended to be dominated by strong women and marriage practices often tended to be matrilocal.[3]

It is important to understand, however, that at least in the nineteenth century, there is no real evidence of Straits Chinese actually marrying Malays. It appears that the cultural patterns that latterly characterised the group were already coming to be fixed by the time Singapore was founded and that the Straits Chinese tended to marry the daughters of other Straits Chinese, rather than to marry women from the local indigenous communities. Moreover, women of the Baba community were valuable as marriage partners for China-born men seeking both a mate and local kin connections. In most cases, Straits Chinese families could pick and choose among the most successful and prosperous of the newcomers as their sons-in-law. As Clammer points out, generally, these men were then socialised into the Baba culture.

The *sinkehs* came from a variety of ethnic and linguistic backgrounds. In Singapore, the various ethno-linguistic groups are known as the "five groups of Chinese" or the *wu bang*: Hokkien, Teochew, Cantonese, Hakka and Hainanese. While their numbers included coolies, craftsmen and both large and small merchants, they also included thugs, pirates, gangsters, secret society members and other less desirable elements. These were, in an economic sense, the raw material for Singapore's economic prosperity. Since economic relations and affiliations tended to follow linguistic lines, cultural characteristics mattered in the market place. *Bang* affiliation was important in Singapore, and those who crossed *bang* lines were fairly rare. Even the Straits Chinese found it difficult to communicate, let alone do business with many of the newcomers, since they themselves can also be seen to have been representing a *bang* of their own.

The Straits Chinese and the Singapore opium farms

From the time of its founding, the colony of Singapore was swamped with an extraordinary influx of Chinese persons. Arriving in the thousands and tens of thousands annually, during the first five decades of the nineteenth century, their numbers increased even more rapidly in the second half of the century. Soon the Straits-born too had been overwhelmed by thousands of new China-born immigrants, and a number of scholars have suggested that the former found themselves pressured to re-Sinicise to a certain degree. While this scenario has been challenged, I believe that some elements of this process can be seen in the history of the opium revenue farms in Singapore.[4]

Throughout the early nineteenth century, Baba Chinese appear to have been the dominant force in the opium farms of Singapore. Tay Han Long was said to be the first Singapore opium farmer, and he and his son remained important figures in opium farming syndicates until the 1840s. Other prominent members of the fraternity were Cheang Sam Teo and Kiong Kong Tuan. Kiong held the farms until the mid-1840s when he lost them to what seems to have been a newly established clique made up largely of Teochews but led by one Lau Jun Teck, who may have been a Hakka.[5]

Lau Jun Teck's syndicate was boosted to prominence by its domination of the pepper and gambier industry. Even before the founding of Singapore, there had been pepper and gambier planters active on Singapore Island. The agriculture expanded quite rapidly after the British arrived and soon came to engage the labours of a large population of coolies. These individuals were the largest body of opium consumers; however, they were located, for the most part, in the jungles beyond the town limits of Singapore and in areas where even the British did not venture. If we can believe Munshi Abdullah, the entire interior of the island was dominated by pepper and gambier planters who had organised, or perhaps been organised by a powerful secret society.[6] This body was variously known as the Tiandihui, the Ghee Hin Society, or the Ngee Heng Kongsi. Likewise, it appears that the merchants who controlled the agriculture – that is, those who lent money and provisions to planters, those who purchased their products and those who controlled the revenue concessions in the countryside were either China-born Teochews or Hokkiens who could communicate with them. Moreover, they were certainly affiliated with the Ngee Heng Kongsi.

The growth of pepper and gambier agriculture represented an important shift in the economic and demographic centres of gravity in Singapore. Initially, it appears that most of opium shops in Singapore were located in the town itself. Coolies could buy opium when they came into town and sought other amenities among the countrymen in the sections of town dominated by their ethnic group. Nevertheless, being in the town, it was likely possible for the Straits Chinese opium farmers to initially secure their monopoly and maintain control of the retail outlets. As time passed, however, and the plantations came to be located further and further from town, it is clear that an informal version of what has been described as the Kangchu system came into being. Small settlements, probably consisting of a few provision shops, gambling dens, opium shops, and wine or spirits shops sprung up at the places that still bear their names in Singapore today, such as Lim Chu kang, Yeo Chu kang, and Chua Chu kang. These settlements would have been far more difficult to control for the Baba merchants of the town.

In terms of demography, an important shift had taken place. By the late 1840s it appears that Teochews had come to make up the vast majority of planters and coolies in pepper and gambier agriculture. Indeed, they appear to have constituted the largest single group of ethnically and occupationally defined Chinese in Singapore at this time. Seah Eu Chin, in his brief 1848 article on the Chinese of Singapore indicates that there were some 8,000 Teochew pepper and gambier planters in Singapore.[7] There was also a much smaller number of Hokkien planters. As for pepper and gambier dealers, again Teochews predominated, but there was also a considerable number of Hokkiens.[8] Later on, perhaps in the 1850s, the overall population balance began to shift in favour of the Hokkiens.

We should assume a series of events here. At some point, the Teochew merchants who dominated the planting settlements decided that they were wealthier, more numerous and more powerful than the Straits Chinese merchants in the town who controlled the opium concessions. At some point, they must have begun to provide large quantities of opium for individuals who controlled the settlements in the interior. This, however, was a difficult matter since Singapore was a free port and raw opium flowed in and out of it quite freely. Anyone with the basic skills could buy a few balls of opium and a big pot and go off into the jungle and boil it down into *chandu* or smokeable opium. In order to protect his monopoly from possible smuggling, it eventually became necessary for the Straits Chinese opium farmer to bring into partnership the Teochew or other *sinkeh* merchants. The latter were more closely connected to the labourers. Moreover, one of these Teochews named Lau Jun Teck seems to have acquired the appropriate credentials to make himself acceptable to the Europeans and in about 1845 or 1846 the Singapore revenue farms came under his control.[9]

Who was this man? It is of interest that he has no biography in the pages of Song Ong Siang's volume. This suggests that he was not recognised as one of the Straits Chinese community. Indeed, he was in China when he died in about 1859 or 1860. At the time of his death, he was described by a Singapore police official as "the principal monied man of the opium farm".[10] He also seems to have made some sort of deal with at least some elements of the earlier opium farm fraternity since it was also indicated that Cheang Sam Teo was one of his partners. Cheang was a Hokkien and also a recognised Straits Chinese.[11] Thereby there came into being a financial coalition between the most powerful Hokkien and Teochew mercantile cliques which, in the 1860s controlled both the opium and the spirit farms for Singapore and Johor.[12] While this new combination might have represented something of a challenge to the Straits-born/ Hokkien interests, at least a few managed to maintain their involvement and this was important for the community as a whole.[13] For the Teochews and other *sinkeh*, I believe it signified a growing equality with the Hokkiens and the possibility for some of them to gain acceptance into the Straits Chinese community itself.

The combination of Straits-born and *sinkeh* interests in the revenue farms represented an important linkage between the producers of wealth, the holders of capital, and the colonial government. While the actual labourers got little out of it, the small-scale merchants and the larger mercantile firms that lined Boat Quay (the centre for large Teochew pepper and gambier dealers), now gained access to one of the most important instruments of wealth-creation in the colony. The opium farms were one of the things that made capital accumulation possible in nineteenth century Southeast Asia.

This syndicate seems to have been fairly durable. It lasted for almost fifteen years. Lau Jun Teck went back to China where he died (another circumstance suggesting his non-Straits born origins). The field was left open for a new group (or perhaps a new combination of the old group) to seek the prized concession. Matters did not go smoothly. The decade saw one of those spectacular boom and bust cycles that seemed to characterise the colonial economy. The revenue farms of nearby Johor became detached from those of Singapore, leaving the door open to smuggling.[14] There was a division between Hokkiens and Teochews which then lasted for the next decade. Syndicate partners on both sides came and went and bankruptcies were common. Deals were made, only to be followed by double-crosses. The minions of the revenue farmers (the "revenue police" or *chintengs*, smugglers and secret society members) all battled each other in the streets and in the waterways around Singapore. In fact, it appears that the major secret society also fragmented at about the same time and split into warring clan factions.[15]

Peace was not established again until 1870, when Cheang Hong Lim and Tan Seng Poh joined hands with the Johor *taukeh*, Tan Hiok Nee, to form what has been styled "The Great Syndicate": this was the combined opium and spirit farms of Singapore, Johor, Riau and Melaka. Not only did the conflict between mercantile factions come to an end, but the period of the 1870s was one of extraordinary prosperity for Malaya as a whole, as the pepper and gambier industry now spread all over Johor and into Negri Sembilan, Melaka and even Sarawak, and the tin industry of the other western Malay states began to boom under colonial "protection" and major infusions of Chinese capital from the Straits Settlements. With the end of the Hokkien/Teochew feud in Singapore, the competition over the farms also ended. The rental for the farms rose by only a few hundred dollars during the entire decade of the 1870s. This would have made the farms doubly lucrative for the shareholders and the partners, but it was not very good for the colonial government.

It is of interest that of the major partners in the syndicate, two were now clearly seen as locally born and considered to be leading members of the Baba community, albeit of the two wings: Hokkien and Teochew. Cheang Hong Lim, the son of Cheang Sam Teo, emerged as one of the pre-eminent figures in Singapore's Hokkien society and continued to be prominent for the remainder of the century. He held official and quasi-official positions and distinguished himself with charitable works and the support of temples and other community endeavours. Today, he is commemorated by the Chinatown park which bears his name, as does the district of Singapore in which it is located. Tan Seng Poh, the Teochew, was the son of a Perak opium farmer, and was also the brother-in-law of Seah Eu Chin. He appears to have taken over the management of Seah's business interests in the mid-1860s and run them until Seah's sons had attained their majority. In the meantime, he grew extremely wealthy, owning the gunpowder magazine, some ships, and ten shares in the new Tanjong Pagar Dock Company.

Today, only a small street is named after him. Nonetheless, his two sons went on to become leading lights of Singapore's Straits Chinese society. Unfortunately, Tan died young. He was only in his late 40s when he died in 1879, the same year in which his Great Syndicate lost the Singapore farms to a new interloper.[16]

The point of this story is, among other things, that it was the "old money" that prevailed over time. Even though it took a couple of decades, the newcomers were not only brought into the farming syndicate but, socially and culturally, they and their families became part of the Baba community, or perhaps communities. It should be understood that Cheang and his interests were still essentially linked to the Hokkien community while those of Tan Seng Poh and his Seah in-laws were affiliated with the Teochew community. In terms of wealth, each represented a great deal of the accumulated capital of their respective communities. While it is not entirely clear how and what vehicles carried the resources of the Cheang/Hokkien grouping, the Teochews were clearly dominated by the Seahs and their Ngee An Kongsi, a hegemony which lasted until the turn of the century.[17]

Singapore, Saigon and Hong Kong

The next set of events brought this trend into sharper focus. In 1878, Cheang Hong Lim, one of the key partners in the Singapore opium syndicate, joined forces with the Saigon opium syndicate to take over the Hong Kong opium farms.[18] There are two issues here that need to be understood. One is that the Saigon farmers were also Singapore-born Straits Chinese. Gan Wee, also known in Cantonese as Ngan Chan Wai and generally known by his "chop" or trademark as Banhap, seems to have been the key figure in this venture. He was joined by his partners in the Saigon/Cochin-china farms, Tan Keng Seng, and Tan Keng Hoa, who was possibly the latter's brother.[19] There can be little question that this was a venture organised primarily by Singapore-born Straits Chinese.

The second issue concerns the stakes for which they were playing. A syndicate holding the opium farms of Hong Kong, Saigon and Singapore would have had tremendous financial and political power. The Singapore farmers already dominated the pepper and gambier areas of the lower Straits including Singapore, Johor, Riau and Melaka. They probably also had controlling interests in Negri Sembilan and Sarawak. In addition, they dominated the flow of coolie labour through Singapore, and it was the labourers who were the main consumers of opium. The Saigon farmers controlled all of French Cochin-china, Cambodia and perhaps parts of Vietnamese-controlled Annam. They also dominated the all-important rice trade of the Mekong Delta.

The Hong Kong farmers also controlled the flow of labour out of Guangdong as well as Macau. What is more important is that they controlled the flow of prepared opium to those labourers, most of whom had gone to California, Hawaii, Australia and other parts of the Pacific rim. Christopher Munn has noted that the New World sales of opium from Hong Kong constituted 70 per cent of the opium processed there, or about five chests per day.[20] Clearly it was this market that Banhap and Cheang Hong Lim were hoping to steal away from the Cantonese merchants of the Wo Hang and the Yan Wo Companies that had controlled it until that time. There is also the possibility that the Singapore/Saigon combination could have controlled the traffic in smuggled opium that was then moving into China. Unfortunately for these daring entrepreneurs, the whole scheme came unstuck almost as quickly as it was put together.

The first sign of trouble came from another Straits Chinese, this time from Penang. Koh Saeng Tat was the scion of one of the oldest, most well-established Straits Chinese families of Penang. Saeng Tat was the great-grandson of one of the first Chinese Kapitans of Penang. Not only was he English-educated, as were many of the Baba Chinese of his day, he had travelled widely in Europe. He also had a sharp mind and an intuitive sense of money and value. According to a European classmate of his, when he toured Rome, rather than admire the artistic and architectural grandeur of the ruins, he spent his time calculating the cost of materials and labour to build the monuments.[21]

In 1879, he bid successfully for the Singapore opium farm, thus cutting the ground out from under the Great Syndicate. In order to sweeten the deal, he later included Cheang Hong Lim, Lim Quee Eng (Cheang's son-in-law) and Tan Keng Swee, the son of Tan Seng Poh, as partners. Thus, for a brief moment it may have appeared that this group of Straits Chinese were the holders of a network of opium farms stretching from Penang and Singapore, to Saigon and Hong Kong. Between them they controlled a network that actually included much of Sumatra and the Malay Peninsula (including southern Siam). Moreover, their reach now extended to the west coast of the US and to Australia. But the loss of the farms was a blow for Cheang Hong Lim, his son-in-law and Tan Keng Swee. They were apparently not willing to let the Penang *taukehs* into the deal and they proceeded to undercut the Singapore farms by buying smaller farms in Sumatra and Riau and smuggling opium into Singapore.

Unfortunately for Cheang and Banhap, the ex-Hong Kong farmers did the same thing to them. They acquired the Macau farms and proceeded to sabotage the Hong Kong farms. Moreover, they refused to give up the rights they held on the preferred "chops" of prepared opium which were favoured in the off-shore markets. At the same time, Banhap was under attack from the French colonial government in Saigon and by 1881, he had lost the rights to the Cochin-Chinese farms, as the colonial government had decided to run them as a state monopoly. Finally, the opium markets in California and Australia collapsed with the rise of white settler opposition to Chinese mining ventures and the immigration of Chinese labour. The US Congress passed the first Oriental Exclusion Act in 1882 and the beginnings of the White Australia policy also began to appear. By 1881 the Banhap syndicate appears to have collapsed. They also found themselves caught in crossfire between feuding Cantonese farmers, their erstwhile partners and rivals, some of whom attempted to sue for fraud and damages.[22]

The long-term success of this venture was minimal, but it did signal a new era for Southeast Asia's Chinese revenue farmers. From this time until the early twentieth century, Penang and Singapore Chinese continued to be actively involved in the opium farms of Hong Kong and the Treaty Ports. It seems somewhat ironic, that the most "assimilated" and desinicised of the Straits Chinese were the ones to go to China with the expertise and capital which they had gained in the Nanyang.

The enormous ambition of their grand scheme seems to be a forerunner of some of the grandiose but fragile financial empires that have continued to characterise the Overseas Chinese economies of Southeast Asia and Hong Kong. The incident also seems to reflect some of the long-term inherent weaknesses of Chinese capital ventures. The economy seems characterised by great schemes or the dreams of some visionary which were built on a foundation of segmented, loosely connected ventures where the organisational infrastructure was really quite weak and the slightest pressure could have seen the entire edifice collapse back into its regional components.

What can it tell us about the nature of Chinese capitalism in the late nineteenth century? First of all, it demonstrates the mobility of Chinese capital, which had been built up in the Southeast Asian colonies during the earlier decades of the century. Now, perhaps in search of an arena where they could break out of the "middleman" syndrome and perhaps break free of the colonial constraints upon their activities they were "returning" to China. Unfortunately, they never broke free of the colonial infrastructure. Indeed, the entire edifice was premised upon the structures of British rule, and when the British became frustrated with one group of Chinese middlemen, they could, at least at this time, usually find some others.

The story also demonstrates some of the strengths of the Straits Chinese network during the nineteenth century. Since the 1840s or 1850s, Chinese born to established Baba families in Singapore had been migrating out of the colonial port. They established businesses and found careers as compradores and clerks throughout Southeast Asia, and even migrated "back" to China, particularly to the Treaty Ports. Singapore Chinese were among the instigators of the Xiao Dao Hui (Small Sword, or Dagger Society) uprising in Shanghai and Xiamen in 1849–50. By the 1880s, a Singapore Chinese person could travel from Batavia to Kobe, and his Baba kinsmen and business associates could be found in virtually every port of call.[23]

I believe, however, that the account here does pose something of a challenge to the "middleman" stereotype of overseas Chinese capitalism. At least, it suggests that some Chinese understood its limitations and sought to break out of the role. Unfortunately, it also shows some of the difficulties that the breakout entailed, given the segmented nature of Chinese economic organisation and the inherent disunity of cliques and combinations. It also shows some of the contradictions in the system where one still needed local on-the-ground knowledge and control to make a venture work, and at the same time required access to global networks; linkages to European administrative leadership; and all of the infrastructure that colonialism had built.

Notes

1. I have looked at these events in an earlier study – C. A. Trocki, "The Internationalization of Chinese Revenue Farming Networks", in *Water Frontier: Commerce and the Chinese in the Lower Mekong Region, 1750–1880*, ed. N. Cooke and Li Tana [Singapore: Rowan and Littlefield Publishers Inc. and Singapore University Press, 2004], pp. 159–73) – but in this chapter I would like to look at some of the same events from a somewhat different perspective.
2. Song Ong Siang, *One Hundred Years' History of the Chinese in Singapore* (Singapore: University of Malaya Press, 1923), pp. 10–26.
3. John Clammer, *Straits Chinese Society: Studies in the Sociology of the Baba Communities of Malaysia and Singapore* (Singapore: Singapore University Press, 1980), Chapter 3.
4. John Clammer and a number of authors have argued that the dominance of Straits Chinese in Singapore was called into question with the rise of Chinese nationalism and the increasing numbers of *sinkehs* arriving in Singapore. Mark Frost, however, has pointed out that it was the Straits Chinese themselves such as Lim Boon Keng and Song Ong Siang and others who led the movement to establish Chinese schools teaching in Mandarin and also were the first to support Sun Yat Sen and reform and later revolutionary movements in China. See M. R. Frost, "Emporium in Imperio: Nanyang Networks and the Straits Chinese in Singapore, 1819–1914", *Journal of Southeast Asian Studies* 36, 1 (2005): 29–66.
5. Carl A. Trocki, *Opium and Empire: Chinese Society in Colonial Singapore 1800–1910* (Ithaca, New York: Cornell University Press, 1990).
6. Abdullah bin Abdul Kadir, *The Hikayat Abdullah* (Kuala Lumpur: Oxford University Press, 1970).
7. Siah U Chin, "The Chinese in Singapore, General Sketch of the Numbers, Tribes and Avocations of the Chinese in Singapore". *Journal of the Indian Archipelago and Eastern Asia* 2 (1848): 283–90.
8. This seems to have been a pattern of association that, like pepper and gambier agriculture itself, was imported from nearby Riau (Bentan Island) where the agriculture had been established since the mid-eighteenth century. In Riau, the Hokkien merchants dominated the town area of Tanjong Pinang while the Teochews lived across the harbour in the village of Senggarang. See Carl A. Trocki, *Prince of Pirates: The Temenggongs and the Development of Johor and Singapore, 1784–1885* (Singapore: Singapore University Press, 1979).
9. There are some questions regarding Lau Jun Teck's ethnic origins. Circumstantial evidence suggests an affiliation with the Teochew merchants, but David C. K. Ch'ng (personal communication) believes that he was a Hakka. In support of this there is evidence of a considerable settlement of Hakka planters in Singapore during this period, some of whom were associated with the Roman Catholic mission.
10. Trocki, *Opium and Empire*.
11. There may be some doubt about Cheang's status at this time, but ultimately he and his descendants have come to be considered as being part of Baba society. Certainly, his son, Cheang Hong Lim, was Singapore-born and a major figure in Hokkien-Straits born society. See Song Ong Siang, *One Hundred Years' History of the Chinese in Singapore*.
12. The question of whether Lau Jun Teck was a Teochew or a Hakka, seems irrelevant here since it seems that his main backers, or partners were Teochews associated with Seah Eu Chin.
13. It should be understood that the farms were of significance to the wealthier section of society since they represented a relatively safe, yet profitable place to place one's savings. The farmers were men of parts. They had the respect and trust of the government and, given the financial requirements of the farm, they could not possibly have

Revenue farming and the Chinese economy 313

reached into their own pockets for the large amounts of capital to manage the farms. They had to sell shares to the community at large. These functioned as the blue-chip holdings of the era and from the little evidence that exists, had retailed for about $1,000 in the 1880s.

14 The Singapore opium and spirit farms had been amalgamated with those of Johor since the 1840s, but Governor Orfeur Cavanagh had decided to separate them, because he believed that the farmer was paying too much for the Johor farms. Unfortunately, this ignored the "nuisance value" of the Johor concession and led to smuggling and conflict.

15 Trocki, Opium *and Empire*.

16 Carl A. Trocki, "The Rise of Singapore's Great Opium Syndicate, 1840–1886", *Journal of Southeast Asian Studies* 18 (March 1987): 58–80; and Trocki, *Opium and Empire*.

17 Yen Ching-hwang 顏清煌, "Power Structure and Power Relations in the Teochew Community in Singapore, 1819–1930", In *Chaozhouxue guoji yantaohui lunwenji* 潮州學國際研討會論文集 (Essays from the First International Conference on Teochew Studies), ed. Tay Lian-Soo 鄭良樹. Guangzhou, China: Jinan University Press, 1994, vol. 2, pp. 685–732.

18 *Straits Times Overland Journal*, 1 February 1879.

19 The Tan brothers of Saigon were contractors to the French colonial government of Cochinchina according to the *Chronicle and Directory for China, Corea, Japan, the Philippines* (1872, p. 331). It gives their names as Tan Keng Sing & Brothers, Chief Contractors to Government: Tan Keng Sing, Tan Keng Ho, and Tan Keng Hoa. In another listing in the same directory, we find, "Tan Keng Sing & Co., Storekeepers, Quai de Commerce". I am grateful to Dr Li Tana for bringing this reference to my attention. See also, C. A. Trocki, "The Internationalization of Chinese Revenue Farming Networks". Song Ong Siang mentions Tan Keng Hoon, who had died in 1877, when his will was contested by his "adopted son", Tan Hoon San in 1891. See Song Ong Siang, *One Hundred Years' History of the Chinese in Singapore*, p. 271.

20 In 1883, when Hong Kong had a mostly Chinese (preponderantly male) population of about 160,000, the government finally obtained the production figure of 2 chests per day prepared for local consumption (reduced through boiling into about 2,000 taels of prepared smokable opium): Ayres's calculations suggested that this would supply between 40,000 and 60,000 addicts. By the 1870s and 1880s, the more important market for the colony's prepared opium was not the local population but the overseas Chinese communities in California, Australia, and elsewhere. In 1882 more than 70 per cent of opium prepared in Hong Kong (or five out of seven chests processed every day) went to these destinations. Managed by Hong Kong-based Chinese companies, which made use of European and American steamships and banks, the export of prepared opium from Hong Kong to the Chinese communities in the New World intersected neatly with the two great trades that sustained Hong Kong's early economy: the import of opium into China and the export of labour out of China. See C. Munn, "The Hong Kong Opium Revenue, 1845–1885", in *Opium Regimes: China, Britain and Japan, 1839–1952*, ed. T. Brook and B. T. Wakabayashi (Berkeley, Los Angeles and London: University of California Press, 2000), pp. 105–26.

21 J. T. Beighton, *Betel-Nut Island: Personal Experiences and Adventures in the Eastern Tropics* (London: The Religious Tract Society, 1888).

22 The testimony from this trial can be found in the *Hong Kong Daily Press*, 1–8 December 1880. I am grateful to Dr Li Tana for informing me of this source.

23 Claudine Salmon, "Sur les traces de la diaspora des Baba des Détroits: Li Qinghui et son 'Récit sommaire d'un voyage vers l'Est' (1889)", *Archipel* 56 (1998): 71–120.

14 Towards a connected history of Asian Communism

The case of early Sino-Vietnamese revolutionary overlaps

Christopher E. Goscha

Introduction

The anti-Communist "Red Scares" in the United States and parts of Asia obsessed with Chinese Communist "expansionism", the Vietnam War and its radicalisation of intellectual and political circles, and especially the violent meltdown of Asian Communism in the late 1970s have never made it easy to study Asian Communism in cool-headed ways. During the height of the Cold War, only anti-Communists and defenders of the "domino theory" spoke of the "spread" or "expansion" of Chinese and Vietnamese Communism into East and Southeast Asia. Anti-Communist states in Southeast Asia often transformed long-standing Chinese communities into "Fifth Columns" working secretly for Beijing. The "Overseas Chinese" were often equated with "Communists" by Indonesian officials, while the Thais adopted remarkably similar policies towards the "overseas Vietnamese" concentrated in northeast Thailand. If the Sino-Vietnamese Communist alliance in the early 1950s convinced many Western leaders that the Asian dominos would fall to the Chinese communists, the violent fall-out between Vietnamese and Chinese Communists in 1979 saw Chinese and Vietnamese Communist allies break, violently, over the control of former French Indochina and purge their longstanding interactions from the official historical record. He or she who writes on Asian Communism in transnational ways must still tread very carefully because official and not so official historiographies of the Cold War in Asia remain mined. It is only recently, thanks to our distancing from the wars for Indochina, the end of the Cold War and the concomitant opening of new Communist archives, that the de-mining of the field has begun, and scholars can venture into heretofore dangerous areas of the past.

Aware of the risks, I would like to revisit the regional or transnational nature of early Asian Communism. If a variety of scholars have provided sophisticated, multidisciplinary and transnational studies of the spread of Western and Asian religions on the ground and in peoples' heads, the study of the expansion of major secular belief systems into and throughout Asia lags behind. This is particularly the case for Communism, in large part for the reasons outlined above. A plethora of studies exists on Communism, to be sure. But they almost always focus on national Communisms and concentrate largely on politics and state-building. Rare

are the specialists who examine the spread of Communism in a wider geographical and historical context than the modern nation state. Even rarer are those who try to look at how communism worked itself out on the ground and in people's heads: how it was accepted, rejected or adapted as it moved throughout the region. If religions have rightly received important attention, many scholars would, I think, still scoff at the idea of studying Communism on the same level as say Buddhism or Islam.

While Communism is not a religion, I would nonetheless suggest that conceptually and methodologically there is a need to rethink our study of Communism in wider geo-historical terms than simple national Communism. We might examine Communism seriously as another layer of historical, social and even cultural experience that arrived, spread or challenged many Asian societies in the twentieth century. For many, this secular religion was a "modern" answer to under-development and a roadmap out of colonial domination to national liberation. For some it was a source of individual salvation. For others it was a heretical credo to be combatted.[1]

In this chapter, I would like to try to examine the spread and the expansion of Asian Communism from the bottom-up and in a wider regional context than the nation-state or even regional strait-jackets like "East" or "Southeast Asia". I adopt a geographical and historical approach[2] in order to track, across a longer stretch of time and a wider spatial swath, that which would connect Chinese and Vietnamese Communisms running between East and Southeast Asia. Rather than assuming that Southeast Asia and China existed independently in time and space or that they were cut off by the formation of Western and Japanese colonial states, I would like to suggest that regional linkages flowing out of the "pre-colonial period" continued to exist in the late nineteenth and right into the twentieth century; and that such links are crucial to understanding how this secular religion moved into and throughout Asia. To track this wider context, I focus on how Sino-Vietnamese revolutionary links developed in the southern Chinese provinces of Yunnan, Guangxi and Guangdong *and* how they would extend into the "Nanyang" (South Seas) region via Chinese and Vietnamese émigré communities, and the overland and overseas routes connecting East Asia and Southeast Asia by way of southern China. In many ways, southern China and Vietnam are parts of both East and Southeast Asia. While this chapter does not draw upon a mass of new research as such, it tries to sketch out an alternative way of rethinking Asian Communism beyond the polemics of the past and the borders of the day. The Sino-Vietnamese connection is my way of running between East and Southeast Asia.

Early Sino-Vietnamese overlaps in Southern China

Exchanges between southern China and northern Vietnam have ancient roots. Tributary relations certainly ensured diplomatic contacts. So did war. During these times, peoples, goods, ideas, and technologies moved across borders, as chapters in this volume demonstrate diversely. For example, if the immigration of Chinese merchants southwards into Vietnam is well known, Vietnamese could also move northwards into the Middle Kingdom. In the early fifteenth century, during the Ming occupation of Đại Việt, the Chinese commander Zhang Fu sent over 7,000 Vietnamese artisans to the Chinese capital of Nanjing, where their technical talents were much appreciated. Ming records reveal that in 1408 Vietnamese were already working in various Chinese government ministries. A certain Lê Trừng was Vice-Minister of Public Works in Nanjing. Some Vietnamese carpenters or architects would even join in the building of the imperial fortress in Beijing, to where the Chinese capital was moved in the 1420s.[3] Many centuries later, other Vietnamese would find their way to Hong Kong, Macao, and elsewhere in southern China as part of larger, overland and overseas trading networks, run by Chinese, Europeans, and sometimes Vietnamese. Far from shutting down pre-existing Asian movements, Western colonialism built upon them from the nineteenth century for their own state-building and economic purposes. Beginning in the late nineteenth century, French colonialism would accelerate Vietnamese immigration northwards into the southern Chinese provinces bordering on their new colonial creation, French Indochina. Between 1903 and 1913, for example, the French would send around 25,000 northern Vietnamese into Yunnan province to help build, staff, and run the railway linking northern Vietnam to Kunming.[4]

Similar exchanges extended southwards into what the Chinese called the *Nanyang*, a space extending roughly from southern China to Singapore and linked by maritime routes, commerce, and increasingly overseas Chinese sojourners (*Huaqiao*) trading and/or living outside China. China's trade with the region and Vietnam is treated by other authors in this collection. What needs to be stressed for our purposes here is that long before the twentieth century, the nature of Chinese immigration to Southeast Asian coastal cities had always provided Chinese political refugees with bases from which they had sought shelter, collected funds, regrouped and tried, as best they could, to oppose their opponents in China. Many of these political refugees stayed on in Nanyang countries to make important historical contributions to local states. On the run, the famous Mạc family played a notable role in the economic, political, and cultural development of the Hà Tiên region, long before the ethnic Vietnamese got there. Similar things can be said for the Chinese in the Gulf of Thailand.[5] "Triad Societies" and "Heaven and Earth Associations" originally seeking to restore the Ming emerged from the seventeenth century in Taiwan and throughout most of the Nanyang. The Vietnamese king Tự Đức would turn to these secret societies for help as the French consolidated their hold on southern Vietnam.[6]

Vietnamese regional movements were much more limited in time and space than those of their Chinese counterparts. Compared to the Chinese, Vietnamese regional immigration was mainly overland and southwesterly in its geographical flow. Its offshoots into Laos, Cambodia and Thailand were parts of the larger Vietnamese overland colonisation of what eventually became today's southern Vietnam. By the turn of the twentieth century, small, overland Vietnamese sojourners (*Việt Kiều*) could be found living and working in Bangkok, Phnom

Penh, Nakhon Phanom, and a few as far away as Singapore.[7] As in southern China, the French would build upon these pre-existing patterns of Vietnamese immigration to build an Indochinese colonial state with ethnic Viet bureaucrats, workers, and customs agents at the helm on the ground. Just as the British stepped up Chinese immigration to Malaya from southern China (and Indian movement to Burma), so too did the French continue moving Vietnamese into the western parts of French Indochina (Laos and Cambodia) and into parts of southern China. To my knowledge, there were very few Malay, Burmese, Thai, Lao or Khmer being moved to eastern parts of French Indochina or the southern provinces of China to work on plantations or in the bureaucracy. There were, however, thousands of Chinese who continued to move to colonial Vietnam, particularly to the southern port city of Saigon-Cholon.

Western colonial domination of Asia elicited diverse responses throughout the region. If many Asians looked to the West for the keys to "modernity", others focused on how to oppose the West in order to regain their independence (without necessarily abandoning the quest for Western-styled "modernisation"). In China, Sun Yat-sen (Sun Zhongshan) would lead followers in a bid to overthrow the Qing dynasty, modernise the country, and reverse Western imperial encroachments into China. The Vietnamese had it even worse: France had occupied the country by force, shackled the monarchy, and incorporated Vietnam into a wider Indochinese colonial State, together with Cambodia and what would eventually become Laos. The French colonial police, in collaboration with their Dutch, Japanese, and British counterparts, would follow anti-colonialists with some of the most modern surveillance techniques of the time (the telegraph being one of the most important). But they also used ancient channels: Infiltrating the long-standing routes of Chinese and Vietnamese immigration across Asia was key to colonial police success.

At the turn of the twentieth century, Chinese and Vietnamese (and many others from across the colonised Afro-Asian world) looked to Japan for help. Meiji's western modernisation of Japan in record time, without direct Western colonisation, and her remarkable military defeat in 1905, of Russia, a Western power, held out the possibility of an "Asian road" to independence and modernisation. Like Sun Yat-sen, the Vietnamese scholar-patriot, Phan Bội Châu, travelled to Japan at this time, enthusiastic about gaining Japanese assistance in expelling the "barbarian" French, though determined to use their techniques to modernise Vietnam. He even created something of a Vietnamese study abroad programme, the Đông Du (Go East Movement). He was particularly interested in enrolling his young Vietnamese students in newly built Japanese military academies, so that they could learn modern Western military science via a successful Asian importer.[8] One of Phan Bội Châu's young students, Hồ Học Lãm, was an excellent example. Not only was he trained in a Japanese military academy; but he also studied with ranking Chinese nationalists of the time, including Chiang Kai-shek (Jiang Jieshi). Such early Sino-Vietnamese connections in Japan were limited, of course. Tokyo's expulsion of Chinese and Vietnamese anti-colonialists in favour of correct relations with the West, as well as

Japan's own colonising mission in Asia (Japan colonised Korea in 1910), badly weakened early Asian anti-colonialist trust in Japan and denied nationalists a sanctuary safe from colonial surveillance.

Chinese and Vietnamese anti-colonialists looked back to the Asian mainland. As they did, they would pick up on ancient socio-geographical linkages running from southern China across the Nanyang. For example, following his expulsion from Japan in 1907, Sun Yat-sen formed branches of the Tongmenghui (TMH, a patriotic association first formed in Japan and precursor to the Guomindang) among the increasing number of *Huaqiao* living and working in Nanyang port cities, especially in colonial Singapore, Malaya and Vietnam and often by winning over pre-existing secret societies. Rich Chinese merchants often helped finance Sun Yat-sen's revolutionary activities, contributing in part to the Republican victory in 1911–1912. That Sun Yat-sen opposed the Qing from the Nanyang, where the *Huaqiao* lived, and that he set up his powerbase in southern Chinese provinces, especially Guangdong and Guangxi, ensured that the paths of Vietnamese and Chinese nationalists would cross.

Similarly, once the French had colonised most of Indochina and the Japanese accepted it by expelling the *Đông Du*, Vietnamese anti-colonialists led by Phan Bội Châu,[9] turned to *Việt Kiều* communities in southern China and Siam (Thailand) for shelter, funds, and external bases for retaking Vietnam from the outside. With a blind eye from Bangkok and regional authorities keen on one day getting parts of western Indochina "back", *Đông Du* disciples set up revolutionary organisations among Vietnamese living in the Bangkok-Ayutthaya area, in Phichit province and, by the early 1930s, among the large overseas Vietnamese communities living in the Mekong provinces of Nakhon Phanom, Nong Khai and Udon Thani. Following the 1911 Chinese Revolution, Phan Bội Châu and his followers could transfer their operations to southern Chinese provinces, strategically positioned just to the north of French Indochina and the centre of Sun Yat-sen's power base in southern China.

However, compared to Sun Yat-sen, Phan Bội Châu's success rate was much more limited. With the French in control of western Indochina, Chau only had the *Việt Kiều* in Siam at his potential disposal. Moreover, the Vietnamese in Siam could hardly match the donations of much richer Chinese in the Nanyang. Southern China was thus most important to the Vietnamese at this time. Following Sun Yat-sen's successful taking of southern China in 1911–1912 and the subsequent formation of the Guomindang (GMD, Chinese Nationalist Party) shortly thereafter, Vietnamese nationalists saw a possible revolutionary model to emulate. Indeed, based on the Chinese Republican model, Phan Bội Châu created a similar Vietnamese government-in-waiting just outside French Indochina, complete with ministers, ministries and domestic and foreign policies. It was called the "Vietnamese Restoration Society" (*Việt Nam Quang phục Hội*). Phan Bội Châu considered it the real government of an uncolonised, national Vietnam. Yet it had to operate outside colonial Indochina, in Asia and above all in southern China. Like its Korean counterpart, it was still very much imagined.

The Chinese revolution of 1911 opened the way to a host of Sino-Vietnamese anti-colonial connections. A rapidly developing sense of nationalism and common opposition to Western domination was at the root of it; military co-operation and the overlapping of early Vietnamese and Chinese Communisms would emerge from it. There was also an historically important international conjuncture after WWI: Communists had taken power in what soon became known as the Soviet Union and were keen on supporting Asian anti-colonialists as part of a larger movement spanning the Eurasian continent. Anti-colonialism was seen as an essential building block and a natural part of this new ideology. Lenin, in his colonial theses, would make this linkage. Moreover, Communism, not unlike Catholicism and Islam, saw itself in universal terms, as the formation of the Comintern (Communist International) in 1919 demonstrated. The Soviet Union, as the leader of this growing internationalist Communist world, had the duty to help the colonial and semi-colonial countries in a larger bid to create a Communist utopia. For the first time since the introduction of Catholicism to Asia in the sixteenth and seventeenth centuries, the diffusion of a new ideology from the West was about to make itself felt in Asia. And the Vietnamese and Chinese (and Korean) nationalists interested in this new secular religion were positioned to play leading roles as intermediaries in its diffusion into peninsular Southeast Asia from the north.

Moreover, for a number of Chinese, Vietnamese and Korean anti-colonialists and nationalist intellectuals active at this juncture, Communism and its victory in the Soviet Union offered a promise, an explanation of the world, and of their subjugation to and domination by the West. It offered the promise of national liberation and a way out of Social Darwinism. Indeed, in their eyes (and those of many others) Communism represented another road to "modernisation". Last, many Asians coming out of WWI and disappointed by the West's refusal to reverse the humiliating colonial state of Asia[10] saw in Communism the possibility of joining a larger global network, one which would, they believed, rework the world in their favour and link them concretely to the successful Soviet Union. While this is not the place to try to argue the real impact of this universalist promise on Chinese and Vietnamese revolutionary minds, it would be wrong to succumb to the sentiments which gave rise to the recent break in Sino-Vietnamese relations by writing off Communist internationalism as mere hocus pocus. It was certainly not so at the time, as Zhou Enlai, Hồ Chí Minh, and even Mao Zedong would have readily acknowledged. Having made the leap of faith, Vietnamese and Chinese converts believed in Marxism-Leninism and its message of dual liberation from capitalist and imperial domination.[11] They were emboldened by the dispatch of European advisors to help them, and elated to receive military training and even arms for the Republican government and army of Sun Yat-sen, at a time when no other Western power was willing to risk its own colonial interests in a divided and weak China, let alone adopt a premature policy of decolonisation. The Soviet Union supported an alliance between the GMD and the Chinese Communist Party, formed in 1921 with the direct assistance of the Soviets at Shanghai (Chinese Communism was also conceived in a maritime context). From its headquarters in Moscow, the Comintern began dispatching its own European advisors to southern China, where it was felt that the most favourable conditions for revolution existed among the workers and dockers located in coastal cities. Among them were General Vasili K. Blyuker (V. Galen), Grigori Voitinsky, Mikhail Markovich Borodin, and Otto Braun. A number of Asian converts, not least of all Li Lisan, Zhou Enlai and Nguyễn Ái Quốc (later known as Hồ Chí Minh), travelled to Moscow themselves before returning to Guangzhou (Canton) where Sun Yat-sen and Chiang Kai-shek's GMD and Comintern advisors were then based. By the mid-1920s, Guangzhou – not Paris, not Tokyo – was the most important Asian forward base through which anti-colonial Communism began to enter the Nanyang region, extending from southern China to Singapore.[12]

Viewed in this larger geographical context, it was no accident that Nguyễn Ái Quốc arrived in Guangzhou in late 1924 to work as an interpreter to Mr Borodin and with Zhou Enlai, who administered military affairs in Guangxi and Guangdong provinces and whom Nguyễn Ái Quốc had met briefly in France. Nguyễn Ái Quốc was part of larger Communist movements, of which, in the Comintern's eyes, the Chinese – not the Vietnamese – were the most important component. Between 1924 and 1927, thanks to this wider triple entente between the GMD, the Chinese Communist Party (CCP), and the USSR, Guangzhou became a revolutionary laboratory for young Vietnamese whom Quốc could bring there via a gamut of secret routes, most importantly via the overland *Việt Kiều* communities of the *Đông Du* in northeastern Thailand and Bangkok. He could also draw upon the pre-existing anti-colonialists and nationalist bases set up by Phan Bội Châu.

Indeed, Nguyễn Ái Quốc wanted to exploit these favourable conditions in southern China and pre-existing immigration networks in Asia to begin work on training a group of youths who would constitute the foundation of a Vietnamese Communist party, its ruling elite, and the military officers needed for a future, postcolonial Vietnamese army. There was an added overlap at work for the Vietnamese anti-colonialist movement in southern China: Just as the CCP and the GMD worked in a fragile alliance in Guangzhou until Sun Yat-sen's death in 1925 led to its demise, so too did Nguyễn Ái Quốc find that his Communist building had stiff competition from non-Communist Vietnamese anti-colonialists with their own ties to the GMD, who wanted nothing to do with Communism. Nonetheless, both Vietnamese Communism and anti-Communism sprang from the same historical transnational context; and both groups sought to gain from the favourable southern Chinese conjuncture. And like the Chinese, the ideological seeds of the Vietnamese civil war between Communists and non-Communists began in southern China in the 1920s, not in Hanoi in 1945 or Saigon in the 1950s.[13]

In this larger anti-colonial context, Nguyễn Ái Quốc quickly formed a youth organisation, the *Thanh niên Cách mạng Đồng chí Hội* (Vietnamese Revolutionary Youth Group), from which he could pick the best and the brightest of his anti-colonial nationalist elite to undergo revolutionary and military training.

From there, he sent them to the Whampoa Military Academy outside Canton for an education in military science (see below) and, for the best, on to Moscow for advanced communist training. To this end, Nguyễn Ái Quốc relied on earlier anti-colonial connections and *Viet kieu* living in north-eastern Siam and southern China. In southern China, he turned to Hồ Học Lãm, a Vietnamese patriot who had already met with Chiang Kai-shek in Japan and who, by this time, was working for the GMD's General Staff in Nanjing and Nanning. In Siam, Nguyễn Ái Quốc could trust Đặng Thúc Hứa to send him youths from upper central Vietnam via the maritime route linking Bangkok to Guangzhou and Hong Kong.

Nowhere is the evolution of Sino-Vietnamese twentieth-century overlaps better seen than in the Vietnamese and Chinese alliances forged in the "Politico-Military Academy of Whampoa" in Guangzhou. Created in 1924, this Chinese military officer's training school was run by the GMD and, to a lesser extent, the CCP, with Soviet advisors overseeing much of the organisation, administration, and training. Based on the Soviet model created by Leon Trotsky, Whampoa sought to form political elites and military officers to run China's government and army. This would be essential to running a modern and unified state and defeating powerful warlords still controlling large parts of China. The Soviets understood that the CCP was still in its infancy and they obligated Chinese Communists to join the first "United Front" with the GMD on the bet that they could eventually take hold of its revolutionary direction from the inside. To them, the GMD was the best revolutionary force going at the time.

Communist or not, Vietnamese anti-colonialists found much needed anti-colonialist sympathy and support from GMD, CCP, and Soviet officers in the Whampoa military academy, which had officially opened on 16 June 1924. This Chinese link to modern military science being taught by hundreds of Soviet, European and even Japanese instructors in Guangzhou was particularly important to early Vietnamese military science.[14] In control of Vietnam, the French were obviously opposed to the idea of creating hundreds of political and military elites keen on regaining Vietnamese independence, let alone diffusing communism. Between 1925 and early 1927, Nguyễn Ái Quốc and other nationalist leaders enrolled at least 200 Vietnamese students in the Whampoa academy to study politics and above all military science.[15] The names of those selected by Nguyễn Ái Quốc for training at Whampoa reads like a *Who's Who* of the Vietnamese Communist Party and its future army: Lê Hồng Phong, Lê Hồng Sơn, Trương Vân Lĩnh, Hoàng Đình Giong, Phùng Chí Kiên, Nam Long, Lê Quảng Ba, Nguyễn Sơn, Lê Thiết Hùng, and many more. Besides Borodin, budding Vietnamese communists in Guangzhou also heard lectures from ranking CCP leaders such as Zhou Enlai, Liu Shaoqi, Li Fuchun, Chen Yannian, and Peng Pai, all of whom were among the highest-ranking members of the CCP elite. Even Nguyễn Ái Quốc participated in and executed the orders of the CCP between 1924 and 1927.

In this wider geo-historical context, we should not be surprised to find that young Vietnamese nationalists trained in southern China took part in Chinese political and revolutionary movements. One of the best examples of such overlaps was the participation of young Vietnamese revolutionaries in the "Canton Commune", the outbreak of civil war between Chinese communist and non-communist nationalists. Of the dozen or so Vietnamese who took up arms alongside the CCP were some of the future leaders of revolutionary Vietnam: Lê Thiết Hùng, Nguyễn Sơn, Lê Hồng Sơn, Phùng Chí Kiên, Lê Hồng Phong, Trương Văn Lệnh, Lý Tự Trọng, Hồ Tùng Mậu and Vụ Hồng Anh among others. Vụ Hồng Anh led Chinese workers against Chinese nationalist attacks. Phùng Chí Kiên fled with the CCP to Jiangxi, where he joined in the fight against the GMD and helped build new Chinese revolutionary bases in southern central China. Kiên became an officer in the Chinese Red Army.[16] Thanks to the earlier work of Nguyễn Ái Quốc, Hồ Tùng Mậu became a member of the CCP and would serve as a crucial intermediary for Chinese and especially Vietnamese communists running revolutionary networks between East and Southeast Asia. Mậu was based in Hong Kong in the early 1930s.[17]

The Vietnamese Communist Party (renamed the Indochinese Communist Party) was created outside Vietnam in 1930, in Hong Kong. The location made perfect sense. And that the Comintern and the CCP played a role in the formation of the nationalist party for the Vietnamese should not be denied on nationalist grounds, so common since the Sino-Vietnamese conflict of 1979. Rather the establishment of the party must be situated in the geo-historical context of Asian Communism as it developed at the time and along maritime routes. The fact that one of Vietnam's most famous generals, Nguyễn Sơn, took part in the Canton Commune in 1927, joined the CCP Central Committee, participated in the Long March and became a general in the Chinese Red Army also points up nicely that the "special relationship" in the history of Asian Communism is the Sino-Vietnamese one and not the "Indochinese" one pushed by Vietnamese Communists from the late 1970s and condemned by the Chinese.[18] Despite his neglect until recently by Vietnamese official historians smarting from the war with China in 1979, the fact the Nguyễn Sơn became a ranking member of the Chinese Communist Party and Army has little, if anything, to do with "pro-Chinese" sentiments in Vietnamese nationalism. It has everything to do with the geographical and historical evolution of Asian anti-colonialism and Communism over decades and within this wider regional context, one in which the Vietnamese, the Chinese and Koreans played a leading role. Indeed, there were few, if any, Lao or Khmer nationalists running these revolutionary networks between East and Southeast Asia. But again, rather than ascribing this to the 'underdeveloped' nature of Lao and Khmer revolutionary nationalism, let us continue to follow the spread of communism *beyond* southern China into what the Chinese still called the Nanyang region.

The Sino-Vietnamese origins of continental Southeast Asian Communism[19]

The regional intersection between Vietnamese and Chinese Communists was not limited to southern China. For twentieth century communism, the violent break between the GMD and the CCP in southern China from 1927 was perhaps the crucial turning point. It pushed Chinese (mainly Hainanese) and Vietnamese (largely Nghệ Tĩnh) radicals out of southern China and further into the Nanyang countries. The Comintern, relying mainly on its pre-existing Chinese and Vietnamese Asian delegates, tried to compensate by extending its communist activities into peninsular Southeast Asia by tapping into the transnational networks of these two countries in the form of *Huaqiao* and *Việt Kiều* patterns of long-standing emigration. On the run in the Nanyang, many Chinese communists began forming new and/or break-away CCP branches in opposition to the older GMD organisations, as the civil war between Nationalists and Communists in Guangzhou manifested itself throughout Chinese (and Vietnamese) patriotic organisations across Southeast Asia. Chinese communists were naturally attracted to the growing Chinese working classes in the region's major urban centres in Singapore, Rangoon, Bangkok, and Saigon. In Singapore, Chinese radicals transformed the "South Seas [Nanyang] Branch Committee" of the CCP into the "South Seas [Nanyang] Communist Party" (SSCP), whose "First Congress" was held in 1927. Directed by CCP headquarters, now relocated briefly to Shanghai, the SSCP was given permission "to gradually expand its activities to all parts of the South Seas".[20] CCP members tried to form entirely independent CCP branches in Saigon and Bangkok in 1927 and 1928. However, the success of Chinese Communists in Saigon in the late 1920s was less than impressive, due to the long-standing GMD presence there, tight European surveillance, and limited *Huaqiao* commercial interest in proletarian revolution. It was only in September 1938, as the Sino-Japanese war expanded in southern China, that a CCP "section" appeared in southern Vietnam among a growing ethnic Chinese urban working class.[21]

Nguyễn Ái Quốc left China in the wake of the GMD crackdown in 1927. After a brief trip to Moscow, he too reoriented his work to the Nanyang. But whereas the CCP focused on the *Huaqiao* in Saigon, Bangkok and Singapore, Quốc travelled to northeast Siam where large *Việt Kiều* populations lived along both sides of the Mekong. Adept in Chinese, he also maintained the logic of Sino-Vietnamese communist networks dating from Guangzhou by entering into contact with CCP Nanyang leaders in Bangkok and Singapore. At the same time, the Comintern, through its Far Eastern Bureau, assigned Chinese and Vietnamese revolutionaries the task of converting the local, "indigenous" populations of the countries in which they were working. The CCP, for example, would need to "indigenise" their largely ethnic Chinese organisations in Malaya and Singapore, while the Vietnamese would have to recruit ethnic Thai, Lao and Khmer into their mainly ethnic Viet patriotic organisations aimed at Vietnamese independence, not "Indochinese" liberation.

Obviously the Comintern's Far Eastern Bureau had to be run by Asians familiar with the region, its languages, and geography. While Nguyễn Ái Quốc was not Moscow's first choice, nor its main Comintern pointman there,[22] he was nonetheless well-suited to linking the Nanyang's revolutionary networks. He had the language skills, the major Asian contacts of the *Đông Du* and Youth League, knew the leading patriotic émigré leaders in north-eastern Siam (Đặng Thúc

Hứa) and in southern China (Hồ Học Lãm), and had essential contacts within the French Communist Party and above all in the CCP. Nguyễn Ái Quốc's instructions were to place the VCP/ICP under the direction of the Comintern's Singapore office; transform the South Seas [Nanyang] Communist Party into the Communist Party of Malaya; attach the Nanyang's central committee in charge of South Seas' Communist movements to the Singapore Section of the Comintern; and to create a Siamese Communist party by combining Chinese communists attached to the Nanyang branch in Bangkok with their Vietnamese Youth League counterparts in the northeast. These decisions were in line with Comintern internationalist directives calling for a party in each regional state, whether colonial or national.[23]

Revealingly, Nguyễn Ái Quốc disagreed with the Comintern's desire to attach the Vietnamese party to the SSCP Secretariat based in Singapore.[24] He argued that Vietnam's proximity to China made it wiser to place the Vietnamese organisation under the "Far Eastern Bureau" (FEB) in southern China, together with Communist parties from China, Japan and Korea.[25] Geographically, Quốc explained, Vietnam was more closely linked to southern China, given the long-standing maritime and land links connecting the two countries and the revolutionary collaboration that had existed since the mid-1920s. In a letter to the Comintern, dated 18 February 1930, he stressed that northern Vietnam was propitiously positioned at the tip of a revolutionary thrust extending southwards from Russia across China to Tonkin.[26] Nguyễn Ái Quốc was clearly putting his finger on the special, geo-historical linkages uniting Vietnamese Communism to its Chinese brother in southern China. To put it another way, Vietnam's unique geographical position could allow it to be linked to both China and Southeast Asia, without having to be all one or all the other. National and regional constructions do not do justice to these transnational movements.

Indeed, even if Quốc tilted towards southern China for building Vietnamese Communism (with the CCP's and Comintern's presence in Shanghai and Hong Kong firmly in mind),[27] the civil war in China and the Nanyang nature of his internationalist tasks ensured that his movements would have to be linked to Singapore. But this did not exclude continued Sino-Vietnamese revolutionary collaboration in Southeast Asia. For this reason, Quốc was quick to add, "I ask the Chinese C[ommunist] P[arty] [for] a letter of introduction so that we may send an Annamese comrade to work with Singapore".[28] Sino-Vietnamese overlaps were thus extended from southern China into the Nanyang. Given the level of Sino-Vietnamese co-operation in Guangzhou, Quốc counted on the CCP's overseas organisations to execute the Comintern's directives in the Nanyang. Sometime around March or April 1930, he returned to Bangkok for the second time. He met with overseas Chinese Communists first before moving inwards to *Việt Kiều* strongholds in northeastern Thailand.[29] Like his seventeenth-century Catholic predecessors, Nguyễn Ái Quốc and others started where their chances of success were greatest: among the *Huaqiao* and *Việt Kiều* emigrants and the pre-existing patriotic organisations abroad.

The transnational origins of Siamese Communism

On the backside of Indochina, Nguyễn Ái Quốc transformed the Youth League's "Udon Provincial Committee" into the "North-Eastern Siamese Territorial Committee" (*Xứ uỷ Đông Bắc Xiêm*).[30] He explained to his followers the international situation; the recent creation of the VCP in Hong Kong; and relayed the Comintern's desire to establish a Siamese Communist party. He made it clear that the Comintern had issued instructions calling for the participation of all cadres in the proletarian revolution in whichever Asian state they might reside, regardless of ethnic distinctions. For this reason, he insisted, Vietnamese radicals in Siam, based among and relying upon the *Việt Kiều*, now had the responsibility of helping the Siamese "masses" undertake a revolution in the "spirit of international proletarianism". Quốc called on his men to select appropriate members from the "Youth League" section – all ethnic Viet – to become communists and to create a "Siamese" communist party, separate from the VCP.[31]

Back in Bangkok, Nguyễn Ái Quốc joined with CCP cadres of the South Seas Communist Party to form the "Siamese Communist Party" (SCP). Vietnamese and, above all, Chinese ran its central committee. Fu Ta Chang, a Chinese member of the CCP's Southern Bureau, helped jump-start weak Siamese Communism,[32] for at the outset the SCP was a remarkable Nanyang construction. Of the SCP's 325 party members, most were Chinese industrial and estate workers who were said to be "of weak quality", unable to carry out their tasks effectively. Ethnically, there were 55 Vietnamese and 20 Cantonese. The rest were Hainanese.[33] "As for authentic Siamese comrades", a high-ranking Vietnamese cadre in Udon Thani tells us, "there just weren't that many in reality". The best "indigenous" recruits, he claims, came from the offspring of Thai-Viet mixed marriages in the north-east.[34] Revealingly, this cadre, Hoàng Văn Hoan, says that he spent most of his time translating Chinese revolutionary tracts produced by the CCP in the Bangkok area. Even the language of the communist message in Siam was Sino-Vietnamese.

The trans-Mekong nature of Lao Communism

If Chinese and Vietnamese immigrant networks helped introduce Communism to Siam for the first time, the overland patterns of Vietnamese immigration to upper north-east Siam led Vietnamese Communists to play the leading role in spreading Communism to western Laotian urban centres. As in Bangkok and Udon Thani, Nguyễn Ái Quốc was present at the creation. In fact, during his first trip to Thailand in 1928–29, he had already ordered the expansion of the "Youth League" to *Việt Kiều* communities concentrated in Laotian urban centres directly opposite his Siamese bases. He even made a brief trip to Laos in 1929 to evaluate the revolutionary potential there and to form liaisons with central Vietnam.[35] Given that the Vietnamese constituted the majority of the urban population in Laos, as well as its working class in the mines, in its road construction crews, and in the Indochinese bureaucracy, it is hardly surprising that the "Youth League's" graft in Laos occurred along strictly ethnic Viet lines.

Returning to the Mekong in 1930, Nguyễn Ái Quốc personally ordered the transformation of the (few) "Youth League" organisations in Laos into communist cells. According to Hoàng Văn Hoan, Nguyễn Ái Quốc himself may well have formed the first "Lao communist cell" in early 1930, separate from an "Indochinese" one given that the ICP did not yet exist in early 1930.[36] In any case, Vietnamese communists would form a "Laotian Territorial Committee" (*Xứ uỷ Ai-Lao*) in September 1934, linked to the Siamese one he had created in Udon, another in central Vietnam and to the ICP's headquarters now transferred to Macao under the Comintern, and possibly subject to the CCP's supervision. As of 1934, though, Vietnamese communists had yet to recruit an ethnic Lao. They would, however, convert two in 1935–36.[37] The rest were all Vietnamese. Even the mysterious first Lao communist, Khamseng, appears to have been a Viet-Lao *métis*, born in Nakhon Phanom and recruited among the mainly Viet workers in the mines of Phontiou. It appears that he was taken by Hoàng Văn Hoan to southern China in 1935 under the name of "Van". There, Hoan left him with none other than the future general Lê Thiết Hùng for revolutionary training and possible dispatch to Moscow.[38] What is certain is that by the mid-1930s, Sino-Vietnamese-brokered Communism had extended itself from southern China (Guangzhou) to Bangkok and northeastern Thailand (Udon Thani), to make its way into Indochina's Laotian backdoor by way of *Việt Kiều* and *Huaqiao* networks. It was a fascinating, clandestine connected exercise.

The weakness of early Cambodian Communism?

To the southeast, another young Vietnamese radical named Trần Văn Giàu hoped to use the *Việt Kiều* concentrated in Phnom Penh and south-eastern Cambodia to form a parallel ICP "Cambodian Territorial Committee" (*Xứ uỷ Cao Miên*). He had first attempted this in 1934. Unlike his northern counterparts, though, Trần Văn Giàu had no bases among the mainly Catholic *Việt Kiều* situated in southeastern Cambodia since the seventeenth century. Second, Giàu was much more interested in organising the workers in the cities than the peasants in the countryside; therefore, any interest he had in finding a "Cambodian working class" had to focus, again, on the *Việt Kiều* and *Huaqiao* majority "proletariats" in Phnom Penh or the Vietnamese coolies working the rubber plantations of eastern Cambodia. Third, the fact that Trần Văn Giàu, a young southerner trained in France and Moscow, was always in much closer contact with the French Communist Party's (FCP) Asian liaisons and agents running through Saigon would not have helped. Further, Trần Văn Giàu was largely an unknown quantity to Nguyễn Ái Quốc's Guangzhou – Udon Thani graduates like Nguyễn Sơn or Lê Thiết Hùng.[39] Indeed, Trần Văn Giàu's Whampoa- and Youth League-trained rival, Nguyễn Văn Tây (Nguyễn Thanh Sơn), may have been the one dealing with communist affairs in Cambodia in the 1930s. According to the French, Nguyễn Văn Tây had first converted the future "father" of Cambodian communism, Sơn Ngọc Minh, to the ICP's internationalist cause in the 1930s. And if Khamseng came from a Viet-Lao family in northeast Siam, Sơn Ngọc

Minh was a Viet-Khmer *métis* from the Cambodian minority of southern Vietnam.

The Nanyang nature of the early Malaya Communist Party

After having worked with the CCP to form the Vietnamese Communist Party in Hong Kong in early 1930, a "Lao communist cell" in Nakhon Phanom shortly thereafter, and the Siamese Communist Party in Bangkok in April 1930, Nguyễn Ái Quốc took a boat to Singapore, where he attended, on behalf of the FEB, the Third Representative Conference of the "South Seas Communist Party". Under his direction, the South Seas Communist Party was dismantled, as ordered by the Comintern, and re-christened as a separate "Communist Party of Malaya" (MCP). The MCP was also put in charge of fellow communist parties in Siam, British North Borneo, and the Netherlands East Indies until the latter could stand on their own feet under the direction of the Far Eastern Bureau. "The whole aim of this reorganisation" of "Nanyang communism", a Special Branch report said, "was to free the South Seas movement from the direct 'Central' control which was making of it a purely Chinese movement". Under the FEB, "it was hoped that each individual state would progress along racial lines". According to the Special Branch, the Comintern's idea in creating the FEB was to establish more direct contact with each regional country rather than relying entirely on the CCP's Nanyang networks running from Shanghai to Singapore, "which hitherto had been the main instrument in the dissemination of communism in Eastern Colonial countries".[40] Relying on captured SSCP documents, the British reported that the Comintern's failure to promote indigenous communism via CCP channels was one of the main reasons for the dispatch of Serge Lefranc (alias Ducroux) and the allocation of 100,000 Straits dollars to reorganise the Nanyang parties "along racial lines."[41] In his address to the Third Representative Conference of the SSCP, Nguyễn Ái Quốc pointed out to his Chinese listeners the need to study the Malay language and to enlist ethnic Malay recruits in the party, all the more so since there were no Malay or Indians present at Quốc's "nationalist" transformation of the SSCP into the MCP for the "internationalist cause".[42]

The irony of all this could not have been lost on Nguyễn Ái Quốc. Nowhere is this better seen than in the selection of the Secretary General of the MCP. For if Quốc had lamented Chinese domination of Malay radicalism in 1930, chronic organisational and structural problems and police repression of the Chinese allowed an ethnic Vietnamese, known by the pseudonym of "Lai Te", (also known as "Lai Teck") to take over the MCP. Lai Te arrived in Singapore in late 1932 and became the Secretary General of the MCP in 1938. He held this office until 1947.[43] In August 1945, British military intelligence sources confirmed that Lai Te, known secretly as "Mr. Wright" to the Allies during the war, was the former Secretary General of the MCP prior to WWII and was still a member of the Central Committee after the war. The British identified him as an ethnic Vietnamese, as well as the MCP's "most secret and revered personality. [...] He is a shrewd and clever man, but no fanatic".[44] Lai Te was apparently an informer passed by the French *Sûreté* to the British Special Branch in 1934 or 1935. A veteran Vietnamese communist, Dương Quang Đông, recently revealed that during an arms mission to Kuala Lumpur after WWII (to receive weapons donated by the MCP to the Vietnamese), he was shocked when he met the General Secretary of the MCP: It was an old friend with whom he had studied at the Petrus Ky *lycée* in Saigon.[45]

In the wider view of Sino-Vietnamese ideological overlaps in the Nanyang, Vietnamese and Chinese Communists, relying on their *Huaqiao* and *Việt Kiều* connections, had formed the Vietnamese Communist Party in Hong Kong in early 1930, the Siamese Communist Party, a "Lao communist cell", and the Communist Party of Malaya, and had begun Communist proselytising in Cambodia. To the north, Nguyễn Sơn would reach the highest levels of power within the CCP, while Hồ Học Lãm worked as a colonel in Chiang Kai-shek's General Chiefs of Staff in Nanjing and his nephew was an officer of the GMD army, member of the ICP, and mole for the CCP.

It is only by viewing Sino-Vietnamese military and ideological overlaps in this larger regional context and over a longer period of time that one can begin to truly appreciate the degree to which peninsular Communism running from southern China to Malaya was, to an important extent, a Sino-Vietnamese transnational phenomenon. There was no Lao, Khmer, Thai, Burmese or Malayan working in the CCP, GMD or ICP or taking the initiative to build communism in Vietnam for the Vietnamese. In September 1932, the MCP Central Committee admitted that it had "not been able to organise other races and our activities have been confined to a section of the Chinese people". As of 1934, 90 per cent of the MCP was Hainanese.[46] The Vietnamese importation of radicalism to Laos was running up against a similar form of indigenous disinterest and ethnic Viet de facto domination. Frustrated, a Vietnamese cadre conceded in 1934 that Communism in Laos was "nothing other than a subsection of the Vietnamese Communist party".[47] Even Thai writers have acknowledged that the Communist Party of Thailand, the descendant of the Siamese Communist Party of 1930, "was conceived from the womb of the CCP in 1942", the official national birthday of *Thai* Communism.[48] According to a high-ranking Vietnamese communist official raised in Laos, the General Secretary of the Thai Communist Party in the 1980s was a Viet-Thai *métis*, a descendant of the Đặng Thúc Hứa family in north-eastern Siam, a nice parallel to Hồ Học Lãm's work in southern China.[49]

Explaining Sino-Vietnamese domination of peninsular Communism

Sino-Vietnamese domination of early Asian Communist networks was less due to ideological "under-development" or "weak nationalism" in Laos, Cambodia or Malaya than to the long-standing mechanics of Sino-Vietnamese migration running across the peninsula for centuries; the indispensable, transnational role of *Huaqiao* and *Việt Kiều* revolutionaries in the early (internationalist) "stock" of the Comintern's (national) "grafts" in the Nanyang; and their related faith in the universal Communist message. This, in turn, might be analysed in terms of the Chinese and Vietnamese constituting the majority working classes in the colonial plantation economies and urban centres of mainland Southeast Asia during the period of "colonial modernisation", especially in Laos, Cambodia, and Malaya. Meanwhile, at that time, the majority local populations remained overwhelmingly concentrated in the rural areas. There was thus little chance for these two currents (national and transnational) to converge at the outset. Given the proletarian shift in the internationalist line in the late 1920s, the Comintern obviously had little choice but to turn to the existing Vietnamese and Chinese majority working classes and ancient patterns of Sino-Vietnamese immigration to spread Communism into peninsular Southeast Asian urban centres from southern China following the violent break in Guangzhou in 1927. Attention also needs to be paid to how the intellectuals in Vietnam, China and Korea seemed to respond in parallel ways to Western domination and the challenges of Western modernisation.

Vietnam, however, was in a unique position in these Nanyang revolutionary movements; for it was both an exporter of the *Việt Kiều* workers and bureaucrats vital to the French colonial administration of Laos and Cambodia in western Indochina and home to a large *Huaqiao* "national minority" that was itself playing an important modernising role in colonial Vietnam and Cambodia.[50] The Comintern's focus on urban workers may explain why it was that, in Nguyễn Ái Quốc's report to the FEB in early 1931, it was noted that of the 1,740 members of the ICP, 190 (11 per cent) were Chinese and that, of the 1,370 union workers, 300 (18 per cent) were Chinese. Two central committee positions in the ICP had been reserved for *Huaqiao* Communists in Indochina.[51] While Vietnamese held important leadership positions in the Siamese, Cambodian and Lao party sections, the transnational nature of *Huaqiao* immigration in the Nanyang ensured that Chinese immigrant Communists helped build Communism in Vietnam, especially in the south where Chinese immigration had historically been concentrated. Two Chinese communists, "Lam Lap Dao" and "A Duyen", held ranking positions in the Central Committee of the ICP during its shift to southern Vietnam after the outbreak of the Chinese civil war in 1927 and the French repression of Vietnamese revolutionaries in upper Vietnam from 1930. This Sino-Vietnamese revolutionary link was such that a dozen or so *Huaqiao* Communists joined in the failed ICP Nam Kỳ uprising in 1940. Most of them were killed or arrested; but some escaped to Thailand.[52] Just as Vietnamese revolutionaries participated in the CCP's uprisings in Guangzhou in 1927, so too did the Chinese see no nationalist contradiction in helping out in a battle against French colonialism in southern Vietnam. However, there were no Lao, Siamese or Malay revolutionary intellectuals crossing the Ai-Lao pass in 1930–1931 to help out Vietnamese communists during the Yen Bay or Soviet Nghệ-Tĩnh "uprisings". Nor did the ethnic Khmer "revolutionaries" in southern Vietnam pick up arms during the

Nam Kỳ "uprising" in 1940. Early Communism in peninsular Southeast Asia was essentially a Sino-Vietnamese affair.[53]

Conclusion

Of course, these pre-WWII Sino-Vietnamese overlaps and networks running between East and Southeast Asia did not remain static. Indeed, one of the major post-war challenges was to be the "nationalisation" of these profoundly transnational revolutionary networks as decolonisation advanced across Asia and modern nation-states emerged in its wake. Many of the postcolonial nation-states in Southeast Asia were non-Communist or even anti-Communist. These pre-war revolutionary connections would be lost in the creation of fierce nationalist historiographies that stressed the indigenous over the foreign and purged all that was Communist or associated it, often falsely, with overseas Chinese and Vietnamese. Even the Communist states in Asia would lose sight of the wider connections of Asian Communism as internationalism melted down in favour of virulent nationalism and racism. For example, Vietnamese Communist brothers sent tens of thousands of overseas Chinese packing in the 1970s.[54] By the late 1970s, Vietnamese, Chinese, Lao and Cambodian Communist xenophobes recast the history of Communism in absurdly nationalist or, in the case of Vietnam, even timeless Indochinese terms. This historiography is misleading, unfortunate and outdated. For if there is a "special relationship" in the history of Asian Communism, it is the Sino-Vietnamese one emerging out of the nineteenth century, and not the one linking Vietnamese and Lao communists in a "special relationship" à l'indochinoise at the end of the twentieth century. Future studies of the expansion of Asian Communism should not lose sight of the wider geo-historical and maritime nature of Asian Communism over the long term and beyond the colonial and nation states and their strait-jacketing of the past.

Last, while this reflection focuses on geographical and historical connections and overlaps, the question of how people accepted, rejected or adapted to Communism – above in party circles and below in people's heads – remains a largely unstudied question. To what extent did military force and the favourable conjuncture explain, in the end, the spread of Communism? To what extent did Lao and Khmers workers (or peasants) embrace the revolutionary word? How did they convert? What attracted them? What repulsed them? How did Chinese and Vietnamese missionaries tailor the Communist message? In this chapter, I have argued for the need to rethink our approaches to the study of Asian Communism. To this end, I have tried to propose one way – a connected one. But it is most certainly not the only one. It is hoped that future studies of Asian Communism will be able to explore social, cultural and anthropological aspects. Let us also hope that such new approaches will be free of the earlier attacks of a narrow nationalist kind or the hot-headed ones of the Cold War, coming from the ideologues on the Far Right and Left. It's time to move on.

Notes

1 It would be interesting to examine more closely and in equally cool-headed ways the origins of Asian anti-communism and its regional, indeed, global context.
2 The importance of "geo-history" is well known in Europe. Its analytical importance has long been shown by the likes of Fernand Braudel, Denys Lombard, and Roderich Ptak among others. See Fernand Braudel, *La méditerranée et le monde méditerranéen à l'époque de Philippe II*, 3 vols., 9th edn (Paris: Armand Colin Editeur, 1990); Denys Lombard, *Le carrefour javanais*, 3 vols. (Paris: Éditions de l'École des Hautes Études en Sciences Sociales, 1990); Denys Lombard, "Une autre «Méditerranée» dans le Sud-Est Asiatique", *Hérodote* 88 (1st trimester 1998): 184–93; Roderich Ptak, "The Northern Trade Route to the Spice Islands: South China Sea-Sulu-Zone-North Moluccas (14th to 16th Century)", *Archipel* 43 (1992): 27–56; and "Braudel et l'Asie", *Annales*, no. 1 (January–February 2001a): 5–50.
3 Geoff Wade, trans., "Ming Taizong Shilu" juan 71.1b–3b 11–0988/92, in *The Ming Shi-lu (Veritable Records of the Ming Dynasty) as a Source for Southeast Asian History – 14th to 17th Centuries*, PhD diss. (Hong Kong: University of Hong Kong, 1994); and Zhang Xiumin, "Mingdai Jiaozhiren zai Zhongguo neidi zhi gongxian" (my thanks to Geoff Wade for this reference and translation of some excerpts).
4 Vice-Consulat de France, "Le gerant du Vice-Consulat au Gouvernement general de l'Indochine", no. 24, 12 June 1913, grouping Indochine, *Rebelles annamites en Chine*, Serie III (January–August 1914), (France: Archives of the Ministry of Foreign Affairs).
5 Chingho A. Chen, "Mac Thien Tu and Phrayataksin: A Survey on Their Political Stand, Conflicts and Background", *Proceedings of the Seventh IAHA Conference* (Bangkok: Chulalongkorn University Press, 1979); and Nguyễn Thế Anh, "L'immigration Chinoise et la Colonisation du Delta du Mékong", *The Vietnam Review*, no. 1 (Autumn–Winter 1996): 157.
6 Nguyễn Thế Anh, "Secret Societies: Some Reflections on the Court of Hue and the Government of Cochinchina on the Eve of Tu Duc's Death (1882–1883)", *Asian Affairs* IX, part 2 (June 1978): 179–85.
7 "La présence viêtnamienne au royaume du Siam du XVIIe au XIXe siècle: Vers une perspective péninsulaire", in *Guerre et paix en asie du sud-est*, ed. Nguyễn Thế Anh and Alain Forest (Paris: Editions L'Harmattan, 1998), pp. 211–43.
8 Christopher E. Goscha, "Building Force: Asian Origins of 20th Century Military Science in Vietnam, (1905–1954)", *Journal of Southeast Asian Studies* 34, 3 (2003): 535–60.
9 Phan had met Sun Yat-sen and other Chinese nationalists in Japan.
10 It is no accident that the Vietnamese, Koreans and Chinese all placed their hopes in President Wilson's 1918 call for "self-determination" and that they all came away from Versailles convinced that liberation would not come via negotiations and gradual decolonisation. The fact that many Koreans, Chinese and Vietnamese nationalists, not least of all Hồ Chí Minh, turned to Communism at this juncture needs to be situated in this larger spatial and temporal analysis of the history of anti-colonialism, communism and decolonisation. For an America-centric approach and focus on Wilsonianism as the source of anti-colonial nationalism, see Erez Manela, *The Wilsonian Moment: Self-Determination and the International Origins of Anticolonial Nationalism* (Oxford: Oxford University Press, 2007).
11 On the importance of ideology for Chinese Communists, see Chen Jian, *Mao's China and the Cold War* (Chapel Hill: The University of North Carolina Press, 2001).
12 This is not to say that this was the sole avenue. I am aware of the Western networks introducing Communism into the Dutch Indies and the role of the Communist Party of Indonesia (PKI). My point here, however, is that Communism arrived in peninsular Southeast Asia via this southern Chinese route during the early 1920s.

13 One could also argue that the Vietnamese civil war between Communist and non-Communist nationalists began in prison cells in the colonial prison in Indochina from the early 1930s. Non-Communist Vietnamese and Chinese revolutionary and nationalist overlaps deserve a separate study. Again, it would perhaps be useful to study Asian anti-Communism in wider spatial and temporal contexts, going beyond my focus on its Sino-Vietnamese component.
14 Bruce A. Elleman, *Modern Chinese Warfare, 1795–1989* (London: Routledge, 2001), pp. 154–63.
15 Goscha, "Building Force".
16 Thanh Đạm, "Các nhà cách mạng Việt Nam tham gia khởi nghĩa Quảng Châu", *Nghiên cứu lịch sử*, no. 6, 253 (1990): 73–5.
17 Hoàng Thanh Đạm and Phan Hữu Thịnh, *Đời nối đời vì nước: kể chuyện gia tộc Hồ Tùng Mậu* (NXB Nghe An, 1996), p. 124 and "Entrevue avec 'Pinot' chez M. le Directeur, 1ère partie", file Lê Hồng Phong, Rapports d'agents, box 383, Service de Protection du Corps Expeditionnaire [hereafter cited SPCE], Centre des Archives d'Outre-Mer [hereafter cited CAOM]. Lê Hồng Son was a member of the CCP, as were Trương Văn Lenh, Trương Phước Dat and Lê Hồng Phong. See Nguyễn Q Thắng and Nguyễn Bá Thế, *Từ điển nhân vật lịch sử Việt Nam* (Hanoi: NXB Khoa Hoc Xa Hoi, 1992), pp. 392–93, 931; "Document no. 115, Envoi no. 70 du 18 novembre 1932, du SR Changhai", d. 3, c. 385, SPCE, CAOM; and *Đồng chí Lê Hồng Phong* (Hanoi: NXB Chinh Tri Quoc Gia, 1997), pp. 32 (note 2), 69.
18 On Nguyễn Sơn, see Goscha, "Building Force".
19 This section on peninsular Communism draws in part on Christopher Goscha, "Vietnamese Revolutionaries and the Early Spread of Communism to Peninsular Southeast Asia: Towards a Regional Perspective", *The Copenhagen Journal of Asian Studies*, no. 14 (2000): 1–41.
20 Cheah Boon Kheng, *From PKI to the Comintern, 1924–1941: The Apprenticeship of the Malaya Communist Party* (Ithaca, Cornell: Southeast Asia Program, 1992), p. 14 and Yong Ch'ing Fatt, *Chinese Leadership and Power in Colonial Singapore*, 2nd edition (Singapore: Times Academic Press, 1994), pp. 233–4.
21 The CCP appeared in southern Vietnam in 1927, when Ho Pe Siang tried unsuccessfully to form the "Association of Overseas Revolutionary Partisans" in Saigon. In 1932, an effort was made by a colleague to revive it in another form, but to no avail. "Note sur les activités chinoises du Sud Vietnam", April 1952, p. 27, box 10H659, Service Historique de l'Armée de Terre [hereafter cited as SHAT] and "Note sur les activités politiques chinoises en Indochine", September 1946, file Communistes chinois, 5, box 104, grouping Conseiller Diplomatique, CAOM, Aix-en-Provence.
22 Sophie Quinn-Judge, *Ho Chi Minh: The Missing Years (1919–1941)* (London: Christopher Hurst, 2003).
23 Furuta Motoo, "The Vietnamese Political Movement in Thailand: Legacy of the Dong-du Movement", in *Phan Boi Chau and the Dong-Du Movement*, ed. Vinh Sinh (New Haven: The Lac-Viet Series, no. 8, 1988), p. 158.
24 This plan had been presented to Comintern representatives in Hong Kong by the Chinese delegate of the "special branch of the CCP in Singapore". Dương Hạc Đính, "Schéma des liaisons possibles entre différents groupements communistes d'Extrême-Orient", in box 365, SPCE, CAOM.
25 Dương Hạc Đính, "Schéma des liaisons de la III Internationale communiste avec les divers partis nationaux ... (Projet de Nguyễn Ái Quốc et des délégués)", c.365, SPCE, CAOM.
26 Furuta Motoo, "The Vietnamese Political Movement in Thailand", pp. 159–60 and Nguyễn Ái Quốc, "Báo cáo gửi Quốc tế Cộng sản" [Report to the Comintern], dated 18 February 1930, in *Hồ Chí Minh toàn tập*, vol. III (Hanoi: NXB Chinh Tri Quoc Gia, 1995), pp. 15–16.

27 Nguyễn Ái Quốc wrote: "I propose that the VCP be directed from Shanghai by way of Hong Kong".
28 Furuta Motoo, "Vietnamese Political Movement in Thailand", pp. 159–60 and Nguyễn Ái Quốc, "Báo cáo gửi Quốc tế Cộng sản", p. 16.
29 Hoàng Văn Hoan, *Giọt nước trong biển cả. (Hồi Ký Cách Mạng)* (Beijing: NXB Tin Viet Nam, 1986), p. 60; "La fusion des associations anti-françaises en Indochine"; and personal dossier on Nguyễn Ái Quốc in file Nguyen Ai Quoc: Documents emportés par M. Nevon [sic, Néron] lors de sa mission à Hong Kong, box 364, SPCE, CAOM.
30 Xuan An, "Đồng chí Trần To Chan", *Tạp chí lịch sử Đảng*, no. 5 (1994): 58.
31 Hoàng Văn Hoan, *Giọt nước*, pp. 61–3.
32 Cheah Boon Kheng, *From PKI to the Comintern*, pp. 32, 61, note 39 and Dennis J. Duncanson, "Ho-chi-Minh in Hong Kong, 1931–1932", *The China Quarterly*, no. 57 (January/March 1974): 87.
33 "Siamese Executive Committee to the Malaya Communist Party", 20 September 1932, k. t. 39/13–30, Communists 2473–2480 [1930–1937], Box 2 (Bangkok: Thai National Archives) and "Annual Report, 1932", p. 11, FO371/17178/F1558/1558/40 (Great Britain: Public Records Office).
34 Hoàng Văn Hoan, *Giot Nuoc*, p. 93.
35 Nguyễn Tai, "Nho lai Ngay dua Bac Ho tu Thái Lan sang gây dựng cơ sở cach Mang o Lao", *Tạp chí Cộng San*, no. 12 (December 1986): 80–2 and Hoàng Văn Hoan, *Giot Nuoc*, p. 59.
36 Hoàng Văn Hoan, *Giot Nuoc*, p. 63.
37 MacAlister Brown and Joseph J. Zasloff, *Apprentice Revolutionaries: The Communist Movement in Laos, 1930–1988* (Stanford: Hoover Institution Press, 1986), p. 15.
38 Hoàng Văn Hoan, *Giot Nuoc*, pp. 89, 117–18 and "Parti communiste [laotien], Comité central N.LH.S", 10 October 1958 and 1 February 1958, file 75, box G14–7, Laos, 1945–1965, Jean Deuve papers (France: Caen Memorial). Hoang Van Hoan refers to this person as "Van" and as a Communist from Thailand, whereas the French source speaks of "Khamseng". Both sources, however, confirm that this person was entrusted to future General Lê Thiết Hùng in 1935, leading me to hypothesise that this "Van" was most probably "Khamseng", who joined the ICP in 1936.
39 However, Trần Văn Giàu may have collaborated with (Moscow-trained?) Chinese internationalists in Shanghai, some of whom were forced into southern Vietnam following the fall of Shanghai to the Japanese in mid-1937.
40 Straits Settlements Police, "Communism in Malaya in 1931 and 1932", *Police Intelligence Journal*, supplement no. 4 to issue no. 11, 31 November 1932, p. 2 (Singapore: Special Branch) 23 November 1932, file 65560, grouping Gouverneur General de l'Indochine, CAOM.
41 "Communism in Malaya in 1931 and 1932", pp. 1, 5–6 and "Communist Propaganda among Malay and Indians", Supplement no. 12 to no. 10, 31 October 1934, Special Branch, in Ibid.
42 Yong Ch'ing Fatt, *Chinese Leadership and Power in Colonial Singapore*, 2nd edition (Singapore: Times Academic Press, 1994), p. 236 and Chin Peng, *My Side of History* (Singapore: Media Masters, 2003), p. 57.
43 Chin Peng, *My Side of History*, p. 58; Yoji Akashi, "Lai Teck, Secretary General of the Malayan Communist Party, 1939–1947", *Journal of the South Seas Society* 49 (1994): 57–102; C. F. Yong, *The Origins of Malayan Communism* (Singapore: South Seas Society, 1997), pp. 128–51; and Cheah Boon Kheng, *From PKI*, pp. 25–8, for more details on this Vietnamese person.
44 HQ Force 136 to Kandy, "Memorandum by Head of Malaya Country Section, Force 136, on Resistance Forces in Malaya on the Eve of the Japanese Capitulation", 21 August 1945, WO203/5767, PRO.
45 Nguyễn Ngọc, *Có một con đường mòn trên biển Đông* (Hanoi: NXB Ha Noi, no date), p. 28.

46 "A Review of the Condition of the Malaya Communist Party in Malaya during the Years 1932 and 1933: Compiled by Mr. J. C. Barry from the original records of the Party's representative Conferences held in 1932 and 1933", Special Branch, Straits Settlements, 30 June 1934, pp. 1–2, in file 65560, GG, CAOM.
47 "Résolutions prises par la Conférence régionale des Représentants du Laos du 6 au 9 septembre 1934", box 54, SLOTFOM, III, CAOM.
48 Nopporn Suwanpanich and Kraisak Choonhavan, "The Communist Party of Thailand and Conflict in Indochina" (The Hague: Institute of Social Studies, 1980), p. 18.
49 This former, high-ranking Vietnamese official was active politically and diplomatically in Vietnamese revolutionary networks in Thailand after WWII. This person insisted on anonymity.
50 The Chinese population in Cochin-china increased from 156,000 in 1921 to 205,000 in 1931. Tsai Maw-Kuey, *Les Chinois au Sud-Vietnam* (Paris: Bibliothèque Nationale, 1968), p. 41, Table III.
51 Translated and reproduced in "Gouverneur général de l'Indochine à Ministre des Colonies", no. 2758/SG, Hanoi, 11 August 1932, file Bureau d'Extrême-Orient, box 127, SLOTFOM, III, CAOM and Nguyễn Ái Quốc, "Báo cáo gửi Quốc tế Cộng sản", dated 18 February 1930.
52 H. D., "Phong trào nguoi Hoa ở Do thì Sài Gòn", *Mùa thu rồi ngày hăm ba*, volume II, 3rd section (Hanoi: NXB Chính trị quốc gia, 1996), pp. 468–9; "Note sur les activités chinoises du Sud Vietnam" April 1952), p. 27, box 10H659, SHAT; and Secteur Saigon-Cholon, S/Secteur Cholon, no. 1339/SSC/S, "Rapport sur l'activité des Chinois à Cholon", file BR58, box 10H4358, SHAT.
53 This is in contrast to the Cao Đài faith, which attracted Vietnamese and Cambodians regardless of ethnicity in areas up along the Mekong River.
54 During this period, General Nguyễn Sơn's participation in the Chinese Communist Party's Long March and the Red Army was side-lined until Vietnamese historians rehabilitated him in the wake of improving Sino-Vietnamese relations in the 1990s.

Bibliography

Primary sources

Archives

"A Review of the Condition of the Malaya Communist Party in Malaya during the Years 1932 and 1933: Compiled by Mr. J. C. Barry based on the original records of the Party's representative Conferences held in 1932 and 1933." Special Branch, Straits Settlements, 30 June 1934, pp. 1–2, in file 65560, GG, Centre des Archives d'Outre-Mer, Aix-en-Provence, France.

Châu Ban Triều Nguyễn, Vol. 1. Triều Gia Long (The files of the Gia Long reign). Kept in the National Archives no. 1, Hanoi.

"Document no. 115, Envoi no. 70 du 18 novembre 1932, du SR Changhai." c.385, SPCE, Centre des Archives d'Outre-Mer, Aix-en-Provence, France.

Dương, Hạc Đính. "Schéma des liaisons possibles entre différents groupements communistes d'Extrême-Orient." In box 365, SPCE, Centre des Archives d'Outre-Mer, Aix-en-Provence, France.

Dutch Documents from Melaka in the India Office Records. R/9/20 and R/9/22. The British Library, London, United Kingdom.

"Entrevue avec 'Pinot' chez M. le Directeur, 1ère partie." File Le Hong Phong, Rapports d'agents, box 383, Service de Protection du Corps Expeditionnaire, Centre des Archives d'Outre-Mer, Aix-en-Provence, France.

"Gouverneur général de l'Indochine à Ministre des Colonies." No. 2758/SG, Hanoi, 11 August 1932, file Bureau d'Extrême-Orient, box 127, SLOTFOM, III, Centre des Archives d'Outre-Mer, Aix-en-Provence, France.

HQ Force 136 to Kandy, "Memorandum by Head of Malaya Country Section, Force 136, on Resistance Forces in Malaya on the Eve of the Japanese Capitulation", 21 August 1945, WO203/5767, Public Records Office, United Kingdom.

Junjichu lufu zouzhe waijiaolei: Taiguo (軍機處錄副奏摺外交類：泰國 Copies of Memorials of the Qing period kept in the Council of State, Diplomatic Documents: Thailand. Unpublished Archives). Beijing: National First Historical Archive.

Maingy, A. D. "Report by Mr. A. D. Maingy on the Provinces of Mergui and Tavoy." Straits Settlements Records. L-16 (Penang: Mergui and Tavoy). Reports by Commissioners. Vol. I. Singapore National Archives. Singapore, 1826.

Ming shilu (Veritable Records of the Ming Dynasty). Taipei: Institute of History and Philology, Academia Sinica, 1962–66.

"Nguyen Phuc Tran to Wei Jiuguan", 11 August 1673 as cited in Ming Do Su, Vol. 7.

336 *Bibliography*

"Note sur les activités politiques chinoises en Indochine." September 1946, file Communistes chinois, 5, box 104, grouping Conseiller Diplomatique, Centre des Archives d'Outre-Mer, Aix-en-Provence, France.

"Note sur les activités chinoises du Sud Vietnam." April 1952, box 10H659, Service Historique de l'Armée de Terre.

Overgekomen brieven en papieren, Archives of the Dutch East India Company (VOC), National Archives of the Netherlands, the Hague, Netherlands.

"Parti communiste [laotien], Comité central N.LH.S." 10 October 1958 and 1 February 1958, file 75, box G14–7, Laos, 1945–1965, Jean Deuve papers, France: Caen Memorial.

Personal dossier on Nguyen Ai Quoc in file Nguyen Ai Quoc: Documents emportés par M. Nevon [sic, Néron] lors de sa mission à Hong Kong.Box 364, SPCE, Centre des Archives d'Outre-Mer, Aix-en-Provence, France.

"Résolutions prises par la Conférence régionale des Représentants du Laos du 6 au 9 septembre 1934." Box 54, SLOTFOM, III, Centre des Archives d'Outre-Mer, Aix-en-Provence, France.

RMAS, "Rakhine Mìn-raza-grì Areì-daw Sadan." [Palm-leaf manuscript, number 1632] AMs [copied in 1784], National Library, Ministry of Culture, Yangon, Union of Myanmar, 1775.

Secret Palace Memorials of the Ch'ien-lung Period: Ch'ing Documents at the National Palace Museum (Taipei: National Palace Museum, 1983), no. 15 (August 1756–December 1756), pp. 485–6.

Secteur Saigon-Cholon, S/Secteur Cholon, no. 1339/SSC/S, "Rapport sur l'activité des Chinois à Cholon", file BR58, box 10H4358, Service historique de l'armée de terre, France.

"Siamese Executive Committee to the Malaya Communist Party." 20 September 1932, k. t. 39/13–30, Communists 2473–2480 [1930–1937]. Box 2, Bangkok: Thai National Archives.

Straits Settlements Police. "Communism in Malaya in 1931 and 1932." *Police Intelligence Journal*, supplement no. 4 to issue no. 11, 31 November 1932. Singapore: Special Branch, 23 November 1932, file 65560, grouping Gouverneur General de l'Indochine, Centre des Archives d'Outre-Mer, Aix-en-Provence, France.

Straits Settlements Police. "Communist Propaganda among Malay and Indians", *Police Intelligence Journal*, Supplement no. 12 to no. 10, 31 October 1934, Singapore: Special Branch.

Vice-Consulat de France. "Le gerant du Vice-Consulat au Gouvernement general de l'Indochine." no. 24, 12 June 1913, grouping Indochine, *Rebelles annamites en Chine*, Serie III (January–August 1914). France: Archives of the Ministry of Foreign Affairs.

VOC 1141, p. 212r, letter from Johan van Twist, Governor of Melaka, to the Governor-General and his Council in Batavia, 17 December 1642, National Archives of the Netherlands.

Published archival documents and court records

Ban, Gu 班固 and Ban Zhao 班昭. *Qian Han Shu* 前漢書 (History of the Former Han Dynasty). *c.*100. Beijing: Zhonghua shuju, 1975 reprint.

Cai, Yurong 蔡毓榮 (1681–1686). "Chou Dian di ba shu 籌滇第八疏 (The Eighth Memorial Presenting Plans for Yunnan)", 1691, *Yunnan Tongzhi* (雲南通志 Local Topography of Yunnan), juan 29, *yiwen* 藝文 3, 35b–39b.

Cao, Xuân Dục 高春育, Lưu Đức Xứng 劉德稱 and Trần Xán 陳燦 compil. *Đại Nam Nhất Thống Chí* 大南一統志 (Gazetteer of the Unified Dai Nam), 12 Volumes, MS. A. 853 (VHN). 1882. Hue: Nhà Xuất Bản Thuận Hóa, 1996 reprint.

Chen, Menglei 陳夢雷 and Jiang Tingxi 蔣廷錫. compil. *Qingding gujin tushu jicheng* 欽定古今圖書集成 (Imperial Encyclopaedia). 1726. Shanghai: Zhonghua shuju, 1934 reprint.

Chen, Zilong 陳子龍 et al compil. *Ming jingshi wenbian* 明經世文編 (Collected Essays on Statecraft of the Ming Dynasty), Beijing: Zhonghua shuju reprint, 1962.

Colecção de Documentos Sincos do Ian/TT Referentes a Macau durante a dinastia Qing (A Collection of the Qing Archives on Macau, held in Torre do Tombo, Portugal). Macau: Macau Foundation, 1999.

Da, Shan 大汕. *Haiwai Jishi* 海外紀事 (Travel Account of Nguyễn Viet-Nam). 1699, Beijing: Zhonghua shuju, 1987 reprint.

Đại Nam Liệt Truyện Tiền Biên 大南列傳前編 (Biographies of the Nguyễn Court). 6 juan 1852. Tokyo: Keio University Press, 1961 reprint.

Đại Nam Thức Lục Tiền Biên 大南寔錄前編 (The Primary Compilation of the Veritable Records of Đại Nam). 5 volumes, 1844. Tokyo: Keio University Press, 1961 reprint.

Dai, Xi 戴熺 and Ouyang Can 歐陽燦. *Qiongzhou fuzhi* 瓊州府志 (Gazetteer of Hainan Island). Wanli edition, 1617.

DMY. *Duti-ya Maha-ya-zawin-daw-gyì*. Mandalay, 1919.

Đồng chí Lê Hồng Phong. Hanoi: NXB Chính trị Quốc gia, 1997.

Duti-ya Na-wa-dè, Tayoub-than-yauk Maw-gùn. Edited by U Nyun. Publication series no. 31. Burma Research Society, 1933.

Fan, Chengxun 范承勳. "Tuyi Guicheng Kenqing Shouzhi Shu 土彝歸誠懇請授職疏 (A memorial on the Local Yi barbarians who have pledged allegiance and earnestly request the conferral of official titles)." 1691. In *Yunnan Tongzhi* 雲南通志 (Local Topography of Yunnan), juan 29, *yiwen* 藝文3, 67a–70a.

Fan, Ye 范曄. *Hou Han Shu* 後漢書 (History of the Later Han Dynasty). Beijing: Zhonghua shuju, 1973 reprint.

Fan, Ye 范曄. *Yunnan Tongzhi* 雲南通志 (Local Topography of Yunnan), Preface dated 1691.

Fei, Xin 費信. *Xingcha Shenglan* 星槎勝覽 (The Overall Survey of the Star Raft). c.1436. Annotated by Feng Chengjun 馮承鈞. Taipei: Commercial Press, 1970.

Gong, Zhen 鞏珍. *Xiyang fanguozhi* 西洋番國志 (Record of the Barbarian Countries in the Western Ocean), 1434. Beijing: Zhonghua shuju, 1961 reprint, annotated by Xiang Da 向達.

Government of India. *Report on the Census of British Burma*. Rangoon: Government Press, 1875, 1881.

Government of India. *Census of 1891: Burma Report*. Rangoon: Superintendent, Government Printing, Burma, 1892.

Government of India. *Report on the Census of Burma 1901*. Rangoon: Superintendent, Government Printing, Burma (C. C. Lowis), 1902.

Government of India. *Selected Correspondence of Letters Issued from and Received in the Office of the Commissioner Tenasserim Division for the Years 1825–26 to 1842–43*. Rangoon: Superintendent, Government Printing and Stationery, Burma, 1928.

Government of India. *Report on the Census of Burma 1931*. Rangoon: Office of the Superintendent, Government Printing and Stationery, Burma, 1933.

Gu, Yanwu 顧炎武. *Tianxia junguo libing shu* 天下郡國利病書 (Merits and Drawbacks of All the Countries in the World), 120 *juan* 1662. Guangzhou: Tushu jichengju, 1901 reprint.

Gu, Yingxiang 顧應祥. *Jingxuzhai xiyinlu* 靜虛齋惜陰錄 (Works Drafted at the Jingxu Study). c.1550, Sikuquanshu cunmu congshu edition, Jinan: Qilu shushe, 1996 reprint.

Gu, Zuyu 顧祖禹. *Dushi fangyu jiyao* 讀史方輿紀要 (Essentials of Historical Geography), 1667. Beijing: Zhonghua shuju, 1955 reprint.

Guoli gugong bowuyuan 國立故宮博物院. *Shi-liao xun-kan* (史料旬刊 Historical Materials Published Every Ten Days). Beijing: National Palace Museum, 1930–31.

Guoli zhongyang yanjiuyuan lishi yuyan yanjiusuo 國立中央研究院歷史語言研究所 compil. *Mingqing shiliao* 明清史料, Taipei: Zhongyang yanjiuyuan lishi yuyan yanjiusuo, 1953–1975, 10 series and each series contains 10 books.

Guoshiguan 國史館 compil. *Qing Shi Gao Jiao Zhu* 清史稿校注 (Annotated Draft History of the Qing Dynasty). Taipei: Guoshiguan, 1986–1990.

Hayashi, Harunobu 林春勝 and Hayashi Nobuatsu 林信篤 compil. *Kai Hentai* 華夷變態 (Collected Records on China and Foreign Countries as Submitted by the Chinese Captains at the Customs Office of Nagasaki and Hirado), 1732, 3 Volumes, Tokyo: Toyo Bunku, 1958–60 reprint.

He, Qiaoyuan 何喬遠. *Mingshan cang* 名山藏 (Anectotal History of the Ming Dynasty). c.1620. Nanjing: Jiangsu guangling guji keyinshe, 1993 reprint.

HNY, *Hman-nàn Maha-ya-zawin-daw-gyì*. 4 vols. Mandalay: Royal Press, 1883.

Huang, Zuo 黃佐. *Taiquan ji* 泰泉集 (Complete Works of Huang Zuo). c.1540. Sikuquanshu edition.

Huang, Zuo 黃佐. *Guangdong tongzhi* 廣東通志 (Gazetteer of Guangdong). 1561. Hong Kong: Dadong tushu gongsi, 1977 reprint.

Kala, Ù. *Maha-ya-zawin-gyì*. c.1730, 3 vols. Rangoon: Hanthawaddy Press, 1960 reprint.

Lê, Quý Đôn 黎貴惇. *Phủ Biên Tạp Lục* 撫邊雜錄 (Miscellaneous Records of the Pacification of the Frontiers). 1776, Saigon: Ủy Ban Dịch Thuật, Phủ Quốc Vụ Khanh Đặc Trách Văn Hoá, 1972–3 reprint, 2 volumes.

Li, Dongyang 李東陽 and Shen, Shixing 申時行. comp. *Da Ming huidian* 大明會典 (Compilation of State Regulations of the Great Ming Dynasty). 5 books. Taipei: Huawen shuju, 1964.

Li, Tiaoyuan 李調元. *Nanyue biji* 南越筆記 (Hanhai 函海, in Baibu congshu jicheng 百部叢書集成 37/11, comp. by Yan Yiping 嚴一萍). Taipei: Yiwen yinshuguan, 1964–70 reprint.

Li, Wenxuan 李文烜 and Zheng Wencai 鄭文彩 comp. *Qiongshan xianzhi* 瓊山縣誌 (Gazetteer of the Qiongshan County), 1857. *Zhongguo fangzhi congshu* 中國方志叢書. Taipei: Chengwen chubanshe, 1974 reprint.

Li, Xiling 李熙齡. *Pu'er fuzhi* 普洱府志 (Gazetter of the Pu'er Prefecture). Preface 1851.

Li, Xian 李賢 and Peng Shi 彭時. (comp.). *Da Ming yitong zhi* 大明一統志 (Comprehensive Geography of the Ming Empire). c.1450. Taipei: Wenhai chubanshe, 1965 reprint.

Liu, Wenzheng 劉文征. *Dianzhi* 滇志 (Gazetteer of Yunnan). Tianqi 天啓 (1621 to 1627) edition, Kunming: Yunnan jiaoyu chubanshe, 1991 reprint.

Liu, Xifan 劉錫蕃. *Lingbiao Jiman* 嶺表記蠻 (Narrative of the Barbarians in Guangdong and Guangxi). Shanghai: Shangwu Yinshuguan, 1934 reprint.

Lou, Yao 樓鑰. *Gongkui ji* 攻媿集. c.1210. Wuyingdian juzhen edition 武英殿聚珍版.

Ma, Huan 馬歡. *Yingyai Shenglan* 瀛涯勝覽 (Triumphant Visions of the Ocean Shores). 1451. Annotated by Feng Chengjun 馮承鈞. Taipei: Commercial Press, 1970 reprint.

Mao, Ruizheng 茅瑞徵. *Huangming xiangxulu* 皇明象胥錄 (Account of Relations with Countries Overseas). Preface 1629. Beijing: Guoli Beiping tushuguan, 1937 reprint.

Mao, Yuanyi 茅元儀. *Wubei Zhi* 武備志 (*A Treatise on Military Defense*). 1624 edition, Shanghai: Shanghai guji chubanshe, 1995 reprint.

Min, Hongxue 閔洪學. *Fu Dian Zoucao* 撫滇奏草 (Drafts of Memorials While Serving as the Grand Coordinator of Yunnan). 1626 edition held in the Naikaku Bunko 內閣文庫 in Tokyo.

Ming shi-lu 明實錄 (Veritable Records of Ming Dynasty). Taipei: Guoli zhongyang yanjiuyuan lishi yuyan yanjiusuo, 1966 reprint.

Ming, Yi 明誼 (comp.), *Qiongzhou fuzhi* 瓊州府志. 1841. In *Zhongguo fangzhi congshu* 中國方志叢書 47, 2 vols., ed. Zhang Yuesong 張岳松, Taipei: Chengwen chubanshe, 1967 reprint.

Ni, Tui 倪蛻. *Dian Yun Linian Zhuan* 滇雲歷年傳 (A Chronological Record of Events in Yunnan). 1846. Kunming: Yunnan daxue chubanshe, 1992 reprint.

Qian, Wei 錢薇. "Yu dangdao chuwoyi 與當道處倭議 (On Dealing with the Japanese Pirates)." *Ming Jingshi Wenbian* 明经世文编, juan 214. Zhonghua shuju, 1967 reprint.

Qinchuan jushi (琴川居士) compil. *Huangqing zouyi* 皇清奏議 (Memorials of the Qing Dynasty). 1902. Taipei: Wenhai chubanshe, 1967 reprint.

Qing shilu 清實錄 (Veritable Records of Qing Dynasty). Beijing: Zhonghua shuju, 1986 reprint.

Quốc Sử quán Triều Nguyễn 阮朝國史館. *Đại Nam Thực Lục Tiền Biên* 大南實錄前編 (Chronicle of Greater Vietnam, Premier Period of the Nguyễn). Tokyo: Keio Institute of Linguistic Studies, 1961 reprint.

Rangoon Gazette and Weekly Budget. Newspaper based in Rangoon, 1887–9, 1894–6.

Shi, Fan 師範. *Dian Xi* 滇繫 (Local Gazetteer of Yunnan). *c.*1808. Taipei: Chengwen chubanshe, 1967 reprint in 4 books.

Sima, Guang 司馬光. *Zizhi tongjian* 資治通鑒 (Comprehensive Mirror of History for Aid in Government). 1084. Beijing: Zhonghua shuju, 1956 reprint.

Song, Lian 宋濂. *Yuan shi* 元史 (History of the Yuan Dynasty). 1370. Beijing: Zhonghua shuju, 1976 reprint.

Taipei National Palace Museum 台北故宮博物院 ed. *Gongzhongdang Yongzhengchao Zouzhe* 宮中檔雍正朝奏摺 (Secret Palace Memorials of the Yongzheng Reign). Taipei: National Palace Museum Press, 1977–1980.

Taipei National Palace Museum 台北故宮博物院 ed. *Gongzhongdang Qianlongchao zouzhe* (宮中檔乾隆朝奏摺 Secret Palace Memorials of the Qianlong Reign). Taipei: National Palace Museum, 1982.

Tan, Cui 檀萃. *Dianhai Yuheng Zhi* 滇海虞衡志 (A Record of the Topography and Products of Yunnan). Wenyinglou yudi congshu 問影樓輿地叢書 edition. Preface by Tan Cui dated 1799 and published in 1804.

Tang, Zhou 唐胄. *(Zhengde) Qiong tai zhi* (正德)瓊台志 (Account of Hainan Island). *c.*1520. *Tianyi ge cang Mingdai fangzhi xuankan* 天一閣藏明代方志選刊. Shanghai: Shanghai guji chubanshe, 1964 reprint.

Tao, Zongyi 陶宗儀. *Nancun chuo geng lu* 南村輟耕錄. *c.*1366. Beijing: Zhonghua shuju, 1959 reprint.

The Chronicle and Directory for China, Corea, Japan, the Philippines. Hong Kong: Daily Press, 1870–95.

Tin, Ù (Mandalay), *Kòn-baung-zet Maha-ya-zawin-daw-gyì*. 3 vols. Rangoon: Hanthawaddy Press, 1968.

Trịnh, Hoài Đức 鄭懷德. *Gia Định thông chí* [嘉定通志 Gia Định Gazetteer]. Saigon: Phủ Quốc vụ khanh đặc trách văn hoá, 1972.

Trịnh, Hoài Đức 鄭懷德. "Jiading tongzhi: chengchi zhi"《嘉定通志》城池志. In *Lingnan zhiguai deng shiliao sanzhong* 嶺南摭怪等史料三種 (Three primary Vietnamese sources of *Lĩnh Nam trích quái*, *Gia Định thông chí* and *Hà Tiên trấn diệp trấn Mạc thị gia phả*), eds. Dai Kelai 戴可來 and Yang Baoyun 楊保筠. Zhengzhou: Zhongzhou guji chubanshe, 1991.

Tuo, Tuo 脫脫 and Ouyang Xuan 歐陽玄. *Song shi* 宋史 (History of the Song Dynasty). 1345. Beijing: Zhonghua shuju, 1977 reprint.

Wang, Xiangzhi 王象之. *Yudi jisheng* 輿地紀勝 (The Geographical Wonders of China). 1221. In *Songdai dili shu shi zhong* 宋代地理書十種. 2 books. Taipei: Wenhai chubanshe, 1963 reprint.

Wang, Xianqian 王先謙. *Qianlongchao Donghua xulu* (乾隆朝東華續錄 Supplementary Imperial Records from the Dong-hua Hall: Qianlong Reign). 1884, Shanghai: Shanghai guji chubanshe, 1995 reprint.

Xu, Fuyuan 許孚遠. *Jinghetang Ji* 敬和堂集 (Private Collection of Xu Fuyuan Prepared at Jinghe Hall). 1594, 8 juan, in Siku quanshu cunmu congshu 四庫全書存目叢書: Jibu 集部, juan 136. Jinan: Qilu shushe 齊魯書社, 1997 reprint.

Xu, Song 徐松 compil. *Song huiyao jigao* 宋會要輯稿 (Drafts for the Administrative Statutes of the Song Dynasty). 1809, in 8 books. Beijing: Zhonghua shuju, 1957 reprint.

Yan, Congjian 嚴從簡. *Shuyu zhouzilu* 殊域周咨錄 (Record of Despatches Concerning Different Countries). 1520. Beijing: Zhonghua shuju, 1993.

Yang, Bowen 楊博文. *Zhufan zhi jiaoshi* 諸蕃志校釋 (Zhao Rugua's Zhufanzhi with Annotations). Beijing: Zhonghua shuju, 1996.

Zhang, Tingyu 張廷玉 Ji Huang嵇璜, Liu Yong劉墉, and Ji Yun紀昀. ed. *Huangchao Wenxian Tongkao* 皇朝文獻通考 (Comprehensive Study of the History of Qing Dynasty). 1787. Taipei: Taiwan shangwu yinshuguan, 1984 reprint.

Zhang, Tingyu 張廷玉, Zhu Yizun朱彝尊, You Tong尤侗, Mao Qiling毛奇齡, Wan Sitong萬斯同, and Wang Hongxu王鴻緒. ed. *Ming shi* 明史 (History of the Ming Dynasty). 1739. Beijing: Zhonghua shuju, 1974 reprint.

Zhang, Xi 張嶲, Xing Dinglun邢定綸, and Zhao Yilian趙以濂compil. *Yanzhou zhi* 崖州志 (Account of Hainan Island). 1914. Guangzhou: Guangdong renmin chubanshe, 1983 reprint, annotated by Guo Moruo 郭沫若.

Zhang, Xie 張燮. *Dongxiyang Kao* 東西洋考 (Treatise on the Eastern and Western Oceans). 1617. Beijing: Zhonghua shuju, 1981 reprint.

Zheng, Shungong 鄭舜功. *Riben yijian* 日本一鑑 (Account of Japan). 1565. Shanghai, 1937 reprint.

Zheng, Wencai 鄭文彩 ed. *Qiongshan xianzhi* 瓊山縣志 (Gazetteer of Qiongshan County). 1857. Haikou: Hainan renmin chubanshe, 2004 reprint.

Zhou, Daguan 周達觀. *Zhenla Fengtuji* 真臘風土記 (Notes on the Customs of Cambodia). c.1312. Beijing: Zhonghua shuju, 1981 reprint with annotation by Xia Nai 夏鼐. English version translated from the French version of Paul Pelliot by J. Gilman D'Arcy Paul, Bangkok: Social Sciences Association Press, 1967.

Zhou, Qufei 周去非. *Lingwai daida jiaozhu* 嶺外代答校注 (Information on What is Beyond the Passes with Annotations). 1178. ed. and annotated by Yang Wuquan 楊武泉. Beijing: Zhonghua shuju, 1999 reprint.

Zhu, Mengzhen 朱孟震. *Xinan yi fengtuji* 西南夷風土記 (Descriptions of the Customs and Geography of Southwestern Natives). c.1584. Beijing: Zhonghua shuju, 1985 reprint.

Zhu, Shunshui 朱舜水. *Annan Gongyi Jishi* 安南供役記事 (Narrative of Experience in Annam). c.1660, Beijing: Zhonghua shuju, 1981 reprint.

Zuikei, Shuho 瑞溪周鳳. *Zenrin Kokuhōki* 善鄰國寶記 (*Japan's Foreign Relations 1200 to 1392 A.D.*). Tokyo: Kokusho Kankokai 國書刊行會, 1975 reprint.

Books and articles

Abdullah bin Abdul Kadir. *The Hikayat Abdullah*. Kuala Lumpur: Oxford University Press, 1970.

Adhyatman, S. *Notes on Green Wares Found in Indonesia*. Jakarta: Ceramic Society of Indonesia, 1983.

Akashi, Yoji. "Lai Teck, Secretary General of the Malayan Communist Party, 1939–1947." *Journal of the South Seas Society* 49 (1994): 57–102.

Al-Sufri, Pehin Jamil. "Wenlai sudan ershi 汶萊蘇丹二世 (The Second Sultan of Brunei)," in *Zouxiang haiyang de zhongguoren* 走向海洋的中國人 (Seafaring Chinese), (ed.) Nanjing Zheng He yanjiuhui 南京鄭和研究會, Beijing: Haichao chubanshe, 1996, pp. 228–36.

Albuquerque, Afonso de. *The Commentaries of Great Alfonso Dalboquerque, Second Viceroy of India*. London: Hakluyt Society, 1875–84.

Allan, James Wilson. *Islamic Metalwork: The Nuhad Es-Said Collection*. London: Sotheby's; Totowa, N.J., USA: Biblio Distribution Centre [distributor], 1982.

Altman, Ida. *Transatlantic Ties in the Spanish Empire: Brihuega, Spain, and Puebla, Mexico, 1560–1620*. Stanford: Stanford University Press, 2000.

Andaya, Barbara. *To Live as Brothers: Southeast Sumatra in the 17th and 18th Centuries*. Honolulu: University of Hawaii Press, 1993.

Anderson, James A. and John K. Whitmore (ed.). *China's Encounters on the South and Southwest: Reforging the Fiery Frontier*. Leiden: Brill, 2015.

Andrade, Tonio and Xing Hang (ed.). *Sea Rovers, Silver, and Samurai: Maritime East Asia in Global History, 1550–1700*. Honolulu: University of Hawaii Press, 2016.

Anonymous. "The Trade of Ava." 1826. In Horace Hayman Wilson, *Documents Illustrative of the Burmese War with an Introductory Sketch of the Events of the War and an Appendix*. Calcutta: Government Gazette Press, 1827, pp. xlvi–xlvii.

Anonymous. "Chronicles of the Portuguese Discovery and Conquest of India." *Revista de Cultura*, Macau: Instituto Cultural do Governo da R.A.E. de Macau, 2nd Series, 31 (April–June 1997): 30–2.

Anonymous. "Carta masa sejarah kesultanan Terengganu," in *Seminar darul iman 2001: Persejarahan Terengganu sehingga abad ke-18*, 13–14 October 2001, Muzium Negeri Terengganu.

Aoyagi, Yoji. "Production and Trade of Champa Ceramics in the 15th Century," in *Commerce et Navigation en Asie du Sud-Est (XIVe-XIXe siècle)*. Nguyên Thê Anh and Yoshiaki Ishizawa (eds.). Paris and Montreal: L'Harmattan, 1999, pp. 91–100.

Arasaratnam, S. "Merchants of Coromandel in Trade and Entrepreneurship *circa* 1650–1700," in *Emporia, Commodities and Entrepreneurs in Asian Maritime Trade, c.1400–1750*, Roderich Ptak and Dietmar Rothermund (eds.). Stuttgart: Franz Steiner Verlag, 1991, pp. 37–52.

Armitage, David and Michael J. Braddick (eds.). *The British Atlantic World, 1500–1800*. Basingstoke: Palgrave Macmillan, 2002.

Aung-Thwin, Michael. *Myth and History in the Historiography of Early Burma: Paradigms, Primary Sources, and Prejudices*. Athens, Ohio: Ohio University Center for International Studies, 1998.

Aziz, A. *The Imperial Treasury of the Indian Mughals*. Delhi: Idarah-i-Adabiyāt-i-Delli, 1972.

Badenoch, Nathan and Tomita Shinsuke 富田晋介. "Mountain People in the Muang: Creation and Governance of a Tai polity in Northern Laos." *Southeast Asian Studies* 2, 1 (April 2013): 29–67.

Bibliography

Bailyn, Bernard. *Atlantic History: Concept and Contours*. Cambridge Mass: Harvard University Press, 2005.

Barretto, W. L. *Heroes of Burma: A Compilation of Lectures*. Rangoon: Burma Union Press, 1930.

Barretto, W. L. "Maha Thiha Thura: The Saviour of Burma from the Chinese Invasion (Which Lasted From 1765 to 1769)," in W. L. Barretto, *Heroes of Burma: A Compilation of Lectures*. Rangoon: Burma Union Press, 1930, pp. 38–54.

Bauck, Sönke and Thomas Maier. "Entangled History." www.uni-bielefeld.de/cias/wiki/e_Entangled_History.html.

Bauer, R. S. "Identifying the Tai substratum in Cantonese", in *The Fourth International Symposium on Language and Linguistics*, Thailand, Institute of Language and Culture for Rural Development, Mahidol University, 1996, pp. 1806–44.

Baxter, I. A. "Dutch Records from Malacca in the India Office Records." *Journal of the Malaysian Branch of the Royal Asiatic Society* 56, 2 (1983): 105–33.

Bayly, Christopher. *The Birth of the Modern World, 1780–1914: Global Connections and Comparison*. Oxford: Blackwell, 2004.

Beaujard, Philippe. *Les Mondes de l'Océan Indien*, 2 volumes. Paris: Armand Colin, 2012.

Beighton, J. T. *Betel-Nut Island: Personal Experiences and Adventures in the Eastern Tropics*. London: The Religious Tract Society, 1888.

Benedict, Carol. *Bubonic Plague in Nineteenth-Century China*. Stanford: Stanford University Press, 1966.

Bentinck, William Cavendish. *The Correspondence of Lord William Cavendish Bentinck: Governor-General of India 1828–1835*. Vol. I, edited and with an introduction by C. H. Philips. Oxford: Oxford University Press, 1977.

Berger, Joachim, Jennifer Willenberg, and Lisa Landes. "EGO | European History Online: A Transcultural History of Europe on the Internet." www.ieg-ego.eu/introduction-2010-en Beveridge, A. S. (trans.). *The Baburnama in English*. 2 vols, 1922. Mainz: Institute of European History, 2010.

Bielenstein, Hans. *Diplomacy and Trade in the Chinese World, 589–1276*. Handbook of Oriental Studies/Handbuch der Orientalistik, Section Four, China. Vol. 18. Leiden, Boston: Brill, 2005.

Blackmore, Thaung. "British Quest for China Trade by the Routes Across Burma (1826–1876)." In *Symposium on Historical Archaeological and Linguistic Studies on Southern China, South-East Asia and the Hong Kong Region: Papers Presented at Meetings held in September 1961 as part of the Golden Jubilee Congress of the University of Hong Kong*, F. S. Drake and Wolfram Eberhard eds. Hong Kong: Hong Kong University Press, 1968, pp. 180–90.

Blussé, Leonard. "The Rise and Fall of a Chinese Colonial Town." *Journal of Southeast Asian Studies* 12 (1981): 159–78.

Blussé, Leonard. *Strange Company: Chinese Settlers, Mestizo Women and the Dutch VOC Batavia*. Dordrecht, the Netherlands: Foris Publications, 1986.

Blussé, Leonard. "Testament to a Towkay: Jan Con, Batavia and the Dutch China Trade." In *All of One Company*, ed. Anonymous. Leiden: Leiden University Press, 1986, pp. 3–41.

Blussé, Leonard. "In Praise of Commodities: An Essay on the Crosscultural Trade in Edible Bird's-Nests." In *Emporia, Commodities and Entrepreneurs in Asian Maritime Trade, c. 1400–1750*, R. Ptak and D. Rothermund. Stuttgart (eds.). Stuttgart: Franz Steiner Verlag, 1991, pp. 317–35.

Blussé, Leonard. "No Boats to China. The Dutch East India Company and the Changing Pattern of the China Sea Trade, 1635–1690." *Modern Asian Studies* 30, 1 (1996): 51–76.
Blussé, Leonard. *The Bitter Bonds: A Colonial Divorce Drama of the Seventeenth Century*. Princeton: Markus Wiener, 1997.
Blussé, Leonard. "Chinese Century: The Eighteenth Century in the China Sea Region." *Archpel* 58 (1999): 107–29.
Blussé, Leonard and Chen Menghong eds., *The Archives of the Kong Koan of Batavia*. Leiden: Leiden University Press, 2003.
Bort, Balthasar, trans. M. J. Bremner, "Report of Governor Balthasar Bort on Malacca, 1678." *Journal of the Malayan Branch of the Royal Asiatic Society* 5 (1927): 39–44.
Boudet, Paul. "La conquête de la Cochinchine par les Nguyễn et le rôle des émigrés chinois." *Bulletin de l'École française d'Extrême-Orient* 42 (1942): 115–32.
Boxer, Charles R. "Notes on Chinese Abroad in the Late Ming and Early Manchu Periods: Compiled from Contemporary European Sources, 1500–1750." *T'ien Hsia Monthly* 9, 5 (December 1939): 218–68.
Boxer, Charles R. *The Great Ship from Amacon: Annals of Macao and the Old Japan Trade, 1555–1640*. Lisbon: Centro de Estudos Históricos Ultramarinos, 1959.
Boxer, Charles R. *The Portuguese Seaborne Empire*. London: Hutchinson & Co. Ltd., 1969.
Braudel, Fernand. *The Wheels of Commerce*. London: Collins, 1982.
Braudel, Fernand. *La Méditerranée et le monde méditerranéen à l'époque de Philippe II*. 3 tomes, 9th ed. Paris: Armand Colin Editeur, 1990.
Brown, MacAlister and Joseph J. Zasloff. *Apprentice Revolutionaries: The Communist Movement in Laos, 1930–1988*. Stanford: Hoover Institution Press, 1986.
Brown, Rajeswary Ampalavanar. *Capital and Entrepreneurship in Southeast Asia*. New York: St. Martin's Press, 1994.
Brown, Roxanna M. *The Ceramics of South-East Asia, Their Dating and Identification*. Kuala Lumpur: Oxford University Press, 1977.
Bulbeck, David, Anthony Reid, Lay Cheng Tan and Yiqi Wu. comp. *Southeast Asian Exports since the 14th Century: Cloves, Pepper, Coffee and Sugar*. Singapore: ISEAS, 1998.
Burger, D. H. *Het Ontsluiting van Java's Binnenland voor het Wereldsverkeer*. Wageningen: H. Veenman, 1939.
Burney, Henry. "Some Account of the Wars between Burmah and China. Together with the Journals and Routes of Three Different Embassies Sent to Peking by the King of Ava: Taken from Burmese Documents." *Journal of the Asiatic Society of Bengal* 6 (1837): 542–59.
Cadiere, L. "Les Elephants Royaux." *Bulletin des Amis de Vieux Hue* 9, 1 (1922): 41–102.
Cai, Peter. "Understanding China's Belt and Road Initiative." Sydney: Lowy Institute, 2017.
Calanca, Paola. "Aspects spécifiques de la piraterie à Hainan sous les Ming et au début des Qing." In *Hainan: de la Chine à l'Asie du Sud-Est; von China nach Südostasien*, eds., Claudine Salmon and Roderich Ptak (eds.), Shing Müller (ass. ed.)., *South China and Maritime Asia* 10. Wiesbaden: Harrassowitz Verlag, 2001, pp. 113–23.
Campbell, Gwyn (ed.). *Early Exchange Between Africa and the Wider Indian Ocean World*. New York: Palgrave McMillan, 2016.
Carswell, J. "China and Islam: A Survey of the Coast of India and Ceylon." *Transactions of the Oriental Ceramic Society* 42 (1977–78): 24–69.

Carswell, J. "The Port of Mantai, Sri Lanka." In *Rome and India: The Ancient Sea Trade*, V. Begley and R. D. de Puma (eds.). Madison and Delhi: Manohar, 1992, pp. 197–203.

Carswell, J. *Blue and White. Chinese Porcelain around the World*. London: British Museum Press, 2000.

Carswell, J., Siran Deraniyagala and Alan Graham. *Mantai. City by the Sea*. Colombo: Archaeological Department of Sri Lanka, Aichwald, Linden Soft Verlag, 2013.

Casale, Giancarlo. *The Ottoman Age of Exploration*. Oxford: Oxford University Press, 2010.

Chan, Hok-lam 陳學霖. "The 'Chinese Barbarian Officials' in the Foreign Tribute Missions to China During the Ming Dynasty." *Journal of the American Oriental Society* 88 (1968): 411–8.

Chandavij, N. *Chinese Ceramics from Archaeological Sites in Thailand*. Bangkok: Department of Fine Arts, 1986.

Chang, Pin-tsun 張彬村. *Chinese Maritime Trade: The Case of Sixteenth-Century Fuchien (Fukien)*. PhD diss., Princeton University, 1983.

Chang, Pin-tsun 張彬村. "The First Chinese Diaspora in Southeast Asia in the Fifteenth Century." In *Emporia, Commodities and Entrepreneurs in Asian Maritime Trade, c.1400–1750*, R. Ptak and D. Rothermund (eds.). Stuttgart, Germany: Franz Steiner Verlag, 1991, pp. 13–28.

Chang, Pin-tsun 張彬村. "The Formation of a Maritime Convention in Minnan (Southern Fujian), *c.*900–1200," in *From the Mediterranean to the China Sea: Miscellaneous Notes*, eds. Claude Guillot, Denys Lombard and R. Ptak, South China and Maritime Asia 7, Wiesbaden: Harrassowitz Verlag, 1999, pp. 143–56.

Chang, Pin-tsun 張彬村. "Dutch VOC and the Rise of Chinese Mercantile Power in Maritime Southeast Asia in the Seventeenth Century." *Journal of the South Seas Society* 56 (2002): 88–97.

Chang T'ien-tse. *Sino-Portuguese Trade from 1514 to 1644: A Synthesis of Portuguese and Chinese Sources*. Leiden: Brill, 1934.

Chang, Tseng-hsin 張增信. *Mingji dongnan Zhongguo de haishang huodong* 明季東南中國的海上活動 (Maritime Activities on the Southeast Coast of China in the Latter Part of the Ming Dynasty). Vol. 1. Taipei: Sili dongwu daxue zhongguo xueshu zhuzuo jiangzhu weiyuanhui, 1988.

Chang, Tseng-hsin. "Commodities imported to the Chang-chou Region of Fukien During the Late Ming Period: A Preliminary Analysis of the Tax Lists Found in Tung-hsi-yang k'ao," in *Emporia, Commodities, and Entrepreneurs in Asian Maritime Trade, c.1400-1750*, Roderich Ptak and Dietmar Rothermund (eds.). Stuttgart: Steiner Verlag, 1991, pp. 159–194.

Charney, Michael W. "Problematics and Paradigms in Historicizing the Overseas Chinese in the Nineteenth- and Twentieth-century Straits and Burma." *Journal of the South Seas Society* 54 (1999): 93–106.

Charney, Michael W. "The External and Internal Sides of Chinese-ness: Colonial Historiography and the 'Overseas Chinese' in Burma." Seminar given at the East Asian Institute, Singapore, 29 September 2000.

Charney, Michael W. "Chinese Business in Penang and Tenasserim (Burma) in the 1820s: A Glimpse from a Vietnamese Travelogue." *Journal of the South Seas Society* 55 (2002a): 48–60.

Charney, Michael W. "Centralizing Historical Tradition in Precolonial Burma: The Abhiraja/Dhajaraja Myth in Early Kòn-baung Historical Texts." *South East Asia Research* 10, 2 (2002b): 185–215.

Charney, Michael W. *Chinese Migrants Abroad: Cultural, Educational, and Social Dimensions of the Chinese Diaspora*. Singapore: Singapore University Press, 2003.

Charney, Michael W. and Brenda S. A. Yeoh, and Tong Chee Kiong (eds.) "Esculent Bird's Nests, Tin, and Fish: The Overseas Chinese and Their Trade in the Eastern Bay of Bengal (Coastal Burma) in the First Half of the Nineteenth Century," in *Maritime China in Transition 1750–1850*, Wang Gungwu and Ng Chin-Keong (eds.). Wiesbaden: Harrossowitz Verlag, 2004, pp. 245–59.

Chaudhuri, K. N. *The Trading World of Asia and the English East India Company, 1660–1760*. Cambridge: Cambridge University Press, 1978.

Chaudhuri, K. N. *Trade and Civilization in the Indian Ocean: An Economic History from the Rise of Islam to 1750*. Cambridge: Cambridge University, 1985.

Cheah, Boon Kheng. *From PKI to the Comintern, 1924–1941: The Apprenticeship of the Malaya Communist Party*. Ithaca, Cornell: Southeast Asia Program, 1992.

Chen, Chingho 陳荊和. "Zheng Huaide zhuan Jiading tongzhi chengchi zhi zhushi 鄭懷德撰嘉定通志城池志注釋" (Annotations on Gia Định gazetteer: Towns). In *Nanyang xuebao* 12, 24 (1956a): 1–31.

Chen, Chingho 陳荊和. "Hexianzhen Yezhen Moshi Jiapu Zhushi 河仙鎮葉鎮鄚氏家譜注釋" (Notes on the Genealogy of the Mac Family from Hà Tiên). *Wenshizhe xuebao (Bulletin of the College of Arts of Taiwan National University)*, 7 (1956b): 77–140.

Chen, Chingho 陳荊和. "Chengtian mingxiangshe yu qinghepu 承天明香社與清河舖" [The Minh Hương Village and Thanh Hà Pho in Thừa Thiên (Central Viet-Nam)]. *Xinya xuebao* 3, 1 (August 1959): 305–29.

Chen, Chingho 陳荊和. (ed.), *Shiqi shiji guangnan zhi xin shiliao* 十七世紀廣南之新史料 (New Sources on Seventeenth Century Guangnan). Taipei: Zhonghua chongshu, 1960a.

Chen, Chingho 陳荊和. "Shiqi ba shiji Huian zhi tangrenjie jiqi shangye 十七、八世紀會安之唐人街及其商業" (The Chinese Town of Faifo (Hội An) and its Trade during the 17th and 18th Centuries). *Xinya xuebao*, Hong Kong, 13, 1 (1960b): 273–332.

Chen, Chingho 陳荊和. ed., *A Brief Study of the Trần Family Register, A Ming Refugee Family in Minh-Huong-Xa Thua-Thien (Central Vietnam)*, Southeast Asian Studies Section, New Asia Research Institute, Chinese University of Hong Kong, Hong Kong, 1964.

Chen, Chingho 陳荊和. "Qingchu Zheng Chenggong canbu zhi yizhi nanqi 清初鄭成功殘部之移殖南圻" (The Migration of the Cheng Partisans to South Vietnam). *Xinya xuebao*, 8, 2 (August 1968a): 413–85.

Chen, Chingho 陳荊和. *The Chinese Community in the 16th Century Philippines*. Tokyo: Centre for East Asian Cultural Studies, 1968b.

Chen, Chingho 陳荊和. *Historical Notes on Hoi-An (Faifo)*. Carbondale: Center for Vietnamese Studies, Southern Illinois University, 1974.

Chen, Chingho 陳荊和. "Mac Thien Tu and Phrayataksin: A Survey on Their Political Stand, Conflicts and Background." In *Proceedings of the Seventh IAHA Conference*. Bangkok: Chulalongkorn University Press, 1979, pp. 1534–75.

Chen, Dasheng 陳達生 and Claudine Salmon. "Rapport préliminaire sur la découverte de tombes musulmanes dans l'île de Hainan." *Archipel* 38 (1989): 75–106.

Chen, Gaohua 陳高華 and Wu Tai 吳泰. *Song Yuan shiqi de haiwai maoyi* 宋元時期的海外貿易 (Overseas Maritime Trade of the Song and Yuan Dynasties). Tianjin: Tianjin renmin chubanshe, 1981.

Chen, Gaohua 陳高華 and Wu Tai 吳泰. "Yuandai de Haiwai Maoyi 元代的海外貿易" (Foreign Maritime Trade in Yuan Dynasty), in Chen Gaohua, *Yuanshi Yanjiu Lungao (Collected Essays on Yuan History)*. Beijing: Zhonghua shuju, 1991, pp. 99–112.

Chen, Gaohua 陳高華 and Wu Tai 吳泰. *Yuanshi Yanjiu lungao* 元史研究論稿 (*Collected Essays on Yuan History*). Beijing: Zhonghua shuju, 1991.
Chen, Jian. *Mao's China and the Cold War*. Chapel Hill: The University of North Carolina Press, 2001.
Chen Yi-Sein 陳孺性. "The Chinese in Upper Burma before A.D. 1700." *Journal of Southeast Asian Researches* 2 (1966a): 81–93.
Chen Yi-Sein 陳孺性. "The Chinese in Rangoon During the 18th and 19th Centuries," in *Essays Offered to G. H. Luce By his Colleagues and Friends in Honour of His Seventy-Fifth Birthday*. Ba Shin, Jean Boisselier and A. B. Griswold (eds.). Ascona, Switzerland: Artibus Asiae, 1966b, I, 107–11.
Chen Yi-Sein 陳孺性. "The Chinese Revolution of 1911 and the Chinese in Burma." *Journal of Southeast Asian Researches* 2 (1966c): 95–102.
Chen Yongzhi (ed.), *Porcelain Unearthed from Jininglu Ancient City Site in Inner Mongolia*. Inner Mongolia Institute of Cultural Relics and Archaeology, 2004.
Chen Zhiwu 陳志武. "Women as Insurance Assets in Traditional Societies: A study of Bride Prices during 18th ~19th Century China," Presentation at Hong Kong University of Science and Technology, 6 May 2015.
Cheong, Weng Eang 張榮洋. *Hong Merchants of Canton*. Surrey: Curzon, 1997.
Cherian, P. J. and J. Menon. *Unearthing Pattanam. Histories, Cultures, Crossings*. New Delhi: National Museum, and Kerala Council for Historical Research, 2014.
Chin, Kong James 錢江. *Merchants and Other Soujourners: The Hokkiens Overseas, 1570–1760*, unpublished PhD diss., University of Hong Kong, 1998.
Chin, Peng 陳平. *My Side of History*. Singapore: Media Masters, 2003.
Chung, Yang-mo. *Cultural Relics Found off the Sinan Coast*. Seoul. National Museum of Art, 1977.
Clammer, John. *Straits Chinese Society: Studies in the Sociology of the Baba Communities of Malaysia and Singapore*. Singapore: Singapore University Press, 1980.
Clark, Hugh. "Muslims and Hindus in the Culture and Morphology of Quanzhou from the Tenth to the Thirteenth Century." *Journal of World History* 6, 1 (1995): 49–74.
Colenbrander, H. T. and W. Ph. Coolhaas (eds.), *Jan Pietersz. Coen. Bescheiden omtrent zijn bedrijf in Indie* (Jan Pietersz. Coen: Documents Concerning His Activities in the Indies), 7 volumes in 8 parts. The Hague: Nijhoff, 1919–53.
Cooke, Nola. "Regionalism and the Nature of Nguyễn Rule in Seventeenth Century Đàng Trong (Cochinchina)." *Journal of Southeast Asian Studies* 29, 1 (March 1998): 122–61.
Cooke, Nola. and Li Tana (eds.). *Water Frontier: Commerce and the Chinese in the Lower Mekong Region, 1750–1880*. Lanham: Rowman & Littlefield Publishers, Inc. and Singapore University Press, 2004.
Cordier, Henri. "L'arrivee des portugais en Chine." *T'oung Pao*. Second Series, 12, 4 (1911): 483–543.
Cortesão, Armando. *The Suma Oriental of Tomé Pires*. 2 volumes. London: Hakluyt Society, 1944.
Courmont, Barthélémy, Frédéric Lasserre and Éric Mottet (ed.) *Assessing Maritime Disputes in East Asia: Political and Legal Perspectives*. Abingdon, Oxon: Routledge, 2017.
Cox, Hiram. *Journal of a Residence in the Burman Empire*. London: Colburn, 1821.
Crawfurd, John. *Journal of an Embassy from the Governor-General of India to the Court of Ava, in the Year 1827*. 2nd ed. 2 volumes. London: K. Bentley, 1834.
Crawfurd, John. *Journal of an Embassy to the Courts of Siam and Cochin China*. Singapore: Oxford University Press, 1967 reprint.

Cross, Harry E. "South American Bullion Production and Export 1550–1750." In *Precious Metals in the Later Medieval and Early Modern Worlds*, (ed.) J. F. Richards. North Carolina: Carolina Academic Press, 1983, pp. 397–423.

Cushman, Jennifer Wayne. *Fields from the Sea: Chinese Junk Trade with Siam During the Late Eighteenth and Early Nineteenth Centuries*. PhD diss., Cornell University, 1975. Formally published with the same title, Ithaca: Cornell University Southeast Asia Program, 1993.

Cushman, Jennifer Wayne. *Family and State: The Formation of a Sino-Thai Tin-mining Dynasty, 1797–1932*. Oxford: Oxford University Press, 1991.

Cushman, Jennifer W. and Wang Gungwu (ed.), *Changing Identities of the Southeast Asian Chinese Since World War II*. Hong Kong: Hong Kong University Press, 1988.

Dai, Yingcong. "A Disguised Defeat: The Myanmar Campaign of the Qing Dynasty." *Modern Asian Studies* 38, 1 (2004): 145–89.

Dai, Yixuan 戴裔煊. *Mingshi Folongjizhuan jianzhu* 明史佛郎機傳箋注 (Annotation of the History of Ming Dynasty: Legend of Portugal). Beijing: Zhongguo shehui kexue chubanshe, 1984.

Daniels, Christian. "Shōsū Minzoku no Rekishi wo Dō Miru no ka: Kinnen no Kenkyū Shōkai wo Kanete 少数民族の歴史をどうみるのか-近年の研究紹介をかねて" (How do we View the History of the Minority Peoples: A Review of Recent Research). *Ajia Yūgaku* (アジア遊学 Intriguing Asia) 9 (1999): 12–32.

Daniels, Christian. "The Formation of Tai Polities between the 13th and 16th Centuries: The Role of Technological Transfer." Tokyo: *The Memoirs of the Toyo Bunko* 58 (2000a): 51–98.

Daniels, Christian. "Seinan Chūgoku Shan Bunkaken ni okeru Hikanzoku no Jiritsu teki Seiken: Shipuson Pannaa Ohkoku no Kaido Kiryū wo Jitsurei ni 西南中国・シャン文化圏における非漢族の自律的政権—シプソンパンナー王国の改土帰流を実例に—" (Autonomous Non-Han Political Regimes in South-west China and the Tai Cultural Area; the case of *gaitu guiliu* in Sipsong Panna). *Tōyō Daigaku Ajia Afurika Bunka Kenkyūjo Kenkyū Nenpō* 東洋大学アジア・アフリカ文化研究所研究年報 34 (2000b): 56–70.

Daniels, Christian. "Historical Memories of a Chinese Adventurer in a Tay Chronicle; Usurpation of the Throne of a Tay Polity in Yunnan, 1573–1584." *International Journal of Asian Studies* 3, 1 (January 2006): 21–48.

Daniels, Christian. "Blocking the Path of Feral Pigs with Rotten Bamboo: The Role of Upland Peoples in the Crisis of a Tay Polity in Southwest Yunnan, 1792 to 1836." *Southeast Asian Studies* 2, 1 (April 2013): 133–70.

Dars, Jacques. "La marine chinoise du Xe siècle au XIVe siècle." *Études d'histoire maritime 11*. Paris: Economica, 1992.

Delisle, Jacques. "China's Territorial and Maritime Disputes in the South and East China Seas: What Role for International Law?" in Jacques Deslisle and Avery Goldstein (ed.), *China's Global Engagement: Cooperation, Competition, and Influence in the 21st Century*. Washington, D.C.: Brookings Institution Press, 2017, pp. 235–90.

Dermigny, Louis. *La Chine et l'Occident: le commerce à Canton au XVIIIe siècle, 1719–1833*. 3 tomes. Paris: S.E.V.P.E.N., 1964.

Des Granges, Baron Otto. "Short Survey of the Countries Between Bengal and China, Showing the Great Commercial and Political Importance of the Burmese Town of Bhanmo, on the Upper Irawady, and the Practicability of a Direct Trade Overland Between Calcutta and China." *Journal of the Asiatic Society of Bengal* 17 (1848): 132–7.

Dhiravat, Na Pombejra. "Administrative and Military Roles of the Chinese in Siam during an Age of Turmoils, circa 1760–1782." In *Maritime China in Transition 1750–1850*, eds. Wang Gungwu and Ng Chin-keong. Wiesbaden: Harrassowitz Verlag, 2004, pp. 335–53.

Dick, Howard, Michael Sullivan and John Butcher (ed.). *The Rise and Fall of Revenue Farming: Business Elites and the Emergence of the Modern State in Southeast Asia.* Basingstoke: Palgrave Macmillan, 1993.

Digby, S. "The Literary Evidence for Painting in the Delhi Sultanate." *Bulletin of the American Academy of Banares* (1967): 47–58.

Diller, Stephan. "The Participation of the Danish Companies in Euro-Asiatic and Intra-Asiatic Trade." In *From the Mediterranean to the China Sea*, Claude Guillot, Denys Lombard and Roderich Ptak (eds.). Wiesbaden, Germany: Harrassowitz Verlag, 1998, pp. 215–32.

DMY. *Duti-ya Maha-ya-zawin-daw-gyì*. Mandalay, 1919.

Dong chi Le Hong Phong 1902–1942 (Comrade Le Hong Phong 1902–1942). Hanoi: NXB Chinh Tri Quoc Gia, 1997.

Doveton, F. B. *Reminiscences of the Burmese War in 1824–5–6.* (Originally published in the *Asiatic Journal*), London: Allan and Co., 1852.

Drabble, John H. *An Economic History of Malaysia, c.1800–1990.* London: Macmillan, 2000.

Duara, Prasenjit. *Rescuing History from the Nation: Questioning Narratives of Modern China.* Chicago: The University of Chicago Press, 1995.

Duncanson, Dennis J. "Ho-chi-Minh in Hong Kong, 1931–1932." *The China Quarterly*. 57 (January/March 1974): 84–100.

Duti-ya Na-wa-dè. *Tayoub-than-yauk Maw-gùn*. U Nyun (ed.). Publication series no. 31. Burma Research Society, 1933.

Edwards, Penny. "Relocating the Interlocutor: Taw Sein Ko (1864–1930) and the Itinerancy of Knowledge in British Burma." *South East Asia Research* 12, 3 (2004): 277–335.

Ehmke, Eva. *Das Hai-cha yu-lu als eine Beschreibung der Insel Hainan in der Ming-Zeit*. Mitteilungen der Gesellschaft für Natur- und Völkerkunde Ostasiens 115. Hamburg, 1990.

Elleman, Bruce A. *Modern Chinese Warfare, 1795–1989*. London: Routledge, 2001.

Emmerson, Donald. "Southeast Asia–What's in a Name?" *Journal of Southeast Asian Studies* 15, 1 (1984): 1–21.

Eredia, Manuel Godinho de. "Report on the Golden Chersonese." Transl. J. V. Mills, *Journal of the Malaysian Branch of Royal Asiatic Society* 8, 1 (1930): 227–55.

Fairbank, J. K. *Trade and Diplomacy on the China Coast*. Cambridge: Cambridge University Press, 1953.

Fairbank, J. K. (ed.) *The Chinese World Order: Traditional China's Foreign Relations.* Cambridge, Massachusetts, Harvard University Press, 1968.

Fairbank, J. K. "A Preliminary Framework" in John King Fairbank (ed.) *The Chinese World Order: Traditional China's Foreign Relations*. Cambridge, Mass.: Harvard University Press, 1968, pp. 1–19.

Fairbank, John King. "The Chinese World Order" (Chinese translation) in Tao Wenzhao (comp.), Lin Hai *et al.* (trans.) *Works of Fei Zhengqing* [John King Fairbank]. Tianjin: Tianjin People's Publishing House, 1992.

Fairbank, J. K. and E. O. Reischauer. *China: Tradition and Transformation* [Chinese translation]. Nanjing: Jiangsu renmin chubanshe, 1996.

Felix, A. Jr., (ed.) *The Chinese in the Philippines, 1570–1770*. 2 volumes. Manila: Solidaridad Publishing, 1966.

Ferguson, Donald. *Letters from Portuguese captives in Canton, written in 1534 and 1536*. With an introduction on Portuguese intercourse with China in the first half of the sixteenth century. Bombay: Educ. Steam Press, Byculla, 1902.

Fernando, M. R. and D. Bulbeck (eds.). *Chinese Economic Activity in Netherlands India*. Singapore: ECOHSEA, ANU/Institute of Southeast Asian Studies, 1992.

Fernando, M. R. (eds.). "Early Settlers in the Land of Promise: Chinese Traders in the Malay Archipelago in the Seventeenth and Eighteenth Centuries." In *Maritime China in Transition 1750–1850*, eds. Wang Gangwu and Ng Chin-keong. Wiesbaden: Harrassowitz Verlag, 2004, pp. 227–44.

Fernando, M. R. (eds.). "The Lost Archives of Melaka: Is It Really Lost?" *Journal of the Malaysian Branch of Royal Asiatic Society* 78, 1 (2005): 1–36.

Ferrars, Max and Bertha Ferrars. *Burma*. London: Sampson Low, Marston and Company. New York: E. P. Dutton & Co., 1901.

Finlay, Robert. "The Treasure Ships of Zheng He: Chinese Maritime Imperialism in the Age of Discovery." In *Terrae Incognitae* 23 (1991): 1–12.

Fitzgerald, C. P. *The Southern Expansion of the Chinese People: 'Southern Fields and Southern Ocean'*. Canberra: Australian National University Press, 1972.

Fonseca, Father Manoel da. "Father Manoel da Fonseca, S. J., in Ava (Burma) (1613–1652)." *Journal of the Asiatic Society of Bengal* (New Series) 5 (1835): 19–48.

Foster, W. *Early Travels in India, 1583–1619*. Oxford: Oxford University Press, 1921.

Franke, Wolfgang and Chen Tieh Fan 陳鐵凡. *Chinese Epigraphic Materials in Malaysia*. 3 volumes. Kuala Lumpur: University of Malaya Press, 1982–7.

Fraser, Alexander. "Report on a Route from the Mouth of the Pakchan to Krau, and Thence Across the Isthmus of Krau to the Gulf of Siam." 1861, *MPRIC 1886*, I, 285–97.

Frost, M. R. "*Emporium in Imperio:* Nanyang Networks and the Straits Chinese in Singapore, 1819–1914." *Journal of Southeast Asian Studies* 36, 1 (2005): 29–66.

Fung Ping Shan Museum. *Ceramic Finds from Tang and Song Kilns in Guangdong*. Hong Kong: University of Hong Kong Press, 1985.

Furber, Holden. *Rival Empires of Trade in the Orient, 1600–1800*. Minneapolis: University of Minnesota Press, 1976.

Gerini, G. E. *Old Phuket: Historical Retrospect of Junkceylon Island*. Reprinted from the *Journal of the Siam Society*. Bangkok: The Siam Society, 1986.

Gibb, H. A. R. transl. *Ibn Battuta. Travels in Asia and Africa 1325–1354*. London: Routledge Kegan Paul, 1929.

Giersch, C. Pat. "'A Motley Throng:' Social Change on Southwest China's Early Modern Frontier, 1700–1880." *The Journal of Asian Studies* 60, 1 (February 2001): 67–94.

Giersch, C. Patterson. *Asian Borderlands: The Transformation of Qing China's Yunnan Frontier*. Cambridge MA: Harvard University Press, 2006.

Giersch, C. Patterson. "Cotton, Copper, and Caravans: Trade and the Transformation of Southwest China." In *Chinese Circulations: Capital, Commodities, and Networks in Southeast Asia*, Eric Tagliacozzo and Wen-Chin Chang (eds.), pp. 37–61. Durham and London: Duke University Press, 2011.

Giles, H. A. *The Travels of Fa-hsien (399–414 A.D.) or Record of the Buddhistic Kingdoms*. London, Routledge & Kegan Paul, 1923.

Gipouloux, François. *The Asian Mediterranean: Port Cities and Trading Networks in China, Japan and Southeast Asia, 13th–21st Century*, translated by Jonathan Hall and Dianna Martin. Cheltenham and Northampton, MA: Edward Elgar Publishing, 2011.

350   Bibliography

Glamann, Kristof. *Dutch-Asiatic Trade, 1620–1740*. The Hague: Martinus Nijhoff, 1958.

Goitein, S. D. *A Mediterranean Society. The Jewish Communities of the Arab World as Portrayed in the Documents of the Cairo Geniza*. 5 vols. Berkeley: University of California Press, 1967–88.

Gong, Yin 龔蔭. *Zhongguo Tusi Zhidu* 中国土司制度 (The Native Chieftain System of China). Kunming: Yunnan minzu chubanshe, 1992.

Goodrich, L. Carrington and Fang Chaoying eds. *Dictionary of Ming Biography, 1368–1644*. 2 volumes. New York and London: Columbia University Press, 1976.

Goscha, Christopher E. *Thailand and the Southeast Asian Networks of the Vietnamese Revolution (1885–1954)*. London: Routledge/Curzon, 1999.

Goscha, Christopher E. "Vietnamese Revolutionaries and the Early Spread of Communism to Peninsular Southeast Asia: Towards a Regional Perspective." *The Copenhagen Journal of Asian Studies* 14 (2000): 1–41.

Goscha, Christopher E. "Building Force: Asian Origins of 20th Century Military Science in Vietnam (1905–1954)." *Journal of Southeast Asian Studies* 34, 3 (2003): 535–60.

Goscha, Christopher E. and Christian Ostermann (ed.), *Connecting Histories: Decolonization and the Cold War in Southeast Asia 1945–1962*. Stanford, Stanford University Press, 2009.

Gotuaco, Larry, Rita C. Tan and Allison I. Diem. *Chinese and Vietnamese Blue and White Wares Found in the Philippines*. Manila: Bookmark Inc. 1997.

Gouger, Henry. "Deposition." In *Documents Illustrative of the Burmese War with an Introductory Sketch of the Events of the War and an Appendix*, 1826, Horace Hayman Wilson (ed.). Calcutta: Government Gazette Press, 1827, pp. 219–22.

Goldstein, Avery. "A Rising China's Growing Presence: The Challenges of Global Engagement," in Jacques Deslisle and Avery Goldstein (ed.), *China's Global Engagement: Cooperation, Competition, and Influence in the 21st Century*. Washington, D.C.: Brookings Institution Press, 2017, pp. 1–34.

Graaf, H. J. de and Th. G. Th. Pigeaud (edited by M. C. Ricklefs). *Chinese Muslims in Java in the 15th and 16th Centuries*. Melbourne: Monash Papers on Southeast Asia, 1984.

Grabowsky, Volker. "Forced Resettlement Campaigns in Northern Thailand during the Early Bangkok Period." *Journal of the Siam Society* 87, 1 and 2 (1999): 45–86.

Grabowsky, Volker. "The Northern Tai polity of Lan Na (Babai-Dadian) between the Late 13th and Mid-16th Centuries: Internal Dynamics and Relations with Her Neighbours." Paper presented at Workshop on Southeast Asia in the 15th Century and the Ming Factor, 18–19 July 2003, Asia Research Institute, National University of Singapore.

Grabowsky, Volker. "Population and State in Lan Na Prior to the Mid-Sixteenth Century." *Journal of Siam Society* 93 (2005): pp. 1–68.

Gray, Basil. "The Export of Chinese Porcelain to India." *Transactions of the Oriental Ceramic Society* 36 (1964–66): 21–36.

Gray, Basil. "The Export of Chinese Porcelain to the Islamic World: Some Reflections on its Significance for Islamic Art before 1400." *Transactions of the Oriental Ceramic Society* 41 (1975/76–1976–77): 231–61.

Griffiths, Arlo. "The Problem of the Ancient Name Java and the Role of Satyavarman in Southeast Asian International Relations around the Turn of the Ninth Century CE." *Archipel* 85 (2013): 43–81.

Grimsditch, Mark. "Chinese Agriculture in Southeast Asia: Investment, Aid and Trade in Cambodia, Laos and Myanmar." Bangkok: Heinrich-Böll-Stiftung Southeast Asia, June 2017. https://th.boell.org/en/2017/06/22/chinese-agriculture-southeast-asia-investment-aid-and-trade-cambodia-laos-and-myanmar.

Guldi, Jo and David Armitage, *The History Manifesto*. Cambridge: Cambridge University Press, 2014.

Gunn, Geoffrey. *History Without Borders: The Making of an Asian World Region, 1000–1800*. Hong Kong: Hong Kong University Press, 2011.

Gupta, Ashin Das. "Changing Faces of the Maritime Merchant." In *Emporia, Commodities and Entrepreneurship in Asian Maritime Trade, c.1400–1750*, Roderich Ptak and D. Rothermund (eds.). Stuttgart: Franz Steiner, 1991, pp. 353–71.

Guy, John. *Oriental Trade Ceramics in South East Asia: Ninth to Sixteenth Centuries*. Singapore: Oxford University Press, 1986.

Guy, John. *Ceramic Excavation Sites in South-East Asia. A Preliminary Gazetteer*. Adelaide: University of Adelaide, 1987.

Guy, John. "The Vietnamese Wall Tiles of Majapahit." *Transactions of the Oriental Ceramic Society* 53 (1988–9): 27–46.

Guy, John. *Ceramic Traditions of South-East Asia*. Singapore: Oxford University Press, 1989.

Guy, John. "Tamil Merchant Guilds and the Quanzhou Trade." In *The Emporium of the World: Maritime Quanzhou, 1000–1400*. A. Schottenhamer (ed.) Leiden: Brill, 2001, pp. 283–317.

Guy, John. "Early Asian Ceramic Trade and the Belitung 'Tang' Cargo." *Transactions of the Oriental Ceramic Society* 66 (2001–2): 13–27.

Guy, John. "Early Ninth Century Chinese Export Ceramics and the Persian Gulf Connection: The Belitung Shipwreck Evidence." In *Chine – Méditerranée, routes et échanges de la céramique jusqu'au XVIe siècle, TAOCI* 4 (2006): 9–20.

Guy, John. "Rare and Strange Goods: International Trade in Ninth-Century Asia." In *Shipwrecked. Tang Treasures and Monsoon Winds*. Regina Krahl, John Guy and J. Keith Wilson. (eds.). Washington D.C., Sackler Gallery, 2010: 19–28.

Guy, John. "Tamil Merchants and the Hindu Buddhist Diaspora in Early Southeast Asia." In *Early Interactions between South and Southeast Asia: Reflections on Cross-Cultural Exchange*. Pierre-Yves Manguin and A. Mani (eds.). Singapore: Institute of Southeast Asian Studies and New Delhi: Manohar Publishers and Distributors, 2011, pp. 243–62.

Guy, John. "The Phanom Surin Shipwreck, a Pahlavi Inscription, and their Significance for the History of Early Lower Central Thailand." *Journal of the Siam Society* 105 (2017a): 179–96.

Guy, John. "Shipwrecks in Southeast Asia: Southern China's Maritime Trade and the Emerging Role of Arab Merchants in Late First Millennium Indian Ocean Exchange," in Angela Schottenhammer (ed.), *Exchange, Transfer, and Human Movement Across the Indian Ocean World*. London, Palgrave Macmillan, 2017b.

H. D. Phong trào nguoi Hoa ở Do thỉSài Gòn, *Mùa thu rồi ngày hăm ba*, volume II, 3rd section (Hanoi: NXB Chính trị quốc gia, 1996), pp. 468–9.

Haijun haiyang cehui yanjiusuo 海軍海洋測繪研究所 and Dalian Haiyun xueyuan hanghaishi yanjiushi 大連海運學院航海史研究室 compil. *Xinbian Zheng He hanghaitu ji* 新編鄭和航海圖集 (A New Atlas of Zheng He Voyages). Beijing: Renmin jiaotong chubanshe, 1988.

Hall, D. G. E. *A History of South-East Asia*. London, Macmillan, 1970, Third edition.

Hall, Kenneth R. "Economic History of Early Southeast Asia," in *The Cambridge History of Southeast Asia* vol. 1, (ed.) Nicholas Tarling. Cambridge: Cambridge University Press, 1992, pp. 183–275.

Hamashita, Takeshi 濱下武志. "The Tribute Trade System and Modern Asia." *Memoirs of the Research Department of the Toyo Bunko* 46 (1988): 7–23.

Hamashita, Takeshi 濱下武志. "The Intra-Regional System in East Asia in Modern Times," in *Network Power: Japan and East Asia*, Peter Kaatzenstein and Takashi Shiraishi (eds.). Ithaca: Cornell University Press, 1997, pp. 113–35.

Hamashita, Takeshi 濱下武志. *Jindai Zhongguo de guoji qiji: chaogong maoyi tixi yu jindai yazhou jingjiquan* (近代中國的國際契機: 朝貢貿易體系與近代亞洲經濟圈 The International Turning Point of China in Modern Times – Tributary Trade System and Sphere of Asian Economy in Modern Times). Beijing: Zhongguo shehui kexue chubanshe, 1999.

Han, Zhenhua 韓振華. *Zhufan zhi zhubu* 諸蕃志注補 (Zhao Rugua's Zhufanzhi with Annotations). In *Han Zhenhua xuanji* 韓振華選集 (Selected Works of Han Zhenhua). Vol. 2. Hong Kong: Centre of Asian Studies Occasional Papers and Monographs 134, the University of Hong Kong, 2000.

Hang, Xing. *Conflict and Commerce in Maritime East Asia: The Zheng Family and the Shaping of the Modern World, c.1620–1720*. Cambridge: Cambridge University Press, 2015.

Harrell, Stevan. (ed.) *Cultural Encounters on China's Ethnic Frontiers*. Seattle: University of Washington Press, Seattle, 1995.

Hartwell, Robert M. *Tribute Missions to China, 960–1126*. Philadelphia: author's edition, 1983.

Harvey, G. E. *History of Burma: From the Earliest Times to 10 March 1824 The Beginning of the English Conquest*. London: Longmans, Green, 1925.

Harvey, G. E. *British Rule in Burma 1824–1942*. London: Faber & Faber, 1946.

Hasegawa, Kiyoshi 長谷川清." Sip Song Panna Ohkoku (Shari) no Seiji Shihai Soshiki to Sono Tochi Ryoiki; Unnan Taizoku *Kenkyū* no Ikkan to shite 西雙版納王国（車里）の政治支配組織とその統治領域－雲南幾族研究の一環として" (The Organisation of Political Control in the Sipsong Panna Kingdom (Cheli) and the Extent of its Rule; A Study of the Dai Nationality in Yunnan). *Tōnan Ajia- Rekishi to Bunka* 東南アジア一歷史と文化 11 (1982): 132–36.

Hayes, James. "The Pattern of Life in the New Territories in 1898." *Journal of the Hong Kong Branch of the Royal Asiatic Society* New Series, 2 (1962): 75–102.

Heidhues, Mary S. *Bangka Tin and Mentok Pepper: Chinese Settlement on an Indonesian Island*. Singapore: Institute of Southeast Asian Studies, 1992.

Heilbron, J. L. "In Diaspora," in *The Chinese Diaspora: Selected Essays*, Wang Ling-chi and Wang Gungwu (eds.). Singapore: Times Academic Press, 1998, pp. xii–xiv.

Herman, John. "The Cant of Conquest: Tusi Offices and China's Political Incorporation of the Southwest Frontier'," in *Empire at the Margins*, Pamela Crossley, Helen Siu, and Donald Sutton (eds.). Berkeley: University of California Press, 2006, pp. 136–57.

Hicks, G., (ed.) *Overseas Chinese Remittances from Southeast Asia 1910–1940*. Singapore: Select Books, 1993.

Hill, Ann Maxwell. *Merchants and Migrants; Ethnicity and Trade among the Yunnanese Chinese in Southeast Asia*. New Haven: Monograph 47, Yale University Southeast Asian Studies, 1998.

Hirth, F. and W. W. Rockhill. *Chau Ju-kua, His Work on the Chinese and Arab Trade in the Twelfth and Thirteenth Centuries, Entitled Chu-fan-chï*. St. Petersburg: Imperial Academy of Sciences, 1911. Taipei, 1967 reprint.

Hồ, Chí Minh 胡志明. *HồChíMinh toà tậ* (The Complete Writings of Ho Chi Minh). 12 volumes. Hanoi: NXB Chíh triquố gia, 1995–96.

Hoàng, Văn Hoan 黃文歡. *Giọt nước trong biển cả (Hồi Ký Cách Mạng)*. Beijing: NXB Tin Viet Nam, 1986.

Hoàng, Thanh Đạm and Hữu Thỉnh Phan, *Đời nối đời vì nước: kể chuyện gia tộc Hồ Tùng Mậu*. NXB Nghe An, 1996.

Hong, Yongbin 洪用斌. "Yuandai de mianhua shengchan he mianfangye 元代的棉花生産和棉紡業." *Zhongguo shehui jingjishi yanjiu* 中國社會經濟史研究 3 (1984): 55–63.

Huang, Wei and Huang Qinghua. "Yuan qinghua ciqi zaoqi leixing de xin faxian – cong shizheng jiaodu lun Yuan qinghua ciqi de qiyuan" [New discoveries of Yuan blue-and-white ceramic types – an evidentiary investigation into the origin of Yuan blue-and-white porcelain], *Wenwu* 11 (2012): 79–88.

Huang, Yao 黃堯. *Xingma huaren zhi* 星馬華人志 (History of the Chinese in Malaysia and Singapore). Hong Kong: Mingjian chubanshe, 1967.

Huang, Yuanzhi 黃元直 and Liu Dashi 劉達式 compil. *Yuanjiang zhigao* 元江志稿 (The Draft Gazetteer of Yuanjiang). 1922, Taipei: Chengwen chubanshe, 1968 reprint.

Huber, Edouard. "La Fin de la Dynastie de Pagan." *Bulletin de l'École française d'Extrême-Orient* 9 (1909): 663–80.

Hucker, Charles. "Hu Tsung-hsien's Campaign Against Hsu Hai, 1556," in *Chinese Ways in Warfare*, (ed.) John K. Fairbank. Cambridge, MA: Harvard University Press, 1974, pp. 273–307.

Hucker, Charles O. "Entry on Chu Chan-chi" in *Dictionary of Ming Biography*, (eds.) L. Carrington Goodrich and Chaoying Fang (eds.). New York: Columbia University Press, 1976, pp. 279–89.

Hunt, E. H. "Old Hyderabad China." *Journal of the Hyderabad Archaeological Society*, 1916.

Iijima Akiko 飯島明子. "'Taijin no seiki' saikō: shoki Raannaa shijō no Sho mondai (「タイ人の世紀」再考—初期ラーンナー史上の諸問題 A Re-Examination of the 'Tai Century': Some Issues in Early Lanna history)," in Ishizawa Yoshiaki 石澤良昭, *Iwanami Kōza Tōnan Ajia Shi Dai 2 Kan Tonan Ajia Kodai Kokka no Seiritsu to Tenkai* 岩波講座東南アジア史 第2巻、東南アジア古代国家の成立と展開 (The Iwanami Series of Studies of Southeast Asian History, volume 2, The Formation and Development of Ancient States in Southeast Asia), Tokyo: Iwanami Tōnan 岩波書店, 2001, pp. 257–86.

Ishii, Yoneo 石井米雄. *The Junk Trade from Southeast Asia: Translation from the Tosen Fusetsu-gaki, 1674–1723*. Singapore: Institute of Southeast Asian Studies and Research School of Pacific and Asian Studies, Australian National University, 1998.

Jiang, Boqin 姜伯勤. *Qingchu lingnan chanxue shi yanjiu chubian: Shilian Daxian yu Aomen chanshi* 清初嶺南禪學史研究初編：石濂大汕與澳門禪史 (Thach Liem Daxian and the Development of Zen in Macau). Shanghai: Xuelin chubanshe, 1999.

Jiang, Yingliang 江應樑. *Daizu Shi* 傣族史 (A History of the Dai Nationality). Chengdu: Sichuan minzu chubanshe, 1983.

Jiang, Zuyuan 蔣祖緣 and Fang Zhiqin 方志欽. (eds.) *Jianming Guangdong shi* 简明廣東史 (A Brief History of Guangdong). Guangzhou: Guangdong renmin chubanshe, 1987.

Jin, Guoping 金國平. *Zhongpu guanxi shidi kaozheng* 中葡關係史地考證 (A Textual Examination of History and Geography in Early Sino-Portuguese Relations). Macau: Macau Foundation, 2000.

Jones, Russell. *Chinese Loan-Words in Malay and Indonesian. A Background Study*. Kuala Lumpur: Universiti Malaya, 2009.

Judson, Adoniram. *A Memoir of the Life and Letters of the Rev. Adoniram Judson, D. D*. Compiled by Francis Wayland. Boston: Philips, Sampson & Company, 1853.

Kambe Teruo 神戸輝夫. "E'ertai to Unnan (鄂爾泰と雲南 E'ertai and Yunnan)," *Shigaku Ronshū* (Beppu Daigaku Shigaku Kenkyūkai 史学論叢 (別府大学史学研究会) 21 (1990), pp. 95–128.

Kang, David C. *East Asia Before the West: Five Centuries of Trade and Tribute*. New York: Columbia University Press, 2010.

Karashima, Noboru. "Trade Relations between South India and China During the 13th and 14th Centuries." *Journal of East–West Relations* 1 (1989): 59–81.

Kathirithamby-Wells, Jeyamalar and John Villiers (ed.). *The Southeast Asian Port and Polity: Rise and Demise*. Singapore: Singapore University Press, 1990.

Katō, Kumiko 加藤久美子. "Changes in Sipsongpanna in the Eighteenth Century: Focusing on the 1720s and 1730s." *Nagoya Daigaku Bungakubu Kenkyu Ronshu* 名古屋大学文学部研究論集 (*Shigaku*史学) 43 (1997): 1–18.

Katō, Kumiko 加藤久美子. *Bonchi Sekai no Kokkaron: Unnan, Shipusonpanna no Taizoku Shi* 盆地世界の国家論ー雲南、シプソンパンナーのタイ族史 (The Polities of the World of Basins: A History of the Tai People of Sipsong Panna). Kyoto: Kyoto Daigaku Gakujutsu Shuppankai 京都大学学術出版会, 2000.

Katō, Kumiko 加藤久美子. "Sipsong Pannā Mun Kenryoku no kōeki e no kakawari: 'Goyō Shōnin' Naay Hoy wo Megutte (シプソンパンナー、ムン権力の交易への関わりー御用商人ナーホイをめぐって The Relationship Between Mäng Political Power and Trade in Sipsong Panna: Naay Hoy 'the government contractors'," Nagoya Daigaku Tōyōshi Kenkyū Hōkoku 名古屋大学東洋史研究報告 No. 25, 2001, pp. 388–403.

Kauz, Ralph. "Die Insel Hainan in persischen und arabischen Quellen," in *Hainan: de la Chine à l'Asie du Sud-Est; von China nach Südostasien*, eds. Claudine Salmon and Roderich Ptak, Wiesbaden: Harrassowitz Verlag, 2001, pp. 139–52.

Kayoko, Fujita, Momoki Shiro, and Anthony Reid (ed.). *Offshore Asia: Maritime Interactions in Eastern Asia Before Steamships*. Singapore: Institute of Southeast Asian Studies, 2013.

Kelley, Liam C. "Thoughts on a Chinese Diaspora: The Case of the Macs of Ha Tien." *Crossroads* 14, 1 (2000): 71–98.

Kikuchi, Hideaki 菊池秀明. *Kōsei Imin Shakai to Taihei Tengoku* 広西移民社会と太平天国 (The Migrant Society of Guangxi and the Kingdom of Heavenly Peace). Tokyo: Fūkyōsha 風響社, 1998, 2 volumes.

Kōbata, Atsushi 小葉田淳. *Chūsei Nantō Tsūkō Bōekishi no Kenkyū* 中世南島通交貿易史の研究 (Studies on the History of Trade and Communication in Southern Islands). Tokyo: Nihon Hyōronsha, 1939.

Kōbata, Atsushi 小葉田淳. *Hainandao shi* 海南島史 (A History of Hainan Island). 1943, Chinese trans.; Taibei: Xuehai chubanshe, 1979 reprint.

Kōbata, Atsushi 小葉田淳 and Mitsugu Matsuda. *Ryukyuan Relations with Korea and South Sea Countries. An Annotated Translation of Documents in the Rekidai Hôan*. Kyoto: Higashiyamaku, 1969.

Kong, Yuanzhi 孔遠志. *Zhongguo yindunixiya wenhua jiaoliu* 中國印度尼西亞文化交流. Beijing: Beijing daxue chubanshe, 1999.

Kong, Yuanzhi 孔遠志. *Muslim Tionghoa Cheng Ho, Misteri Perjalanan Muhibah di Nusantara Pustaka*. Jakarta: Populer Obor, 2000.

Krahl, R. *Chinese Ceramics from the Topkapi Saray Museum, Istanbul, A Complete Catalogue*, ed. J. Ayers. 3 vols. London: Sotheby's, 1986.

Kuwabara, Jitsuzô 桑原隲藏. "On P'u Shou-kêng ... a Man of the Western Regions, Who Was the Superintendent of the Trading Ships' Office in Ch'üan-chou ... Towards the End of the Sung Dynasty, Together with a General Sketch of Trade of the Arabs in China during the T'ang and Sung Eras." *Memoirs of the Research Department of the Toyo Bunko* 2 (1928): 1–79; 7 (1935): 1–104.

Kwame Sundaram, Jomo and Brian C. Folk (ed.). *Ethnic Business: Chinese Capitalism in Southeast Asia*. New York: Routledge, 2003.

Lahuzu jianshi bianxiezu 拉祜族简史編寫組. *Lahuzu Jianshi* 拉祜族简史 (A Short History of the Lahu). Kunming: Yunnan Renmin Chubanshe, 1986.

Laird, John. "Deposition." 1826. In *Documents Illustrative of the Burmese War with an Introductory Sketch of the Events of the War and an Appendix*, ed. Horace Hayman Wilson. Calcutta: Government Gazette Press, pp. 223–9.

Lê, Thành Khôi. *Histoire du Viêt Nam des origines à 1858*. Paris Sudestasie, 1992.

Lee, James Z. *The Political Economy of a Frontier: Southwest China, 1250–1850*. Cambridge: Harvard University Asia Center, 2002.

Lee, Lung-wah 李龍華. "Mingdai de kaizhongfa 明代的開中法" (The Kaizhong System during the Ming Dynasty), in *Zhongguo wenhua yanjiusuo xuebao* 中國文化研究所學報, Hong Kong, 4, 2 (1972): 371–493.

Le Strange, Guy. transl. *Ruy Gonzalez de Clavijo. Embassy to Tamerlane 1403–1406*. London: George Routledge and Sons, 1928.

Legge, James. *A Record of Buddhistic Kingdoms; Being an Account by the Chinese Monk Fâ-Hien of his Travels in India and Ceylon, A.D. 399–414 A Record of Buddhist Kingdoms ... Fa-Hien (399–414)*. Oxford: Clarendon Press, 1886, Dover, 1965 reprint.

Lewis, D. *Jan Compagnie in the Straits of Malacca*. Ohio, Athens: Ohio University Press, 1995.

Liaw, Yock Fang. *Undang-undang Melaka*. The Hague: Nijhoff, 1976.

Lieberman, Victor B. "Ethnic Politics in Eighteenth-Century Burma." *Modern Asian Studies* 12, 3 (1978): 455–82.

Lieberman, Victor B. *Burmese Administrative Cycles: Anarchy and Conquest, c.1580–1760*. Princeton, New Jersey: Princeton University Press, 1986.

Lieberman, Victor B. "An Age of Commerce in Southeast Asia? Problems of Regional Coherence: A Review Article." *Journal of Southeast Asia* 54, 3 (1995): 796–807.

Liew, Foon Ming 劉奮明. "The Luchuan-Pingmian Campaigns (1436–1449) in the Light of Official Chinese Historiography." *Oriens Extremus* 39, 2 (1996): 162–203.

Li, Guoxiang 李國祥 and Yang Chang 楊昶 (eds.) *Ming shilu leizuan. Guangdong Hainan juan* 明實錄類傳: 廣東海南卷. Wuhan: Wuhan chubanshe, 1993.

Li, Jinming 李金明. "Shilun Mingdai haiwai chaogong maoyi de neirong yu shizhi" 試論明代海外朝貢貿易的內容與實質, *Haijiaoshi yanjiu* 海交史研究 13 (1/1988): 172–81.

Li, Jinming 李金明 and Liao Dake 廖大珂. *Zhongguo gudai haiwai maoyi shi* 中國古代海外貿易史 (Maritime History of Imperial China). Nanning: Guangxi renmin chubanshe, 1995.

Li, Kangying. *The Ming Maritime Trade Policy in Transition, 1368 to 1567*. Wiesbaden: Harrassowitz, 2010.

Li, Mo 李默. *Guangdong fangzhi yaolu*. 廣東方志要錄 (A Catalogue Summary of Local Gazzetteers of Guangdong). Guangzhou: Guangdongsheng difangzhi bianzuan weiyuanhui bangongshi, 1987.

Li, Rongxi. "The Journey of the Eminent Monk Faxian," in BDK English Tripitaka, *Lives of Great Monks and Nuns*. Berkeley, Numata Center, 2002.

Li, Tana 李塔娜 and Anthony Reid, (ed.) *Southern Vietnam under the Nguyen*. Singapore: EHSEAP, ANU/ASEAN Economic Research Unit, ISEAS, 1993.

Li, Tana 李塔娜. *Nguyễn Cochinchina: Southern Vietnam During the Seventeenth and Eighteenth Centuries*. Ithaca: SEAP, Cornell University Press, 1998.

Li, Tana 李塔娜. "The Late 18th century Mekong Delta and the World of the Water Frontier." In *Vietnam: Borderless Histories*, (ed.) Nhung Tuyết Trần and Anthony Reid. Madison, Wisconsin: The University of Wisconsin Press, 2005, pp. 147–62.

Lin, Tien-wai (Lin Tianwei 林天蔚). *Songdai xiangyao maoyi shigao* 宋代香藥貿易史稿. Hong Kong: Zhongguo xueshe, 1960.

Lin, Ying 林英, Zhu Yihui 朱逸輝 and He Hongsheng 何洪生 eds. *Hainan mingren zhuanlüe* 海南名人傳略. Guangzhou: Guangdong lüyou chubanshe, 1993.

Liu, Hong 劉宏. "Old Linkages, New Networks: The Globalization of Overseas Chinese Voluntary Associations and Its Implications." *China Quarterly* 155 (September 1998): 582–609.

Liu, Hong 劉宏. "Sino-Southeast Asian Studies: Toward a New Analytical Framework". Paper presented at the "Approaching Asia from Asia" Workshop, Sariska, India, 20–22 February 2000.

Liu, Xifan 劉錫蕃. *Lingbiao Jiman* (嶺表記蠻 A Record of the Barbarians of Guangdong and Guangxi), Shanghai: Shangwu Yinshuguan 商務印書館, 1934.

Liu, Xinyuan, "Imperial Export Porcelain from Late Yuan to Early Ming." *Oriental Art* XLV 3 (1999): 48–54.

Lo, Hsiang Lin 羅香林. "Islam in Canton in the Sung Period: Some Fragmentary Records," in *Symposium on Historical, Archaeological and Linguistic Studies on Southern China, South-East Asia and the Hong Kong Region*, (ed.) F. S. Drake. Hong Kong: Hong Kong University, 1967: 176–9.

Lo, Jung-pang 羅榮邦. "The Decline of the Early Ming Navy." Chinese translation by Chen Xiyu, *Zheng He Studies* 鄭和研究, 3rd Issue (1998): 52–61.

Lombard, Denys. *Le carrefour javanais.* 3 vols. Paris: Éditions de l'École des Hautes Études en Sciences Sociales, 1990.

Lombard, Denys. "Une autre « Méditerranée » dans le Sud-Est Asiatique." *Hérodote* 88 (1st trimester 1998): 184–93.

Lu Wei 盧葦. "Lishi shang de Hainan zai guoneiwai maoyi zhong de diwei he zuoyong 歷史上的海南在國內外貿易中的地位和作用." *Guangdong shehui kexue* 22, 4 (1989): 79–87.

Lu Wei 盧葦. "Mingdai Hainan de 'haidao', bingbei he haifang 明代海南的海盜、兵備和海防." *Ji'nan xuebao* 45, 4 (1990): 99–108.

Lubo-Lesnichenko, E. "The Blue-and-white Porcelain of Yuan Period from Khara-Khoto." *International Symposium on Ancient Chinese Trade Ceramics: Collected Papers*. Taipei: National Museum of History, 1994.

Luce, G. H. "Chinese Invasions of Burma in the 18th Century." *Journal of the Burma Research Society* 15, 2 (1925): 115–28.

Ma Huan. *Ma Huan's Ying-yai Sheng-lan* (The Overall Survey of the Ocean's Shores, 1433), trans. by J. V. Mills. Cambridge: Hakluyt Society, 1970.

MacLeod, T. E. "Abstract Journal of an Expedition to Kiang Hung on the Chinese Frontier. Starting from Moulmein on the 13th December, 1836." *Journal of the Asiatic Society of Bengal* 6 (December 1837): 989–1005.

Majumdar, R. C. *Champa. History and Culture of an Indian Colonial Kingdom in the Far East, 2nd–16th Century A.D.* Delhi: Gian Publishing House, 1985 reprint.

Mak, Phoeun. *Histoire du Cambodge, de la fin du XVIe siecle au debut du XVIIIe*. Paris: Ecole Francaise d'Extreme-Orient, 1995.

Malcom, Howard. *Travels in the Burman Empire*. Edinburgh: William and Robert Chambers, 1840.

Mancall, Mark (ed.). *China at the Center: 300 Years of Foreign Policy* (Transformation of Modern China series). NewYork: Free Press, 1984.

Manela, Erez. *The Wilsonian Moment: Self-Determination and the International Origins of Anticolonial Nationalism*. Oxford: Oxford University Press, 2007.

Bibliography 357

Manguin, Pierre-Yves. *Les Portugais sur les côtes du Viêt-Nam et du Campa. Étude sur les routes maritimes et les relations commerciales, d'après les sources portugaises (XVIe, XVIIe, XVIIIe siècles)*. Publications de l'École Française d'Extrême-Orient 81. Paris: École française d'extrême orient, 1972.

Manguin, Pierre-Yves. "Études Cam. II: L'introduction de l'Islam au Campa." *Bulletin de l'École française d'Extrême-Orient* 66 (1979): 255–87.

Manguin, Pierre-Yves. "The Southeast Asian Ship: An Historical Approach." *Journal of Southeast Asian Studies* 11, 2 (1980): 266–76.

Manguin, Pierre-Yves. "Relationships and Cross-influences between Southeast Asian and Chinese Shipbuilding Traditions." *SPAFA Final Report on Maritime Shipping and Trade Networks in Southeast Asia*, 1984, pp. 197–212.

Manguin, Pierre-Yves. "The Vanishing *Jong*: Insular Southeast Asian Fleets in Trade and War (Fifteenth to Seventeenth Centuries)," in *Southeast Asia in the Early Modern Era: Trade, Power and Belief*, (ed.) Anthony Reid. Ithaca: Cornell University Press, 1993, pp. 197–213.

Mani, B. R. *Delhi – Threshold of the Orient* (Studies in Archaeological Investigations). New Delhi: Archaeological Survey of India, 1997.

Manning, Patrick. *Navigating World History: Historians Create a Global Past*. New York: Palgrave Macillan, 2003.

Matthew, K. S. "Kwaja Shams-ud-din Giloni: A Sixteenth Century Entrepreneur in Portuguese India." In *Emporia, Commodities and Entrepreneurship in Asian Maritime Trade, c.1400–1750*, Roderich Ptak and D. Rothermund (eds.). Stuttgart: Franz Steiner Verlag, 1991, pp. 363–72.

Maung, Htin Aung. *A History of Burma*. New York: University of Columbia Press, 1967.

Maw, Henry Lister. *Memoir of the Early Operations of the Burmese War: Addressed to the Editor of the United Service Journal*. London: Smith, Elder, 1832.

McKeown, Adam. "Conceptualizing Chinese Diasporas, 1842–1949." *Journal of Asian Studies* 58, 2 (1999): 306–37.

McNeill, William. *The Rise of the West: A History of the Human Community*. Chicago: University of Chicago Press 1992 [1963].

Mei Tsu-lin and Jerry Norman. "The Austroasiatics in Ancient South China: Some Lexical Evidence." *Monumenta Serica* 32 (1976): 274–301.

Meilink-Roelofsz, M. A. P. *Asian Trade and European Influence in the Indonesian Archipelago between 1500 and about 1630*. The Hague: Martinus Nijhoff, 1962.

Miksic, John. "Chinese Ceramic Production and Trade." *Oxford Research Encyclopaedia of Asian History*, Oxford: Oxford University Press, http://asianhistory.oxfordre.com/view/10.1093/acrefore/9780190277727.001.0001/acrefore-9780190277727-e-218, 2017.

Mills, J. V. G., (trans. and ed.) *Ma Huan: Ying-yai Sheng-lan. The Overall Survey of the Ocean's Shores [1433]*. Cambridge: Cambridge University Press for the Hakluyt Society, Extra Series No. XLII, 1970.

Mills, J. V. G. "Arab and Chinese Navigators in Malaysian Waters in about A.D. 1500." *Journal of the Malaysian Branch of the Royal Asiatic Society* 47, 2 (1974): 1–82.

Mills, J. V. G., (trans. and ed.) "Chinese Navigators in Insulinde about A.D. 1500." *Archipel* 18 (1979): 69–93.

Mills, J. V. G., (trans. and ed.) trans., revised, annotated and edited by Roderich Ptak, *Fei Hsin, Hsing-ch'a sheng-lan: The Overall Survey of the Star Raft*. Wiesbaden: Harrassowitz Verlag, 1996.

Millward, James A. *Beyond the Pass: Economy, Ethnicity, and Empire in Qing Central Asia, 1759–1864*. Stanford: Stanford University Press, 1998.

Minh Chi, Ha Van Tan and Nguyễn Tai Thu. *Buddhism in Vietnam*. Hanoi: The Gioi Publishers, 1993.
Misugi, T. *Chinese Porcelain Collections in the Near East, Topkapi and Ardebil*. 3 vols. Hong Kong: University of Hong Kong Press, 1981.
Miyazaki, Ichisada 宮崎市定. "Yōsei Tei; Chūgoku no Dokusai Kunshu 雍正帝－中国の独裁君主 (The Yongzheng Emperor: The Chinese Despotic Monarch)," in *Miyazaki Ichisada* Zenshū 宮崎市定全集 (The Collected Works of Miyazaki Ichisada). Tokyo: Iwanami Shoten, 1991.
Mogensuo 摩根索 (Hans Joachim Morgenthau), *Guojia jian de zhengzhi: wei quanli yu heping er douzheng* 國家間的政治：為權力與和平而鬥爭 (Politics among Nations: The Struggle for Power and Peace). New York: Knopf, 1954, Chinese translation, Beijing: Shangwu yinshuguan, 1993.
Momoki, Shiro 桃木至郎. "Đại Việt and the South China Sea Trade: From the 10th to the 15th Century." *Crossroads* 12, 1 (1998): 1–34.
Morse, Hosea B. *The Chronicles of the East India Company Trading to China, 1635–1834*. Clarendon: Oxford University Press, 1926.
Mote, Frederick W. and Denis Twitchett. *The Cambridge History of China – Volume 7: The Ming Dynasty 1368–1644* Part 1. Cambridge: Cambridge University Press, 1988a.
Mote, Frederick W. and Denis Twitchett. "The Rise of the Ming Dynasty 1330–1367," in *Cambridge History of China*. Cambridge: Cambridge University Press, Vol. 7, 1988b, pp. 11–5.
Mote, Frederick W. and Denis Twitchett. *Imperial China 900–1800*. Cambridge Massachusetts: Harvard University Press, 1999.
Motoo, Furuta, "The Vietnamese Political Movement in Thailand: Legacy of the Dong-du Movement." In *Phan Boi Chau and the Dong-Du Movement*, (ed.) Vinh Sinh. New Haven: The Lac-Viet Series, no. 8, 1988, pp. 150–81.
Mourão, Isabel Tavares. "L'île de Hainan à travers quelques récits portugais des XVIe et XVIIe siècles," in *Hainan: de la Chine à l'Asie du Sud-Est; von China nach Südostasien*, (ed.) Claudine Salmon and Roderich Ptak, (ass. ed.) Shing Müller, South China and Maritime Asia 10. Wiesbaden: Harrassowitz Verlag, 2001, pp. 153–77.
Muljana, Slamet. *A Story of Majapahit*. Singapore: Singapore University Press, 1976.
Munn, C. "The Hong Kong Opium Revenue, 1845–1885." In *Opium Regimes: China, Britain and Japan, 1839–1952*, (ed.) T. Brook and B. T. Wakabayashi. Berkeley, Los Angeles and London: University of California Press, 2000, pp. 105–26.
Mya, Than. "The Chinese in Myanmar," in *Ethnic Chinese as Southeast Asians*, (ed.) Leo Suryadinata. Singapore: Institute of Southeast Asian Studies, 1997, pp. 115–57.
Needham, Joseph. *Science and Civilisation in China*. Cambridge: Cambridge University Press, 1954–2008.
Netolitzky, Almut. *Das Ling-wai tai-ta von Chou Ch'ü-fei. Eine Landeskunde Südchinas aus dem 12. Jahrhundert. Münchner Ostasiatische Studien 21*. Wiesbaden: Franz Steiner Verlag, 1977.
Ng, Chin-Keong 吳振強. *Trade and Society: The Amoy Network on the China Coast, 1683–1735*. Singapore: Singapore University Press, 1983.
Nguyễn, Ái Quốc. "Báo cáo gửi Quốc tế Cộng sản" [Report to the Comintern], dated 18 February 1930, in *Hồ Chí Minh toàn tập*. Vol. III. Hanoi: NXB Chinh Tri Quoc Gia, 1995, pp. 15–6.
Nguyễn, Đình Đầ*u. Nghiên cứu địa bà triều Nguyễn: Biên H*òa (Cadastral registers study of Nguyen dynasty: Bien Hoa). Hochiminh City: Hochiminh City Publishing House, 1994.

Nguyễn, Long. *Việt Nam Phật Giáo Sử Luận* (History of Buddhism in Vietnam). Hanoi: Nhà xuất bản văn học, 1992.

Nguyễn Ngọc, *Có một con đường mòn trên biển Đông*. Hanoi: NXB Ha Noi, undated.

Nguyễn, Q. Thắng and Nguyễn Bá Thế. *Từ diễn Nhân vật Lịch sử Việt Nam*. Hanoi: NXB Khoa học xã hội, 1992.

Nguyễn, Tai. "Nho lai Ngay dua Bac Ho tu Thái Lan sang gây dựng cơ sở cach Mang o Lao." *Tạp chí Cộng Sản* 12 (December 1986): 80–2.

Nguyễn, Thanh Nha. *Tableau économique du Viêt Nam aux XVIIe et XVIIIe siècles*. Paris: editions Cujas, 1870.

Nguyễn, Thế Anh. "Secret Societies: Some Reflections on the Court of Hue and the Government of Cochinchina on the Eve of Tu Duc's Death (1882–1883)." *Asian Affairs* 9, 2 (June 1978): 179–85.

Nguyễn, Thế Anh. "Le Nam Tiến dans les texts Vietnamiens," in *Les frontières du Viet Nam: Histoire des frontières de la Péninsule indochinoise*. (ed.) P. B. Lafont, Paris: L'Harmattan, 1993, pp. 121–27.

Nguyễn, Thế Anh. "L'immigration Chinoise et la Colonisation du Delta du Mékong." *The Vietnam Review*, 1 (Autumn–Winter 1996): 154–77.

Nguyễn, Thế Anh and Alain Forest (eds.) *Guerre et paix en asie du sud-est*. Paris: Editions L'Harmattan, 1998.

Nguyễn, Thế Anh and Alain Forest eds. "Hainan et les marchands hainanais dans les sources vietnamiennes," in *Hainan: de la Chine à l'Asie du Sud-Est; von China nach Südostasien*, in *Hainan: de la Chine à l'Asie du Sud-Est; von China nach Südostasien, South China and Maritime Asia 10*. Wiesbaden: Harrassowitz Verlag, 2001, (ed.) Claudine Salmon and Roderich Ptak, ass. ed. Shing Müller, South China and Maritime Asia 10. Wiesbaden: Harrassowitz Verlag, 2001, pp. 179–94.

Nigata Prefecture Museum of Modern Art. *Tō Kōtei kara no okurimono* (*Gifts of the Tang Emperors: Hidden Treasures from the Famen Temple*). Tokyo: Niigata Prefecture Museum of Modern Art, 1999.

Nishikawa Kazutaka 西川和孝. *Unnan Chūka Sekai no Bōchō: Pūarucha to kōzan kaihatsu ni miru ijū senryaku* 雲南中華世界之膨張—プーアル茶と鉱山開発にみる移住戦略 (The Expansion of the Chinese World into Yunnan by Han Migration: Their strategies as seen in the cultivation of Pu'er Tea and the opening of markets). Tōkyō, Keiyūsha 慶友社, 2015.

Nomoto Takashi 野本敬 and Nishikawa Kazutaka 西川和孝. "Kanzoku Imin no Katsudō to Seitai Kankyō no Kaihen 漢族移民の活動と生態環境の改変 [The activities of Han migrants and changes to the ecological environment]," in *Ronshū Monsūn Ajia no Seitai Shi, Vol. 2: Chiiki no Seitai Shi* 論集モンスーンアジアの生態史，第二巻：地域の生態史 [Articles on the ecological history of Monsoon Asia, Vol. 2: Regional ecological history], edited by Christian Daniels. pp. 15–34. Tokyo 東京: Kōbundō 弘文堂, 2008.

North, Douglass C. *Institutions, Institutional Change, and Economic Performance*. Cambridge: Cambridge University Press, 1991.

Nowell, Charles E. *A History of Portugal*. New York: Van Nostrand, 1952.

Oliveira e Costa, João Paulo de and Vítor Luís Gaspar Rodrigues. *Campanhas de Afonso de Albuquerque: Conquista de Malaca, 1511*. Lisbon: Tribuna da Historia, 2011.

Ollé, Manel. *Estrategias filipinas respecto a China: Alonso Sánchez y Domingo Salazar en la empresa de China (1581–1593)*. 2 vols. Ph.D. diss., Barcelona: Universitat Pompeu Fabra, 1998.

Ollé, Manel. *La invención de China. Percepciones y estrategias filipinas respecto a China durante el siglo XVI*. South China and Maritime Asia 9. Wiesbaden: Harrassowitz Verlag, 2000.

Olson, Mancur. "Big Bills Left on the Sidewalk: Why Some Nations are Rich, and Others Poor?" *Journal of Economic Perspectives* 10, 2 (1996): 3–24.

Origo, Iris. *The Merchant of Prato*. Harmondsworth: Penguin, 1963.

Osterhammel, Jürgen. *The Transformation of the World: A Global History of the Nineteenth Century*. Princeton: Princeton University Press, 2014.

Palat, Ravi. *The Making of an Indian Ocean World-Economy, 1250–1650: Princes, Paddy fields, and Bazaars*. New York: Palgrave Macmillan, 2015.

Pang, Keng-Fong. "Being Hui, Huan-nang, and Utsat Simultaneously: Contextualizing History and Identities of the Austronesian-Speaking Hainan Muslims," in *Negotiating Ethnicities in China and Taiwan*, (ed.) Melissa J. Brown. Berkeley: Institute of East Asian Studies, 1996, pp. 183–207.

Panikkar, K. M. *Asia and Western Dominance: A Survey of the Vasco da Gama Epoch of Asian History*. London, Allen and Unwin, 1953.

Parker, E. H. *Burma with Special Reference to Her Relations to China*. Rangoon: Rangoon Gazette Press, 1893.

Pearn, Bertie Reginald. *A History of Rangoon*. Rangoon: Baptist Mission Press, 1939.

Pearson, Michael (ed.) *Trade, Circulation, and Flow in the Indian Ocean World*. New York: Palgrave Macmillan, 2015.

Pelliot, Paul. "Les grands voyages maritimes chinois au début du XVe siècle." *T'oung Pao* 30 (1933): 305–11.

Phalgunadi, Gusti Putu. *The Pararaton. A Study of the Southeast Asia Chronicle*. New Delhi: Sundeep Prakashan, 1996.

Phayre, Arthur P. *A History of Burma including Burma Proper, Pegu, Taungu, Tenasserim, and Arakan: From the Earliest Times to the End of the First War with British India*. London: Trübner, 1883.

Poivre, Pierre. "Description de la Cochinchine (1749–1759)." *Revue d'Extreme-Orient*, Tome III (1887): 81–121.

Pope, J. A. *Fourteenth Century Blue and White: A Group of Chinese Porcelain in the Topkapi Sarayi Muzesi, Istanbul*. Washington: Freer, 1952 (revised ed. 1970).

Pope, J. A. *Chinese Porcelain from the Ardebil Shrine*. Washington: Freer, 1956 (2nd ed. 1981).

Prakash, Om. "Restrictive Trade Regimes: VOC and Asian Spice Trade in the Seventeenth Century," in *Emporia, Commodities and Entrepreneurs in Asian Maritime Trade, c.1400–1750*, Roderich Ptak and D. Rothermund (eds.). Stuttgart: Franz Steiner Verlag, 1991, pp. 107–26.

Ptak, Roderich. "Pferde auf See. Ein vergessener Aspekt des maritimen chinesischen Handels im frühen 15. Jahrhundert." *Journal of the Economic and Social History of the Orient* 34 (1990): 199–233.

Ptak, R. and D. Rothermund (eds.), *Emporia, Commodities and Entrepreneurs in Asian Maritime Trade, c.1400–1750*. Stuttgart: Franz Steiner Verlag, 1991.

Ptak, Roderich. "The Northern Trade Route to the Spice Islands: South China Sea-Sulu-Zone-North Moluccas (14th to early 16th Century)." *Archipel* 43 (1992): 27–56.

Ptak, Roderich. "Piracy along the Coasts of Southern India and Ming-China: Comparative Notes on Two Sixteenth Century Cases." In *As relações entre a Índia portuguesa, a Ásia do Sueste e o Extremo Oriente. Actas do VI Seminário Internacional de História*

Indo-Portuguesa, eds. Artur Teodoro de Matos and Luís Filipe F. Reis Thomaz. Macau and Lisbon: Instituto de Cultura, 1993a, pp. 255–73.

Ptak, Roderich. "China and the Trade in Cloves, c.960–1435." *Journal of the American Oriental Society* 113, 1 (1993b): 1–13.

Ptak, Roderich. "Yuan and Early Ming Notices on the Kayal Area in South India." *Bulletin de l'École Française d'Extrême-Orient 80* (1993c): 137–56.

Ptak, Roderich. "Merchant and Maximization: Notes on Chinese and Portuguese Entrepreneurship in Maritime Asia, c.1350–1600." In *Maritime Asia: Profit Maximization, Ethics and Trade Structure*, Karl A. Sprengard and Roderich Ptak (eds.). Wiesbaden: Harrassowitz Verlag, 1994, pp. 29–35.

Ptak, Roderich. "Images of Maritime Asia in Two Yuan Texts: *Daoyi zhilue* and *Yiyu zhi*." *Journal of Song-Yuan Studies* 25 (1995): 47–75.

Ptak, Roderich. "Die Paracel- und Spratly-Inseln in Sung-, Yüan- und frühen Ming-Texten: Ein maritimes Grenzgebiet?" In *China and Her Neighbours. Borders, Visions of the Other, Foreign Policy. 10th to 19th Century*, Sabine Dabringhaus and Roderich Ptak (eds.), South China and Maritime Asia 6. Wiesbaden: Harrassowitz Verlag, 1997, pp. 159–81.

Ptak, Roderich. "Südostasiens Meere nach chinesischen Quellen (Song und Yuan)." *Archipel* 56 (1998a): 5–30.

Ptak, Roderich. "Ming Maritime Trade to Southeast Asia, 1368–1567: Visions of a System." In *From the Mediterranean to the China Sea*, Claude Guillot, Denys Lombard and Roderich Ptak (eds.), with the assistance of Richard Teschke. Wiesbaden, Germany: Harrassowitz Verlag, 1998b, pp. 157–91.

Ptak, Roderich. *China and the Asian Seas: Trade, Travel, and Visions of the Other (1400–1750)*. Aldershot, Singapore, Sydney: Ashgate, 1998c.

Ptak, Roderich. "From Quanzhou to the Sulu Zone and Beyond: Questions Related to the Early Fourteenth Century." *Journal of Southeast Asian Studies* 29, 2 (September 1998d): 269–94.

Ptak, Roderich. *China's Seaborne Trade with South and Southeast Asia 1200–1750*. Aldershot, Singapore, Sydney: Ashgate, 1999.

Ptak, Roderich. "Braudel et l'Asie." *Annales*, 1 (January–February 2001a): 5–50.

Ptak, Roderich. "Hainans Außenbeziehungen während der frühen Ming-Zeit (Hongwu bis Hongzhi)." In *Hainan: de la Chine à l'Asie du Sud-Est; von China nach Südostasien*, Claudine Salmon and Roderich Ptak (eds.), Shing Müller (ass. ed), South China and Maritime Asia 10. Wiesbaden: Harrassowitz Verlag, 2001b, pp. 107–8.

Ptak, Roderich. "Jottings on Chinese Sailing Routes to Southeast Asia: Especially on the Eastern Route in Ming Times." In *Portugal e a China. Conferências nos encontros de história luso-chinesa*, (ed.) Jorge M. dos Santos Alves. Lisbon: Fundação Oriente, 2001c, pp. 107–31.

Ptak, Roderich. "China's Medieval *fanfang* – A Model for Macau under the Ming?" *Anais de História de Além-Mar* 2 (2001d): 47–71.

Ptak, Roderich. "Hainan in the Letters by Cristóvão Vieira and Vasco Calvo." In *D. João III e o Império. Actas do Congresso Internacional Comemorativo do seu Nascimento (Lisboa e Tomar, 4 a 8 de Junho de 2002)*, Roberto Carneiro and Artur Teodoro de Matos (eds.). Lisbon: Centro de História de Além-Mar und Centro de Estudos dos Povos e Culturas de Expressão Portuguesa, 2004a, pp. 485–99.

Ptak, Roderich. "Chinesische Wahrnehmungen des Seeraumes vom Südchinesischen Meer bis zur Küste Ostafrikas, c.1000–1500." In *Der Indische Ozean. Das afroasiatische Mittelmeer als Kultur- und Wirtschaftsraum*, Dietmar Rothermund and

Susanne Weigelin-Schwiedrzik (eds.), Edition Weltregionen 9. Vienna: Verein für Geschichte und Sozialkunde, ProMedia, 2004b, pp. 37–59.

Ptak, Roderich. *China, the Portuguese, and the Nanyang: Oceans and Routes, Regions and Trade (c.1000–1600)*. Aldershot: Ashgate, 2004c.

Ptak, Roderich. "Hainan and the Trade in Horses (Song to Early Ming)," in *Pferde in Asien: Geschichte, Handel und Kultur/Horses in Asia: History, Trade and Culture*, Bert G. Fragner and Ralph Kauz, Bert G. Fragner, Ralph Kauz, Roderich Ptak and Angela Schottenhammer (eds.). Vienna: Verlag der Österreichischen Akademie der Wissenschaften, 2009; Veröffentlichungen zur Iranistik 46, pp. 219–28.

Ptak, Roderich and Claudine Salmon (eds.). *Hainan: de la Chine à l'Asie du Sud-Est; von China nach Südostasien*, South China and Maritime Asia 10. Wiesbaden: Harrassowitz Verlag, 2001.

Purcell, Victor. *The Chinese in Southeast Asia*. 2nd edn. London: Oxford University Press, 1965.

Quinn-Judge, Sophie. *Ho Chi Minh: The Missing Years (1919–1941)*. London: Christopher Hurst, 2003.

Raben, Remco and Dhiravat na Pombejra (eds.). *In the King's Trail: An 18th Century Dutch Journey to the Buddha's Footprint Theodorus Jacobus van den Heuvel's Account of His Voyage to Phra Phutthabat in 1737*. Bangkok: Royal Netherlands Embassy, 1997.

Ravenstein, E. G. (trans and ed.). *A Journal of the First Voyage of Vasco da Gama, 1497–1499*. London: Hakluyt Society, 1898.

Ray, H. "The South East Asian Connection in Sino-Indian Trade." In *South East Asia and China: Art, Interaction and Commerce*, R. Scott and J. Guy (eds.). London: Percival David Foundation of Chinese Art Colloquies on Art and Archaeology, no. 17, University of London, 1995: 41–54.

Reid, Anthony. "Economic and Social Change, c.1400–1800," in *The Cambridge History of Southeast Asia*. Vol. 1, Part 2, (ed.) Nicholas Tarling. Cambridge: Cambridge University Press, 1992, pp. 116–63.

Reid, Anthony. *Southeast Asia in the Age of Commerce, 1450–1680*. 2 vols. New Haven: Yale University Press, 1993a and 1995.

Reid, Anthony. "The Unthreatening Alternative: Chinese Shipping in Southeast Asia, 1567–1842." *Review of Malaysian and Indonesian Affairs* 27, 1–2 (1993b): 13–32.

Reid, Anthony (ed.). *Southeast Asia in the Early Modern Era: Trade, Power, and Belief*. Ithaca, New York: Cornell University Press, 1993c.

Reid, Anthony (ed.). *Sojourners and Settlers: Histories of Southeast Asia and the Chinese in Honour of Jennifer Cushman*. St Leonards, NSW: Allen & Unwin, 1996.

Reid, Anthony (ed.). *The Last Stand of Asian Autonomies*. London: Macmillan, 1997.

Reid, Anthony. "The Rise and Fall of Sino-Javanese Shipping," in Anthony Reid (ed.), *Charting the Shape of Early Modern Southeast Asia*. Chiang Mai: Silkworm Books, 1999, pp. 56–84.

Reid, Anthony. *Charting the Shape of Early Modern Southeast Asia*. Chiang Mai, Thailand: Silkworm Books, 1999; Singapore: ISEAS, 2000 reprint.

Reid, Anthony. "Hybrid Identities in the Fifteenth-Century Straits of Malacca," Asia Research Institute Working Paper Series No. 67 (Singapore: Asia Research Institute, 2006). www.ari.nus.edu.sg/wps/wps06_067.pdf.

Remer, Charles Frederick. *Foreign Investment in China*. New York: Macmillan, 1931.

Remmelink, W. *The Chinese War and the Collapse of the Javanese State, 1725–1743*. Leiden: KILTV, 1994.

Reynolds, Craig. "Review Article: Tai-land and Its Others," in *South East Asia Research* 11, 1 (March 2003): 113–30.
Reynolds, Sian. *The Mediterranean and the Mediterranean World in the Age of Philip II*, 2 vols. Berkeley: University of California Press, 1995.
Richards, Dick. *South-East Asian Ceramics: Thai, Vietnamese, and Khmer, from the Collection of the Art Gallery of South Australia*. Kuala Lumpur: Oxford University Press, 1995.
Richardson, D. "An Account of some of the Petty States Lying North of the Tenasserim Provinces, Drawn up From the Journal and Reports of Dr. Richardson, Esq., Surgeon of the Commissioner of the Tenasserim Provinces." *Journal of the Royal Asiatic Society of Bengal* 5 (October 1836): 601–25; 5 (November 1836): 668–707.
Robequain, Charles, James Russell Andrus, and Katrine R. C. Greene. *The Economic Development of French Indo-China*, tran. Isabel Ward. London and New York: Oxford University Press, 1944.
Rockhill, W. W. "Notes on the Relations and Trade of China with the Eastern Archipelago and the Coast of the Indian Ocean during the Fourteenth Century." *Tu'ong Pao* 15 (1914): 419–47; 16 (1915): 61–159, 236–71, 374–92.
Rogers, A. (trans.) and H. Beveridge (ed.). *The Tuzuk-i-Jahangiri or Memoirs Jahangir from the First to the Twelfth Year of His Reign*. London: Royal Asiatic Society, 1909–14.
Rossabi, Morris (ed.). *China Among Equals: the Middle Kingdom and Its Neighbors 10th–14th Centuries*. Los Angeles: University of California Press, 1983.
Rouffaer, G. P. and J. W. Ijzerman (eds.). *De Eerste Scheepvaart der Nederlanders naar Oost-Indie onder Cornelis Houtman 1595–1597*. 2 Volumes. The Hague: Nijhoff, 1915.
Salmon, Claudine. *Literary Migrations, Traditional Chinese Fiction in Asia (17–20th Centuries)*. Chinese translation, Beijing: International Culture Publishing Corporation, 1987.
Salmon, Claudine. "Regards de quelques voyageurs chinois sur le Vietnam du XVIIe siècle," in *Asia Maritima: Images et réalité Bilder und Wirklichkeit, 1200–1800*, eds. Denys Lombard and Roderich Ptak, South China and Maritime Asia 1. Wiesbaden: Harrassowitz Verlag, 1994, pp. 117–46.
Salmon, Claudine. "Sur les traces de la diaspora des Baba des Détroits: Li Qinghui et son 'Récit sommaire d'un voyage vers l'Est' 1889." *Archipel* 56 (1998): 71–120.
Salmon, Claudine and Roderich Ptak (eds.) *Hainan: de la Chine à l'Asie du Sud-Est; von China nach Südostasien*, South China and Maritime Asia 10. Wiesbaden: Harrassowitz Verlag, 2001.
Samphantharak, Krislert. "The Rise of China and Foreign Direct Investment from Southeast Asia." *Journal of Current Southeast Asian Affairs* 30, 2 (2011): 65–75.
Sastri, K. A. N. *Foreign Notices of South India: From Megasthenes to Ma Huan*. Madras: University of Madras, 1939.
Sauvaget, J. *Aḥbār aṣ-Ṣīn wa l-Hind. Relation de la Chine et de l'Inde rédigée en 851*. Paris: Belles Lettres, 1948.
Schafer, Edward H. *The Golden Peaches of Samarkand: A Study of T'ang Exotics*. Berkeley: University of California Press, 1963.
Schafer, Edward H. *Shore of Pearls*. Berkeley: University of California Press, 1970.
Schottenhammer, Angela. *Quanzhou, Fujian, in der Song-Zeit (960–1279): Die Verknüpfung zwischen zentralstaatlicher Politik und regionaler wirtschaftlicher Entwicklung und deren Auswirkung auf den maritimen Handel*. Unpublished habil. thesis, Munich, 2000.

Schottenhammer, Angela (ed.). *The Emporium of the World: Maritime Quanzhou, 1000–1400*. Leiden: Brill, 2001a.

Schottenhammer, Angela. "Hainan's politisch-ökonomische Anbindung an das chinesische Festland während der Song-Dynastie." In *Hainan: de la Chine à l'Asie du Sud-Est; von China nach Südostasien*, eds. Claudine Salmon and Roderich Ptak, 2001b, pp. 35–81.

Schottenhammer, Angela (ed.). *The East Asian Mediterranean: Maritime Crossroads of Culture, Commerce and Human Migration*. Wiesbaden: Harrassowitz Verlag, 2008.

Scott, James C. *The Art of Not Being Governed: An Anarchist History of Upland Southeast Asia*. New Haven and London: Yale University Press, 2009.

Shaffer, Lynda N. *Maritime Southeast Asia to 1500*. New York: M. E. Sharp, 1996.

Shambaugh, David. "China Engages Asia: Reshaping the Regional Order." *International Security* 29, 3 (Winter 2004/05): 64–99.

Shepherd, John Robert. *Statecraft and Political Economy on the Taiwan Frontier, 1600–1800*. Stanford: Stanford University Press, 1993.

Shiba, Yoshinobu 斯波義信. *Sōdai Shōgyōshi Kenkyū* 宋代商業史研究 (*Commercial Activities during the Sung Dynasty*). Tokyo: Kazuma shoten, 1969.

Shiba, Yoshinobu 斯波義信. *Commerce and Society in Sung China*. Translated by Mark Elvin. Michigan: University of Michigan, 1970.

Shin, Leo. *The Making of the Chinese State: Ethnicity and Expansion on the Ming Borderlands*. Cambridge: Cambridge University Press, 2006.

Shintani, Tadahiko 新谷忠彦 (ed.) *Ohgon no Yonkaku Chitai-Shan Bunkaken no Rekishi, Gengo Minzoku* 黄金の四角地帯—シャン文化圏の歴史・言語・民族 (The Zone of the Golden Quadrangle: The History, Language, and Ethnic Groups of the Tai Cultural Area). Tokyo: Keiyūsha 慶友社, 1998.

Shintani, Tadahiko 新谷忠彦 (ed.), *Shan (Tay) go On'in Ron to Moji Hō* シャン (Tay) 語音韻論と文字法 (The Phonology and Writing System of Shan [Tay]). Tokyo: Ajia Afurika Gengo Bunka Kenkyūjo アジア・アフリカ言語文化研究所, 2000.

Siah, U Chin. "The Chinese in Singapore, General Sketch of the Numbers, Tribes and Avocations of the Chinese in Singapore." *Journal of the Indian Archipelago and Eastern Asia* 2 (1848): 283–90.

Silva, Chandra Richard de. *Sri Lanka: A History*. New Delhi, Vikas Publishing House, 1987.

Singh, Jatswan. "The Origins of British Burma: Arakan and Tenasserim, 1826–1852." M.A. Thesis, University of Malaya, 1992.

Sishier meijushi. *Zheng Zhao zhuan* (四十二梅居士: 鄭昭傳 Biography of Chao Taksin). *Shan Hu Fortnightly* (珊瑚半月刊) 3, 2 (August 1939) [no page numbers].

Skelton, Robert. "The Shah Jahan Cup." *Victoria and Albert Museum Bulletin*, vol. II, no. 3 (July 1966): 109–10.

Skinner, G. William. *Chinese Society in Thailand: An Analytical History*. Ithaca, New York: Cornell University Press, 1957.

Smart, Ellen. "Fourteenth Century Chinese Porcelain from a Tughlaq Palace in Delhi." *Transactions of the Oriental Ceramic Society* 41 (1975–77): 199–230.

Smith, Anthony D. *The Ethnic Origins of Nations*. Cambridge, MA: Blackwell, 1986.

Smith, Ronald Bishop. *Siam or the History of the Thais from 1569 A.D. to 1824 A.D.* Bethesda, Maryland: Decatur Press, 1967.

So, Billy K. L 蘇基朗. *Prosperity, Region, and Institutions in Maritime China: The South Fukien Pattern, 946–1368*. Cambridge MA: Harvard University Press, 2000.

Solheim, Wilhelm G. II. "'Southeast Asia:' What's in a Name: Another Point of View." *Journal of Southeast Asian Studies* 16 (1985): 141–7.

Sơn, Nam. *Đồng bằng Sông Cửu Long* (The Mekong Delta). Ho Chi Minh City: Ho Chi Minh City Press, 1993.
Song, Ong Siang 宋旺相. *One Hundred Years' History of the Chinese in Singapore*. Singapore: University of Malaya Press, 1923.
Soudavar, A. "A Chinese Dish from the Lost Endowment of Princess Sultanum (925–69/1519–62)," in Kambiz Eslami ed., *Iran and Iranian Studies in Honor of Iraj Afshar*. Princeton, 1998: 125–34.
Spry, Henry Harper. "A Three Weeks Sail in Search of Health." *Journal of the Asiatic Society of Bengal* (1841): 143–8.
Stargardt, Janice. "Burma's Economic and Diplomatic Relations with India and China from Early Medieval Sources." *Journal of the Economic and Social History of the Orient* 14 (1971): 38–62.
Steensgaard, Niels. *The Asian Trade Revolution of the Seventeenth Century*. Chicago: The University of Chicago Press, 1973.
Stern, S. M. "Ramisht of Siraf, a Merchant Millionaire of the Twelfth Century." *Journal of the Royal Asiatic Society* (1967): 10–4.
Subrahmanyam, Sanjay. *Explorations in Connected History: From the Tagus to the Ganges*. Delhi: Oxford University Press, 2004.
Suebsaeng, Promboon. *Sino-Siamese Tributary Relations, 1282–1853*. Ph.D. diss., University of Wisconsin, 1971.
Sun, Laichen 孫來臣. "Yongli's Refuge in Burma and its Implications for Burmese History." Burma Colloquium, Northern Illinois University, 7–9 October 1994.
Sun, Laichen 孫來臣. "Chinese Historical Sources on Burma: A Bibliography of Primary and Secondary Works." *Journal of Burma Studies* 2 (1997): 1–116.
Sun, Laichen 孫來臣. *Ming-Southeast Overland Interactions, 1368 to 1644*. Unpublished PhD diss., Ann Arbor: University of Michigan, 2000.
Sun, Laichen 孫來臣. "*Chinese Military Technology and Dai Viet:* c.*1390–1497*, Asia Research Institute Online Working Paper No. 11 (September 2003a), www.ari.nus.edu.sg/docs/wps/wps03_011.pdf.
Sun, Laichen 孫來臣. "Military Technology Transfers from Ming China and the Emergence of Northern Mainland Southeast Asia (c.1390–1527)." *Journal of Southeast Asian Studies* 34, 3 (October 2003b): 495–517.
Sun, Laichen 孫來臣. "Chinese Gunpowder Technology and Dai Viet: c.1390–1497," in *Viet Nam: Borderless Histories*, Nhung Tuyết Trần and Anthony Reid (eds.). Madison, Wisconsin: University of Wisconsin Press, 2006, pp. 72–120.
Sutherland, Heather. "Southeast Asian History and the Mediterranean Analogy." *Journal of Southeast Asian Studies* 34, 1 (February 2003): 1–20.
Sutton, Donald S. "Violence and Ethnicity on a Qing Colonial Frontier: Customary and Statutory Law in the Eighteenth-Century Miao Pale." *Modern Asian Studies* 37, 1 (2003), pp. 41–80.
Suwanpanich, Nopporn and Kraisak Choonhavan. *The Communist Party of Thailand and Conflict in Indochina*. The Hague: Institute of Social Studies, 1980.
Syamananda, Rong. *A History of Thailand*. Bangkok: Chulalongkorn University Press, 1973.
Symes, Michael. *An Account of an Embassy to the Kingdom of Ava*. London: Nicol & Wright, 1800.
Tagliacozzo, Eric and Wen-chin Chang (ed.). *Chinese Circulations: Capital, Commodities, and Networks in Southeast Asia*. Durham: Duke University Press, 2011.
Takeuchi, Fusaji 武内房司. "Taihei Tengoku no Byōzoku Hanran ni tsuite: Kishū Tōnanbu Byōzoku Chiku wo chūshin ni 太平天国期の苗族反乱について―貴州東

南部苗族地区を中心に (Miao Rebellions in South-east Guizhou during the Kingdom of Heavenly Peace Period)." *Shichō* 史潮 (*Shin* 新), 12 (1982): 26–56.

Takeuchi, Fusaji 武内房司. "Byōzoku Tōnanbu no Kan ni tsuite; Shindai Shōsei Byōzoku Shakai ni okeru Ketsumei shūzoku 苗族の款について—清代湘西苗族社会における結盟習俗 (The Kuan [Consensual Pacts] of the Miao People; the Alliance Forming Customs of Miao Society in Western Hunan during the Qing Period)." *Rao Bai Shin no Sekai* 老百姓の世界, 5, (December 1987): 52–70.

Takeuchi, Fusaji 武内房司. "*Kindai Unnan Suzugyō no Tenkai to Indoshina* 近代雲南錫業の展開とインドシナ [The expansion of the tin mining industry in modern Yunnan and Indochina]." *Tōyō Bunka Kenkyū* 東洋文化研究 5 (2003): 1–33.

Takeuchi, Fusaji 武内房司. "19 Seiki Zenhan Unnan Nanbu Chiiki ni okeru Kanzoku Ijū no Tenkai to Sanchimin Shakai no Henyō 一九世紀前半，雲南南部地域における漢族移住の展開と山地民社会の変容 [The Expansion of Han Migration and the Transformation of Hill People's Society in Southern Yunnan During the First Half of the Nineteenth Century]." In *Chūgoku Kokkyō Chiiki no Idō to Kōryū: Kingendai Chūgoku no Minami to Kita* 中国国境地域の移動と交流—近現代中国の南と北 [Movement and Interaction in Chinese International Border Areas: South and North in Modern and Contemporary China], edited by Shigeyuki Tsukada 塚田誠之, pp. 117–43. Tokyo: Yūshisha 有志舎 (2010).

Tan, Qixiang 譚其驤 et al. compil. *Zhongguo lishi ditu ji* (中国歷史地圖集 The Historical Atlas of China). Shanghai: Ditu chubanshe, 1987.

Tang, Kaijian 湯開建. "Yuandai dui Hainandao de kaifa yu jingying 元代對海南島的開發與經營." *Ji'nan xuebao* 45, 4 (1990): 131–45.

Tao, Wenzhao 陶文釗 (ed.) *Fei Zhengqing ji* 費正清集 (*Works of John Fairbank*). Tianjin: Tianjin renmin chubanshe, 1992.

Tapp, Nick. "A New Stage in Tai Regional Studies: The Challenge of Local Histories." In *Civility and Savagery: Social Identity in Tai States*, (ed.) Andrew Turton. Richmond Surrey: Curzon Press, 2000, pp. 351–59.

Tarling, Nicholas (ed.) *The Cambridge History of Southeast Asia*. 2 volumes, Cambridge: Cambridge University Press, 1992.

Taw, Sein Ko. "The Chinese in the Tharawaddy District." In *Burmese Sketches*. 2 vols. Rangoon: British Burma Press, 1920a, vol. 2, pp. 128–31.

Taw, Sein Ko. *Burmese Sketches*. 2 vols. Rangoon: British Burma Press, 1920b.

Taylor, Keith. "Nguyen Hoang (1525–1613) and the Beginning of Viet Nam's Southward Expansion," in *Southeast Asia in the Early Modern Era: Trade, Power and Belief*, (ed.) Anthony Reid. Ithaca: Cornell University Press, 1993, pp. 42–65.

Terwiel, B. J. *A History of Modern Thailand, 1767–1942*. St. Lucia: University of Queensland Press, 1983.

Thanh Đạm. "Các nhà cách mạng Việt Nam tham gia khởi nghĩa Quảng Châu." Nghiên cứu lịch sử, no. 6, 253 (1990): 73–5.

Thành, Thế Vỹ. *Ngoài Thương Việt-Nam: Hồi Thế Kỷ XVII, XVIII và đầu XIX*. Hanoi: Sử Học, 1961.

Thein, Jocelyn Co. "The Resilience of an Immigrant Community: The Chinese-Burmans in Twentieth-Century Rangoon Chinatown." Unpublished B.A. thesis, Department of East Asian Languages and Civilizations. Harvard College, Cambridge, Massachusetts, 1997.

Thomaz, Luís Filipe F. Reis. *Nina Chatu and the Portuguese trade in Malacca*, translated from the Portuguese by M.J. Pintado; with a foreword by A. Kalimuthu. Melaka: Luso-Malaysian Books, 1991.

Thomaz, Luís Filipe F. Reis. *Early Portuguese Malacca*. Macau: CTMCDP/IPM, 2000.
Thompson, Virginia. *French Indo-China*. First published New York: Macmillan, 1937. New York: Octagon Books, 1968 reprint.
Thornton, John K. *Africa and Africans in the Formation of the Atlantic World, 1400–1680*. 2d expanded edn. Cambridge: Cambridge University Press, 1998.
Tibbetts, G. R. *A Study of the Arabic Texts Concerning Materials on South-East Asia*. London: Royal Asiatic Society, 1979.
Tibbetts, G. R. *Arabic Navigation in the Indian Ocean before the Coming of the Portuguese*. London, Royal Asiatic Society, 1981.
T'ien, Ju-k'ang 田汝康. "Cheng He's Voyages and the Distribution of Pepper in China." *The Journal of the Royal Asiatic Society of Great Britain and Ireland* 2 (1981): 186–97.
Tin, Ù (Mandalay). *Kòn-baung-zet Maha-ya-zawin-daw-gyi*. 3 vols. Rangoon: Hanthawaddy Press, 1968.
Toynbee, Arnold. *A Study of History*. Oxford: Oxford University Press, 1934–39.
Trocki, Carl A. *Prince of Pirates: The Temenggongs and the Development of Johor and Singapore, 1784–1885*. Singapore: Singapore University Press, 1979.
Trocki, Carl A. "The Rise of Singapore's Great Opium Syndicate, 1840–1886." *Journal of Southeast Asian Studies* 18 (March 1987): 58–80.
Trocki, Carl A. *Opium and Empire: Chinese Society in Colonial Singapore 1800–1910*. Ithaca, New York: Cornell University Press, 1990.
Trocki, Carl A. "Chinese Pioneering in Eighteenth-Century Southeast Asia," in *The Last Stand of Asian Autonomies*, (ed.) Anthony Reid. London and New York: MacMillan and St. Martins Press, 1997a, pp. 83–101.
Trocki, Carl A. "Boundaries and Transgressions: Chinese Enterprise in Eighteenth- and Nineteenth-Century Southeast Asia." In *Ungrounded Empires: The Cultural Politics of Modern Chinese Transnationalism*, Aihwa Ong and Donald M. Nononi (eds.). New York: Routledge, 1997b, pp. 61–90.
Trocki, Carl A. "The Internationalization of Chinese Revenue Farming Networks," in *Water Frontier: Commerce and the Chinese in the Lower Mekong Region, 1750–1880*, N. Cooke and Li Tana (eds.). Singapore: Rowan and Littlefield Publishers Inc. and Singapore University Press, 2004, pp. 159–73.
Tsai, Maw-Kuey. *Les Chinois au Sud-Vietnam*. Paris: Bibliothèque Nationale, 1968.
Ts'ao, Yung-ho 曹永和. "Zhongguo Haiyang Shihua 中國海洋史話" (A Discourse on Chinese Maritime History). In Ts'ao Yung-ho, *Zhongguo Haiyangshi Lunji* (*Collected Essays on Chinese Maritime History*). Taipei: Lianjing Press, 2000a, pp. 1–147.
Ts'ao, Yung-ho 曹永和. *Zhongguo Haiyangshi Lunji* 中國海洋史論集 (*Collected Essays on Chinese Maritime History*). Taipei: Lianjing Press, 2000b.
Tun, Than (ed.) *The Royal Order of Burma, A.D. 1598–1885*. Kyoto: Kyoto University Center for Southeast Asian Studies, 1988.
Turpin, M. *History of the Kingdom of Siam*. Translated by B. O. Cartwright, Bangkok: American Presbyterian Mission Press, 1908.
Van Dyke, Paul "The Canton-Vietnam Junk Trade in the 1760s and 1770s: Some Preliminary Observations from the Dutch, Danish, and Swedish Records." Paper for the International Workshop "Commercial Vietnam: Trade and the Chinese in the 19th Century South," Ho Chi Minh City, Vietnam, December 1999.
Van Goor, Jurrien "A Hybrid State: The Dutch Economic and Political Network in Asia," in *From the Mediterranean to the China Sea*, eds. Claude Guillot, Denys Lombard and Roderich Ptak, with the assistance of Richard Teschke. Wiesbaden: Harrassowitz Verlag, 1998, pp. 193–214.

Van Leur, J. C. *Indonesian Trade and Society: Essays in Asian Economic and Social History*. The Hague: W. van Hoeve, 1955.

Vermeulen, J. Th. *De Chinezen te Batavia en de Troebelen van 1740*. Leiden: E. Ijdo, 1938.

Viraphol, Sarasin. *Tribute and Profit: Sino-Siamese Trade, 1652–1853*. Cambridge, Massachusetts: Harvard University Press, 1977.

Von Glahn, Richard. *The Country of Streams and Grottos: Expansion, Settlement, and the Civilising of the Sichuan Frontier in Song Times*. Harvard University Council of East Asian Studies, Cambridge, 1987.

Wade, Geoff. "On the Possible Cham Origin of the Philippine Scripts." *Journal of Southeast Asian Studies* 24, 1 (1993): 44–87.

Wade, Geoff. *The Ming Shi-lu (Veritable Records of the Ming Dynasty) as a Source for Southeast Asian History – 14th to 17th Centuries*. 7 vols. Ph.D. diss., University of Hong Kong, 1994a.

Wade, Geoff. "Melaka in Ming Dynasty Texts." *Journal of the Malayan Branch of the Royal Asiatic Society* 70, 1 (1997): 31–69.

Wade, Geoff. "The Spread of the Theravada Tradition in the Tai Polities of Yunnan 14th – 18th Centuries." Paper presented at the Third Euro-Japanese Symposium on Southeast Asian History – Religious Diffusion and Cultural Exchange in Southeast Asia, University of Hamburg, 7–9 September 1998.

Wade, Geoff. "The *Ming shi-lu* as a Source for Thai History – Fourteenth to Seventeenth Centuries." *Journal of Southeast Asian Studies* 31, 2 (2000): 249–94.

Wade, Geoff. "The Southern Chinese Borders in History," in *Where China Meets Southeast Asia: Social and Cultural Change in the Border Regions*, Grant Evans, Christopher Hutton, and Kuah Khun Eng (eds.). Bangkok: White Lotus, and Singapore: The Institute of Southeast Asian Studies, 2000, pp. 28–50.

Wade, Geoff. "The Portuguese as Represented in Some Chinese Sources of the Ming Dynasty," in *Portugal e a China. Conferências nos Encontros de História Luso-Chinesa*, ed. Jorge M. dos Santos Alves. Lisbon: Fundação Oriente, 2000.

Wade, Geoff. "The Zheng He Voyages: A Reassessment." *Journal of the Malaysian Branch of the Royal Asiatic Society*, 77, 1 (2005): 37–58.

Wade, Geoff. "Early Muslim Expansion in Southeast Asia, Eighth to Fifteenth Centuries," in David O. Morgan and Anthony Reid (eds.), *The New Cambridge History of Islam, Vol 3: The Eastern Islamic World Eleventh to Eighteenth Centuries*. Cambridge: Cambridge University Press, 2010, pp. 366–408.

Wade, Geoffrey P. "Ming Colonial Armies in 15th-Century Southeast Asia," in *Colonial Armies in Southeast Asia*, Karl A. Hack and Tobias Rettig (eds.). London: Routledge Curzon, 2005, pp. 73–104.

Wade, Geoffrey P. "Domination in Four Keys: Ming China and its Southern Neighbours 1400–1450," in Craig Clunas, Luk Yu-Ping and Jessica Harrison-Hall (ed.). *Ming China: Courts and Contacts 1400–1450*. London: British Museum Press, 2016.

Wahyono Martowikrido. "Preliminary Notes on the Technique of the Making of the Wonoboyo Hoard," in *Precious Metals in Early Southeast Asia*, W. H. Kal (ed.) Amsterdam, Royal Tropical Institute, 1999: 73–82.

Walsh, Warren. "The Yunnan Myth." *Far Eastern Quarterly* 2, 3 (May 1943): 272–85.

Wan, Ming 萬明. *Zhongguo rongru shijie de bulu: Ming yu Qing qianqi haiwai zhengce bijiao yanjiu* 中國融入世界的步履：明與清前期海外政策比較研究 (China's Integration into the World: A Comparative Studies on the of Overseas Policies in Ming and Early Qing). Beijing: Shehui kexue wenxian chubanshe, 2000.

Wang, Dayuan 汪大淵. *Daoyi Zhilue* 島夷誌略. *c.* 1350. Annotated by Su Jiqing 蘇繼廎. Beijing: Zhonghua shuju, 1981 reprint.
Wang, Gungwu 王賡武. "The Nanhai Trade: A Study of the Early History of Chinese Trade in the South China Sea." *Journal of the Malayan Branch of the Royal Asiatic Society* 31, 2 (1958): 1–135; Singapore: Times Academic Press, 1998 reprint.
Wang, Gungwu 王賡武. "The Opening of Relations between China and Malacca." In *Malayan and Indonesian Studies: Essays Presented to Sir Richard Winstedt*, J. S. Bastin and R. Roolvink (eds.). Oxford: Clarendon Press, 1964, pp. 87–104.
Wang, Gungwu 王賡武. "Early Ming Relations with Southeast Asia: A Background Essay," in *The Chinese World Order*, (ed.) John K. Fairbank. Cambridge MA: Harvard University Press, 1968a, pp. 35–62.
Wang, Gungwu 王賡武. "The First Three Rulers of Malacca," in *Journal of the Royal Asiatic Society Malaysian Branch* 41 (1968b): 11–22.
Wang, Gungwu 王賡武. "China and Southeast Asia 1402–24," in *Social History of China and Southeast Asia*, J. Chen and N. Tarling (eds.). Cambridge 1970, pp. 375–402.
Wang, Gungwu 王賡武. *Community and Nations: Essays on Southeast Asia and the Chinese*. Sydney: Heinemann Educational Books (Asia); Kuala Lumpur and Sydney: George Allen & Unwin, 1981.
Wang, Gungwu 王賡武. "Merchants without Empire: The Hokkien Sojourning Communities," in *The Rise of Merchant Empires: Long Distance Trade in the Early Modern World*, (ed.) James D. Tracy. Cambridge: Cambridge University Press, 1990, pp. 409–21.
Wang, Gungwu 王賡武. *China and the Chinese Overseas*. Singapore: Times Academic Press, 1991a.
Wang, Gungwu 王賡武. "Public and Private Overseas Trade in Chinese History," in Wang Gungwu, *China and the Chinese Overseas*. Singapore: Times Academic Press, 1991b, pp. 130–46.
Wang, Gungwu, "China and Southeast Asia 1402–24," in Wang Gungwu, *Community and Nation: China, Southeast Asia and Australia*. Sydney: ASAA in conjunction with Allen and Unwin, 1992.
Wang, Gungwu 王賡武. "Sojourning: The Chinese Experience in Southeast Asia," in Anthony Reid (ed.), *Sojourners and Settlers: Histories of Southeast Asia and the Chinese*. Sydney, Australia: Allen and Unwin, 1996, pp. 1–14.
Wang, Gungwu. "China and Southeast Asia: Myths, Threats and Culture." EAI Occasional Paper No. 13. Singapore: World Scientific, 1999.
Wang, Gungwu. *The Chinese Overseas: From Earthbound China to the Quest for Autonomy*. Cambridge, MA: Harvard University Press, 2000.
Wang, Gungwu. *The Nanhai Trade: Early History of Chinese Trade in the South China Sea*. Singapore: Eastern Universities Press, 2003.
Wang, Gungwu and Ng Chin-keong (ed.). *Maritime China in Transition 1750–1850*. Wiesbaden: Harrassowitz, 2004.
Wang, Huijun 王會均. "Ming Qing 'Qiongzhou fuzhi' yanjiu" 明清《瓊州府志》研究, in *Hainan ji Nanhai xueshu yanjiuhui lunwenji* 海南暨南海學術研究會論文集, (ed.), Guoli zhongyang tushuguan Taiwan fenguan 國立中央圖書館台灣分館. Taipei: Guoli zhongyang tushuguan Taiwan fenguan, 1996, pp. 41–52.
Wang, Jiazhong 王家忠. "Mingdai Hainan renkou lun" 明代海南人口論, *Zhongguo bianjiang shidi yanjiu* 中國邊疆史地研究 28, 2 (1998): 24–33.
Wang Yuan-kang. *Harmony and War: Confucian Culture and Chinese Power Politics*. New York: Columbia University Press, 2010.

Watanabe, Hiroshi. "An Index of Embassies and Tribute Missions from Islamic Countries to Ming China (1368–1644) as Recorded in the *Ming Shih-Lu*, Classified According to Geographic Area." *Memoirs of the Research Department of the Toyo Bunko* 33 (1975): 285–347.

Watt, James C. Y. (ed.), *The World of Khubilai Khan. Chinese Art in the Yuan Dynasty*, Metropolitan Museum of Art/Yale University Press, 2011.

Wheatley, Paul. "Geographical Notes on Some Commodities Involved in Sung Maritime Trade." *Journal of the Malasian Branch of the Royal Asiatic Society* 32, 2 (1959): 1–140.

Whitmore, J. K. *Vietnam, Hồ Quý Ly and the Ming (1371–1421)*. New Haven: Yale University Press, 1985.

Wiethoff, Bodo. *Die chinesisiche Seeverbotspolitik und der private Überseehandel von 1368 bis 1567*, Wiesbaden, 1963.

Williams, C. "Memorandum on the Question of British Trade with Western China via Burmah." *Journal of the Asiatic Society of Bengal* 33 (1864): 407–33.

Wills, John, E. "Chinese Further Shores: Continuities and Changes in the Destination Ports of China's Maritime Trade, 1680–1690." In *Emporia, Commodities and Entrepreneurs in Asian Maritime Trade, c.1400–1750*, eds. Roderich Ptak and Dietmar Rothermund. Stuttgart: Franz Steiner Verlag, 1991, pp. 53–80.

Wilson, Horace Hayman. *Documents Illustrative of the Burmese War with an Introductory Sketch of the Events of the War and an Appendix*. Calcutta: Government Gazette Press, 1827.

Winstedt, R. and P. E. De Josselin De Jong. "The Maritime Laws of Melaka. Edited with an Outline Translation." *Journal of the Malayan Branch of the Royal Asiatic Society* 29, 3 (1956): 22–59.

Wolfgang, F. and Chen T. F. *Chinese Epigraphic Material in Malaysia*. Kuala Lumpur: University of Malaya Press, 1985.

Wolters, Oliver W. *Early Indonesia Commerce*. Ithaca and London: Cornell University Press, 1963.

Wolters, Oliver W. *The Fall or Srivijaya in Malay History*. Ithaca: Cornell University Press, 1970.

Wong, Grace. *A Comment on the Tributary Trade between China and Southeast Asia*. Singapore: Southeast Asian Ceramic Society, Transactions 7, 1979.

Wong Lin-Ken 黃麟根. "The Trade of Singapore, 1819–69." *Journal of the Malayan Branch of the Royal* Asiatic Society 33, 4 (1960).

Wong Lin-Ken 黃麟根 "The Revenue Farms of Prince of Wales Island, 1805–1830." *Journal of the South Seas Society*, 19, i (1964): 56–127.

Wong Lin-Ken 黃麟根. *The Malayan Tin Industry to 1914*. Tucson: University of Arizona Press, 1965.

Wong Wai-yee, Sharon. "A Preliminary Study on some Economic Activities of the Khmer Empire: Examining the Relationship between the Khmer and Guangdong Ceramic Industries during the 9th–14th Centuries" PhD. dissertation, National University of Singapore, 2009. http://scholarbank.nus.edu.sg/handle/10635/17643.

Wood, Betty and Martin Lynn (eds.), *Travel, Trade and Power in the Atlantic, 1765–1884*. Cambridge: Cambridge University Press, 2003.

Wood, William Alfred Rae. *A History of Siam from the Earliest Times to the Year A.D. 1781, with a Supplement Dealing with More Recent Events*. Bangkok: The Siam Barnakich Press, 1933.

Wright, Arnold, H. A. Cartwright and Oliver T. Breakspear. *Twentieth Century Impressions of Burma: Its History, People, Commerce, Industries, and Resources*. London: Lloyd's Greater Britain Publishing Company, 1910.

Wyatt, David K. *Thailand: A Short History*. New Haven: Yale University Press, 1982.

Xu, Rongsong 許榮頌. compil. *Dingan xian wenwu zhi* 定安縣文物志 (Cultural and Historical Relic of Ding'an County). Guangzhou: Zhongshan daxue chubanshe, 1987.

Xuan An. "Đồng chí Trần To Chan" [Comrade Tran To Chan, 1900–1948], *Tạp chí lịch sử Đảng* 5 (1994): 50–8.

Yang, Baoyun 楊保筠. *Contribution a l'histoire de la Principaute des Nguyễn au Vietnam Meridional, 1600–1775*. Geneve: editions Olizane, 1992.

Yang, Bin. "Horses, Silver, and Cowries: Yunnan in Global Perspective." *Journal of World History* 15, 3, (September 2004): 281–322.

Yang, Dechun 楊德春. *Hainandao gudai jianshi* 海南島古代簡史 (A Brief History of Ancient Hainan Island). Changchun: Dongbei shifan daxue chubanshe, 1988.

Yang, Hanqiu 楊翰球. "Shiwu zhi shiqi shiji zhongye zhongxi hanghai maoyi shili de xingshuai 十五至十七世紀中葉中西航海貿易勢力的興衰" (The Rise and Fall of the Sino-Western Seafaring and Trading Forces from the 15th to the mid-17th Centuries). Beijing: *Lishi yanjiu* 歷史研究 5 (1982): 93–105.

Yen, Ching-hwang. *The Chinese in Southeast Asia and Beyond: Socioeconomic and Political Dimensions*. New Jersey: World Scientific Publishing, 2008.

Yen, Ching-hwang 顏清煌. "Power Structure and Power Relations in the Teochew Community in Singapore, 1819–1930," in *Chaozhouxue guoji yantaohui lunwenji* 潮州學國際研討會論文集 (Essays from the First International Conference on Teochew Studies), (ed.) Tay Lian-Soo 鄭良樹. Guangzhou, China: Jinan University Press, 1994, vol. 2, pp. 685–732.

Yeung Wai-Chung, Henry. *Chinese Capitalism in a Global Era: Towards Hybrid Capitalism*. London: Routledge, 2004.

Yong, Ch'ing Fatt 楊進發. *Chinese Leadership and Power in Colonial Singapore*, 2nd edition. Singapore: Times Academic Press, 1994.

Yong, Ch'ing Fatt 楊進發. *The Origins of Malayan Communism*. Singapore: South Seas Society, 1997.

Yu, Changsen 喻常森. *Yuandai haiwai maoyi* 元代海外貿易 (Maritime Trade of Yuan Dynasty). Xi'an: Xibei daxue chubanshe, 1994.

Yule, Henry. *A Narrative of the Mission Sent by the Governor-General of India to the Court of Ava in 1855, With Notices of the Country, Government, and People*. London: Smith, Elder, and Co., 1858.

Yule, Henry and Arthur Coke Burnell. *Hobson Jobson: Glossary of Colloquial Anglo-Indian Words & Phrases, & of Kindred Terms Etymological, Historical, Geographical & Discursive*. J. Murray, 1903. New edition edited by William Crooke, fourth edition, Delhi: Munshiram Manoharlal Publishers, 1984.

Yunnan Tongzhi (雲南通志 The Comprehensive Gazetteer of Yunnan), Preface dated 1691 (Kangxi康熙 10). Textual references to edition held in the Toyo Bunko 東洋文庫, Tokyo 東京.

Zhang, Dexin 張德信. (ed.) *Mingshi Hai Rui zhuan jiaozhu* 明史海瑞傳校注. Xi'an: Shaanxi renmin chubanshe, 1984.

Zhang, Haipeng 張海鵬 and Zheng Shanyu 鄭山玉 (eds.) *Zhongpu guanxishi ziliaoji* 中葡關係史資料集 (Collection of Records on the History of Sino-Portuguese Relationship). Chengdu: Sichuan renmin chubanshe, 1999.

Zhang, Xiumin 張秀民. "Mingdai jiaozhiren zai Zhongguo neidi zhi gongxian 明代交趾人在中國之貢獻," in *Xue Yuan* 學原, Beijing, 1949, 3 (1); *Mingdai guoji guanxi* 明代國際關係 (Foreign Relations of Ming Dynasty), Taipei: Xuesheng shuju, 1968 reprint, pp. 61–87.

Zhang, Xiumin 張秀民. *Zhong Yue guanxishi lunwenji* 中越關係史論文集 (Collected Studies on the History of Sino-Vietnamese Relations). Taipei: Wenshizhe chubanshe, 1992.

Zheng, Changshi 鄭昌時. *Hanjiang jianwenlu* (韓江見聞錄 In and about the Hanjiang Area), no publisher, 1824.

Zheng, Hesheng 鄭鶴聲 and Zheng Yijun 鄭一鈞 (eds.) *Zheng He xiaxiyang ziliao huibian* 鄭和下西洋資料彙編 (Collected Records on Zheng He's Voyages to the West Ocean). Jinan: Qilu shushe, 1980, 3 volumes.

Zheng, Yongchang 鄭永常. "Ming Yongle nianjian (1407–1424) Zhongguo tongzhi xia de Annam 明永樂年間 (1407–1424) 中國統治下的安南" (Annam under the Ming Rule, 1407–1424). In *Zhongguo haiyang fazhanshi lunwenji* 中國海洋發展史論文集. Vol. 5. ed. Zhang Bincun 張彬村 and Liu Shiji 劉石吉. Taipei: Zhongyang yanjiuyuan Zhongshan renwen shehui kexue yanjiusuo, 1993, pp. 61–109.

Zhuang, Weiji 莊為璣 and Zheng Shanyu 鄭山玉 (eds.) *Quanzhou pudie huaqiao shiliao yu yanjiu* 泉州譜牒華僑史料與研究 (A Collection of Clan Genealogies from Quanzhou), Beijing: Zhongguo huaqiao chubanshe, 1998.

Zhu, Jieqin 朱傑勤, *Dongnanya Huaqiao shi* 東南亞華僑史 [A History of the Overseas Chinese in Southeast Asia]. Beijing: Tertiary Education Publishers, 1990.

Index

Page numbers in **bold** denote tables, those in *italics* denote figures.

Abdul Jalil, Tun 255
Abu'l Fazl 74
A'fif Tarikh-I-Firuzshahi 61
"Age of Commerce" 116
Akbar al-Sin wa'l-Hind 50
Akbar, emperor 58, *73*, 74
Akbarnama 74
Alagakkonara (Ya-lie-ku-nai-er) 97, 136
Alaungpaya, King 184
Albuquerque, Afonso de 139–40, 143, 149
Ali al-Ridha, shrine 68, 78
al-Malik az-Zahir 60
Álvares, Jorge 140
anchasi (surveillance commission) 33
Andrade, Fernão Peres de 141
Anglo-Burmese War 283–4, 286, 290, 293
Annam 137; *see also* Đại Việt
Arabic, as *lingua franca* 50
Ardabil Shrine 68–9
Armitage, David 1
Arya Huang Fu-xin 111
Arya Xu-li-man 111
ASEAN (Association of Southeast Asian Nations) 2
Asian communism 6, 314–15, 322, 330
"Asian Mediterranean" 2
"Association of Overseas Revolutionary Partisans" 332n21
Ayutthaya 174–5, 177–9, 182, 184–5, 265–6, 318

Baba Chinese 4, 256, 285, 303–6, 308–11, 312n11; *see also* Straits Chinese
Babur 58, *59*, 74
Baburnama 57, 74
Bang Giao Luc 161
Banhap 309–10

Ba Yansan 183
"Belt and Road Initiative" 10
bendahara of Johor 255
Biographies of Exemplary Women 92, 119
blue-and-white porcelain 53–6, *54–5*, 60–2, 76–7, 81, 83n32
Blundell, Edmund Augustus 285, 290–1
Blyuker, Vasili K. 320
Boelen, David 253
Book burning 118
Borodin, Mikhail Markovich 320–1
Boromakot, King 174
Braudel, Fernand 1
Braun, Otto 320
bride-price market 213
Brief Description of the Island Foreigners (Daoyi zhilüe) 51, 59–60
British Museum 56
British rule, over Hong Kong 225
Brunei king 135, 137
Buddha King 215
Buddhism 9–10, 162–4, 167, 315
Burma 3, 6–7, 94, 99, 101, 107–9, 132, 137, 149, 184, 186, 188, 190–1, 193, 205, 211, 215, 225, 243, 317; Anglo-Burmese War 283–4, 286, 290, 293; Ayutthaya, conquest of 174–5, 178; China relations 178, 282–3; Chinese migrants in 282–97; threats to 97
Burma Pacification Commission 137
Burma with Special Reference to Her Relations to China 294

Cai Han 179–80
Cai Yurong 199, 202, 204
Cambodian communism 326–7
"Canton Commune" 322

Cao Yujun 201
capitalism 311
Capital Museum, Beijing 84n59
Captains of Chinese 254–7
Catholicism 319
Cavanagh, Orfeur 312n14
Caw Ing Mäng 193
CCP (Chinese Communist Party) 319–23, 326–8, 330, 332n21, 334n54
celadon dishes *62, 63*
ceramic trade 4, 8, 25, 29–30, 44, 47, 50, 52–3, 58–60, 69; glazed ceramics 49–51, 118; *see also* Chinese porcelain
Chamber of Orphans 259
Champa Muslims 26, 30
Chang Pin-tsun 27
Chao Phraya Chakri 174
Cheang Hong Lim 308–10, 312n11
Cheang Sam Teo 304, 306–8, 312n11
Cheli Pacification Superintendency 103
Cheli Xuanweishi (Cheli Pacification Commissioner) 193, 195–6, 205, 216n30
Cheng Ho *see* Zheng He
Chenghua reign 102–3, 148
Cheng Zhe 179
Cheng Wei 137
Chen Jin 141
Chen Junqin 181, 187n29
Chen Wansheng 181
Chen Wenfang 179
Chen Mei 175–7
Chen Tian-ping (Trần Thiên Bình) 92
Chen Wuzhi 213
Chen Yongbin 109
Chen Yue 103
Chen Zhi 135
Chen Zuyi 96, 136
Cheng Wei 137
Chiang Kai-shek 317, 320–1, 328
Chief Military Commission 89
Chihl Sutun 69
China: Burma relations 178, 282–3; India, engagement with 44–50, 56; Portuguese occupation of Melaka, response to 140–50; remittances to **265**; Sipsong Panna relations 193–206; Southeast Asia relations 2–10; Tai polities, and 190–2; Taksin, relations with 175–86
"China-and-Barbarians Order" 130, 132
China Room (*Chinikhana*) 68, 74
Chinese Baba *see* Baba Chinese
Chinese Buddhist pilgrims 44
Chinese Chamber of Commerce 296

Chinese Communist Party *see* CCP
Chinese communities, in Southeast Asia **228**
Chinese *kongsi* 261n3
Chinese immigration: Burma, in 282–97; Mekong delta 265–8, **274n8**, 268–9; *see also* Hokkien migration
Chinese languages, adoption of 8–9
Chinese mercantile activities **246–7, 249–51**, 259
Chinese Muslims 9, 120
Chinese National Academy 158
Chinese Nationalist Party *see* Guomindang
Chinese people, massacre of 50, 206, **207**, 265–7, 269–73
Chinese population, in Melaka **244**
Chinese porcelain *45–7, 49,* 50, 56, *57, 58, 59–61, 63–73,* 74, *75–80,* 81, 83n32, 84n51, 224; blue-and-white 53–6, *54–5,* 60–2, 76–7, 81, 83n32; *see also* ceramic trade
Chinese trading, patterns of 244–9
Chinese Water Frontier 267
Choa Chong Long 304
Christianity 191
Chronological Record of [Events] in Yunnan, A (Dian Yun linian zhuan) 197, 209–10, 212
Chua Su Cheong 257–8
Chuyet Chuyet 162
"circulating official" 90
Clavijo, Ruy Gonzalez de 57
code of maritime laws 262n11
coinage, tin and copper 50
Cold War 2, 314, 331
"colonial modernisation" 329
Comintern (Communist International) 319–20, 322–7, 329
communism: Asian communism 6, 314–15, 322, 330; Cambodian communism 326–7; Lao communism 325–6; Siamese communism 325; Southeast Asian communism 322–5
Communist Party of Indonesia (PKI) 332n12
Communist Party of Malaya *see* MCP
Confucianism 5, 191, 237n21; Neo-Confucianism 147–8
Confucian schools 8, 92, 102, 118–19, 164
contraband trade 33
Council of State 175
Covilhã, Pêro da 139
cowries, as currency 25
Cox, Hiram 284

Crawfurd, John 284
credit system 271
Cultural Revolution 296

Da Gama, Vasco 139, 229
Đại Nam Thực Lục Tiền Biên 158–63
Đại Việt, invasion of 92–3, 99, 115, 125n141, 316
Daizong, Emperor: foreign policies of 100–2
Đặng Thúc Hứa 321, 324
Dao Ganmeng 90
Dao Guanghuan 205
Dao Jinbao (Taw Kin Paw) 196–8, 216n30
Dao Ruzen 199
Dao Xingguo 212, 217n48
Daoyi zhilue (*Brief Description of the Island Foreigners, A*) 51, 59–60
Dao Zhengyan 197–8, 206, 210–11, 214, 216n30
Da Shan 9, 158–60, 163–7, 170, 173n63
Datini, Francesco 254
decolonisation 2, 319, 330, 331n10
Delhi Sultanate 61–2, 68–9, 74, 81n1
Deng Xiaoping 10
depression, in 1930s 277n64
Dian Yun linian zhuan (*Chronological Record of [Events] in Yunnan, A*) 197, 209–10, 212
divide-and-rule policy 90, 109–10
"domino theory" 314
Đông Du (Go East Movement) 317–18, 320, 324
Dongxiyang Kao 167
Doveton, F.B. 286
Dutch control of Melaka 243–4, 264
Dutch United East India Company (VOC) 76, 221, 225, 229–35, 239n46, 241–3, 245, 257–9
Duti-ya Maha-ya-zawin-daw-gyì 283

East India Company, British (EIC) 233–4, 284
Eastern Ocean 94
"eastern trade route" 23, 29, 52
E'ertai 6, 189–90, 194, 196–7, 206, 209–11, 214
Ekathat, King 177–8
Embroidered-Uniform Guard 110
"enfeoffment" 88–9, 130–1, 176, 180, 182
Estado da India (State of India) 231–2
European East India Companies 239n42
Europe–Asia trade 230–1
examination system 191

Fair Winds for Escort (*Shunfeng Xiangsong*) 52
Fairbank, John King 5
Fan Chengxun 202, 214
Far Eastern Bureau (FEB) 324, 327, 329
Farquhar, William 303
Faxian 44, 47
Ferghana 44, 56
Fernandez, Duarte 149
feudalism 130, 148
"Fifth Columns" 314
firearms 7–8, 117–18
Firuz Shah Tughlaq 61–2, 68
"four barbarians" 130
free trade 35
French Communist Party (FCP) 324, 326
French Indochina 317

gaitu guiliu policy 107, 189, 195–6
Gan Enchi 175, 180–1
Gan Wee *see* Banhap
Gao Qizhuo 189, 204–5, 217n48
Genealogy of the Mo Family in the Towns of Ha-tien and Ye 177
General Administrative Office of the Pu'er and Simao Border (*Pusi Yanbian Xingzheng Zongju*) 195
General Tea Store 206, 208–10
Ghee Hin Society 306
Gia Định thông chí 268–9, 271–2
Goa, fall of 231
Go East Movement (*Đông Du*) 317–18, 320, 324
gold dinar 50, 53
Gong Xiang 100, 110
Gouger, Henry 284
Great Ming 87–8, 133, 141
Great Syndicate, The 308–10
Great Wall 102
guanben system 28, 35
Guihai yu heng zhi 21
Gui Lin 183
Gulai, prince 32
Gulf of Siam 22
Gulf of Tonkin 22
Guldi, Jo 1
Gulistan Museum 69
Guangdong tongzhi (*GDTZ*) 21
Guomindang (GMD) 317–18, 320–3, 328

Hainan maritime trade: Ming period 30–5; Song period 23–7; Yuan period 27–30
Hai Rui 32
Hai Wai Ji Shi (*HWJS*) 163–4

Hamashita Takeshi 5
Han dynasty 89, 131–2
Han institutions and assimilation 191–2
Han migrants, massacre of 206, **207**
Han Zhenhua 37n14
Hao Yulin 196, 198
harbour-master's list 241, 249, 252–3, 261n4
Harrell, Stevan 191
Harvey, Godfrey Eric 292
Hasegawa Kiyoshi 194, 213
He Ao 142
"Heaven and Earth Associations" 316
"Heavenly court" 148
"Heavenly Kingdom" 132
Heeren XVII documents 241
Hinduism 149
History of Burma, The 294
History Manifesto, The 1
History of Rangoon 295
History of the Han Dynasty 132
History of the Ming Dynasty 135, 145–6
History of the Song Dynasty, The 132
Hoang Chen 158
Hoàng Văn Hoan 325–6
Hồ Chí Minh 319–21, 323–7, 329, 331n10
Hồ Học Lãm 317, 321, 324, 328
Hokkien migration 266–7, **268**, 281, 285, 287, 290, 297, 305; *see also* Chinese immigration
Hong Đực Code of Law 162
Hong Kong, under British rule 225
Hongwu, emperor 48, 56, 70, 90, 102, 108, 110, 114, 133–7, 147
Hongxi Emperor 93
Hongzhi reign 104–5
horses, as tribute 25–6, 32, 34, 37n16
Hou Xian 94, 97
Huang Xingzeng 52
Huang Zuo 32
Huaqiao 316, 318, 323, 325–6, 328–9; *see also* overseas Chinese
Humayan 74
Hu Qizao 201
Hu Weiyong 91, 122n25

Ibn Battuta 59–61, 68
Ibn Khurdadhbih 44
India: engagement with China 44–50, 56
"imperial monopoly trade" 116
"Indianization" 223
Indochinese Communist Party (ICP) 322, 326–9
intra-Asia country trade 230
Isfahan rebellion 30

Iskandar Shah 138
Islam 9, 53, 120, 223, 315, 319; Champa Muslims 26, 30; Chinese Muslims 9, 120; Muslim traders 26
Islamic conservatism 61
Islamic India 4
Islamization 223

Jahangir, emperor 74
James I 76
Japan, modernisation of 317
Java, violence in 96
Jiang Bin 141, 144
Jiang Gui, general 100
Jianwen Emperor 91
Jiajing, Emperor 150–1
Ji Qing 112
Jiu Tang shu 48
Judson, Adoniram 284
Jue Linh 167

Kaizhong system 113–14, 127n192
Kang, David 5
Kangchu system 306
Kangxi emperor 214
kanhe system 134
Kataoka Tatsuki 215
Katō Kumiko 190, 193–5, 198, 213
Ke Shuxun 195
Khajeh Jahan 70
Khoja Hassan 141–2, 144
kinship network 257–8
Kromphra' Damrong Ratchanuphap 184
Khamseng 326–7, 333n38
Khurrum, Prince 76
Kikuchi Hideaki 191
King of Đong Phố 160
Kiong Kong Tuan 304, 306
Kitab al-Masalik 44
Koh Saeng Tat 310
Kökö Temür 87
Kong Yuanzhi 120
Kotla Firoz Shah palace complex 61–2, 81
Krung Phra Nakhon Sri Ayudhya 88
Kuwabara, Jitsuo 26

Laird, John 284
Lai Te 327–8
Lao communism 325–6
Lau Jun Teck 306–8, 312n9
Lê Court 157–9, 170
Lê Dynasty 157, 159, 162, 165
Lê Lợ'I 112
Lê Quý Dôn 159

Lê Thánh Tông 162
Lê Văn Khôi rebellion 273
Liang Daoming 96
Liang Shangxuan 181, 187n29
Liang sigong ji (Memoirs of the Liang Dynasty) 47
Li, ethnic group 25, 28, 30, 35
Li Guan 101
Li Hu 183
Li Lisan 320
Lim Boon Keng 312n4
Lim Quee Eng 310
Lingwai daida 21, 24, 51
Lin Yi 177
Li Shiyao 175, 177–81
Li Sizhong 201
Liu Chongli 201
Liu Daxia 148
Liu Hongdu 199
Liu Jin 105
Liu Sifu 160
Liu Qing 166
Li Wenguang (Lý Văn Quang) 160–1, 266–7, 269
Longchuan Pacification Commission 100, 137
Long March 322, 334n54
lord–vassal relationship 192, 212, 214–15
Low Tiev, position of 272–3
Luang Phijaya Saneha 183
Lukui Mountain, outlaws of 199–202, **203**, 204–5
Lu Wei 24

Mạc family 157, 316
Ma Chengwang 27
MacLeod, T.E. 291
Maha-ya-zawin-gyì 297
Mahin Banu Khanumas, princess 68, 77–8
Ma Huan 51–2
Mahmud Shah, Sultan 140
Maingy, Anthony de la Combe 285–90
Majapahit 88, 96, 116
Malacca *see* Melaka
Malay noblemen, and patronage 255–6
Malik Fasula 253
Manchu *see* Qing
Mäng Ham, revolt of 197–8, 210
Mao Zedong 319
Ma Qi 93, 112
maritime forces 94, 97–8
"Maritime Great Wall" 226
maritime prohibitions 91, 111, 151, 226–7, 229, 235

maritime trade 4, 7, 21, 24, 27, 30, 52–3, 91–3, 104–6, 110, 112, 116, 119, 134, 151–2, 185, 223–6, 228–32, 234–5
Maritime Trade Supervisorate 92–3
maritime vessels, used by traders 251, 252, 253–4
massacres: Chinese people 50, 206, **207**, 265–7; Saigon massacre 269–73
Mas'udi 50
Maung Htin Aung 292
MCP (Malayan Communist Party) 324, 327–8
Mekong delta: Chinese migration to 265–8, **274n8**; Chinese occupations in 268–9
Melaka: Chinese population **244**; Portuguese occupation of 5, 139–40, 231; sultanate 5, 7
"Memorandum on the Question of British Trade with Western China via Burma" 293
Mencius 148
mercantile dominance, by South and West Asians 221–5
Miao rebellion 189
Military and Civilian Pacification Superintendencies 94
military farm (*tuntian*) system 28
'military revolution' 8
military technology 117–18
Mindon, King 283
Ming dynasty 5–9, 21–3, 44, 51, 56, 76, 78, 87, 130, 163, 167–70, 189, 316; foreign policy 88–106; Hainan maritime trade, and 30–5; maritime policy 221, 226–9, 235; migration policy 113–14, 127n196; political expansion 107–8; Southeast Asia, and 112–21; world order, and 133–9
Ming law code 87
Ming shilu (*MSL*) 21, 30–2, 41n53, 95, 98, 100, 104
Ming Taizu *see* Zhu Yuanzhang
Min Gui 105
Min Hongxue 134
Minh Chính Công 169
Ming Wuzong *see* Wuzong
Ming Xianzong *see* Xianzong
Ming Xiaozong *see* Xiaozong
Ming Xuanzong *see* Xuanzong
Ming Yingzong *see* Yingzong
Ming Daizong *see* Daizong
Minister of Personnel 103
Minister of War 103

378 *Index*

Ministry of Revenue 94, 102, 104–5, 110, 142, 148
Ministry of Rites 92, 105, 134, 142, 144
Ministry of Works 95
Ministry of War 106, 144
Miscellaneous Records of the Frontiers (Phủ Biên Tạp Lục) 158–9
Mo Guangyi 181
Mo Shilin 177, 179, 186
Mon rebellion 287
money economy 101, 206–13
money-lending 206, 210
Mongol ancestry 44
Mughal India 44, 76, 77, 81
Muhammad bin Tughlaq, Sultan 61–2, 74
Munshi Abdullah 306
Mu Sheng 94, 100
Muslim traders 26

Nakhoda 249, 253
Na-luo-ta 97, 137
Narasimhavarman II, King 46, 48
nasta'liq script 76–8, 80
"native offices" 90, 94, 99, 102–3, 106–7, 189
Native Officials and Native Administrators 189, 192
"native troops" 93, 109, 113
Neo-Confucianism 147–8
networks, kinship 257–8
Ngan Chan Wai *see* Banhap
Ngee Heng Kongsi 306
Nguyễn Ái Quốc *see* Hồ Chí Minh
Nguyễn Hoàng 157–8
Nguyễn Phúc Chu 158–61, 163–7, 169
Nguyễn Phúc Khoat 160–1, 164
Nguyễn Phúc Nguyên 157
Nguyễn Phúc Tần 165, 168–9
Nguyễn Phúc Trăn 9, 162–3, 168
Nguyễn Quang Tiền 159
Nguyễn rule: court and administration 167–9; government-to-government relations 157–62; religious development, and 162–7; Vietnam, southern 156, 171n12; *see also* Vietnam
Nguyễn Sơn 321–2, 326, 328, 334n54
Ni Tui 197
Nok-iang 174

Offices of Scrutiny 88
Old Port, attack on 96, 110
Olson, Mancur 221
"One Belt, One Road" 10

opium 4–5, 288–9, 295, 303–11, 312n14, 313n20
Oriental Exclusion Act 310
Ortega, Francisco de 34
outlaws, of Lukui Mountain 199–202, **203**, 204–5
Overall Survey of the Ocean's Shores (*Yingyai Shenglan*) 51
Overgekomen Brieven en Papieren documents 261n4
overland Chinese 7, 191, 282, 287, 315–16
overland trade 10, 44, 57, 74, 284, 291, 293, 316
overseas Chinese 6–7, 287, 311, 314; *see also Huaqiao*
Overseas Customs Officer 50
"Overseas Vietnamese" 314, 316, 320, 325

pacification office 27
"pacification superintendency" 96
Palembang 9, 96, 110, 114, 120, 137
Pallava dynasty 46
Parameswara 136
Parker, Edward H. 294
patriarchal clan system 130
Pearn, B.R. 295
peasant revolt 56
Penang Riots 285
Peranakan *see* Baba Chinese
Peregrinação 21
Phạm Ngàn 269
Phan Bội Châu 317–18, 320
Phayre, Arthur 292, 294
Phraya Sin *see* Taksin
Phraya Sundhon Aphai 182–3
Phủ Biên Tạp Lục (Miscellaneous Records of the Frontiers) 158–9
Pinto, Fernão Mendes 21
pirates 33–4, 96, 104–5, 147, 226, 272
Pires, Tomé 140–1, 145, 153n36
PKI (Communist Party of Indonesia) 332n12
Poivre, Pierre 160
porcelain *see* Chinese porcelain
Portuguese, occupation of Melaka 5, 139–40, 231; China's response 140–50; implications of 150–2
Portuguese trade 34, 153n36
private trade 28, 34, 91, 110–12, 114, 159, 225–7, 229, 235
Pu "clan" 27
Pu Sheng 32

Pusi Yanbian Xingzheng Zongju (General Administrative Office of the Pu'er and Simao Border) 195
Pu Youcai 205

Qianlong, emperor 175, 177–80, 183
Qian-wen-ji 99
Qin Dynasty 131
Qin Shihuang, Emperor 147
Qing dynasty 3, 6, 21–3, 107, 112, 158, 185, 188–9, 191, 317
Qingho she 273
Qing Shi 160
Qiong tai zhi 21–2, 26, 29, 31–2, 34, 41n53
Qiu Daolong 142
Qiu Mingyang 198

Raffles, Thomas S. 303
Records of the Tributary Countries in the Western Ocean (*Xiyang chaogong lu*) 52
Red Army 322, 334n54
"Red Chinese" 297
"Red Scares" 314
religions, spread of 9
remittances, to China **265**
Renzong emperor 98, 148
revenue farming 4, 303, 308
"revenue police" 308
Revolution of 1911 296, 318–19
Roe, Thomas 76
Royal Asiatic Society of Bengal, Journal 291–2

Safavid royal family 69
Saigon massacre 269–73
Salar Jung Museum 84n51
Samudera, attack on 98
Sarasin Viraphol 187n29
Sayyif Beg 73
Seah Eu Chin 307–8, 312n12
sea trade *see* maritime trade
Second World War *see* World War II
secret societies 305–6, 308, 316
Sequeira, Diogo Lopes de 139
Shah 'Abbas I, emperor 69, 81
Shah Jahan, emperor 74, 76–7, 79, 81, 84n58
Shambaugh, David 5
Shang Dynasty 130
Shang Lu 103
Shaykh safi al-Din 69
Shore of Pearls 22

shibosi office 24, 27–8, 30–1, 39n35
Shi Heshang 205
Shintani Tadahiko 188
ship-building 7, 29, 94–5, 117, 151, 269
shipping toll 24
Shizong, Emperor 144–5
Shunfeng Xiangsong (Fair Winds for Escort) 52
Siah U Chin 285
Siamese communism, origins of 325
Siamese Communist Party 324–5, 328
Si Die 104
Si Jifa 100–1, 108, 110
Si Kenfa 101
silk-for-silver trade 34
Silk Road 44, 56
Si Lu 104, 110
Si Lunfa 89–90, 100, 108–9
Singapore, Straits Chinese in 303–9
silver exports 230
Simao Tongzhi 194
Sinan shipwreck 83n32
"Sinicization" 223, 224
*sinkeh*s 303–5, 307, 312n4
Sino-Burmese war 178
Sino-Indian relations 49
Sino-Japanese war 323
Sino-Javanese shipping 7
Sino-Vietnamese Communist alliance 314, 323–4, 329–30; early relations 315–22
Sipsong Panna 6, 90, 109, 190, 213–4; annexation of 196–7; during the 1720s and 1730s 193–6; relations with China 193–206; revolt in 188–9
Si Renfa 100, 102, 107–8, 110, 114, 125n139
Social Darwinism 319
Song dynasty 4, 21, 23, 35, 51, 53, 132, 147–8, 184, 191; Hainan maritime trade, and 23–7
Song huiyao jigao 21
Song Ong Siang 304, 307, 312n4
Song shi 51
"Son of Heaven" 130, 136–7
South and West Asians, mercantile dominance 221–5
Southeast Asia: China relations 2–10; Chinese communities in **228**; communism 322–5; Ming dynasty, and 112–21; topography, changes in 114–21
"Southeastern Asia" 12n14
"Southern Silk Road" 12n14
"South Seas [Nanyang] Communist Party" (SSCP) 323–5, 327

380   Index

Soviet Union 319–21
Special Branch 327–8
spice trade 140, 222–3, 230–1, 233, 236n3, 239n46
Spring and Autumn Annals 132
Sri Lanka, attack on 97
Sri Narasimha Potavarman 48
Srivijaya 137
State Archaeology Museum, Hyderabad 84n51
State of India (*Estado da India*) 231–2
Straits Chinese: middlemen 304, 311; in Singapore 303–9; *see also* Baba Chinese
Straits of Malacca 95, 115
Straits Settlements 5, 284–5, 293, 308
Sultanate India 56–7, 61
Su-gan-la 98
Sun An 113
Sun Hongben 217n35
Sun Laichen 117
Sun Yat Sen 312n4, 317–18, 320
Superintendent of Shipping 53
surveillance commission (*anchasi*) 33
Su Shi 21
syahbandar 243
Symes, Michael 282–4
"Synas, the land of " 139

Tai Cultural Area (TCA), 12n14, 188, 191–2
Tai polities 6, 8, 90, 94, 102, 104, 107, 110, 114–15, 118; area of 188; Chinese state, and 190–2
Taiping huanyu ji 21
Taizu, Emperor 133–5, 147
Taksin, King 6, 275n27; relations with China 175–86; early years 174–80
Tamerlane 57
Tam Ty system 165
Tan Che Sang 304
Tang Dynasty 44, 49
Tạ Nguyên Thiều (Xie Yuan Shao) 163
Tan Hiok Nee 308
Tanjong Pagar Dock Company 308
Tan Keng Hoa 309
Tan Keng Seng 309
Tan Keng Sing & Brothers 313n19
Tan Keng Swee 310
Tan Seng Poh 308–10
Tan Tock Seng 304
Taw Kin Paw (Dao Jinbao) 196–8, 216n30
Tay Han Long 304, 306
"Tayoub" 282–3
Tây Sơn massacre *see* Saigon massacre

Tea Mountains 194, 196–7, 199, **203**, 206, 208–11, 217n35, 217n48
textiles trade 39n40, 50–1, 166, 222, 230–1, 233–4, 236n3
Thanh niên Cách mạng Đồng chí Hội (Vietnamese Revolutionary Youth Group) 320
Thonburi, king of 175
Tiandihui 306
Tiền Biên see Đại Nam Thức Lục Tiền Biên
T'ien Ju-k'ang 227
Timurid royal house 44, 74
tin and copper coinage 50
Tongmenghui 318
Tong Shiyin 212
Topkapi Saray Museum 69
trade model **222**, **223**
trade monopoly 116, 221, 229–35, 239n46
Trần Dương Thuận 169
Trần Hung 169
Trần Thiên Bình (Chen Tian-ping) 92
Translator's Institute 106
Trần Văn Giàu 326–7, 333n39
"treasure ships" 31, 33, 95, 135–6
Treaty of Yandabo 286
Treaty Ports 311
"Triad Societies" 316
tribute goods 25, 27, 211
"tribute missions" 98, 131, 226–8
tribute tea 211
tribute trade 30, 35, 88–91, 110–12, 126n165, 134, 138, 185, 226–9, 235
tributary system 5, 14n31, 14n34, 32–4, 88, 133–40, 149–51, 159, 282; origins of 130–2
Trotsky, Leon 321
Ts'ao Yung-ho 224
Trịnh family 157, 160–1
Tuao Alemancet 145
Tuao Mafame 144–5
Tuao Nacem Mudaliar 143
Tự Đức, king 316
Tughlaq Sultanate 56
tuntian (military farm) system 28
Turkic-Mongol descent 44
Tuzik-i-Jahangiri, memoirs 74, 76

ultra-nationalism 148
Ulugh Beg 74
"Universal Tribute Decree" 130

Veritable Records of the Ming Dynasty 141, 143, 150

Việt Kiều communities 318, 320–1, 323–6, 328–9
Vietnam: Chinese population in 264–6, 272–3; warfare against 31; *see also* Nguyễn rule
Vietnamese civil war 320, 332n13
Vietnamese Communist Party (VCP) 320–2, 325, 327–8
"Vietnamese Restoration Society" 318
Vietnamese Revolutionary Youth Group (*Thanh niên Cách mạng Đồng chí Hội*) 320
Vietnam War 314
VOC (*Verenigde Oostindische Compagnie*) *see* Dutch United East India Company
Voitinsky, Grigori 320
"voyages of friendship" 95
Vườn Trầu (Betel Nut Gardens) 269

Walsh, Warren 292
Wang Dayuan 47, 51, 60
Wang Guitong 94
Wang Gungwu 5
Wang Ji, general 100–1
Wang Jinghong 97, 120
Wang Yuan-kang 5
"water frontier" 7
Wei Jiuguan 168–9
Wei Xiying 143
weights and measures 9–10, 120, 122n22, 123n72
"Western Ocean" 70, 94–5, 97
"western trade route" 22, 26–7, 29, 52
Whampoa 304
Whampoa Military Academy 321
"White Chinese" 297
White, Richard 211
Whitmore, John 92, 118
Williams, C. 293–4
Wilson, President 331n10
wokou groups 33–4
world order, Ming dynasty and 133–9
World War II 281, 296–7, 319, 328, 330
Wudi, Emperor 131–2, 147
Wu Sangui 202–4, 214
Wuzong, Emperor 141; foreign policies of 105–6, 141–2, 144

Xia Yuanji 148
Xie-du-yan-da 180
Xie Yuan Shao (Tạ Nguyên Thiều) 163
Xi Jinping 10
Xiyang chaogong lu (Records of the Tributary Countries in the Western Ocean) 52
Xianzong, Emperor: foreign policies of 102–4
Xiao Dao Hui uprising 311
Xiaozong, Emperor: foreign policies of 104–5
Xing Che 158
Xuande emperor 31, 52–3, 149, 227
Xuanzong, Emperor 148; foreign policies of 98–9
Xu Quan 178
Xu Liang 112
Xu Wen 107

Ya-lie-ku-nai-er (Alagakkonara) 97, 136
Yang Jingsu 181–2, 187n29
Yang Ling 159
Yang Pan 137
Yang Yingju 178
Yangzi River, as marker 12n14
Yi Ji 133
Yin Jishan 209–10
Yingyai Shenglan (Overall Survey of the Ocean's Shores) 51
Yingzong, Emperor 148; foreign policies of 100–2
Yongle, Emperor 31, 52–3, 70, 91–2, 94, 96–7, 103, 110, 135–40, 147–9, 214–15, 227
Yongzheng, emperor 189, 198
Yuan dynasty 21, 23, 44, 51, 53, 56, 60, 62, 68, 133, 221, 225, 227; decline of 87; Hainan maritime trade, and 27–30
Yuanfeng jiuyu zhi 21
Yudi jisheng 21, 23
Yun Xian 99, 112
Yunnan, as "country" 89–90, 107, 125n138; invasion of 93–4, 100–1
"Yunnan Myth" 292–4
Yunnan Provincial Administration Commission 99
Yunnan Regional Military Commission 93

Zainuli Abidin 98, 115
Zhang Fu 316
Zhang Jingzhi 135
Zhang Qian 94
Zhao Cui 176–7
Zhao Rugua 21, 24–7, 50–3
Zhao Sai 110
Zhao Shichang 176–7
Zhao Wangji 176

Zhao Wenbin 160
Zhejiang 94
Zhengde reign 21, 105–6, 141–2, 144, 150–1
Zheng He 6, 9, 31, 51–2, 70, 135–6, 148; voyages of 94–9, 120, 123n64, 138, 227–8
Zheng Rui 179
Zhengtong reign 110
Zheng Yong 174
Zheng Zhao 181

Zhou Dynasty 130–1, 202
Zhou Enlai 319–21
Zhou Qufei 21, 25, 51
Zhou Rituals 131
Zhu Di 91–2
Zhufan zhi 21, 24, 50–2
Zhu Shunsui 168, 170
Zhu Yuanzhang 87; policies of 89–91, 121n1, 133
Zhu Yunming 99
Ẕiyā' al-Dīn Baranī 61

Printed in the United States
By Bookmasters